Political Theory, History, and Modern Practice for the Common Good

Antonio Cortijo Ocaña
University of California, Santa Barbara, USA

Vicent Martines
Universitat d´Alacant, Spain

IGI Global
Scientific Publishing
Publishing Tomorrow's Research Today

Vice President of Editorial	Melissa Wagner
Director of Acquisitions	Mikaela Felty
Director of Book Development	Jocelynn Hessler
Production Manager	Mike Brehm
Cover Design	Jose Rosado

Published in the United States of America by
IGI Global Scientific Publishing
701 East Chocolate Avenue
Hershey, PA, 17033, USA
Tel: 717-533-8845 | Fax: 717-533-7115
Website: https://www.igi-global.com E-mail: cust@igi-global.com

Library of Congress Cataloging-in-Publication Data

LCCN: 2025027523 (CIP Data Pending)
ISBN13: 979-8-3373-2332-9
Isbn13Softcover: 979-8-3373-2333-6
EISBN13: 979-8-3373-2334-3
British Cataloguing in Publication Data
A Cataloguing in Publication record for this book is available from the British Library.

Table of Contents

Detailed Table of Contents

This chapter seeks to tackle Plutarch's work on good governance (the normally known as Praecepta gerendi reipublicae) to note the role it plays in his political thinking. We shall focus on the exempla virtutis that the author proposes to teach good government to young people. These virtues have their roots in classical Greece and Rome, and in the polis system, but the context of the Roman Empire leads Plutarch to reinterpret them and place them within their proper limits. The figure of the emperor acts as a bond of union between the citizen elites and the senatorial elites and Plutarch preaches both the freedom and autonomy of the Greek cities and the submission to the empire as the architect of the pax Romana. The exempla of the past, of the classical polis, are admired, but discouraged by Plutarch as risky and a possible cause of confrontation with the Romans.

The aim of this chapter is to describe, according to Dio Chrysostom's speeches on monarchy, the importance of these two institutions, the monarchy and the city, as well as to assess both the role that each of them plays in his political thinking and the relationship that exists between them, particularly -but not only-in the eastern part of the empire. The first has a tradition in Hellenistic political theory that Dion himself introduced, to a large extent, into the political thought of Rome; the second underpins Greco-Roman political theory as a model of civilisation and a privileged means of human development. The provincial elites and the senatorial elite agree in exalting the emperor in order to maintain as far as possible realities that represent a great deal for both: the libertas of the Romans and the polis of the Greeks.

This study analizes the contributions of medieval and Renaissance civic humanism to Political Science (with special attention to the theory of good government) and how current they can be effectively today; how useful they can be today. The analysis focuses on the contribution of Francesc Eiximenis´s Regiment de la cosa pública ['Government of the public'] as part of his Dotzè del Crestià. We make a brief anthology of fragments (in the original version and in translation into Spanish to make it more accessible to a wider audience, especially, if possible, active politicians) that include advice and teachings that can show how useful Francesc Eiximenis' conceptual proposal can be today.

This chapter investigates the role of education in rethinking territory, community, and citizenship as essential forms of the common good. Within a pedagogical perspective, it emphasizes how these dimensions are not merely physical or administrative constructs, but relational and symbolic spaces where identity, inclusion, and participation are negotiated. In the face of growing inequalities and the privatization of public spaces, the text calls for an educational commitment to reclaim and care for shared places, fostering democratic life and social justice. The concept of the educating community emerges as a concrete response to contemporary crises, promoting active citizenship and collective responsibility. By linking bodies to spaces and people to places, pedagogy becomes a transformative force capable of reimagining the public sphere, strengthening social bonds, and sustaining forms of coexistence based on solidarity, accessibility, and shared belonging.

The sharing economy is nothing new in principle. Its beginnings date back to the times of the creation of social communities. In the dimension of the urban economy, we can identify it with the municipal economy or, as in the case of Poland, an attempt to enfranchise Polish citizens under the Universal Privatization program. Today, the sharing economy is understood as an economic model based on sharing broadly understood resources with other people. Examples of such an economy in the context of the urban economy include sharing mainly broadly understood municipal goods (for example, excess energy from solar panels) or, in the authors' understanding, also co-participation in the creation of some such goods. This co-participation can be understood, among others, as the possession by residents of a settlement unit of shares, for example, in a water treatment plant, if the legal structure allows for such an organizational and legal form.

This chapter analyzes nature literature in the United States as a form of embodied political thought that impinges on current debates about ecological justice and the common good. It examines the evolution of this tradition from classic authors such as Thoreau, Muir, and Leopold to contemporary voices, highlighting the shift from the self-sufficient individual to a relational ethic of interdependence, reciprocity, and care of place. It addresses feminist, ecocritical and indigenous critiques of the contemplative model and proposes an alternative framework where writing acts as a symbolic technology that reconfigures ecological sensibilities and forms of community. The common good is redefined as a living network between humans, more-than-humans, memories, territories and possible futures. Thus, environmental literature is presented as an ethical and political tool for imagining and building livable worlds.

This essay explores the role of intercultural education in promoting the common good, emphasising its importance in fostering pluralistic, equitable and democratic societies. The essay posits that,alongside education for peace and global citizenship, intercultural education nurtures democratic values by encouraging dialogue, critical reflection, and ethical awareness. Drawing on the work of thinkers such as Dewey and Freire, it also emphasises education's transformative power in combatting hate speech, racism and discrimination. Schools are presented as pivotal institutions in cultivating respect, tolerance, and solidarity, particularly in contexts of diversity and conflict. Through a case study on Global Civic Education, the essay lastly demonstrates how reflective educational practices can empower individuals to recognise and value cultural differences, thereby contributing to a more inclusive and sustainable society based on mutual understanding and shared responsibility.

Imagine an Ishikawa diagram (also known as a fishbone diagram or cause-and-effect diagram) where the word "introduction" and the reference to technological humanism appear at the tail end, providing the framework for development. The upper segments contain headings on the society of uncertainty (sharing a question for current education: who will guarantee that what is taught or learned will be useful for students in their future?); and artificial intelligence (cross-sectional layout); and in the lower parts, influencers (or people who offer another way of learning) and microlearning (as a training strategy inspired by brevity and precise granularity) are named. At the front, there are some final considerations that invite reflection on a reality that is constantly under construction, with actions and aspirations.

The work provides a comprehensive analysis of the concept of good administration, which is connected with the idea of the common interest or good, its legal framework, and its practical implications, drawing comparisons between the European and U.S. legal traditions. The core argument is that good administration is not merely a desirable moral goal, how it was until the end of the 20th century, but a current legal requirement that can be enforced through various mechanisms, including judicial review and administrative procedures. The document also explores the relationship between good administration, transparency, and the need to address cognitive biases in regulatory decision-making.

This paper analyses good administration in Spanish law, exploring its development in legislation and some implications. It is assumed that good administration is a new or third generation right, of fundamental right in the European Union. It is a new generation right, whose function is to permeate the functioning of public administrations, and citizens. In construing the right to good administration, we recognize it as a subjective right and we align ourselves is a new or third-generation right. This right has acquired the category of a new generation fundamental right, as stated by the Supreme Court. It is a basic and essential right of citizens, which includes, as a minimum, the right of the individual to have public administrations respond within a reasonable period of time to the requests made to them, responding to them in an explicit, consistent and well-reasoned manner. It is also a cross-cutting right.

Artificial Intelligence (AI) has begun to significantly influence the shaping of strategies and policies in the field of education, offering new opportunities and challenges. One of the main impacts of AI is its ability to enable personalized learning. Through adaptive learning systems, AI can analyze the needs and abilities of each student, providing tailored educational material and support. This not only improves educational outcomes but also helps reduce inequalities, as students with different skill levels can progress at their own pace. Moreover, AI assists in improving the management of educational institutions. By automating tasks such as grading, attendance tracking, and resource management, educators can focus more on teaching and creating quality educational experiences. At the same time, AI can be used to predict trends and analyze data, helping schools and policymakers make informed decisions about resource allocation and the development of new curricula.

The dual philosophical frameworks of Utilitarianism and Distributive Justice, This chapter critically examines the indispensable contributions of Myanmar migrant workers to Thailand's socio-economic structure through. Chapter argues that improving labor conditions to ensure equitable wages, and grant legal protections to migrant workers do not merely benefit the workers themselves but also serve the broader common good. By strengthening economic productivity, fostering social cohesion, and promoting sustainable development, Myanmar migrants could play a pivotal role in labor-intensive industries such as agriculture, construction, and manufacturing sectors of Thailand in long term. Depend on Thailand's economic growth in Migrant workers, paper argue that precarious working conditions and limited legal protections are still a matters for migrant development.

The administration of Vocational High Schools (EPAL) in Greece has undergone significant transformations due to the influence of contemporary political theories. These theories have shaped the policies and governance models adopted by school administrators, affecting decision-making processes, leadership styles, and institutional priorities. The impact of these theories can be observed in areas such as democratic governance, neoliberal reforms, inclusivity, and social justice. One of the most prominent political theories influencing the administration of EPALs is democratic governance. Rooted in liberal democratic thought, this approach emphasizes participatory decision-making, accountability, and transparency. School administrators are expected to involve teachers, students, and parents in the governance process, ensuring that policies are developed through consultation and collective input. This participatory model aligns with broader European Union directives that encourage stakeholder engagement in educational administration.

This chapter per the authors examines how political theories—neoliberalism, social democracy, and Marxism—influence school building funding in Europe and Greece, highlighting the European Union's dual role as promoter of cohesion and neoliberal reform. A comparative analysis of eight European countries and a Greek case study reveals systemic inequalities worsened by austerity, decentralization, and ideological conflicts. Key challenges include climate adaptation, digital divides, and demographic changes. The chapter advocates for context-sensitive, equitable, and sustainable infrastructure solutions, emphasizing the need to balance market efficiency with social justice in educational investment.

This chapter scrutinizes the context and the critical conditions that shaped the Greek digital governance, and its impact on Greek educators. A critical review of the longitudinal digital culture of policymakers and unions will shed light on the country's digital agenda, the trajectory of its digital transition and the ecosystem in which the contemporary Greek educators' professional identity has been forged. Greece still lags behind in digital maturity, consistently ranking among Europe's lowest. The establishment of educational institutions and structured initiatives, such as Pedagogical Guidance Counselors-Mentors in teacher induction and official lifelong professional development teacher training programs through the formation of virtual professional learning communities and networks, can foster a culture of digital connectivism, peer collaboration, co-creativity and innovation. However, the country needs to accelerate the cultivation of a holistic and coherent digital culture that goes beyond the mere acceptance or cursory adoption of new technologies by professional capital.

Preface

INTRODUCTION

The pursuit of the common good has long been a central concern of political theory, threading its way through centuries of philosophical and humanistic inquiry. In assembling this volume, *Political Theory, History, and Modern Practice for the Common Good*, our aim has been to foreground a particular tradition within that broader intellectual landscape—one that places the reflections of humanists and writers, rather than solely jurists or political theorists, at the heart of political thought.

From the late medieval period through early modernity and into the modern era, thinkers across the humanities have engaged with the question of how best to realize the common good. This tradition, rooted in the rebirth of classical learning and the enduring legacy of humanism, positioned the educated individual not merely as a scholar, but as a civic actor—a participant in the shaping of public life and the moral fabric of society, a *uomo civico* and *uomo rinascimentale*. Humanists viewed the interweaving of ethical, philosophical, and political reflection as essential to their intellectual vocation. The humanist was, by nature, a political being, with both the capacity and the responsibility to consider the well-being of the broader community.

While much attention in the study of political ideas has focused on legal theorists, political philosophers, and constitutional thinkers, this volume turns its gaze toward another cohort of influential figures. We examine the contributions of humanists and writers who, throughout the pre-modern and modern periods, reflected on governance, civic virtue, and the ideals of collective life—not from within formal political treatises, but through literature, moral philosophy, and cultural commentary. Their reflections, we argue, are no less vital to understanding the evolution of the concept of the common good.

This book is intended for a specialized audience, including university students and scholars in the fields of political theory, intellectual history, and the humanities more broadly. At the same time, we hope it will speak to a wider readership—anyone with an interest in the history of ideas, and in the enduring challenge of imagining a just and flourishing society.

ORGANIZATION OF THE BOOK

This volume opens with a return to antiquity in **Chapter 1**, which explores Plutarch's *Praecepta gerendae reipublicae* as a foundational text in classical political thought. The chapter analyzes how Plutarch employs *exempla virtutis*—moral exemplars drawn from Greece and Rome—as tools for instructing the political elites of his time. While rooted in the civic ideals of the classical polis, Plutarch reinterprets these virtues within the framework of the Roman Empire, advocating both the autonomy of Greek cities and their loyalty to imperial authority. His vision of the common good balances nostalgic admiration for classical values with a pragmatic acceptance of imperial order.

Continuing the classical thread, **Chapter 2** focuses on the political thought of Dio Chrysostom during the High Roman Empire. Through his orations on monarchy and civic life, Dio articulates a nuanced relationship between the authority of the emperor and the autonomy of the city. Drawing from Hellenistic and Roman traditions, he champions both monarchy and the *polis* as complementary institutions central to human flourishing. The chapter highlights how provincial and senatorial elites reconciled these two forces to preserve Roman *libertas* and Greek civic identity, situating their synthesis as a model of good governance in a pluralistic empire.

In **Chapter 3**, the focus shifts to the late medieval and early Renaissance context with a study of Francesc Eiximenis, a Catalan thinker whose *Regiment de la cosa pública* offers a vibrant contribution to civic humanism. Rooted in theological and philosophical traditions, Eiximenis develops a theory of governance deeply concerned with moral integrity and the dangers of tyranny and corruption. The chapter presents an accessible anthology of key passages—in translations both into English and Spanish— to demonstrate the enduring relevance of his thought, particularly for contemporary political actors and civic leaders.

Chapter 4 turns to the educational dimension of the common good, framing pedagogy as a means to reclaim community, territory, and citizenship as active and relational constructs. In the face of neoliberal privatization and social fragmentation, the chapter argues for an "educating community" model, in which schools and civic institutions become spaces for democratic participation and social justice. Education is not only a site of knowledge transmission, but a political and ethical force for reimagining public life and fostering shared responsibility.

The evolving forms of collective life are further explored in **Chapter 5**, which reconsiders the sharing economy through the lens of political theory. While often discussed in terms of market innovation, this chapter repositions the sharing economy as a contemporary iteration of older communal practices tied to municipal governance and social solidarity. Drawing on examples such as citizen co-ownership of local infrastructure, it proposes a vision of the economy where civic participation and public good converge, reframing economic exchange as a form of democratic co-creation.

In **Chapter 6,** we move into the environmental humanities with an analysis of American nature writing as a vehicle for political reflection on ecological justice. From Thoreau to contemporary voices, nature writing emerges as a tradition that links care of place to care of community. Challenging the myth of individual self-sufficiency, the chapter foregrounds relational ethics and environmental interdependence, presenting literature as both a mirror and a catalyst for reshaping political imaginaries around sustainability and the common good.

Chapter 7 revisits the transformative potential of education, this time through the lens of intercultural and global civic education. Drawing from thinkers like Dewey and Freire, the chapter highlights the capacity of schools to nurture democratic values, especially in contexts of cultural diversity and social tension. By promoting empathy, dialogue, and critical engagement, intercultural education becomes a foundation for a more inclusive, tolerant, and just society. A case study on global civic education illustrates how reflective pedagogy can empower individuals to embrace pluralism as a civic virtue.

Chapter 8, a meditation on technological humanism and the changing landscape of contemporary education. Structured metaphorically around an Ishikawa (fishbone) diagram, the chapter diagnoses the challenges of the "society of uncertainty," from the rapid rise of artificial intelligence to the influence of digital microlearning and online personalities. It calls for a reimagining of educational practices in light of these dynamics, proposing a humanistic approach that remains agile, ethical, and committed to building meaningful learning experiences in a world in constant flux.

Chapter 9 introduces a comparative legal analysis between the European right to good administration and the U.S. "hard look" doctrine, grounded in the evolving field of behavioral law and economics. The chapter argues that good administration has transitioned from a normative ideal to a legally enforceable right, increasingly tied to democratic transparency, administrative accountability, and the correction of cognitive biases in public decision-making. In doing so, it expands the concept of the common good to include procedural fairness and rational governance, emphasizing the legal and institutional mechanisms that ensure public administration serves the citizen effectively.

Chapter 10 builds on this legal foundation by exploring the development of good administration in the context of Spanish administrative law. Defined as a third-generation fundamental right in the European legal framework, good administration is shown to have significant practical implications for how citizens interact with state institutions. The chapter identifies key aspects of this right—timely, coherent, and reasoned responses from public authorities—as essential components of democratic legitimacy and social trust. As such, the legal construction of good administration directly shapes citizens' experience of justice and collective governance.

Shifting to the intersection of governance and technology, **Chapter 11** explores the transformative impact of artificial intelligence on educational policy and institutional strategy. AI's capacity for personalized learning and data-informed decision-making opens new pathways for addressing educational inequalities and improving administrative efficiency. However, the chapter also invites critical reflection on how AI reshapes the public good in education—highlighting the need for inclusive policies that balance innovation with ethical safeguards, equitable access, and pedagogical integrity.

Chapter 12 applies the philosophical lenses of utilitarianism and distributive justice to the lived experiences of Myanmar migrant workers in Thailand. The chapter foregrounds the central role these workers play in Thailand's economic development and argues that ensuring their rights—through fair wages, legal protections, and humane working conditions—is not only a matter of justice, but also integral to the broader common good. In so doing, it offers a compelling account of how migration, labor policy, and economic justice converge within the frameworks of political theory and practical governance.

In **Chapter 13**, the influence of contemporary political theories—such as democratic governance, neoliberalism, and social justice—on the administration of Greece's Vocational High Schools (EPAL)—is examined. This chapter reveals how administrative decisions in education are not merely technical but deeply political. It illustrates how participatory governance models, encouraged by EU directives, are reshaping school leadership and stakeholder involvement, aligning educational administration more closely with democratic values and inclusive practices.

Chapter 14 continues this line of inquiry by examining the funding of school infrastructure in Europe and Greece through the prism of political theory. Drawing from neoliberal, social democratic, and Marxist frameworks, the chapter investigates how ideologies influence investment strategies, particularly during periods of austerity. It critically analyzes the role of the EU in promoting both cohesion and market-based reforms, and calls for equitable, context-sensitive solutions that prioritize social justice, environmental sustainability, and educational equity.

Chapter 15 deepens the focus on Greece by assessing how digital governance reforms have influenced the professional identity and development of educators.

Despite ongoing digital transitions, Greece continues to lag in overall digital maturity. This chapter explores the tension between policy aspirations and practical implementation, arguing for a more coherent, culturally embedded digital agenda. It highlights the potential of professional learning networks, peer collaboration, and mentorship programs in fostering an adaptive and innovation-driven educational culture aligned with the common good.

In a unique blend of literature and political reflection, **Chapter 16** turns to the ancient *Greek Tales on Papyrus*, where mythical dynasties pass on the values of good governance through storytelling. These tales, which include figures such as Ninus, Semiramis, and Calligone, are not only literary artifacts but also pedagogical tools, transmitting civic virtues from one generation to the next. Reimagined as card game characters, these figures serve as imaginative vehicles for discussing continuity, leadership, and ethical governance, underscoring the enduring power of narrative in shaping political consciousness.

Chapter 17 addresses the urgent need for adult informatics educators in the Greek and European public sectors. Through the lens of human capital theory and lifelong learning frameworks, this chapter positions adult education as a critical lever for economic resilience, social inclusion, and democratic participation in the digital age. Informatics educators, in particular, play a pivotal role in equipping citizens with the skills needed to navigate technological change and engage meaningfully in the labor market and civil society alike.

Together, these final chapters reinforce the central theme of the volume: that the common good is not a static ideal, but a dynamic and evolving principle that must be continually reinterpreted in light of legal reforms, educational strategies, labor realities, technological transformations, and historical traditions. Through diverse case studies and theoretical engagements, this book affirms the enduring importance of political theory—both classical and contemporary—in guiding modern practices for a more just, inclusive, and humane society.

CONCLUSION

As editors of *Political Theory, History, and Modern Practice for the Common Good*, we have sought to curate a volume that not only spans time and geography, but also disciplines and perspectives. From classical antiquity to contemporary debates on digital governance, from humanist reflections to legal innovations and educational reform, and spanning a large swath of European geography, each chapter contributes to a shared inquiry: How has the idea of the common good been imagined, contested, and redefined across different political and cultural contexts?

This book demonstrates that the common good is neither a static concept nor a purely theoretical ideal. It is a living principle—one shaped by historical experience, political imagination, and institutional practice. It requires both memory and innovation, drawing on past wisdom while remaining attentive to the demands of a changing world. Whether expressed through civic humanism, legal rights, educational policy, or environmental ethics, the common good challenges us to think beyond individual interest and to consider the conditions under which collective life can flourish.

We hope that this volume will serve not only as a resource for scholars and students, but also as a contribution to ongoing public debates about justice, governance, and the responsibilities we share as members of political communities. In bringing together voices from different disciplines, traditions, and regions, our goal has been to foster a dialogue that is at once critical and constructive—one that affirms the enduring relevance of political theory in shaping modern practice for the good of all.

Chapter 1
Plutarch's Praecepta Gerendae Reipublicae: The Exempla Virtutis as a Theory of Good Governance

Aránzazu Calzada
https://orcid.org/0000-0002-6061-6523
Universidad de Alicante, Spain

ABSTRACT

This chapter seeks to tackle Plutarch's work on good governance (the normally known as Praecepta gerendi reipublicae) to note the role it plays in his political thinking. We shall focus on the exempla virtutis that the author proposes to teach good government to young people. These virtues have their roots in classical Greece and Rome, and in the polis system, but the context of the Roman Empire leads Plutarch to reinterpret them and place them within their proper limits. The figure of the emperor acts as a bond of union between the citizen elites and the senatorial elites and Plutarch preaches both the freedom and autonomy of the Greek cities and the submission to the empire as the architect of the pax Romana. The exempla of the past, of the classical polis, are admired, but discouraged by Plutarch as risky and a possible cause of confrontation with the Romans.

INTRODUCTION

Certainly, political theory for the common good has occupied philosophers, writers and humanists, not only in the modern era, but also, fundamentally, in classical antiquity. Concern for the good of rulers and the pursuit of the common good has

DOI: 10.4018/979-8-3373-2332-9.ch001

been a preoccupation since ancient times, especially, as far as we are concerned, in the Greco-Roman world.

Plutarch, the great Greek polygraph, born in Chaeronea (Boeotia), around 50 AD, when Greece was part of the Roman Empire, famous for his *Parallel Lives* and, as far as this site is concerned, for his *Moral Works* (*Moralia*), had a notable influence, through his prolific work, on the thinking of authors such as Montaigne and Shakespeare; it is even said that Napoleon always carried one of his books with him, together with Goethe's *Werther*. Be that as it may, if humanism represented a renaissance of the interrelation between philosophical reflection and politics, the classical authors who laid the foundations for the later renaissance cannot be ignored.

Plutarch is not only an extremely influential figure in our culture, but his value as an educator has placed him even earlier among the poets than among the philosophers. The figure of the polymatician of Chaeronea was thus interpreted in Shelley's famous *Defence of Poetry*. This is, in a way, our starting point. Here the romantic poet vindicates the function of poetry as a social reformer and the role of the poet as prophet and educator at the same time. Plutarch is included among the poets along with Plato or Herodotus, while, paradoxically, Shakespeare or Milton are among the philosophers. This idea of Shelley's reflects in part the pedagogical value that Plutarch's works have assumed, particularly in the training of politicians and soldiers. Plutarch, like Plato, exalts life, beauty, understood also as moral beauty, (Sanders, 1994).

If this exaltation of moral beauty can be seen in anything, it is in the use of *exempla virtutis* as a means of educating in ethics. This instrument, which originated in rhetoric and was taken up by the Stoics, permeates Plutarch's entire work and is one of the factors that most contributes to linking him to Roman culture. Or, if you like, this element of Greek origin was so intimately taken over by Roman culture that it endowed it with new characteristics, increased its importance and thus contributed to being a link between East and West.

To do so, we will focus our analysis on one of his texts: *Political councils (Praecepta gerendae reipublicae),* considered a reference in terms of good government. Written in the author's maturity and in the form of a diatribe, it forms part, together with three other works, of a *corpus politicum* plutarqueo, compiled at the end of the 13th century by Maximus Planudes under the title *Moralia*. We shall see how the division of Plutarch's work is less radical than it seems, and it is precisely the use of *exempla* that demonstrates this most clearly.

At the request of a wealthy young man, Menemachus, who wishes to enter politics and seeks his advice, Plutarch writes a treatise on the actions of the ruler and summarises the motives that encourage a young man to devote himself to public life, the ways to get there, the most appropriate behaviour whatever the position attained, and the need to place the common good above all other pretensions.

In the following lines we will try to define what the *exemplum virtutis* is, outline its importance in Roman culture and highlight how it appears throughout Plutarch's work as the main eloquent resource. More importantly, we will highlight how this resource became integrated into the Roman world and served as a means of defining good government through the exaltation of moral virtues. All of this, of course, reinterpreted according to the demands of 2nd century AD politics. To sum up, we aim to assess to what extent the moral example has, apart from a pedagogical value, the function of incardinating the Greek or Roman citizen within his own community, while allowing him to take charge of his own history, and, not least, how good government and the common good are recognized in the practice of these civic virtues, initially conceived for a city state, but in Plutarch's time, reinterpreted to justify the *pax Romana*.

PLUTARCH AND THE *EXEMPLA VIRTUTIS* AND THESE AS AN ELEMENT OF UNITY IN HIS WORK

From the very first chapter Plutarch refers to the *exempla* (*paradeigmata*) as the central motif of what is presented as a letter to a noble young man with a political vocation.

> *ρ ν ο ν σε παρωρμημένον ξίως τ ς ε γενείας ν τ πατρίδι μύθων τε ητ ρ΄ μεναι πρηκτ ρά τε ργων, πειδ χρόνον ο κ χεις νδρ ς φιλοσόφου βίον παιθρον ν πράξεσι πολιτικα ς κα δημοσίοις γ σι κατανο σαι κα γενέσθαι παραδειγμάτων ργ μ λόγ περαινομένων θεατής, ξιο ς δ παραγγέλματα λαβε ν πολιτικά, τ ν μ ν ρνησιν ο δαμ ς μαυτ προσήκουσαν ε ναι νομίζω, τ δ΄ ργον ε χομαι κα τ ς σ ς ξιον σπουδ ς κα τ ς μ ς προθυμίας γενέσθαι· το ς δ παραδείγμασι ποικιλωτέροις, σπερ ξίωσας, χρησάμην.*
> (*"Therefore, seeing that the desire has been aroused in you a*
> *Speaker of speeches to be, and also a doer of actions)*

In your native State, as befits your noble birth, since you have not time to gain an understanding of a philosopher's life in the open among affairs of State and public conflicts or to be a spectator of examples worked out in deed, not merely in word, Cand since you ask for some precepts of statecraft, I think it is not at all fitting that I should refuse, and I pray that the result may be worthy of your zeal and of my goodwill; and, as you requested, I have made use of a rather large variety of examples." (We make use of the translation by H. N. Fowler, published in the Loeb Classical Library edition (1936) and now in the public domain. The translations we quote are also in the public domain and can be accessed online.

Glossing a quotation from Homer (Il. IX 443), a very common rhetorical procedure, Plutarch refers to the exempla he is going to use, revealing that they are not just a matter of words, vain rhetoric, but an incitement to do good. This underlines the idea that moral exemplars are an essential reference in political life and the way to achieve the common good of society.

As pointed. out above, the method of the *exempla* in Plutarch is more than a pedagogical model or a narrative framework. In the *exempla* the author's attention is focused on certain biographies to which he confers a model value, a value for shaping the conduct of new generations by following the actions of the greatest figures of past ages. This method can be found, naturally, in the *Parallel Lives*, but it is also present in that group of works which are grouped together in the Middle Ages under the title of *Moralia* (θικά). This is the case of the *Praecepta gerendae reipublicae*, a work to train future politicians in the moral canons valued by the elites of the 2nd century AD.

Recently, the Italian philologist Alberto Barzanò has paid attention to this aspect of Plutarch's work, the use of *exempla*, and has even related them to hagiography, (Barzanò 1994). This is not entirely new, at least as applied to other authors. We know, for example, how hagiographic texts are influenced in some way (not as much as might be claimed at first sight) by third century authors such as the Lives of the philosophers and sophists by Eunapius of Sardis or the well-known Life of Apollonius of Tyana, by Philostratus. The novelty of Barzanò's approach, in our opinion, is to relate political ethics to the examples of the rhetoricians and the relationship he establishes between the common good and the cultivation of such virtues. This, especially in the following centuries, links Plutarch's way of narrating with the hagiographers. In Plutarch's biographical works, the use of *exempla* has been a much-studied topic in recent years. Regardless of the genre cultivated by the author, the use of *exempla* as a role model is a common defining feature of his work.

Although minor differences can be noted between the role played by *exempla* in biographies and in moral opuscules, the separation between these two types of works is completely arbitrary. We know that in the late Byzantine period, as early as the 13th century and by the hand of Maximus Planudes, the so-called *Moralia* were compiled and that when they reached the West in the Middle Ages and especially after the first Aldine edition (1509) both types of works were published separately. This obscures many common features and ignores the unity of Plutarch's work, (Geiger, 2008).

Even if small differences can be noted between the role played by *exempla* in biographies and in the moral tracts, the separation between these two types of works is completely arbitrary. We know that in the late Byzantine period, as early as the 13th century and by the hand of Maximus Planudes, the so-called *Moralia* were compiled, and that when they reached the West in the Middle Ages, and especially from the first Aldine edition (1509) onwards, both types of works were published separately. This hides many common features and ignores the unity of Plutarch's work, (Geiger, 2008).

The difference is that in a biography Plutarch announces the *exemplum* he is going to develop right from the foreword and, in many cases, he contrasts the positive example with a negative one, as in the case of Agesilaus and Pompey, (Jacobs, 2017). In one of his moral opuscules he dwells on a multitude of examples, from which he draws certain conclusions about the political conduct appropriate to his historical moment, and this links him to other authors of Greek literature from the Roman period, as well as Latin literature.

This is the case of the *Praecepta gerendae reipublicae*, which has recently been studied precisely in connection with the *Parallel Lives*, (Alexiou, 2008). Plutarch's approach in the work we are about to discuss focuses on *eunoia* as a virtue and examines its influence on the political career. *Eunoia* is to be understood as *philanthropia* (Alexiou, 2008) and in Greek it means something more than goodwill, because its semantic content includes elements such as predisposition to help, benevolence. It is a concept that dominates the political theory of Isocrates (De Romilly 1958 p. 92) and influences Plutarch through this author. Good government for Plutarch is in some way linked to the exercise of this virtue, i.e., *eunoia*.

In the biographies, on the other hand, the problem is considered from another, more realistic point of view, since the subject is success in the political and military career, in which *eunoia* and its relation to virtue is essential, but also the dealings with the members of the community. It is not about advising a young man interested in a political career, but rather about the description of the character and the actual conditions of his career, (Alexiou, 2008).

THE CONSOLIDATION OF *EXEMPLA VIRTUTIS* IN ROMAN CULTURE: RHETORIC AND POLITICAL *PAIDEIA* FOR GOOD GOVERNMENT

Brenk has recently pointed out a trend in the use of this rhetorical device in which both Greek and Roman authors agree in the 2nd century AD. In fact, in Rome the use of *exempla* had a remarkable tradition at that time in history, going back to classical Greece. Aristotle (Arist. *Rhet.* II 20 1394a) presents the *exemplum* (in Greek *paradeigma*, the Latin version is due to Cicero) as a real or invented story that serves to persuade. Seneca *(ad Luc.* VI 5) goes so far as to contrast *principia* and *exempla* and confers more effectiveness to the latter if principles are to be transmitted, (Chaplin, 2000; Brenk, 2008). Of course, the nature of what is real and what is invented does not correspond to our standards.

Mittam itaque ipsos tibi libros et ne multum operae inpendas, dum passim profutura sectaris, inponam notas, ut ad ipsa protinus, quae probo et miror, accedas. Plus tamen tibi et viva vox et convictus quam oratio proderit. In rem praesentem venias oportet, primum, quia homines amplius oculis quam auribus credunt; deinde, quia longum iter est per praecepta, breve et efficax per exempla.
("I shall therefore send to you the actual books; and in order that you may not waste time in searching here and there for profitable topics, I shall mark certain passages, so that you can turn at once to those which I approve and admire. Of course, however, the living voice and the intimacy of a common life will help you more than the written word. You must go to the scene of action, first, because men put more faith in their eyes than in their ears, and second, because the way is long if one follows precepts, but short and helpful, if one follows patterns" Translation by Richard Mott Gummere).

Aristotle reminds us that historical facts are more effective in politics than invented history, although fables, which are by nature fiction, can be useful in an assembly. This is the context in which Plutarch's work is set. Both he and other authors of the Second Sophistic would, for example, draw on Homer to reflect on politics, the human condition and destiny, to cite just a few examples. And, as far as historical material is concerned, from the beginning of the imperial era there is a desire to collect exemplary cases or anecdotes with moral value, such as Valerius Maximus or Veleius Paterculus.

We have seen how the presence of *exempla* unites the *Moralia* and the Parallel Lives. Despite the title, this phenomenon can be clearly observed in the *Praecepta*. Mayer (1991) starts from a too radical separation of the two genres, but he detects very correctly that the use of *exempla* increases in Roman authors and that Plutarch was influenced by them. The technical use of *exemplum* in Latin is, as we have stated, earlier, but it was Seneca (Ep. XCVIII 12) who coined it definitively, (Litchfield, 1914), who, in using moral exempla, stated that he wanted to be seen in this way by posterity *(Ep.* 98 13):

Nos quoque aliquid et ipsi faciamus animose; simus inter exempla.
("Let us also, therefore, carry out some courageous act of our own accord; let us be included among the ideal types of history.")

But this statement is part of a list of *exempla* of obvious moral value in the field of politics:

Dic tibi, ex istis, quae terribilia videntur, nihil est invictum. Singula vicere iam multi: ignem Mucius, crucem Regulus, venenum Socrates, exilium Rutilius, mortem ferro adactam Cato; et nos vincamus aliquid! Rursus ista, quae ut speciosa et felicia trahunt volgum, a multis et saepe contempta sunt: Fabricius divitias imperator reiecit, censor notavit. Tubero paupertatem et se dignam et Capitolio iudicavit, cum fictilibus in publica cena usus ostendit debere iis hominem esse contentum quibus di etiam nunc uterentur. Honores reppulit pater Sextius, qui ita natus ut rem publicam deberet capessere, latum clavum divo lulio dante non recepit; intellegebat enim quod dari posset, et eripi posse. Nos quoque aliquid et ipsi faciamus animose: simus inter exempla. Quare deficimus ? quare desperamus ? quicquid fieri potuit, potest.
("Of all these experiences that seem so frightful, none is insuperable. Separate trials have been overcome by many: fire by Mucius, crucifixion by Regulus, poison by Socrates, exile by Rutilius, and a sword-inflicted death by Cato; therefore, let us also overcome something." Again, those objects which attract the crowd under the appearance of beauty and happiness, have been scorned by many men and on many occasions. Fabricius when he was general refused riches, and when he was censor branded them with disapproval. Tubero deemed poverty worthy both of himself and of the deity on the Capitol when, by the use of earthenware dishes at a public festival, he showed that man should be satisfied with that which the gods could still use. The elder Sextius rejected the honors of office; he was born with an obligation to take part in public affairs, and yet would not accept the broad stripe even when the deified Julius offered it to him. For he understood that what can be given can also be taken away. Let us also, therefore, carry out some courageous act of our own accord; let us be included among the ideal types of history. Why have we been slack? Why do we lose heart?").

Since the use of *exempla*, although earlier, developed mainly among the Stoics, it is believed that it is the influence of Posidonius that determines this rhetorical turn in favour of *exempla* and their use in Rome. Undoubtedly, the influence of Panaetius is present in Cicero *(De off.* II 16; 76), (Sedley, 1999).

Cic. (*De off.* II 76)

Laudat Africanum Panaetius, quod fuerit abstinens. Quidni laudet? Sed in illo alia maiora; laus abstinentiae non hominis est solum, sed etiam temporum illorum.
("Panaetius praises Africanus for his integrity in public life. Why should he not? But Africanus had other and greater virtues. The boast of official integrity belongs not to that man alone but also to his times").

As we can see, Panaetius' quotation refers to a Roman *exempluum*. The exempla would become a feature of Roman culture, as can be seen in Cicero (Rambaud 1953 pp. 25-34) or in Titus Livy, (Chaplin, 2000). Exempla become much more than a rhetorical exercise, for they signify the development of *virtus* through the generations, since their repetition creates the imago virtutis which persuades by itself, (Mayer, 1991).

THE *EXEMPLA VIRTUTIS* IN THE *PRAECEPTA GERENDAE REIPUBLICAE* BY PLUTARCH: GOOD GOVERNANCE FROM THE PERSPECTIVE OF THE PROVINCIAL ELITES ALLIED WITH ROME

At no point should it be forgotten that the context of the Second Sophistic has much to do with the Greek elites of the cities, who justify its existence as a means of communication with the Roman authorities. These authors, and especially Plutarch, are well acquainted with Roman culture and indifferently resort to *exempla* that correspond to it alongside those of their own tradition. Good government is presented as the main consequence of virtue, originally understood as military virtue (derived from the term *vir*), later also as both political and moral virtue. With the onset of Christianity, the consideration of virtue from an aspect even more closely linked to morality did not marginalize the *exempla* of Roman history or their civic value; on the contrary, they maintained their role in the pedagogy of politicians and in the ideal of good government. St. Augustine himself will say:

Aug. *Civ. Dei*, V I6:

> *Merces autem sanctorum longe alia est etiam hic opprobria sustinentium pro ueritate Dei, quae mundi huius dilectoribus odiosa est. Illa ciuitas sempiterna est; ibi nullus oritur, quia nullus moritur; ibi est uera et plena felicitas, non dea, sed donum Dei; inde fidei pignus accepimus, quandiu peregrinantes eius pulchritudini suspiramus; ibi non oritur sol super bonos et malos, sed sol iustitiae solos protegit bonos; ibi non erit magna industria ditare publicum aerarium priuatis rebus angustis, ubi thensaurus communis est ueritatis. Proinde non solum ut talis merces talibus hominibus redderetur Romanum imperium ad humanam gloriam dilatatum est; uerum etiam ut ciues aeternae illius ciuitatis, quamdiu hic peregrinantur, diligenter et sobrie illa intueantur exempla et uideant quanta*

dilectio debeatur supernae patriae propter uitam aeternam, si tantum a suis ciuibus terrena dilecta est propter hominum gloriam.
("And, therefore, it was not only for the sake of recompensing the citizens of Rome that her empire and glory had been so signally extended, but also that the citizens of that eternal city, during their pilgrimage here, might diligently and soberly contemplate these examples, and see what a love they owe to the supernal country on account of life eternal, if the terrestrial country was so much beloved by its citizens on account of human glory".)

Within the Stoic tradition, Roman elites used certain virtues with civic value and developed a properly Roman scheme around them. As Litchfield (1914) explains:

"Of the distinctively moral virtues, those most often enforced by exemplary citation appear to be: *iustitia (aequitas)*; *fides*; *pietas erga deos, patriam, parentes, ceteros*; *severitas (disciplina militaris); fortitudo; constantia (et in morte propinquorum) = patientia; continentia; paupertas X luxuria; dementia; moderatio X ambitio (petulantia)* - with their opposites, the less obvious of which I have indicated. Less frequently cited are *amicitia (concordia); gratia; observantia; gravitas; munificentia (liberalitas) X avaritia*. Someone of these qualities, and of these only, forms the theme of nearly every appeal to the exemplum in Latin authors".

The procedure of identifying specific civic virtues and glossing concrete *exempla* of them is a rhetorical device which, as we have noted above, Plutarch uses throughout his work. In the case of the *Praecepta* the reference to virtues and their protagonists is more extensive but less intense than in the biographies dedicated to a certain character, but in reality, to highlight the virtues of that particular character, which implies going deeper into his character. But the idea that good government depends on the cultivation of certain virtues is the foundation of both types of plutarchic work.

One of the causes of this exaltation of civic moral examples in antiquity and especially in Rome is the presence of war in political life, which demands a heroic or at least a calm and reflective attitude at all times. The examples to which the author resorts place us, moreover, in the real context of his time, which relativises to a large extent the scope of certain *exempla* or reduces them to their limits.

In order to comment on the main features of Plutarch's opuscule, we believe it is necessary to comment directly on some of its most important fragments. We shall begin by commenting on a particularly long text, but in our opinion necessary to understand the context in which we are moving, and also to observe how Plutarch integrates the *exempla* and reinterprets them according to the political situation of his time.

We refer to chapter 10, where the advice on political life for good governance and personal success is based both on glorious historical moments highly valued by the Greek civic elites, and on the imperatives of the reality of the moment.

10 ο μ ν γ ρ ε θ ς σπερ ξ κραςπελαγ ου πρ ξεως πιφανο ς κα μεγ λης χο σης δ τ λμαν ραντες φ καν π τ ν πολιτε αν, γο μενοι λ γειν ρθ ς τ ν Π νδαρον ς ρχομ νου δ΄ ργου πρ σωπον χρ θ μεν τηλαυγ ς· κα γ ρ δ χονταιπροθυμ τερον ο πολλο κ ρ τιν κα πλησμον τ ν συν θων τ ν ρχ μενον, σπερ γωνιστ ν θεατα , κα τ ν φθ νον κπλ ττουσιν α λαμπρ ν χουσαι κα ταχε αν α ξησιν ρχα κα δυν μεις. ο τε γ ρ π ρ φησιν ρ στων καπν ν ποιε ν ο τε δ ξαν φθ νον, ν ε θ ς κλ μψ κα ταχ ως, λλ τ ν κατ μικρ ν α ξανομ νων κα σχολα ως λλον λλαχ θεν πιλαμβ νεσθαι· δι πολλο πρ ν νθ σαιπερ τ β μα κατεμαρ νθησαν. που δ΄, σπερ π το Λ δαλ γουσιν, ψ φος ν σπληγος ν ο ασιν, νθα κ στεφανο τοπρεσβε ων θριαμβε ων στρατηγ ν πιφαν ς, ο θ΄ ο φθονο ντεσ ο θ΄ ο καταφρονο ντες μο ως π τοιο των σχ ουσιν. ο τωπαρ λθεν ε ς δ ξαν ρατος, ρχ ν ποιησ μενος πολιτε ας τ ν Νικοκλ ους το τυρ ννου κατ λυσιν· ο τως λκιβι δης, τ Μαντινικ συστ σας π Λακεδαιμον ους. Πομπ ιος δ κα θριαμβε ειν ξ ου μ πω παρι ν ε ς σ γκλητον· ο κ ντος δ Σ λλα, "πλε ονες" φη "τ ν λιον νατ λλοντα προσκυνο σιν δυ μενον"· κα Σ λλας πε ξε το τ΄ κο σας. κα Σκιπ ωνα δ Κορν λιον ο κ φ΄ ς τυχεν ρχ ς ωμα ων δ μος γορανομ αν μετερχ μενον ξα φνης πατον π δειξε παρ τ ν ν μον, λλ θαυμ σας α το μειρακ ου μ ν ντος τ ν ν βηρ μονομαχ αν κα ν κην, μικρ ν δ΄ στερον τ πρ ς Καρχηδ νι χιλιαρχο ντος ργα, περ ν κα Κ των πρεσβ τερος νεφ νησεν ο ος π πνυται, το δ σκια σσουσιν.

There are two entrances to public life and two paths leading to it: one the quick and brilliant road to reputation, by no means without risk, the other more prosaic and slower, but safer. For some men launch out at once into political life with some conspicuous, great, and daring action, like men who launch a vessel from a promontory that juts out into the sea; they think Pindar is right in saying:

> To a work's beginning we needs must set
> A front that shines afar,

for the masses are more ready to accept the beginner because they are so palled and surfeited with those to whom they are accustomed, just as spectators at a show are glad to accept a new performer; and authority and power that has a brilliant and rapid growth takes envy's breath away. For, as Ariston says, fire does not cause smoke, nor reputation envy, if it blazes up quickly at the start, but those who grow great gradually and slowly are attacked one from one side, another from another;

hence many men before coming to full bloom as public speakers have withered away. But if, as is said of Ladas,

> The noise o' the barrier's fall was in his ears

even when he has been crowned for his brilliant success on an embassy, for a notable triumph, or for achievement as a general, in such instances neither those who envy a man nor those who despise him have so much power as before. In this way Aristion arrived at fame, beginning his public life with the destruction of the tyrant Nicocles; so Alcibiades, by making the Mantinean alliance against the Lacedaemonians. Pompey demanded a triumph although he had not yet been admitted to the senate, and when Sulla voted against it, he said, "More worship the rising than the setting sun"; and Sulla, when he heard this, withdrew his opposition. And take the case of Cornelius Scipio; it was not because of any chance beginning that the Roman people suddenly and contrary to law appointed him consul when he was a candidate for the aedileship, but rather because they admired his victorious single combat in Iberia when he was a mere youth, and his deeds a little later at Carthage as military tribune, about which Cato the Elder exclaimed

> He and he only has sense, the rest are mere flickering shadows").

Exemplifying the text with a quotation from Pindar *(Ol.* VI 4) and another from Homer *(Od.* XI.495), as usual in the authors of the Second Sophistic, Plutarch compares the quick and risky access to the political career with the calm but more pedestrian access to it. The *exempla* to which he resorts are, as usual, first Greeks and then Romans: Aratus and Alcibiades; Pompey, Sulla and Scipio.

Aratus was able to overthrow Nicocles, tyrant of Sicyon when he was very young, and Plutarch himself devoted a more extensive biography to this character, who is also well remembered in Latin sources (Cic. *de off.* II 23). Alcibiades too, as we know from Thucydides, in his youth promoted an aggressive policy against Sparta and achieved an alliance with Argos, Ellis, Mantineia and other cities of the Peloponnese. This was a rapid rise, but the reader of the time was well aware that this alliance was fatal for Athens and cost Alcibiades his first ostracism. Plutarch attributes to Cato the Elder the quotation from Homer celebrating Scipio despite his youth and precisely because of his military victories at Carthage. Earlier he refers to Pompey, whom Sulla had prevented from celebrating his triumph because of his youth and, according to Plutarch, Pompey himself replied that he owed more adoration to the rising sun than to the setting sun: τ ν λιον νατ λλοντα προσκυνο σιν δυ μενον.

To this anecdote we can add that of Scipio, who was promoted to the consulship for his military victories in Hispania when he should have been eligible to become aedile because of his age, and the praise of Cato the Elder by means of a quotation from Homer.

As is usual in the *Moralia*, the *exempla* - Greek and Roman - are apparently reduced to an anecdote, but this is significant enough to describe a character and, in the process, underline those qualities on which good rulership depends. In Plutarch's biographies, these virtues are explored in depth, but in works such as the one we are discussing they are reduced to an anecdote, as we have said, a significant one. In the *Vita Aemilii Pauli* Plutarch says that he sets aside every vice and will focus on the *exempla(paradeigma)* that are most useful to lead our thinking towards the most beautiful examples: πρ ς τ κ λλιστα τ ν παραδειμ των (Plut. *Aem.* 1.5).

This is emphasised in the *Moralia*, because in the *Vitae* there is more room for contrast with anti-heroes or greater psychological depth, (Barzanò 1994).

The second part of the text is in our opinion even more interesting because it serves in some way as a counterpoint to what we have seen so far: Plutarch, who understands that good government is due to the cultivation of certain civic virtues that he believes must be instilled in the young (in fact, the opuscle is conceived as an epistle) places here the freedom and the position of the citizens of the Greek *poleis* at the limit that could be expected from the Roman Empire. The aim is to realistically situate the political career in the 2nd century AD, when the cities did not have the importance, they had had in classical Greece, if we stick to the Greek models, or to the period of the Punic Wars if we think of the Roman *exempla.*

ν νο ν τε τ πρ γματα τ ν π λεων ο κ χει πολ μων γεμον ας ο δ τυρανν δων καταλ σεις ο δ συμμαχικ ς πρ ξεις, τ ν΄ ν τις ρχ ν πιφανο ς λ βοι κα λαμπρ ς πολιτε ας α δ και τε λε πονται α δημ σιαι κα πρεσβε αι πρ ς α τοκρ τορα νδρ ς διαπ ρου κα θ ρσος μα κα νο ν χοντος δε μεναι. πολλ δ΄ στι κα τ νπαρειμ νων ν τα ς π λεσι καλ ν ναλαμβ νοντα κα τ ν ξ θους φα λου παραδυομ νων π΄ α σχ ν τιν τ ς π λεως βλ β μεθιστ ντα πρ ς α τ ν πιστρ φειν. δη δ κα δ κη μεγ λη καλ ς δικασθε σα κα π στις ν συνηγορ πρ ς ντ δικον σχυρ ν π ρ σθενο ς κα   παρρησ α πρ ς γεμ να μοχθηρ ν π ρ το δικα ου κατ στησεν ν ους ε ς ρχ ν πολιτε ας νδοξον. ο κ λ γοι δ κα δι΄ χθρας η ξ θησαν, πιχειρ σαντες νθρ ποις π φθονον χουσιν ξ ωμα κα φοβερ ν· ε θ ς γ ρ το καταλυθ ντος σχ ς τ κρατ σαντι μετ   βελτ ονος δ ξης π ρχει. τ   μ ν γ ρ νδρ χρηστ κα δι΄ ρετ ν πρωτε οντι προσμ χεσθαι κατ φθ νον, ς Περικλε Σιμμ ας, λκμ ων δ Θεμιστοκλε , Πομπη   δ Κλ διος, παμειν νδ δ Μενεκλε δης   τωρ, ο τε πρ ς δ ξαν καλ ν ο τ΄ λλως συμφ ρον· ταν γ ρ ξαμαρτ ντες ο πολλο πρ ς νδρα χρηστ ν, ε θ΄ γ γνεται ταχ ως π΄ ργ μετανο σωσι, πρ ς το τ ν στην πολογ αν δικαιοτ την νομ ζουσιν, πιτρ ψαι τ ν ναπε σαντα κα   καταρξ μενον. τ   μ ντοι φα λον νθρωπον, πονο δ κα δειν τητι πεποιημ νον φ΄ α τ τ ν π λιν, ο ος ν Κλ ων θ νησι κα Κλεοφ ν, παναστ ντα καθελε ν κα ταπειν σαι λαμπρ ν ποιε ται τ ν π ροδον σπερ δρ ματος τ ς πολιτε ας. ο κ γνο δ΄ τι κα βουλ ν τινες παχθ κα λιγαρχικ ν κολο σαντες, σπερ φι λτης θ νησι κα Φορμ ων παρ΄ λε οις, δ ναμιν μακα δ ξαν σχον· λλ μ γας ρχομ ν πολιτε ας ο τος κ νδυν ς στι. δι κα βελτ ονα Σ λων λαβεν ρχ ν, διεστ σης ς τρ α μ ρη τ ς π λεως, τ τ ν Διακρ ων λεγομ νων κα τ τ ν Πεδι ων κα τ τ ν Παραλ ων· ο δεν γ ρ μμ ξας αυτ ν, λλ κοιν ς ν π σι κα π ντα λ γων κα πρ ττων πρ ς μ νοιαν ρ θη νομοθ της π τ ς διαλ σεις κα κατ στησεν ο τω τ ν ρχ ν. μ ν ο ν πιφανεστ ρα π ροδος ε ς τ ν πολιτε αν τοσα τας χει κα τοια τας ρχ ς.

("Nowadays, then, when the affairs of the cities no longer include leadership in wars, nor the overthrowing of tyrannies, nor acts of alliances, what opening for a conspicuous and brilliant public career could a young man find? There remain the public lawsuits and embassies to the emperor, which demand a man of ardent temperament and one who possesses both courage and intellect. But there are many excellent lines of endeavour that are neglected in our cities which a man may take up, and also many practices resulting from evil custom, that have insinuated themselves to the shame or injury of the city, which a man may remove, and thus turn them to account for himself. Indeed, in past times a just verdict gained in a great suit, or good faith in acting as advocate for a weak client against a powerful opponent, or boldness of speech in behalf of the right against a wicked ruler, has opened to some men a glorious entrance into public life. And not a few also have grown great through the enemies they have made by attacking men whose position made them enviable or caused them to be feared; for when such a man is overthrown his power passes at once, and with better reputation, to the man who overcame him. For attacking, through motives of envy, a good man who, on account of his virtue, is leader of the state, as Pericles was attacked by Simmias, Themistocles by Alcmeon, Pompey by Clodius, and Epameinondas by Menecleides the orator, is neither conducive to a good reputation nor advantageous in any other way; for when the people have committed a wrong against a good man and then (which happens quickly) repent of their anger, they think the easiest way to excuse themselves for this offence is the most just, namely, to destroy the man who was the author of it and persuaded them to commit it. On the other hand, to revolt against a bad man who by shameless audacity and cunning has made the city subject to himself, such as Cleon and Cleophon were at Athens, and to pull him down and humble him provides a glorious entrance upon the stage of public life. And I am not ignorant of the fact that some men by curtailing the power of an oppressive and oligarchical senate, as Ephialtes did at Athens and Phormio at Elis, have gained at the same time both power and glory; but to one who is just entering upon public life there is a great risk in this. Therefore Solon made a better beginning, when the State was divided into three factions called the Diacrians ("hill-folk"), the Pedieans ("plainsfolk"),

and the Paralians ("coastfolk"); for he entangled himself with none of them, but acted for all in common and said and did everything to bring about concord among them, so that he was chosen lawgiver to reconcile their differences and in this way established his rule. So many, then, and of such kinds are the more conspicuous ways of entering upon a public career").

We say that this is perhaps the most revealing quotation and that is why we have preferred to comment on it in its entirety because this paragraph qualifies what is expressed in the previous one. It is not possible in our time (ν νο ν), says Plutarch, to think that a young man can begin his political career as in those days:

ν νο ν τε τ πρ γματα τ ν π λεων ο κ χει πολ μων γεμον ας ο δ τυραννδων καταλ σεις ο δ συμμαχικ ς πρ ξεις, τ ν΄ ν τις ρχ ν πιφανο ς λ βοι κα λαμπρ ς πολιτε ας

The author wonders how, in the circumstances of the time, young people can excel in political careers. It is significant that he focuses on the city as the ideal means of development of the individual and speaks of the affairs of cities (τ πράγματα τ ν πόλεων) as a way of referring in general to politics. Young people in our day must discard wars and alliances as a means of beginning to achieve notoriety. There remain matters before the courts and - most telling of what the autonomy of the cities means - embassies to the emperor. The emperor played a decisive role in this new situation, for the *pax romana* was interpreted as a good to be served. That is why the cities defended their independence as a means of helping the emperor in the fight against his enemies. This is why Veyne (1999) says that these councils are both resigned and favourable to Roman domination. This scholar gives us other quotations (Aristides, Apollonius of Tyana...) where praise for the Romans, who are counterposed together with the Greeks to the barbarians, is also present.

Plutarch then reviews the merits of defending a weak person against a powerful person in court and points out that in the past others also began their careers in this way. He then elaborates on envy and cites examples (three Greek and one Roman) of how the most illustrious were attacked by the envy of others (Pericles by Simmias, Themistocles by Alcmeon, Pompey by Clodius, and Epameinondas by Menecleides).

This is followed by a pessimistic meditation on the people and democracy. Although the connection between the two themes is not clear, envy is the theme that serves to introduce this one. He states that the people, when they see an injustice, they have committed against a good man, try to repair it by destroying the cause of that injustice, the one who persuaded them to commit it. The problem of demagogy and populism that democracy entails is undoubtedly in Pericles' mind. and who persuaded them to commit it.

The *exempla* to which he resorts are again two characters from the Peloponnesian War, Cleon and Cleophon, proposed as models for those who begin by confronting a powerful person who acts unjustly. He then cites the case of Ephialtes, the reformer against the oligarchy, but Plutarch discourages such behavior and cites the conciliatory example of Solon.

The following statement serves to deepen the basic ideas of this opuscle.

[17] Φ σει μ ν ο ν ρχων ε π λεως πολιτικ ς σπερ γεμ ν νμελ τταις, κα το το χρ διανοο μενον χειν τ δημ σια δι χειρ ς
("Now the statesman is always by nature ruler of the State, like the leader bee in the hive, and bearing this in mind he ought to keep public matters in his own hands").

The term "stateman" is translating archon and states of him that by nature he is the one who must rule and draws on the image of the bees, whose queen (Plutarch speaks of the ruler of the bees: γεμ ν νμελ τταις) keeps control of the power.

ε σι ντα δ΄ ε ς πασαν ρχ ν ο μ νον κε νουςδε προχειρ ζεσθαι το ς λογισμο ς, ο ς Περικλ ς α τ ν πεμ μνησκεν ναλαμβ νων τ ν χλαμ δα, "πρ σεχε, Περ κλεις· λευθ ρων ρχεις, λλ νων ρχεις, πολιτ ν θηνα ων"· λλ κ κε νο λ γειν πρ ς αυτ ν, " ρχ μενος ρχεις, ποτεταγμ νηςπ λεως νθυπ τοις, πιτρ ποις Κα σαρος· ' 'ο τα τα λ γχη πεδι ς,'ο δ΄ α παλαια Σ ρδεις ο δ΄ Λυδ ν κε νη δ ναμις"·ε σταλεστ ραν δε τ νχλαμ δα ποιε ν, κα βλ πειν π το στρατηγ ου πρ ς τ β μα, κα τ στεφ ν μ πολ φρονε ν μηδ πιστε ειν, ρ ντα το ς καλτ ους π νω τ ς κεφαλ ς· λλ μιμε σθαιτο ς ποκριτ ς, π θος μ ν διον κα θος κα ξ ωμα τ γ νιπροστιθ ντας, το δ΄ ποβολ ως κο οντας κα μ παρεκβα νοντας το ς υθμο ς κα τ μ τρα τ ς διδμ νης ξουσ ας π τ νκρατο ντων.
17 ("And when entering upon any office whatsoever, you must not only call to mind those considerations of which Pericles reminded himself when he assumed the cloak of a general: "Take care, Pericles; you are ruling free men, you are ruling Greeks, Athenian citizens," but you must also say to yourself: "You who rule are a subject, ruling a State controlled by proconsuls, the agents of peace; 'these are not the spearmen of the plain,' nor is this ancient Sardis, nor the famed Lydian power." You should arrange your cloak more carefully and from the office of the generals keep your eyes upon the orators' platform and not have great pride or confidence in your crown, since you see the boots of Roman soldiers just above your head. No, you should imitate the actors, who, while putting into the performance their own passion, character, and reputation, yet listen to the prompter and do not go beyond the degree of liberty in rhythms and metres permitted by those in authority over them").

Again, the ideal of good government is the freedom that the Greeks consider their own, and refers to what Pericles was told when he took over military command, as opposed to other communities that were also under his command.

Plutarch frequently uses the image of music to indicate that the government of the Greek cities is subject to Roman rules and regulations, and here he compares political action to the idea of rhythm and coordination.

In the same chapter Plutarch parodies those who want to understand civic life in the same way as the ancients. To this end he draws on moral examples from the Athens of the Ionian War, specifically the loss of Miletus.

Τ μ ν γ ρ μικρ παιδία τ ν πατέρων ρ ντες πιχειρο ντα τ ς κρηπ δας ποδε σθαι κα το ς στεφάνους περιτίθεσθαι μετ παιδι ς γελ μεν, ο δ΄ ρχοντες ν τα ς πόλεσιν νοήτως τ τ ν προγόνων ργα κα φρονήματα κα πράξεις συμμέτρους το ς παρο σι καιρο ς κα πράγμασιν ο σας μιμε σθαι κελεύοντες ξαίρουσι τ πλήθη, γέλωτά τε ποιο ντες ο κέτι γέλωτος ξια πάσχουσιν, ν μ πάνυ καταφρονηθ σι. πολλ γ ρ στιν λλα τ ν πρότερον λλήνων διεξιόντα το ς ν ν θοποιε ν κα σωφρονίζειν, ς θήνησιν πομιμνήσκοντα μ τ ν πολεμικ ν, λλ΄ ο όν στι τ ψήφισμα τ τ ς μνηστίας π το ς τριάκοντα· κα τ ζημι σαι Φρύνιχον τραγ δί διδάξαντα τ ν Μιλήτου λωσιν· κα τι, Θήβας Κασάνδρου κτίζοντος, στεφανηφόρησαν· τ ν δ΄ ν ργει πυθόμενοι σκυταλισμόν, ν πεντακοσίους κα χιλίους ν ρήκεσαν ξ α τ ν ο ργε οι, περιενεγκε ν καθάρσιον περ τ ν κκλησίαν κέλευσαν· ν δ το ς ρπαλείοις τ ς ο κίας ρευν ντες μόνην τ ν το γεγαμηκότος νεωστ παρ λθον. τα τα γ ρ κα ν ν ξεστι ζηλο ντας ξομοιο σθαι το ς προγόνοις· τ ν δ Μαραθ να κα τ ν Ε ρυμέδοντα κα τ ς Πλαταιάς, κα σα τ ν παραδειγμάτων ο δε ν ποιε κα φρυάττεσθαι διακεν ς το ς πολλούς, πολιπόντας ν τα ς σχολα ς τ ν σοφιστ ν. ("Furthermore when we see little children trying playfully to bind their fathers' shoes on their feet or fit their crowns upon their heads, we only laugh, but the officials in the cities, when they foolishly urge the people to imitate the deeds, ideals, and actions of their ancestors, however unsuitable they may be to the present times and conditions, stir up the common folk and, though what they do is laughable, what is done to them is no laughing matter, unless they are merely treated with utter contempt. Indeed there are many acts of the Greeks of former times by recounting which the statesman can mold and correct the characters of our contemporaries, for example, at Athens by calling to mind, not deeds in war, but such things as the decree of amnesty after the downfall of the Thirty Tyrants, the fining of Phrynichus for presenting in a tragedy the capture of Miletus, their decking their heads with garlands when Cassander refounded Thebes; how, when they heard of the clubbing at Argos, in which the Argives killed fifteen hundreds of their own citizens, they decreed that an expiatory sacrifice be carried about in the assembly; and how, when they were searching the houses at the time of

Harpalus's frauds, they passed by only one, that of a newly married man. By emulating acts like these it is even now possible to resemble our ancestors, but Marathon, the Eurymedon, Plataea, and all the other examples which make the common folk vainly to swell with pride and kick up their heels, should be left to the schools of the sophists. ")

The comparison between the children playing at being adults and the magistrates of the cities who want their fellow citizens to repeat the deeds of the past could not be more revealing. In this context the *exemplum* is set in the Athens of the thirty tyrants and the famous anecdote of the tragic Phrynicus, who was fined for having rekindled the grief of the Athenians over the loss of Miletus in the Ionian war. It is possible to honor the heroes of the past and the victories of Marathon and Platea, Plutarch concludes, "but by no means to imitate them". Revealingly, he says that such attitudes are typical of the Sophists, that is, of the schools of rhetoric. The sentence with which he closes the chapter is very expressive: πολιπόντας ν τα ς σχολα ς τ ν σοφιστ ν, in the sense of schools where oratory is learnt and where one of the usual exercises was the evocation of yesterday's deeds. It should be borne in mind that at that time the confrontation between rhetoric and philosophy was still being discussed, and that this was a recurring theme in the literature of the time. We find it in Lucian, in Philostratus, in Plutarch himself. Scholastic exercises are presented here as necessary but elementary and somewhat trivial. But it is also true that at that time rhetoric integrated aspects of philosophy or political theory without great conflict. As Nock (1933) showed, the idea of conversion to philosophy is later used to explain conversion to Christianity, but this occurs in a context where the confrontation between rhetoric and philosophy that we know in Plato has no real parallel.

The moment of the Second Sophistic has, therefore, little to do with the frontal opposition between the two educational projects (*paideia*), that of Isocrates and that of Plato. Rhetoric was simply in complete coexistence with philosophy, which in turn integrated political theory. Plutarch's advice is no more than a series of sensible warnings in a world that is known to be far removed from the heroic age of the *polis*, even further from the heroes of myth.

Plutarch, in a clear allusion to Roman rule, considers that the politician must not only show himself and his country to be irreproachable before his governors, but must also procure some friends among the most powerful and in high positions, as a firm defence of his political performance. Politics and the achievement of the common good are in the hands of certain elites who must help each other. Hence Plutarch's important advice.

[18] Ο μ νον δ δε παρ χειν α τ ν τε κα τ ν πατρ δα πρ ς το ς γεμ νας να τιον, λλ κα φ λον χειν ε τινα τ ν νωδυνατωτ των, σπερ ρμα τ ς πολιτε ας

β βαιον· α το γ ρ ε σι ωμα οι πρ ς τ ς πολιτικ ς σπουδ ς προθυμ τατοι το ς φ λοις· κα καρπ ν κ φιλ ας γεμονικ ς λαμβ νοντας, ο ον λαβε Πολ βιος κα Πανα τιος τ Σκιπ ωνος ε νο πρ ς α το ς μεγ λα τ ς πατρ δας φελ σαντες, ε ς ε δαιμον αν δημοσ αν ξεν γκασθαι καλ ν. ρει ντε Κα σαρ, τε τ ν λεξ νδρειαν ε λε, δι χειρ ς χων κα μ ν προσομιλ ν τ ν συν θων συνεισ λασεν, ε τα το ς λεξανδρε σι τ σχατα προσδοκ σι κα δεομ νοις φη διαλλ ττεσθαι δι τε τ μ γεθος τ ς π λεως κα δι τ ν ο κιστ ν λ ξανδρον, "κα τρ τον," φη, "τ φ λ μου το τ χαριζ μενος." ρ γ΄ ξιον τ χ ριτι τα τ παραβαλε ν τ ς πολυταλ ντους πιτροπ ς κα διοικ σεις τ ν παρχι ν, ς δι κοντες ο πολλο γηρ σκουσι πρ ς λλοτρ αις θ ραις, τ ο κοι προλιπ ντες· τ ν Ε ριπ δην πανορθωτ ον δοντα κα λ γοντα, ς ε περ γρυπνε ν χρ κα φοιτ ν π΄ α λειον τ ρου κα ποβ λλειν αυτ ν γεμονικ συνηθε , πατρ δος π ρι κ λλιστον π τα τα χωρε ν, τ δ΄ λλα τ ς π το ς σοις κα δικα οις φιλ ας σπ ζεσθαι κα φυλ ττειν

("And not only should the statesman show himself and his native State blameless towards our rulers, but he should also have always a friend among the men of high station who have the greatest power as a firm bulwark, so to speak, of his administration; for the Romans themselves are most eager to promote the political interests of their friends; and it is a fine thing also, when we gain advantage from the friendship of great men, to turn it to the welfare of our community, as Polybius and Panaetius, through Scipio's goodwill towards them, conferred great benefits upon their native States. And Caesar, when he took Alexandria, drove into the city holding Areius by the hand and conversing with him only of all his friends, then said to the Alexandrians, who were expecting the most extreme measures and were begging for mercy, that he pardoned them on account of the greatness of their city and for the sake of its founder Alexander, "and thirdly," said he, "as a favour to my friend here. Is there any comparison between such a favour and the procuratorships and governorships of provinces from which many talents may be gained and in pursuit of which most public men grow old haunting the doors of other men's houses and leaving their own affairs uncared for? Or should we correct Euripides when he chants the sentiment that if a man must spend sleepless nights and haunt another man's court and subject himself to an intimacy with a great man, it is best to do so for the sake of his native land, but otherwise it is best to welcome and hold fast friendships based on equality and justice?")

Nevertheless, even if the politician determines and procures the obedience of his country to its sovereigns, he must not humiliate it too much, nor, if the chains already hold the foot, put the neck under as well. Some, Plutarch maintains, by denouncing before the authorities everything, the small and the great, make their bondage more ignominious, or, moreover, completely destroy the constitution of their city. The result is that the Council, the People's Assembly, the courts, and all the magistracies lose their authority. This warning by Plutarch is extremely important, because it shows the extent to which the traditional institutions of the poleis had to maintain their dignity in a context in which they were respected only for what they meant historically and for the idea - common in Greco-Roman culture - that the city was the ideal environment for the development of the individual, and therefore education in civic politics was the most desirable path to politics.

> **19**) *Ποιο ντα μ ντοι κα παρ χοντα το ς κρατο σιν ε πειθ τ νπατρ δα δε μ προσεκταπειvο ν, μηδ το σκ λους δεδεμ νουπροσυποβ λλειν κα τ ν τρ χηλον, σπερ νιοι, κα μικρ κα με ζωφ ροντες π το ς γεμ νας ξονειδ ζουσι τ ν δουλε αν, μ λλον δ΄ λως τ ν πολιτε αν ναιρο σι, καταπλ γα κα περιδε κα π ντων κυρον ποιο ντες.*
> *("However, the statesman, while making his native State readily obedient to its sovereigns, must not further humble it; or, when the leg has been fettered, go on and subject the neck to the yoke, as some who do, by referring everything, great or small, to the sovereigns, bring the reproach of slavery upon their country, or rather wholly destroy its constitutional government, making it dazed, timid, and powerless in everything".)*

In these manifestations Plutarch wants to save the appearance of civic freedom, while at the same time warning of the reality of Roman rule. The ideal political community, the city, should try to act as autonomously as possible, to be self-governing in obedience to the emperor and not turn to him for matters that can be solved by internal mechanisms. This is a further consequence of what has been stated in the previous paragraphs. The city must make itself respected for what it symbolically means, behave as freely as possible, but all this without believing that the historical and political panorama of the classical polis is possible.

> *[20] ερ ν δ χρ μα κα μ γα π σαν ρχ ν ο σαν κα ρχοντα δε μ λιστα τιμ ν, τιμ δ΄ ρχ ς μοφροσ νη κα φιλ α πρ ςσυν ρχοντας πολ μ λλον στ φανοι κα χλαμ ς περιπ ρφυρος. ο δ τ συστρατε σασθαι κα συνεφηβε σαι φιλ ας ρχ ν τιθ μενοι, τ δ συστρατηγε ν κα συν ρχειν χθρας α τ αν λαμβ νοντες, ν τ ν τρι νκακ ν ο διαπεφε γασιν· γ ρ σους γο μενοι το ς συν ρχοντας α το στασι ζουσιν κρε ττονας φθονο σιν ταπεινοτ ρουςκαταφρονο σι. δε δ κα θεραπε ειν τ ν κρε ττονα κα κοσμε ν τ ν ττονα κα τιμ ν τ ν μοιον, σπ ζεσθαι δ κα φιλε ν παντας, ς ο δι τραπ ζης ο δ κ θωνος, ο δ΄ φ΄ στ ας, λλ κοιν κα δημοσ ψ φ φ λους γεγον τας κα τρ πον τιν πατρ αν τ ν π τ ςπατρ δος ε νοιαν χοντας.*
> *("And deeming every public office to be something great and sacred, we must also pay the highest honour to one who holds an office; but the honour of an*

office resides in concord and friendship with one's colleagues much more than in crowns and a purple-bordered robe. But those who consider that serving together in a campaign or in the school for young citizens is the beginning of friendship, but regard joint service in the generalship or other office as the cause of enmity, have failed to avoid one of the three evils; for either they regard their colleagues as their equals and are themselves factious, or they envy them as their superiors, or despise them as their inferiors".)

The group solidarity that Plutarch will defend in the following section cannot be separated from its first theoretical foundation, expressed in the previous paragraph: the sacral nature of the magistracies, which demand such solidarity. Such is the meaning of μοφροσύνη κα φιλία, which appears in the text.

The two examples lead one to consider the importance of companionship in politics, and the second concerns Plutarch himself in his youth. In Rome, Scipio was criticized because he had not invited Mumius, a fellow officer, to the banquet he gave to his friends at the consecration of a temple to Heracles. in fact, although the two men did not generally consider themselves friends, the Romans believe that, in such circumstances, one should honor and be courteous to one's fellow officers by reason of their office. In short, the omission of such a small act of courtesy earned a man like Scipio, admirable in other ways, Plutarch points out, a reputation for pride and haughtiness. The second of the *exempla* involves Plutarch who as a young man shared an embassy with someone who failed to do his duty. Following his father's advice in the report he spoke in the plural, as if both had acted.

This exaltation of solidarity is a group solidarity, typical of the curial class to which Plutarch and the rest of the elite citizens of the eastern part of the Roman Empire belong.

[21] λ γουσι δ΄ ο πλε στοι κα νομ ζουσι πολιτικ ς παιδε ας ργον ε ναι τ καλ ς ρχομ νους παρασχε ν· κα γ ρ πλ ον στ το ρχοντος ν κ στ π λει τ ρχ μενον· κα χρ νον καστος ρχει βραχ ν, ρχεται δ τ ν παντα χρ νον ν δημοκρατ πολιτευ μενος· στε κ λλιστον ε ναι μ θημα κα χρησιμ τατον τ πειθαρχε ν το ς γουμ νοις, κ ν ποδε στεροι δυν μει κα δ ξ τυγχ νωσιν ντες.
("Most people say and believe that it is the business of political teaching to cause men to be good subjects; for, they say, the subject class is in every State larger than the ruling class; and each official rules but a short time, whereas he is ruled all the time, if he is a citizen of a democracy").

Most people say and think that the proper work of political education is to train obedient subjects; for in every city the governed class is more numerous than the governing class, and in a democratic regime each one governs for a short time, but is governed for a lifetime. This is another of the fundamentals of good government: it is in one's own interest to be just in government, for then one can demand that those who are responsible for it should be just to one's own.

2 ο τε γ ρ π΄ ργασί κα χρηματισμ προσιτέον το ς κοινο ς, ς ο περ Στρατοκλέα κα Δρομοκλείδην π τ χρυσο ν θέρος, τ β μα μετ παιδι ς ο τως νομάζοντες, λλήλους παρεκάλουν· ο θ΄ ο ον πιλήπτους π πάθους φυω γενομένους, ς Γάιος Γράκχος π θερμο ς το ς περ τ ν δελφ ν τυχήμασιν πωτάτω τ ν κοιν ν τ ν βίου θέμενος, ε θ΄ βρει τιν ν κα λοιδορί πρ ς α τ ν ναφλεχθε ς π΄ ργ ς, νέπεσε το ς κοινο ς· κα ταχ μ ν πλήσθη πραγμάτων κα δόξης, ζητ ν δ παύσασθαι κα δεόμενος μεταβολ ς κα συχίας ο χ ε ρε καταθέσθαι τ ν δύναμιν α το δι μέγεθος λλ προαπώλετο·

"But the man who has entered upon public life from conviction and reasoning, as the activity most befitting him and most honourable, is not frightened by any of these things, nor is his conviction changed. For neither is it right to enter upon public life as a gainful trade, as Stratocles and Dromocleides and their set used to invite each other to come to the golden harvest (for so they called the orators' platform in jest); nor ought we to enter upon it as if we were suddenly seized by an onset of strong emotion, as Gaius Gracchus did, who, when his brother's misfortunes were still fresh, withdrew so far as possible from public affairs and then, inflamed by anger because certain persons insulted and reviled him, rushed into public life. And although he was quickly satiated with public affairs and fame, yet when he tried to stop and wished for a change and a quiet life, he found that his power was too great to be laid down but before he could lay it down, he perished. And those who make themselves up for political."

We have chosen this passage from the beginning of the *Praecepta* because it deals with the ups and downs of political life and draws on two lesser-known Greek examples Stratocles and Dromocleides, both from Athens, but the Roman is none other than the brother of Gaius Gracchus. The lesson Plutarch wants us to draw is that even if a politician is vocational once he has begun his career it is very difficult to leave it. There is something mysterious about politics that subjugates human behavior.

CONCLUSION

After having introduced the meaning of the *exemplum* as the backbone of Plutarch's rhetoric and after having highlighted its pedagogical value for the local elites, we have dealt with the real socio-cultural context in which this theory of good government based on civic virtues is formulated. This context implies the maintenance of the values that once underpinned the life of the classical *polis*, but accepting its integration into the Roman Empire.

This attitude of basing good government on the cultivation of these civic virtues dates back to the Hellenistic period and implies a realistic attitude that seeks to combine both principles, that of submission to the *pax Romana* and the maintenance of civic autonomy based on the idea that the *polis* is the ideal environment both for the development of a political career and for the development of individuals in various areas of the person.

The *exemplum*, both of Greek and Roman characters, is therefore the rhetorical device used by Plutarch not to idealize an era he considers to be in the past, but to save the values compatible with the new situation of these cities in the eastern part of the empire. It makes no sense, in this context, to contrast rhetoric and philosophy or, on the other hand, rhetoric and political theory. In fact, we are at a time when rhetoric encompasses all other spheres of knowledge. We know that in the Second Sophistic the boundaries between these spheres of knowledge were not very precise.

The fact that these *exempla* integrate Greek and Roman characters is the result of the Greek elites' acceptance of the Roman world as homologous to the Hellenic world and in contrast to the barbarian one. The authors of the Second Sophistic, whether or not they are more inclined towards the Roman Empire, recognize its dominance as definitive. The apogee of the Principate is a period of great political and ideological stability that is perceived by those who lived through it as definitive. This precludes exaltations of the past that contravene the existing political order.

At the same time, Plutarch sees a political career as something that dominates the personality of the person who commits himself to it and advises moderation. It is significant, in our opinion, that from the beginning he refers to the figure of the second of the Gracchi, who enters politics to vindicate the figure of his brother. In all of Plutarch's work, and in all his work in general, we must bear in mind that the intention is to maintain the exaltation of the values of Greek culture, but always with a clear slant towards realism. The presence of the Roman Empire is seen in some way as an end of those times of civic independence which the scholastic oratory of the time exalts so much and from which he distances himself.

REFERENCES

Alexiou, E. (2008). *Eunoia* bei Plutarch: von den *Praecepta gerendae reipublicae* zu den Viten, (pp. 365–386).

Barzanò, A. (1994). Biografia pagana come agiografia. Il caso della vita plutarchea di Lucio Emilio Paolo. *Rivista dell'Istituto Lombardo, 128*, 403–424.

Brenk, F. E. (2008). Setting a good exemplum: Case studies in the *Moralia*. The *Lives* as case-study. In Nikolaidis, A. (Ed.), *The unity of Plutarch's work* (pp. 237–253). De Gruyter. DOI: 10.1515/9783110211665.5.237

Chaplin, J. D. (2000). *Livy's exemplary history*. Oxford University Press. DOI: 10.1093/oso/9780198152743.001.0001

De Romilly, J. (1958). *Eunoia* in Isocrates or the political importance of creating goodwill. *The Journal of Hellenic Studies, 78*, 92–101. DOI: 10.2307/628928

Geiger, J. (2008). Lives and Moralia: How Were Put Asunder. What Plutarch Hath Joined Together. *De Gruyter EBooks*, 5–14. DOI: 10.1515/9783110211665.1.5

Jacobs, S. S. (2017). *Plutarch's pragmatic biographies: Lessons for statesmen and generals in the Parallel Lives*. Brill. DOI: 10.1163/9789004276611

Litchfield, H. W. (1914). National *exempla virtutis* in Roman literature. *Harvard Studies in Classical Philology, 25*, 1–71. DOI: 10.2307/310381

Nock, A. D. (1933). *Conversion*. Oxford University Press.

Mayer, R. G. (1991). Roman historical exempla in Seneca. In Reverdin, O., & Grange, H. (Eds.), *Seneca and Latin prose* (pp. 141–169). Fondation Hardt.

Rambaud, M. (1953). *Cicéron et l' histoire romaine*. Les Belles Lettres.

Sanders, A. (1994). *The Short Oxford history of English literature*. Clarendon Press.

Sedley, D. (1999). The Stoic–Platonist debate on *kathêkonta*. In Ierodiakonou, K. (Ed.), *Topics in Stoic philosophy* (pp. 128–152). Clarendon Press. DOI: 10.1093/oso/9780198237686.003.0006

Veyne, P. (1999). L' identité grecque devant Rome et l'empereur. *Revue des Études Grecques, 112*, 510–567. DOI: 10.3406/reg.1999.4382

Chapter 2

Monarchy and Cities in the Political Views of Dio of Prusa:

Good Governance in the High Roman Empire According to Second Sophistic

Carlos Sánchez-Moreno Ellart
https://orcid.org/0000-0001-6896-8091
University of Valencia, Spain

ABSTRACT

The aim of this chapter is to describe, according to Dio Chrysostom's speeches on monarchy, the importance of these two institutions, the monarchy and the city, as well as to assess both the role that each of them plays in his political thinking and the relationship that exists between them, particularly -but not only-in the eastern part of the empire. The first has a tradition in Hellenistic political theory that Dion himself introduced, to a large extent, into the political thought of Rome; the second underpins Greco-Roman political theory as a model of civilisation and a privileged means of human development. The provincial elites and the senatorial elite agree in exalting the emperor in order to maintain as far as possible realities that represent a great deal for both: the libertas of the Romans and the polis of the Greeks.

DOI: 10.4018/979-8-3373-2332-9.ch002

INTRODUCTION

We propose to comment briefly on some aspects that we consider particularly significant in Dio of Prusa's famous speeches on the monarchy *(Or.* I-IV) that concern the ideal of good government. Our intention is to frame the ideas that the orator conveys in the context of the Principate, at a time when this political system was consolidated and, consequently, has defined the status of the emperor, in order to evaluate what impact they have in the foundation of this regime. This is a first approach to the subject, as required by the rules of this book, since the subject is complex and requires the handling of a multitude of sources, from legal to literary, from numismatic to epigraphic, and covers an enormously long period.

Dio's life takes place at a particularly revealing time, that of the Flavian and Antonine dynasties, with which he had intense relations respectively, (Sidebottom, 1996). The assassination of Domitian and the arrival of a new dynasty are events that undoubtedly influenced his theory of the good king and the contrast he makes between him and the tyrant, (Gangloff, 2009). In this he does not differ from other authors such as Pliny the Younger.

We shall briefly make a couple of remarks about the limitations that, in our opinion, have affected the assessment of Dio's speeches as a source of knowledge of the political theory of that historical moment, that of the Principate. First, we shall mention a very pertinent point by John Ma on the basic topic, monarchy in the Greco-Roman world; then we shall refer to the treatment of rhetorical sources for the knowledge of political theory, which in general -we believe- have been overlooked.

Commenting on the main features of the way kingship has been studied in the Greek world, John Ma (2003) recently resorts to parody to unveil the prejudices that have hindered an objective study of this question. There have been attempts to limit the existence of kingship to the Archaic and Hellenistic periods, and even within the latter there have been different positions as to whether it is in fact a Greek institution or an Eastern influence. In the case of Rome -we point out- the prejudices in understanding the true meaning of the monarchical ideal during the Principate have been far more marked, perhaps because many scholars still want to interpret this regime exclusively on the basis of Augustus' statements in a masterly propaganda text such as the *Res Gestae* and forget that the regime itself had already evolved towards a peculiar form of monarchy since at least the end of the Julio-Claudian dynasty and that this objective was present from the beginning of Augustus' reign.

Regarding the value of rhetorical sources, especially those of the High Empire, we can affirm that a veil of disinterest has fallen over them, at least for scholars of public law. They have been seen mostly as mere exercises in style, of great formal beauty, but merely known as propaganda texts, (Méthy, 2000; Manolarakis, 2008). This has been stated specifically of Pliny the Younger's Panegyricus to Trajan, the text we have to refer to in these pages, but the comparison is also useful in our case, since Dio is exalting the same emperor with very similar reasons and all this has been understood as mere praise, (Moles, 1990).

For these grounds, we believe that certain prejudices about Dio's work and his relationship with Rome should be, at best, questioned. His speeches are interpreted as mere rhetorical exercises, as brilliant in style as they are hollow, and the political thought that underlies them all tends to be undervalued as a result. Indeed, it is recent studies on the Second Sophistic that lead us to think that the importance of this author's political reflection has been trivialised. To sum up, we do not believe, as Barbara Cassin (2003) claimed, that the Second Sophistic is limited to being a literary movement, nor that these discourses of Dio are exhausted in mere propaganda texts in the service of power.

The integration of the Greek world into the Roman empire and the role of the cities is, as we shall see, closely linked to the role of the emperor as a bond of union. Some contributions, such as Veyne's, brilliant in other respects, make the mistake, in our opinion, of presenting Dion as anti-Roman. If this were so, his reflection on monarchy as good government would be of little significance for the political theory of the Principate, because it would reflect prejudices deeply rooted in the Greek mentality, specifically from the Hellenistic monarchies. We will try to show that this is not exactly the case. The Greek mentality re-emerges from a peculiar, but no less authentic, integration into the Roman Empire.

In this sense, and to advance our conclusions somewhat, the role played by the emperor in the provinces, and particularly in the East, cannot be explained only by what the provincials say, but the influence which Rome and its political powers symbolise in the conception of those ideas which took root in the provinces must be taken into account. It is not so much, therefore, a mere reception of Greek ideas into Roman political theory, but rather a double and mutual influence.

We shall try to keep our paper to the following outline: first we shall tackle the essential theses that Dion of Prusa explains in his four discourses (I-IV) about the monarchy. Then we will deal with the legitimising part that Dion gives to the virtues of the good king. In the third section we will assess to what extent the monarchy as good government had already been taken into account in the theories of the mixed constitution and in what way we believe it can be included in a reflection on the Roman constitution that was recognised by the Romans themselves in the Principate period, always following the rhetorical *topos* of the imperial virtues. To conclude, we shall summarise the main corollaries of our position on the subject, especially the role that the emperor played as a link between the eastern and western half of the empire (1999), especially with the Greek world, and the necessary exaltation of his figure for this purpose. This point is of considerable importance in understanding these four speeches, as they reflect to a large extent the official political thinking of the regime at the time and the rhetorical clichés in which the regime indulged.

As a matter of fact, the kingship in Dion is treated under the influence of various philosophical schools (mainly Cynic and Stoic) and, no doubt, of the neo-Pythagorean authors who dealt with the monarchy in the Hellenistic period. Gangloff (2009), for example, stresses the author's background is essentially Stoic, but he comes from a Cynic-influenced Stoic like Musonius Rufus, the so-called 'Roman Socrates'. As is well known, according to the author's own confession, he himself disguised himself as a beggar and led the typical life of a cynical philosopher: (*Or.* XIII.10-11)

> *Ο τω δ παρακελευσάμενος μαυτ μήτε δεδιέναι μήτε α σχύνεσθαι τ πρ γμα, στολήν τε ταπειν ν ναλαβ ν κα τ λλα κολάσας μαυτ ν λώμην πανταχο . 11 ο δ ντυγχάνοντες νθρωποι ρ ντες, ο μ ν λήτην, ο δ πτωχ ν κάλουν, ο δέ τινες κα φιλόσοφον. ντε θεν μο συνέβη κατ' λίγον τε κα ο βουλευσάμενον α τ ν ο δ φ' αυτ μέγα φρονήσαντα τούτου το νόματος τυχε ν. ο μ ν γ ρ πολλο τ ν καλουμένων φιλοσόφων α το ς νακηρύττουσιν, σπερ ο λυμπίασι κήρυκες· γ δ τ ν λλων λεγόντων ο κ δυνάμην ε κα π σι διαμάχεσθαι.*
> *("So, after exhorting myself in this way neither to fear or be ashamed of my action, and putting on humble attire and otherwise chastening myself, I proceeded to roam everywhere. And the men whom I met, on catching sight of me, would sometimes call me a tramp and sometimes a beggar, though some did call me a philosopher. From this it came about gradually and without any planning or any self-conceit on my part that I acquired this name. Now the great majority of those styled philosophers proclaim themselves such, just as the Olympian heralds proclaim the victors; but in my case, when the other folk applied this name to me, I was not able always and, in all instances to have the matter out with them," (Dio & Cohoon, 2002).*

All this is evident in the mere mention of the virtues of the king, a theme which Dion would elaborate on, and which was from the beginning of the Principate regime a fundamental motif of propaganda. Nor should this be understood apart from the personal relationship that Dion had with the different emperors. It is important to consider that the speeches under discussion are from the Antonine dynasty, during the reigns of Nerva and especially Trajan. The dating proposed by Arnim has also been disputed, but this fact has been proven. In the treatment of the king/tyrant contrast in these speeches by Dio, it is worth remembering the complex relationship he himself maintained with the Flavian dynasty, ranging from enthusiastic collaboration with Vespasian and even Titus, to the persecution and banishment ordered by Konstan and Netlibrary (1996).

BACKGROUND

The cultural origins of Dio: the idea of monarchy as good government in the Hellenistic and Roman world. The reception of the catalogue of royal virtues

Valdenberg pointed out that a distinction had to be made between monarchy and the monarchical principle. This scholar began by commenting on the much-used contrast between monarchy and freedom, which would prevent the existence of a true monarchy in the classical Greek world and, we would point out, also in the Roman world if we take into account the original meaning of the term *libertas*. Monarchy as such would only have existed in the Hellenistic period, but - contrary to this reductionist view of the question - the monarchical idea, Valdenberg goes on to say, had already had an important development in classical Greek thought, (Valdenberg, 1927). It is a matter of interpreting these authors in the political and social context in which they developed their theses, specifically at the time of the decline of the classical *polis*.

Indeed, as is widely known, in classical Greek literature there was already a significant treatment of the subject of monarchy, especially in authors who were little or not at all enthusiastic about Athenian democracy and, consequently, admirers of Persia, (Ma, 2003), as is the case of Xenophon or Plato himself, with his theory of the philosopher-king.

This point naturally became central during Hellenism and was favoured by various factors, such as hero worship, the policy of mixing with the local populations, encouraged by Alexander the Great himself, and perhaps the fact that the Macedonian monarchy itself retained features of heroic-era kingship, such as the divine origin of the monarch, or the personal attachment of subjects and generals to the king. But the model cannot be exclusively the background of the Macedonian monarchy, (Champion, 2004), for it also has important differences with the Hellenistic monarchies, for the Macedonian king had various limitations on his powers that the Hellenistic monarchs were unaware of, e.g. the Macedonian king was elected by the army and from the army, ultimately, derived the legitimacy of power (Tarn 1967 47). But here, too, some similarity can be seen, for, as we shall see, the command of the army is a title of legitimacy of royal power in all Hellenistic monarchies.

Because of the complexity of the problem, we shall not go into whether the Hellenistic monarchy has a more Eastern than Greek origin or into the influence that hero worship may have had on its conception, but we stress that the Greek elements of this institution are not alien to this political ideal either. Nor shall we deal with the complex issue of characterising the various monarchies of that period, because these differences have recently been pointed out to the extent that forgetting that may lead to the reductionism of believing that Hellenistic monarchy is a political category applicable to all the kingdoms that emerged from Alexander's empire,

(Eckstein 2009). We accept, however, as a starting hypothesis that of Eckstein, i.e. that there are certain common features among the different types of Hellenistic monarchy, notably the characteristic that all Hellenistic kings lack any real dynastic link with Alexander the Great, whom they otherwise use propagandistically. Their real power is based on the successful command of the art of war, and this is even recognised as an element of political legitimacy. We believe that in the Roman world this characteristic is fundamental to understand the use of certain themes of Greek political theory and propaganda.

As for the treatises on kingship written at the time of the Hellenistic kingdoms, these are undoubtedly a determining influence on Dio and his treatment of kingship, but we must bear in mind that these materials are known to us only in fragmentary form, (Goodenough, 1928; Delatte, 1942) and mainly through the work of Iohannes Stobaeus. There is no certainty as to their date. The earliest chronology dates them to the 3rd century BC, but Delatte believes that they all date from the 1st century BC. In any case, Delatte's annotated edition of the sources we can rely on offers a very useful overview that allows us to link what Dio says with the tradition received from such authors.

According to what we can deduct from the material collected by Delatte, these authors, all of neo-Pythagorean influence, emphasize the exceptional personality of the monarch, who has been somehow distinguished by the gods. In this, fortune plays a fundamental role, which is emphasized in the philosophy of this period. In the philosophy of history of late Stoicism it plays the role of providence, as in Posidonius, who conceives history as a teleological process, (Reinhardt, 1921). We will limit ourselves to analyzing a few texts where the exceptionality of the king's personality is appreciated in Dio of Prusa, in order to understand what role these ideas played (and had previously played) in the Roman political world.

But how does Dio describe the ideal king? In some paragraphs of these speeches, it can be seen how the virtues he points out are very similar to those pointed out by the Roman authors, not only because they use the same material, but also because the elites of the provinces essentially coincide with those of Rome.

Or. III 45-47

τρία γ ρ ε δη, τ φανερώτατα, πολιτει ν { νομάζεται} γιγνομένων κατ νόμον κα δίκην μετ δαίμονός τε γαθο κα τύχης μοίας· μία μ ν πρώτη κα μάλιστα συμβ ναι δυνατή, περ ς ν ν λόγος, ε διοικουμένης πόλεως πλειόνων θν ν ξυμπάντων νθρώπων ν ς νδρ ς γαθο γνώμ κα ρετ · (46) δευτέρα δ ριστοκρατία καλουμένη, ο τε ν ς ο τε πολλ ν τινων, λλ λίγων τ ν ρίστων γουμένων, πλε ον πέχουσα δη το δυνατο κα το συμφέροντος· {το το μοιγε δοκε κα μηρος ε πε ν διανοηθείς, ο κ γαθ ν πολυκοιρανίη· ε ς κοίρανος στω, ε ς βασιλεύς, δωκε Κρόνου πα ς γκυλομήτεω.} (47) τρίτη δ πασ ν δυνατωτάτη σχεδ ν σωφροσύν κα ρετ δήμου προσδοκ σά ποτε ε ρήσειν κατάστασιν πιεικ κα νόμιμον, δημοκρατία προσαγορευομένη, πιεικ ς νομα κα πρ ον, ε περ ν δυνατόν.

(The three most conspicuous forms of government —governments based on law and justice and enjoying the favour of heaven and fortune—are expressly named. One is the first to come into existence and the most practicable — that which forms the subject of the present address—where we have a city, or a number of peoples, or the whole world, well ordered by one good man's judgment and virtue; second, the so-called " aristocracy," where not one man, nor a considerable number of men, but a few, and they the best, are in control—a form of government, at length, far from being either practicable or expedient. It seems to me that Homer too had this in mind when he said: " The rule of the many is not well. One must be chief in war, and one the king, to whom the son of Cronus, crafty in counsel, the sceptre doth give." Third, possibly the most impracticable one of all, the one that expects by the self-control and virtue of the common people some day to find an equitable constitution based on law. Men call it " democracy " —a specious and inoffensive name, if the thing were but practicable.)

Dio expresses himself within the theory (Aristotelian, taken up by Polybius and, as such, received in Rome) of the three classical forms of government. There is a treatment of monarchy that often goes unnoticed and which is a decisive influence on how the Romans conceived their own political constitution: the theory of the mixed constitution. One of the most favourable treatments of the monarchical institution is to be found in a Peripatetic, heavily influenced by the Stoics, Dicaearchus of Messina, who, in setting out what would later be called a ‘mixed constitution’, refers to the Spartan political system and highlights monarchy as one of its three constituent elements[1]. As we shall see, it is in this context that Polybius and Cicero move when speaking about the Roman constitution, and Dion himself uses this scheme to exalt the figure of the emperor.

In the context of the three main forms of government, Dio refers to one-man rule, which he understands as the oldest and easiest to put into practice (πρώτη κα μάλιστα συμβ ναι δυνατή) and contrasts it with aristocracy and democracy, which, with pessimism, he characterises as hardly conceivable, i.e. as a government of which one hopes with significant mistrust, that it can be constituted by the people themselves. Dio, commenting on Homer when he says that the government of all is not good because someone must rule, comments on the mere name of the government of all: for him it is as inoffensive as it is misleading, because it is something impossible (πιεικ ς νομα κα πρ ον, ε περ ν δυνατόν).

Pessimism plays an important role in Dio's dismissal of democracy as impossible: someone must lead the political community. This pessimism, which Valdenberg points out in Dio as a consequence of his time, was already present in the doctrine of the mixed constitution itself, specifically in Polybius' thought, who was extremely influential in Roman political theory. He started from the inevitable degeneration of all forms of government(*anacyclosis*), as Aristotle had pointed out and Cicero subsequently will mention, which in turn was included in a pessimistic conception of the cosmic order.

Starting from the common cliché of quoting Homer, traditional since classical times and very common in the Second Sophistic, (Moles, 1990; Cassin, 2003; Kim, 2022), Dio concludes that one's government is the most favourable. Homer, apart from his importance in Greek *paideia*, is the benchmark of wisdom about the divine and the human, and that quality implies the art of government. From him Dio takes various images to exalt the monarchy. Thus, it can be affirmed that the identification of good government with imperial power moves within the parameters of the Roman constitution, reinterpreted on the basis of the monarchical principle, but adapted to the schemes that the Principate created from its origins.

Dio follows this pattern of idealising the figure of the monarch on the basis of a catalogue of virtues, he goes deeper into it and adapts it to his own time, that is, to the Roman Empire under the regime of the Principate. From his speeches on kingship, we can derive a concrete image of the ideal king that Dion postulates, and the fact that they were delivered before Trajan is not exactly anecdotal, (Valdenberg, 1927; Ubierna, 2006). These speeches follow the author's exile, from which he was allowed to return after Domitian's death. That signified a turning point in Dion's political thought: at the moment when the Principate, during the reign of Trajan, was at its height, Dio became the regime's apologist, (Arnim, 1898).

The four speeches on kingship focus on differentiating the king from the tyrant (a fundamental theme already in Dicaearchus), on presenting the virtues expected of a good king, particularly philanthropy, exemplary life and serenity, and, above all, on defending that the king, paraphrasing Homer, as superior to the rest of mortals, is the son of Zeus *(Or.* II.65) and derives his power from him. This idea is repeated incessantly throughout the four discourses dedicated to kingship: Or. I 37-41; 45; 59; 64-67; 73; 83; Or. II 72; Or. III 50-54; Or. IV. 21-23; 27; 31; 38-43 (Moles 1990).

Or. I.11

φέρε ε πωμεν τά τε θη κα τ ν διάθεσιν το χρηστο βασιλέως, ν βραχε περιλαμβάνοντες ς νεστιν,
δωκε Κρόνου πα ς γκυλομήτεω
σκ πτρόν τ δ θέμιστας, να σφίσι βουλεύ σιν.

("Let me state, then, what are the characteristics and disposition of the ideal king, summarizing them as briefly as possible — the king
'To whom the son of Saturn gives the sceptre, making him
The lawgiver, that he may rule the rest'.")

With this reference to Homer (Il.II. 205-206), the speaker deals with the virtues of a king, a decisive theme in his defence of monarchy, and this allows him to focus the theme on the distinction between the king and the tyrant. Dio (Or. I 15) refers to Homer's conception of the ideal king as a source of truth (ο κο ν λέγωμεν π ρ το καθ μηρόν τε κα τ ληθεί βασιλέως). The king is devoted to the gods, worships them, strives to serve his subjects, being more concerned with good government than with his own pleasures, precisely because of the position he occupies (δι τ ν ρχήν Or. I 21), which implies having the virtue of work.

We find it significant that next, when he speaks of the good king being loved by his friends and feared by his enemies, he concludes that the king is characterised by being 'by nature a lover of his companions, a lover of his citizens and, at the same time, of his soldiers':(Or. I 28) Φιλέταιρος δ κα φιλοπολίτης κα φιλοστρατιώτης μοίως πέφυκεν. The term companion (τα ρος) relates to the idea of friendship which he has invoked above by referring to the good king's friends loving him, the term φιλοστρατιώτης emphasises, for its part, the relationship with the army and particularly with the soldiers, but most revealing is the term φιλοπολίτης, because in a context of power concentrated in a king (an idea which the Romans held to be identical with tyranny) the term "citizen" and the values it embodies, analogous to the Roman libertas, are maintained.

Earlier (Or. I 22), Dio has referred to the nature of royal power as a lord of freemen and slaves. An ancient society was made up of both types of men, but symptomatically he links freedom with the nature of being a subject of a good king:

δεσπότην δ ο χ πως τ ν λευθέρων, λλ μηδ τ ν δούλων χαίρειν καλούμενον·

This undoubtedly means that the ancient ideals of freedom were, for various reasons, subsumed in the royal power. Likewise, in his commentary on Homer, Dio compares the situation of the king, who derives his power from Zeus and adapts his conduct to the will of Zeus, with that of the king who does not comply with the designs of the gods. This serves to bring the comparison into the realm of the Roman empire, which reveals, in our opinion, the true context of the discourse.

σπερ ο ν σοι στρατηγοί τε κα ρχοντες στρατοπέδων κα πόλεων κα θν ν, στις ν τ ν σ ν μάλιστα μιμ ται τρόπον κα το ς σο ς θεσιν μοιον α τ ν ς δυνατ ν φαίνηται παρέχων, ο τος ν ε η σο πάντων ταιρότατος κα προσφιλέστατος·

ε δέ τις ναντίος κα νόμοιος γίγνοιτο, δικαίως ν τυγχάνοι μέμψεώς τε κα τιμίας κα α τ ς γε τ ς ρχ ς ταχ παυθείς, παραχωρήσειεν τέροις μείνοσί τε κα μεινον δυναμένοις διοικε ν· 45 ο τω δ κα τ ν βασιλέων, τε ο μαι παρ το Δι ς χόντων τ ν δύναμιν κα τ ν πιτροπήν, ς μ ν ν πρ ς κε νον βλέπων πρ ς τ ν το Δι ς νόμον τε κα θεσμ ν κοσμ κα ρχ δικαίως τε κα καλ ς, γαθ ς τυγχάνει μοίρας κα τέλους ε τυχο ς· 46 ς δ' ν παραβ κα τιμάσ τ ν πιτρέψαντα δόντα τ ν δωρε ν ταύτην, ο δ ν πώνατο τ ς πολλ ς ξουσίας κα δυνάμεως τοσο τον μόνου σον φανερ ς π σι γενέσθαι το ς καθ' α τ ν κα το ς στερον πονηρ ς κα κόλαστος ν, τ ν μυθευόμενον Φαέθοντος ναπληρώσας πότμον, τε σχυρο κα θείου παρ μο ραν πιβ ς ρματος, ο χ καν ς ν νίοχος.

"Therefore, just as among generals and commanders of legions, cities or provinces, he who most closely imitates your ways and shows the greatest possible conformity with your habits would be by far your dearest comrade and friend, while he who showed antagonism or lacked conformity would justly incur censure and disgrace and, being speedily removed from his office as well, would give way to better men better qualified to govern; so too among kings, since they, I ween, derive their powers and their stewardship from Zeus; the one who, keeping his eyes upon Zeus, orders and governs his people with justice and equity in accordance with the laws and ordinances of Zeus, enjoys a happy lot and a fortunate end, while he who goes astray and dishonours him who entrusted him with his stewardship or gave him this gift, receives no other reward from his great authority and power than merely this: that he has shown himself to all men of his own time and to posterity to be a wicked and undisciplined man, illustrating the storied end of Phaethon, who mounted a mighty chariot of heaven in defiance of his lot but proved himself a feeble charioteer".

Just as the emperor is above the governors of provinces and generals, and disloyal conduct by them authorises the monarch to remove them from office, so is the relationship of Zeus to the king (Moles 1990 p. 317.). Within the king/tyrant contrast, the role of Zeus is to legitimise the power of the king who conforms to the virtues that a king should have.

The myth of Phaeton, which he announces at the end of paragraph 26, has a high symbolic meaning, for the hybris that power generates implies losing the status of virtuous king and falling into tyranny. As Moles underlines, the subtext contrasts Trajan (good king) with Domitian (tyrant). What in Dio is a clear distance between the gods and the king, in Pliny is even more explicit because the reference to Domitian is obvious in condemning that the emperor wants to act as a living god (Pliny Pan. II 3; XI 3; XXXIII 4).

Something similar happens in Pliny's Panegyricus, where the contrast between what the author calls princeps optimus (Trajan) and tyrant (Domitian) is tacitly expressed by the contrast between the virtues of the good king and the vices of the tyrant:

Plin. Pan. III 3-5

Magna et inusitata Principis gloria, cui gratias acturus, non tam vereor, ne me in laudibus suis parcum, quam ne nimium putet. Haec me cura, haec difficultas sola circumstat: nam merenti gratias agere facile est, Patres Conscripti. Non enim periculum est, ne, quum loquar de humanitate, exprobrari sibi superbiam credat; quum de frugalitate, luxuriam; quum de clementia, crudelitatem; cum de liberalitate, avaritiam; cum de benignitate, livorem; cum de continentia, libidinem; cum de labore, inertiam; cum de fortitudine, timorem. Ac ne illud quidem vereor, ne gratus ingratusve videar, prout satis aut parum dixero. Animadverto enim, etiam deos ipsos non tam accuratis adorantium precibus, quam innocentia et sanctitate, laetari; gratioremque existimari, qui delubris eorum puram castamquem mentem, quam qui meditatum carmen intulerit.
("Rare and great is the glory of an emperor, whose panegyrist fears less appearing frugal than lavish with his praise! That is my only concern, the only difficulty I feel today; for it is easy, conscript fathers, to express gratitude when it is deserved. To name gentleness will never be, for the one I praise, a reproach of pride; economy, of luxury; clemency, of cruelty; liberality, of avarice; kindness, of malice; continence, of debauchery; activity, of sloth; courage, of cowardice. I do not even fear to please or displease, depending on whether I have said enough or too little. I look to the gods, and I see that eloquent prayers move them less than the innocence and holiness of their worshippers; and that, to find favour in their sight, it is better to bring to their temples a chaste and pure soul than hymns ingeniously composed. ").

Pliny himself concludes his speech with praise based on the contrast between king and tyrant, in parallel to the king appointed by Zeus and who follows his designs, as opposed to the tyrant, who derives his power from Zeus but rebels against the will of the gods. On the political level he sums it up in this way:

Plin. LXXII

Fuit tempus, ac nimium diu fuit, quo alia adversa, alia secunda principi et nobis: nunc communia tibi nobiscum tam laeta, quam tristia: nec magis sine te nos esse felices, quam tu sine nobis potes. (...) Adeo nihil tibi amore civium antiquius, ut ante a nobis, deinde a diis, atque ita ab illis amari velis, si a nobis ameris. (*"There were times, and too long, (fuit tempus, ac nimium diu fuit) when adversity and prosperity were not the same for the prince as for us: now, both joys and sorrows are common to you and us, and we cannot be happier without you than you can be without us [...]. Indeed, the end of previous princes has shown that only those whom men love are loved by the gods"*).

The panegyric again alludes to Domitian without mentioning him, recalling a time that was inauspicious and too long, that of his tyranny. Starting from the comparison between a luminous present and that execrable past, Pliny refers to the cliché of the good king loved by his people that we have seen in Dio and takes it to the hyperbole of identifying his happiness with that of his subjects. Thus, he states from the outset that the function of the praise prescribed by the senate for the new consul is both to exalt the good prince and to mark the path of the bad ones (Plin Pan. IV 1: Sed parendum est Senatusconsulto, quo ex utilitate publica placuit, ut Consulis voce, sub titulo gratiarum agendarum, boni principes, quae facerent, recognoscerent; mali, quae facere deberent.). The catalogue of virtues assumes here, apart from its role of legitimising power and providing a basis for good government, a function of persuading the emperor to adjust his conduct to the demands and values of the elite.

The problem of tyranny is central to Roman political thought, where monarchy was traditionally identified (in the sense of 'power of one', not properly speaking of having a king) and where, within traditional rhetoric, it was difficult to exalt monarchy as Dio does in these speeches.

A very common rhetorical commonplace in the Roman tradition is precisely that happiness distinguishes the good ruler (the king, for example) from the tyrant, who is hated and not loved by his people. Dio also develops this cliché with his usual mastery, which had already been dealt with, for example, by Seneca in his de Clementia (I.7-9), addressed, ironically, to Nero. Manolaraki (2008) p. 170 points out that this work probably had an influence on later texts praising emperors, such as the Panegyricus a Trajan:

7. Magnam adibat aleam populus Romanus, cum incertum esset, quo se ista tua nobilis indoles daret; iam vota publica in tuto sunt; nec enim periculum est, ne te subita tui capiat oblivio. Facit quidem avidos nimia felicitas, nec tam temperatae cupiditates sunt umquam, ut in eo, quod contigit, desinant; gradus a magnis ad maiora fit, et spes improbissimas conplectuntur insperata adsecuti; omnibus tamen nunc civibus tuis et haec confessio exprimitur esse felices et illa nihil iam his accedere bonis posse, nisi ut perpetua sint. 8. Multa illos cogunt ad hanc confessionem, qua nulla in homine tardior est: securitas alta, adfluens, ius supra omnem iniuriam positum; obversatur oculis laetissima forma rei publicae, cui ad summam libertatem nihil deest nisi pereundi licentia. 9. Praecipue tamen aequalis ad maximos imosque pervenit clementiae tuae admiratio; cetera enim bona pro portione fortunae suae quisque sentit aut exspectat maiora minoraque, ex clementia omnes idem sperant; nec est quisquam, cui tam valde innocentia sua placeat, ut non stare in conspectu clementiam paratam humanis erroribus gaudeat.

("The Roman people faced a great hazard, when it was (still) uncertain in what (direction) that noble nature of yours would take itself; now the prayers of the community are assured; for there is no danger that forgetfulness of yourself should take you by surprise. Too much prosperity makes (men) greedy, nor are our desires ever so moderate that they cease at the point when there has been success; (this) creates stepping(-stones) from great to (even) greater (successes), and, once they have gained unexpected (things), they embrace the most perverse of hopes; yet now, this confession is extorted from all your citizens, both that they are happy, and this as well, that nothing can be added to their blessings, except that they should be continuous. (8) Many (circumstances) force them to (make) this admission, and nothing less hasty than this is (likely to be said) among men: (there is) a security deep (and) abounding, (and) justice (has been) placed above all wrong; the most welcome form of government is to be seen by the eyes (of men), from which nothing is lacking to (provide) the highest degree of liberty, except the power of (self-)destruction. (9) Above all, however, admiration of your (quality of) mercy, extends from the highest to the lowest (of your subjects); for each man experiences or expects a larger or smaller (measure) of other blessings in proportion to his luck, (but) from your mercy they all expect the same; nor is there any man whose own innocence is so greatly satisfying, that he does not rejoice that your mercy remains in view, ready (to accommodate) human errors". Translation by John W. Basore, available on the Perseus site).

The very safety of a ruler, according to Seneca, consists precisely in ruling justly, unlike the tyrant, who rules arbitrarily. The philosopher points out, therefore, something very important in the political legitimacy of the Principate, which is the legitimacy of exercise. The same theme is present in Dio, for he relates the ruler's justice to his own security and links that justice to the origin of power in Zeus himself.

Dio echoes these ideas, for, apart from extolling justice in an even utilitarian way, he expands on it to differentiate the king from the tyrant. What is important for understanding the context in which these statements are made is precisely the comparison with Pliny the Younger's Panegyricus.

Dio Or. I. 45-46

[45] ο τω δ κα τ ν βασιλέων, τε ο μαι παρ το Δι ς χόντων τ ν δύναμιν κα τ ν πιτροπήν, ς μ ν ν πρ ς κε νον βλέπων πρ ς τ ν το Δι ς νόμον τε κα θεσμ ν κοσμ κα ρχ δικαίως τε κα [46] καλ ς, γαθ ς τυγχάνει μοίρας κα τέλους ε τυχο ς: ς δ ν παραβ κα τιμάσ τ ν πιτρέψαντα δόντα τ ν δωρε ν ταύτην, ο δ ν πώνατο τ ς πολλ ς ξουσίας κα δυνάμεως τοσο τον μόνον σον φανερ ς π σι γενέσθαι το ς καθ α τ ν κα το ς στερον πονηρ ς κα κόλαστος ν, τ ν μυθευόμενον Φαέθοντος ναπληρώσας πότμον, τε σχυρο κα θείου παρ μο ραν πιβ ς ρματος, ο χ καν ς ν νίοχος.

(So too among kings, since they, I ween, derive their powers and their stewardship from Zeus; the one who, keeping his eyes upon Zeus, orders and governs his people with justice and equity in accordance with the laws and ordinances of Zeus, enjoys a happy lot and a fortunate end, 46 while he who goes astray and dishonours him who entrusted him with his stewardship or gave him this gift, receives no other reward from his great authority and power than merely this: that he has shown himself to all men of his own time and to posterity to be a wicked and undisciplined man, illustrating the storied end of Phaethon, who mounted a mighty chariot of heaven in defiance of his lot but proved himself a feeble charioteer.)

Kings derive their powers from Zeus himself, and it is Zeus himself who compels the king to rule according to that model, i.e. in such a way that the ruler rules by contemplating (βλέπω) Zeus' way of ruling, i.e. with justice and in accordance with what is right, as opposed to tyranny. Only in this way will the ruler enjoy a happy destiny (ς μ ν ν πρ ς κε νον βλέπων πρ ς τ ν το Δι ς νόμον τε κα θεσμ ν κοσμ κα ρχ δικαίως τε κα καλ ς, γαθ ς τυγχάνει μοίρας κα τέλους ε τυχο ς).

Dio Or. III. 83-85

83] τα τα δ λογιζόμενος ο κ χθεται καρτερ ν. κατανοε δ το ς μ ν πόνους γίειάν τε παρέχοντας κα σωτηρίαν τι δ δόξαν γαθήν, τ ν δ α τρυφ ν παντα τούτων τ ναντία. τι δ ο μ ν πόνοι α το ς λάττους ε ποιο σι κα φέρειν λαφροτέρους, τ ς δ δον ς μείζους κα βλαβεστέρας, ταν γίγνωνται μετ το ς πόνους. δέ γε τρυφ το ς μ ν πόνους ε χαλεπωτέρους ποιε φαίνεσθαι, τ ς δ δον ς πομαραίνει κα σθενε ς ποδείκνυσιν. [84] γ ρ ε τρυφ ν νθρωπος, μηδέποτε δ πτόμενος πόνου μηδενός, τελευτ ν πόνον μ ν ο κ ν ο δένα νάσχοιτο, δον ς δ ο δεμι ς ν α σθοιτο, ο δ τ ς σφοδροτάτης. στε φιλόπονος κα γκρατ ς ο μόνον βασιλεύειν καν ώτερός στιν, λλ κα διον βιοτεύει πολ τ ν ναντίων. 85] γρηγόρσεως δ κα πνου το ς μ ν στρατιώταις ξ σου μέτεστι, τ ν μ ν φυλαττόντων ν μέρει, τ ν δ ναπαυομένων: δ στρατηγ ς γρυπνότερός στι τ ν ε φυλαττόντων. ("Reasoning thus, the good king endures without repining. He realizes too that toil brings health and salvation and goodly report as well; while, on the other hand, luxurious ease brings quite the opposite. Then again, toil endured ever grows less and easier to support, the while it makes pleasure greater and less harmful if it follows the toil. Ease, on the other hand, makes toil appear more and more difficult in that it lessens pleasure and blunts its edge. 84 The man who lives in the lap of luxury and never puts his hand to a single task, ends by being unable to endure any task or to feel any pleasure at all, however intense. 85 Consequently, he who loves to toil and exercises self-control is not only better qualified to be king but is able to live a much more pleasant life than those in the opposite case").

The influence of Hellenistic treatises is obvious, but - as we can see from the Roman sources cited above - the reformulation of these principles can only be understood in a Roman context. First of all, the anthropological pessimism already detectable in the civil wars is a spur for the Romans to distrust democracy, whatever its concrete reality in their political system, and this attitude has a precedent in Plato himself (Valdenberg 1927 145). Dio considers democracy impossible, resorting to a well-established rhetorical topos: the people are like the passage of a ship and it is the pilot, the king, who sees to it that they reach port.

Or. II.2.65

πολλ δ κα λλα χοι τις ν ε πε ν παρ΄ μ ρ παιδε ματα κα διδ γματα νδρε α κα βασιλικ , π ρ ν σως μακρ τερον το ν ν πεξι ναι. πλ ν τι γε τ ν α το γν μην πασαν ποδε κνυται σαφ ς, τι π ντων ριστον ο εται δε ν τ ν βασιλ α ε ναι, μ λιστα δ π το γαμ μνονος, τε τ πρ τον παρατ ττει τ ν στρατι ν κα το ς γεμ νας σ μπαντας καταλ γει κα τ πλ θος τ ν νε ν.(66) κε γ ρ ο δ μιλλαν τ ν λλων ο δεν καταλ λοιπεν ρ ων πρ ς α τ ν, λλ΄ σον τα ρος γ λης περφ ρει κατ μην κα μ γεθος, τοσο τον διαφ ρειν φησ τ ν βασιλ α, ο τως λ γων· τε βο ς γ ληφι μ γ΄ ξοχος πλετο π ντων τα ρος· γ ρ τε β εσσι μεταπρ πει γρομ ν σι· το ον ρ΄ τρε δην θ κε Ζε ς ματι κε ν , κπρεπ ΄ ν πολλο σι κα ξοχον ρ εσσιν. ("There are many other lessons and teachings in Homer, which might be cited, that make for courage and the other qualities of a king, but perhaps their recital would require more time than we now have. I will say, however, that he not only expresses his own judgment clearly in every instance — that in his belief the king should be the superior of all men — but particularly in the case of Agamemnon, in the passage where for the first time he sets the army in array, calls the roll of the leaders, and gives the tale of the ships. 66 In that scene the poet has left no room for any other hero even to vie with Agamemnon; but as far as the bull surpasses the herd in strength and size, so far does the king excel the rest, as Homer says in these words: "And as a bull amid the horned herd/ Stands eminent and nobler than the rest,/So Zeus to Agamemnon on that day/Gave to surpass in manly port and mien/The heroes all" (Il. II 482-483)".

Again, Dio resorts to the quotation from Homer to extol the virtues of the king, and by means of the rhetorical figure of preterition he merely refers to the image of the bull leading the herd, present in the Iliad. The image of Agamemnon as the king leading the army is not chosen by chance, when the emperor holds a title already of a quasi-regal nature, but which was originally based on military command (imperium). As we have said, this was the case in the Principate and had also been the case in the Hellenistic monarchies.

At different times, as we have already seen in the previous text, Dio resorts to the tradition accepted in Hellenism of quoting Homer as an exegetical key and in this case to define the good king, the basic condition of good government.

What is presented as a scholarly digression has an indisputable political intention, as it helps to legitimise the figure of the emperor as a superior being, relating him to the gods and precisely in relation to the command of the army.

Or. III.55-57

τ ν τε τ ν νθρ πων πιμ λειαν ο π ρεργον ο δ σχολ αν λλως νεν μικεν, βαρυν μενος ο μαι τ ς φροντ δας, λλ ργον α το κα τ χνην τα την. κα ταν μ ν λλο τι ποι , ο δ ν γε ται σπουδα ον ο δ τ ν α το πρ ττειν· ταν δ νθρ πους φελ , τ τε νομ ζει τ προσ κον ποτελε ν, τε π το μεγ στου θεο ταχθε ς π το το τ ργον, πειθε ν ο θ μις ο δ ν ο δ χθεσθαι.(56){ τε προσηκο σας α τ νομ ζων τ ς ε εργεσ ας}. ο δε ς γ ρ ο τω μαλακ ς ο δ φιλ δονος ς ο χ δεται τ α το πρ ξει, κ ν τ χ π πονος· ς κιστα μ ν κυβερν της ν χθεσθε η το ς ν θαλ ττ π νοις, κιστα δ γεωργ ς το ς περ γεωργ αν ργοις, κιστα δ κυνηγ της ο ς δε θηρ ντα κ μνειν· κα τοι σφ δρα μ ν π πονον γεωργ α, σφ δρα δ κυνηγεσ α.(57) ο μ ν παξιο τ κ μνειν κα νοχλε σθαι τ ν λλων νεκεν, ο δ τα τ χε ρον πρ ττειν νεν μικεν, ν δ πλε στους α τ ν ν χεσθαι π νους κα πλε στα πρ γματα χειν. (Then, the care bestowed on his subjects he does not consider an incidental thing or mere drudgery, when weighed down, let us say, by cares, but as his own work and profession. And when he is otherwise engaged, he does not feel that he is doing anything worthwhile or that he is attending to his own business; it is only when he helps men that he thinks he is doing his duty, having been appointed to this work by the greatest god, whom it is not right for him to disobey in aught nor yet to feel aggrieved, believing, as he does, that these tasks are his duty. For no one is so effeminate or enslaved to pleasure as not to like his own occupation even if it chance to be laborious. A sea-captain, for example, never finds his toil at sea irksome, nor a farmer his work in tilling the soil; never is the huntsman wearied by the hardships of the chase; and yet both farming and hunting are most laborious. No indeed, the king does not object to toil and discomfort, in behalf of others, nor does he deem his lot any the worse simply because he has to face the most tasks and have the most troubles. For he sees that the sun, too, although inferior to none of the gods, frets not because, to preserve man and life, he must accomplish all his many tasks throughout the ages.)

As regards the divine nature of royal power, Dio resorts to the image of the sun, which would later be so important under the Severan dynasty and even later for Aurelian, but the image has a clearly Stoic origin and not only in its cosmological aspect, because the sun represents the creative fire, (Rist, 1978), which symbolizes virtue and it is in the catalogue of virtues that the emperor seeks to legitimize his power. The use of the solar symbol has already been pointed out by several authors, who give it different interpretations as to its origin, but not as to its later influence, both in the Hellenistic and Roman worlds2.

The catalogue of virtues and its reinterpretation in Rome.

In the tradition of monarchical thought in classical Athens and in Xenophon we find a catalogue of five virtues that adorn the king, which in Stoic thought are usually four. This tendency was accentuated in the Hellenistic kingdoms and eventually arrived in Rome.

What does this list of virtues add to our understanding of the Principate as a political regime? Traditionally, this list is often seen as a mere propagandistic device, a clever rhetoric no doubt, but without much substance. We disagree with this. It is significant that, when discussing the nature of the Principate, many authors remain with the texts that are considered foundational, especially the Res gestae divi Augusti and its assertion that the princeps did not surpass other magistrates in potestas, but only in auctoritas.

If we say that research on the nature of the Principate often suffers from these prejudices, it is because we know, as the so-called lex de imperio Vespasiani testifies, that already at the beginning of the Flavian dynasty, the role of the emperor was much more decisive than was recognized in the declarations of the Res Gestae divi Augusti. This is a brilliant example of political propaganda that has probably overshadowed other documents, which, moreover, are not abundant. But a completely different picture emerges from the lex de imperio Vespasiani and various literary sources, of which we are all aware, but which from the point of view of public law has probably not the object of enough attention.

The catalogue of virtues is never the same, each reign highlights some or emphasises others, but the root of the matter is that the charismatic power of the emperor increasingly underlies the entire political system, but at the same time the fiction that the Roman libertas is still alive is to be maintained. This objective was shared by the elites in the western and eastern parts of the empire, some because they wanted to maintain as much of the senatorial libertas as possible, others because the emperor's allegiance to the figure of the emperor allowed them to retain some of the Greek civic autonomy.

Perhaps this is the point of view to adopt in order to understand the ideological mechanism underlying Dio and which, in some respects, coincides with that of other Roman authors who use the catalogue of virtues not only to flatter the emperor, but also to guide him in the fulfilment of his function and thus to somehow maintain libertas and thus achieve good government.

In this respect there are parallels with Pliny the Younger's Panegyricus to Trajanus, to which we have briefly referred above. In this speech we note something that was already evident in the lex de imperio Vespasiani, that the emperor was the one who held all the political power and who, for example, intervened in the appointment of magistrates. this is something that is clearer in the Panegyricus, because not only are the candidates he proposes given preference, as was the case in the lex de imperio Vespasiani, but they are directly appointed by the emperor himself, (Paladini, 1960). This example serves to illustrate the point.

It is obvious that the common element that unites both panegyrics is that the difference between the two texts, Pliny's and Dio of Prusa's, which are practically contemporary and addressed to the same emperor, is minimal. This is that Pliny represents an aristocratic group that recovers the traditions of the Roman constitution in order to prevent the emperor from becoming a tyrant (i.e. the idea of libertas), while Dio focuses on the figure of the emperor as the guarantor of political order (an idea shared by Pliny), but also as the protector of civic life in the eastern half of the empire.

Certain features of Roman political thought, such as the obsession with avoiding tyranny, are undoubtedly equivalent in the Greek world, but it is a defining feature of the conception of good government defended by the senatorial elites of the time. Power derived from Zeus requires to be exercised according to his designs. This theme is also present in Roman authors of the time. Pliny also assumes that the emperor is appointed by Jupiter(Iuppiter Optimus Maximus), in a similar way to what Dio affirmed with respect to the king and Zeus (Pl. Pan. I 36; V 1; VII 5; VIII 1 3LXXXVIII 8), but with some significant differences.

Plin. Pan. I.36

Quo magis aptum piumque est, te, Iupiter optime maxime, antea conditiorem, nunc conservatorem imperii nostri, precari, ut mihi digna consule, digna senatu, digna principe contingat oratio: utque omnibus, quae dicentur a me, libertas, fides, veritas constet: tantumque a specie adulationis absit gratiarum actio mea, quantum abest a necessitate.
("It is therefore all the more fitting that I should turn in prayer to thee, Jupiter, most mighty and good, and ask that my address may prove worthy of me as consul, worthy of our senate, and worthy of our prince; that my words may bear the stamp of freedom, faith, and truth, and lack as much the sem- blance, as they do the need, of flattery" Trans. by F. P. Garland, from Masterpieces of Eloquence, ed. Mayo (2016).

Within the exordium the speaker invokes Jupiter as the inspirer of himself, the Senate and the emperor. He then turns to the topos of the list of virtues: libertas, fides, veritas. It is no coincidence that the first is one of the backbone and justifying elements of the speech.

The beginning of Chapter VIII seems to us to be more significant:

Sedulo ergo vitavit hunc casum, nec iudicia hominum, sed deorum etiam in consilium assumsit. Itaque non tua in cubiculo, sed in templo; nec ante genialem torum, sed ante pulvinar Iovis optimi maximi, adoptio peracta est: qua tandem non servitus nostra, sed libertas et salus et securitas fundabatur.
("He therefore carefully avoided this pitfall and took counsel, not only from men, but from the gods. Thus, it was not in the core of the palace, but in a temple; before the imperial bed, but before the sacred cushion of Jupiter Optimus Maximus, that an adoption was consummated which did not establish our slavery, but our freedom, our happiness, our security.")

Indeed, as we have repeatedly pointed out, from the beginning of the new regime the list of imperial virtues had a legitimising effect on the status of the emperor. As Wallace-Hadrill says, the monarch's legitimacy derived from different sources, but persuasion played a fundamental role (Wallace-Hadrill 1981 p. 298). Being the emperor, in Max Weber's terms, a largely (but not only) charismatic ruler the importance of extraordinary virtues must be deemed as essential. That is why Dio, as we have amply shown, deals with this question in detail.

As Wallace-Hadrill sums up: "The vehicle for propagation of belief was the official coinage, which frequently bore on its reverses the depictions of various 'virtues' personified. The choice of the virtues so advertised depended on assumptions about what the 'ideals' of a ruler were, which ultimately flowed from Greek philosophical thought about kingship, and which became 'canonised' in the Golden Shield presented to Augustus," (Wallace-Hadrill, 1981).

The author's criticism is not the one we are going to formulate, insofar as Wallace-Hadrill focuses on discussing the propagandistic value of numismatics, while we believe that, although there are undoubted roots in Greek philosophy and the so-called catalogue of virtues, the development of these ideas cannot be understood if we disregard the Roman substratum where they are used. In Dio, in particular, we cannot speak only of the use of Greek political theory in a Roman setting, but of a use of Greek doctrine already influenced by the Roman context. Even if the author comes from the Greek world, it is obvious that he is already embedded in Roman political theory, even if the latter was conceived on the basis of Greek philosophy.

And something similar can be stated of Greek political philosophy as used in the propaganda of the Principate regime. Wallace-Hadrill points out that the traditional Stoic virtues do not coincide exactly with those which Augustus vindicated in his Res Gestae and which were the object of a symbolic shield given to him by the Senate. Of course, this is so, because, for example, at that historical moment when a new regime is presented as a continuation of the previous one, it is more important to emphasize the emperor's observance of the official religion(pietas) than to speak of his wisdom. It is also more appropriate to stress clementia than sophrosyne, but in every reign he will emphasize other virtues. What is important is that both Dio and Pliny base the emperor's qualification for being the good king the community needs on a catalogue of virtues.

By the 2nd century AD nobody in his right mind expected the restoration of the previous political system and this meant that the great ideas on which Roman political education was based, such as libertas, would be reinterpreted in a way that was compatible with personal power and that personal power was legitimised both by its divine origin (originating in Zeus, says Dio, accepted by Jupiter, says Pliny) and by its exercise and in this the role of the virtues was fundamental for the legitimacy of the regime.

Wallace-Hadrill's critique, while reflecting that the coincidence with Greek political theory and Roman usage does not coincide, does not stop to point out the reasons or does not always get them right: "By the time of Cicero this is firmly established, and he constantly rehearses the four as an assumed fact of moral philosophy: he renders them as fortitudo (not virtus), temperantia/continentia, iustitia, and prudentia/sapientia. What canonised this group perhaps more effectively than Stoic systematisation were the rigid prescriptions of rhetoric: in rhetorical handbooks, whether Cicero and Quintilian, or the arid imperial tracts collected in Spengel's Rhetores, the prescription is constant, that to praise a man, in particular a king, the orator must demonstrate the four virtues".

It is true that there is a canon of Stoic origin, although also earlier, of the four royal virtues and that a canon is in principle difficult to alter, but this does not mean that the Roman political system and its propaganda must reproduce it exactly and mechanically. Precisely one of the characteristics of Roman culture is the creativity with which they received the Greek influence, far removed from the servile, unthinking imitation that many scholars take as granted, and which is based on an unjustified prejudice. Firstly, as Wallace-Hadrill (1981) acknowledges, one virtue can encompass others, as is the case with Cicero: "The first book of de officiis is based on the four virtues of the good citizen: among these magnitudo animi replaces fortitudo, but this, as Cicero explains, is because magnanimity also includes patientia, passive as well as active bravery, and should therefore be regarded as the leading species".

But also, and this is no minor objection, each dynasty and often each emperor needed to resort to certain virtues to support his propaganda, and they were not always the same. For example, Tiberius follows Augustus in giving a very important role to iustitia, but in the technical Roman sense of this term in that historical period, that is, the virtue of doing something in accordance with the law, in other words, by raising iustitia as a banner, the emperor exalts the rule of law and this serves to affirm that the new regime is being respectful of the traditional Roman constitution. This same virtue assumes the sense of material justice in other reigns, also that of justice as lawful revenge in a just war (Vespasian in the case of the war in Palestine). It is Hadrian who uses iustitia in the sense of material justice and, perhaps, iustitia in the sense of legislative policy, alluding to the codification of the edict or the organisation of the consilium Principis and the formal beginning of the promulgation of imperial constitutions. It is not easy, on the other hand, to distinguish between this meaning of the term and the reign of Augustus, when the emperor reformed the criminal and civil process. In other words, the canon was adapted to the propaganda of the time.

CONCLUSION

Having viewed the catalogue of virtues as an element of political legitimacy, we shall try to conclude the function that the monarchy plays in the Roman political system of the Principate (and which shall be accentuated in the later period, the so-called Dominate) and how it is valued from the two approaches, a Greek perspective and a strictly Roman one. We believe that, for various reasons, there has been a very similar way of justifying the new regime in both, with differences that we shall try to highlight.

We must start from an undeniable fact that can be seen in the Second Sophistic, namely, that the provincial elites of Hellenistic origin coincide with the senatorial elites in that the figure of the monarch is necessary. The Greeks often addressed the emperor as king and the Romans maintained the title of Princeps in order to feign a constitutional continuity which, as we know and as we have shown, was purely theoretical and empty of real content, because the emperor, as early as Augustus, held much more power than was recognised in the propaganda of the regime.

The element that binds the interests of both elites is the senatorial libertas and the civic eleutheria of the Greeks. It is significant that a text by Plutarch (Praecepta gerenda reipublicae X) compares the political life of the cities of the time with that of the past:

> *ν νο ν τε τ πρ γματα τ ν π λεων ο κ χει πολ μων γεμον ας ο δ τυραvν δων καταλ σεις ο δ συμμαχικ ς πρ ξεις, τ ν΄ ν τις ρχ ν πιφανο ς λ βοι κα λαμπρ ς πολιτε ας α δ και τε λε πονται α δημ σιαι κα πρεσβε αι πρ ς α τοκρ τορα νδρ ς διαπ ρου κα θ ρσος μα κα νο ν χοντος δε μεναι.*
> *(Nowadays, then, when the affairs of the cities no longer include leadership in wars, nor the overthrowing of tyrannies, nor acts of alliances, what opening for a conspicuous and brilliant public career could a young man find? There remain the public lawsuits and embassies to the emperor, which demand a man of ardent temperament and one who possesses both courage and intellect".)*

The contrast between the life of the politician who ruled the cities in the past, when tyrants had to be overthrown or wars had to be won, is seen by Plutarch as something that was never to return. Significantly, apart from court functions, embassies to the emperor (πρεσβε αι πρ ς α τοκρ τορα) are mentioned as very important. The monarchy, embodied in the Roman emperor, must be channelled through philosophy and persuaded by rhetoric so that the emperor is the guarantor of the only freedom that can be conceived within the empire, the autonomy of the cities. The role of the king as a link between the central power and the cities is something that already existed in the Hellenistic world (Ma 2003 pp. 177-179) and not only intensifies in Roman times, but it is precisely in the relationship with the cities that the emperor finds one of his main sources of political legitimacy.

The polis is still seen as a grouping of free citizens and Dio's discourses insist on this aspect, an idea that, created by Aristotle (Pol. III) (Rhodes 2009 p. 57), spread already in Hellenistic times and survived, as a hallmark of Greek identity, in the Roman empire. Citizens, under Roman power, can expect to perform functions within the government of those cities, a fact that is identified with freedom. On the other hand, the imperial cult from the end of the 2nd century and definitely in the 3rd century insists not only on the link between the emperor and the local elites but also with the divinities, particularly the local divinities, which gives the emperor the role of a unifying force with the civic structures. In the late Byzantine period, it could rightly be said that the presence of the monarchy serves to reinterpret the entire political system, which is articulated around the emperor. The ceremonial that develops at court and in the cities more and more externalises this new reality of political power (Cameron 1987 106-136).

The exaltation of the monarch in the Roman political thought of the Principate, already consolidated as a form of government, is presented as a guarantee of libertas by the senatorial elite, who want to establish the idea of the optimus princeps or the princeps civilis as a model of ethics. Libertas remains under the protection of the monarch and the panegyrics, whether Pliny's or Dio's, have the function of guiding the emperor's behavioral norms. They are both an exaltation and a way of guiding his political action.

REFERENCES

Arnim, H. v. (1898). *Leben und Werke des Dio von Prusa.* Weidmannsche Buchhandlung.

Cameron, A. (1987). The Construction of Court Ritual. The Byzantine Book of Ceremonies. In *D. Carradine / S. Price, Rituals of Royalty* (pp. 106–136). Cambridge University Press.

Cassin, B. (2003). Sophists. In *J. Brunschwig & G. Lloyd, A Guide to Greek Thought* (pp. 435–453). The Belknap Press of Harvard University Press.

Champion, C. B. (2004). *Cultural Politics in Polybius' Histories.* University of California Press.

Delatte, L. (1942) Les traités de la royauté d' Ecphante, Diotogène et Sthénidas, Liège (Bibliothèque de lla Faculté de Philosophie et Lettres de l' Université de Liège XCVII).

Dio, C., & Cohoon, J. W. (2002). *Dio Chrysostom. 1. Discourses 1-11.* Harvard Univ. Press.

Eckstein, A. M. (2009). Hellenistic Monarchy in Theory and Practice. In Balot, R. K. (Ed.), *Greek and Roman Political Thought* (pp. 247–265). Wiley-Blackwell.

Gangloff, A. (2009). Le sophiste Dion de Pruse, le bon roi et l'empereur. *Revue Historique*, *9*, 3–38.

Goodenough, E. R. (1928). The Political Philosophy of Hellenistic Kingship. *Yale Classical Studies*, *1*, 55–102.

Henkel, H. (1887). *Studien zur Geschichte der griechischen Lehre vom Staat.* Teubner.

Kim, L. (2022). Homer in the Second Sophistic. In Manolea, C.-P. (Ed.), *Brill's Companion to the Reception of Homer from the Hellenistic Age to Late Antiquity* (pp. 164–188). Brill.

Konstan, D. & Netlibrary, I. (1996). *Friendship in the classical world.* Cambridge University Press.

Ma, J. (2003). Kings. In Erskine, A. (Ed.), *A Companion to the Hellenistic World* (pp. 178–195). Blackwell.

Manolarakis, E. (2008). Political and Rhetorical Seascapes in Pliny's Panegyricus. *Classical Philology*, *103*, 374–394.

Mayo. (2016). Masterpieces of Eloquence; Famous Orations of Great World Leaders from Early Greece to the Present Time. Palala Press.

Méthy, N. (2000). Éloge rhéthorique et propagande politique sous le Haut Empire: L'exemple du Panégyrique de Trajan. *Mélanges de l'École Française de Rome*, *112*, 365–411.

Mirhady, D. D. (2001). Dicaearchus of Messina. The Sources. In Fortenbauch, W. W., & Schutrumpf, E. (Eds.), *Dicaearchus of Messina* (pp. 1–142). Routledge.

Moles, J. (1990). The Kingship Orations in Dio Chrysostom. *Papers of the Leeds International Latin Seminar*, *6*, 297–375.

Osann, F. (1837). *Beiträge zur griechischen und römischen Literaturgeschichte*. Verlag Eduard Heil.

Paladini, M. L. (1960). Elezioni dei magistrati al tempo di Plinio il giovane. In *Hommages à Léon Hermann* (pp. 571–583). Latomus.

Reinhardt, K. (1921). Poseidonios. München C.H. Beck. https://archive.org/details/poseidonios00reinuoft

Rist, J. M. (1978). *The Stoics*. University of California Press.

Sidebottom, H. (1996). Dio of Prusa and the Flavian Dynasty. *Classical Quarterly*, *46*, 447–456.

Tarn, W. W. (1967). *Hellenistic Civilisation*. Meridian Books.

Ubierna, P. (2006). La idea de Bizancio en la tradición intelectual rusa y soviética 1840-1970. *Byzantion Nea Hellás*, *25*, 183–203.

Valdenberg, V. (1927). La théorie monarchique de Dion Chrysostome. *Revue des Études Grecques*, *40*, 142–162.

Veyne, P. (1999). L'identité grecque devant Rome et l'empereur. *Revue des Études Grecques*, *112*, 510–567.

Wallace-Hadrill, A. (1981). The Emperor and His Virtues. *Historia (Wiesbaden, Germany)*, *30*, 298–323.

ENDNOTES

1 Henkel (1887) p. 102 refers to Osann (1837) pp. 8-34, who explains that the sources from which we can deduce the treatment of the mixed constitution in Dicaearchus are Cic. *ad Att.* XIII 32 and Ath. IV.19. Today the sources on the thought of this author are collected in Mirhady (2001) and specifically that of Athenaeus on p. 102.

2 Goodenough (1928) pp. 80-82 insists on the Eastern origin of this image, but that does not necessarily exclude Stoicism as its source.

Chapter 3
Against Corruption and Tyranny:
The Political Relevance of 14th–15th-c. Francesc Eiximenis

Vicent Martines
https://orcid.org/0000-0002-2186-4815
University of Alicante, Spain

ABSTRACT

This study analizes the contributions of medieval and Renaissance civic humanism to Political Science (with special attention to the theory of good government) and how current they can be effectively today; how useful they can be today. The analysis focuses on the contribution of Francesc Eiximenis´s Regiment de la cosa pública ['Government of the public'] as part of his Dotzè del Crestià. We make a brief anthology of fragments (in the original version and in translation into Spanish to make it more accessible to a wider audience, especially, if possible, active politicians) that include advice and teachings that can show how useful Francesc Eiximenis' conceptual proposal can be today.

INTRODUCTION: CIVIC HUMANISM AGAINST TYRANNY AND IN FAVOR OF GOOD PUBLIC GOVERNANCE

In the Middle Ages and during Humanism, that is, from the last quarter of the 13th to the 16th century, a line of thought developed that was compatible with Humanism from the beginning and with a vocation, practically from its seminal stage, towards the transfer of knowledge to the civic sphere (Anchústegui Igarturi and Lázaro Pulido 2021; Arquero Caballero 2023; Baron 1955, 2014; Blythe 2000;

DOI: 10.4018/979-8-3373-2332-9.ch003

Freeden / Stears (eds.) 2013; Hankins, 2000). This is, in short, a true praise of the civic and it will not be surprising that it is so if we take into account that so many of the thinkers that we will indicate below held responsibilities of government or advice to government bodies (royal, municipal, ecclesiastical) and their writings have clear traces of influences from the model or fundamental reference that was Plato's *Republic* (Butinyà 2016, 2018, 2020; Butinyà / Cortijo (Eds.) 2011, 2012; Cortijo 2018; Hankins 2009; Hernando 1994; Nederman 2019; Olives 2000). The praise of the civic is accompanied by an obvious "praise" of the word (oral and written), and that becomes a crucial element for cultural identity. These are relevant figures, who establish a line of thought that is ultimately coherent, such as: Saint Thomas Aquinas, Blessed Ramon Llull, Dante Alighieri, Francesc Eiximenis, Joan Fernández d'Heredia, Saint Vincent Ferrer, Bernat Metge, Coluccio Salutati, Ferran Valentí, Niccolò Machiavelli, Saint Thomas More and Juan Luis Vives (Barceló Crespí and Ensenyat Pujol 1996; Butinyà 2016, 2018, 2020; Butinyà / Cortijo (eds.) 2011; Martines 2014, 2024; Pocock 2010).

Francesc Eiximenis embodies the common factor of the social pedagogy strategy of these authors: he aims at a specific target learning audience, that is, individuals, a collective, a society with whom they relate to make either sermons (properly) or writings precisely oriented to provide a guidance towards public virtues (and morals) in order to seek the Public Good and the General Interest for the sustainability of society and good government; explicitly against tyranny (Baron 1955; Berlin 1969; Evangelisti 2017; Hankins 2019, 2022; Martines 2022; Peterson 2011; Pettit 2002; Souza/ Bayona Aznar 2013; Ullmann 1961). In this collective it is assumed that, during the moment one reads their books, there is a high degree of preparation that allowed their recipients to read and understand complex texts; in other cases, the authors become a kind of "officiant", rhetorician, 'orator', who addresses a multiple target audience, very diverse and that shows great differences in terms of their cultural level and social status. These treatises, ars and "manuals", even fiction novels, are true examples of "polyacroasia" (Cortijo (ed.) 2018; Hernández i Dobón 2024; Martinez-Roig / Merma / Gavilán 2021; Roig-Vila 2015).

These intellectuals can be coherently understood as stations on a conceptual line (too often a *via crucis*) that tends, from the few – those who are *καλοκ γαθός*, according to the Platonic qualifier, which contains the qualities of "beautiful", "noble", "good", which are those of ριστος, "excellent", which, although at the time it referred to 'noble', is now qualified by the quality of *ρετή*, that is, "excellence", "virtue" – towards the majority... (Camps 2019; Costa 2009; Dagger 1997; Hankins 2019).Although it does not always (or almost never) happen with the majority. It is about promoting good practices of government and subjugation to power (in rulers and subjects) that will come to inspire great figures of the Enlightenment (Rousseau, Voltaire, Diderot, Grimm, Madame d'Épinay, etc.), and includes rulers who, like

Catherine II the Great of Russia, drank from the sources of the Enlightenment, and, like her, from the sources of it. In short, it is the formulation of the foundations of the modern State.

FRANCESC EIXIMENIS (GIRONA, *ca.* 1328/32-1409, PERPIGNAN), PROGRAMATIC COINCIDENCES WITH COLUCCIO SALUTATI (STIGNANO, BUGGIANO, 1331-FLORENCE, 1406) AGAINST TYRANNY.

We will highlight, from the aforementioned series of authors, two, who also coincide in their postulates (servants of power with a vocation for the general interest), between the 14th and 15th centuries: Francesc Eiximenis, with his *Regiment de cosa pública* ["Government of the public"] in the *Dotzè del Crestià*, coincides greatly with a concept by the great Coluccio Salutati and his, for example, *De tyranno* (De Rosa 2017; Hankins 2009, 2012, 2019, 2022; Poloni 2020; Pastore Stocchi 2014).

He was a Franciscan, Bishop of Elna and Patriarch of Jerusalem, trained in some of the most important higher education centers and universities of the time. He was in the service of the Crown of Aragon, Peter the Ceremonious, John the Poet or the Hunter, and Martin the Human; he was the confessor of Queen Mary, wife of King Martin, as well as advisor to the Jury of Valencia, the Marquis of Villena and Count of Gandia and Ribagorça, Alfonso of Aragon, the Archbishop of Valencia and Pope Benedict XIII, Pope Luna. He was one of the most important intellectuals in Europe at the turn of the 15th century. He is indispensable in the thinking of the time and essential to understand the threshold of the paradigm shift towards the Renaissance with the (Civic) Humanist moviment (Brines 2018; Escolà 2023; Martí Castellà / Renedo Puig (eds.) 2021).

In the *Dotzè del Crestià*, there is the *Regiment de la cosa pública* ['The Government of the Public'] (Eiximenis 2024, 2023; Regiment/Gobierno 2009), in which he condenses his concern (and teaching) for the common good (or general interest), based on his knowledge of politics (civil –municipal and royal – and religious – secular, regular, diocesan and papal) and its relations with religion and the models and teachings that the classics, not only the Fathers of the Church, can contribute (Bayona Aznar 2019; Escolà (Coord) 2000; Gascón Urís 1990; Giner 2010; Guixeras 1998, 2013; Guixeras Olivet 2021; Hauf Valls 2007; Juncosa i Bonet 2021; López Amo 1946; Maravall 1967; Pedretti 2021; Renedo Puig 2021; Tormo Camallonga 2021; Tostes 2021; Viera 1980; Webster 1968; Wittlin 2003, 2008, 2010).

This work cannot be ignored as a precedent for Machiavelli or, if one does not want it to be a "precedent" in terms of textual affiliation, then a precedent in the treatment of the issue (Canfora 2005; Pocock 2010). In this sense, it is very significant that the Treatise on Good Political Practices which is the *Regiment…* by Francesc Eiximenis, is a work destined to be a *vademecum* for the juries of Valencia. It is the civic power that renews the ideology and political praxis. Humanism becomes, without a doubt, civic. Eiximenis also makes his contribution in a "civic" sense in the linguistic sense. Eiximenis uses the Romance language, as Leonardo Bruni, a contemporary of Eiximenis, but much younger, would later suggest (Rogers 1991a, 1991b).

In the same way that, shortly afterwards (in fact almost simultaneously) we find in a fundamental work, *De Tyranno* (1400) by another key figure in (civic) Humanism, Coluccio Salutati, Chancellor of Florence, that he is very concerned about good government and the purity of the principles and values that should guide the rulers (the prince and his officers) and the vices that they should avoid (De Rosa 2017; Martines 2023)

EXAMPLES OF EIXIMENIS'S SUPERB ADVICE FOR GOOD GOVERNANCE, INCLUDING IN THE CURRENT CIRCUMSTANCES

Below we offer a brief anthology of advice from Eiximenis that current (Valencian) rulers should pay heed to. The following excerpts have been translated into English by Prof. Antonio Cortijo (Center for Catalan Studies, UCSB) and are a foretaste of his complete English translation of the work from the Catalan version established by Hauf and the Spanish translation by Martines / Justiniano (*Regiment/Gobierno* 2009). In each example, we provide first the English translation, followed by the aforementioned Spanish translation.

Eiximenis and the Public Good

> CCCLVII. In which it explains what is the public (common) (Regiment/Gobierno 2009: 93)

[...]

The first [proposition] is that the public is a community of people gathered together who live under the same law, government and customs, if you want such a union to be a kingdom, city or town, castle or any similar community, but not a single house. Because it seems that the domestic union that represents a single house or a part of some community cannot be called a "public thing", but that it is called a "private or own thing". This is how the Philosopher explains this topic in his *Politics*.

The second is this: that each community must be composed of different people who help each other according to their needs. This is so because the relationship of each good community has to be the unity and well-being of the inhabitants, and it has to be founded and bound in love and harmony, and each one cannot get what he needs by himself. Therefore it is necessary, for the preservation of the community, that one helps the other according to his need.

CCCLVII. Que explica qué es lo público (Regiment/Gobierno 2009: 93)

[...]

La primera es que lo público es una comunidad de gentes reunides que viven bajo una misma ley, gobierno y costumbres, si se quiere que tal unión sea reino, ciudad, villa, castillo o cualquier comunidad semejante, que no sea una casa sola. Porque parece que la unión doméstica que representa una casa sola o parte de alguna comunidad no se puede llamar "cosa pública", sino que se llama cosa particular, privada o propia; así lo explica el filósofo hablando de este tema en su *Política*.

La segunda es ésta: que cada comunidad debe estar compuesta por distintas personas que se ayuden unes a otras según sus necesidades. Esto es así porque la relación de cada buena comunidad tiene que ser la unidad y bienquerencia de los habitantes, y tiene que estar fundada y atada en el amor y la concordia, y cada uno no puede obtener por sí mismo lo que necesita. Por eso es necesario, para la preservación de la comunidad, que uno ayude al otro según su necesidad.

Eiximenis on Law and Justice

CCCLXIV. How good government of the public requires that the laws be made in favor of it and that they be obeyed by all (Regiment/Gobierno 2009: 105)

Public government still requires for its conservation to be ordered and governed by noble and beneficial laws, and this is its second main foundation. That is why it should be known here that Tullius tells in the first book of his *Rhetoric* that the judges must always guide the laws for the preservation of the public, because that is mainly why they have have been made. Just as medicine has not been made for the profit of the doctor, but only to provide health to the sick, so the law should not be made for the personal profit of the prince or anyone in particular, but for the profit of the public government, to which many or all offend if the prince, who must be a good doctor, does not succeed with good laws and with good customs to restore health, that is, the good state. [...] these laws must be founded on charity and justice, and then those who want to do evil cannot be excused under the shadow of the law.

[...]

The dignity and nobility of a good law must also move men to the observance of the laws, *fueros* and good ordinances, because the great philosopher Demosthenes says that laws are the exaltation of the public, and also Papinianus in book II, *De natura de homine*, indicates that the condition of the true law is that it by itself and through it is the destruction of crimes, persecution of evildoers and declaration of the understanding of men; so that the law is for all a mirror of truth, a rule of justice and a firm foundation for all those who love the community.

> CCCLXIV. Cómo el buen gobierno de lo público requiere que las leyes sean hechas a su favor y que sean bien observadas por todos (Regiment/Gobierno 2009: 105)

Requiere todavía el gobierno público para su conservación, que sea ordenado y regido por nobles y provechosas leyes, y éste es su segundo fundamento principal. Por eso se debe aquí saber que Tulio cuenta en el primer libro de su *Rethorica* que los jueces siempre deben orientar las leyes para la preservación de lo público, porque para eso se han hecho principalmente. Así como la medicina no se ha hecho para provecho del médico, sino que es solamente para procurar la salud del enfermo, así la ley no debe ser hecha para provecho personal del príncipe ni de nadie en particular, sino para provecho del gobierno público, al cual muchos o todos ofenden, si el príncipe, que debe ser el buen médico, no consigue con buenas leyes ni con buenas costumbres devolverle la salud, es decir, el buen estado. [...] deben estas leyes estar fundadas en la caridad y en la justicia, y entonces aquellos que quieran hacer el mal, no se puedan excusar bajo la sombra de la ley.

[...]

La dignidad y nobleza de una buena ley debe además mover a los Hombres a la observación de las leyes, fuero y buen ordenamiento, porque cuenta de las leyes aquel gran filosofo Demóstenes que son exaltación de lo público, y también cuenta Papinianus *libro II, De Natura de homine*, que la condición de la verdadera ley es que ella y por ella sea la destrucción de crímenes, persecución de malhechores y declaración del entendimiento de los Hombres; de manera que ella sea para todos espejo de verdad, regla de justicia y firme fundamento de todos los que aman la comunidad.

> CCCLXVIII. That teaches the third foundation of the public thing, to rigurously maintain justice (Regiment/Gobierno 2009: 109-110)

The third main foundation of public government is that it is governed by a righteous justice. The reason why the profit and the good condition of the whole community requires that it be governed by justice, is because from justice, as well as from true virtue, comes all the connection, support and strength of the public [...] By these words you can see how justice mainly protects the general interest of the community and then pretends to do good to each one in particular, because the general interest is the particular interest of each one of the community as long as he is a member of the public.

And if you want to see how justice protects the general interest, listen to how Saint Bernard declared it in an Advent *sermon*, where he says: "Justice teaches to give to each one what is his and what belongs to him. Therefore, and in the same way, it teaches that to each one, that is, to the elders, honor, reverence and obedience; to equals, love and help in their case; and support and patience to the minors, piety, advice and order according the possibilities of the just person. If these things are maintained by all, the public remains highly governed". That's why Aristotle said, in the fifth book of *Ethics*, that justice is such a wonderful virtue that the stars of the sky should not be compared to it.

[...] for the public government it is completely necessary for all communities to observe justice if we do not want all of us to end up in nothing. Because of this he says [Saint Augustine in *The City of God*] that the community must beware of entrusting justice to people who do not know how to observe it and do not want to do it, as is the case of young people, men corrupted by the love of money, negligent or lazy people, those who are too much in love with themselves, or soft people who have no virtue, no capacity for sacrifice and no strength. [...] On the contrary, know that to those who have zeal for the justice of the public and suffer tribulation, God in this life and in the next gives them special honors, graces and privileges.

> CCCLXVIII. Que enseña el tercer fundamento del gobierno público, que es mantener rigurosamente la justicia (Regiment/Gobierno 2009: 109-110)

El tercer fundamento principal del gobierno público es que esté regido por una recta justicia. La razón por la cual el provecho y el buen estamento de toda la comunidad requiere que esté regida por la justicia, es, porque de la justicia, así como de la verdadera virtud, sale toda la ligazón, sostenimiento y Fortaleza de lo público [...] Por estas palabras se puede ver cómo la justicia principalmente protegí el interés general de la comunidad y después pretende hacer el bien a cada uno en particular, porque del interés general se sigue el interés particular de cada uno de la comunidad en cuanto que se es miembro de lo público.

Y si se quiere ver de qué manera la justicia protegí el interés general, atended a cómo lo ha declarado san Bernardo en un *sermón de Adviento*, donde dice: "La justicia enseña a dar a cada uno lo suyo y lo que le pertenece. Por consiguiente y del mismo modo enseña a dar a cada uno, esto es, a los mayores, honores, reverencia y obediencia; a los iguales, amor y ayuda en su caso, y apoyo y paciencia a los menores, Piedad, consejo y orden según las posibilidades de la persona justa. Si estas coses son mantenidas por todos, lo público permanece altamente gobernado". Por eso decía Aristóteles, en el quinto libro de las *Éticas*, que la justicia es una virtud tan maravillosa que las estrelles del cielo no se deben comparar con ella.

[...] para el gobierno público es completamente necesario a toda la comunidad observar la justicia si no queremos todos caer finalmente en la nada. A causa de esto se dice que se debe guardar la comunidad de encomendar la justicia a persones que no la sepan observar y no la quieran hacer, así como son los jóvenes, los hombres corrompidos por el amor al dinero, las persones negligentes o perezosas, aquéllas que sean demasiado amantes de sí mismas, o persones blandes que no tengan ninguna virtud, ni capacidad de sacrificio ni ninguna fuerza. [...] Por el contrario, sabed que a aquellos que tienen celo por la justicia de lo público y sufren tribulación, que Dios en esta vida y en la otra les concedí especiales honores, gracias y privilegios.

Eiximenis Against Disloyalty

> CCCLXIX. Which exposes the fourth foundation of the public thing, and it is loyalty (Regiment/Gobierno 2009: 113)

The fourth foundation of the public is the loyalty of men. The reason is, just as persevering with unfaithful people takes away the courage, in the same way the audacity to do justice and the hard things and of value to the one to whom it belongs; and that the regent feels fidelity and loyalty with those among whom he lives, they fortify his heart to do virtuously and without fear everything that corresponds to his charge.

In the same way, if any member in the Council by which the public government is governed sees that there are great forgers and deceivers there, who with their tricks and bad ways can spoil his good judgment or reveal it improperly, such a man will never be able to advise fully and perfectly, because he will think: "This is so; and why do I have to give this good advice since it will not be followed at all by these, who will spoil it with falsehoods, but will be harmed by them, because they themselves will reveal my advice to those who will always be my enemies?" See how through fear of disloyalty a good council has been lost, which in the presence of loyal men would go forward and be of great benefit. And so when a man gets into the habit of being disloyal, never or very late will he want to make an effort.

> CCCLXIX. Que explica el cuarto fundamento de lo público, que es la lealtad (Regiment/Gobierno 2009: 113)

El cuarto fundamento de lo público es la lealtad de los hombres. La razón es, porque así como perseverar con personas desleales quita el coraje, la audacia de hacer justicia y las cosas arduas y de valor a aquel a quien pertenece hacerla; y que el regente sienta fidelidad y lealtad entre quienes habita, hace que el corazón se le fortifique para hacer virtuosamente y sin miedo todo lo que le corresponda a su cargo.

Del mismo modo, si quien interviene en el Consejo por el que se rige el gobierno público ve que allí hay grandes falsarios y engañadores, que con sus mañas y malas maneras le pueden estropear su buen juicio o lo revelarán indebidamente, nunca tal hombre podrá aconsejar íntegra y perfectamente, porque pensará: "Esto es así; y ?por qué tengo yo que dar este buen consejo puesto que no se seguirá en absoluto por éstos, que falsamente lo estropearán, sino que se hará mal, porque ellos mismos revelaran mi consejo a aquellos que siempre serán mis enemigos?" Ved cómo por el temor a la deslealtad se ha perdido un buen consejo, el cual en presencia de hombres leales iría adelante y sería de gran provecho. Y es así que cuando el hombre toma por costumbre ser desleal, nunca o muy tarde se querrá esforzar.

Eiximenis Against Bad Advisers

> CCCLXXI. That the rulers must be loyal to the people and in what matters, and about the bad advisers of the rulers (Regiment/Gobierno 2009: 119-123)

So that the subjects had more loyalty, they wanted the princes to keep this to their the vassals until death. And they said that the prince is as treacherous to his vassal when he lacks trust, as the vassal is to the lord; and it is worthy of greater pain in that more loyalty and virtue must appear in the prince than in the vassal, and the public will never be well governed if the prince does not keep loyalty to his vassals and subjects. In this case the prince loses the heart of the subjects, and therefore the government of the public falls to the ground, since the head is not united to the members: just as the body of the man is dead if the head is removed, and the head also dies if it is separated from the body.

It is true that the bad and crazy princes, since no one wants to give them a displeasure and no subject is able to challenge them for the loyalty they owe them, no matter how great are the disloyalties they commit they will not consider them as such, but they are so crazy that they do not believe that they can be disloyal to anyone, as if they were gods who do not sin by nature; and as if they were gods, they believe that everything they do is theirs to do, and so they go to perdition. And their bad advisers are to blame for suggesting such follies to them; and for that they have their prize finally, because God turns the winds and the heart of the princes against them, and finally they kill them, and they also take away everything they have gathered in their service.

[...]

As for the loyalty that exists among the members of the community, know that it is very necessary and priceless. [...] This loyalty also requires that ones go directly and sincerely to the other, and that he supports him in his passions, if his ways are not unbearable, like the passions of madmen and manifest rogues, unless they are so ugly that it brings one shame to have such a bad friend. On the other hand, if it is supportable, he must consent to it to preserve the public government, especially if he is loyal in all his acts.

> CCCLXXI. Que los gobernantes al pueblo deben guardar lealtad entre sí y en qué coses, y sobre los malos consejeros de los gobernantes (Regiment/ Gobierno 2009: 119-123)

Para que los súbditos tuviesen más lealtad, querían que los príncipes la guardasen a los vasallos hasta la muerte. Y decían que tan traidor es el príncipe a su vasallo cuando le falta a la confianza, como el vasallo al señor; y es digno de mayor pena en cuanto que debe aparecer más lealtad y virtud en el príncipe que en el vasallo, y lo público nunca estará bien gobernado si el príncipe no guarda lealtad a sus vasallos y súbditos. En este caso el príncipe pierde el corazón de los súbditos, y por consiguiente, entonces, el gobierno de lo público cae a tierra, puesto que la cabeza no está unida a los miembros: así como el cuerpo del hombre está muerto si se le quita la cabeza, y la cabeza también se muere si se la separa del cuerpo.

Es verdad que los malos y locos príncipes, puesto que nadie les quiere dar un disgusto ni ningún súbdito es capaz de retarlos por la lealtad que les deben, por grandes deslealtades que cometan no las tendrán por tales, sino que están tan locos, que no creen que ellos puedan ser desleales a nadie, como si fueran dioses que no pecan por naturaleza; y como si fueran dioses, creen que todo lo que hacen les toca hacerlo, y así van a la perdición. Y tienen culpa sus malos consejeros que les dan a entender tales locuras; y por eso tienen su premio finalmente, porque Dios gira los vientos y el corazón de los príncipes contra ellos, y finalmente los hacen matar, y les quitan asimismo todo cuanto han reunido en sus servicios.

[...]

En cuanto a la lealtad que hay entre los Hombres de la comunidad, sabed que es muy necesaria y no tiene precio. [...] Requiere además esta lealtad que el hombre vaya directo hacia el otro y sin ficción, y que lo soporte en sus pasiones, si sus maneras no son insoportables, como las pasiones de los locos y de los granujas manifiestos, a no ser que sean tan feas que conlleven para el hombre una vergüenza tener un amigo tan malo. De otro modo, en caso de que el otro sea llevadero, se le debe consentir para conservar el gobierno público, principalmente si es leal en todos sus actos.

CCCLXXI. Which explains that the fifth foundation of public government is to be governed by good advisers (Regiment/Gobierno 2009: 123)

The fifth foundation of public government is to be governed by good counselors. [...] although much good advice is useful for the public government, nevertheless such advice does not come from the most of men, because normally they are not good to advise on high things; and because of this most of the good advice comes from few men. Wisdom is found only in a few, according to the Holy Scriptures, for just as good advice only comes from wise men, only a few men have most of the good advice. Therefore, to deal with high, great and dangerous matters, a multitude of people should not be called, but should only be dealt with by a few and chosen people. And this is how all the communities in the world normally do it: everything that belongs to the government of the public is dealt with by a few who are reputed to be the wisest and the best in the community.

And that this is necessary, it is also clear in that the communities when they come together they immediately riot and their members are soon ready to fight with each other when they contradict each other, and they immediately make noise when they don't understand each other. It is dangerous for the people to riot against those who are the highest members of the community, against whom the community and the crowds are normally moved before.

CCCLXXI. Que explica que el quinto fundamento del gobierno de lo público es que sea regido por buenos consejeros (Regiment/Gobierno 2009: 123)

El quinto fundamento del gobierno de lo público es que sea regido por buenos consejeros. [...] aunque muchos buenos consejos sean provechosos para el gobierno público, sin embargo tales consejos no salen del conjunto de los hombres, porque normalmente no es bueno para aconsejar en cosas altes; y por eso la multitud de los buenos consejos está en unos pocos Hombres. La sabiduría no se encuentra sino en unos pocos, según dicen las Sagradas Escrituras. pues, como los buenos consejos solamente salen de los hombres sabios, solamente en unos pocos hombres está la multitud de los buenos consejos. Por ello, para tratar altos asuntos, grandes y peligrosos, no se debe llamar a multitud de gentes, sino que solamente deben ser tratadas por pocas y elegidas persones. Y así lo hacen normalmente todas las comunidades del mundo: todo lo que pertenece al gobierno de los público es tratado por unos pocos que son reputados como las más sabios y los mejores de la comunidad.

Y que así sea necesariamente, se manifiesta además porque las comunidades reunides se alborotan inmediatamente y sus miembros pronto están dispuestos a pelear entre sí mismos en cuanto se contradice a otro, y arman inmediatamente ruido cuando no se entienden. Es peligroso que el pueblo se alborote contra aquéllos que son principales, contra quienes la comunidad y la multitud normalmente se conmueve antes.

Eiximenis Against Speculators, Usurers and Swindlers

> CCCXCI. How the speculator damages the public government (Regiment/Gobierno 2009: 157)

[...] the speculator must be persecuted and expelled from the community as capital enemy. Because the speculator always wishes for bad weather and scarcity, he buys wholesale with the hope of making the land more expensive, he is totally opposed to the good merchant, and he never stops trading or exchanging unless it is for his own profit. Because of this, God confuses them because of the curses that they justly receive by the people and because of the affliction that He causes them.

Against these in particular, the regents of the public government must make a common front and take care, setting laws and limits that they do not dare to exceed without great pain, for them and for the other resellers who make the community more expensive; and if they fall into penalties, that they execute them without delay.

> CCCXCI. Cómo el especulador daña en mucho al gobierno público (Regiment/Gobierno 2009: 157)

[...] el especulador debe ser perseguido y expulsado de la comunidad como capital enemigo. Porque el especulador siempre desea el mal tiempo y la carestía, compra al por mayor con la esperanza de encarecer la tierra, es totalmente contrario al buen mercader, y nunca para ni cesa de trasegar o de cambiar si no es para su propio provecho. A causa de esto los confunde Dios por las maldiciones que el pueblo justamente les da y por la aflicción que les procura.

Contra éstos en especial se deben reunir y cuidar mucho, los regentes del gobierno público, poniéndoles leyes y límites que no se atrevan a exceder sin grandes penas, para ellos y para los otros revendedores que encarecen la comunidad; y si caen en las penas, que las ejecuten sin dilación.

> CCCXCII. It says that usurers and swindlers must be expelled from the community […] (Regiment/Gobierno 2009: 158)

[...] that usurers, those lending at interest or any fraudsters be expelled from the community, so that the people and the community are not burdened with debts for nothing. [...] cut-price shopkeepers take the money, and swindlers are the death of the merchants. Because the good merchant is always clear and direct to everyone.

They must be avoided, moreover, because such swindlers deceive innocent people and burden them with sin; and when people are fake, they lose their love for the community and act according to their own interests.

> CCCXCII. Que dice que de la comunidad sean expulsados los usureros y los estafadores. [...] (Regiment/Gobierno 2009: 158)

[...] que de la comunidad sean expulsados los usureros, de intereses y de cualquier estafa, para que la gente y la comunidad no se carguen de deudas por nada. [...] los barateros se llevan el dinero, y los estafadores son la muerte de los mercaderes. Porque el buen mercader siempre va claro y directo a todo el mundo.

Se les debe esquivar, además, porque tales estafadores hacen falsa a la gente inocente y la cargan de pecado; y cuando la gente es falsa pierde el amor a la comunidad y obra según su propio interés.

Eiximenis Against Princes and Great Lords Who Are Fearful

> DLXXVI. That it is absolutely wrong for the ruler to be fearful (Regiment/Gobierno 2009: 177-179)

That it is worse for princes and great lords to be fearful than for all other men in the world, it is taught by Sempronius, when he writes *ad Lacedomium Regem Parchie* thus, because he says here: "That in the prince there is nobility of lineage, civil power, abundance of riches and just cause, and that he is afraid of confronting someone, of attacking his opponent or of making him come to his senses, clearly shows that he is not a knight or a man fit for government. Secondly, because the cowardly prince is not fit to defend himself or his subjects, and, therefore, it is as if they had no lord. Thirdly, because such a prince is not good at imparting justice, nor to do anything related to his office, and, consequently, he must be ashamed of being called king or lord. Fourthly, because fear always makes men think of themselves and closes their understanding so that they neither know how to advice, nor perceive or consider anyone's advice, and they not know it nor can they put it into practice; it makes men tremble, and, consequently, makes them be totally overcome and terrified." Think, well, in what state is the kingdom that has such a lord, and it would be better if he had none, because then they would name someone else who would govern them better and with courage.

> DLXXVI. Que al gobernante le queda absolutamente mal ser miedoso (Regiment/Gobierno 2009: 177-179)

Que para los príncipes y los grandes señores esté peor que para todos los otros hombres del mundo ser miedosos, lo enseña así Sempronius, cuando escribe *ad Lacedomium regem Parchie* así, porque él dice aquí: "Que en el príncipe haya nobleza de linaje, potencia civil, abundancia de riquezas y causa justa, y que tanga miedo de enfrentarse a alguien, de atacar a su contrario o de hacerlo entrar en razón, claramente muestra que no es caballero ni hombre apto para el gobierno. En segundo lugar, porque el príncipe miedoso no es apto para defenderse a sí mismo ni a sus súbditos y, por consiguiente, para los súbditos es como si no tuvieran señor. En tercer lugar, porque asimismo tal príncipe no es bueno para impartir justicia, ni para hacer nada relacionado con su oficio, y, por consiguiente, debe tener gran vergüenza de llamarse rey o señor, y el pueblo no debe consentir estar en tan mala situación. En cuarto lugar, porque el miedo hace al hombre pensar siempre en sí mismo y le cierra el entendimiento de manera que ni sabe aconsejarse, ni percibe ni considera el consejo de nadie, ni lo sabe ni lo puede poner en ejecución; hace al hombre temblar, y, por consiguiente, hace al hombre estar totalmente vencido y aterrado." Piensa, pues, en qué estamento está el reino que tiene tal señor, y más le valdría no tener ninguno, porque entonces nombrarían a cualquier otro que los gobernase mejor y con valentía.

Eiximenis Against Tyranny

DCII. That the ruler is not a tyrant, and what is tyranny (Regiment/Gobierno 2009: 189)

All the aforementioned cautions are reduced by Aristotle, in his Politics, to four, and they are these. The first is: that tyrants do everything possible to make their subjects ignorant and rude, so that they do not know how to attack them. The second: let them be fearful, so that no one dares to rise up against them. The third: that they be poor, so that they cannot make war on him. The fourth: that they are not united, so that they cannot plot anything against him.

DCII. Que el gobernante no sea tirano, y qué es la tiranía (Regiment/Gobierno 2009: 189)

Todas las cautelas dichas las reduce Aristóteles, en su Política, a cuatro, y son éstas. La primera es: que los tiranos hacen lo posible para que sus súbditos sean ignorantes y groseros, de manera que no sepan encontrar la manera de atacarlos. La segunda: que sean miedosos, para que nadie se atreva a alzarse contra ellos. La tercera: que sean pobres, para que no puedan hacerle guerra. La cuarta: que no estén unidos, para que no puedan tramar nada contra él.

DCIII. How many evils does the tyrant (Regiment/Gobierno 2009: 195)

In seventh place: because they are never satisfied with those goods that they desire, that is to say, to have enough money, since they incur infinite expenses and expect to incur more every day, and there are those who have done more with love than they with terror, although those obtain it in a fair way, while the tyrants do it unjustly and against the commandments of God. And it comes that in spite of all their tricks they cannot manage to be safe in their governments, neither they themselves nor their children, as the kings are; and they think that if they leave their lordships to their children, that they will inherit what is not theirs and, consequently, they will be condemned and they will have themselves and their children condemned for that same reason. If they don't give them power, they will leave them poor and without anything, despised and persecuted, while the people will throw them all out. You can see if the unfortunates tyrants were born in a bad place, because neither in this life nor in the next do they expect anything but evil and sorrows, pains and torments.

DCIII. Cuántos males obra el tirano (Regiment/Gobierno 2009: 195)

En séptimo lugar: porque jamás se ven satisfechos con aquellos bienes que desean, es decir, tener bastante dinero, ya que hacen gastos infinitos y esperan hacer más cada día, y hay quien ha hecho más con amor que ellos con terror, aunque aquellos lo obtienen de modo justo, mientras que los tiranos lo hacen injustamente y en contra de los mandamientos de Dios. Y ven que a pesar de todas sus artimañas no pueden conseguir estar seguros en sus gobiernos, ni ellos mismos ni sus hijos, así como están los reyes; y piensan que si dejan sus señorías a sus hijos, que ellos heredarán lo que no es suyo y, por consiguiente, serán condenados y se harán condenar a sí mismos y a sus hijos por esa misma razón. Si no les dejan el poder, ven que los dejarán pobres y sin nada, despreciados y perseguidos, en tanto que el pueblo los echará a todos. Ya veis si los desgraciados de los tiranos han nacido en mal punto, porque ni en esta vida ni en la otra les esperan sino males y dolores, penas y tormentos.

Eiximenis Against Corruption

DCLXXXVII. That shows in what evils incurs the official of the ruler who voluntarily accepts gifts. (Regiment/Gobierno 2009: 227)

[...] the officer of the lord who accepts gifts or donations falls into the following evils. [...] The third [our emphasis]: because the bad official, due to his corruption, takes away his fame, since he is not at all appreciated by anyone, and gives a very bad example of himself, while if he is a high office, as well as a chancellor, a governor or similar, he provokes other lesser officials to do the same, and also provokes the people to despair completely and to take justice into their hands. The fourth: that by receiving gifts he becomes so blind that he thinks that injustice is justice and will defend it fearlessly and without shame in public, since he is used to this evil [...] The fifth evil is this: that the man who accepts gifts agrees that he loses the right to speak and to promote justice; the reason is because the man who accepts gifts sells himself to those from whom he accepts them, while, like a captive, he has to do what is in favor of those from whom he accepts them; therefore he does not dare to speak to them, but if he sees that something is unjust he has to remain silent, and, if he speaks, he will pervert the right of the other and direct justice in favor of the one who has corrupted him, and he will do justice in his own way until he brings it in his favor.

> DCLXXXVII. Que enseña en qué males cae el oficial del gobernante que acepta voluntariamente donaciones. (Regiment/Gobierno 2009: 227)

[...] el oficial del señor que acepta regalos o dádivas cae en los siguientes males. [...] El tercero *[negrilla nuestra]*: porque el mal oficial, por su corrupción, se quita la fama, en tanto que, no es en absoluto apreciado por nadie, y da de sí mismo muy mal ejemplo, en tanto que si es un alto cargo, así como un canciller, un gobernador o semejante, provoca a los otros cargos menores a hacer lo mismo, y también provoca al pueblo a desesperarse por completo y a tomarse la justicia por su mano. El cuarto: que por recibir dádivas él se vuelve tan ciego que le parece que la injusticia sea justicia y la defenderá sin miedo y sin vergüenza en público, puesto que está acostumbrado a esta maldad [...] El quinto mal es así: que el hombre que acepta dádivas conviene que pierda el derecho a hablar y a favorecer la justicia; la razón es porque el hombre que acepta dádivas se vende a aquéllos de quienes las acepta, en tanto que, como un cautivo, él tiene que hacer lo que está a favor de aquéllos de quienes las acepta; de lo que se sigue que no se atreva a hablar ellos, sino que si ve que algo es injusto él tiene que callar, y, si habla, pervertirá el derecho del otro y dirigirá la justicia en pro de aquél que lo ha corrompido, y hará justicia a su guisa hasta que la lleve a su favor.

CONCLUSION

We have carried out an analysis of the contributions of medieval and Renaissance civic humanism to political science (with special attention to the theory of good government) and how effective they can be today. We have focused on the contribution of Francesc Eiximenis with the *Regiment de la cosa publica* as part of his *Dotzè del*

Crestià. We have proposed a brief anthology of fragments (in the original version and in translation into Spanish – in order to make it more accessible to a wider audience, especially, if possible, active politicians) that offer advice and teachings that can show how useful Francesc Eiximenis' conceptual proposal can be today.

We have seen, from the examples in Eiximenis' work, how deeply rooted it is in the principles of civic humanism. It is a coherent contribution in the context of Western Europe, where humanism developed. Humanism is not just about a philological passion for the Greco-Roman classics themselves. Based on a deep knowledge of the classics, Humanism aims to improve (civic) government and the social education of the people. The works of civic Humanism are a true eulogy to the word that teaches how to make laws, how to apply them, how to educate (not just train) rulers, public servants and the people for the common good.

We would like to highlight two sentences from the excerpts we have emphasized. It refers to the fact that just laws encourage the people to respect them: "laws must be founded on charity and justice, and then those who want to do evil cannot be excused under the shadow of the law," (Regiment/Gobierno, 2009); "the law is for all a mirror of truth, a rule of justice and a firm foundation for all those who love the community," (Regiment/Gobierno, 2009). That should be enough, for Eiximenis and civic humanism, to promote good government and avoid the evils of tyranny and corruption (see above for examples of the evils of tyranny and corruption).

The vocation of service to the "public thing" of Eiximenis is very similar to that which animates the (public) University as a category. It is about putting knowledge, research, innovation, the development of knowledge, methods, concepts, theories, skills, practices and their transfer at the service of society and its rulers. As the Mallorcan humanist, doctorate in Civil and Canon Law in Bologna, Ferran Valentí, would say in the prologue of his Catalan translation of Cicero's *Paradoxa*, it is about making it possible for many to benefit from knowledge, (Barceló Crespí / Ensenyat Pujol 1996; Martines, 2014).

This is also shown by the Second *Partida* of Alfonso X the Wise (Nanu, 2013), dedicated to treating "Of the studies in which knowledge is learned and of teachers and of schoolchildren" (31.1-11, Arquero Cabellero 2023). If the Wise King of Castile, son-in-law of James I the Conqueror, concludes his important Second *Partida* – that encompasses 31 titles and 359 laws, in which he deals with temporal (that of the government) and spiritual power and, above all, their respective duties – by paying attention to "the studies" it is because they should not have been and should not be a minor thing for good government, as the rulers of that time knew and those of today should keep in mind. The Wise King of Castile says: "And because men and lands and kingdoms take advantage of wise men, and are protected and guided by their advice, therefore we want to talk at the end of this *Partida* about studies, teachers and students, who work to teach and learn this knowledge" (31.1-11).

Therefore, whoever governs should always pay attention to “the wise men” and “their advice”. Eiximenis gave and can still give excellent advice to those in power, as he did in the 14th and 15th centuries to the Juries of Valencia. It would be necessary for the current rulers of any country to still heed the advice of Eiximenis. There should be a need for more Eiximenis and a greater commitment to the general interest.

ACKNOWLEDGMENT

This study has been developed within the Higher Institute of Cooperative Research IVITRA [ISIC-IVITRA] [Program for the Constitution and Accreditation of Higher Institutes of Cooperative Research of Excellence of the Generalitat Valenciana, Ref. ISIC/2012/042] and within the framework of the following projects, networks and research groups: «El catalán antes y después de Pompeu Fabra (s. XVII-XXI). Impacto de la normalización sobre la evolución de la lengua catalana» [PID2021-128381NB-I00]; «Multilingual Observatory for the Linguistic Variation» [CIPROM/2023/6] within the frame of the Prometeo Program of the Valencian Regional Government for Research Groups of Excellence; the UA Research Group VIGROB-125; and the Research Group on Educational Technology in Cultural History, Linguistic Diachrony and Translation [University of Alicante, Ref. GITE-09009-UA].

REFERENCES

Anchústegui Igartua, E., & Lázaro Pulido, M. (Eds.). (2021). Aportaciones franciscanas al republicanismo político. *Araucaria: Revista Iberoamericana de Filosofía, Política, Humanidades y Relaciones Internacionales* [Monográfico I: La creatividad en la filosofía, en la educación y en las artes para hacer las paces: nuevos horizontes interdisciplinarios. Monográfico II: Integración, Derechos Humanos y Ciudadanía Global], 23, 48, 9-31.

Arquero Caballero, G. F. (2023). Alfonso X y el ideal universitario: el final de la Segunda Partida (título XXXI). In Vergara Ciordia, J., Comella Gutiérrez, B., & Arquero Caballero, G. (Eds.), *Aulas, libros y bibliotecas en la Edad Media y Moderna* (pp. 97–126). Dykinson.

Barceló Crespí, M., & Ensenyat Pujol, G. (1996). *Ferrando Valentí i la seva família*. Departament de Filologia Catalana i Lingüística General de la Universitat de les Illes Balears / Publicacions de l'Abadia de Montserrat.

Barceló Crespí, M., & Ensenyat Pujol, G. (2000). *Els nous horitzons culturals a Mallorca al final de l'Edat Mitjana*. Edicions Documenta Balear.

Baron, H. (1955). *The crisis of the early italian Renaissance: civic humanism and republican liberty in an age of classicism and tyranny*. Princeton University Press.

Baron, H. (2014). *In search of Florentine civic humanism: Essays on the transition from medieval to modern thought*. Princeton University Press.

Bayona Aznar, B. (2019). *Pactismo y Teocracia. Las dos caras del pensamiento político de Francesc Eiximenis*. Tecnos.

Berlin, I. (1969). *Four Essays On Liberty*. Oxford University Press.

Blythe, J. (2000). 'Civic humanism' and medieval political thought. In Hankins, J. (Ed.), *Renaissance civic humanism: reappraisals and reflections* (pp. 30–74). Cambridge University Press.

Brines, L. (2018). Biografia documentada de Francesc Eiximenis, OFM. València: Brines.

Butinyà, J., & Cortijo, A. (Eds.). (2011). *L'Humanisme a la Corona d'Aragó (en el context europeu i hispànic)*. Scripta Humanística.

Butinyà, J. (2016). En el pas de la filosofia cristiana a l'ètica en l'Edat Mitjana: l'humanisme català. In A. de Benedetto & E. Bou (Eds.), *Novecento e dintorni. Grilli in Catalogna. Rassegna Iberistica,* 3 (pp. 57-78), Ca'Foscari: Venice.

Butinyà, J. (2018). Metge i Llull front als sarraïns. *Mirabilia*, *26*(1), 194–215.

Butinyà, J. (2020). Ramon Llull i els primers Humanistes. *eHumanista/IVITRA*, 18, 166-187.

Butinyà, J., & Cortijo, A. (Eds.). (2012). Monogràfic: L'humanisme a la Corona d'Aragó, *eHumanista/IVITRA, 1*, 1-246.

Camps, V. (2019). *Virtudes públicas*. Arpa.

Canfora, D. (2005). *Prima di Machiavelli. Politica e cultura in età umanistica*. Laterza.

Cortijo, A. (Ed.). (2018). *Chivalry, the Mediterranean and the Corown of Aragon*. Juan de la Cuesta Hispanic Monographs.

Costa, M. V. (2009). Neo-republicanism, freedom as non-domination, and citizen virtue. *Politics, Philosophy & Economics*, *8*(4), 401–419.

Dagger, R. (1997). *Civic virtues: rights, citizenship, and republican liberalism*. Oxford University Press.

De Rosa, D. (2017) SALUTATI, Lino Coluccio, *Dizionario biografico degli italiani*. Istituto dell'Enciclopedia Italiana: Roma.

Eiximenis, F. (2021). Regiment de la cosa pública, ed- by D. Guixeras Olivet. Barcino (Els Nostres Clàssics. Autors medievals, 40).

Eiximenis, F. (2024). Die Regierung des Gemeinwesens (Regiment de la cosa pública) [translation into German] Alexander Fidora (trad.), Alexander Fidora (ed. lit.). Freiburg im Breisgau: Herder.

Escolà, M. B. (2023). Reflexions entorn d'Eiximenis. Regir la cosa pública. Eiximenis encara. Quaderns Francesc Eiximenis. *Revista de Dret Públic de Catalunya, 1*(1), 11–19.

Escolà, M. B. (Coord) (2000). *Idees de poder.* Barcelona: Institut d'Estudis Humanístics Miquel Coll i Alentorn.

Escolà, Marc. B. (1994). Sobre la teoria del poder en el tractat de Francesc Eiximenis: Regiment de la cosa pública. *Finestrelles [Centre d'Estudis Ignasi Iglésias]*, 6, 189-204.

Evangelisti, P. (2017). La legittimità del potere ed il suo esercizio: Elementi comparativi nella testualità politica francescana del XIV secolo. *Horizonte: revista de Estudos de Teologia e Ciências da Religiao* [Dossiê: Ordens Religiosas Medievais: Poder e Sociedade], 15, 48, 1299-1323

Freeden, M., & Stears, M. (Eds.). (2013). *Oxford handbook of political ideologies.* Oxford University Press.

Gascón Uris, S. (1990). Francesc Eiximenis, 'Tractat d'usura'. *Llengua i literatura: Revista anual de la Societat Catalana de Llengua i literatura*, 28, 554-556.

Giner, S. (2010). Francesc Eiximenis i els orígens del republicanisme. La significació de Lo regiment de la cosa pública. *L'Espill, 34*, 26–33.

Guixeras Olivet, D. (2021). Consideracions sobre els procediments judicials en el Regiment de la cosa pública, de Francesc Eiximenis. In J. Serrano Daura (ed.), *Francesc Eiximenis: en homenatge, Miscel·lània, 4.* Societat Catalana d'Estudis Jurídics, filial de l'Institut d'Estudis Catalans, 223-237.

Guixeras, D. (1998). La tradició textual del Regiment de la cosa pública de Francesc Eiximenis: una aproximació. In A. Chas Aguión, M. Pampín Barral, N. Pena Sueiro, B. Campos, C. Parrilla García, M. Campos Souto (eds.), *Edición y anotación de texos, Actas del Primer Congreso de Jóvenes Filólogos*. Universidade de A Coruña, 323-337.

Guixeras, D. (2013). Edició crítica i estudi del Regiment de la cosa pública de Francesc Eiximenis, Tesi doctoral sota la dirección de Xavier Renedo. Girona: Universitat de Girona.

Hankins, J. (2000). *Renaissance civic humanism: reappraisals and reflections.* Cambridge University Press.

Hankins, J. (2009). *La riscoperta di Platone nel Rinascimento italiano-* Edizione della Normale (Scuola Normale Superiore): Pisa.

Hankins, J. (2012). Coluccio Salutati e Leonardo Bruni. In Ciliberto, M. (Ed.), *Il contributo italiano alla storia del pensiero* (pp. 85–94). Treccani.

Hankins, J. (2019). *Virtue políitics: soulcraft and statecraft in Renaissance Italy.* The Belknap Press of Harvard University Press.

Hankins, J. (2022). *La politica della virtù. Formare la persona e formare lo Stato nel Rinascimento italiano.* Viella Libraria Editrice.

Hauf Valls, A. (2007). El poder espiritual y terrenal de la Iglesia. Las "Allegationes" de Francesc Eiximenis como síntesis de su pensamiento teocrático. Res Publica: revista de filosofía política, 18, 59-82.

Hernández i Dobón, F. (2024). Una nota sobre l'aprenentatge i l'amistat. *Creativity and Educational Innovation Re view (CEIR)*, 8, 67-70.

Hernando, J. (1994). *El poder polític a l'edat mitjana: de la sacralització a la secularització.* Universitat de Barcelona.

Juncosa i Bonet, E. (2021). Eiximenis i el poder reial. Entre la teoría i la praxi. In J. Serrano Daura (ed.), *Francesc Eiximenis: en homenatge, Miscel·lània, 4.* Barcelona: Societat Catalana d'Estudis Jurídics, filial de l'Institut d'Estudis Catalans, 11-50.

López-Amo, A. (1946). El pensamiento político de Eiximeniç en su tratado de "Regiment de princeps. *Anuario de Història del Derecho Español, 17*, 5–139.

Maravall, J. A. (1967). *La corriente democrática medieval en España y la fórmula quod homnes tangit. Estudios de historia del pensamiento español: Serie primera. Edad media.* Cultura Hispánica.

Martí Castellà, S., & Renedo Puig, X. (Eds.). (2021). *Francesc Eiximenis. Vida. Obra, transmissió.* Universitat de Girona, Institut de Llengua i Cultura Catalanes, Secció Francesc Eiximenis.

Martines, V. (2014). Una clave humanista de mediados del siglo XV para el Humanismo de la Corona de Aragón desde fines del siglo XIV: Ferran Valentí y el Prólogo a su traducción de las *Paradoxa* de Cicerón. *Estudios Hispánicos*, *22*, 105–114.

Martines, V. (2022). The pandemic of tyranny. The virus of hatred and other dangers faced by democracy during a pandemic: The Thirty Tyrants of Athens and the prevention of tyranny by Civic Humanism. In Cortijo, A., & Martines, V. (Eds.), *Handbook of research on historical pandemic analysis and the social implications of COVID-19* (pp. 142–152). IGI-Global.

Martines, V. (2023). El tirà, corruptor de lleis, enemic de la saviesa: De la tirania segons Francesc Eiximenis i Coluccio Salutati. Humanisme Cívic contra la tirania. In M.T. del Olmo Ibáñez, M. Soledad Villarrubia Zúñiga, I. Sánchez-López (eds.), Investigación interdisciplinar: Educación y construcción del conocimiento. Valencia: Tirant lo Blanch, 369-382.

Martines, V. (2024). L'actualitat de la ciència política proposada per Francesc Eiximenis (*ca.* 1328/32-1409): el Regiment de la cosa pública i el Dotzè del Crestià al servei dels polítics (actuals). *SCRIPTA. Revista Internacional De Literatura i Cultura Medieval i Moderna, 24*(24). https://doi.org/10.7203/scripta.24.30056 (consulta: 10-5-2025).

Martinez-Roig, R., Merma, G., & Gavilán-Martín, D. (2020). Proposals for social pedagogy and the best political practices. Contribution from the Crown of Aragon: Francesc Eiximenis and his *Regiment de la cosa pública*. In Cortijo, A., & Martines, V. (Eds.), *History of Catalonia*. IGI-Global: IGI Global.

Nanu, I. (2013). *La Segunda Partida de Alfonso X el Sabio y la tradición occidental de los* specula principum. PhD directed by Prof. Marta Haro. Valencia: Universitat de València. https://roderic.uv.es/items/c0ab9d59-b20e-4afe-8719-8242dd841bcb (consulta: 10-10-2024).

Nederman, C. (2019). *Civic humanism*. Stanford Encyclopaedia of Philosophy.

Olives, J. (2000). Poder i reialesa. In *Escolà, Marc. B. (coord.). Idees de poder* (pp. 39–70). Institut d'Estudis Humanístics Miquel Coll i Alentorn.

Pastore Stocchi, M. (2014). *Pagine di storia dell'Umanesimo italiano*. FrancoAngeli.

Pedretti, M. (2021). Els jueus en el Primer del Crestià. In J. Serrano Daura (ed.), *Francesc Eiximenis: en homenatge, Miscel·lània, 4*. Barcelona: Societat Catalana d'Estudis Jurídics, filial de l'Institut d'Estudis Catalans, 89-115.

Peterson, A. (2011). *Civic republicanism and civic education: The education of citizens*. Springer.

Pettit, P. (2002). *Republicanism: a theory of freedom and government*. Oxford University Press.

Pocock, J. G. A. (2010). *Machiavelli and Rome: the republic as ideal and as history. The Cambridge Companion to Machiavelli.* Cambridge University Press.

Poloni, A. (2020). Oltre Coluccio Salutati. La florentina libertas nel contesto del conflitto politico interno nella Firenze del XIV secolo [Monograph on "Libertad, autonomía y orden político a fines de la Edad Media], *Edad Media: revista de historia*, 21, 31-55. https://revistas.uva.es/index.php/edadmedia/article/view/4478 (Consulta: 12-10-2024).

Martines, V. & Justiniano, M. (eds.) (2009). *Regiment Gobierno.* Francesc Eiximenis. *El regiment de la cosa pública en el Dotzé del Crestià, El gobierno de lo público en el Duodécimo del Cristiano*, Pròleg d'A. Hauf, Introducció i notes de V. Martines, Trad. a l'espanyol de V. Martines & M. Justiniano. Palas Atenea: Madrid.

Renedo Puig, X. (2021). Del Dotzè del Crestià al Llibre dels àngels. In J. Serrano Daura (ed.), *Francesc Eiximenis: en homenatge, Miscel·lània, 4.* Barcelona: Societat Catalana d'Estudis Jurídics, filial de l'Institut d'Estudis Catalans, 363-404.

Rogers, D. M. (1991a). La llengua oral al "Regiment de la cosa pública" de Francesc Eiximenis. In J. Mas i Vives, J. Miralles i Montserrat, P. Rosselló Bover (eds.*), Actes de l'Onzè Col·loqui Internacional de Llengua i Literatura Catalanes*, vol. 1, Palma (Mallorca). Publicacions de la Abadia de Montserrat, 431-438.

Rogers, D. M. (1991b). Legal terms in Eiximenis "Regiment de la cosa pública"Termes legals i Eiximenis "Regiment de la cosa pública". *Revista de llengua i dret*, 15, 35-41.

Roig-Vila, R. (2015). Elogio de la palabra en la formación y enseñanza en algunos clásicos de la literatura catalana medieval: Llull, Eiximenis y San Vicente Ferrer. *Crítica Hispánica, 37*(1), 97–116.

Schadee, H. (2018). A Tale of Two Languages: Latin, the Vernacular and Leonardo Bruni's "Civic Humanism". *Humanistica lovaniensia: journal of neo-latin studies*, 67, 1, 10-46.

Souza, J. A., & Bayona Aznar, B. (Eds.). (2013). *Doctrinas y relaciones de poder en el Cisma de Occidente y en la época conciliar (1378-1449).* Prensas de la Universidad de Zaragoza.

Tormo Camallonga, C. (2021). Eiximenis i el dret, a propòsit de les noves ciutats cristianes. In J. Serrano Daura (ed.), *Francesc Eiximenis: en homenatge, Miscel·lània, 4.* Societat Catalana d'Estudis Jurídics, filial de l'Institut d'Estudis Catalans, 51-88

Tostes, R. (2021). Que multiplicació de juristes... posa en lo cor dels hòmens gran terror. Francesc Eiximenis diante do saber jurídico, um ensaio. In J. Serrano Daura (ed.), *Francesc Eiximenis: en homenatge, Miscel·lània, 4.* Societat Catalana d'Estudis Jurídics, filial de l'Institut d'Estudis Catalans, 277-363.

Ullmann, W. (1961). *Principles of government and politics in the Middle Ages.* Methuen.

Viera, D. J. (1980). *Bibliografia anotada de la vida i obra de Francesc Eiximeis (1340?-1409?).* Fundació Salvador Vives Casajoana.

Webster, J. R. (1968). La república cristiana y el rey en el siglo xiv según Francesc Eiximenis (1340?-1409?). *Estudios Franciscanos: Publicación Periódica de Ciencias Eclisiásticas de las Provincias Capuchinas Ibéricas*, *69*, 111–118.

Wittlin, C. (2003). És veritat que Francesc Eiximenis «inventava autors, títols de llibres, i noms de reis i d'altres persones» i que patia d'una "ingenuïtat i credulitat sense limits"? In Martí Castellà, S., Cabré Ollé, M., Feliu Torrent, F., Iglésias Franch, N., & Prats, D. (Eds.), *Actes del Tretzè Col·loqui Internacional de Llengua i Literatura Catalanes* (Vol. 3, pp. 35–55). Universitat de Girona.

Wittlin, C. (2008). El que Francesc Eiximenis sent dels romans que "han elegit antipapes" ("Regiment de la cosa pública" cap. 5, "Dotzè" cap.361). In Massot i Muntaner, J. (Ed.), *Miscel·lània Joaquim Molas* (pp. 29–47). Publicacions de l'Abadia de Montserrat.

Wittlin, C. (2010). Era cristià, *Lo Crestià* de Francesc Eiximenis? Història d'un error de paleografia. *Caplletra: Revista Internacional de Filologia*, *48*, 163–177.

Chapter 4
Pedagogical Reflections on the Common Good: Territories, Communities, and Global Citizenship

Massimiliano Fiorucci
https://orcid.org/0000-0002-9927-6095
Roma Tre University, Italy

Lisa Stillo
https://orcid.org/0000-0002-9271-8495
Roma Tre University, Italy

Aurora Bulgarelli
Link Campus University, Italy

Francesca Gabrielli
https://orcid.org/0009-0003-5012-2540
Niccolò Cusano University, Italy

Alessandra Casalbore
Roma Tre University, Italy

ABSTRACT

This chapter investigates the role of education in rethinking territory, community, and citizenship as essential forms of the common good. Within a pedagogical perspective, it emphasizes how these dimensions are not merely physical or administrative constructs, but relational and symbolic spaces where identity, inclusion, and participation are negotiated. In the face of growing inequalities and the privatization of public spaces, the text calls for an educational commitment to reclaim and

DOI: 10.4018/979-8-3373-2332-9.ch004

care for shared places, fostering democratic life and social justice. The concept of the educating community emerges as a concrete response to contemporary crises, promoting active citizenship and collective responsibility. By linking bodies to spaces and people to places, pedagogy becomes a transformative force capable of reimagining the public sphere, strengthening social bonds, and sustaining forms of coexistence based on solidarity, accessibility, and shared belonging.

INTRODUCTION

In the current context, both globally and locally, we are witnessing a crisis of humanity that manifests itself in multiple forms: the weakening of democracies around the world and the rise of hate speech and extremism; the escalation of conflicts and wars with a consequent widening of global socio-economic inequalities; the resurgence of racism and the loss of spaces for active participation; and climate change linked to processes of unlimited exploitation of primary resources (Aime, 2020; AA.VV., 2024; Chancel et al., 2022; IDCM, 2024). These are just some of the ongoing processes that call for deep reflection and urgent responses not only on a political level, but also on an educational and cultural one.

Pedagogy, both in the past and today, has played a crucial role in reflecting on the processes of human development and the various social structures in which individuals live and act. As well defined by Dewey, philosopher and pedagogue of the early twentieth century, education is closely connected and inherent to human development and its social and governmental structures, establishing that fundamental link between education and politics, and between education and society (Dewey, 1899, 1916), as affirmed by many modern scholars, but which can already be found in fundamental philosophical works such as Plato's *The Republic*, and more generally in the Hellenistic tradition.

Every educational act is a political act, as it is both orientative and intentional, not the result of chance or fate but historically and socially inscribed, capable of shaping the individual and collective actions of subjects while simultaneously being influenced by specific value systems or worldviews (Freire, 1996).

Therefore, reflecting on current processes and the complexity of the world as it is today implies adopting an interdisciplinary perspective, equipping us with various contributions to knowledge and understanding through a critical posture.

Pedagogy, understood as critical reflection on educational and social processes, has always had a fundamental role in attempting to deconstruct dangerous narratives and to dismantle the weight of political ideologies within the developmental paths of individuals and future citizens. In particular, the increasing complexity of life and development processes forces us to direct our efforts toward the ability to interconnect issues and processes. A complex world is one in which a small and local event can have global consequences, where the proportionality between cause and effect breaks down.

Moreover, it is essential to reflect on the dominant neoliberal economic-political framework, which has generated a series of further transformations, such as the acceleration and alienation of human life, both individual and social (Rosa, 2010; Valzania, 2016). This orientation is based on a logic of progress understood solely in terms of profit, privatization at the expense of the "public good," competition and individualism in contrast with community and solidarity-based forms of life, and the wealth and well-being of a few at the expense of the many.

In strictly educational terms, this economic-political framework resulted in various and complementary forms: significant reductions in investment in public education, an increase in children living in conditions of educational poverty, the growing corporatization of educational and cultural institutions (from primary schools to universities), the standardization of learning paths, and the disintegration of civic participation and community sentiment. According to UNESCO's 2024 Global Education Monitoring Report, over 244 million children and youth worldwide remain out of school, with the highest rates concentrated in sub-Saharan Africa and South Asia (UNESCO, 2023). Moreover, in low-income countries, only 20% of children complete secondary education, compared to 80% in high-income countries, highlighting persistent global disparities in access and completion (OECD, 2024).

All these trends have long risked promoting a simplification- and specialization-oriented mindset, rather than directing knowledge toward complexity and the capacity to interconnect information and envision responses appropriate to the challenges of the present and the near future. In this regard, the reflections of Morin, along with those of Martha Nussbaum, seem particularly significant. In his work "The Well-Made Head: Rethinking Reform, Reforming Thought" (1999), the French sociologist invites us to rethink the organization of the cognitive process starting from an awareness of the interconnection between knowledge, contexts, processes, and individuals. She proposes an "ecologization of knowledge" (Bateson, 1972), fostering systemic reflection and action skills based on the construction of a real planetary consciousness resulting from a responsibility and an ethics of human understanding.

On these same themes, Martha Nussbaum, in her book *Cultivating Humanity: A Classical Defense of Reform in Liberal Education* (1997), reflects on the necessity to support a "cosmopolitan" education, in which imagination, the plurality of languages and knowledge, and the development of critical thinking serve as means to foster feelings of collective belonging and a renewed sense of co-responsibility and recognition of the other in a fully intercultural perspective (Catarci, Fiorucci, 2015). In another work (Nussbaum, 2010), she returns to these themes, questioning the role that humanistic knowledge can and must still play in countering dangerous anti-democratic tendencies and intolerance toward otherness, asserting that education must assume a guiding role in combating the process of alienation and dehumanization, as well as the loss of fundamental rights for individuals.

Within this framework of meaning, and in light of the escalation of violence and wars around the world – in the name of religious conflicts, territorial claims, disputes over borders and energy resources, or more "banally," struggles for domination and power – it seems crucial to recover a culture of *co-existence* (Langer, 2001), capable of rehumanizing our choices and our ability to live together, by valuing plurality and nurturing coexistence and reciprocity. To achieve this, it is clear that we must operate on multiple levels, intervening across various areas of action that can offer a renewed perspective on the idea of community and the common good, starting from the local context and extending to embrace a global outlook.

THE COMMON GOOD AS AN EDUCATIONAL PREROGATIVE

Reasoning in terms of collectivity and coexistence, both locally and globally, requires a complex and non-trivial effort. It demands a willingness to question and critically examine one's own values and epistemic positioning, as well as emotional dispositions and behaviors. From a broad perspective, the concept of collectivity and the common good has assumed, and continues to assume, varied forms and meanings that reflect the many ways to conceive human development and contemporary and future society.

Historically, interest in what we define as the common good has inspired a multitude of reflections across diverse fields of study, ranging from philosophy to sociology, law, economics, and pedagogy, intertwining questions and disciplines. Within a pedagogical paradigm, the common good can be understood as both a means and an end of education, as an "ethical-political" horizon of human development (Dewey, 1927; Cambi, 2006, 2021) and as an intentional project to be built and enacted, rather than as a pre-existing reality. This is intrinsically linked to the social value of education in a reciprocal relationship between educational processes and social structures (Natorp, 1899; Dewey, 1899), and to their historically situated definitions.

From this perspective, although the common good has taken on different forms, it has always been connected to and articulated through concepts such as community, participation, democracy, and sharing. They represent, on the one hand, the prerequisites for achieving the common good and, on the other, essential elements of what it means to promote it: they define some of its properties or manifestations of existence.

Based on this premise, then, in a global context marked by a deep crisis in participation and democracy, we can also speak of a crisis of the "common good." If the well-being of a community cannot be derived simply by summing up individual goods but is instead defined as something different, where individual needs and desires are transcended, then the realization of the common good necessarily involves attention to otherness and the ability to orient oneself toward broad, democratic, participatory, and communal sharing.

This forces us to question the kind of relationships we can build with others, whoever they may be, and to reflect on the concepts of identity/alterity, coexistence, and reciprocity.

Numerous scholars have already pointed out the urgency of a growing intolerance rooted in a form of identity-based extremism, or more precisely, "identitarianism" (Aime, 2020), which frames dynamic and complex concepts within static, one-dimensional perspectives. The result is a dangerous extremism that generates discriminatory and exclusionary behaviors, undermining and denying plural forms of belonging and broad community sentiments, which are instead the very preconditions and direct consequences of both globalization and migratory flows, as well as increasing global interdependence.

While pluralism is a concrete reality of the world, we must act intentionally and systematically to build societies that elevate plurality to a universal value, to design a world that belongs to all. This means ensuring full participation of every individual in their life context, in a vision where individual well-being is aligned with the construction of collective well-being, one that arises from the recognition of each person's subjectivity, potential, capabilities, and dignity. Only through such a process of mutual discovery of the other (Bhabha, 2003; Granata, 2018) can we envision and pursue a more equitable society and contrast long-standing inequalities.

There are many critical issues to be addressed and processes to be dismantled: power dynamics between individuals and groups stemming from both "classical" colonialism and epistemic colonialism (de Sousa Santos, 2014); the logics of profit and privatization; and the unlimited use of resources which, despite global technological, cultural, and economic advancement, continues to produce a highly unequal world, where only a few have full access to a healthy life.

Without addressing these factors and identifying less exclusionary forms of community life, it is not possible to reimagine the common good, which is fundamentally a process of interaction between individuals who must truly be recognized as such by assuming the role of participatory citizens (Dewey, 1927; Amadini, 2012), capable of building dialogue and initiating processes of reciprocal negotiation. This can only happen if there are no acts of domination or oppression, but instead a sense of belonging that is no longer merely local, and which presupposes the possibility of choice and the freedom of existence for all individuals.

This condition is the only real way toward enabling human beings to develop their life contexts from a perspective of collective good, one that is supra-individual, born from reciprocity, recognition, opportunity, accessibility, and grounded in co-existence, sharing, and community growth.

It involves activating processes that are opposed to the dominant neoliberal paradigm, which fosters a society based on consumption and competition at the expense of conviviality (Illich, 1973a, 1973b), individualism, and isolation in contrast to solidarity and communal living, privileging the rights of the few to the detriment of the many, and intolerance of pluralism – an element embedded in the DNA of both the Earth and its inhabitants.

In light of such a configuration, that rejects the construction of a global community of destiny, "non è possibile, soprattutto in prospettiva pedagogica, non auspicare il primato di un'economia della cooperazione (Calame, 2019) in grado di promuovere la costruzione di una co-scienza planetaria su basi umanitarie (Morin, 2004)"[1] (Martino, 2020, p. 215). The real challenge today, more than ever before, is to rethink the common good on a global scale, fully aware of the increasingly complex interdependencies that govern life in societies around the world, and of the need to care for and take responsibility for these issues beyond simplistic localisms or narrowly defined interests.

This becomes possible only through an education that fosters planetary consciousness repeatedly invoked by figures such as Edgar Morin (1999), which establishes a plural and shared sense of identity "because the common good encompasses all conditions that make each person or group reach her fullness and work together to interpret the good life" (Irawan, 2016, p. 4). From this perspective, grounding our reflections on the common good as the result of an anthropological, philosophical, social, and pedagogical construction of humanity, it is possible to identify it as a polysemic concept that defines an ongoing process, the result of relationships among individuals, a system of opportunities and possibilities for those who belong to a given society (Riordan, 2008), aimed at fair development and progress for all, within a democratic framework.

In this regard, several international initiatives offer concrete examples of how education can be mobilized to promote the common good. The UNESCO Global Network of Learning Cities (Osborne et al., 2013; UNESCO, 2017, 2023), for instance, provides a model of lifelong learning that fosters social inclusion, economic development, and cultural vitality through community-based educational strategies. Cities such as Cork (Ireland), Medellín (Colombia), and Osan (South Korea) have implemented inclusive policies that link education to urban regeneration and civic engagement.

Moreover, the digital transformation of education opens new avenues for promoting the common good. Online learning platforms, virtual communities of practice, and open educational resources (OERs) can democratize access to knowledge and foster global collaboration. Projects such as Coursera for Refugees (Coursera, 2023) or the Khan Academy's multilingual outreach (Khan Academy, 2024) exemplify how digital tools can support marginalized populations and facilitate intercultural dialogue. However, these opportunities must be critically examined in light of the digital divide and unequal access to infrastructure, which risk reproducing existing inequalities. A pedagogical approach to digital education must therefore prioritize inclusivity, ethical engagement, and the co-construction of knowledge across diverse contexts (Selwyn, 2016; Warschauer, 2004).

In this sense, education emerges as the very precondition for its realization, and its field of action necessarily becomes "una società aperta e pluralista che rispetta la dignità delle persone e consente il dialogo"[2] (Isidori et al., 2017, p. 70). From this perspective, it becomes clear that a constant redefinition and renegotiation of the common good is necessary, one that must involve an ever-broader range of individuals who can speak up and inhabit the spaces and places of social life.

Only in this way is it possible to activate real forms of participation and support shared collective identities in which pluralism is a core value, cutting across the many ways and forms in which the common good can be promoted.

In this regard, the intercultural pedagogical perspective, focused on rehabilitating and redefining relationships between individuals and groups, can support the delicate task of educating us to communal and plural existence, to the negotiation of values, to conflict management, and to rethinking particularistic interests and structural asymmetries. The common good, as we intend it here, is indeed a "un sistema valoriale che rimanda a una globalizzazione umanizzante: esprime la relazione uomo-mondo, giustizia-solidarietà, diritti-doveri, condivisione-partecipazione, libertà-democrazia, in una prospettiva pedagogica di "lifelong education" e di "long wide learning"[3] (Simonetti, 2017, p. 213).

For these reasons, this contribution aims to develop reflections starting precisely from the "corporeality" of education and its spatial dimensions, in full awareness of the inseparable link between education, the construction of community, and spatial regulation, which become both prerequisites and tools for constructing a common good that places at its core a society rooted in relationships and solidarity. This is a continuous challenge that, in light of ongoing social and human complexity, demands an urgent and organic pedagogical reflection on the purposes and objectives of education.

The lifelong learning perspective has long raised questions about the ways, times, and spaces necessary to make the aspiration to "learn to live together" (Delors, 1997, p. 18–19) a concrete reality, rather than mere rhetoric that clashes with increasing inequalities, including in education. The knowledge society, which is gradually transforming into what has been defined as a post-truth society, requires us to adopt a serious and critical perspective toward lifelong learning processes. Although these processes represent a foundational pillar of the present and the near future, they must be situated within an ecological and systemic framework, capable of revealing existing contradictions. Within this horizon of reflection and action, the common good – though not definable once and for all – must take root in the very contexts in which social life is built, for it is a relational and dialogical process, the outcome of encounters and clashes between individuals and groups in search of possibilities for being and acting. In this view of education as a form of liberation, the common good transcends egocentrism and is rooted in community values that must be able to express the heterogeneity of the world to avoid falling into empty formalism and dangerous relations of subordination.

Accordingly, intercultural and critical pedagogical reflection supports this approach with a decentered gaze – one capable of engaging in dialogical relationships, discovery, and respect for otherness, with attention to today's "heterogeneous" and highly complex socio-cultural contexts. This includes a recognition of the challenging processes of mediation that the encounter between different interpretive and epistemic paradigms of the world can generate.

The tension between universalistic and relativistic dimensions – at the heart of intercultural reflection – thus becomes a training ground for cultivating what we might call "migrant" thinking (Pinto Minerva, 2002): a dynamic mindset capable of stepping outside one's viewpoint and activating new forms of recognition and understanding of the other.

Starting from such efforts, it becomes possible to reimagine the construction of the common good as grounded in inclusive community forms, capable of embracing complexity and plurality as essential features of becoming a community, not in abstract or rhetorical terms but rooted in real contexts and life spaces.

The common good, in fact, can be translated into diverse forms and expressions, in which spaces and community-building processes are both potential expressions and essential prerequisites of the common good – domains where to act with a critical pedagogical perspective.

THE PEDAGOGICAL PERSPECTIVE ON URBAN SPACE

Numerous pedagogical perspectives have addressed the role of space in either generating community or, conversely, fostering exclusion and discrimination. Among these, social pedagogy emerges as a relatively young field whose founder is considered to be Paul Natorp, with his text *Sozialpädagogik*, published in 1899. This work initiated pedagogical and educational reflection on themes related to social transformations and the ever-evolving needs of citizens. The main themes addressed by social pedagogy include education for sociality, the analysis of social conditions that directly or indirectly influence individual and community educational pathways, and, lastly, the analysis and recognition of the educational responsibility shared by various social actors. As outlined in the previous paragraph, another relevant perspective is that of intercultural pedagogy, a pedagogical approach to social phenomena that took shape in Europe in the 1980s, following the rising wave of migratory flows. Intercultural pedagogy explores how to manage cultural diversity and how to relate to those who are perceived as "other." Although in a less direct way than social pedagogy, this approach also reflects on the educational value of space and territory, considering them key elements in the cultural exchanges that occur between individuals with migratory backgrounds and the native population.

However, it is in *urban pedagogy* that the relationship between education and space becomes central. Although numerous educational reflections already exist that interpret the city as a *large classroom* (Dewey, 1899, 1916; Malaguzzi, 2010), linking learning processes to the socio-spatial dimension, urban pedagogy constitutes an interdisciplinary, structured, and specific approach to these themes. This field emerges from the intersection of various disciplines, including urban planning, geography, psychology, social pedagogy, and sociology. Through these interdisciplinary connections, it seeks to analyze how the city can be considered an educational context in its own right. Thus, informal and non-formal educational experiences—those that take place outside structured institutional environments—also become important, as they value everyday experiences and social relationships (Molina-Guenante, Ríos-Peters & Santi-Vargas, 2022). Moreover, community coexistence, urban culture and the culture of place, and the social and cultural history of cities all gain relevance, as education about public space assumes a renewed centrality in educational planning (Cuesta Moreno, 2010).

By adopting urban pedagogy as an interpretive lens for reality, it becomes possible to read urban spaces – and their adaptation to global social, economic, and political changes, along with the effects these changes produce on the population – as essential indicators of the dynamics of social inclusion and exclusion. First and foremost, it is necessary to distinguish the concept of *space* from that of *place*. The former refers to the material aspects of the environment, implying a purely sensory perception of its elements; in contrast, the latter incorporates both individual and collective perception, granting the environment a unique symbolic meaning. This latter dimension is particularly valuable from both a pedagogical and social perspective for analyzing processes of marginalization and global social transformations, as places have increasingly become contested resources between communities and processes of privatization.

Contemporary society is characterized by a dual relationship with spaces: on the one hand, there is the need to preserve public places as free, creative, collective, and inclusive environments; on the other, there is a drive to create exclusive spaces reserved for just a few, establishing a stark, though often invisible, boundary between privilege and exclusion. To better understand the implications of this duality, it is helpful to consider a concrete example of a process of privatization that particularly marks this millennium, namely, *overtourism*, defined as:

> *a regime, meaning a complex and deeply entrenched system that exerts control over urban landscapes, economies, and social dynamics in which tourism economics start to be the main source of income, transforming cities into perpetual holiday destinations. More specifically, the overtourism regime can be understood as a multifaceted and self-perpetuating system that prioritises economic growth through mass tourism and a visitor economy, gradually replacing existing economic activities. In such a context, the touristification processes unleash questionable unfair practices, such as rent expropriation, labour exploitation, indigenous community displacement and expulsion and natural resources extraction, to name just a few (Milano, Novelli & Russo, 2024, p. 1318).*

Venice represents a paradigmatic example of this urban transformation process, marked by increasing touristification and the privatization of public and cultural spaces. This is evident in the introduction, beginning in 2024, of an access fee to visit the city from April to July, the peak tourist season. According to the official website of the City of Venice, if the ticket is purchased at least four days in advance, the cost is €5; after that deadline, the price rises to €10. Although originally conceived as an economic deterrent to reduce the overwhelming number of tourists, the absence of a maximum entry limit and the positive financial return of the initiative—which led to a gain of €2.2 million[4] in 2024—suggest that the "privatization" of the city is yet another consequence of urban touristification driven by overtourism.

Venice is just one example of this ongoing transformation, which affects not only the city as a physical space, but also its inhabitants. The growing exclusivity of urban spaces has, in fact, rekindled public interest in space not merely as a lived and inhabited environment, but as a meaningful communal place, a collective good worth protecting. In this regard, numerous actions in recent years have seen broad citizen participation aimed at defending cities as shared places. Many of these movements originated in the previous century as housing rights movements in response to financial expropriation and eviction and have since evolved also to assume an anti-tourism character. Consider, for example, the Spanish organization *Sindicat de Llogateres* and *Plataforma de Afectats per la Hipoteca* (PAH). The former was officially established in 2017, although early meetings between tenants and housing rights activists in Barcelona took place the year before, intending to fight rent increases, demand longer contracts, and eliminate abusive clauses[5]. The latter was founded in 2009 as a response to the housing crisis and maintains that housing, once a fundamental right, has now become a market commodity that condemns people to precarity, eviction, and exclusion[6]. Both organizations denounce how the impact of mass tourism on Spanish cities is a significant cause of the housing crisis, fueling dynamics of precarization, exclusion, and marginalization of residents (Milano, Novelli & Russo, 2024).

Beyond the phenomenon of touristification, another alarming process that redefines access to urban space is the privatization of cities, which are increasingly destined to become luxury goods reserved for economic elites. One example of this evolution of urban space is the disturbing proposal made by Donald Trump during his 2023 presidential campaign, in which he announced his intention to establish ten *Freedom Cities*[7] - new modern cities built from scratch on federal land. These envisioned cities would be characterized by massive technological development, essentially functioning as *smart cities*, facilitated by exemptions from numerous federal regulations in order to encourage innovation in fields such as artificial intelligence, biotechnology, and nuclear energy. However, this would come at the expense of environmental sustainability, civic participation, and labor protections. What emerges is a model based on the exploitation of labor and resources, leading to new forms of exclusion that would marginalize low-income people, migrants, vulnerable groups, and those not politically aligned with Trump's vision. These cities – although currently just a fantasy – are openly designed for the wealthy, educated, highly skilled, and politically aligned, leaving little room for the vulnerable, the marginalized, or those ideologically opposed. They represent "a fantasy of spatial cleansing [...] prosperity and safety abound, while elements that have been cast as undesirable, abject, and anti-American are forcibly kept out through intensive policing and state protection" (Woodworth, 2024, p. 50). Urban space would thus become a laboratory for deeply exclusionary economic and social experiments, where democracy is replaced by the interests of private economic entities, and the logic of profit overrides those of social equity, environmental justice, and collective rights. Precisely for these reasons, it is essential to promote forms of urbanization that are genuinely inclusive, capable of countering exclusionary models of the city that sacrifice social justice in the name of economic growth and risk institutionalizing segregation and selective access to rights. It is important to stress that urban projects centered on technological innovation and presented as social projects of freedom and progress often conceal mechanisms of systematic exclusion of the most vulnerable, reinforcing economic, social, and cultural barriers within urban spaces. In opposition to such elitist and divisive visions, it is crucial to promote urban visions capable of including and representing those currently marginalized, ensuring active participation in decision-making processes and equitable access to urban resources.

Overtourism and urban privatization processes – of which Trump's proposal is just one example – transform shared space from a common and indispensable good into a luxury commodity, reserved for those with economic and social privilege. In both cases, urban segregation and the reproduction of structural inequalities already present in our societies are exacerbated within cities that are reduced to mere consumer goods. As a result, marginalized groups are physically excluded from urban spaces and symbolically distanced from the possibility of participating in public life – that is, from exercising active citizenship.

The phenomena analyzed so far mainly focus on the urban center, which is increasingly the target of privatization processes that transform it into an exclusive, consumption-oriented space, inaccessible to marginalized segments of the population. This dynamic directly contributes to the *peripherization* of the city, fueling a process of spatial segregation that extends beyond mere physical distance to encompass profound social, symbolic, and political meaning.

It is therefore necessary to focus on a central dichotomy in the reflection on urban issues: the center-periphery relationship. These two poles do not merely define geographical distance; they are also symbolic spaces that carry opposing narratives: on one hand, the center is associated with services, well-being, quality of life, and access to active citizenship; on the other hand, the periphery is often perceived as a place of absence, decay, exclusion, and mismanagement. In this opposition, the center functions as a legitimized and recognized space, while the periphery becomes a residual area – expelled and marginalized – hosting those whom the urban and social system has excluded and continues to exclude.

Peripheries, then, are not simply marginal zones or areas physically distant from the vibrant heart of the city. They are both material and symbolic embodiments of marginality, the result of specific political and economic choices and socio-spatial demarcations. These are places where spatial marginality coincides with the social exclusion of those who inhabit and live in these contexts. This gives rise to a high level of complexity, both sociopolitical and individual, that results in a perspective often far from the dominant one. This is because peripheries represent actual ruptures in the established order, shaped by an intersection of multiple spheres: socioeconomic, cultural, racial, gender-based, related to citizenship, and local welfare systems. In this sense, intersectional studies (Hill Collins, 2019) provide a valuable interpretive lens: every individual identity is composed of multiple identity axes that influence how one inhabits urban space, whether one is included or excluded, visible or invisible. It thus becomes clear that space is never neutral but rather a site of relationships, power, and conflict – yet also of encounter, exchange, and possibility.

Following a generative vision of urban space – and particularly of peripheral space – it is essential to reference bell hooks (1990), who identifies the margins as:

much more than a site of deprivation [...] that is also the site of radical possibility, a space of resistance [...] a central location for the production of a counter-hegemonic discourse that is not just found in words but in habits of being and the way one lives [...]. Spaces can be real and imagined. Spaces can tell stories and unfold histories. Spaces can be interrupted, appropriated, and transformed" (pp. 149-150, 152).

Thus, the world's peripheries, even though marked by conditions of hardship, exclusion, and vulnerability, are also places of potential transformation, learning, and social regeneration. We must avoid thinking of the *banlieues* in Paris, the *barrios* in Latin America, or the *favelas* only as spaces defined by economic poverty, educational deprivation, deviance, and segregation, but also as generative spaces of change – highly creative and innovative (Musaio, 2021; Stillo, 2023; Zizioli, Stillo & Franchi, 2024). While these areas are undeniably marked by precariousness, high unemployment, and media and institutional stigmatization (Maurin, 2004; Stebé & Marchal, 2009; Paone, 2010), they are also strongholds of solidarity, belonging, and cultural resistance. The binary of exclusion/inclusion becomes more complex here: peripheries are both spaces of ghettoization and of encounter, often tense, but inevitable, with otherness and those deemed "different." A symbolic figure of this encounter is the migrant, who notably occupies peripheral space, deeply transforming both the culture they encounter and the urban fabric itself (Castells, 1972; Harvey, 2012). Migrations, like other forms of relationship with those perceived as "other," redraw not only spatial boundaries but also those of citizenship and coexistence. It is evident, then, that the margins of society, the peripheries, are simultaneously places of experimentation and tension that require a new pedagogy of urban space: one that can recognize complexity, promote inclusive practices, transform prevailing narratives, and open new possibilities for active citizenship, even in areas furthest from the centers of power. Thanks to these characteristics, peripheries stand out for the social and cultural initiatives emerging from the bottom up, aiming to generate new ideas and social change "contrastando il disagio e restituendo un'altra immagine dei contesti marginali e di quelle piazze dello spaccio che diventano palestre di formazione per i più giovani quando non si danno alternative"[8] (Zizioli, 2024, p. 31).

The journey across different semantic dichotomies – center/periphery, inside/outside, citizenship/tourism, exclusion/inclusion – supports a pedagogical reflection focused on incorporating spatial issues into educational planning. What emerges from this analysis is the need to consider territory as a place, inseparably linked to its communitarian dimension. By recognizing this connection, urban space can be redefined not just as a public good, but as a common good. As such, it is essential that all members of a community be able to inhabit, live in, shape, and make use of that place: "community can be built on: spaces and common services shared and opened to their neighborhoods; local resources and skills connected to a wider network; initiatives aimed at promoting the value of a place" (Meroni & Trapani, 2011, p. 386).

Public space as a common good thus carries profound pedagogical significance: it can only be constructed through the active participation of community members. In this way, it is not simply a commodity to be consumed, speculated upon, privatized, or taken away. Instead, it becomes a symbolic entity rooted in the act of identifying oneself as a member of a community, forging bonds of belonging between places and society. It is therefore imperative to reflect on the future of urban space so that we may effectively anticipate, counter, and prevent forms of economic exclusion, exploitation, oppression, and domination. It becomes clear that space is a *pedagogical device* (Mantegazza, 1995; Massa, 1975), a deeply heterogeneous device composed of multiple dimensions (institutional, architectural, administrative, moral, philosophical, etc.) that inevitably impacts educational processes (Quinto, 2021). For this reason, it is essential to value approaches such as urban pedagogy, which uses territorial socio-educational practices to offer a fresh perspective on today's challenges. This allows work on multiple fronts: the management of social problems in educational spaces, the promotion of civic education, community participation, environmental and sustainability education, socio-cultural animation, the prevention and combat of exclusion, and education regarding cultural and urban heritage (Nájera Martinez, 2008). In doing so, urban planning will no longer benefit the few at the expense of the many, but rather aim at the empowerment of all, local democratization, and a vision of cities as genuine spaces for social inclusion.

TERRITORY AS A CAPACITATING COMMON GOOD: COMMUNITY EMPOWERMENT STRATEGIES THROUGH PARISH MAPS

As previously noted, territory, in its connotation as *place*, is not merely a physical space: it acts not only as a container for individual experiences but also as a "quotidiano e complesso sistema di vita dei soggetti"[9] (Tramma, 1999, p. 81), rich with pedagogical meaning (Catarci, 2013). It represents a "ambito di riferimento teorico e operativo per l'iniziativa di formazione"[10] (*ivi*, p. 79), characterized by pedagogical dimensions that must be taken into account when designing educational actions aimed at impacting the reality in which they are implemented.

For an educational initiative to have a positive impact on the social fabric into which it is inserted, it must be pedagogically oriented – that is aimed at developing the competencies necessary to act consciously in today's society and to fully exercise one's citizenship. It should foster the formation of a personal sense-making perspective concerning life and the world, or, in short, focus on empowering the individual. From this viewpoint, the educational experience must be critical, creative, transformative, problematizing, and liberating—geared toward emancipation, conscientization, and self-determination, and committed to freeing individuals from all forms of oppression (Freire, 1996).

In this sense, the territorial context can be understood as a *common good* and plays a fundamental role. Referring to the Capability Approach developed by Nobel Prize-winning economist Amartya K. Sen (Sen, 1999) and philosopher Martha C. Nussbaum (2011), the territory can be defined as *enabling*: it can influence what people are able to be and to do, that is "[...] the *actual living* that people manage to achieve (or going beyond that, on the *freedom* to achieve actual livings that one can have reason to value)" (Sen, 2000, p. 73, italics in the original). The place where educational initiatives take place carries significant weight in shaping individual destinies: educational experiences, mediated and facilitated by the territory, are the starting point for pathways that can be inclusive or, conversely, lead to marginalization. The context strongly influences an individual's right to learn, to develop skills and competencies, to cultivate aspirations, to make conscious choices, to have control over one's life, and to pursue personal life goals.

It is important to highlight that this concept implies all educational agents within a given environment: school, family, and territory. This calls for overcoming the narrow view of education as confined to the classroom and instead promotes a pedagogical responsibility extended to the entire territorial community, involving all actors who contribute to education. Such a perspective requires full recognition of the role of every educational subject within a specific territory, recalling Frabboni's idea of a "sistema formativo integrato"[11] (Frabboni, 1989), defined as a "rete sistemica di agenzie formative nel contesto locale"[12] (Catarci, 2013, p. 100), characterised by the "integrazione e interconnessione razionale e democratica delle risorse intenzionalmente educative presenti sul territorio"[13] (*ibidem*). This constitutes a political project for developing a shared educational vision, nurtured by the diverse educational actors in a given context, within a democratic and inclusive framework.

From this perspective, the integrated education system also functions as a "strategia di empowerment territoriale"[14] (Catarci, 2013, p. 100), enabling the community within a specific territory to increase its capacity for self-determination and self-efficacy. It is not the individual alone, but the community as a whole, in its complexity, that gains the ability to develop greater control over its own identity and to redesign its future. This fosters greater decision-making autonomy concerning its destiny and the dynamics that shape it.

Although deeply rooted in their territories, communities find their true meaning in the relationships formed within them. In this context, a strong interconnection emerges among territories, services, and collectives. When these elements remain in constant dialogue, they can generate what, in educational theory, is referred to as an *educating community*.

The *educating community* represents a true protective factor (Curti et al., 2020), acting as a social stronghold that enables the entire community to exercise self-determination: "la comunità educa perché è spazio di partecipazione, educa perché abilita all'esercizio di alcuni valori, educa perché vigila sul compito educativo ed educa perché in molti casi assume direttamente responsabilità ed iniziative educative"[15] (Del Gottardo, 2016, p. 7). The concept of community can be reinterpreted as a dynamic relationship in constant evolution, emphasizing mutual exposure as an ontological element (Curti et al., 2020): in this view, the community functions as an educational agent in formation, expressing its essence by pursuing its form – translated into competence and the generation of collective well-being. "In questo continuo processo di trasformazione, la comunità educe, tira fuori la sua essenza"[16] (Curti et al., 2022, p. 48). The goal is to work on the community itself and on its ability to express its essence, in the "idea di un noi responsabile del proprio percorso formativo, trasformativo e migliorativo"[17] (*ivi*, p. 60).

One tool for territorial empowerment, which treats *place* as a common good and enables the community within a specific context to increase its capacity for self-determination and self-efficacy, is the Parish Map.

The Parish Map originated in England in the mid-1980s, thanks to the initiative of Common Ground[18], a non-profit organization founded in 1983 by urban planner Sue Clifford, designer Angela King, and writer Roger Deakin. The association was created to promote the appreciation of community heritage, the relationship between humans and nature, and a sense of environmental responsibility toward the surrounding environment. These goals are rooted in the concept of *Local Distinctiveness* (Clifford & King, 1993), which holds that both material elements - such as buildings, train stations, rivers - and intangible ones - like traditions, dialects, legends, or recipes - though often overlooked or taken for granted, may represent unique features of a place and carry deep, irreplaceable meaning for the community that inhabits it. As the organization states:

> *everywhere means something to someone. You don't have to own it, or even see it every day, for a place and its stories to be important to you. The combination of commonplace histories and ordinary nature makes places what they are. Things do not have to be spectacular, rare or endangered for people to value them and want them about their everyday lives*[19].

The goal, therefore, is to give value to what makes a specific area unique by recognizing and highlighting the elements that residents know intimately, identify with, and feel responsible for. One of the core features of the Parish Map is the direct involvement of the community in constructing local knowledge, aimed at both recovering and reinterpreting the places people live in. Sue Clifford and Angela King have pointed out how traditional cartographic tools fail to adequately represent the essence of a territory (Cozzi, 2023), its uniqueness, and the familiarity contained in the concept of *sense of place* (Seddon, 1972), which, in Seddon's sense, well expresses the deep sense of belonging and identification with a specific place. Parish Maps, in fact, depict places as they are perceived and experienced daily by those who live there. This is a collective process of reflection on the distinctive features of the territory, whether material or immaterial, that takes shape in the creation of a visual representation of the community and its identity. They can thus be defined as *participatory community maps*. The representations, often created with the support of artists, do not follow conventional cartographic formats. Instead, they take subjective and sometimes critical forms, expressed through creative media such as collages, texts, photographs, sculptural installations, or digital tools[20].

Similar participatory mapping initiatives have emerged worldwide, confirming the transformative potential of community-based cartography. In Kenya, the *Map Kibera Project*[21] (founded in 2009) enabled residents of Nairobi's largest informal settlement to collectively map their neighborhood, reclaiming visibility and agency in urban planning decisions. Likewise, in Canada, the *Indigenous Mapping Workshops*[22] foster collaborative creation of territorial maps integrating traditional knowledge with digital technologies, strengthening both cultural heritage and community self-determination.

From this perspective, the adoption of Parish Maps can serve as a powerful educational, inclusive, and transformative tool. Through participatory and community-based experiences oriented toward co-constructing one's living environment, these maps foster the questioning of dominant narratives and promote a decolonial reinterpretation of territory and social relationships (hooks, 2003). By actively engaging communities in knowledge production rooted in lived experiences, perspectives, and both individual and collective needs, Parish Maps foster critical thinking, challenge stereotypes, expose power dynamics, and value cultural identities and diversity.

In this sense, their use constitutes a form of territorial empowerment, as it enables the community to strengthen its capacity for self-determination and self-efficacy. It is not the individual alone, but the community in all its complexity that develops greater control over its own identity and the power to redesign its existence, achieving greater decision-making autonomy over its destiny and the dynamics that shape it.

To echo a famous passage from *Pedagogy of the Oppressed*, a seminal work by Brazilian educator Paulo Freire, "no one teaches another, nor is anyone self-taught. People teach each other, mediated by the world" (Freire, 1996, p. 80), thereby acknowledging two essential dimensions of education: its communal and planetary nature. From an educational and pedagogical perspective, these are inseparable and indispensable elements that anticipate an awareness in educational action, both rooted in the local context, about one's own community, and simultaneously oriented toward an awareness of global interdependence, as will be further explored in the continuation of this discussion.

EDUCATING FOR GLOBAL CITIZENSHIP

Following the pedagogical and educational considerations developed thus far, it is essential to reflect on a conception of the common good that, starting from a local and territorial, community-based understanding grounded in collective participation, prompts us to question which form of citizenship should be promoted. It is therefore important to support a global vision of citizenship, oriented toward the common good and the pursuit of more equitable societies. Before delving into the specific features of global citizenship and its almost visceral connection with the notion of the common good, it is necessary to reflect on the very definition of citizenship, in order to highlight its social, political, and pedagogical implications.

The notion of citizenship has been the subject of a long and complex international debate that, over time, has shifted focus from the traditional definition of citizenship as legal belonging to a nation-state (Marshall, 1950), toward a more dynamic and inclusive vision rooted in a sense of broad communal belonging, based on a "planetary consciousness" and a shared sense of responsibility toward global challenges (Reimers, 2020). In this regard, Edgar Morin's words are particularly illuminating: "la minaccia nucleare e la minaccia ecologica che gravano sulla biosfera impongono all'umanità una comunità di destino. Così è diventata vitale la consapevolezza di questo destino planetario che stiamo vivendo"[23] (Morin, 2004, pp. 7–8), or again: "Une intelligence incapable d'envisager le contexte et le complexe planétaire, rend aveugle, inconscient et irresponsable"[24] (Morin, 1999b, pp. 6–7).

For the French sociologist, planetary union is the common denominator of an increasingly interconnected and interdependent world. Such a union requires:

> *Conscience et le sentiment de notre appartenance et de notre identité terrienne sont aujourd'hui vitaux. C'est la progression et l'ancrage de cette conscience d'appartenance à notre patrie terrestre qui permettront le développement, par des canaux multiples, dans les diverses régions du globe, d'un sentiment de reliance et d'intersolidarité nécessaire pour civiliser les relations humaines*[25] *(Morin, 1999b, p. 72).*

The notion of *Terra-Patria* (Earth-Homeland) evokes a form of identity-based belonging which is capable of embracing all human beings as members of the same community of destiny (Morin, 2004). Yet for Morin, *terrestrial identity* is not the only possible form of belonging. Identity itself must always be seen in the plural:

> *Qui suis-je ? Je réponds: je suis un être humain. C'est mon substantif. Mais j'ai plusieurs adjectifs, d'importance variable selon les circonstances ; je suis français, d'origine juive sépharade, partiellement italien et espagnol, amplement méditerranéen, européen culturel, citoyen du monde, enfant de la Terre-Patrie. Peut-on être tout cela en même temps? Non, cela dépend des circonstances et des moments où tantôt l'une tantôt une autre de ces identités prédomine"* [26] *(Morin, 2021, p. 8).*

Naturally, not all these identities carry the same weight at all times:

> *dépend des circonstances et des moments où tantôt l'une tantôt une autre de ces identités prédomine [...] Chacun a l'identité de sa famille, celle de son village ou de sa ville, celle de sa province ou ethnie, celle de son pays, enfin celle plus vaste de son continent. Chacun a une identité complexe, c'est-à-dire à la fois une et plurielle"*[27] *(Morin, 2021, pp. 8-9).*

This layered view of identity strongly resonates with the thought of Lebanese writer Amin Maalouf, (2001) who states: "ciascuno di noi dovrebbe essere incoraggiato ad assumere la propria diversità, a concepire la propria identità come la somma delle sue diverse appartenenze, invece di confonderla con una sola, eretta ad appartenenza suprema e a strumento di esclusione"[28] (p. 175). This *concentric model of identity*, composed of overlapping circles that extend from the local to the global, is also endorsed by Italian educator Ettore Gelpi, who makes it his own:

> *Je suis Milanaise, Italienne, Européenne, Mondiale. Je ne veux nier aucune de ces identités, mais le compléter, car elles s'enrichissent les unes les autres. C'est une grande aventure et une grande joie d'être chez soi à Rio ou à Varsovie, à Pékin comme à Cotonou, à Milan ou à Mexique; de pouvoir se fâcher ou se réjouir dans quelques pays que ce soit avec desgens sans préjugés ni complexes... et en même temps, j'aime ma maison, mon quartier, mes cinéma... mes salles*[29] *(Gelpi, 1987, p. 12).*

In his writings, Gelpi often linked *terrestrial identity* to two global priorities that he considered essential: reconciliation with the Earth – understood as the protection and preservation of the natural heritage – and reconciliation among the people who inhabit the planet, who must see themselves as part of the same terrestrial community. According to Gelpi: "identità e coscienza del mondo non sono in contraddizione: un mondo unito è il risultato della varietà e della ricchezza delle lingue e delle culture e non di un processo di omologazione che porterebbe alla perdita progressiva delle identità delle popolazioni più deboli"[30] (Riccardi, 2019, p. 121). In this light, to be a global and terrestrial citizen means "comprendere le forze che uniscono il mondo a una velocità accelerata ed essere capaci di operare concretamente oltre i confini di una singola nazione per affrontare le sfide che esse creano, o per catturare le opportunità che offrono"[31] (Reimers, 2018, pp. 15-16). Global citizenship, therefore, is a form of belonging that both incorporates and transcends the local and national dimensions in favor of a unified *world-system* that presupposes, within each individual, the coexistence of multiple identities that do not necessarily align but rather *complement one another*, gaining different significance depending on the context.

To feel part of a broader community, called Earth, leads the global citizen to center the common good in their actions, exercising rights and responsibilities not solely as a member of a state, but as a citizen of the world (MacIntyre, 1984).

Adopting this perspective involves making a conscious choice—a stance that calls for the implementation of an educational approach that must not be undertaken solely by the individual, inspired by a universalist vocation, but must instead be directed to the entire community, which must recognize itself as part of a larger entity bound by a common destiny. Becoming aware of our interconnectedness and interdependence with the rest of the world—regardless of place of origin—leads us to face global challenges with a shared sensibility, one that touches every individual, even when the issue at hand may seem, at first glance, unrelated to their daily life. In this regard, the well-known *"butterfly effect"* described by physicist Edward Lorenz is emblematic: "the flap of a butterfly's wing in Brazil can set off a cascade of atmospheric events that, weeks later, spurs the formation of a tornado in Texas".

The school is the first designated space for building education around global citizenship, which carries the complex responsibility of preparing individuals capable of facing today's global challenges consciously and responsibly. This involves commitment on multiple levels (UNESCO, 2017):

- "cognitive", aimed at understanding global dynamics by highlighting both critical issues and strengths within the educational community;
- "social and emotional", focused on fostering empathy, awareness, and respect for others;
- "behavioral", directed at promoting social change (Diller, 2001; Adler & Goggin, 2022) through civic engagement, understood as activism and participation in public life, particularly by younger generations (Pontes et al., 2019).

Two particularly significant documents that highlight the strategic role of education in fostering global citizenship are The Earth Charter (1987–2000) and the UNESCO Declaration (2015).

The first document, The Earth Charter, developed through a decades-long process of global consultation, was approved at UNESCO headquarters in Paris in 2000. The declaration outlines the fundamental ethical principles for building a just, sustainable and peaceful global society. The Charter "It seeks to inspire in all people a new sense of global interdependence and shared responsibility for the well-being of the whole human family, the greater community of life, and future generations. It is a vision of hope and a call to action" (preamble). Of particular relevance is Principle 14 of the Earth Charter "Integrate into formal education and life-long learning the knowledge, values, and skills needed for a sustainable way of life"[32], which examines the contribution that schools can offer from the perspective of global responsibility, addressing themes such as environmental protection, human rights, equitable human development, and peace. The Charter also highlights the importance given to the "Promote the contribution of the arts and humanities as well as the sciences in sustainability education". Philosopher Martha Nussbaum, in *Cultivating Humanity: A Classical Defense of Reform in Liberal Education* (1997), similarly stresses the crucial role of humanistic knowledge in building a *cosmopolitan education*—one capable of resisting anti-democratic tendencies and attitudes of intolerance toward the other. In this context, imagination, multilingualism, plural forms of knowledge, and the developement critical thinking become essential tools for cultivating and strengthening a shared sensibility, rooted in the feeling of compassion, understood in its Latin etymology (*cum–patior*) as *suffering with*, the act of participating in another's pain by shifting one's perspective away from the self. This sense of solidaristic union is captured in the concept of *planetary understanding*, a core idea for Morin, who also sees the humanities as key in developing planetary consciousness:

> *Littérature, poésie, cinéma, psychologie, philosophie devraient converger pour devenir écoles de la compréhension. L'éthique de la compréhension humaine constitue sans doute une exigence clé de nos temps d'incompréhension généralisée: nous vivons dans un monde d'incompréhension entre étrangers mais aussi entre membres d'une même société"*[33] *(Morin, 1999b, p. 74).*

The second document, the UNESCO Declaration (2015), is a global action plan for people, planet, and prosperity, signed by the member states of the United Nations. It consists of 17 goals (divided into 169 targets) aimed at building a planetary consciousness capable of addressing "issues related to poverty, the right to health and education, access to water and energy, work, inclusive and sustainable economic growth, climate change and environmental protection as global issues that affect anyone, anywhere in the world". From this perspective, the 2030 Agenda can be considered one of the most important global tools for constructing global citizenship.

What emerges is the strategic role of schools in shaping future citizens with a *well-made head*, capable of managing complex thinking that allows them to navigate consciously an increasingly "narrow" world (Fortini, 1984). This entails the necessity for a pedagogy that fosters the ability to contextualize and globalize knowledge, by adopting an *ecologizing mindset*, one that can "*Il* s'agit en même temps de reconnaître l'unité au sein du divers, le divers au sein de l'unité, de reconnaître par exemple l'unité humaine à travers les diversités individuelles et culturelles, les diversités individuelles et culturelles à travers l'unité humaine"[34] (Morin, 1999b, p. 30).

A fundamental task of education is to instill in new generations an ethic based on care for and preservation of the Common Good, understood as a Heritage of Humanity and, consequently, a "moral" property of every inhabitant of the Earth: "Solidarité et responsabilité ne peuvent venir d'exhortations pieuses ni de discours civiques, mais d'un sentiment profond d'affiliation (affiliare, de filius, fils), sentiment matri-patriotique qui devrait être cultivé de façon concentrique sur la France, l'Europe, la Terre"[35] (Morin, 1999b, p. 73).

The school, of course, cannot be left alone in this task but must cooperate with a network of other educational actors (family; peer groups; sports; secular, religious, and political associations; etc.) who, whether consciously or not, play an active role in global citizenship education by offering experiences that are different yet complementary to those provided by schools, and equally significant (Francesconi, 2021) From the perspective of fostering dialogue between formal education and extracurricular contexts, a promising approach is offered by service learning, a pedagogical strategy that promotes students' active participation in their communities, creating a virtuous cycle between learning and solidarity-based service. However, service learning should not be viewed as just another subject or a form of voluntary work—it is a form of experiential learning that enables knowledge acquisition *through and thanks to* the solidarity actions undertaken (Fiorin, 2016).

The aspiration is to educate "cittadini consapevoli della loro possibilità di immaginare futuri alternativi e di incidere sulle sorti del pianeta, attraverso l'esercizio dei propri diritti e doveri in un mondo fortemente interrelato"[36] (UNESCO, 2017, p. 8), rooted in principles of equality and social justice (Tarozzi, 2015), within an increasingly glocal dimension (Bauman, 2008).

CONCLUDING REFLECTIONS FOR A PEDAGOGY OF THE COMMON GOOD

The objective of this paper has been to contribute to the discourse on the common good through the analytical and observational lens of pedagogy. This approach entails looking to the past, present and future with a vision aimed at designing increasingly inclusive societies. In this regard, alignment with the principle of *Leave No One Behind* is essential – a core value promoted within the 2030 Agenda and the Sustainable Development Goals, which perfectly embodies the spirit of community, the fight against social exclusion, and the promotion of a global citizenship approach. The principle *Leave No One Behind*:

> *compels us to focus on discrimination and inequalities (often multiple and intersecting) that undermine the agency of people as holders of rights. Many of the barriers people face in accessing services, resources and equal opportunities are not simply accidents of fate or a lack of availability of resources, but rather the result of discriminatory laws, policies and social practices that leave particular groups of people further and further behind*[37].

In this light, reflecting on the *common good* today means thinking about and designing actions that counteract the global and multidimensional dynamics of exclusion and exploitation. In particular, we have highlighted how dominant economic models favor individual well-being and self-interest, deeply wounding the values of communitarianism and each person's responsibility toward the collective. In contemporary urban contexts, the principle of *leaving no one behind* intersects with the valorization of the common good, conceived not merely as a shared resource but as a relational fabric that nurtures social cohesion within neighborhoods and cities. Urban commons – such as public spaces, educational services, and cultural or community venues – are essential elements in the construction of inclusive and solidarity-based communities, where all individuals can fully exercise their rights and participate in collective life. Urban space thus takes on an educational and generative function, contributing to the formation of aware citizens who can recognize themselves as part of a broader community. When these spaces are governed through participatory processes, with the active involvement of those who inhabit them, transformative dynamics are activated that promote inclusion, combat inequality, and resist systemic forms of exclusion and marginalization. Participating in the processes of care, regeneration, and shared management of common goods is not merely a civic act – it is a key means of implementing the *Leave No One Behind* principle. It ensures that public policies are not imposed from above, but co-constructed with communities, recognizing local knowledge, diversity, and the specific needs of each territory. In this way, participation becomes a tool for social justice, capable of including even those who have too often been made invisible or silenced:

> *A democracy is more than a form of government; it is primarily a mode of associated living, of conjoint communicated experience. The extension in space of the number of individuals who participate in an interest so that each has to refer his own action to that of others, and to consider the action of others to give point and direction to his own, is equivalent to the breaking down of those barriers of class, race, and national territory which kept men from perceiving the full import of their activity (Dewey, 1916, p. 101).*

However, within this framework, we must also acknowledge the failures that continue to demand a renewed and more committed effort to ensure that *Leave No One Behind* becomes a real process of building societies based on the full recognition of everyone's potential, while actively deconstructing and challenging the limitations and contradictions that still permeate national and supranational policy agendas. From a pedagogical perspective, which cannot be disconnected from both local and global political and cultural concerns, attention must be focused on participation and learning processes that still risk excluding some in favor of others. Disparities in access to educational opportunities and high-quality learning experiences directly affect people's ability to fully exercise their agency in the world, and overcoming these inequalities is a challenge that must be addressed both in terms of relational and educational offerings, and by rethinking places, cities, and neighborhoods themselves.

In the framework of *learning cities*, the city becomes a space of humanity and a concrete laboratory of lifelong learning, where "la cultura intesa come diritto di cittadinanza, nel senso più esteso del termine, deve diventare motore di aggregazione civica"[38] (Teti, 2020, p. 48), and more broadly a foundation for collective well-being the result of encounters and mediation among different paradigms, identities, and possibilities. Achieving the *common good*, then, means reaching a new way of thinking about humanity – one that is open, dynamic, dialogical, and transformative, capable of feeling and teaching tenderness and solidarity, recognizing oneself in the other, whoever they may be.

AUTHOR'S NOTE

The contribution *Pedagogical Reflections on the Common Good: Territories, Communities and Global Citizenship* is the result of a collaborative effort among the authors. Solely for the purpose of identifying individual sections (where required), authorship should be attributed as follows: Massimiliano Fiorucci – 1. Introduction; Lisa Stillo – 2. The Common Good as an Educational Prerogative; Aurora Bulgarelli – 3. The Pedagogical Perspective and Urban Space: Cities, Places, Communities, and Educational Challenges *and* 6. Concluding Reflections for a Pedagogy of the Common Good; Francesca Gabrielli – 4. Territory as an Enabling Common Good: Community Empowerment Strategies through Parish Maps; Alessandra Casalbore – 5. Educating for Global Citizenship.

REFERENCES

AA.VV. (2024). *Global Multidimensional Poverty Index 2024. Poverty Amid Conflict*. UNDP and OPHI.

Adler, R. P., & Goggin, J. (2022). What do we mean by "civic engagement"? *Journal of Transformative Education*, *3*(3), 236–253. DOI: 10.1177/1541344605276792

Aime, M. (2020). *Classificare, separare escludere. Razzismi e Identità* [Classifying, Separating, Excluding: Racisms and Identity]. Einaudi.

Amadini, M. (2012). *Crescere nella città. Spazi, relazioni, processi partecipativi per educare l'infanzia* [Growing Up in the City: Spaces, Relationships, and Participatory Pathways for Childhood Education]. La Scuola.

Bambang Irawan, P. (2016). A capability to promote the common good. *JURNAL TEOLOGI*, *05*(01), 1–14. DOI: 10.24071/jt.v5i1.477

Bateson, G. (1972). *Steps to an Ecology Mind*. Chandler Publishing Company.

Bauman, Z. (2008). *Missing Community*. Harvard University Press.

Bhabha, H. K. (2003). The Other Question: Difference, Discrimination and the Discourse of Colonialism. In Barker, F., Hulme, P., Iversen, M., & Loxley, D. (Eds.), *Literature Politics & Theory* (pp. 194–211). Routledge.

Cambi, F. (2006). *Abitare il disincanto. Una pedagogia per il postmoderno* [Living Disenchantment: A Pedagogy for the Postmodern]. UTET.

Cambi, F. (2021). *Scuola e cittadinanza. Per la formazione etico-politica dei giovani* [School and Citizenship: For the Ethical-Political Education of Youth]. Studium Edizioni.

Castells, M. (1972). *La question urbaine* [The urban question: A marxist approach]. François Maspero.

Catarci, M. (2013). *Le forme sociali dell'educazione. Servizi, territori, società* [The Social Forms of Education: Services, Territories, and Society]. FrancoAngeli.

Catarci, M., & Fiorucci, M. (Eds.). (2015). *Intercultural Education in the European Context. Theories, Experiences, Challenges*. Ashgate.

Chancel, L., Piketty, T., Saez, E., & Zucman, G. (2022). *World Inequality Report 2022*. World Inequality Lab. DOI: 10.4159/9780674276598

Clifford, S., & King, A. (Eds.). (1993). *Local Distinctiveness: Place, Particularity and Identity*. Common Ground.

Coursera. (2023). Coursera for Refugees Program. Retrieved from https://www.coursera.org/refugees

Cozzi, D. (2023). Un approccio etnografico nel lavoro educativo. Le mappe di comunità partecipate. [An Ethnographic Approach in Educational Work: Participatory Community Mapping] In Zoletto, D. (Ed.), *Migrazioni, complessità, territori. Prospettive per l'azione educativa* [Migrations, Complexity, and Territories: Perspectives for Educational Action]. (pp. 209–219). Carocci editore.

Cuesta Moreno, O. J. (2010). Pedagogìa urbana, convivencia ciudana y aprendizaje por reglas [Urban Pedagogy, Civic Coexistence, and Learning Through Rules]. *Revista Educatiòn y Desarrollo Social*, *2*, 176–188.

Curti, S., Fornari, S., & Moroni, E. (2020). Educating Communities as a Protection Network Against Educational Poverty [Le comunità educanti come rete di protezione contro la povertà educative]. *QTimes webmagazine*, 12(4), 332-344.

Curti, S., Fornari, S., & Moroni, E. (2022). *Sociologia della povertà educativa. Concetti, metodi, politiche e pratiche* [Sociology of Educational Poverty: Concepts, Methods, Policies, and Practices]. Meltemi editore.

De Sousa Santos, B. (2014). *Epistemlogies of the South. Justice against Epistemicide*. Routledge.

Del Gottardo, E. (2016). *Comunità educante, apprendimento esperienziale, comunità competente* [Educating Community, Experiential Learning, Competent Community]. Giapeto editore.

Delors, J. (1997). Learning: the treasure within; report to UNESCO of the International Commission on Education for the Twenty-first Century.

Dewey, J. (1899). *The School and Society*. University of Chicago Press.

Dewey, J. (1916). *Democracy and Education: An Introduction to the Philosophy of Education*. The McMillan Company.

Dewey, J. (1927). *The Public and Its Problems* (Vol. H). Holt and Company.

Diller, E. C. (2001). *Citizens in service: The challenge of delivering civic engagement training to national service programs*. Corporation for National and Community Service.

Fiorin, I. (2016). *Oltre l'aula* [Beyond the Classroom]. Mondadori.

Forbes Breaking News. (2023, March 3). Trump Proposes Building Ten New US 'Freedom Cities,' Offering 'Baby Bonuses' [Video]. Youtube. https://www.youtube.com/watch?v=dJA_GBhCGgE&t=23s

Fortini, F. (1984). *Paesaggi con serpente* [Landscapes with Serpent]. Einaudi.

Frabboni, F. (Ed.). (1989). *Il sistema formativo integrato: una nuova frontiera dell'educazione* [The Integrated Education System: A New Frontier in Education]. EIT.

Francesconi, D. (2021). Enactive networks, sustainable development and civic engagement. The case of FridaysforFuture. *Pedagogia oggi*, 19(2), 116-123.

Freire, P. (1996). *Pedagogy of Autonomy: Necessary Knowledge for Educational Practice*. Paz e Terra.

Gelpi, E. (1987). *Un meccano international. Crisi et crèation* [An international Meccano. Crisis and creation]. Clancier-Guernaud.

Granata, A. (2018). *La ricerca dell'altro. Prospettive di pedagogia interculturale*. Carocci.

Harvey, D. (2012). *Rebel cities. From the right to the urban revolution*. Verso.

Hill Collins, P. (2019). *Intersectionality as Critical Social Theory*. Duke University Press.

hooks, b. (1990). *Yearning. Race, Gender, and Cultural Politics*. South End Press.

hooks, b. (2003). *Teaching Community. A Pedagogy of Hope*. Routledge.

IDCM (2024). *Global Report on Internal Displacement-GRID 2024*. IDMC, NRC.

Illich, I. (1973a). *Tools for Conviviality*. Harper & Row.

Illich, I. (1973b). *Deschooling Society*. Penguin.

Irawan, B. (2016). The Common Good and Global Citizenship. *Journal of Citizenship Studies*, *4*(1), 1–10.

Isidori, E., Migliorati, M., Maulini, C (2017). Lo sport come bene comune: tra politica ed educazione [Sport as a Common Good: Between Politics and Education]. MeTis. *Mondi educativi. Temi, indagini, suggestioni*, 7(2), 48-72.

Khan Academy. (2024). Language Expansion Initiative. Retrieved from https://www.khanacademy.org

Langer, A. (2001). *La scelta della convivenza* [The choice of living together]. Edizioni E/O.

Maalouf, A. (2001). *L'identità* [Identity]. Bompiani.

MacIntyre, A. (1984). *After virtue: A study in moral theory*. University of Notre Dame Press.

Malaguzzi, L. (2010). *I cento linguaggi dei bambini. L'approccio di Reggio Emilia all'educazione dell'infanzia* [The Hundred Languages of Children: The Reggio Emilia Approach to Early Childhood Education]. Edizioni Junior.

Mantegazza, R. (1995). *Teoria critica della formazione* [Critical Theory of Education]. Unicopli.

Marshall, T. U. (1950). *Citizenship and social class, and other essays*. Cambridge University Press.

Martino, P. (2020). Educare all'inoperosità. Oltre l'antropologia del capitale umano: bioeconomia, pedagogia e valore dell'inutile [Educating for Inoperosity: Beyond the Anthropology of Human Capital: Bioeconomy, Pedagogy, and the Value of the Useless]. *Metis. Mondi educativi. Temi, indagini, suggestioni,* 10 (2), 213-230.

Massa, R. (1975). *La scienza pedagogica. Epistemologia e metodo educativo* [The Science of Pedagogy: Epistemology and Educational Method]. La Nuova Italia.

Maurin, E. (2004). *Le ghetto français. Enquête sur le séparatismesocial* [The French Ghetto: An Investigation into Social Separatism]. La Seuil.

Meroni, A., & Trapani, P. (2011). Public spaces as common good. The role of creative communities and collaborative networks. In Y. Lou & X. Zhu (eds.*), Cumulus Proceedings. ShangHai. Young Creators For Better City & Better Life 2010* (pp. 386-392), School of Art and Design, Aalto University.

Milano, C., Novelli, M., & Russo, A. P. (2024). Anti-tourism activism and the inconvenient truths aboutmass tourism, touristification and overtourism. *Tourism Geographies. VoL., 26*(8), 1313–1337.

Molina-Guenante, M., Ríos-Peters, R., & Santi-Vargas, A. (2022). Pedagogía Urbana como una herramienta de resistencia curricular: Aprendizaje para trascender la pandemia [Urban Pedagogy as a Tool of Curricular Resistance: Learning to Transcend the Pandemic]. *REVISTA SABERES EDUCATIVOS*, (8), 46–68.

Morin, E. (1999a). *Seven Complex Lessons in Education for the Future*. UNESCO.

Morin, E. (1999b). *La tête bien faite. Repenser la réforme, réforme la pensée* [The Well-Made Head: Rethinking Reform, Reforming Thought]. Éditions du Seuil.

Morin, E. (2004). Prefazione. Educare all'era planetaria. [Preface: Educating for the Planetary Era] In Bocchi, G., & Ceruti, M. (Eds.), *Educazione e globalizzazione* [Education and Globalization]. (pp. VII–X). Raffaello Cortina.

Morin, E. (2021). *Leçons d'un siècle de vie* [Lessons from a Century of Life]. Éditions Denoël.

Musaio, M. (Ed.). (2021). *Ripartire dalla città. Prossimità educativa e rigenerazione delle periferie* [Restarting from the City: Educational Proximity and the Regeneration of Peripheries]. Vita & Pensiero.

Nájera Martinez, E. (2008). Esbozos para una pedagogía urbana pertinente a los desarrollos educativos en las ciudades [Outlines for an Urban Pedagogy Relevant to Educational Developments in Cities]. *Polis, 20*, https://journals.openedition.org/polis/3421

Natorp, P. (1899). *Sozialpädagogik* [Social Pedagogy]. F. Frommann (E. Hauff).

Nussbaum, M. C. (1997). *Cultivating Humanity. A Classical Defense of Reform in Liberal Education*. Harvard University Press.

Nussbaum, M. C. (2010). *Not for Profit. Why Democracy Needs Humanities*. Princeton University Press.

Nussbaum, M. C. (2011). *Creating Capabilities: The Human Development Approach*. Harvard University Press. DOI: 10.4159/harvard.9780674061200

Osborne, M., Kearns, P., & Yang, J. (2013). Learning cities: Developing inclusive, prosperous and sustainable urban communities. *International Review of Education, 59*(4), 409–423. DOI: 10.1007/s11159-013-9384-y

Paone, S. (2010). La città fra marginalità ed esclusione sociale [The City Between Marginality and Social Exclusion]. *SocietàMutamentoPolitica*, 1(2), 153–164. DOI: 10.13128/SMP-9280

Pinto Minerva, F. (2002). *L'intercultura* [Interculture]. Laterza.

Pontes, A. I., Henn, M., & Griffiths, M. D. (2019). Youth political (dis)engagement and the need for citizenship education: Encouraging young people's civic and political participation through the curriculum. *Education, Citizenship and Social Justice, 14*(1), 3–21. DOI: 10.1177/1746197917734542

Quinto, A. (2021). An urban pedagogy or the implicit pedagogy of urban spaces *MeTis. Mondi educativi. Temi, indagini, suggestioni,* 11(1), 358-372

Reimers, F. M. (2018). Educare alla cittadinanza globale: le emergenze e gli approcci possibili. Proposte per costruire percorsi operativi. [Educating for Global Citizenship: Emergencies and Possible Approaches. Proposals for Building Practical Pathways] In Reimers, F. M., Barzanò, G., Fisichella, L., & Lissoni, M. (Eds.), *Cittadinanza globale e sviluppo sostenibile. 60 lezioni per un curriculum verticale* [Global Citizenship and Sustainable Development: 60 Lessons for a Vertical Curriculum]. (pp. 13–37). Pearson.

Reimers, F. M. (2020). *Educating students to improve the world: Global citizenship education for the 21st century.* Springer. DOI: 10.1007/978-981-15-3887-2

Riccardi, V. (2019). Scuola italiana e cittadinanza terrestre: alcune considerazioni a partire dai dati ICCS 2016. [Italian School and Earthly Citizenship: Some Considerations Based on ICCS 2016 Data] In Nanni, S., & Vaccarelli, A. (Eds.), *INTERCULTURA E SCUOLA. Scenari, ricerche, percorsi pedagogici* [Interculturalism and School. Scenarios, Research, and Pedagogical Pathways]. (pp. 103–121). Franco Angeli.

Riordan, P. (2008). A Grammar of the Common Good: Speaking of Globalisation. *Continuum.*

Rosa, H. (2010). *Alienation and Acceleration: Towards a Critical Theory of Late-Modern Temporality*. NSU Press.

Seddon, G. (1972). *Sense of Place. A Response to an Environment. The Swan Coastal Plain*. University of Western Australia Press.

Selwyn, N. (2016). *Education and Technology: Key Issues and Debates*. Bloomsbury Academic.

Sen, A. K. (2000). *Development as Freedom*. Knopf.

Simonetti, C. (2017). Bene comune: la sfida sociale ed educativa dei nostri tempi [Common Good: The Social and Educational Challenge of Our Times]. *MeTis. Mondi educativi. Temi, indagini, suggestioni,* 7(2), 212-224

Stebé, J. M., & Marchal, H. (2009). *Mythologie des cités-ghettos* [Mythology of the Ghettoized Cities]. Le Cavalier Bleu Editions. DOI: 10.3917/lcb.stebe.2009.01

Stillo, L. (2023). *Periferie dell'esclusione. Contesti, soggettività, riflessioni in prospettiva pedagogico-sociale* [Peripheries of Exclusion: Contexts, Subjectivities, and Reflections in a Socio-Pedagogical Framework]. Pensa MultiMedia.

Tarozzi, M. (2015). *Dall'intercultura alla giustizia sociale. Per un progetto pedagogico e politico di cittadinanza globale* [From Interculturalism to Social Justice. Toward a Pedagogical and Political Project for Global Citizenship]. FrancoAngeli.

Teti, V. (2020). *La restanza* [Ethics of remaining]. Einaudi.

Tramma, S. (1999). *Pedagogia sociale* [Social Pedagogy]. Guerini studio. UN Sustainable Development Group. Universal Values Principle Two: Leave No One Behind. https://unsdg.un.org/2030-agenda/universal-values/leave-no-one-behind

UNESCO. (2015). *UNESCO and Sustainable Development Goals*. UNESCO.

UNESCO. (2017). *Learning City e OSS: Guida all'Azione. UNESCO and International Cooperation Centre (2018). Educazione alla cittadinanza globale: temi e obiettivi di apprendimento* [Global Citizenship Education: Topics and Learning Objectives]. UNESCO.

UNESCO. (1987–2000). *The Earth Charter*. UNESCO

UNESCO Institute for Lifelong Learning. (2023). Global Network of Learning Cities. Retrieved from https://uil.unesco.org/learning-cities

Valzania, A. (2016). *Tempo sociale e neoliberismo. Velocità, competizione e nuove forme di alienazione* [Social Time and Neoliberalism: Speed, Competition, and New Forms of Alienation]. Carocci.

Warschauer, M. (2004). *Technology and Social Inclusion: Rethinking the Digital Divide*. MIT Press.

Woodworth, M. D. (2024). 'Freedom Cities': Trump and an American global new city. *Urban Geography*, *45*(1), 45–52. DOI: 10.1080/02723638.2023.2263121

Zizioli, E. (2024). L'esclusione nei contesti urbani: alla ricerca dell'identità delle scuole popolari. [Exclusion in Urban Contexts: In Search of the Identity of Popular Schools] In Zizioli, E., Stillo, L., & Franchi, G. (Eds.), *L'altra scuola. L'educazione popolare tra apprendimento e riscatti sociale* [The Other School: Popular Education Between Learning and Social Redemption]. (pp. 29–52). Donzelli Editore.

Zizioli, E., Stillo, L., & Franchi, G. (Eds.). (2024). *L'altra scuola. L'educazione popolare tra apprendimento e riscatti sociale* [The Other School: Popular Education Between Learning and Social Redemption]. Donzelli Editore.

KEY TERMS AND DEFINITIONS

Community: It is a polysemous concept that has evolved over time, acquiring diverse forms and interpretations. It may denote a network of solidaristic relationships among individuals unified by a shared purpose and the recognition of common needs. Within certain academic discourses, it is conceptualized as a condition encompassing the entirety of human existence, whereas in other theoretical frameworks, it is construed as a locally situated entity, embedded within a specific territorial and socio-cultural context.

ECG (Global civic education): An educational approach that fosters the development of knowledge, competencies, values, and dispositions essential for the active and responsible exercise of global citizenship, grounded in the principles of social equity, inclusion, and sustainability.

Education: The process of cultural transmission – shaped differently by each specific historical and cultural context – through which human personality is formed and integrated into society within certain social institutions such as the family, school, and others.

Glocal: The approach that fosters a dialogue between the global and local dimensions, promoting complex and systemic thinking supported by actions rooted in the local context. Such an approach enables the effective engagement with the challenges of an increasingly interconnected and interdependent world.

Social Inclusion: The multidimensional process that exists in a dialectical relationship with processes of exclusion and seeks to promote the full participation of all individuals in every sphere and dimension of life—social, political, economic, and cultural.

Territory: Extends far beyond its geographical definition; it constitutes a complex context encompassing the physical environment, social relationships, and cultural dynamics in which both individuals and communities grow and develop. In this sense, territory functions as an active learning environment, shaped through direct experience, engagement in community life, and the creation of social relationships

Urban Pedagogy: Disciplinary field that examines the city as an educational environment, with particular attention to the interrelations among public space, learning processes, and the formative function of education in enhancing urban quality of life. It also provides a critical framework for interpreting the social cartographies of the city, revealing how mechanisms of inclusion and exclusion operate within urban spaces to produce both vibrant social centers and zones of marginalization.

ENDNOTES

1 English translation: it is not possible, especially from a pedagogical perspective, not to hope for the primacy of a cooperative economy (Calame, 2019), capable of promoting the construction of a planetary consciousness grounded on humanitarian grounds (Morin, 2004).

2 English translation: an open and pluralist society that respects the dignity of individuals and enables dialogue

3 English translation: value system that refers to a humanising globalisation". It expresses the relationship between man and the world, justice and solidarity, the rights and duties, sharing and participation, as well as freedom and democracy in a pedagogical perspective of 'lifelong education' and 'long wide learning

4 Journalistic Editorial Staff (2024, July 24). Ticket d'accesso, paganti al minimo. Si chiude con 2,2 milioni raccolti. *Venezia Today.* https://www.veneziatoday.it/cronaca/ticket-accesso-ultimi-weekend.html#:~:text=Ticket%20d'accesso%2C%20paganti%20al,con%202%2C2%20milioni%20raccolti&text=Finita%20oggi%2C%20alle%2016%2C%20la,di%20sperimentazione%2C%20per%20il%202024. (last accessed on 28/05/2025).

5 https://sindicatdellogateres.org/historia/ (last accessed on 28/05/2025)

6 https://afectadosporlahipoteca.com/que-es-la-pah/ (last accessed on 28/05/2025).

7 Forbes Breaking News (2023, March 3). Trump Proposes Building Ten New US 'Freedom Cities,' Offering 'Baby Bonuses' [Video]. Youtube. https://www.youtube.com/watch?v=dJA_GBhCGgE&t=23s. (last accessed on 28/05/2025).

8 English translation: "countering hardship and offering a new image of marginal contexts and of those drug-dealing squares that become the only training grounds for young people when no alternatives are provided."

9 English translation: "daily and complex system of life for individuals".

10 English translation: "theoretical and operational frame of reference for educational initiatives".

11 English translation: "integrated educational system".

12 English translation: "systemic network of educational agencies in the local context".

13 English translation: "rational and democratic integration and interconnection of intentionally educational resources within the territory".

14 English translation: "territorial empowerment strategy".

15 English translation: "the community educates because it is a space of participation, educates because it enables the practice of certain values, educates because it oversees the educational mission, and educates because in many cases it directly assumes educational responsibilities and initiatives".

16 English translation: "in this ongoing process of transformation, the community educates, brings forth its essence".

17 English translation: "a *we* that takes responsibility for its own educational, transformative, and developmental path".

18 See https://www.commonground.org.uk for a comprehensive overview of the association's history, vision, and projects (last accessed on 28/05/2025).

19 https://www.commonground.org.uk/parish-maps/ (last accessed on 28/05/2025).

20 For a gallery of Parish Maps, see https://www.commonground.org.uk/parish-maps-gallery/ (last accessed on 28/05/2025).

21 https://www.mapkibera.org (last accessed on 06/10/2025).

22 https://www.indigenousmaps.com/ (last accessed on 06/10/2025).

23 English translation: "The nuclear threat and the ecological threat that weigh on the biosphere impose a community of destiny on humanity. Thus, awareness of this planetary destiny that we are experiencing has become life".

24 English translation: "An intelligence incapable of considering the context and the planetary complex, makes one blind, unconscious and irresponsible".

25 English translation: "Awareness and a sense of belonging and our earthly identity are vital today. It is the progression and anchoring of this awareness of belonging to our earthly homeland that will allow the development, through multiple channels, in the various regions of the globe, of a sense of connection and inter-solidarity necessary to civilize human relations".

26 English translation: "Who am I? I answer: I am a human being. That is my noun. But I have several adjectives, of varying importance depending on the circumstances; I am French, of Sephardic Jewish origin, partly Italian and Spanish, largely Mediterranean, culturally European, citizen of the world, child of the Earth-Homeland. Can one be all of these at the same time? No, it depends on the circumstances and the moments where sometimes one, sometimes another of these identities predominates".

27 English translation: "depends on the circumstances and the moments where sometimes one and sometimes another of these identities predominates [...] Everyone has the identity of their family, that of their village or town, that of their province or ethnic group, that of their country, and finally the broader identity of their continent. Everyone has a complex identity, that is to say, one that is both one and plural".

28 English translation: "Each of us should be encouraged to embrace our own diversity, to conceive our own identity as the sum of our different belongings, instead of confusing it with a single one, erected as a supreme belonging and an instrument of exclusion".

29 English translation: "I am Milanese, Italian, European, global. I don't want to deny any of these identities, but to complement them, because they enrich each other. It is a great adventure and a great joy to be at home in Rio or Warsaw, in Beijing as in Cotonou, in Milan or Mexico; to be able to get angry or happy in any country with people without prejudices or complexes... and at the same time, I love my home, my neighborhood, my cinemas... my theaters".

30 English translation: "identity and world consciousness are not in contradiction: a united world is the result of the variety and richness of languages and cultures and not of a process of homologation that would lead to the progressive loss of the identities of the weakest populations".

31 English translation: "understand the forces that unite the world at an accelerating speed and be able to operate effectively beyond the borders of a single nation to address the challenges they create, or to capture the opportunities they offer".

32 Title of one of the goals described in point 14 of the Earth Charter.

33 English translation: "Literature, poetry, cinema, psychology, and philosophy should converge to become schools of understanding. The ethics of human understanding is undoubtedly a key requirement in our times of widespread incomprehension: we live in a world of incomprehension between strangers but also between members of the same society".

34 English translation: "It is at the same time a matter of recognising unity within diversity, diversity within unity, of recognising, for example, human unity through individual and cultural diversity, individual and cultural diversity through human unity".

35 English translation: "solidarity and responsibility cannot come from pious exhortations or civic speeches, but from a deep feeling of affiliation (affiliare, from filius, son), a matri-patriotic feeling that should be cultivated concentrically on France, Europe, the Earth".

36 English translation: "citizens aware of their ability to imagine alternative futures and to influence the fate of the planet, through the exercise of their rights and duties in a highly interrelated world".

37 UN Sustainable Development Group. Universal Values Principle Two: Leave No One Behind. https://unsdg.un.org/2030-agenda/universal-values/leave-no-one-behind (last accessed on 28/05/2025)

38 English translation: culture - understood as a right of citizenship in the broadest sense - must become the driving force of civic aggregation

Chapter 5
Sharing Economy From the Political Perspective and Common Good

Zbigniew Grzymala
https://orcid.org/0000-0001-8861-8486
SGH-Warsaw School of Economics, Poland

Agnieszka Jadwiga Wójcik-Czerniawska
https://orcid.org/0000-0002-9612-1952
SGH-Warsaw School of Economics, Poland

Jacek Adamczak
https://orcid.org/0009-0007-9417-240X
SGH-Warsaw School of Economics, Poland

ABSTRACT

The sharing economy is nothing new in principle. Its beginnings date back to the times of the creation of social communities. In the dimension of the urban economy, we can identify it with the municipal economy or, as in the case of Poland, an attempt to enfranchise Polish citizens under the Universal Privatization program. Today, the sharing economy is understood as an economic model based on sharing broadly understood resources with other people. Examples of such an economy in the context of the urban economy include sharing mainly broadly understood municipal goods (for example, excess energy from solar panels) or, in the authors' understanding, also co-participation in the creation of some such goods. This co-participation can be understood, among others, as the possession by residents of a settlement unit of shares, for example, in a water treatment plant, if the legal structure allows for such an organizational and legal form.

DOI: 10.4018/979-8-3373-2332-9.ch005

INTRODUCTION

The sharing economy or the sharing economy has accompanied humanity since the creation of social communities, starting with the clan communities. Mutual physical and economic protection constituted the first foundations of what we can define as the sharing economy. As a result of the growth of urban settlements, social division and municipalization of social life, the municipal economy within the urban economy became an element of the sharing economy in cities. The next stage is the transformation of local communities into so-called civil societies. In the dimension of civil society, we can talk about participation in creating, for example, the directions of development of the settlement unit, mutual protection of neighbors or generally about co-decision-making. Another dimension is the sharing of resources at their disposal by individual members of society. This last phenomenon, combined with the communal functions of the settlement unit, favors a pro-ecological and resource-efficient way of life. In practice, this process also means the circular economy.

THE EVOLUTION OF THE SHARING ECONOMY CONCEPT

Nowadays, the sharing economy is understood as an economic model that involves sharing unused or unused resources, products or services with other participants in economic and social circulation, for a fee or free of charge, on the basis of mutual exchange of resources or assistance in action, and the basic determinant of the success of this exchange is the human factor. The concept of *sharing economy* It was first used in 2008 by L. Lessig, ethicist and professor of law at Harvard Law School, advocate of copyright reform, and founder and former chairman of the *nonprofit organization* Creative Commons. L. Lessig defined the sharing economy as follows: *There is not only trade economics, which measures access on a simple price method, but also the sharing economy, where access to culture is regulated not by price, but through a complex set of social relations* (Lessig, 2008; Nadolska, Nadolski, 2019).

Rachel Botsman, recognized as a world authority in the field of cooperation and trust supported by modern technologies, defines the concept *of sharing economy:* "systems that facilitate the sharing of underutilized resources or services – for a fee or free of charge – directly between individuals or organizations. Their key feature includes the process of sharing (sharing, making available)" (Poniatowska Jaksch, Sobiecki, 2017). The essence of *sharing understood in this way economy* refers to "sharing", or "giving something to someone", which requires, that the entity sharing (not only individual entities) has a given resource ownership or had the rights to use the resource that is shared (Botsman, 2015; Nadolska, Nadolski, 2019). In practice This is due to the fact that these resources are not fully utilized (in terms of time or in terms of "production capacity"), i.e. having certain "surpluses" and the will to share them with others. This concept already outlines the problem of the costs of this sharing at the definitional stage. For example, technical wear and tear of the shared device, depreciation, costs of transmitting energy surpluses, using internet platforms to promote various forms of sharing activities economy, etc. The question also arises: who should cover these costs or most of them in the case of lending, i.e. free sharing of a given good or service, the person sharing or the person being shared, or maybe it depends only on the arrangements made between the parties? It seems that the legislation in this area partly addresses these problems, however, due to the emergence of new forms *of sharing economy* the legislation of individual countries as well as international organizations should additionally regulate this phenomenon.

However, before understanding *sharing economy* took the above form, the idea of the sharing economy was present already at the stage of creating social communities. The basic need was the need to defend against attackers such as wild animals, hostile other people, help in building defensive fortifications, shelters, etc. Mutual protection against such dangers was a manifestation of the broadly understood sharing economy. In addition, there were other social needs that in some respect reflected the meaning of the sharing economy. "For example, such social needs as the need for housing, heating, lighting, transport or sanitary and hygienic needs at the early stages of social development were satisfied within households. The gradual social division of labor created conditions for the development of various forms of settlement and the satisfaction of some of these needs through exchange" (Dziembowski, 1991). However, in the initial phase, many of these needs were satisfied on the basis of sharing. This sharing was conditioned by the need to survive. This needs to survive probably led to the expansion of settlement units. "Cities arose from small settlements, where the population began to specialize in various types of activities. A gradual division of labor occurred, and the phenomenon of sharing slowly disappeared in many areas of social and economic life. However, elements of *the sharing economy* can be seen in the case of meeting the so-called municipal needs, i.e., sanitary needs, including sewage disposal, waste disposal, and water supply. "It was increasingly difficult to meet these needs on a single household scale. Building the necessary infrastructure to provide all these municipal services was extremely expensive from the point of view of an average single household. Therefore, the construction and provision of such services was the responsibility of communes. This process was called "communalism of life" by theoreticians of local government" (Rzeczkowski, 1938). Today, it can be described as rational sharing. For example, it is easier to share the costs of infrastructure investments among themselves using an organization such as a commune than to burden an individual or a specific group of people with them. Thanks to the industrial revolution in the 19th century, rational sharing was also possible in the process of providing heating using district heating networks, street lighting or transport within housing estates, as well as telecommunications.

As a result of the further development of social life, some areas of public utility began to take on a more commercial character. The economic reason for their creation, i.e. the high capital intensity of investments, ceased to play a fundamental role. Technical possibilities for introducing competition appeared. This determined the existence of the opposite direction, i.e. the "decommunalization of life". This phenomenon affected primarily telecommunications and the power industry, and later also the heating industry. In such a situation, the non-profit principle and the character of public utility in relation to the municipal economy began to lose their original dimension (Grzymała, 2011, p. 17). In this way, the perception of some public utility services through the prism of the sharing economy was blurred.

Certain social models are more conducive to the concept *of sharing economy*. Such a model may be the concept of civil society. "Different meanings of the term "citizenship" have been shaped in historical development, and the oldest of them have their source in antiquity. In the Greek polis, a citizen was someone who had political rights and participated in the political process. In turn, in ancient Rome, an understanding of citizenship as formal and legal status was formed: "citizens were persons legally recognized as members of a sovereign political community and therefore had rights that were to be protected by the government of a given community, and these could, but did not have to, be political rights. Citizenship in ancient Rome began to refer to a greater extent to the equal protection of individuals by law than to their active participation in establishing and implementing the political order in the state" (Trzciński, 2006; Pudzianowska, 2015). Similarly, in the 20th century, this concept was developed by the British sociologist TH Marshall, who believed that "modern citizenship is created by a triad of rights: personal, political and social" (Marshall, 1950). The latest, only in the last hundred years, was another basic understanding of the term "citizenship" formed - as belonging to any community with which an individual identifies and within which bonds of solidarity are created between people. In this approach, "citizenship" expresses a sense of identity, an experience of psychological identification with a community (in this sense, one can be, for example, a "citizen" of a sports club) (Isin & Turner, 2002; Pudzianowska, 2015).

This society, in addition to participation, for example, in determining the strategic directions of local development or even legal participation of residents in selected municipal infrastructure, as is the case in some municipalities in Sweden with regard to water supply infrastructure, has begun to show demand for co-management of the settlement unit. We can therefore speak here of the so-called economy of shared management. Often, the rulers of settlement units that prefer a consultative or participatory style of management encourage society to such cooperation, not only in Europe or the USA, which can be seen, among others, in Singapore. The basis for shaping such an attitude of sharing management was to draw attention to joint responsibility for the natural environment, natural resources, climate change, socio-economic development, etc. "The sharing economy changes the current paradigm of constant economic growth based on the production of new goods even at the expense of limited resources. It can therefore be assumed that from this point of view, the basic principle of this concept is the assumption that there are unused resources that can be reintroduced into the economic or social circulation by maximizing the life cycle of these resources. "This entrepreneurship can be seen in the category of social innovation, which contributes to a better, more ecological and sustainable development distribution of goods and services. The sharing economy can therefore be seen as a supplement to the mainstream economy with a segment of socially responsible business," (Poniatowska-Jaksch & Sobiecki, 2015). "The sharing economy assumes that Instead of buying a product, good or service, we rent or share this product or service with others. The condition for running a sharing economy is not ownership of resources, but only access to them," (Poniatowska-Jaksch & Sobiecki, 2015). New technologies help us in this technologies such as the Internet and mobile phones, which enable us to maintain continuous, interactive contact with other users of economic turnover and social life, (Adamczak, 2022).

A certain proposed solution referring to the concept *of sharing economy* in Poland was the General Privatization Program undertaken in the 1990s, contained in the Act on National Investment Funds and Their Privatization. In general, this program was about sharing with the Polish society the ownership of the national wealth developed by Polish citizens during the period of so-called socialism. "This program covered 512 enterprises grouped in 15 National Investment Funds (NFI) with the initial value of net assets close to PLN 6 billion. The Act also guaranteed citizens' participation in the ownership structure through so-called share certificates subject to exchange of these certificates for NFI shares. These certificates were made available for a symbolic amount of PLN 20 at the time. The following persons in particular had the right to these shares:

- employees employed in state budgetary units from 1 July 1991 to 31 December 1991,
- soldiers and officers of the Police, Prison Service, Office for State Protection and Border Guard who served from 1 July 1991 to 31 December 1991,
- persons who held the positions of judges, prosecutors and managerial state positions in the period from 1 July 1991 to 31 December 1991,
- retirees and pensioners.

Share certificates were bearer securities. They could therefore be exchanged for selected shares of National Investment Funds through an existing brokerage house according to the following key: one certificate for one share of each NFI. In this way, NFI shares became subject to stock exchange trading, where they could be sold or purchased, thus becoming a shareholder of partnerships and a stock market investor. In practice, the right to NFI shares through share certificates was taken over mainly by banks purchasing certificates from people who were not familiar with the procedures of the privatization program. As a result of these actions, public participation in NFIs, as an expression of universal privatization, failed," (Grzymała, 2010). The reason for the lack of success in such a understood *sharing economy* can be seen in the great immaturity of the then representatives of the Polish government, banks, business groups and to some extent also citizens towards such an idea introduced on such a large scale. This immaturity was probably accompanied and also expressed by the tendency of decision-making stakeholders towards corruption. The following conclusion can be drawn from this example: the given instruments *sharing economy* and their scale depend on the degree of openness of society to such an idea. In other words, the introduction of certain solutions with *sharing economy* will be possible in one society and will be successful, and not in the other and will end in failure. One can also find here a certain allegory to the Marxist socio-economic model and its implementation in the former Soviet Union and in European countries after the Second World War, for example in the Scandinavian countries.

The concept *of sharing economy* as already mentioned is connected with two approaches: sharing goods or services for free or for a fee. The first one approach he responds ideas *Homo Curans* . " *Homo Curans* refers to the very humanness as essentially caring, which in itself has various dimensions of self-care, care for community, ecological care, planetary care, and transcendental care (...) Care is a multilayers concept, crossing several fields of knowledge, each of which with their specific interpretation and implication human flourishing, societal well-being, and sustainability. To understand the notion of care, it is necessary to consider the variety of its meanings in academic, professional, traditional, indigenous, and literary aspects. This inter- and transdisciplinary perspective will serve to deepen our understanding and highlight how central care is in the building of a sustainable and equitable future (....) Care is a complex term studied across disciplines, each contributing in its own way. It considers the well-being of individual as viewed by positive psychology, systemic equity as observed by feminist theories, innovation, and sustainability in fields related to science, technology, engineering, and mathematics (STEM). Irrespective of the emphases, all these views express care as a significant basis for human flourishing and advancement of society.

The " care " aspect in the sense of sharing without payment is expressed in the idea of *Homo Curans* also through religious tradition. Religious traditions frame care as a moral imperative linked to ethical living. Christian agape love, Buddhist karuna (compassion), and Islamic zakat (charity) all link care to spiritual development and concern for others, (McGrath, 2001; Esposito, 2002; Hermandes, 2024). From a philosophical perspective, one can consider the existentialist emphasis on authenticity in relationships, (Sartre, 2018; Hermandes, 2024), the utilitarian assessment of care's societal impact (Mill, 1863; Hermandes, 2024, p. 6), and the Confucian ideals of ren (benevolence) and familial duty (Confucius, 1979; (Hermandes, 2024).

The concept of the sharing economy is also associated with the concept of moving away from traditionally understood economic growth. It is assumed that zero or even negative economic growth is possible. Within this concept, there is even a need to stop or limit economic growth , due to the side effects of this growth, such as excessive exploitation of natural resources, environmental pollution or even its destruction. Therefore, striving for continuous economic growth may result in a threat or even destruction of man himself. "An alternative to traditional economic growth that takes place without respect for the environment is also the concept of green growth, which consists in using environmental resources in a sustainable manner " (Attenborough , 2020, p. 283). Therefore, economic growth may result in greater costs than social benefits. In addition to the aforementioned consumption of limited natural resources, there are also costs of competition on a global scale, as well as between human beings, resulting in constant stress, loss of both physical and mental health. "Development models should be developed in local contexts and reflect regional social and cultural conditions. According to Onofrio Romano, instead of a utilitarian attitude that promotes instrumentalism and the interests of individuals, an anti-utilitarian attitude should be followed, taking into account the value of social bonds and the diversity of forms of life" (Romano, 2020, pp. 61-65).

The Indian concept of Eco- Svaraj, also referred to as radical economic democracy, is of a similar nature. It "proclaims a biocenotic vision of nature, of which man is only one part. Instead of progress and development, it speaks rather of a satisfying social and spiritual life, which should be combined with economic justice. Strong emphasis is placed here on both socio-political decentralization (making important decisions at the most local level possible) and economic democracy, which is to consist in strengthening the processes in which producers and consumers hold control over the means of production, distribution and exchange," (Kothari, Demaria, & Acosta, 2014; Minker, 2022).

In some sense, *sharing economy* fills the gap of untapped capital potential. Peruvian economist Hernando de Soto noticed the existence of untapped or dead capital. He claimed that "in Haiti, for example, one of the poorest countries, the value of the wealth of the poor is four times greater than the value of the 123 largest (legal) enterprises, including subsidiaries of American and French corporations. It is similar in Egypt - there, unlegalized, "wild" and therefore "dead capital" that cannot be used, is worth 30 times more than the assets of enterprises listed on the Cairo Stock Exchange. In Mexico - outside the legal economic circulation, and therefore outside the control or influence of the government - up to 70 percent of private assets operate. In Russia, until recently, the wealth of the poor was the source of over 50 percent of gross national income. I told President Putin a year ago that if he leaves this underground economy to its fate, the mafia will take care of it. The alternative for the underground is to include the grey zone in the legal economy. In the Third World countries, in the hands of the poorest, who make up over 80 percent of their population, there is wealth worth $10 trillion. That is enormous wealth! What does it matter if this capital is partly wasted and partly "dead"? In Egypt, the poor have 55 times more assets in their hands than the value of all foreign investments made in this country over the last 200 years. At the same time, over 90 percent of Egyptians live in poverty, unable to formally use this capital to increase their wealth. They do not have mortgages, property titles, permits, etc. They cannot insure it, pledge it, legally sell it or use it in any other way. Every slum has potential value..." (Fijor, 2002). Although de Soto argued with the advantages and disadvantages of the capitalist system, he rightly noticed the untapped potential that is present in almost every country. He saw the reason for its untapped potential mainly in the legal system that limits its legal, lawful use. Such untapped capital can be found everywhere, according to the idea of *sharing economy* . Its owners are citizens of a given country and they are not even aware of the possibilities offered by the implementation of the *sharing concept enonomy*.

Sharing economy in this understanding also responds to the accusations against the approach discussed above, which focuses on zero or even negative economic growth. The concepts of zero and negative economic growth are criticized, among others, due to potential production limitations or reductions in the provision of existing services, which are components of the classic measure of economic growth such as GDP or even HDI. *Sharing economy* in the light of de Soto's achievements indicates better use of existing assets, better use of their production capacity with simultaneous greater involvement of the human factor, i.e. work. Hence, on a global scale, but also regionally or locally, a decrease in the production of new goods as a result of a decrease in demand for these goods does not necessarily mean an economic slowdown. Thanks to the stimulation of creativity of residents and the construction of a favorable legal environment, as well as increasing the use of production and service capacities of existing capital, even classic measures of economic growth do not have to indicate a decrease in growth, and with an appropriate *share strategy economy* there may even be an increase in these measures of economic development.

FORMS AND MODELS *SHARING ECONOMY*

The sharing economy is therefore manifested in the market in the form of various forms and models. It can be both *non-profit* and profitable for one of the cooperating parties. Above all, however, it is based on an exchange between one person and another, which is why it is often referred to as a *peer -to- peer economy.* (P2P). Hence the discussed idea is also referred to as *peer economy* (so-called peer economy) , *on demand economy* (so-called on-demand economy) *mesh economy* (mixed economy) . However, it is worth noting that these are not identical concepts and therefore cannot be used interchangeably (Sobiecki, 2016). This group also includes *collaborative consumption.* Other similar concepts that give rise to different forms and structures of the sharing economy are (Botsman, 2015):

1. *Collaborative Economy* - Systems that unlock value from underused assets* by matching 'needs' and 'haves' in ways that bypass traditional intermediaries and distribution channels.
2. *Gift Economy*: Systems that enable goods or services to be given without any immediate payment or expectation of future quid pro quo.
3. *Gig Economy*: Systems that break up a traditional company 'job' into individual 'gigs' that independent workers are paid to do for a defined time.
4. *On-Demand Economy*: Systems that instantly match buyers and sellers to deliver goods and services immediately when people need them.
5. *Peer Economy*: Systems that connect buyers and sellers facilitating the exchange of assets directly between individuals.
6. *Rental Economy*: Systems that enable people to rent assets for a fee rather than needing to own them outright.

Collaborative concept *consumption* creates a specific structure and model. " When using this term, consider the behavior around exchanging assets changes and becomes more efficient through technology. For example, Airbnb enables people to rent out their homes and unused spare rooms to guests. Zopa allows people to borrow money from not just their family or friends but from beyond their social circle. And eBay elevates the "garage sale" allowing people to sell their unwanted things to people not just in their locality but to people with access to the internet," (Botsman 2015).

Collaborative economy model arises "when using this term, consider whether the example focuses on bypassing the traditional intermediaries to change the dynamics of supply and demand. For example, Vandebron enables people to buy their power directly from independent energy producers. Food Assembly allows people to buy their fresh produce from local farmers. Upcounsel allows people to select and hire an attorney directly from a marketplace. Uber enables people to get car rides directly from Uber drivers in the vicinity." In turn, gi *ft economy* considers whether the example facilitates true gifting of a product or service. For example, Freecycle enables networks of people who want to give and get stuff for free, Impossible enables people to give away their time, skills and objects within the social network, and Couchsurfing enables people to connect with locals to stay on their couch for free, (Botsman 2015).

When using the term of *gig economy*, "Consider whether the example changes the nature of work, and the worker relationship between the provider, customer and intermediary platform. For example, TaskRabbit pays task runners for every singular task they fulfil. Uber pays drivers per ride they give passengers. Postmates pays workers per delivery they are able to take." A different structure creates the "on-demand economy" model. "When using this term, consider whether the example is on time-based benefits such as immediate focused convenience or instant gratification. Instacart allows people to get their groceries delivered in an hour. Drizly allows people to get liquor delivered in under an hour. Amazon Prime membership expedites shipping and enables people to receive their orders within the hour if they are in the metropolitan area," (Botsman 2015).

When using *peer economy* term, "consider the example uses a genuine peer-to-peer mechanism. For example, Transferwise matches people based on the currency they have and require in order to make a currency swap. Etsy connects makers of crafts with buyers looking for unique or handmade products. Lyft connects people looking for a car ride with everyday drivers offering services. When using the term of "rental economy", consider whether the example asks for a fee in exchange for rental of a good. For example, Rent The Runway allows people to rent designer clothes, Chegg allows people to rent textbooks, and Getable allows companies to rent construction equipment, (Botsman 2015).

Sharing economy can create a socio-economic model based on sharing tangible and intangible resources. "The approach appropriate for *sharing economy* has become the basis for many business models in industries as diverse as IT, transport, hotel industry, and education. All kinds of companies and institutions are increasingly willing to incorporate elements of the sharing economy into their business practices and organizational culture, among other things because of their compatibility with the *lean method,* i.e. emphasizing savings and flexibility. The idea *of sharing economy* occurs in various areas of human life. It should be emphasized that the concept *of sharing economy* is not limited to material things, because people's resources also include their skills and free time, which they can share with other people" (Nadolska, Nadolski, 2019, p. 10).

In conclusion, *sharing economy* is primarily the unused resources of goods available to households. Goods produced and sold on the market very often remain unused or are used extremely rarely. The reason for this state of affairs is both the nature of the objects themselves and the way and possibilities of using goods and services by people. An important area of resources that are also unused or inefficiently used are human labor resources. Although there should be a balance between the demand and supply of labor resources in existing labor markets, very often transaction costs are so high that they eliminate the possibility of using human labor resources. In the sharing economy markets, unused resources are released, and the efficiency of their use is improved by eliminating excessive transaction costs, (Paczkowski, Kamela, & Szyl, 2020).

Therefore, it is so important that the regulations governing this new economic model, which, however, does not fully comply with the applicable tax law, reactively follow the development of this model and support, rather than restrict, its development in its various forms and structures, both the non-profit one and the one bringing a specific financial benefit to one of the parties.

LEGAL ASPECTS OF THE SHARING ECONOMY

The principle of lending is associated with the sharing economy in legal terms. In Polish law, this principle is regulated in the Civil Code (Civil Code, 1964, articles 710-719). In general, this is a fairly universally defined concept, which defines lending as a loan agreement, where the lender undertakes to allow the borrower, for a specified or unspecified period, to use the thing given to him for this purpose free of charge. From a social point of view, lending is an act of goodwill and a different approach to functioning in a social community. However, the aforementioned code indicates that if the thing lent has defects, the lender is obliged to repair the damage he caused to the borrower by not notifying him of the defects while being aware of them. This provision does not apply when the borrower could have easily noticed the defect. In addition, if the agreement does not specify the manner of using the thing, the borrower may use the thing in a manner that is appropriate to its properties and purpose. Without the

In the European Union countries, recommendations for the formulation of law emerging in the EU bodies are important. Legal standardization regarding different models *of sharing economy* was regulated in the European Union in the Resolution of the European Parliament of 15 June 2017 on a European agenda for the collaborative economy (Resolution of the European Parliament, 2017). This Resolution was drawn up taking into account, among others, the Resolution of 19 January 2016 on the Digital Single Market Act (Resolution on the Digital Single Market, 2016) and the Communication from the Commission of 25 May 2016 entitled "Online Platforms and the Digital Single Market. Opportunities and challenges for Europe, (Commission Communication, 2016).

The 2017 resolution emphasizes, among other things, that the collaborative economy has grown rapidly in recent years in terms of users, transactions and revenues, changing the way products and services are provided and challenging established economic models in many sectors. The collaborative economy is socially beneficial for EU citizens. According to a study conducted by the Commission, 17% of European consumers use services provided by the collaborative economy and 52% are aware of such services being offered. The resolution argues that, if developed responsibly, the collaborative economy creates many opportunities for citizens and consumers, who benefit from more competition, tailored services, greater choice and lower prices; emphasizes that the growth in this sector is consumer-driven and enables them to play a more active role. It also encourages Member States to ensure legal clarity and calls for the collaborative economy not to be seen as a threat to the traditional economy; Stresses the importance of regulating the sharing economy in a way that facilitates and enables rather than restricts (European Parliament Resolution, 2017).

The resolution recognizes that the collaborative economy creates new and interesting business opportunities, generates jobs and growth and often plays an important role not only in improving the efficiency of the economic system but also in making it more socially and environmentally sustainable and enabling a better allocation of resources and assets that would otherwise be underutilized, thus contributing to the transition towards a circular economy. At the same time, it recognizes that the collaborative economy can have a profound impact on long-established business models in many strategic sectors such as transport, accommodation, catering, services, retail and finance; understands the challenges resulting from the existence of different legal standards for similar economic entities; considers that the collaborative economy empowers consumers, creates new employment opportunities and can facilitate tax compliance, but emphasizes the importance of ensuring a high level of consumer protection and compliance with workers' rights and tax regulations; recognizes that the collaborative economy affects both urban and rural environments (European Parliament Resolution, 2017).

The Resolution draws attention to the lack of clarity among businesses, consumers and authorities on the application of existing regulations in certain areas and therefore to the need to address regulatory grey areas, and expresses concern about the risk of fragmentation of the single market; is aware that, if not properly managed, these changes may result in legal uncertainty as to existing rules and restrictions on the exercise of individual and consumer rights; believes that regulation must be fit for purpose in the digital age and is deeply concerned about the negative impact of legal uncertainty and regulatory complexity on European start- ups and non-profit organizations involved in the collaborative economy. It also emphasizes the need to see the collaborative economy not only as a set of new business models for offering goods and services, but also as a new form of integration between the economy and society, where the services offered are based on a diversity of relationships that enable economic and social relations to be combined and create new forms of communities and new business models (European Parliament Resolution, 2017).

In assessing the legal solutions, the Resolution notes that while some sectors of the collaborative economy are regulated, including at local and national level, other sectors may fall into a regulatory grey area, as it is not always entirely clear which EU rules apply, which in turn leads to significant differences between Member States due to national, regional and local rules and case law, and fragmentation of the single market. It also calls on the Commission to clarify further and as soon as possible the liability regime within collaborative platforms in order to encourage responsible conduct and promote transparency and legal certainty, thereby increasing user trust; in particular, it notes the uncertainty as to whether an underlying service is provided by a platform or whether the platform is merely offering an information society service within the meaning of the e-Commerce Directive; it therefore calls on the Commission to provide additional guidance on these aspects and to consider whether further action is needed to improve the effectiveness of the regulatory framework; at the same time, it encourages collaborative platform operators to take appropriate measures to this end on a voluntary basis (Resolution of the European Parliament, 2017).

In relation to solutions for the dissemination of the idea *of sharing economy* in the urban economy, The Resolution notes that an increasing number of local authorities and municipalities are already actively involved in regulating and promoting the collaborative economy, focusing on community practices both as the subject of their policies and as a fundamental principle of new forms of collaborative governance and participatory democracy. It adds that national, regional and local authorities have sufficient scope to adopt measures tailored to their circumstances in order to respond to clearly defined public interest objectives with proportionate measures that are fully compliant with EU legislation; calls on the Commission, therefore, to support Member States in shaping policies and adopting regulations that are consistent with EU law . Cities are pioneers, as urban conditions, such as population density and physical proximity, are conducive to the spread of community practices, which extend not only to smart cities but also to sharing cities, and facilitate the transition towards more citizen-friendly infrastructures; also believes that the collaborative economy can be a real opportunity for peripheral, rural and disadvantaged inner regions, and can lead to new and inclusive forms of development, have a positive socio-economic impact and help marginalized communities through indirect benefits for the tourism industry (European Parliament Resolution, 2017).

In relation to *sharing business models economy* "based on the provisions of Polish law, for example, it is possible to indicate a law other than Polish as applicable to the assessment of a given legal relationship. The result of such indication will be the necessity to assess the correctness of the service provision based on the provisions of law other than Polish law. For Polish users of sharing economy services, this may cause uncertainty as to the consequences of their actions and the risk of incurring liability to a broader extent than would result from the provisions of Polish law. It should be noted that despite the choice of foreign law, certain elements of the relations between the participants of the sharing economy will still be assessed on the basis of Polish law, e.g. consumer protection law, tax law or personal data protection law. Some groups of provisions of Polish law are applicable regardless of the choice of foreign law (Wolters Kluwer, 2016).

The concept of the sharing economy has a wide application, also in relation to financial services. Due to the nature of the idea of sharing economy the legal framework for such activities is relatively difficult to establish for both national regulators and stakeholders. The legal framework for individual business models may differ due to the nature of the model.

Contemporary examples of the sharing economy

The sharing economy is one of the fastest growing economic segments today. The car sharing system is developing very well in larger cities, *where* you can use cars using a special application on your phone, which shows you where to park your free vehicles, and also allows you to complete all registration formalities and payments. Instead of buying new things, you can buy used ones (*Ebay, Allegro*), set off in one car with other people in the same direction, sharing the fuel costs (*BlaBlaCar*), rent an apartment for a few days whose tenant has left (*Airbnb*). We also have an online platform that allows you to hire people to provide various services, from standing in line at the store to walking dogs to performing services such as mowing gardens or assembling furniture (*TaskRabbit*). We also have a social platform that helps match ordinary people with free funds with people in need of financial support (*LendingClub*). On other platforms, you can share your leftover food with others (*Taste & Share)*, raise money to finance various innovative projects (*KickStarter*) or start cooperation in the process of designing and jointly solving social problems (*OpenIdeo*). Probably the most environmentally friendly solution in the area of the sharing economy is the self-service urban bike rental systems that fit into the ecological image of cities and reduce exhaust emissions (bike sharing). Applications that enable collaboration are simple and intuitive to use, so it is no wonder that they are gaining huge popularity. Although this is still a niche area, it arouses great interest among consumers, businesses and increasingly also the authorities (Adamczak, 2022).

Crowdfunding websites are platforms that allow for fundraising (crowdfunding). Kickstarter is considered the largest English - language website of its kind. As part of the crowdfunding business model, funds raised using the online platform are then used to implement previously defined projects. These projects concern almost all areas of life, from card games, through music albums, to modern technologies. In exchange for the funds obtained, the originators offer (depending on the type of platform and project) share rights, copies created on the basis of the projects, sometimes it happens that the financing remains without any benefit to the user - investor. Since its inception, the Kickstarter platform has gathered a community exceeding 9 million user - investors, who have supported over 96,426 projects contributing over USD 2 billion to them (...). It should be pointed out that currently within crowdfunding we can distinguish the so -called equity financing, which largely involves the originator of a specific project offering, in exchange for financing, an unspecified group of recipients shares in a special purpose entity (commercial law company) that will implement a specific project, (Wolters Kluwer, 2016).

Another innovation based on the sharing economy can be considered social insurance services. Their idea is implemented on the basis of cooperation between *people* who *trust* each other and who " insure each other " against the risk of a specific event (so - called peer - to - *peer insurance*). These people use the appropriate internet service to collect funds, which are then kept in selected accounts. In the event of an appropriate random event affecting one of the financiers, an appropriate part of the funds collected in this way is transferred to the account of this financier in order to cover its losses resulting from the event. Such services have been developed mainly in relation to car insurance, e.g. heyguevara.com, (Wolters Kluwer, 2016).

An innovation in the field of financial services, which bases its functioning on the sharing economy, are services enabling the sale of receivables via online platforms. Currently, one of the start- up projects enabling entrepreneurs to sell unpaid invoices in order to receive receivables before their due date (so - called peer to peer factoring) is, for example, *the* service *marketinvoice.com,* (Wolters Kluwer, 2016).

Another example of the sharing economy is exchanging services and skills pooling. "This approach to the sharing economy is about exchanging services or skills. For instance, one can repair someone's computer but instead of paying cash for this service, the payment will be an exchange for, let's say, some free yoga classes. Someone needed gardening advice that offers he's painting skills or having German lessons in exchange for surf lesson… The possibilities are infinite.

Co-working spaces are a successful example of skills sharing. By having a variety of freelancers, medium-small companies or civil society organizations working under the same room it gets easier to exchange skills. A sustainability consultancy firm might, for instance, offer advice to an e-commerce startup that in exchange mentions them as partners and increases their SEO. A civil engineer freelancer working on a construction project might ask a circular economy expert for advice on compostable materials and in exchange help with his coding skills. "Again, the possibilities of exchanging know-how are Infinite" (Sharing Economy: Definition, Examples and Figures, 2025).

According to reports from Statista the value of the global shared services market is expected to grow from $19.5 billion in 2018 to over $330 billion in 2025. Behind this phenomenon there is already money, new organizations, marketing and, above all, people who, by establishing companies, have the ambition to create a new quality. It is natural that shopping takes place on the Internet, and everything happens quickly, conveniently, at a good price, based on recommendations from friends and, of course, using a mobile phone. Part of this trend of philosophy is also a kind of minimalism, which assumes that "possession" can be replaced with "use", "use" and "borrowing". We find in it the process of exchanging goods, sharing, focusing on resources available "here and now", placing emphasis on building bonds and a sense of group satisfaction (Business Insider).

It should be emphasized once again that *sharing economy* is directly related to the circular economy model. Its main area is the use of existing resources, which creates a social system that is friendly to the environment and protects its natural resources. This is a completely new quality of economic relations in which mutual cooperation and trust replace the desire for constant product competition and profit maximization (Adamczak, 2022).

SHARING ECONOMY IN THE URBAN ECONOMY

The urban economy is one of the best areas where the sharing economy should be applied in order to improve the quality of life of the local community with the direct participation of the local society. Most areas that the urban economy is interested in are related to the sharing economy. The basis of the activities of the urban economy related to the concept of the sharing economy is the high concentration of population in small areas, rapid technological development and creative social capital. The introduction of the principles of the sharing economy into the areas of the urban economy is the result of IT evolution and a systemic approach to the comprehensive organization of community life in a given area. The advantage of the concept of the sharing economy in the area of the urban economy is undoubtedly the planned sustainable development of these areas by promoting high quality of life, combined with the use of knowledge in the introduction of available solutions aimed at rational management of natural resources. Such practice is also related to the concept of smart city, especially in the dimension of city digitization and the possibilities offered by modern technological solutions.

One of the most important ways of introducing the principles of the sharing economy in urban areas is to use the potential of the local community through the influence of residents on the development of these areas in ecological and social terms, not only as a dimension of civil society but also in terms of the concept of a smart society. The concept of the sharing economy is based on the widest possible access to information through IT systems that very quickly collect and process the information needed to exchange or share raw materials that can be reused. One such example of sharing is the possibility of sharing excess electricity produced in individual households. In practice, current solutions do not guarantee that the power company will receive excess electricity produced by individual solar panels. Especially during the so-called " energy picks ". This is due, among other things, to the high load on the power grid and its relatively poor quality. In such cases, thanks to the IT system, owners of excess energy can transfer it on agreed terms to owners of electric vehicles (electric scooters, bicycles, electric motors, electric cars and buses), who could thus recharge this fleet. The initiator of such a solution could be municipal companies, especially those owned by the city, which increasingly use photovoltaics and other renewable energy sources to produce electricity and heat for their needs. They are also not free from dilemmas related to energy peaks and in this way could contribute to reducing the losses of energy produced during such peak periods. One cannot fail to notice serious changes in the understanding of the role and importance of municipal economy companies by the local community. Municipal companies in many cities have taken on the role of initiating pro-ecological attitudes among the local community.

The first example and proposal of such a solution, which in the sharing economy uses human potential both socially and economically, may be in the areas of urban economy in forest areas, the cleaning of which is the responsibility of municipalities, unless the land belongs to a private owner, building points and equipping them with bags and containers for municipal waste for selective collection. People staying in forests and using various physical activities such as running, walking with poles in the forest, also known as Nordic walking or cycling, could collect the waste left there by taking bags from such a point and leave it at those points where it would be collected by municipal services responsible for municipal waste management. In 2023 alone, as reported by the State Forests, 80.6 thousand cubic meters of waste were collected and removed from Polish forests. waste, which was cleaned up at a cost of PLN 32.5 million. Waste left in the forest creates a fire hazard in forests, pollutes ecosystems and can be deadly traps for insects and small animals. (Business Insider, 2025). The sharing economy in this area could therefore bring many benefits, both social in the form of protecting forests, plants and animals, and economics in the form of a significant reduction in the costs generated by the activities that need to be performed to clean them up.

The second example, as a proposal for establishing relationships related to the sharing economy in the area of connecting the urban economy with the local community, which has both a social and economic dimension, is the construction and equipment of points in city parks that will be equipped with bags for selective collection of municipal waste and cleaning tools such as brooms, rakes and shovels, where people spending their active leisure time could also clean up these areas from waste and leaves. Such areas are very often visited by the local community, because they are very popular places for rest and recreation, which offer the possibility of all kinds of physical activity, but also what is probably most important, namely contact with nature. Such areas often also determine the attractiveness of the place of residence. Therefore, the quality of their maintenance and ongoing care should be a priority in the relations between the urban economy and the local community. The sharing economy in this example would also bring social benefits in the form of creating friendly places for active recreation, maintained with significant help from the local community, and in the economic dimension, where the care, maintenance and arrangement of urban greenery is the responsibility of the municipalities, and the participation of the local community in these areas would significantly relieve the budgets of the municipalities. The sharing economy in these relationships will allow for the perception of mutual benefits in both the economic and socio-environmental dimensions. Such symbiosis will help create new spaces where it will be possible to meet new people, as well as establish new relationships.

Among the areas of the urban economy, waste management is gaining increasing importance in partnership relations between municipal enterprises and the local community and thus in building a shared economy. New IT tools and technologies, which are the basis of social communication, are of fundamental importance in the management and organization of municipal enterprises. The need to improve the management of the municipal sector results from its strategic area of activity for local communities, which is also directly related to the activities of institutions and other economic entities (Adamczak, 2022). Another possibility of creating a sharing economy with the participation of waste management may be the improved organization of collection, storage and distribution of waste generated by households. Thanks to the mentioned technological possibilities, the collected and segregated waste, for example in the "segregation at source" formula in the proposed Eko-AB houses in Poland by engineer A. Bartoszkiewicz, would no longer be perceived as waste, but would become raw materials. There are many companies on the market that can see raw materials in waste. Barriers to the application of this solution lie, among other things, in the still weak flow of information about such possibilities and logistics costs. Thanks to information effectively provided to potential interested parties via the IT system, waste collected, for example, in such houses or other municipal waste management installations could be taken over as raw material in an optimized manner in a relatively short period of time. This would of course require appropriate design and implementation of such a solution. In this way, what is wasted for one person becomes raw material for another, even within the same local community. Of course, this solution refers in some way to the concept of second hand.

In general, the sharing economy in the area of the urban economy is related to the sphere of meeting the current municipal needs of the local community, hence, what is obvious, the area of creating appropriate infrastructural potential is very important here, which will be important for the functioning and activity of the local community precisely in the relations of sharing resources for reuse. This is one of the strategic areas where the sharing economy can contribute to taking joint responsibility for reducing consumption causing the creation of difficult to manage waste streams. At the same time, we have here an obvious example of a circular economy within the city and its residents. In this way, the concepts of the sharing economy, combined with the circular economy, the concept of smart city and smart society, take on a multidimensional meaning complementing each other.

DISCUSSION AND CONCLUSION

Sharing economy is part of the circular concept economy referring, among other things, to the better use of natural resources, manufactured goods and services. It may have a more social character, referring to the concept of *Homo Curans,* from which a more compassionate approach to the other person and the whole society emerges. Sharing in this case is a reflex of the heart, compassion and creating good interpersonal relations. The ideas of civil society and zero and negative economic growth are closer to this approach. However, due to the fact that we live and function in economic realities, even in the case of such a lofty idea, certain elements *sharing economy* must be of an economic nature, such as covering or contributing to covering the logistics costs of providing sharing services economy and legal regulations related to, among others, the act of lending, using online platforms or paying various types of taxes. We are therefore touching upon the idea of *Homo Economicus.*

By combining these two approaches, business models of sharing were also created. They refer to the idea of better use of the capital around us, so that it does not constitute part of the so-called dead capital. In this case, the revival of such capital requires appropriate legislation allowing for the legal "revival" of such capital and regulating the issues of ownership and access to the given capital. In this way, from an economic point of view, both the existing production capacities of capital and the efficiency of people are better used. This phenomenon can also effectively counteract potential declines in the sales of newly manufactured products as a result of reduced demand for new products, both production and consumption. Appropriate calculation of the use of existing production capacities and human capital will have a positive impact on the compensation of those components of GDP, which as a result of sharing economy will decrease.

In turn, the sharing economy in the urban economy is inextricably linked to the economic, social and environmental development of this area because the development of cooperation in these areas will certainly allow, on the one hand, to meet the needs of local communities, and on the other hand, to create the best possible conditions for the functioning of a certain social symbiosis, the aim of which will be to protect the environment and natural resources of nature. It can be said that the sharing economy in urban areas can also become a certain economic model, which will be aimed at the common good. It is possible to consider expanding sharing. Such a possibility may be an ownership share in municipal enterprises representing, in a way, a common public utility, good shaped from the beginning of the creation of society. This will allow for greater social participation in both the psychological and economic aspect in a common enterprise such as a city, and thus also a common household for residents. *Sharing economy* in the urban economy is also a form of sharing power with citizens in the form of extended social consultations or referenda.

In the sharing economy, it is very important not to lose its original idea, namely sharing resources not only for economic reasons, but primarily social, and in the examples given, also environmental. These are values that have priority significance for the functioning of the local community, in which the urban economy is directly inscribed. Such a relationship should be built in terms of a socio-ecological model. Its subjects are people and the social networks they build, and the objects are tools and their time.

In conclusion, it should be noted that the sharing economy somehow makes society aware of its potential both in terms of shared responsibility for the depletion of natural resources and in creating other socio-economic relations. Today's view of natural resources and their depletion forces communities to increasingly care about the conditions of functioning of future generations, which helps to consolidate the concept of circular economy. In addition, the practice of sharing economy strengthens the idea of civil society also within the framework of what can be understood as smart city and smart society.

REFERENCES

Adamczak, J. (2022). *Restructuring of a municipal enterprise towards a circular economy on the example of the waste management industry*. Oficyna Wydawnicza SGH.

Attenborough, D. (2020). *Life on our planet: My story, your future*. Wydawnictwo Poznańskie.

Botsman, R. (2015, November 12). *The sharing economy: Dictionary of commonly used terms*. CollaborativeConsumption.com. https://www.collaborativeconsumption.com/2015/11/12/the-sharing-economy-dictionary-of-commonly-used-terms/

Business Insider. (2024, January 4). *Sharing economy: Nowa ekonomia wpłynęła na światowy rynek*. https://businessinsider.com.pl/twoje-pieniadze/sharing-economy-nowa-ekonomia-wplynela-na-swiatowy-rynek/l754w2b

Business Insider. (2025, April 26). *Lasy Państwowe: Usuwanie śmieci z lasów coraz kosztowniejsze*. https://businessinsider.com.pl/wiadomosci/lasy-panstwowe-usuwanie-smieci-z-lasow-coraz-kosztowniejsze/3g46p46

Confucius, . (1979). *The analects* (Lau, D. C., Trans.). Penguin Classics. (Original work published 500 BCE)

Dziembowski, Z. (1991). *Municipal public utility enterprises: Organization and principles of operation*. FRDL.

Esposito, J. L. (2002). *What everyone needs to know about Islam*. Oxford University Press.

Fijor, J. M. (2002). The wealth of misery: Interview with Hernando de Soto, Peruvian economist. *Wprost Weekly*, (25/1021).

Grzymała, Z. (2010). *Restructuring of the municipal sector in Poland: Organizational, legal and economic aspects*. Publishing House of the Warsaw School of Economics.

Grzymała, Z. (2011). General characteristics of municipal economy. In Grzymała, Z. (Ed.), *Basics of economics and management in municipal economy*. SGH Publishing House.

Hermandes, A. M. (2024, December). *Reclaiming care – Homo curans as vision for human flourishing and sustainability transformation*. German Institute for Global and Area Studies. DOI: 10.13140/RG.2.2.18854.13123/1

Isin, E. F., & Turner, B. S. (Eds.). (2002). *Handbook of citizenship studies*. Sage. DOI: 10.4135/9781848608276

Kothari, A., Demaria, F., & Acosta, A. (2014). Buen vivir, degrowth and ecological swaraj: Alternatives to sustainable development and the green economy. *Development, 57*(3–4), 362–375. DOI: 10.1057/dev.2015.24

Lessig, L. (2008). *Remix: Making art and commerce thrive in the hybrid economy*. Penguin Press. DOI: 10.5040/9781849662505

Marshall, T. H. (1950). Citizenship and social class. In *Citizenship and social class and other essays* (pp. 1–85). Cambridge University Press. (Original work published 1949)

McGrath, A. (2001). *Christian theology: An introduction* (3rd ed.). Wiley-Blackwell.

Mill, J. S. (1863). *Utilitarianism*. Parker, Son & Bourn.

Minker, K. (2022). Critique and critical concepts of sustainable development. In *OKL_2022_Introduction to sustainable development* (PDF file). *(Source name unclear; format assumed to be internal publication)*

Nadolska, A., & Nadolski, W. (2019). Legal framework of aspects sharing economy in Poland. *Legal Journals of the Sejm Chancellery's Office of Sejm Analyses, 2*(62), 1–15.

Paczkowski, T., Kamela, A., & Szyl, M. (2020). *The sharing economy – The birth of a new economic system? The future, opportunities and threats*. University of Bialystok Publishing House.

Poniatowska-Jaksch, M., & Sobiecki, G. (2017). Sharing economy – Conceptual dilemmas. In Sobiecki, R. (Ed.), *Sharing economy* (pp. xx–xx). SGH Publishing House.

Poniatowska-Jaksch, M., & Sobiecki, Ro. (2015). *Sharing economy: (gospodarka współdzielenia) | SGH | Szkoła Główna Handlowa w Warszawie*. Sgh.waw.pl. https://www.sgh.waw.pl/opublikowane-ksiazki/sharing-economy-gospodarka-wspoldzielenia

Pudzianowska, D. (2015). On the essence of the legal institution of citizenship. *Studia BAS, 4*(44), 9–37.

Romano, O. (2020). Anti-utilitarianism. In D'Alisa, G., Demaria, F., & Kallis, G. (Eds.), *Degrowth: Dictionary of the new era* (pp. xx–xx). LangeL Publishing House.

Rzeczkowski, K. (1938). The commune as an entity of municipal policy. *Samorząd Terenalny, 3*.

Sartre, J.-P. (2018). *Being and nothingness: An essay in phenomenological ontology* (Barnes, H. E., Trans.). Routledge.

Sobiecki, G. (2016). Sharing economy – Conceptual dilemmas. In Poniatowska-Jaksch, M., & Sobiecki, R. (Eds.), *Sharing economy* (pp. xx–xx). SGH Publishing House.

Trzciński, T. (2006). *Citizenship in Europe: From the history of ideas and institutions*. Scholar.

Wolters Kluwer. (2016). Sip.lex.pl. https://sip.lex.pl/komentarze-i-publikacje/czasopisma/panstwo-i-prawo/2016-3

ENDNOTES

1. Commission Communication of 25 May 2016 entitled 'Online Platforms and the Digital Single Market. Opportunities and Challenges for Europe (OM(2016)0288).

2. European Parliament resolution of 15 June 2017 on a European agenda for the collaborative economy, 2017/2003(INI) , Texts adopted - A European agenda for the collaborative economy - Thursday, 15 June 2017

3. Resolution of 19 January 2016 on the Digital Single Market Act, P8_TA(2016)0009 .

4. Act of 23 April 1964, Civil Code, Journal of Laws 2024.1061.

5. Act of 30 April 1993 on national investment funds and their privatization (Journal of Laws of 1993, No. 44, item 202, as amended)

Chapter 6
Rooted in the Earth:
American Nature Writing in the Reimagining of the Common Good

Alfonso Fernández-Manso
https://orcid.org/0000-0002-6255-5904
Universidad de León, Spain

ABSTRACT

This chapter analyzes nature literature in the United States as a form of embodied political thought that impinges on current debates about ecological justice and the common good. It examines the evolution of this tradition from classic authors such as Thoreau, Muir, and Leopold to contemporary voices, highlighting the shift from the self-sufficient individual to a relational ethic of interdependence, reciprocity, and care of place. It addresses feminist, ecocritical and indigenous critiques of the contemplative model and proposes an alternative framework where writing acts as a symbolic technology that reconfigures ecological sensibilities and forms of community. The common good is redefined as a living network between humans, more-than-humans, memories, territories and possible futures. Thus, environmental literature is presented as an ethical and political tool for imagining and building livable worlds.

INTRODUCTION

Today, humanity faces an unprecedented ecological crisis that threatens the stability of ecosystems and the very survival of many species, including our own. Climate change, biodiversity loss, soil degradation, and water and air pollution highlight

DOI: 10.4018/979-8-3373-2332-9.ch006

the urgent need to rethink the concept of the common good, integrating ecological sustainability into the foundation of our political and cultural structures. In this context, nature writing emerges as a key resource for reflecting on our relationship with the environment and imagining more just and sustainable futures. Far from being a mere aesthetic or contemplative exercise, this literature constitutes a profound form of political and ethical thinking that can help us rebuild our communities in times of eco-social crisis (Buell, 1995; Fernández-Manso, 2024a).

Traditionally, nature writing has been perceived as a minor genre, dedicated to describing landscapes and conveying personal emotions. However, this view has evolved significantly in recent decades, largely thanks to developments in ecocriticism, which have highlighted the power of narrative to articulate political and ethical discourses on the environment (Buell, 2005). From the 19th century, with authors such as Thoreau and Muir, to contemporary voices such as Kimmerer, Lauret Savoy, and Gary Snyder, nature writing has operated as a laboratory of ethical imagination, a kind of archive of resistance, and a symbolic space for elaborating the tensions between culture, territory, and community.

This literature is not limited to representing the beauty of natural landscapes but also denounces the environmental and social injustices derived from extractivist and colonialist models of development. In works such as Leopold's A Sand County Almanac (1949), for example, an "ethics of the land" is proposed that expands the moral community to include not only humans, but also soils, waters, plants, and animals. Thus, nature writing raises fundamental questions about how we inhabit the planet and about our responsibilities toward the biotic community.

Thoreau is undoubtedly a key figure in the history of nature literature and environmental thought. In Walden; or, Life in the Woods, Thoreau recounts his experience of living self-sufficiently in a cabin in the woods, as an experiment in simple living and harmony with nature. This gesture, far from being a simple spiritual retreat, becomes a political statement that questions the dominant values of the industrial and capitalist society of his time. For Thoreau, self-sufficiency and simplicity are not ends in themselves, but a way to resist unjust institutions and cultivate an ethical relationship with the environment.

Thoreau links this personal ethic with a critique of slavery and the social injustices of his time, showing us that connection with nature is deeply intertwined with political and moral struggles (Buell, 1995). Thus, Walden is not only a diary of life in the woods, but also a political manifesto that invites us to rethink the meaning of freedom, justice, and individual and collective responsibility.

However, the figure of Thoreau and his commitment to individual self-sufficiency have been the subject of criticism in recent decades. From feminist, decolonial, and environmentalist perspectives, the paradigm of the autonomous and isolated subject, which often reproduces logics of privilege and exclusion, has been questioned

(Plumwood, 1993). Plumwood (1993), for example, denounces how this vision reinforces a dichotomy between the individual and the community, and between culture and nature, which ignores the interdependent relationships that sustain life.

Solnit (2005) also criticizes the romantic idea of the "white man" retreating to the forest as a gesture of freedom, pointing out that this model of self-sufficiency is historically inaccessible to many marginalized groups. From a decolonial perspective, Whyte (2018) emphasizes that this narrative of disconnection has contributed to the invisibility of the reciprocal relationships that many indigenous cultures have maintained with the land. Thus, the paradigm of the self-sufficient subject is insufficient to address current ecological crises, which require frameworks of interdependence and environmental justice.

Based on these contemporary critiques, we can understand nature writing not only as a testimony to individual experiences, but also as a normative device that shapes our collective sensibility and offers us ethical frameworks for thinking about the common good in times of eco-social crisis. Buell (2005) defines this capacity as the "ecology of the imagination," a way of reorganizing our environmental imagination to include the diversity of perspectives and multiple forms of life that cohabit the planet.

This literature teaches us that the common good cannot be reduced to a sum of individual interests but rather implies an understanding of justice as a shared responsibility towards future generations and towards the more-than-human community (Kimmerer, 2013). In this way, ecological narrative becomes a tool of resistance against the logic of uprooting, unlimited consumption, and exploitation of territories.

The power of nature literature lies precisely in its ability to connect sensory experience with critical reflection and political action. Rather than offering technical solutions or models of development, this literature invites us to imagine alternative futures based on sensitivity, care, and solidarity with all forms of life. Thus, nature writing stands at the crossroads between ethics, politics, and aesthetics, offering a space for collective deliberation on the kind of world we want to inhabit.

In this sense, nature literature not only describes landscapes, but also constructs symbolic territories of resistance and hope. As Fernández-Manso (2024b) argues, these texts function as "archives of resistance" that preserve memories of respectful relationships with the earth and propose frameworks of environmental justice that include human and interspecies communities.

In short, nature literature constitutes a cultural practice that articulates ethical and political narratives about our relationship with the earth and with other living beings. From Thoreau to contemporary critical voices, this literature challenges us to rethink the common good in times of ecological crisis, challenging dominant ways of inhabiting the world and proposing alternative horizons of justice, solidarity, and care. At a historic moment when it is urgent to rebuild our ties to the earth and to the communities of which we are a part, nature writing stands as an act of resistance and an invitation to collective transformation.

In contrast to the nomadism and perpetual mobility promoted by globalized capitalism, numerous authors defend an ethic of place as the basis for reimagining the common good. This concept is based on the premise that situated knowledge, permanence, and emotional and material connection to the territory are essential for sustaining just and ecologically responsible communities. Among these thinkers, Berry stands out. In The Art of the Commonplace (Berry, 2002), he develops a profound critique of the productivist and technocratic logic that has fragmented the relationships between people and ecosystems. For Berry, caring for the earth also means caring for the human community that depends on it, so that environmental justice and social justice are inextricably intertwined.

Snyder (1990), for his part, draws on elements of Eastern spirituality and deep ecology to propose a vision of nature as a network of interdependence in which all beings—human and non-human—have agency and moral dignity. In The Practice of the Wild, Snyder argues that knowledge of place is not only geographical, but also spiritual and cultural, and that the ethics of place is an invitation to live responsibly and respectfully with the biosphere as a whole. From this perspective, unbridled mobility and uprooting are seen as threats to the sustainability of life, as they break the bonds of reciprocity and care that sustain communities (Snyder, 1990).

Contemporary nature literature has increasingly incorporated indigenous voices that challenge Western conceptions of land ownership and control. Kimmerer (2013), in Braiding Sweetgrass, offers an extraordinary synthesis between scientific knowledge and the Potawatomi indigenous worldview. For Kimmerer, the relationship with the land cannot be reduced to a relationship of use but rather implies an ethic of gratitude and reciprocity. This vision destabilizes the modern logic of domination and exploitation and reminds us that human beings are part of a community of life that deserves respect and care.

In one of the most significant passages of her work, Kimmerer (2013) argues that true knowledge of the territory comes not only from scientific observation, but also from attentive listening and recognition of the agency of nature. This idea is framed within the notion of "relationality," central to many indigenous epistemologies, which rejects the hierarchical separation between humans and non-humans and promotes ways of life based on cooperation and reciprocity (Kimmerer, 2013).

Incorporating this knowledge into our cultural and political practices represents an epistemological and ethical challenge. It involves, on the one hand, recognizing the value of situated knowledge and, on the other, opening ourselves to the possibility of transforming our institutions to include diverse perspectives on environmental justice. By making these voices and experiences visible, nature literature contributes to reframing the relationship between humanity and the earth, thus broadening the horizon of the common good (Whyte, 2018).

Narrative has the unique ability to reconfigure our ecological imagination, that is, to transform the way we think and feel about our relationship with nature. Lawrence Buell (2005) defines this phenomenon as the "ecology of the imagination," emphasizing that environmental literature not only reflects the ecological crisis but also proposes frameworks of meaning that help us interpret it and seek alternatives. According to Buell, this normative potential of literature lies in its ability to connect the personal with the collective, the aesthetic with the ethical, and the particular with the universal (Buell, 2005).

In a world marked by accelerating climate change and the growing perception of ecological collapse, nature writing can act as a form of mourning and symbolic reparation. Authors such as Lauret Savoy (2015) show how environmental history is deeply intertwined with memories of racism, dispossession, and violence. In Trace: Memory, History, Race, and the American Landscape, Savoy (2015) interweaves her own family history with North American landscapes, revealing how the land bears witness to the historical injustices that have shaped the identities of racialized communities. Her work expands the ethical horizon of nature literature, reminding us that environmental justice must include historical reparation and the dignity of excluded bodies and territories.

Whyte (2018) adds a decolonial dimension to this perspective, denouncing how colonialism and capitalism have eroded sustainable relationships between Indigenous communities and their territories. Whyte (2018) argues that the climate crisis cannot be understood outside the power structures that perpetuate inequality and the oppression of Indigenous peoples. From this perspective, environmental narrative becomes a political tool that challenges the established order and proposes models of climate justice based on self-determination and territorial sovereignty.

Far from being a mere description of landscapes or an individual reflection, nature literature can be understood as a form of active resistance to the extractivist logic that devastates territories and communities. Fernández-Manso (2024b) emphasizes that these texts function as "archives of resistance," where the memories of sustainable practices, collective struggles, and alternative ways of life are preserved and updated. This literature has the capacity to redefine the ecological crisis as an opportunity to rebuild our collective ways of life based on values such as reciprocity, care, and justice.

Thus, nature literature not only denounces the injustices of the present but also imagines possible futures. This political imagination is essential for opening spaces for democratic deliberation where new alliances can be articulated between environmental, feminist, Indigenous, and social justice movements. In this sense, environmental narrative can contribute to the creation of ethical communities that recognize the shared vulnerability and interdependence among all living beings (Haraway, 2016).

Reimagining our collective ways of life from an ethic that does not separate humans from the earth they inhabit implies a radical shift in our ways of thinking, feeling, and acting. Nature literature, by integrating stories of connection, reciprocity, and environmental justice, offers us an invaluable resource for this process of transformation. Through writing, we can build more resilient and supportive communities, capable of confronting the ecological crisis and promoting an inclusive common good that embraces all beings who share the planet. Ultimately, rooting ourselves in mutual care and shared responsibility is the first step toward building a future where the earth and humanity can thrive together.

NATURE WRITING AS POLITICAL THOUGHT

Since its origins in the 19th century, nature writing in the United States has functioned not only as a form of aesthetic expression or spiritual contemplation, but also as a powerful vehicle for intervention in the social, ethical, and political debates of its time. In the words of Buell (1995), it has been "a form of cultural and moral thought that articulates worldviews, ways of life, and ethical orientations in relation to the natural environment." Through diverse genres such as diaries, essays, memoirs, poetry, and fiction, this literary tradition has explored the material and symbolic conditions that shape human and non-human life in contexts of ecological crisis, cultural transformation, and civilizational tensions.

This literature can be understood as an embodied form of political theory. Not in the systematic or academic sense, but as a cultural practice that generates values, representations, and normative horizons about how we should live together: among humans and in relation to the rest of the living world. Gifford (2006) has pointed out that even pastoral literature, often dismissed as escapist, is in fact a space for negotiation between social tensions, where the links between rural and urban, local and global, individual and community are debated.

In the American case, this political function is particularly evident in authors such as Thoreau, Muir, Leopold, and Carson. Their works, beyond their stylistic diversity, share a common concern: the deterioration of the links between society and nature, and the need to imagine forms of habitability that prioritize respect, reciprocity, and ecological limits. Nature literature as a genre that emerged in the 19th century is linked to transcendentalism, a philosophical and spiritual movement that flourished in New England. Inspired by European romanticism, thinkers such as Emerson and Thoreau defended the idea that nature is not a mere resource, but a living manifestation of the spirit, a source of knowledge, and a path to self-realization (Buell, 1995). In Walden (1854), Thoreau describes his experience of self-sufficient living in a lakeside cabin as a vital and philosophical experiment. The forest becomes a place of ethical deliberation and resistance to industrial society. According to Cavell (1972), Thoreau does not write as a systematic philosopher, but as a radical citizen who turns his life into an argument. This gesture inaugurates a form of situated thinking, where observation of the natural world is also a form of self-knowledge and moral responsibility.

The political dimension is intensified in authors such as Muir and Leopold. Muir advocated for the preservation of virgin nature, while Leopold, in A Sand County Almanac (1949), formulated his well-known "land ethic," proposing that the "moral circle" be extended to soils, waters, plants, and animals. For him, an action is right if it tends to preserve the integrity, stability, and beauty of the biological community. Both authors expand on Thoreau's critique toward a systemic view of the impacts of industrialization. Nature ceases to be a backdrop and becomes a moral subject and agent of transformation. As Buell (2001) points out, this literature implies a reconfiguration of the political imaginary toward values of sustainability, interdependence, and ecological justice.

In recent decades, ecological writing has tended to abandon the model of the solitary naturalist, emphasizing instead the interdependence of all forms of life. Along these lines, authors such as Berry and Kimmerer have explored the role of community, care, and reciprocity as the cornerstones of ecological ethics. Berry (2002) advocates for an "economy of rootedness," based on a deep knowledge of place, ecological history, and regenerative practices. In contrast to the compulsive mobility of contemporary capitalism, he proposes permanence as an active commitment to the environment. Kimmerer (2013), in Braiding Sweetgrass, intertwines botany with indigenous worldviews, showing that writing about nature is also a way of giving thanks, giving back, and repairing. This relational shift has also been thematized by ecofeminist theory. Haraway (2016) introduces the idea of "kinning" with humans and more-than-humans as a strategy for resisting individualism and extractivism. Writing, understood as a narrative and affective practice, becomes a means of articulating these new bonds. The evolution of nature writing from contemplative forms to integrative political proposals has also led to a reconfiguration of the common good. It is no longer conceived as the sum of individual interests, but as a network of interdependencies that includes humans and the biosphere.

Latour (2018) argues that the common good cannot be defined without the ground we walk on, that is, without a concrete link to territories. This perspective has direct implications for institutions, cultural practices, and public policies. If the common good requires healthy ecosystems and environmental justice, then ecological writing ceases to be decorative and becomes a political tool. It can serve as an archive of memories, a denunciation of injustices, a laboratory for futures, and a catalyst for new alliances. In this sense, writing is not only an artistic or testimonial practice, but an act of intervention in the world. The way we narrate nature also determines how we value it, how we relate to it, and what kind of future we imagine. Hence, literary language is not a mere adornment, but a means of symbolic reorganization with material consequences.

Environmental narrative, therefore, plays a crucial role in the transformation of interpretive frameworks. It does not merely record the ecological crisis, but influences forms of sensitivity, perception, and collective action. This performative potential of literature is manifested in its ability to articulate emotions, generate empathy, and foster an expanded consciousness that includes non-human beings as part of the moral community. From this perspective, writing about nature becomes a way of cohabiting the world, of forging links with the environment and with others from a position of shared vulnerability. Through its stories, metaphors, and memories, ecological literature contributes to imagining new forms of belonging and justice, new ways of being together on the planet.

In sum, nature writing in the United States has evolved from transcendentalist contemplations of individual conscience to more relational, community-oriented visions of ecological ethics. From Thoreau's experiment in moral autonomy to Leopold's land ethic, and from Carson's environmental advocacy to Kimmerer's ethic of reciprocity, this tradition demonstrates that literature about the natural world is inseparable from ethical and political concerns. Far from being ornamental, environmental narrative operates as a symbolic technology that redefines the common good, shapes collective sensibilities, and guides public imagination toward sustainability and justice. By reframing how we perceive and value nature, these texts act as catalysts for ecological responsibility and offer cultural resources for building more inclusive, resilient, and habitable worlds.

THOREAU AND MORAL AUTONOMY: THE INDIVIDUAL FACING THE WORLD

Thoreau has been one of the most influential figures in American environmental literature and, without a doubt, the quintessential emblem of American transcendentalism. His most famous work, Walden (1854), recounts his two-year experience of voluntary seclusion in a cabin by Walden Pond, on the outskirts of Concord, Massachusetts. This work has been interpreted as a meditation on simplicity, a spiritual quest, a critique of industrialization, and a vindication of life in harmony with nature. However, the most radical core of Walden—and of Thoreau's philosophy in general—lies in his defense of the moral autonomy of the individual in the face of society, institutions, and established norms. This exaltation of individual conscience has been both celebrated and harshly criticized, especially from perspectives that emphasize the need for a common ethic and politics.

In Walden, Thoreau states: "I went to the woods because I wished to live deliberately, to confront only the essential facts of life." The experience he describes is not merely a bucolic contemplation of the landscape, but an existential and philosophical experiment that tests the possibility of a life guided by reason, conscience, and self-sufficiency. Thoreau does not flee the world out of misanthropy, but out of the conviction that only by distancing oneself from alienating social structures is it possible to rediscover an authentic life. This conception responds to a tradition of thought that associates freedom with inner sovereignty, inherited from Rousseau and the Enlightenment ideal of the autonomous subject.

But Thoreau does not limit himself to enunciating an individual ethic; he also proposes a form of political resistance. In his essay Civil Disobedience (1849), written after his refusal to pay taxes in protest against slavery and the Mexican War, Thoreau states: "Under a government which imprisons unjustly, the just man's place is also in prison." In this formulation, the law loses legitimacy if it conflicts with conscience. Supreme authority does not reside in the state, or even in the democratic majority, but in personal ethics. This radical conception has inspired numerous subsequent movements, from Gandhi's pacifism to Martin Luther King's civil rights struggle, both of whom explicitly cited Thoreau as a source of inspiration.

In Thoreau's thinking, individual conscience stands as the only valid moral court. This position is diametrically opposed to liberal contractualism, which considers the state to be the guarantor of the common good through collectively agreed norms. For Thoreau, justice cannot be delegated: each person must exercise their ethical judgment directly and assume the consequences of their actions. "The only duty I have is to do what I believe is right at every moment," he writes in Civil Disobedience. This ethical imperative is absolute and does not allow for mediation.

This position has been the subject of much criticism. From an opposing perspective, Arendt (1972) argues that Thoreau cannot be considered a true civil disobedient because his act of resistance lacks a public and collective dimension. For Arendt, civil disobedience involves the concerted action of a group seeking to change unjust laws in the name of the common good. Thoreau's gesture, on the other hand, is solitary, guided by a logic of personal testimony and internal consistency. Conscience, even if morally irreproachable, remains apolitical in this approach. Arendt argues that "the conscientious objector, though admirable, is outside the political realm because he acts on private grounds that cannot be universalized."

However, recent scholarship has sought to bridge the tension between Thoreau's radical individualism and the pressing need for collective action in addressing contemporary ecological and social challenges. Some authors argue that Thoreau's emphasis on personal conscience can be reinterpreted not as an isolated withdrawal but as a foundational gesture that inspires communal forms of resistance and ethical reflection. In this light, Thoreau's cabin at Walden Pond becomes a symbolic laboratory where the seeds of environmental consciousness, social justice, and democratic responsibility are sown. His commitment to self-examination and principled dissent, though expressed through a solitary experience, resonates with current calls for ecological citizenship and civic engagement in the face of climate collapse and systemic inequality.

Moreover, the relevance of Thoreau's thought today lies in its potential to foster dialogue between individual and collective dimensions of environmental responsibility. While his writings have been criticized for their lack of direct engagement with marginalized communities, they also invite us to consider how acts of moral autonomy can contribute to broader struggles for justice and sustainability. By revisiting Thoreau's legacy through the lenses of feminism, decolonial theory, and environmental justice, we can transform his solitary experiment into a shared horizon of reflection and action. Thus, rather than dismissing Thoreau's contribution as anachronistic, we can reinterpret his defense of moral autonomy as a catalyst for building more inclusive and equitable forms of collective life in a time of ecological crisis.

CRITICISMS OF THE SOLITARY SELF-SUFFICIENT PARADIGM

This criticism highlights a fundamental tension in Thoreau's thinking: his project of personal emancipation risks becoming a narcissistic retreat, a withdrawal from the world rather than a transformation of it. The cabin in the woods can be seen, then, not as a revolutionary gesture, but as a form of escapism. This reading has been reinforced by contemporary ecocritical studies that highlight the class, gender, and race privilege that underlies the very possibility of withdrawing from the world, since Thoreau could afford to go into the woods because he had a family home nearby, friends in Concord, and resources that protected him from precariousness (Cronon, 1995; Buell, 2001).

The figure of Thoreau has also been questioned by feminist authors such as Le Guin and Solnit, who criticize the myth of the self-sufficient individual that dominates the male tradition of nature writing. For Le Guin (1986), this archetype responds to a heroic and patriarchal narrative that extols the conquest of outer space as a form of self-affirmation. In contrast to this view, she proposes a "theory of the carrying bag" in which the narrative focuses on containment, care, and gathering. "Perhaps the first cultural artifact was not a spear, but a container," she writes, inviting us to imagine non-heroic ways of life centered on cooperation and sustainability.

Solnit (2005) goes further by pointing out that the insistence on self-sufficiency can devalue the networks of interdependence that make life possible. Desde el ecofeminismo, Plumwood (2002) desarrolla una crítica estructural al sujeto cartesiano y moderno, del cual Thoreau es heredero. Este sujeto se define por su separación del mundo, su control racional y su pretensión de autonomía. En contraste, Plumwood propone un sujeto relacional, encarnado y vulnerable, cuya agencia no reside en el dominio, sino en la capacidad de responder a otros —humanos y no humanos— en términos de cuidado y respeto.

Despite these criticisms, it would be a mistake to dismiss Thoreau's work as a whole. As Dassow Walls (2017) points out in his biography, he was much more than a romantic hermit. He was a rigorous naturalist, an anti-slavery activist, a defender of indigenous peoples, and a keen observer of environmental degradation processes. His retreat was not an escape, but a laboratory for ethical experimentation. However, it is necessary to reread his legacy in light of current challenges, incorporating dimensions that his thinking left in the shadows.

Contemporary authors such as Kimmerer (2013) propose a form of autonomy that is not based on separation, but on reciprocity. In Braiding Sweetgrass, Kimmerer intertwines personal stories, botanical knowledge, and Potawatomi spirituality to construct an ethic of reciprocity. Unlike Thoreau's contemplative self, the subject that emerges in her work is one who listens, learns, gives thanks, and gives back. "Every gift demands a response," she asserts, emphasizing that ecological knowledge cannot be separated from an emotional commitment to the earth (Kimmerer, 2013, p. 25).

The figure of the solitary, self-sufficient, and contemplative individual has occupied a central place in the tradition of nature writing in the United States, particularly since the canonization of Thoreau's Walden. This image of the subject who withdraws from the social world to live in harmony with nature has been celebrated as an expression of freedom, authenticity, and resistance to the alienating forces of modernity. However, in recent decades, numerous critical voices have questioned the philosophical, political, and cultural assumptions of this model, arguing that it obscures the interdependent relationships that sustain life and perpetuates an aesthetic of detachment that can be ethically problematic.

In this sense, from an ecocritical perspective, Cronon (1995) argues in The Trouble with Wilderness that the idea of nature as a pure space separate from society is a cultural construct that obscures the historical and political processes that shape the landscape. According to Cronon, representing nature as a place of moral regeneration reinforces a dichotomy between nature and culture that prevents us from addressing the real ecological problems where we actually live. Buell (1995), for his part, points out that Walden is fraught with unresolved tensions: although Thoreau preaches self-sufficiency, he maintains ties with his family and friends in Concord. His cabin is not a totally isolated space, but a kind of "outpost" from which he observes and comments on social life, without renouncing his privileges.

The subject who contemplates nature from a distance has also been criticized for promoting an aestheticization of the natural world that strips it of agency. Timothy Morton (2007) proposes the concept of "ecology without nature" to denounce this tendency to represent the environment as something separate from humans. According to Morton, this type of representation reinforces the illusion of a self that dominates from outside, rather than inscribing the subject in a network of shared affections and responsibilities.

In contrast to this model of the solitary observer, other authors such as Plumwood, Kimmerer, and Haraway (2002, 2013, 2016) propose approaches based on interdependence, mutual care, and multispecies cohabitation. Plumwood (2002) argues that the contemporary ecological crisis is rooted in dualistic thinking that places the human subject above nature, legitimizing its exploitation. She proposes instead an "ecological subject" that is situated, vulnerable, and relational. Haraway (2016), in Staying with the Trouble, suggests "making kin" to rethink bonds beyond traditional models, asserting that the urgent task is not to flee the world to purify oneself, but to "stay with the trouble" and weave responsible relationships with humans and nonhumans.

These feminist and ecocritical critiques do not deny the value of introspection or spiritual seeking, but rather denounce the false universality of the proposed model. In societies marked by gender, class, and race inequalities, the gesture of retreating to nature is not available to everyone. As hooks (2009) has pointed out, the experience of connection with the land in Black or Indigenous communities has been marked by the violence of dispossession, slavery, or colonization. Nature has not been a neutral refuge, but a field of dispute, exploitation, and survival.

Criticisms of the self-sufficient loner paradigm have profound epistemological and political implications. Epistemologically, they question the idea that knowledge about nature can be produced by a neutral, isolated, or uprooted subject, proposing instead an embodied, contextual, and relational knowledge generated in interaction with the environment and from situated positions. Politically, they warn of the inadequacy of individual acts of moral consistency to transform the world. The current ecological crisis—characterized by climate change, biodiversity loss, and the collapse of life systems—requires collective action, community alliances, and structural policies. In this context, the gesture of retreating to the forest, while inspiring, is insufficient as a political model.

Reimagining the common good in ecological terms means overcoming the fiction of the sovereign self and embracing an ethic of interdependence. As Latour (2018) points out, the common good is, above all, a question of planetary cohabitation. Writing about nature can thus become an instrument for reconstructing the "us," that shared space where the possibilities of a just and sustainable life for all beings are woven together.

In conclusion, the critiques of Thoreau's solitary model highlight the need to move beyond the figure of the self-sufficient individual toward a more relational and inclusive understanding of ecological subjectivity. Rather than dismissing Thoreau's legacy, contemporary thinkers reinterpret it through the lenses of feminism, decolonial theory, and Indigenous worldviews, emphasizing reciprocity, vulnerability, and interdependence. This shift reframes nature writing not as an act of isolation but as a collective practice of care and political imagination. By questioning the privilege and exclusions embedded in the solitary ideal, these critiques open the door to envisioning nature writing as a shared project of ecological justice, one that integrates diverse voices and experiences into the construction of the common good.

TOWARDS AN ETHICS OF PLACE: PERMANENCE, COMMUNITY, AND RESPONSIBILITY

As contemporary criticism has dismantled romantic images of the self-sufficient individual and revealed the structures of privilege implicit in many classic environmental discourses, an alternative current has emerged that claims ethical and political rootedness in place as the key to reimagining our ways of living together. This current is based on the notion that environmental justice and ecological sustainability cannot be achieved without a deep commitment to inhabited territories, their cycles, memories, and communities. In contrast to the paradigm of individual retreat or occasional access to "wild nature," an ethics of place is proposed that prioritizes permanence, intergenerational responsibility, and situated knowledge.

Wendell Berry is undoubtedly one of the authors who has most systematically developed an ethic of place as an alternative to the alienated and destructive forms of contemporary life. An agronomist, poet, essayist, and farmer, Berry has devoted much of his work to defending the need for a sustainable agrarian economy, strong community life, and a reverent relationship with the land. His philosophy is based on the conviction that uprooting—the loss of ties to place—is one of the main causes of the modern ecological and social crisis (Berry, 2002).

In his essays collected in The Art of the Commonplace (2002), Berry argues that globalized capitalism promotes a logic of mobility, relocation, and consumption that prevents the building of strong communities and destroys local economies. In response to this, he defends the value of "staying put," of knowing the land you inhabit deeply, of working it with respect, and of cultivating lasting relationships with neighbors and ecosystems. In his proposal, living well does not mean consuming more, but living responsibly, mindfully, and gratefully.

Berry argues that a human community that cares for its environment and organizes itself according to the ecological limits of the place is more likely to be fair, democratic, and resilient. His concept of "agrarian stewardship" combines care for the land with the ethics of the common good and offers an alternative vision to the modern ideal of unlimited progress. "We cannot live a healthy life in a sick world," Berry says, summarizing his critique of the ecological and social fragmentation that characterizes our era.

One of the keys to the ethics of place is the recognition that ecological knowledge is not acquired in abstraction, but through direct experience with a particular environment. This idea is also present in the work of Gary Snyder, a poet and essayist linked to Zen Buddhism, counterculture, and the environmental movements of the second half of the 20th century. In his book The Practice of the Wild (1990), Snyder insists that "wisdom begins with geography" (Snyder, 1990), emphasizing that ethical systems must emerge from careful observation and commitment to the specific places where life takes place.

Snyder proposes a form of knowledge based on inhabiting rather than observing, on sensitive contact with the territory rather than its representation. The place, understood not only as physical space but as a network of living relationships, thus becomes a teacher. Along these lines, environmental ethics ceases to be a set of abstract rules and becomes a daily practice, a form of presence and attention. This perspective resonates with the proposals of bioregionalism, a philosophical current that advocates reorganizing social, economic, and political life according to the ecological and cultural characteristics of regions.

Bioregionalism, in the words of Sale (1985), holds that "people cannot live healthily and sustainably if they do not know their bioregion—its flora and fauna, its climate, its watersheds, its seasons, its natural and human history—and do not actively commit to caring for it" (p. 42). This idea, although it emerged in Anglo-Saxon contexts, has parallels with ancestral knowledge and indigenous worldviews that for centuries have conceived of territory as a subject of law and as the basis for community life.

The work of Kimmerer, a member of the Potawatomi people, represents one of the most powerful and hopeful proposals for rethinking the relationship with place from an ethic of reciprocity. In Braiding Sweetgrass (2013), Kimmerer articulates scientific knowledge and indigenous worldview to show that the relationship with the land cannot be reduced to a logic of use or contemplation, but must be based on exchange, care, and gratitude.

One of the central concepts of her thinking is that of the "gift": the earth is not an object to be possessed, but a being that gives, and every gift implies responsibility. Cultivating this awareness transforms the way we relate to food, water, plants, and animals. For Kimmerer, the practice of gratitude is not only a spiritual attitude, but a concrete ethic that organizes our decisions and ways of life. "Giving thanks to the earth is a way of giving back, and giving back is a way of healing" (Kimmerer, 2013).

This conception of place as subject and of humans as part of a network of reciprocities profoundly challenges hegemonic political and economic frameworks. While neoliberalism promotes mobility, competitiveness, and uprooting, Kimmerer's vision points toward a reorganization of life around bonds, care, and regeneration. In this sense, her work offers not only criticism but also a concrete proposal for rebuilding the common good from an ethic of place.

Together, the proposals of Berry, Snyder, Kimmerer, Rose, and other authors who defend the value of rootedness allow us to outline a broader conception of the common good, one that transcends immediate human interests and is based on the health of ecosystems and living communities. This vision of the common good cannot be separated from place: it is in the territory where vulnerability is experienced, where bonds are nurtured, where bodies are reproduced, and where the possibilities of a dignified life unfold.

The ethics of place are neither nostalgic nor essentialist. It is not a question of returning to an idealized past or imposing homogeneous forms of local life. On the contrary, it is a question of imagining new ways of inhabiting the world that recognize biocultural diversity, promote territorial justice, and strengthen solidarity economies. In this sense, reimagining the common good from a place of rootedness also implies a change in our forms of knowledge, our narratives, and our institutions.

As Haraway (2016) reminds us, in times of ecological collapse, it is not enough to "save the planet" from above: we must learn to live well amid the ruins, to compost pain, and to cultivate new alliances. The ethics of place, as a situated, relational, and responsible practice, offers a possible path for rebuilding a common world from the ground we walk on, the water we drink, and the relationships we weave.

WRITING, COMMUNITY, AND THE COMMON GOOD: TOWARDS AN ECOLOGICAL POLITICS OF NARRATIVE

After reviewing critiques of the figure of the self-sufficient individual and proposals for an ethics of place based on reciprocity and care, this section focuses on the role of writing as a means of political and ecological reconfiguration of the collective imagination. Nature literature in the United States has not only been a form of testimony or aesthetic contemplation, but also a cultural praxis with the capacity to articulate new modes of community, new notions of justice, and renewed horizons of the common good.

Far from being a solitary act, writing about nature can become a way of repairing the broken relationship between humanity and the environment, as well as a means of challenging the social structures that perpetuate environmental degradation and exclusion. Environmental narrative thus acts as a fundamental symbolic technology for imagining possible worlds, not just for representing the ecological crisis.

One of the main proponents of this conception is Buell, who proposed a true ecology of the imagination. In The Environmental Imagination (1995), Buell argues that environmental literature has the power to decentralize the human subject, make other forms of agency visible, and restore the complexity of symbolic ecosystems. In Writing for an Endangered World (2001), he delves into the idea that language is an active agent in transforming our sensibility and way of inhabiting the world. From this perspective, ecological narrative is not limited to denouncing the loss of nature but creates new forms of community based on the interdependence between human and more-than-human living beings.

One of the most recurring themes in contemporary literature is ecological grief. In the context of climate collapse and biodiversity loss, environmental writing becomes a space for processing the pain of the disappearance of the living world. Authors such as Moore (Great Tide Rising, 2016), Tempest Williams (Refuge, 2004), and Solnit (A Field Guide to Getting Lost, 2005) understand writing as a practice of symbolic restoration, a tool that generates both individual and collective healing processes. Williams, for example, intertwines her mother's illness with the degradation of the Great Salt Lake, showing how human bodies and landscapes share common wounds. The narrative thus not only records loss but also sustains politics of affect.

For her part, Kimmerer (2013) in Braiding Sweetgrass insists that language can be an act of reciprocity: telling, naming, and giving thanks are ways of connecting with the earth that go beyond representation. Writing, in this framework, is actively participating in a network of relationships that involves responsibility and care. It is, as Haraway would say, a form of kinship (Haraway, 1988).

From a critical perspective, authors such as Savoy have expanded this approach by demonstrating how dominant narratives about nature have systematically excluded racialized voices. In Trace (2015), Savoy reconstructs Black and Indigenous memories linked to the land, challenging the white narrative that has presented nature as a space of purity or redemption, ignoring the historical violence that runs through it. This re-reading of environmental history from subaltern positions is fundamental to a plural and just conception of the common good.

Along these lines, Whyte (2018) points out that, for many indigenous communities, climate change is not an apocalyptic future, but the continuation of colonialism. Writing from these experiences allows us to reconfigure the horizons of environmental justice and incorporate memories of resistance, agency, and worldview.

Contemporary ecological writing is thus understood as a situated practice. Inspired by feminism and postcolonial studies, this perspective holds that there is no such thing as neutral knowledge. As Haraway (1988) proposed with her concept of situated knowledge, every narrative implies a position, a network of relationships, and an embodied responsibility. In this sense, writing about nature does not mean speaking on behalf of other beings, but rather weaving partial and relational narratives that contribute to a common world.

This notion is in tune with Tsing's proposal, who in The Mushroom at the End of the World (2015) suggests that, in a damaged world, we must learn to "listen to the stories that spring from the ruins." It is not a matter of aspiring to totalities, but of narrating from shared fragility, contingency, and situated connection.

Ultimately, writing about nature in the 21st century is an act of cohabiting the world from a place of shared vulnerability and ecological responsibility. It is not only a form of aesthetic or intellectual expression, but a gesture of belonging and action. Hybrid genres—poetic essays, ecological memoirs, autoethnographies, chronicles of activism—are proliferating, blurring the boundaries between science, philosophy, and literature. This ecology of knowledge recognizes the diversity of knowledge as part of the common good and positions writing as an essential tool for imagining and building habitable worlds.

AFFECTIVE ECOLOGIES: FROM MOURNING TO SYMBOLIC REPARATION

In recent decades, nature literature has evolved to incorporate pain, melancholy, and loss as constitutive elements of ecological consciousness. Far from limiting itself to describing idyllic landscapes or invoking nostalgic romanticism, contemporary texts have taken on the task of giving voice to the environmental grief that affects both human and nonhuman communities in the context of the global ecological crisis. Climate change, biodiversity loss, deforestation, desertification, and pollution constitute scenarios of collective loss that have radically transformed the way we conceive the relationship between humanity and nature (Buell, 2005). From this perspective, ecological grief ceases to be a merely individual experience and becomes a collective experience that demands new forms of accompaniment, reparation, and political engagement.

Moore (2016) argues that literature can become a privileged space for processing ecological grief. Through storytelling, authors have the ability to represent environmental wounds, but also to redefine and share them, thus building an affective community that transcends geographical and cultural boundaries. In her work, *Great Tide Rising*, Moore proposes a model of "active mourning" that is not limited to nostalgia or lamentation but rather combines the denunciation of environmental injustices with the ability to imagine more just and sustainable alternatives. This active mourning, according to the author, allows us to confront the ecological crisis not through paralysis, but through collective action and ethical creativity (Moore, 2016).

In this sense, ecological mourning is not an end in itself but rather functions as a gateway to symbolic reparation and, potentially, to social and political transformation. As Kimmerer (2013) emphasizes, thanking the earth and recognizing its generosity are political acts that reshape our relationship with the environment and with other species. This ethic of gratitude, characteristic of many Indigenous worldviews, teaches us that every gift received from the earth—be it food, water, beauty, or shelter—involves a reciprocal responsibility for care and protection. In Braiding Sweetgrass, Kimmerer combines her training as a botanist with her Potawatomi cultural heritage to illustrate how gratitude can be a form of resistance and healing: "The act of giving thanks is a form of recognition that affirms our belonging to the earth community" (Kimmerer, 2013).

This vision of gratitude as a political and ethical act challenges the extractivist and consumerist logic that characterizes the Western development model. Gratitude, in this context, is not a gesture of courtesy, but a transformative practice that challenges power hierarchies between human and nonhuman beings. Rather than conceiving of nature as a passive resource, contemporary nature literature proposes viewing it as a subject of rights and reciprocal care (Bennett, 2010). In this way, mourning becomes an experience of learning and responsibility: recognizing loss compels us to act differently and to rebuild broken relationships with the land and its inhabitants.

Savoy (2015) brings a crucial dimension to this conversation by interweaving ecological mourning with historical and cultural mourning. In Trace: Memory, History, Race, and the American Landscape, Savoy denounces how North American landscapes are steeped in memories of slavery, dispossession, and racial violence. For Black and Indigenous communities, the relationship with the land cannot be understood apart from these legacies of dispossession and environmental racism (Savoy, 2015). Thus, ecological mourning overlaps with historical mourning, and symbolic reparation involves not only healing the wounds of nature but also recognizing and giving voice to the silenced memories of racialized communities.

This interweaving of environmental justice and social justice is fundamental to understanding the ethical potential of nature literature. As Whyte (2018) suggests, climate change and other ecological crises are also crises of historical justice: the communities that suffer the most from the impacts of climate change are often the same ones that have been historically marginalized and exploited. Therefore, ecological grief cannot be separated from the struggle for human rights and social equity. Nature literature, by making these connections visible, becomes a space of resistance and reimagining the relationships between humanity and territory (Whyte, 2018).

Furthermore, this approach to environmental and historical justice compels us to question the dominant narratives about nature.

GLOBAL EXAMPLES AND DIALOGUE WITH AMERICAN NATURE WRITING

The political potential of nature writing becomes clearer when placed in dialogue with concrete examples from other cultural and geographical contexts. A paradigmatic case is Rachel Carson, whose Silent Spring (1962) transformed environmental consciousness in the United States and catalyzed historic regulatory reforms. Although grounded in science, Carson's work is a direct heir to the American tradition of Thoreau, Muir, and Leopold: she uses narrative to link sensory experience, ecological ethics, and political action. In this sense, Carson updates classic nature writing and turns it into a tool of resistance against chemical-industrial extractivism.

The Indigenous perspective in the Arctic, expressed in Sheila Watt-Cloutier's autobiography The Right to Be Cold (2015), adds a dimension of climate justice that critically engages with the U.S. canon. If Thoreau made retreat into Walden a political gesture, Watt-Cloutier shows how melting ice is not voluntary withdrawal but a colonial and climatic imposition threatening cultural survival. Arctic Indigenous literature has been acknowledged by American authors and critics as part of an expanded horizon of nature writing, no longer limited to solitary contemplation but incorporating the voices of communities in resistance.

In Africa, the writings of Wangari Maathai, particularly The Green Belt Movement (2003), embody a narrative practice linking ecology, gender, and democracy. Her voice has been read in the United States as an echo of Leopold and Berry, but from the Global South: where they defended a land ethic and an ethic of place, Maathai demonstrated how reforestation could empower women and rebuild entire communities. Contemporary American nature writing frequently cites Maathai as a reference for thinking about the interdependence of social and environmental justice.

In Oceania, Epeli Hau'ofa reimagines territory by proposing the Pacific not as a scattering of isolated islands but as a "sea of islands" (1993). This narrative redefinition resonates with American nature writing because it challenges the very notion of natural boundaries that supported the U.S. tradition of national parks. Hau'ofa introduces a relational vision of space that connects with the bioregionalist proposals of Snyder or Berry.

In Latin America, authors such as Ailton Krenak (Ideas to Postpone the End of the World, 2020) and Davi Kopenawa (The Falling Sky, 2013, with Bruce Albert) have entered global debates with narratives in which the forest is conceived as a subject of rights. This approach recalls Leopold's "land ethic" but displaces it toward a horizon where reciprocity and Indigenous cosmology are central. U.S. ecocritical scholarship has incorporated these texts into an expanded canon, recognizing that twenty-first-century ecological imagination cannot ignore Indigenous and Global South epistemologies.

Finally, in Europe, writers such as Robert Macfarlane (Underland, 2019) extend the legacy of American nature writing by exploring the geological and symbolic depths of the earth. His attention to memory inscribed in the underground directly resonates with Buell's notion of the "ecology of the imagination," broadening the American tradition toward a planetary framework in which deep time and ecological collapse are intertwined.

These examples show that American nature writing has not remained closed within its national boundaries but has been nourished by global dialogues, recognizing affinities and tensions with other narrative traditions. Carson, Watt-Cloutier, Maathai, Hau'ofa, Krenak, and Macfarlane have been incorporated into the U.S. conversation as references that expand ecological sensibility beyond the limits of Walden, Yosemite, or Wisconsin. In this way, American nature writing has evolved from a national literature into a shared horizon of planetary ethical and political imagination.

PEDAGOGICAL AND PUBLIC POLICY IMPLICATIONS

The analysis of American nature writing, especially when expanded through dialogue with global voices, highlights the potential of environmental literature as more than a cultural artifact: it is also a resource for education and policymaking. By weaving together ecological ethics, historical memory, and political imagination, this body of writing offers practical tools for cultivating ecological citizenship and informing strategies of environmental governance.

In the pedagogical sphere, nature writing can serve as a foundation for interdisciplinary curricula that integrate literature, ecology, history, and civic education. Thoreau's Walden or Carson's Silent Spring, for instance, are not only literary classics but also case studies in the ethical dilemmas of industrialization and environmental regulation. Contemporary works such as Kimmerer's Braiding Sweetgrass or Savoy's Trace allow educators to address issues of reciprocity, Indigenous knowledge, and environmental justice. Incorporating these texts into classrooms at secondary and university levels can foster critical ecological literacy: a capacity not only to interpret natural systems but also to evaluate the cultural narratives and political structures that shape them. Such an approach aligns with the concept of "ecological imagination" (Buell, 1995), encouraging students to see environmental crises as questions of justice, responsibility, and community.

Public policy can also draw lessons from the insights of nature writing. Leopold's "land ethic," for example, has been directly influential in conservation policy, reframing land management as a moral rather than purely technical issue. Carson's exposé of pesticides reshaped U.S. chemical regulation and led to the creation of the

Environmental Protection Agency. Indigenous perspectives articulated by authors such as Watt-Cloutier and Krenak suggest that effective climate policy must integrate cultural sovereignty, traditional ecological knowledge, and intergenerational justice. These insights challenge technocratic or market-based approaches to sustainability, underscoring the need for policies rooted in care, reciprocity, and place.

Another implication lies in public communication. Environmental literature demonstrates the importance of storytelling in shaping public opinion and collective action. Policies addressing climate change or biodiversity loss are often hindered by abstraction and complexity. By translating ecological data into narratives of loss, resilience, and shared responsibility, nature writing provides models for how policymakers might engage citizens more effectively. Works such as Macfarlane's Underland or Williams's Refuge show that the affective dimension of ecological crises—mourning, gratitude, hope—can be mobilized to generate empathy and democratic deliberation.

Finally, both in pedagogy and policy, the global turn in nature writing demonstrates that ecological thought must be plural and inclusive. Just as educational syllabi should include Indigenous, African, Pacific, and Latin American voices alongside the American canon, environmental policy must likewise recognize the diversity of cultural relationships to land and water. The ethics of place advanced by Berry, Snyder, and Kimmerer resonates with bioregional and community-based policy frameworks, suggesting pathways toward governance that is simultaneously ecological and democratic.

In this way, nature writing serves as a bridge between the symbolic and the institutional: its pedagogical value lies in shaping ecological imagination, while its policy relevance lies in offering ethical frameworks and narratives that can guide collective decision-making. Both domains converge in the recognition that the common good is not merely the aggregation of human interests, but the cultivation of a shared world where human and more-than-human communities can thrive together.

CONCLUSIONS

In conclusion, the reflections offered throughout this study highlight the profound potential of nature writing to function as a political, ethical, and imaginative tool in times of ecological crisis. Far from being a purely aesthetic exercise, this literature has demonstrated a unique ability to question, challenge, and reconfigure the ways we understand our placc in thc world and our responsibilities towards the more-than-human community. This transformative power of narrative emerges not only from its capacity to represent environmental problems but also from its ability to intervene in the cultural frameworks that shape our perceptions, emotions, and actions regarding nature.

One of the most significant contributions of nature writing lies in its capacity to dismantle the false dichotomies that have historically separated human beings from their environments. As the text has shown, the figure of Thoreau, while emblematic of the solitary naturalist, embodies both the strengths and limitations of a model of moral autonomy that seeks to resist the alienating forces of modern society. Thoreau's experiment at Walden Pond, interpreted as an act of radical self-sufficiency and critique of capitalist values, undoubtedly opened a path for thinking about the ethical relationship between individuals and nature. However, contemporary criticism reminds us that this model, often underpinned by privileges of race, class, and gender, is insufficient for addressing the complexities of today's environmental crises. These critiques—particularly from feminist, decolonial, and Indigenous perspectives—point to the need to recognize interdependence as a fundamental ethical and political principle.

In this sense, the figure of Thoreau serves as both inspiration and caution. His writings remind us of the importance of cultivating a conscious, deliberate relationship with the world around us, but they also reveal the limitations of an approach that, by emphasizing individual autonomy, risks ignoring the networks of care and interdependence that sustain life. As Plumwood and other ecofeminist theorists have argued, the Cartesian subject that separates itself from the world, seeking mastery and control, is one of the root causes of the ecological and social injustices that persist today. By proposing an "ecological subject" that is relational, embodied, and vulnerable, these perspectives invite us to rethink our ethical frameworks, incorporating responsibility towards other beings and recognition of our own situatedness within ecosystems.

The evolution of nature writing—from its romantic and transcendentalist origins to contemporary forms that integrate Indigenous knowledge, feminist ethics, and decolonial critiques—illustrates the genre's ability to adapt and respond to new historical and political challenges. The incorporation of Indigenous voices, particularly those of authors like Kimmerer, has been essential in transforming the discourse on nature from one centered on observation and contemplation to one based on reciprocity, gratitude, and relationality. This shift is not merely stylistic but represents a profound epistemological change that challenges the extractivist logic of modern development. Kimmerer's notion that "every gift demands a response" is not only a poetic expression but also a radical political statement that redefines the relationship between human beings and the land, proposing an ethic of reciprocity that undermines the instrumentalization of nature.

Likewise, the contributions of authors such as Savoy and Whyte have been fundamental in revealing the historical and racial dimensions of environmental injustices.

By connecting the environmental crisis with the legacies of slavery, colonialism, and dispossession, these authors show that the ecological crisis cannot be understood—or resolved—without addressing the structures of power and inequality that have shaped the history of landscapes and communities. The land, as Savoy powerfully demonstrates, is not a neutral stage on which human actions unfold, but a palimpsest inscribed with memories of violence, resistance, and survival. Recognizing these memories is essential for building a just ecological ethic that includes reparations for historically marginalized communities and territories.

The concept of the "ecology of the imagination," proposed by Buell, emerges as a crucial lens through which to understand the transformative potential of nature writing. Literature, by connecting sensory experience with critical reflection and political imagination, enables us to reconfigure the frameworks that define what is possible and desirable. This performative capacity of narrative is especially relevant in the context of accelerating climate change and biodiversity loss, where technical solutions alone are insufficient. As Moore argues, the ecological crisis is not only a material problem but also an emotional and cultural one, requiring new ways of processing grief and loss. Ecological mourning, far from being a passive lamentation, becomes a space of collective learning and ethical creativity that can lead to new forms of resistance and hope.

In this context, nature writing functions as an "archive of resistance," preserving memories of sustainable practices, respectful relationships with the land, and alternative ways of inhabiting the world. These texts, by combining personal stories with critical analysis, challenge the dominant narratives of progress and development that have driven the ecological crisis. The proposals of authors like Berry and Snyder, who defend an ethic of place based on permanence, community, and responsibility, offer a concrete alternative to the uprooting and mobility promoted by globalized capitalism. Their vision of an agrarian or bioregional stewardship, where ecological knowledge is rooted in direct experience with the territory, is not a nostalgic return to the past but a critical strategy for building more just and sustainable communities.

This ethics of place also challenges the illusion of a universal model of development, recognizing that environmental justice must be adapted to the cultural, historical, and ecological specificities of each territory. Bioregionalism, as proposed by Sale, and the Indigenous epistemologies highlighted by Kimmerer, remind us that the relationship with the land is not only a matter of resources but of identity, memory, and collective life. In this sense, the struggle for environmental justice is inseparable from the struggle for cultural and territorial justice. Recognizing this interdependence is essential for imagining a common good that transcends the sum of individual interests and includes the well-being of all living beings.

The performative power of nature writing lies in its ability to generate new forms of community and political imagination. By representing interdependence, vulnerability, and reciprocity, these narratives challenge the logic of individualism and competition that underpins the current ecological crisis. Writing about nature becomes, then, a way of weaving affective and political bonds that recognize the shared fragility of all beings. This perspective is essential in a time marked by the collapse of life systems, where the challenge is not only to mitigate damage but to rebuild relationships and reweave the social and ecological fabric.

From this perspective, nature writing ceases to be a marginal or decorative genre and becomes a crucial tool for confronting the planetary crisis. Its power does not lie in offering technical solutions but in transforming the ways in which we understand ourselves and our place in the world. By connecting personal experience with collective imagination, by linking grief with gratitude, and by intertwining human and more-than-human stories, environmental literature offers us a path to rethink the common good as a shared and situated responsibility. This transformation is not only cultural but also political, as it challenges the dominant frameworks that legitimize extractivism, dispossession, and environmental injustice.

Ultimately, nature writing invites us to imagine a common world where humans are not the center but part of a network of interdependencies. This vision challenges us to rethink our institutions, our economies, and our relationships, recognizing that the sustainability of life depends on the health of ecosystems and the justice of our social relations. The challenge is enormous, but literature reminds us that change begins with the imagination. As Buell points out, the ecology of the imagination is not an escape from reality but a way of transforming it, by proposing new frameworks of meaning and action.

In the current ecological crisis, the task of imagining new forms of the common good requires integrating historical justice, environmental justice, and interspecies justice. This integration is not merely theoretical but has concrete implications for our forms of governance, our educational systems, and our ways of inhabiting the land. The contributions of authors like Kimmerer, Savoy, Berry, and Whyte show that building a fair and sustainable world means listening to multiple voices, recognizing the value of diverse knowledge systems, and cultivating a sense of gratitude and responsibility towards all beings.

Writing about nature is thus an act of resistance and hope. It is resistance because it denounces injustices, challenges privileges, and exposes the structures that perpetuate inequality and destruction. And it is hope because it opens spaces of possibility, invites us to imagine different futures, and reminds us that other worlds are possible. In a time marked by despair and uncertainty, the act of writing becomes a way of caring for the world and for ourselves, of reweaving the bonds that sustain life.

In conclusion, the extensive exploration of nature writing presented here demonstrates that this literature is much more than a genre or a cultural product: it is a practice of ethical, political, and affective intervention. By connecting history and memory, critique and imagination, personal experience and collective responsibility, nature writing offers us a powerful resource for rethinking the common good in times of eco-social crisis. It is not enough to observe or denounce; it is necessary to build alliances, to recognize interdependencies, and to cultivate new forms of care and justice that embrace the full diversity of life on earth.

In the face of the ecological challenges of the 21st century, the task of reimagining our relationship with nature is not optional—it is a moral and political imperative. Literature, by offering us frameworks of meaning, connection, and resistance, invites us to become active participants in this transformation. Thus, nature writing stands as a call to action, an invitation to inhabit the world responsibly, and a reminder that the fight for environmental justice is inseparable from the fight for human dignity and planetary survival.

REFERENCES

Albert, B., & Kopenawa, D. (2013). *The falling sky: Words of a Yanomami shaman* (J. C. Bruce, Trans.). Harvard University Press.Albrecht, G. (2019). Earth Emotions: New Words for a New World. Cornell University Press.

Arendt, H. (1972). *Crises of the Republic*. Harcourt Brace Jovanovich.

Bennett, J. (2010). *Vibrant Matter: A Political Ecology of Things*. Duke University Press.

Berry, W. (2002). *The Art of the Commonplace: The Agrarian Essays of Wendell Berry*. Counterpoint.

Buell, L. (1995). *The Environmental Imagination: Thoreau, Nature Writing, and the Formation of American Culture*. Harvard University Press.

Buell, L. (2001). *Writing for an Endangered World: Literature, Culture, and Environment in the U.S. and Beyond*. Harvard University Press. DOI: 10.4159/9780674029057

Buell, L. (2005). *The Future of Environmental Criticism: Environmental Crisis and Literary Imagination*. Blackwell.

Carson, R. (1962). *Silent spring*. Houghton Mifflin.

Cavell, S. (1972). *The Senses of Walden*. Viking Press.

Cronon, W. (1995). The trouble with wilderness; or, Getting back to the wrong nature. In Cronon, W. (Ed.), *Uncommon Ground: Rethinking the Human Place in Nature* (pp. 69–90). W. W. Norton.

Dassow Walls, L. (2017). *Henry David Thoreau: A Life*. University of Chicago Press. DOI: 10.7208/chicago/9780226344720.001.0001

Fernández-Manso, A. (2024a). Literature and Nature in the United States of America: History, Ideas, Anthology, and Creative Proposal around its National Parks (Doctoral dissertation, Universitat d'Alacant / Universidad de Alicante). Dirigido por A. Cortijo Ocaña.

Fernández-Manso, A. (2024b). Reinterpreting Walden: A bibliotherapeutic perspective through dialogue with Byung-Chul Han's philosophy. En A. Cortijo Ocaña, V. Martines Peres, & V. Orazi (Coords.), Improving Mental Health and Wellbeing Through Bibliotherapy (pp. 47–70). IGI Global. DOI: 10.4018/979-8-3693-4244-2.ch004

Gifford, T. (2006). *Pastoral*. Routledge.

Haraway, D. (1988). Situated knowledges: The science question in feminism and the privilege of partial perspective. *Feminist Studies, 14*(3), 575–599. DOI: 10.2307/3178066

Haraway, D. (2016). Staying with the Trouble: Making Kin in the Chthulucene. Duke University Press. Hau'ofa, E. (1993). *Our sea of islands.* In Waddell, E., Naidu, V., & Hau'ofa, E. (Eds.), *A new Oceania: Rediscovering our sea of islands* (pp. 2–16). University of the South Pacific.

hooks, b. (2009). Belonging: A Culture of Place. Routledge.

Kimmerer, R. W. (2013). *Braiding Sweetgrass: Indigenous Wisdom, Scientific Knowledge, and the Teachings of Plants.* Milkweed Editions.

Krenak, A. (2020). *Ideas to postpone the end of the world* (Whiteside, A., Trans.). House of Anansi Press.

Latour, B. (2018). *Down to Earth: Politics in the New Climatic Regime.* Polity Press.

Le Guin, U. K. (1986). The carrier bag theory of fiction. In Dancing at the Edge of the World: Thoughts on Words, Women, Places (pp. 165–170). Grove Press.

Leopold, A. (1949). *A Sand County Almanac.* Oxford University Press.

Maathai, W. (2003). *The Green Belt Movement: Sharing the approach and the experience.* Lantern Books.Macfarlane, R. (2019). *Underland: A deep time journey.* W. W. Norton & Company.Merchant, C. (1980). The Death of Nature: Women, Ecology, and the Scientific Revolution. Harper & Row.

Moore, K. D. (2016). Great Tide Rising: Toward Clarity and Moral Courage in a Time of Planetary Change. Counterpoint.

Morton, T. (2007). *Ecology without Nature: Rethinking Environmental Aesthetics.* Harvard University Press.

Plumwood, V. (2002). *Environmental Culture: The Ecological Crisis of Reason.* Routledge.

Sale, K. (1985). *Dwellers in the Land: The Bioregional Vision.* Sierra Club Books.

Savoy, L. (2015). *Trace: Memory, History, Race, and the American Landscape.* Counterpoint.

Snyder, G. (1990). *The Practice of the Wild.* North Point Press.

Solnit, R. (2005). *A Field Guide to Getting Lost.* Viking Press.

Thoreau, H. D. (1993). Civil disobedience. In Bode, C. (Ed.), *Collected Essays and Poems by Henry David Thoreau* (pp. 203–225). The Library of America. (Original work published 1849)

Thoreau, H. D. (2004). *Walden; or, Life in the Woods*. Dover Publications. (Original work published 1854)

Tsing, A. L. (2015). *The Mushroom at the End of the World: On the Possibility of Life in Capitalist Ruins. Princeton University Press.Watt-Cloutier, S. (2015). The right to be cold: One woman's fight to protect the Arctic and save the planet from climate change*. Allen Lane.

Whyte, K. P. (2018). Indigenous climate change studies: Indigenizing futures, decolonizing the Anthropocene. *English Language Notes*, *55*(1–2), 153–162. DOI: 10.1215/00138282-55.1-2.153

Williams, T. T. (2004). *Refuge: An Unnatural History of Family and Place*. Vintage.

Chapter 7

Transformative and Emancipative Pedagogy: Intercultural Education and Global Civic Education for the Promotion of the Common Good

Lavinia Bianchi
https://orcid.org/0000-0002-8721-6589
Università degli Studi Roma Tre, Italy

Giorgio Crescenza
https://orcid.org/0000-0001-6704-8314
Università degli Studi della Tuscia, Italy

Veronica Riccardi
https://orcid.org/0000-0002-0419-9438
Università degli Studi Roma Tre, Italy

Marco Iori
https://orcid.org/0009-0009-7930-9361
Università degli Studi Roma Tre, Italy

Marco Leggieri
https://orcid.org/0009-0004-7058-9663
University of Tuscia, Italy

ABSTRACT

This essay explores the role of intercultural education in promoting the common good, emphasising its importance in fostering pluralistic, equitable and democratic

DOI: 10.4018/979-8-3373-2332-9.ch007

societies. The essay posits that,alongside education for peace and global citizenship, intercultural education nurtures democratic values by encouraging dialogue, critical reflection, and ethical awareness. Drawing on the work of thinkers such as Dewey and Freire, it also emphasises education's transformative power in combatting hate speech, racism and discrimination. Schools are presented as pivotal institutions in cultivating respect, tolerance, and solidarity, particularly in contexts of diversity and conflict. Through a case study on Global Civic Education, the essay lastly demonstrates how reflective educational practices can empower individuals to recognise and value cultural differences, thereby contributing to a more inclusive and sustainable society based on mutual understanding and shared responsibility.

THE COMMON GOOD BETWEEN POLITICAL THEORY, EDUCATIONAL ACTION AND NEW PEDAGOGICAL RESPONSIBILITIES

The concept of the *common good* is a cornerstone of political and social reflection with deep roots in Greek, Roman and medieval tradition. From the Aristotelian idea of the *polis*, which aimed at the "good life", to the Thomistic elaboration that made it the foundation of law and political action, the common good has spanned the centuries and remained relevant. It expresses the cooperative dimension of social life: not a simple sum of individual goods, but a collective horizon that favors the growth and fulfilment of everyone (Possenti, 1992).

With modernity, this concept has undergone profound changes. From Machiavelli to Hobbes to the theorists of contractualism (Locke, Rousseau, Kant), the tension between the individual and the community has led to a redefinition of the purposes of politics, often reducing the common good to issues of freedom, security or collective utility (Quintas, 1979). In the 19th century, philosophical currents such as positivism and socialism contributed to a progressive marginalization of the original concept, shifting attention to economic or statist models (Sturza & dos Santos, 2020). In contrast, traditions such as personalism and the social doctrine of the Church insisted on the intrinsic value of the common good as an ethical and political horizon, oriented towards respect and the promotion of human dignity.

Today, the challenge is to globally rethink this concept and at multiple levels: from local communities to supranational institutions, there is an urgent need to build a new social pact based on justice, solidarity and participation. The rediscovery of the common good requires not only reformed policies and institutions, but also a renewed commitment to education, capable of training conscious citizens and active agents in the construction of a more just and inclusive society (Cadei, 2021; Tomarchio & Mazzara, 2022).

The image of the *common good*, rooted in the philosophical tradition since Aristotle, has maintained its strength and deep meaning over the centuries, even if it has sometimes been emptied of its rhetorical uses. The word *good* recalls the moral end towards which all collective action tends, while *common* underlines the dimension of sharing and co-responsibility. In an era marked by systemic crises and growing inequalities, rediscovering its authentic meaning becomes fundamental to counteracting social fragmentation and recovering a horizon of cooperation and solidarity, as Bauman (2012) recalls, warning against the risks of an increasingly atomised society.

The common good is not the simple sum of individual interests but a collective space, both symbolic and concrete, where resources, values and visions that belong to and benefit everyone are intertwined. In an incisive statement, Carlo Maria Martini highlighted that the term derives from the Latin *cum munus* (shared task), highlighting the close link between individual responsibility and active participation in collective life (Loiodice, 2017).

This idea is articulated in terms of both material goods (environment, natural resources) and intangible ones (rights, democracy, knowledge). Their protection is linked to the very heart of *humanitas*, denouncing the persistent global injustices and inhuman conditions that affect millions of people, evoking scenarios that literature and historical memory have fixed in the collective conscience, as in the verses of Primo Levi (Cambi, 2007).

In this scenario, education takes on a strategic role: it must become an instrument of emancipation and empowerment, capable of forming critical and supportive citizens. Indeed, the educational challenge rests on the pillars of justice, fraternity and inclusion, stimulating the construction of cohesive communities, community economies and forms of social enterprise. Only through continuous and integrated education is it possible to make the common good a concrete and transformative practice, rather than an abstraction.

In the light of this theoretical and historical framework, it is possible to explore how the concept of the common good does not remain an abstract principle but finds a concrete expression in the field of education and training. Indeed, the link between pedagogy and politics is central to understanding how schools and educational institutions contribute to the construction of a just and cohesive society. This is the starting point for a more specific analysis that identifies the common good as the essential foundation of educational practices and social dynamics (Locatelli, 2024).

The concept of the common good has always been at the centre of pedagogical and political debate, understood as that which contributes to the collective good and to the creation of a just and equitable society, indeed. In pedagogy, the common good is defined as the construction of inclusive and participatory educational contexts capable of promoting the integral growth of the individual and social cohesion. From the perspective of political theory, the common good represents the set of conditions that allow each member of the community to develop his or her potential in a fair and supportive environment (Rawls, 1971; Arendt, 2017).

In this context, education emerges as a fundamental tool for social and cultural construction, capable of shaping responsible and aware citizens. The school thus becomes a laboratory of democracy, where not only disciplinary knowledge, but also respect, solidarity and peaceful coexistence are learnt. From this perspective, it is essential to adopt an intercultural approach that allows us to face these challenges with appropriate and innovative tools, in a global context characterised by cultural pluralism, migrations and social tensions. Education has been defined by Dewey (2010) in fact as the main vehicle for the transmission of culture and democracy. Freire (1970) emphasised the emancipatory dimension of education, insisting on the importance of dialogue and awareness for the liberation of the oppressed. Similarly, Morin (2000) emphasised the need for an education for complexity, which prepares individuals to understand and manage the plurality of viewpoints and global interconnections.

Consequently, the value of school as a place for building democratic and global citizenship, active participation and social justice has been reaffirmed in the political sphere. The school is therefore not only an educational institution, but also a political space where consciences are formed and citizenship is cultivated. From this perspective, it is important to explore the concept of peace, understood not simply as the absence of conflict, but as an active commitment to social justice and solidarity between peoples. This perspective highlights the need for schools to commit themselves to creating positive relational environments in which difference is seen as a resource and an opportunity for mutual enrichment.

At the same time, it is essential to underline the importance of neutrality and pluralism in educational institutions. Inter-religious dialogue and religious education are crucial tools for preventing conflicts and promoting a climate of mutual respect and understanding, especially in contexts of great cultural and religious diversity.

This reflection leads us to critically question the role of contemporary Europe, which is often far from the original vision outlined in the Ventotene Manifesto. The promise of a continent united in peace and solidarity now seems betrayed by bureaucratic and neo-liberal drifts, where the political project has been reduced to a monetary union and austerity policies that have eroded welfare and weakened common goods. The growing militarisation and subordination to the interests of the war industry show how Europe has lost its vocation as a "force for peace" and has instead succumbed to the logic of conflict and global competition. In this scenario, education for peace and dialogue becomes even more urgent: we need a pedagogy capable of countering the rhetoric of war and awakening consciences to an active commitment to social justice and international solidarity. Only in this way education can restore meaning to the concept of the common good and contribute to the construction of authentically democratic and peaceful societies.

For example, in this context, the struggle for Palestinian freedom is not only a struggle for a people, but a universal issue that concerns the future of democracy and human rights. For these reasons, memory cannot be reduced to a closed narrative incapable of recognising current oppressions: it must remain a critical tool capable of identifying injustices and exposing the mechanisms of exclusion that still condemn entire communities to invisibility and suffering.

In this sense, pedagogy cannot limit itself to a technical or adaptive role but must recover its critical and transformative function (Frabboni & Pinto Minerva, 2013). Contemporary social and economic challenges, exacerbated by neoliberal logics and the growing commodification of culture and education (Baldacci, 2019), require a radical rethinking of educational purposes. In this context, it is necessary to overcome an idea of education that focuses exclusively on efficiency and technical skills, and to embrace a broader and more inclusive vision capable of putting the person and the community back at the centre. Pedagogy must therefore be rebuilt around the concept of the common good, as a guiding principle for rethinking educational content, methods and purposes (Annacontini, 2017). For this reason, educational sciences are now called upon to rethink their objectives and tools to play a critical and planning role that is equal to the global tensions and challenges. There is a growing urgency to move beyond a concept of education limited to the satisfaction of individual needs or the mere transmission of technical skills. Instead, pedagogical reflection needs to be reoriented towards an idea of education that can respond to the principle of the common good by fundamentally redefining educational practices and purposes. The current crisis in education, aggravated by the spread of sovereignist and economic logics, has in some cases reduced education to a training tool functional to the labour market, devaluing the humanising and community dimension of education. It is therefore necessary to recover the profound meaning of education as a political and cultural practice capable of challenging dominant narratives and contributing to the construction of a more just and caring society. In this perspective, the common good becomes a guiding category that restores meaning and value to education as a collective space for growth and emancipation. The challenge is to design inclusive and participatory training courses that counteract the tendency to privatise public space and promote bonds of reciprocity and social cohesion. Education must be understood not only as an individual process, but as a collective practice that generates meaningful relationships and strengthens community networks (Riva & Crescenza, 2022). Overcoming the utilitarian and individualistic vision means rethinking the school as a privileged place for building active citizenship and as an environment that generates new forms of sociality and solidarity. Here pedagogy can once again assume its full ethical and political responsibility, positioning itself as an engine of change and social transformation, capable of educating individuals who are not only competent, but also aware and committed to caring for other living beings.

Starting from these theoretical premises, it is essential to explore how educational theories can concretely contribute to the construction of a democratic and inclusive coexistence capable of responding to the social and cultural challenges of our time. It is not just a matter of reformulating abstract principles, but of understanding how pedagogical models can be translated into effective daily practices and targeted school policies. It is also essential to focus on the analysis of intercultural educational strategies that promote diversity as a resource and foster spaces for dialogue and shared learning. Particular attention will be paid to the crucial role of the school in countering the phenomena of hate speech, discrimination and radicalisation, which are on the rise after the Covid-19 pandemic, by restoring its function as a garrison of social cohesion and justice. It is lastly interesting to look at educational practices and policies aimed at promoting active citizenship, global citizenship education and democratic participation, through the analysis of significant case studies that show how education can have a real impact on the construction of more just, supportive and participatory societies.

EDUCATIONAL THEORIES FOR DEMOCRATIC COEXISTENCE: A CRITICAL PEDAGOGY PERSPECTIVE ON ETHICAL DIMENSION

Harris (1987) includes education among the basic functions of human society, alongside the production and economic management of goods, defence of territory and supplies, establishment of norms for coexistence, and the sacred domain. It is considered to be intrinsic to life itself (Laporta, 1996 pp. 340-345). In the context of ancestral human societies, education is characterised by its fundamental role in shaping individuals to align with prevailing societal norms. It serves as a means of transmitting acceptable behaviours, delineating the boundaries of permissible conduct to newcomers (Papi, 1978).

Education is primarily the responsibility of the family, which acts as the primary agent of socialisation. Throughout history, education has only entered the public sphere for a limited number of subjects, manifesting in formal contexts and through the establishment of dedicated institutions. While this may not be intentional, the objective remains consistent: *social reproduction* (Massa, 1986; Frauenfelder et al., 2011; Baldacci, 2022). This is therefore evident as a widespread and pivotal activity, referenced in early philosophical works and sacred texts of monotheistic religions.

Education must ensure that newcomers are aware of the community's accepted values and behaviours, and those that would lead to punishment or, in some cases, exclusion. Consequently, the interpretation of education from its origins to the present day can be considered analogous to indoctrination.

The term 'indoctrination' is defined a: «Systematic persuasive communication that aims to generate an uncritical acceptance of a particular worldview or lifestyle, primarily through emotional means» (Baldacci, 2022,).

Indoctrination is defined as the process of instilling a set of beliefs in an individual without their knowledge or consent. In this sense, education, can be considered analogous to conditioning, as a process of social reproduction (Annacontini, 2011; Fabbri, 2020). Essentially, education aims to instil shared values in individuals, fostering the belief that these values are freely chosen, when instead they are predetermined.

According to this perspective, the relationship with the political sphere is characterised by the absolute subjugation of education to the preservation of the prevailing order. From Aristotle (2008) to Dewey (1899,2010), prominent philosophers and educationalists have emphasised the importance of coherence between the government and the education provided to young people. The latter is instrumental in maintaining the former.

From Rousseau (2017) onwards this dynamic was subverted in favour of the expression of the individual and his or her singularity. This approach is seen as more mature and articulate in the field of *critical pedagogy* (Freire, 1970; Colicchi, 2009; Giroux, 2020), which upholds the emancipatory principle of education as its fundamental characteristic. This approach begins with a profound understanding of existing realities, fostering awareness (or 'conscientization', as Freire would describe it) of one's surroundings, the social issues that define them, and the dynamics of oppression. This enables the identification of potential strategies for intervention.

Furthermore, critical pedagogy has the potential to engender a *non-evaluative conception of education* (Colicchi, 2022; D'Antone, 2022), in which the identification of 'educational values' (Colicchi, 2021) to be pursued in every situation — that is, what constitutes *good education* (Papi, 1978) — is relinquished in favour of a contextualised, pragmatic paradigm valid for the individuals involved in that particular educational experience (Colicchi, 2021).

Pedagogy establishes its scientific autonomy by moving away from the promotion of a particular conception of humanity, and consequently of good and evil. This frees pedagogy from the influence of other disciplines that could legitimately claim the right to define the ideal subject to be pursued, such as philosophy and political science (Colicchi, 2022). Therefore, it is important to reject the goal of transmitting a concept of good humanity through education and disavow educational values in order to affirm a precise, profoundly emancipatory concept of education.

When selecting an *emancipatory and transformative approach* (Bertin & Contini, 2004; Biesta, 2012; Catarci, 2023), it is hence essential to consider this fundamental aspect of the educational function, alongside an alternative principle.

It could be argued that understanding the emancipatory potential underlying the construction of democratic societies depends on recognising the inherently power-laden and conditioning nature of education. This awareness involves recognising that education can be a means of indoctrination, promoting an atavistic desire to instil specific beliefs and behaviours.

Indeed, alongside the social function of a human society in reproducing customs, mental habits and practices (Papi 1978; Massa 1986), there can be a principle of individual expression. This creates a balance that allows both the social function of reproducing what has been learnt throughout history and the individual's unique creative input (Iori, 2024b). In her construct of *natality*, Arendt (1958, p. 9) proposed that the actions of individuals entering the world can introduce unexpected and unpredictable elements, generating novelty within a community. In the context of education, this idea gives those responsible for education the task of helping individuals to recognise and express the unique qualities they bring to the world (Arendt, 1991).

Three primary elements emerge in relation to the resonance of these reflections on educational praxis, delineating a pedagogical paradigm in which the emancipatory principle is actualised: 1) receptiveness; 2) conditions that valorise dissent; 3) significant educational experiences.

Firstly, it is evident that establishing material conditions is of paramount importance in facilitating *active listening* to the requests of all subjects involved in the educational experience, irrespective of age (Sclavi, 2003). This process is based on establishing *authentic relationships* (Lipovetsky, 2022; Patalano, 2022), showing interest in and openness towards difference, even if that difference is represented by a child, and relating to them "as equals" (Dahlberg & Moss, 2005; Rinaldi, 2005).

Secondly, to promote free expression, conditions must be structured so that dissent is valued in educational experiences, including with regard to proposals by educational figures and the rules of the situation in question (Ford, 2019).

According to Massa (2000), a meaningful educational experience is characterised by three elements: *performative practices* that provide a genuine opportunity for *self-expression*. These practices are accompanied by a *re-elaboration* of experiences in cognitive and emotional terms so that they can be thoroughly understood and given new meaning (Iori, 2025). Furthermore, these three traits are associated with the formation of a *community* (Fiorucci, 2022), in which individuals are interdependent and engaged in genuine relationships. They share common goals and strategies to achieve them based on rational and informed decisions.

In conclusion, this approach lends itself particularly well to a perspective aimed at democratic coexistence (Fiorucci et al., 2024). This involves a valuable element in the discourse: the question of what constitutes a democratic citizen, and therefore what educational interventions are necessary to achieve this (Tarozzi, 2007; Westheimer, 2015; Fiorucci & Crescenza, 2023).

In this sense, *ethical awareness* (Iori, 2024a, 2025) can be considered an effective construct, which is deeply linked to pedagogical deontology (Contini et al., 2014). It involves the capacity to observe oneself and others, understand one's own thoughts, emotions, motivations and desires, and recognise the coherence between actions and the motivations that generated them. It also involves understanding the reasons, conduct and emotions of others, activating empathy and grasping their intentions, motives and behaviour. This construct is therefore closely related to *personal intelligence* (Gardner, 1983), *agency* (Archer, 2000; Bjerke, 2011) and *emotional intelligence* (Goleman, 1995) but also distinct from them due to its profound ethical perspective, relationship with values, and interrelation between conduct and the motivations that generated it. The issue under discussion pertains to both adults and children. In the former case, the concept is associated with the awareness and intentionality of educational action. In the latter, it is identified in the development of initial ethical concepts (Dahlberg & Moss, 2005; Iori, 2023, 2024c).

A pivotal component in promoting ethical awareness is thematically exploring issues that may be perceived as risky, including issues relating to discrimination based on social class, gender, ethnicity, and skin colour (hooks, 1994).

In an educational context, establishing an ethical climate requires all stakeholders to acknowledge and accept divergent perspectives (Giroux, 1983; Ford, 2019).

In Western society, where there is a lack of dedicated spaces and times for introspection and observation of oneself and others, promoting ethical awareness from a very early age is therefore of paramount importance. This should involve critically analysing practices and facts, expressing oneself in individual and dual relationships and in group settings, and appreciating encounters with otherness, even if it is distant, disturbing or antithetical to one's own views (Michelini, 2016; Paterlini, 2019; Iori, 2024b, 2025). To articulate the values and virtues that inform one's actions and demonstrate their coherence, one must engage in sustained training to adopt a *research stance* (Iori & Liuzzi, 2024). This practice does not happen immediately and requires commitment and consistency from the individual. However, it has the capacity to foster individuals who are conscious, empathic, and reflective. In this sense, intercultural pedagogy can provide effective and inclusive educational approaches.

INTERCULTURAL PEDAGOGY: PROMOTING THE COMMON GOOD THROUGH DIVERSITY

Cultural diversity is embodied by every non-native individual and manifests differently each time. However, in common discourse, this diversity is often associated with negative qualities, and people try to distance themselves from them. Foreigners are unconsciously perceived as a source of loss and change, prompting defences that can easily manifest as verbal or behavioural attacks (Kristeva, 2014). In an era of increasingly complex present-day problems, it is crucial to provide people with a solid education and reference values so they can face everyday life with the ability to continuously mediate and discern, always oriented towards the common good (Portera & Dusi, 2016).

From a pedagogical point of view, this necessity can be summarised as the need to educate people to respect identity in diversity, promote interpersonal dialogue and protect individual peculiarities. Fostering new ways of democratic coexistence is essential, as is the task of safeguarding the originality of each individual while respecting common coexistence norms through appropriate educational paths. This is a difficult but crucial task for pedagogical research (Pizzi, 2006). In this sense, an intercultural approach aims to establish a deliberate project that encourages dialogue and cultural comparison among all members of society, whether they are native or foreign. This educational approach considers all forms of diversity — including cultural, gender-based, class-based, biographical, political and sexual orientation-based diversity — as a valuable perspective in educational processes. It enables everyone to develop based on their unique identity and characteristics (Fiorucci, 2020). While school is not the only setting in which multicultural dialogue can be established, it is a central and privileged location for this political process.

Rather than viewing intercultural education as an additional discipline, it should be considered as a different perspective through which to observe and teach the knowledge currently present in the school curriculum. Adopting this perspective from both disciplinary and transversal standpoints enables an in-depth re-examination of school content and rethinking of the curriculum (Fiorucci, 2011). Alongside dealing with subject-specific content, this means that teachers should also integrate topics that foster an understanding of, and appreciation for, the ‘other’. In a history lesson, for instance, students could discuss the cultural influences between different civilisations. This deconstruction involves a multicultural reinterpretation of school content. Students should be encouraged to view content from different cultural perspectives through thematic and interdisciplinary comparisons. This counteracts the ethnocentric approach that often dominates mainstream education. To give another example, in a literature lesson a text could be analysed not only from the perspective of its culture of origin and but also considering how it might be interpreted by other cultures. Migration is a topic that involves many disciplines, and there are numerous novels, short stories and poems that deal with it in literature. Furthermore, there are works by authors who recount their experiences of migration (Santarone, 2013). Teaching activities on this topic could involve students working with materials such as newspapers, books and films.

However, this does not preclude the implementation of targeted strategies for foreign pupils with special educational needs (Demetrio & Favaro, 2002). It is important for newly arrived students to integrate into regular classes immediately, rather than being separated from other pupils. This fosters an inclusive environment, enabling them to feel part of the school community from the outset. The language issue must be carefully assessed, and specific, well-planned language-teaching sessions must be organised and integrated into the bilingual learning programme. This enables students to continue developing their mother tongue while learning the language of the host country. Furthermore, immigrant pupils' families need to play an active role in the educational project, providing information in different languages and using linguistic and cultural mediators to ensure families are represented in school decision-making processes. In order to foster an inclusive learning environment that respects the different cultures present in the school, it is essential that the entire school community, including students, teachers and administrative staff, is involved in the intercultural project. This involves creating real connections with students, teachers, and associations to enrich the educational experience and promote multicultural understanding through international exchanges and collaborations. It also involves establishing local networks that include families, associations, economic and social actors, and local authorities to support the integration of immigrant students and promote a more cohesive, collaborative community.

A substantial transformation of educational practice is desirable and can be achieved by encouraging cooperative learning and facilitating communication between students from different cultural backgrounds (Santagati & Zanzottera, 2018). Attention should also be paid to students' attitudes, values and choices in relation to different school subjects (Sani, 2020). Teaching methodologies should be active, interactive and participatory to stimulate students' activity and autonomy, creating an open, dialogic school climate that values diversity, promotes equal dignity and counteracts prejudice, racism and discrimination. To this end, it is important to make the unwritten rules of the school environment explicit, opening up reflection on their appropriateness and possible renegotiation (Sclavi, 2003). This process aims to reveal our 'cultural frames', the 'unwritten rules' that influence our perceptions, decisions and expectations. This makes them visible, allowing us to set them aside when dialogue with others requires it. In other words, we should experiment with the method of culture shocks or critical incidents (Cohen-Emerique & Rothberg, 2016) to overcome obstacles to multicultural relations and communication. The aim is to overcome obstacles to intercultural relations and communication by shifting the focus from decentralisation to understanding others' frames of reference. This paves the way for constructive negotiation and mediation. In other words, critical incidents stimulate the acquisition of the necessary skills to manage diversity, encouraging reflection on one's own beliefs and values. It is essential to be able to manage one's emotions, accept ambiguity, suspend judgement, reflect, and try to understand others' cultural imagery. These skills are fundamental to effectively dealing with critical incidents and developing the ability to de-centre and reflect critically on ethnocentrism (De Martino, 1977). Adopting different perspectives and overcoming prejudices enables educators and practitioners to better understand their own interpretations and recognise how their personal motivations influence their judgement of events and their relationships with students. Insufficient intercultural education, characterised by strong ethnocentrism, can lead to students from different backgrounds being neglected, labelled as problematic, and isolated (Gobbo, 2000). Conversely, critical ethnocentrism fosters more effective relationship management and greater professional competence when dealing with diversity.

To promote 'good' intercultural pedagogy, the relationship with territories — understood as local and community contexts — must be recognised as important. Territories, both physical and anthropological, provide fertile ground for fostering a sense of participation and action, which are essential for exercising citizenship. Citizenship is not merely a legal status, but a tangible way of existing in the world (Stillo, 2023). This is realised within a territorial context, and integration — a process desired by and constructed with the involvement of both the migrant population and the host society — implies migrants' access to and use of services, resources and communal spaces within the territory.

The territory is also central to 'operationalising' the principle of continuity in lifelong education. It becomes an educational space for action and participation, as well as a training programme and a socio-educational and cultural district. This counteracts the fragmentation of educational processes, configuring the territory as a place of reunification and recomposition (Fiorucci, 2020). As the development of intercultural competences depends largely on the external environment, adequate time and spaces for encounters and interactions are essential. Educational and cultural activities organised in the area or accessible via local services address the socialisation needs of the migrant population, combatting loneliness and encouraging migrant associations and established communities to get involved in educational initiatives. These associations can then become agents of mediation and change by raising awareness (Portera, 2019).

In conclusion, teachers and educators should understand the basics of three main thematic areas in order to contextualise the challenges of ethnocultural pluralism within the major transformations taking place in modern societies and the phenomena causing them. These areas are: openness to diversity, equality and social cohesion. Alongside these, Ouellet (2007) suggests broadening reflection on citizenship education to include two other fundamental values: critical participation in life and democratic deliberation; the preservation of life on the planet and sustainable development. Therefore, intercultural education cannot be limited to special education for a specific social group. Rather, it must become an innovative pedagogical approach that renews society from the ground up and prepares future citizens to live and act in a complex world where encountering differences is recognised as the norm. The intercultural perspective can therefore be seen as the lens through which to develop concrete educational proposals that foster the development of a 'citizen of the world' (Nussbaum, 1999). This approach promotes an integral vision of reality and those living in it, encouraging ways of thinking, feeling, and acting that foster awareness of being part of a global unity. Furthermore, it provides an opportunity to experience a sense of unity and communion with the entire planet (Baroncelli, 2012). Intercultural pedagogy is therefore oriented towards the common good, as its fundamental principles and goals explicitly aim to build a fairer, more equitable, cohesive, and inclusive society from which the entire community, rather than small, specific groups, benefits. In line with the fair management of common good and the principle of not leaving anyone behind, the phenomenon of hate speech contributes to the discrimination of certain people.

HATE SPEECH AT SCHOOL. AN INTERCULTURAL PERSPECTIVE

In the Netflix series *Adolescence* (Graham & Thorne, 2025), a British pre-teen with misogynistic attitudes is accused of murdering a female peer who allegedly rejected him. The show has the effect of a punch in the chest as it explains that children often live in a parallel world where messages and codes travel relentlessly and quickly on social media, carrying condemnations without appeal: you don't do well. If it is in discomfort that the spark of hatred lurks, the transition from hatred to violence is as short as in this case, in which women perceived as weak become sacrificial victims (Brena, 2025). The virulence of the phenomena of hate speech that are gripping and polluting the globe is confirmed by the latest Intolerance Map published by Vox - Italian Observatory on Rights (2025), which shows that online hate speech is expanding and tending to polarise. There is a worrying increase in anti-Semitism, but women are confirmed as the most affected category for the eighth-year running. Islamophobia and xenophobia are on the rise, reminding us that today's society is pervaded by strong impulses to reject the so-called *foreigner*, the repository of culture, history and customs different from our own, often considered dangerous.

Social media are the ideal arena in which acts of exclusion and violence are increasingly perpetrated against the so-called vulnerable groups, i.e. people who have a different sexual orientation, ethnic origin, religious beliefs or even a disability compared to the majority (Perfetti, 2020). This is a hateful reality that is corroding democracies, legal-political architectures that are now interpreted as obsolete and cumbersome systems compared to the rampant authoritarian and illiberal ambitions that are blowing in from both East and West. If the rule of law is not nourished by the guarantee of the values of respect and tolerance for all, weakens and crumbles under the *brute* force of those who discriminate and hate, indeed (D'Amico, 2023).

And in a historical moment full of bitter conflicts underlying the defence of national identities and territories, images of immigrants in handcuffs, behind walls and barbed wire have gone viral on social networks, disseminated by representatives of institutions that pose as guardians of security and champions of justice, justifying inhuman cleansing crusades against the Other. Racism thus promotes the geography of exclusion and, in the new millennium, takes on different forms. It is no longer based on the historical genetic superiority of races, but appears *disguised*, expressing itself on a cultural level, naturalising the differences in values and customs that separate the majority group (the hater) from the minority group (the hated). However, in a *subtle* form and in the absence of overt negative sentiments, it does not advocate any sense of acceptance, often manifesting itself in the famous phrase "I am not racist, but", where the "but" subtly encompasses a hypocritical and structured intolerance. *Neo-racism* thus seeks a great enemy in the immigrant and the poor foreigner, but also an invader and a violent one, and thus an excellent scapegoat for the racist and populist propaganda of the increasingly established and global far right. Sport, the stadiums and the digital spaces associated with them, represent a favourite arena in which the anti-racist regurgitation flares up, consumed through aggressive posts on social networks, violent choruses and bananas thrown at players not only of African origin, but also Latin American or Italian (Santerini, 2021). This idea is based on a distorted interpretation of culture as an immutable and static hereditary trait; it is in fact a logic of racism based on cultural and ethnic values (Balibar & Wallerstein, 1991). Regardless of specific cultural affiliations, however, the only way to counter the growing barbarisation of customs that we are witnessing is to seek dialogue based on what people have in common and on their needs. The concept of barbarism presupposes a rigid ethnocentrism that sees the Other as a threat and a form of inferiority. Barbarism is based on the failure to recognise the humanity of others, whereas civilisation is the opposite, the ability to understand others as others and to accept their humanity. Overcoming the mistrust associated with negative prejudice requires a cognitive effort, an intercultural approach and a hermeneutic attitude (Fiorucci, 2019).

The increasing attention paid to the spread of such phenomena, even outside school walls and through social media by very young people (Mascheroni & Ólafsson, 2018), also raises strong questions on the educational front: how can pedagogical knowledge actually act to counter the use of such forms of communication?

Rather than an anti-racist education that directly addresses the problem, what is needed is a non-racist and therefore *intercultural* education that would rethink *curricula* (especially those related to citizenship education), training processes and textbooks, promoting inclusion and conflict mediation (Catarci, 2004; Fiorucci, 2020). Educational institutions should promote *a way of thinking about differences* that is more inclusive and carry out a profound critical rethinking of the models of subjectivity and humanity that represent the precipitation of Western thought. Such a model is ethnocentric, anthropocentric and phallocentric (Gallelli, 2024). The concept of the *individual* must therefore be rethought, from an isolated identity to a plural and interdependent reality, i.e. *condividuo* (a person inextricably linked to another) (Remotti, 2021). For this reason, education for peace and non-violence necessarily passes through the *conviviality of differences*, the objective of a pedagogy of inclusion. It makes it possible to harmonize the physiological social frictions underlying the protests of minorities in order to acquire the rights denied, guarantee the demands for a fair right to citizenship (Loiodice, 2020) and counteract the drifts by reaffirming the interrupted humanity (Crescenza, 2024).

To this end, John Dewey had already expressed himself in "School and Society" (1915, 2023), referring to Froebel's principles, including the fact that school's task is to train girls and boys in a life of mutual help and cooperation, to encourage the development of interdependence and thus facilitate those adaptations that will allow these values to be translated into explicit actions. However, the change aimed at developing a more inclusive approach in pupils depends on the ability of teachers to ensure that their training is adapted to social changes. Teacher training is essential to prevent prejudices and stereotypes from being perpetuated in the classroom, because a proper way to strengthen the sense of community in the classroom is to welcome and acknowledge each individual voice. Teachers' fear of changing their paradigms to encourage the development of new ways of teaching cannot be an obstacle, as this would mean perpetuating what Freire called "depository education", in which students merely maintain a passive attitude, sometimes encouraged by the teachers themselves. Thus, one of the objectives of transformative pedagogy to promote an intercultural approach in schools is to make the classroom a democratic environment, open and available to the contribution of all (hooks, 1994).

One of the methodologies that can promote inclusion in the classroom is the *workshop*, understood as a useful and effective "space" for bringing together some fundamental dimensions such as narrative, interpretative and co-constructive knowledge, innovative and collaborative methodologies and active teaching. A characteristic element of this space is the sharing of a pedagogical-didactic vision that places the student at the center of the training process, and knowledge not as the mere reproduction of information, but as narrative, participatory, meaningful knowledge, firmly anchored in the individual history of the subject, in the training experience and in his or her cognitive and emotional abilities (Frabboni, 2004). The workshop methodology protects didactics from the temptations of possible differentialist (exaltation of differences) or assimilationist (exaltation of similarities) approaches and outcomes, educating to observe the *diversities-and-affinities* of a social context as an indissoluble whole, to be grasped as a whole. In order to be transformed into a common good, differences — like similarities and equalities — require their incorporation into the cognitive background of the class group (Lapov, 2019).

Classrooms can therefore be the ground on which to develop strong, peace-oriented social relations over time, investing in a noble value that permeates democratic Constitutions: trust. Trust is an essential resource that strengthens the social bond based on interaction, since the parties involved must "bet" on the actions of others, rely on them, and in this sense, trust is a fragile asset that risks not meeting the expectations placed on it (Pastore, 2007). The need for interaction implies that man's efforts to improve his existence must be based on love, education for peace and non-violence, otherwise they will be in vain (Cives, 1994). Only under these conditions will it be possible to support a broad and universal educational project which, in solidarity and active citizenship, and thus in the development of a correct democratic attitude, identifies the antibodies against hate speech for the young people of today and the generations to come. Now, let us analyze the above principles through a case study of active citizenship and democratic participation.

A CASE STUDY OF EDUCATIONAL PRACTICES AND POLICIES DESIGNED TO PROMOTE ACTIVE CITIZENSHIP AND DEMOCRATIC PARTICIPATION

Introduction

This case study reports on two 'work packages' (WP6 and WP7) of a Research Project of Significant National Interest (PRIN) entitled 'Global Civic Education: Transforming Global Citizenship Education into Practice Through Civic Education (GloCivEd)', which was conducted by three Italian universities: Bologna, Foggia, and Roma Tre. The research project is funded by the European Union's Next Generation EU programme, Mission 4, Component 1, CUP F53D23006180006, PRIN 2022 (project code MUR 20229PZXAF), also known as GloCivEd.

The research aimed to explore how secondary school students understand and engage with global citizenship education.

The general framework envisaged synergistic and iterative co-construction by the three research units. The reference epistemology was systemic-constructivist, and the qualitative methodology used was related to thematic analysis.

Specifically, WP6 aimed to explore representations of global citizenship and global citizenship education by answering the following research questions (RQs):

What representation do secondary school students have of citizenship? What representation do they have of global citizenship? What representation do they have of civic education at school?

For WP7, which is aimed to explore approaches and practices related to Global Citizenship Education and detecting their impact on students' civic engagement, the following guidelines were considered: How are ECG themes and approaches integrated into the secondary school curriculum through the entry point of Civic Education? How do these themes and approaches influence students' civic engagement in different contexts, such as volunteering, associations, environmentalism, and student politics? To what extent can ECG trigger civic engagement in secondary school students through civic education? How can the relationship between school, territory and community enable students to develop civic competencies?

Following the research, an interpretative restitution of the analysed data was drawn up, outlining a complex and challenging panorama. Thematization revealed an urgent need to recover a perspective of global citizenship education through the tools of interculturality and peace education. These tools are useful for thinking about and discussing belonging, plural identities, interdependent relationships, and the processes that connect whole human groups in different ways and forms. This supports a renewed sense of caring for others, capable of transforming 'ideal commitment' into 'real action', that is conscious and participatory.

The research design and *in itinere* analysis adopt a metadisciplinary approach, examining the relationships between emergencies and reference literature based on the shared theoretical and methodological foundations that underpin knowledge construction. Knowledge is therefore peninsular: It is a multifaceted entity governed by the principles of conjunction and extension, which must necessarily be linked to the interpretative framework of which it is a part (Morin, 1985). It is characterised by a constant tension between the quest for non-fragmented, non-reductive knowledge, and the recognition of constitutive incompleteness. It considers the interdependencies that link all fields of knowledge, and avoids binary, linear, deterministic and fragmentary thinking. It enables an understanding of the totality of the elements that 'describe' the overall context of the interconnected structure, generating knowledge processes that interact with and engage in dialogue with the complexity of reality.

As with constructivist grounded theory (Charmaz, 2014), thematic analysis can refer to interacting perspectives such as critical theory, feminist methods, interpretivism, postmodernism, poststructuralism and the philosophy of social science. However, it is important to bear in mind that, in order to investigate reality and achieve social justice, it is necessary to adopt an ethical stance and propose a commitment to an 'epistemology of resistance' (Medina, 2013).

Methodology

In line with the qualitative paradigm, an in-depth examination of the context was chosen using thematic analysis (Braun & Clarke, 2006, 2014; Merriam, 2009; Creswell, 2013). This method of analysis identifies and interprets patterns of meaning in data and it is used to interpret patterns in a dataset for their intrinsic meaning (Braun & Clarke, 2006; Liebenberg et al., 2020; Xu & Zammit, 2020). This allows for the formulation of new interpretative hypotheses and a deeper understanding of the investigated phenomenon under study (Boyatzis, 1998; Elliott, 2018; Thomas, 2006). The focus groups were first transcribed and familiarised with the content.

The primary function of thematic analysis is to organise and simplify complex data into meaningful and manageable codes, categories, and themes. This approach to thematic data analysis suggests that data collection and preliminary analysis occur simultaneously, with analysis intensifying as the research progresses (Merriam, 2009). During data collection, thematic analysis operates iteratively as 'a flexible and useful research tool, potentially providing a rich and detailed, yet complex, account of the data' (Braun & Clarke, 2006).

Specifically, 32 focus groups were conducted in high schools and colleges in the Rome and Viterbo area; 16 for WP6 and 16 for WP7.

The analysis of the material collected through the focus groups is divided into six phases (Braun & Clarke, 2006; Creswell, 2013; Merriam, 2009).

1. Data collection;
2. Working with the data;
3. Encoding of data extracts;
4. Generating code categories from the codes;
5. Conceptualise themes from the coded extracts;
6. Contextualising and presenting the findings.

For both WP, categories were generated in order to identify the initial themes emerging from the code analysis.

Two summary tables are shown below: the first is for WP6 and the second is for WP7.

Table 1. WP6: representations of global citizenship and global citizenship education

Categories	Codes/Categorical Aggregation
1. Citizenship	Belonging Rights and Duties Recognition Opportunities Responsibility Active Citizenship
2. Responsible and Engaged Citizen	Information Awareness Participation Contribution Respect Commitment Work Volunteering
3. Citizenship Education	Ineffectiveness Academic Lack of Depth Repetitiveness Voting Need for Change Current Affairs Method
4. Models of Citizenship	Public Figures Ordinary People Importance of the Example
5. Social media	Double Sided Filters Confusion Propaganda
6. Global Citizenship	Interconnection Respect Inclusivity Awareness Deconstruction

Table 2. W7: approaches on global citizenship education and their impact on students' civic engagement

Categories	Codes/Categorical Aggregation
1. Belonging and Identity	a. Community belonging (sense of belonging to a group, nation, state) b. Local/national identity (attachment to the territory and culture of belonging) c. Global identity (sense of belonging to a global community)
2. Rights and Duties	a. Fundamental rights (right to life, health, education, etc.) b. Political rights (right to vote, freedom of expression, etc.) c. Social duties (respect for the law, participation in the social life of the community)
3. Active Citizenship and Commitment:	a. Participate actively in community life, stay informed, vote responsibly b. Volunteering commitment for the common good c. Political/social activism to promote positive changes in society
4. Civic Education	a. Civic education in childhood (school lessons on citizenship rights/duties) b. Continuing civic education in adulthood (attending courses/seminars on social/cultural/political issues)
5. Multiculturalism	a. Respect for cultural b. ethnic/religious diversity in society
6. Social Media:	a. Responsible use of social media to stay informed/share verified information
7. Global Citizenship:	a. Awareness of global issues such as climate change/poverty/wars
8. Diversity and Inclusion	a. Respect/inclusion of cultural/ethnic/religious diversity

Themes Were Conceptualised From Codes and Code Categories

An attempt is made here to recursively synthesise the categories that emerged from both WP, in order to bring the findings into dialogue. From the coded and categorised extracts, the most coherent and meaningful themes could be conceptualised (Braun & Clarke, 2006) to achieve a higher level of abstraction (Creswell, 2013) and attribute broader meaning to the data (Merriam, 2009). The construction of a conceptual framework (Peel, 2019) was guided by the relevant literature, which played a central role in informing and guiding the thematic analysis of the collected data. In particular, the concept of responsible and engaged citizenship emerged from the data processing. However, this concept has several internal contradictions and often appears to be at odds with its translation into civic engagement practices. Specifically, male and female students interpret the construct differently, according to the following themes:

- Rights and duties as pillars of citizenship;
- Belonging and identity as the basis for civic engagement;

- Active citizenship practice;
- Engagement as an expression of responsibility;
- Global citizenship as an expanded vision of responsibility;
- Diversity and inclusion as core values of responsible and engaged citizenship;
- Civic education as a tool for developing civic engagement;
- Models of citizenship as a source of inspiration;
- Social media as both a tool and a double-edged sword.

A common theme that emerges strongly in both WP is the idea that diversity and inclusion are the core values of responsible and engaged citizenship. According to male and female students, a responsible citizen recognises, respects and values individual, cultural and religious differences, and he/she is committed to building a welcoming and inclusive society for all. This concept is referred to as 'multicultural citizenship' (Kymlicka, 1995).

«A responsible citizen is not only a citizen who respects norms; he/she is also a citizen who respects diversity» (FG9).

«Being a global citizen means feeling part of a cosmopolitan and 'supranational dimension'. Consequently, being a global citizen means recognising affinities in others, as well as differences that nevertheless contribute to collective cultural enrichment» (FG10).

One student emphasises the importance of inclusivity and its impact on feelings of identity and belonging: «Earlier, we talked about inclusivity. I wouldn't feel [...] I don't know, belonging to a place where people don't see me for who I really am, but only for my differences [...]. So, in my opinion, it always comes back to being more aware, looking at others more, and informing myself about what I think. I think I am right» (FG3).

Some Provisional Reflections

In terms of the dimensions affecting civic engagement, there is a general and profound disillusionment on the part of young people about the possibility of bringing about social change, and not only that, which confirms a sense of alienation from their own context of reference. The aspect that seems to be most "affected" by this disposition, however, concerns the difficulty of getting involved in the territories and participating in a transformative sense, due to a low level of trust in processes of collective and individual self-determination (e.g. 'what can I do alone?', 'strikes are useless'); this is less true for political involvement, which seems to remain one of the aspects that is still generally recognised as valid or at least possible (e.g. voting). Alternatively, a response to the passivity observed seems to be translated several times on the part of young people into a call for "violence", which testifies to a possible absence or scarcity of opportunities for confrontation in terms of peaceful demonstrations of dissent and education in non-violent conflict, of which Italy has an important tradition – from Maria Montessori to Aldo Capitani, Alexander Langer and Danilo Dolci, to name but a few examples – perhaps little valorised in civic education courses.

At the same time, school seems to play a marginal role in promoting citizenship at a global level. Issues such as education for sustainability (e.g. waste separation) and legality (e.g. fighting organised crime) are often mentioned, rather than broader reflections on social and/or environmental justice issues (e.g. migration, social exclusion, global conflicts). This seems to be reflected in the actions reported by the research participants (few and lacking awareness). In this sense, recovering a perspective of global citizenship education through the tools of interculturalism and peace education can be important for discussing belonging and plural identities, interdependent relationships and the processes that connect human groups in different ways and forms. This can support a renewed sense of caring for others, transforming 'ideal commitment' into 'real action' that is conscious and participatory.

REFERENCES

Annacontini, G. (2011). Controllo sociale, soggetto consortile, pedagogia nera. In A. Mariani (Ed.), *25 saggi di pedagogia* (pp. 13-24). FrancoAngeli.

Annacontini, G. (2017). Dal "valore soggettivo" al "bene comune". *MeTis. Mondi educativi. Temi, indagini, suggestioni, 7*(2), 35-47.

Archer, M. (2000). *Being human: The problem of agency*. Cambridge University Press., https://doi.org/10.1017/CBO9780511488733

Arendt, H. (1958). The origins of totalitarianism. *Meridian*.

Arendt, H. (1991). *Tra passato e futuro*. Garzanti.

Arendt, H. (2017). *Che cos'è la politica?* Einaudi.

Aristotele (2008). *Politica*. BUR Rizzoli.

Baldacci, M. (2019). *La scuola al bivio. Mercato o democrazia?* FrancoAngeli.

Baldacci, M. (2022). *A socio-ethical education curriculum. Proposals for a democratic school*. Carocci.

Balibar, É., & Wallerstein, I. (1991). *Razza, nazione, classe*. Edizioni Associate.

Baroncelli, C. (2012). *Verso un'educazione planetaria: per un futuro sostenibile*. La Scuola.

Bauman, Z. (2012). *Modernità liquida*. Laterza.

Bertin, G. M., & Contini, M. (2004). *Educazione alla progettualità esistenziale*. Armando.

Biesta, G. J. J. (2012). Doing emancipation differently: Transgression, equality and the politics of learning. *Civitas Educationis. Education. Política y Cultura, 1*(1), 15–30.

Bjerke, H. (2011). It's the way to do it. Expressions of agency in child-adult relations at home and school. *Children & Society, 25*, 93–103. https://doi.org/10.1111/j.1099-0860.2009.00266.x

Boyatzis, R. E. (1998). Transforming Qualitative Information: Thematic Analysis and Code Development. *Sage (Atlanta, Ga.)*.

Braun, V., & Clarke, V. (2006). Using Thematic Analysis analysis in psychology. *Qualitative Research in Psychology, 3*(2), 77–101.

Braun, V., & Clarke, V. (2014). What can "Thematic Analysis analysis" offer health and wellbeing researchers? *International Journal of Qualitative Studies on Health and Well-being*, *9*(1), 26152.

Brena, S. (2025). Se l'odio "brucia" i più giovani. Rete nazionale per il contrasto ai discorsi e ai fenomeni d'odio. https://www.retecontrolodio.org/2025/04/29/se-l-odio-brucia-i-piu-giovani/

Cadei, L. (2021). Pedagogia, nuovo umanesimo e democrazia: La ricerca educativa verso il bene comune. *Pedagogia e Vita*, (79), 18–27.

Cambi, F. (2007). La trilogia della Shoah di Primo Levi: una 'Lectio' pedagogica. In Dei, L. (Ed.), *Voci dal mondo per Primo Levi: in memoria, per la memoria* (pp. 33–40). Firenze University Press.

Catarci, M. (2004). *All'incrocio dei saperi. Una didattica per una società multiculturale*. Anicia.

Catarci, M. (2023). Educazione, coscientizzazione ed emancipazione. *Cultura pedagogica e scenari educativi, 1*(1 supp.), 204-209. https://doi.org/10.7347/spgs-01s-2023-39

Charmaz, K. (2014). Constructing Grounded Theory. *Sage (Atlanta, Ga.).*

Cives, G. (1994). *La pedagogia scomoda*. Nuova Italia.

Cohen-Emerique, M., & Rothberg, A. (2016). *Il metodo degli shock culturali. Manuale di formazione per il lavoro sociale e umanitario*. FrancoAngeli.

Colicchi, E. (Ed.). (2009). *Per una pedagogia critica. Dimensioni teoriche e prospettive pratiche*. Carocci.

Colicchi, E. (2021). *I valori in educazione e pedagogia*. Carocci.

Colicchi, E. (2022). Filosofia dell'educazione e teoria pedagogica. *Paideutika, 35*(12), 55–66. https://doi.org/10.57609/paideutika.vi35.2114

Contini, M., Demozzi, S., Fabbri, M., & Tolomelli, A. (2014). *Deontologia pedagogica. Riflessività e pratiche di resistenza*. FrancoAngeli.

Cousin, G. (2009). *Researching Learning in Higher Education: An Introduction to Contemporary Methods and Approaches*. Routledge.

Crescenza, G. (Ed.). (2024). *Educare in tempo di odio e violenza. Sfide pedagogiche e istituzionali*. Progedit.

Creswell, J. W. (2013). Qualitative Inquiry and Research Design: Choosing Among Five Approaches. *Sage (Atlanta, Ga.).*

Dahlberg, G., & Moss, P. (2005). *Ethics and Politics in Early Childhood Education.* Routledge.

D'Amico, M. (2023). *Parole che separano. Linguaggio Costituzione Diritti.* Raffaello Cortina.

D'Antone, A. (2022). Dal "teatro dell'atroce" al dispositivo educativo. La "pedagogia nera" di Katharina Rutschky tra istanze di potere e percorsi di emancipazione. In A. Mariuzzo (Ed.), *Dalla compassione all'educazione. Vie emancipative comunitarie nel Novecento* (pp. 93-115). Il Mulino.

De Martino, E. (1977). *La fine del mondo. Contributo all'analisi delle apocalissi culturali.* Einaudi.

Demetrio, D., & Favaro, G. (2002). *Didattica interculturale. Nuovi sguardi, competenze, percorsi.* FrancoAngeli.

Dewey, J. (1899). *The school and society. Being three lectures.* The University of Chicago Press.

Dewey, J. (2010). *Democracy and education* [1916]. International Alliance Press.

Dewey, J. (2023). *Scuola e società* (Codignola, E., & Borghi, L., Trans.). Edizioni Conoscenza. (Original work published 1915)

Diller, E. C. (2001). *Citizens in service: The challenge of delivering civic engagement training to national service programs.* Corporation for National and Community Service.

Elliott, V. (2018). Thinking about the Coding Process in Qualitative Data Analysis. *The Qualitative Report, 23*(11), 2850–2861.

Fabbri, M. (2020). Educazione e condizionamento. Le ragioni di un binomio. In Baldacci, M., & Colicchi, E. (Eds.), *I concetti fondamentali della pedagogia. Educazione, istruzione e formazione* (pp. 98–112). Avio.

Fiorucci, M. (Ed.). (2011). *Una scuola per tutti. Idee e proposte per una didattica interculturale delle discipline*. FrancoAngeli.

Fiorucci, M. (2019). Narrazioni tossiche. *MeTis. Mondi educativi. Temi, indagini, suggestioni, 9*(2), 15-34. https://doi.org/10.30557/MT00095

Fiorucci, M. (2020). *Educazione, formazione e pedagogia in prospettiva interculturale*. FrancoAngeli.

Fiorucci, M. (2022). Comunità. Per un'idea di educazione sociale. In M. Amadini, L. Cadei, P. Malavasi, & D. Simeone (Eds.), *Parole per educare. Volume I. Pedagogia generale e sociale* (pp. 45-52). Vita e pensiero.

Fiorucci, M., & Crescenza, G. (2023). Educare alla pace e alla cittadinanza. *MeTis. Mondi educativi. Temi, indagini, suggestioni, 13*(1), 1-17. https://doi.org/10.30557/MT00245

Fiorucci, M., Riccardi, V. & Stillo, L. (2024). Dare corpo alla pace, per la democrazia. *I problemi della pedagogia, LXX*(1), 67-78.

Ford, D. R. (2019). Pedagogy of the "Not": Negation, Exodus, and Postdigital Temporal Regimes. *Postdigital Science and Education, 1*, 104–118. https://doi.org/10.1007/s42438-018-0009-4

Frabboni, F. (2004). *Il laboratorio*. Laterza.

Frabboni, F., & Pinto Minerva, F. (2013). *Manuale di pedagogia e didattica*. Laterza.

Frauenfelder, E., De Sanctis, O., & Corbi, E. (Eds.). (2011). *Civitas educationis. Interrogazioni e sfide pedagogiche*. Liguori.

Freire, P. (1970). *The pedagogy of oppressed*. Herder and Herder.

Gallelli, R. (2024). Educare alle differenze per educare alle relazioni. In Crescenza, G. (Ed.), *Educare in tempo di odio e violenza* (pp. 79–88). Progedit.

Gardner, H. (1983). *Frames of mind. The Theory of Multiple Intelligences*. Basic Books.

Giroux, H. (1983). *Theory and resistance in education. A Pedagogy for the Opposition*. Bergin & Garvey.

Giroux, H. (2020). *On critical pedagogy*. Bloomsbury.

Gobbo, F. (2000). *Pedagogia interculturale. Il progetto educativo nelle società complesse*. Carocci.

Goleman, D. (1995). *Emotional intelligence. Why it can matter more tha IQ*. Bantam Dell Pub Group.

Graham, S., & Thorne, J. (Producers). (2025). *Adolescence* [TV series]. It's All Made Up Productions, Matriarch Productions, One Shoe Films, Plan B Entertainment, Warp Films.

Guba, E. G., & Lincoln, Y. S. (1994). Competing paradigms in qualitative research. In Harris, N. K. (Ed.), *M. (1987). Cultural Anthropology*. Harper & Row.

hooks b. (1994), *Teaching to transgress. Education as the practice of Freedom.* London, Pluto Press.

Iori, M. (2023). Valorizzare l'insegnamento attraverso l'attitudine etica dell'insegnante. *Pedagogia più Didattica, 9*(2), 109-121. https://doi.org/10.14605/PD922308

Iori, M. (2024a). Educare alla cittadinanza attiva e globale: La promozione di consapevolezza etica, a partire dalla scuola dell'infanzia. *Articolo, 33*(5), 66–73.

Iori, M. (2024b). Pensiero riflessivo e consapevolezza etica: promuoverli dalla prima infanzia per contrapporsi alla cultura della discriminazione. *Educazione interculturale, 22*(1), 152-164. https://doi.org/10.6092/issn.2420-8175/18006

Iori, M. (2024c). Ethical illiteracy: Reflecting on values starting from pre-school to counter it, *Q Times, Journal of Education. Technology and Social Studies, 3*, 997–1008.

Iori, M. (2025). Fostering Meaningful Education: Exploring Ethical Awareness and Ethical Literacy in Preschools through Qualitative Research, *DEDiCA. Revista de Educação e Humanidades, 23*, 1–22. https://doi.org/10.30827/dreh.23.2025.31328

Iori, M., & Liuzzi, A. (2024). La postura di ricerca del pedagogista come elemento di qualificazione dei servizi educativi 0-6. *RELAdEI – Revista del Instituto latinoamericano de Estudios sobre la Infancia, 13*(2), 119-132.

Kristeva, J. (2014). *Stranieri a se stessi. L'Europa, l'altro, l'identità.* Donzelli.

Kymlicka, W. (1995). *Multicultural Citizenship: A Liberal Theory of Minority Rights.* Oxford University Press.

Laporta, R. (1996). *L'assoluto pedagogico. Saggio sulla libertà in educazione.* La Nuova Italia.

Lapov, Z. (2019). Laboratorio interculturale per l'inclusione: verso una modellizzazione pedagogica. *Ricerche pedagogiche, 53*(211), 75-94.

Liebenberg, L., Jamal, A., & Ikeda, J. (2020). Extending Youth Voices in a Participatory Thematic Analysis Approach. *International Journal of Qualitative Methods, 19*, 1–13.

Lipovetsky, G. (2022). *La fiera dell'autenticità.* Marsilio.

Locatelli, R. (2024). Bene comune (educazione come). In Simeone, D. (Ed.), *Dizionario di Pedagogia generale e sociale* (pp. 45–52). Scholé-Morcelliana.

Loiodice, I. (2017). *La pregnanza educativa della locuzione "bene comune". MeTis. Mondi educativi. Temi, indagini, suggestioni, 7(2).* I-IV.

Loiodice, I. (Ed.). (2020). *Ripensare le relazioni intergenere. Studi e riflessioni per la pre-venzione e la lotta alla violenza contro le donne*. Progedit.

Mascheroni, G., & Ólafsson, K. (2018). *Accesso, usi, rischi e opportunità di internet per i ragazzi italiani. I primi risultati di EU Kids Online 2017*. EU Kids Online e OssCom.

Massa, R. (1986). *Le tecniche e i corpi. Verso una scienza dell'educazione*. Unicopli.

Massa, R. (2000). Tre piste per lavorare entro la crisi educativa. *Animazione sociale, 30*(140), 60-66.

Medina, J. (2013). *The Epistemology of Resistance: Gender and Racial Oppression, Epistemic Injustice, and Resistant Imaginations*. Oxford University Press.

Michelini, M.-C. (2016). *Fare comunità di pensiero. Insegnamento come pratica riflessiva*. FrancoAngeli.

Merriam, S. B. (2009). *Qualitative research: A guide to design and implementation*. Jossey-Bass.

Mignolo, W. D., & Walsh, C. E. (2024). *Decolonialità. Concetti, analisi, prassi*. Castelvecchi.

Morin, E. (1985). Le vie della complessità. In Bocchi, G., & Ceruti, M. (Eds.), *La sfida della complessità*. Feltrinelli.

Morin, E. (2000). *La testa ben fatta. Riforma dell'insegnamento e riforma del pensiero*. Raffaello Cortina.

Nussbaum, M. C. (1999). *Coltivare l'umanità. I classici, il multiculturalismo, l'ed-ucazione contemporanea*. Carocci.

Ouellet, F. (2007). Le componenti della formazione interculturale. In M. Santerini, & P. Reggio (Eds.), *Formazione interculturale: teoria e pratica* (pp. 129-169). Unicopli.

Papi, F. (1978). *Educazione*. Isedi.

Pastore, B. (2007). *Pluralismo fiducia solidarietà. Questioni di filosofia del diritto*. Carocci.

Patalano, R. (2022). *Autenticità e senso di Sé*. Tab.

Paterlini, M. (2019). *La riflessività in una prospettiva materialista*. Zeroseiup.

Peel, A. K. (2020). A Beginner's Guide to Applied Educational Research using Thematic Analysis. *Practical Assessment, Research & Evaluation, 25*(1), 1–16.

Perfetti, S. (2020). Il fenomeno dell'hate speech e la cultura digitale. La scuola degli affetti come bene comune. *Encyclopaideia – Journal of Phenomenology and Education, 24*(56), 119-132. https://doi.org/10.6092/issn.1825-8670/10749

Pizzi, F. (2006). *Educare al bene commune. Linee di pedagogia interculturale.* Vita e Pensiero.

Portera, A., & Dusi, P. (Eds.). (2016). *Neoliberismo, educazione e competenze interculturali.* FrancoAngeli.

Portera, A. (2019). Modello interattivo di Competenze interculturali. In Portera, A., & Milani, M. (Eds.), *Competenze interculturali e successo formativo* (pp. 195–212). ETS.

Possenti, V. (1992). Bene comune. *Politico (Pavia, Italy)*, •••, 483–496.

Quintas, A. M. (1979). *Analisi del bene comune.* Bulzoni.

Rawls, J. (1971). An egalitarian theory of justice. *Philosophical Ethics: An Introduction to Moral Philosophy*, 365-370.

Remotti, F. (2021). *Sull'identità.* Raffaello Cortina.

Rinaldi, C. (2005). *In dialogue with Reggio Emilia. Listening, Researching and Learning.* Routledge.

Riva, M., & Crescenza, G. (2022). Scuola e famiglia: Comunità educanti per la cittadinanza e la politica come beni comuni. *Pedagogia e Vita*, *3*, 138–145.

Rousseau, J.-J. (2017). *Emilio o dell'educazione.* Armando.

Sani, S. (2020). L'approccio interculturale nella scuola: Le politiche dell'Unione Europea in favore del potenziamento del ruolo e delle competenze degli insegnanti. *Education Sciences & Society*, *2*, 508–529.

Santagati, M., & Zanzottera, C. (2018). Istruzione: una sfida per le città interculturali. In Villa, M. (Ed.), *Le città globali e la sfida dell'integrazione* (pp. 81–108). Ledizioni.

Santarone, D. (2013). *Le catene che danno le ali. Percorsi educativi tra didattica intercultura e letteratura.* Le lettere.

Santerini, M. (2021). *La mente ostile. Forme dell'odio contemporaneo.* Raffello Cortina.

Sclavi, M. (2003). *Arte di ascoltare e mondi possibili. Come si esce dalle cornici di cui siamo parte.* Mondadori.

Stillo, L. (2023). *Periferie dell'esclusione. Contesti, soggettività, riflessioni in prospettiva pedagogico-sociale*. Pensa Multimedia.

Sturza, J. M., & dos Santos, K. E. G. (2020). O bem comum como valor e o acesso à giustiça como compromisso: Implicações sobre o Processo Civil. *Revista Juridica, 1*(58), 410–433.

Tarozzi, M. (2007). Quale formazione per quale cittadino? *Paideutika. Quaderni di formazione e cultura. Nuova Serie, III*(6), 45–59.

Thomas, D. R. (2006). A General Inductive Approach for Analyzing Qualitative Evaluation Data. *The American Journal of Evaluation, 27*(2), 237–246.

Tomarchio, M., & Mazzara, R. (2022). Il tempo della differenza come bene comune. *Pedagogia delle Differenze, 51*(1), 71–81.

Vox – Osservatorio italiano sui diritti (2025). *Mappa dell'intolleranza 8*. https://www.voxdiritti.it/ottava-edizione-mappa-intolleranza/

Westheimer, J. (2015). *What Kind of Citizen? Educating Our Children for the Common Good*. Teachers College Press., https://doi.org/10.15572/ENCO2003.03

Xu, W., & Zammit, K. (2020). Applying thematic analysis to education: A Hybrid Approach to Interpreting Data in Practitioner Research. *International Journal of Qualitative Methods, 19*, 1–9.

Chapter 8
Technological Humanism and Contemporary Education:
Actions and Aspirations

Víctor Amar
https://orcid.org/0000-0001-9036-2651
Universidad de Cádiz, Spain

Flavia Amar
Universidad de Cádiz, Spain

Jorge Amar
Universidad de Cádiz, Spain

ABSTRACT

Imagine an Ishikawa diagram (also known as a fishbone diagram or cause-and-effect diagram) where the word "introduction" and the reference to technological humanism appear at the tail end, providing the framework for development. The upper segments contain headings on the society of uncertainty (sharing a question for current education: who will guarantee that what is taught or learned will be useful for students in their future?); and artificial intelligence (cross-sectional layout); and in the lower parts, influencers (or people who offer another way of learning) and microlearning (as a training strategy inspired by brevity and precise granularity) are named. At the front, there are some final considerations that invite reflection on a reality that is constantly under construction, with actions and aspirations.

DOI: 10.4018/979-8-3373-2332-9.ch008

INTRODUCTION

The principle of education has changed throughout history. It has evolved from a ranking system promoted by states to a sign for citizens of what is valuable in life (Amar, 2024). Interests and intentions that sometimes go beyond education. What's more, certain educational goals are present today, but they are constantly being rewritten. However, it is an essential point, specifically number four on the SDG 20-30 agenda (Sustainable Development Goals), and it is here that education is labeled with the adjective "quality" (López, 2022). This concept of quality is inherently subject to a service or product that can be subjected to a quality system, specified by other entities, sometimes external, and establishing scales of excellence, topics, or powers. And, apparently, because of this or because of its shortcomings, education in the 21st century has been smeared with the nuance of new challenges and new solutions (Rodríguez, 2022), under the umbrella of the concept of quality.

Similarly, education has had allies, some more loyal or interested than others (Puelles, 2004). In this context, we should consider everything from different religious denominations or ideological frameworks to manipulative states or those labeled as benevolent (Naval et al, 2020). In this context, the current concept of presentism emerges. Let us see: an imperfection called presentism that has spread in contemporary times, perhaps due to the prevailing senselessness, devoid of critical thinking and the ability to replicate; an act translated as a fault that develops voluntarily or involuntarily. That is, with a derivative and two ways of exempting or condemning oneself for it. The present is the act of attending to current reality as a protagonist, secondary actor, or contributor. Presentism, on the other hand, is what we enthrone with the here and now that explains everything, without contextualizing or considering its possibilities for understanding and valuing the current world; however, without losing perspective on the past.

But technological humanism (Gunkel, 2018; Kissinger et al., 2023; Mitchel, 2024) is fundamental to understanding the other bastion that sustains this complicated framework, because in the era of history in which we find ourselves, let's call it techno-evo, artificial intelligence is like the compass or the printing press in the West in the Middle Ages. Despite the differences, the compass is being rewritten and we have a new horizon of research to explore. It is no longer just a matter of searching or selecting (which determined a position based on the choice of certain pages offered by search engines); now, with artificial intelligence, the text is generated and becomes the creator of a work that is done, organized, and even substantiated. Likewise, the printing press is reinventing itself and taking on a special role as the new way of recording and amplifying knowledge. In other words, it is manifesting itself as the new printing press of the 21st century, (Piscitelli, 2009).

In this broad context, which could be described as a mixture of phobias and enthusiasm, both founded and unfounded, it is necessary to reflect on the role or prominence of information and communication technologies. Now, we must include the relational nuance that infers in the social and educational sphere, making use of social knowledge, with new epistemologically knowledgeable, effective, and valid subjects. Where technologies, communication, and education function as a triumvirate, while artificial intelligence acts transversally. According to Marta-Lazo and Gabelas-Barroso (2023), everything is covered under the umbrella that activates "the axis that connects the uses, consumption, and interactions that occur in networks, encompassing the three dimensions of the human being (cognitive, emotional, and social) and considering the mediating agents in a triple environment (individual, social, and environmental)."

An extensive network of educational agents, and not just agencies that educate, is working to curb poor education or educational deficits. And, therefore, it is renewed with unwavering enthusiasm through the figure of the teacher, who values the work of the learner in their ability, perhaps, not only to memorize or understand content but also, thanks to the generosity of sharing it; approved, of course, and we insist on this, by the teaching staff. And here we are talking about shared responsibility and a denied or non-existent curriculum that is becoming more evident than ever, because what is needed is available online. What is needed now is an incentive to compare and update it, (Arrieta & Meza, 2001).

Certainly, artificial intelligence can deceive, but it does not perform the task of educating. This is something that occurs between and with people. Artificial intelligence can seduce, but it will not always definitively drive the process. Artificial intelligence deflates in the face of ideal ethical behavior that is motivated by doing things right, with good manners and with not only personal projection but also social and pro-community convictions (Gascón et al., 2024). In this way, the importance of human relationships at this moment in time is underscored. A knowledge society that is evolving by leaps and bounds, but which would become even greater if society developed the concept of knowledge. A knowledge that resembles the work of the wise man; and the wise man is the one who shares knowledge. And knowledge will spread, not only through the magic of technology, but also through the consistency of those who use it, as a universal value.

TECHNOLOGICAL HUMANISM

In this sense, it is important not to lose sight of the humanistic perspective on the horizon, so that human beings remain the central focus of this technologized contemporary world without losing their dignity and value (Bertolosa, 2024). Human beings surrounded by technologies that are innovative and efficient skills that have also generated inequalities, techno-excluded individuals, and neo-illiterates. A human being capable of evolving, perhaps, having taken the step from homo sapiens to homo digitalis (Cendoya, 2018). But one who continues to develop intellectually, without abandoning their communicative, comprehensive, empathetic, learning, and happiness-seeking abilities.

Technological humanism does not provide an answer to the current situation, not even to education, although it may offer partial solutions. It is therefore necessary to define what is meant by technological humanism. In this regard, the strategy is to include technologies at the service of people and not exclusively the other way around. We could talk about the importance of harmonization between humans and technology, without entering into confrontation with technological transformation or establishing brakes inspired by apocalyptic principles. Technological humanism is a path that would explain the current context and crossroads of commercial and ideological interests, where ethics would save a part of this mare magnum, explaining it and dignifying human beings in the face of intolerant phobias (technophobes), others who are confused by delusional situations of enthusiasm (techno-enthusiasts), or a legion of nonconformist addicts who seek solutions when they have not even detected the problem. All in all, how threatened does humanity feel? (Innerarity & Robledo, 2024).

A contemporary universe where technological humanism seeks solutions to abuse, misuse, or overuse. Within this framework, ethics is established to improve people's lives and opportunities (Habermas, 1998). A humanism that presents concepts such as inclusion, care, and diversity. A technology that guarantees well-being or social justice and, therefore, we talk about technological humanism as the result of a long equation and, in this way, put technologies at the service of people for their personal and social, professional, or relational development.

Technological humanism harmonizes technological advances for the well-being of people. A well-being that is synonymous with a set of possibilities necessary for good living, in a comfortable and peaceful manner, away from misfortune that may result in probable somatic or psychological consequences. With technologies, some of which are presented schematically, these could range from:

- Cyberchondria: searching the internet for symptoms of an illness or disorder that can lead a hypochondriac to a state of anxiety.
- Cyberphobia: fear of computers and information technology in general.
- Doomscrolling: A predilection for browsing negative, unpleasant, or disturbing news, producing a feeling of exhaustion or distress.
- Escopophobia: Fear of losing privacy through technology.

- Faster: Listening to audio (WhatsApp, series, podcasts, etc.) at high speed and feeling the need to do something else at the same time.
- Monophobia: Fear of believing that something is happening on the Internet and that you are missing it.
- Morphing: Modification of an image to transform it into another with inappropriate use (for example: a photo of a minor can be modified and acquire connotations, even erotic ones).
- Nomophobia: An irrational fear of being disconnected, either due to a lack of connection or the feeling that you have lost your cell phone, searching for it, connecting, recharging the battery, etc.
- Oversharing: Posting any type of information online (your own or someone else's).
- Phubbing: Ignoring another person online or on a mobile phone. Also known as snubbing.
- Rapid learning: This could be interpreted as skimming through content, viewing it quickly, without reading it carefully.
- Retterophobia: The act of reviewing a message several times before sending it, fueling the fear that it may be poorly written, incomplete, contain spelling mistakes, or be interpreted in an undesirable way.
- Scroll down: Derived from the above, although it is normal to scroll down the screen.
- Infinite scroll: A website design that contains all the information on one page. As you scroll vertically, the content loads automatically.
- Scrolling: The act of moving your finger vertically across the screen to advance quickly, allowing you to see different parts of the document/screen.
- Selfie phobia: Refusal to take or appear in a selfie.
- Selfitis: A persistent desire to share one's image, sometimes at the risk of an accident, endangering one's own life or that of others.
- Sharenting: Posting any type of information about children on social media without considering who will see it and, above all, the possible consequences.
- Shitposting: Intentionally posting content of mediocre quality; sometimes it can be aggressive, useless, or provocative. Sometimes ironic or crude.
- Information fatigue syndrome: A syndrome caused by information overload (IFS) that manifests itself in symptoms such as fatigue due to continuous exposure, excessive consumption, and use/overuse of information on screens.
- FOMO (Fear of Missing Out) syndrome: Anxiety about seeing what others are doing and posting online (stories, profiles, etc.).
- JOMO (Joy of Missing Out) syndrome: The opposite of FOMO, i.e., enjoying being disconnected; not prioritizing the internet.

- Techno-enthusiast: The opposite of the above; being attracted to technology (technophilia).
- Techno-stress: Related to the negative psychosocial effects of ICT use, which manifest themselves in a psychosomatic state of tension caused by stressful situations, or anxiety, distress, etc.
- Technophobia: rejection of technology.
- Telefonophobia: aversion to telephones (landlines or cell phones).
- Troll: a person who presents themselves with an unknown or dubious identity and posts provocative, sometimes unnecessary messages. Sometimes generates controversy
- Vibranxiety: The sensation of feeling or hearing your cell phone vibrate, associated with the arrival of a notification or alert
- Whatsappitis: A particular addiction or exaggerated preference for instant messaging

A technological humanism that must avoid focusing, as far as possible, on what is considered OCD (Fernández & Roussos, 2023). Far from falling into psychological analysis, it is understood as an obvious way of generating:

- Stress (persistent anxiety or unease that can lead to problems such as relationship issues or phobias)
- Temporary persistence (repeated throughout the day and over several days)
- Obsessions (which translate into persistent impulses and a fixed idea)
- Compulsions (repetitive behaviors with stereotypes)
- Anxiety (a state of intense, sometimes excessive, and persistent worry that occurs in everyday situations when a person feels threatened or in danger). And here:
- Physical symptoms (feeling tired, sweating, palpitations, malaise, rapid breathing, etc.) and psychological symptoms (sleep disorders, loss of concentration, lack of appetite, irritability, etc.) may manifest themselves.

Now, it is time for the educator to take action. After a lengthy observation process, they must remain vigilant in the classroom and pay attention in order to warn and repair. Without forgetting the importance of training, so as not to stop learning (in theory and practice in situ). In addition to understanding, in the sense of listening and understanding through the experience of professionals (educators, psychologists, educational psychologists, etc.). And, as it could not be otherwise, with education, so that what is expressed is useful as something that is valuable for life. And at the center of this whole framework of current education, humanistic technology is established as a probable platform for proposing solutions. At the very least, a panel to detect deficits and allow each party to offer their experiences and possibilities for improvement.

SOCIETY OF UNCERTAINTY

In the context of our changing contemporary world, uncertainty stands out as a key factor. However, it is important to distinguish between change and uncertainty. That is, change is leaving something for something else or another situation, and in that transfer, changes occur and it does not have to have the same value, consistency, or form as the original. Meanwhile, uncertainty is the lack of certainty that causes unease and moves away from certainty. It produces, perhaps, a certain uneasiness that translates into insecurity or indecision, causing doubts and concern. Callejo (2020) explains it as follows: "So, uncertainty colonizes certainties. Sometimes, the shadow of uncertainty prevents us from seeing the object that stands between the observer and the light source."

Therefore, technology must have something to offer. It is not considered to be the infallible solution to an unexpected situation that is getting worse, but from a relational perspective, it could mitigate the harmful effects. In this sense, the relational factor "brings together and encompasses many aspects of the social skills that enable individuals to achieve a state of well-being in the community," (Gabelas, Marta, & González, 2015). This is based on the importance of social knowledge, which in turn is an incentive to promote participation and collaborative creation. This would be a continuation of what was presented by Gómez and Zelmalman (2005): "In truth, the context in which we live is characterized by a lack of interest in asking ourselves about the ultimate goals, because knowledge is reduced to the simple preservation or reproduction of what already exists."

All in all, we can start talking about co-creation. Another concept that can be introduced into this debate is that of intermethodology, which sees people as active and participatory agents, with the conviction that they should not only learn content but also be driven by the need to know how to relate to others, listen, defend ideas, and express them with firmness and conviction. In addition, the concept of interlearning, synonymous with reciprocity, could be introduced as an improvement, in the sense of carrying out a proposal to work with a common intention, where students influence each other to benefit from the process to the learning outcomes. With the presence of these three notions (relational factor/co-creation, intermethodology, and interlearning), uncertainty is diluted in the face of improved personal and collective development. Dynamic interaction between students is greatly encouraged.

However, uncertainty is heightened by the advent of so-called artificial intelligence. Artificial intelligence is constantly evolving and should not be viewed as two separate concepts, as they have been linked since their inception. It is seen as a logical and persuasive activity, but one that is unrelated to creativity, beauty, and ethics, even though it is presumed to be capable of reasoning. And this is where we establish the debate as to whether quantity or quality is necessary. This is resolved by Gracián (2003) -in Spanish Baroque- pointing in this direction that "Perfection does not consist in quantity, but in quality."

But this complicated system, concealed by a society of uncertainty, is also marked by a society of risk, based on those who are left behind by a technological society that is far removed from adequate literacy and lacks critical-reflective development. A panoptic society that functions with a concern for observation and surveillance, where attention is focused on the control exercised by new intermediaries. Consequently, a society marked by invisibility and the obscuring of what is important has been promoted. Analytical skills are needed to understand the social and cultural moment in which we find ourselves. This generates a pathological society that inspires continuous fluidity (Bauman, 2021), close to disappointment, in the face of possible fatigue (Han, 2017), as well as close to probable ignorance (Innerarity, 2024), sometimes risk (Beck, 2019) or even ignorance, among other ways of manifesting itself. All these forms of society are leading to a knowledge society, which:

> *"It is nothing more than a new stage in a free market capitalist system that aspires to continue growing thanks to the incorporation of a fourth factor of production, knowledge, to the classic trio of land, labor, and capital. From the liberal democratic perspective in which we find ourselves immersed, we cannot envisage any consistent alternatives to the Knowledge Society" (Brey, 2009, p. 20).*

Certainly, in societies of uncertainty and post-digitalism (Gil, 2023), emerging, emerged, and emergency contexts arise. Two social spheres with relative similarities, but with very specific profiles that generate a networked society. It might be possible to define post-digital society based on the concept coined by Cascone (2000), establishing itself with and among the digital as everyday life, inspired by a connection of many millions of people around the world. A hyperconnection and hypersimplification that facilitates continuous online use, diversified by computers and different wireless devices. Similarly, 5G, 3D, smart watches, and extended realities (which bring together virtual reality, augmented reality, and mixed reality) have become popular. And all under the common denominator of a revolution that continues, strengthening artificial intelligence. Despite everything, it is not exempt from contemporary criticism and questioning (Gardner et al., 2021; Torres, 2024).

A post-digital society that is moving through the contemporary world without abandoning the decisive factor that was the massive expansion of digital technology into everyday life, including work, entertainment, communication, etc. An event marked by ubiquity and connectivity, immediacy and hyper-simplification. In a way, post-digital society should not be interpreted as something that develops in opposition to digital technology, but rather as a cross-cutting manifestation of digital technologies. It is the continuation of an evolution, transformation, and expansion of the unifying sphere of digital technology (Knox, 2019).

And, at the center of it all, education is constantly evolving and inheriting its own evolution. Now, in the 21st century, we are experiencing the fourth industrial revolution, which has robotics and artificial intelligence as its allies. Developed big data moves and interprets massive amounts of data from the perspective of volume, variety, velocity, and veracity (Giró & Sancho, 2022).

ARTIFICIAL INTELLIGENCE

As Santoveña (2021) points out: "We are not smarter or wiser than previous generations, we simply handle more data..." This gives rise to a connection with the most pressing current events. In other words, there may be people who think that the current generation is less intelligent than previous ones. This may be cause for concern, perhaps in the same way as considering this generation to be less supportive, empathetic, or dreamy, or less likely to be excited about learning. However, digital memory and persistent curiosity, which motivate us to seek, select, evaluate, compare, and update knowledge, provide some reassurance. To this we must add artificial intelligence that:

> *"Today, the fascination with AI – including its ethical dimensions – is amplified by its development and real-world applications. (…).*
> *Despite the multitude and diversity of definitions of AI, there is certain consensus, at the most general level, that its two aspects can be distinguished: one usually labelled as 'theoretical' or 'scientific' and the other one as 'pragmatic' or 'technological'." (UNESCO, 2019)*

The definition of intelligence is understood as the ability that living beings have to comprehend. We equate this with understanding or that virtue by which ideas are conceived, enabling us to compare or judge them, as well as deduce them or get to know them better. In other words, it is what we understand as reasoning. Artificial intelligence, on the other hand, is merely a simulation or something purely fictitious. In other words, it may be an intentional activity or have an artificial purpose.

Another issue to bear in mind would be to consider the difference between searching on any search engine or metasearch engine and artificial intelligence. Obviously, search engines present options to choose from, while artificial intelligence generates, relates, and orders information, precisely for use, personalizing the result. We are moving from evolution to a profound revolution. A (re)evolution based on the marked difference that artificial intelligence processes information; in addition, it can be questioned and a dialogue established, thereby increasing the content. The distinguishing feature of processing is related to the possibility of obtaining a product that will be transformed based on prompts (instructions). The most immediate result is a narrative synthesis, which can be presented as a summary or explanation. In this sense, a new academic authority has emerged, known as generative artificial intelligence (GAI). And, continuing with the present development, it would be worth establishing where the limits of intelligence lie:

> *"It is said that humans are an intelligent species: they can talk, solve mathematical problems, have reached the moon... but aren't the other animals that inhabit the planet intelligent too? Indeed, dogs display intelligent behavior and are even capable of expressing feelings. So where do we draw the line between what is and isn't intelligent? (García, 2016)"*

In the 21st century, artificial intelligence has become an essential reference point in today's education (García, Llorens, & Vidal, 2024). It is a way of accommodating this immense wealth of information and converting it into knowledge. And therein may lie another controversy surrounding artificial intelligence, as it gives the impression that it takes the trouble and liberty to do so instead of the user. This is something that worries teachers, for example, who fear the possibility of copying or plagiarism. However, its use should be encouraged, but only after reading and selecting the ideas that appear. Appropriating them may be the beginning of negligence, but it may also be the reason for reading, reflecting, and interpreting a possible solution. This concern should not be focused solely on the search, but also on the fact that they may not read it and simply reproduce it.

A persuasive staging inspired by immediacy and oversimplification. This would be a good excuse to rewrite the need for critical pedagogy, the need to analyze reality and vindicate the figure of the current, qualified teacher to respond to the demands of contemporary society. A society that is connected and willing to value ubiquity. Since it recognizes the meaning of social knowledge and the potential of artificial intelligence.

Artificial intelligence should not be understood as two separate or antagonistic concepts (Ayuso and Gutiérrez, 2022; Cassidy et al, 2023). The shared idea is that of two disciplines forged into a model that aims to perform actions comparable to those that the human mind itself could perform. Of course, it is a simulation that has many possibilities for education, teaching, learning, and reasoning. It is a tool that offers answers when there are questions, inviting us to unlearn (reject what is not valid) and relearn. It is a novel and innovative way of learning.

It could be seen as an ideal pretext for motivation. Where the ability to stimulate is an incentive to learn more and better. And the risk is taken when motivation is lost, which is interpreted as curiosity. Furthermore, the ethical factor must not be deflated and cease to be synonymous with commitment to curb possible abuse, misuse, overuse, or disuse, (Cortina, 2024). An ethic that questions not only the how, (Paguay et al., 2024), but also the where, what, when, and why we continue to rely on it, (Alonso, 2024).

An ethic that is overtaken by endoculture, which instead of being educated by older people (supposedly validated knowledge), anchors us solely in the many possibilities that are determined by that which has, exclusively, a greater capacity to persuasively generate data.

This is reassuring because artificial intelligence, at least for now, cannot educate. It is a generative training tool. Education is established from person to person, between hearts that beat and feel. A mixture to establish effective and affective training (García, Rincón, & Lantarón, 2025). An education inspired by shared responsibility. Opposite this is artificial intelligence, which has its own limitations, (Ribera & Díaz, 2024).

We are facing a powerful contemporary tool. A call to make artificial intelligence enable intelligent learning, (Fernández-Enguita, 2023). All in all, a qualitative step forward for artificial intelligence would be to turn that potential social knowledge into satisfactory knowledge and move away from the feeling of knowing, as it is misleading, (Rossellini, 2001).

In short, these words by Jiménez-García et al (2024) serve to highlight the journey and learning process that must be undertaken with artificial intelligence. However, prior to this, rigorous critical reflection is necessary in order to establish it as an effective and responsible tool, accurate and committed to the truth, moving away from fallacy or artifice:

> *"It is essential to emphasize that, although AI presents ample opportunities for education, it does not provide a comprehensive solution to all educational problems. Therefore, it is essential to use it consciously and thoughtfully, in a manner appropriate to the specific educational context, in order to maximize its potential benefits. Consequently, critical and rigorous reflection is necessary to ensure the effectiveness and responsibility of AI use in education".*

Let's talk about intelligence that is both generative and imaginative, that has the ability to facilitate new ideas, representations, images, intentions, opinions, among other attributes. In short, intelligence that promotes truthful knowledge.

INFLUENCERS

How many people have influenced a human being's educational process? Taking stock, perhaps many would mention several teachers, or teachers outside the classroom who gave private lessons or specific courses, as well as the presence of family, peers, and the media. Similarly, how many times have we encountered the conflict of hearing a child say, "My teacher doesn't teach me that," or perhaps, "When I grow up, I want to be an influencer," (Cortejoso, 2019; Gutiérrez & Ramírez, 2022).

However, the most concise way to define what an influencer is would be to describe them as people who generate "new, more flexible, omnipresent, and anonymous processes, providing the time and space conducive to responding to the need for immediate recognition by others" (Gutiérrez & Ramírez, 2022). Certainly, today, we must consider the presence of influencers through new media (the Internet and wireless devices... social networks). Furthermore, it may be premature, but there may be a KOL (acronym for Key Opinion Leader). In other words, a key person and opinion leader who could be considered an expert on a particular topic and who is recognized or, at least, respected by their audience because they demonstrate a certain consistency, connection, and reputation.

An influencer is someone who creates and recreates content; they act as a guide or source of inspiration (Bazarra & Casanova, 2019). This is where a lengthy debate would begin as to whether they are comparable to a supposed collective intelligence among like-minded people, to whom we grant authority over the content they convey. With varying degrees of artifice, or without it, we turn to them through our screens. Sometimes they are young people with a certain youthful appeal, smiling and carefree, but at other times they present themselves as mature adults whom we would trust.

They use open channels or other more restricted ones. However, in most cases, they are influential people; it would be far from accurate to consider them accredited professionals or to assess their degree of responsibility and prestige. What is remarkable is that they manage to influence, producing a certain effect on those who see or hear them. The problem arises when this presence exerts a significant dominance, whereas the situation would improve if it contributed, with varying degrees of effectiveness and success, to the teaching-learning process. In any case, they could be taken as appropriate contributions for improvement. They are never substitute teachers, but could be considered as possible support.

Therefore, they should not stray from the value of teaching with the tools of the time in which students learn. These influencers speak to them in their own language and allow them to approach social knowledge. However, their role and work will be defended under the auspices of motivated, trained, and qualified 21st-century teachers, (Alvariñas et al., 2025). We are looking at a way to enrich learning perspectives, with a diversification of content and levels that enrich the range of content and student choice.

A (good) influencer knows the possibilities that arise from accessibility inspired by accessing content in an ideal way, but at any time or place, subscribing to the principles of ubiquity. Sometimes, brevity should not only be seen as something that is developed with little length or duration, but should also encourage sharing in a way that facilitates rapid understanding of that content, without neglecting communication skills, (Andrade et al, 2024). It is that promptness or decisive conciseness that, sometimes, teachers do not possess due to certain circumstances, while others do.

Influencers should be seen as a resource. It would be a mistake to label them solely as inspirational figures, without considering them as educated and altruistic individuals, as there are cases where this is true. Bonaga and Turiel (2016) even see it as a quality encouraged by relevant educational and creative figures. According to them, the responsibility of today's teachers also includes knowing and recognizing the main influencers in their fields. They should advise or discourage their students from consulting them, as they not only present explanatory videos but also have a thread of comments, respond to questions asked by students, or provide documents or resources for support or further information. Clearly, we are promoting collaborative learning, endorsing the existence of other people who are epistemologically valid in terms of their contribution to the construction of knowledge. Without losing sight of the fact that this content, shared by experts, must be up-to-date and relevant, as well as accurate and responsive to issues covered by the latest research, trends, and teaching knowledge.

Influencers who primarily operate outside the classroom. They use entertaining resources to liven up the teaching-learning process. They use audiovisual elements, diagrams, and accessible language. The fact that they appear on screens in the comfort of an environment other than the classroom may act as an allí, (Korres & Elexpuru, 2022). This is a way of guiding students that can complement the official curriculum, as it would involve presenting cross-curricular or social content ranging from environmental awareness to education for peace and human rights.

Not everything is without certain risks. Some parents do not approve of screens being part of their children's daily lives. There is also the issue of the shallow content sometimes imposed by the limited time available on platforms such as TikTok, (Ibanez et al, 2022; Hartung et al, 2023). Not to mention the errors that can be transmitted due to a lack of accuracy, ranging from inaccuracies to omissions and misunderstandings. This translates into content quality with certain flaws, inaccurate sections, or biased information. And what was initially presented as a quality in terms of brevity, simplification can now be understood as trivialization, where the aim is to present and make content simply attractive or easier to understand.

Similarly, what was said as a possibility derived from interaction and response may not always be fulfilled, and the user may feel disappointed when there is no reply or counter-reply to a question or clarification, (Márquez & Ardévol, 2018). Faced with the proliferation of influencers, and without prior guidance from the teacher, the learner may feel lost and feed the feeling of wasting time, after fruitless searches or finding someone else who lacks didactic, educational, or content credibility.

It is true that the experience accumulated by influencers means that they are well organized and can hide behind statements such as "edu" to include a large group of people who are dedicated to this work or are inclined towards it. However, it is not always guaranteed that they are, in fact, educational. Perhaps this causes confusion among students who feel let down and, in relation to adults, leads them to distrust this resource.

In this interesting context for creating and recreating content, influencers tend to be good communicators and have the ability to convey messages persuasively, (González & Rojas, 2024). However, they should not be confused with virtual tutors, who guide and accompany students in their teaching and learning process. For some time now, bots have had an important presence in the educational landscape, and their link to artificial intelligence makes them appear to be allies. This is a future that is also developing in today's education. Attractive and proactive voices and designs underpin this host, who usually has and maintains empathic and didactic skills. They tend to be excellent content providers and perform tutoring functions that facilitate learning, as their motto is to clarify and explain the content that students demand. Perhaps we are witnessing the emergence of "new digital artisans in education" (Marcelo et al, 2022). And, for this reason, they develop strategies such as monitoring students' work, providing summaries and outlines, and designing activities to encourage study, achievement, results, etc.

MICROLEARNING

One could say that we are dealing with a training strategy. (Betancur & García-Valcárcel, 2023), or rather, a learning modality where content is fragmented in order to respond to the demands of mosaic culture and the two coordinates on which it is based: brevity (far from fleetingness) and granularity (close to detail and precision). Perhaps priority will be given to the creative exercise of presenting content in an episodic manner, without forgetting that this is a teaching tool (the art of teaching everything to everyone, while respecting each individual's particularities). Microlearning goes beyond simply disseminating content, as it can act as a resource for introducing it, inviting further exploration of a particular topic, focusing action on a specific lesson, supplementing what has been explained, encouraging students to learn more, presenting solutions, or promoting debate, among many other possible actions.

Microlearning is inspired by the spirit of self-management on the part of the learner and, behind it, the management of the teacher who is willing and available to maintain the effect of regularity and present information in an abbreviated form. The content is selected and prepared to offer an acceptable structure, far from being unstructured or presented as something superfluous. This would overcome the intention of incomplete and, at times, incorrect learning that is the result of something merely spontaneous. The priority now is to present the content in segments, in small pieces, always with the intention of promoting autonomous learning, without undermining the value of the students' self-esteem in the digital age, (Cerezo et al, 2023).

We are facing something that should be more than a brief learning exercise, but rather one that becomes effective, where innovation takes over the process; always, and we emphasize this, so that it is synonymous with improvement. Guerschberg & Gutiérrez put it this way:

> *"Among the innovative strategies that have emerged to address these challenges, microlearning has emerged as one of the most promising. This approach is based on breaking down educational content into small, accessible, and digestible units that students can consume in short, flexible sessions. Instead of traditional lengthy lessons, microlearning presents the opportunity to deliver specific content efficiently and tailored to the individual needs of students, which has a direct impact on the learning process, motivation, and information retention," (Guerschberg & Gutiérrez, 2025).*

Therefore, we are dealing with an action with basic educational purposes, with a humanizing bias, and designed to respond to the demands of the 21st century. However, this does not mean that clarity should not prevail in the process and that the digital divide between those who are connected and those who are not should be ignored, nor should the fact that some of those who are connected do not make appropriate use of digital tools.

An action with educational purposes, moving away from exclusive spontaneity and the presentation of fragile content that lacks meaning or significance. It is an elaborate work that provides students with a series of multimedia resources so that they can competently navigate knowledge, selecting material, which entails a desire to choose and, consequently, to take a position on knowledge. And this is where the fragmented view comes into its own, in the sense of offering it as an option that makes learning more than just the acquisition of ideas or knowledge. In other words, it advocates dialogue, gamification, active listening, and complementary outings.

What's more, with a dynamic teacher who, in addition to generating materials, can also work to strengthen relationships between students and the content.

This is the moment when social knowledge, combined with researched knowledge but also with the pedagogy of understanding (grasping the idea expressed) and seduction, becomes powerful, with the intention of bringing it closer (Amar, 2020). But new knowledge acquired is enriched from the moment it is shared, as it is made available to others. And always under the teacher's supervision. All in all, the new nuance that can be added to this discourse on microlearning is the possibility that derives, advantageously, from the benefits of making it customizable (i.e., teachers adapt it to the level of understanding and difficulty of the students).

It is not precisely a complexity of the current moment in education, but rather a qualitative step forward in terms of improvement within the framework of mobile learning, without losing sight of the value of informal education (Cabero et al, 2025). Now that learners study outside the single educational institution, perhaps the end of uniqueness has been consolidated; in the same way that they learn not only formal content (official curriculum versus unofficial curriculum) but also values, habits, skills, etc. Students learn at the same time as they do at school/university, and this positions them before this current, dynamic, and willing learning option.

Next, it could be said that microlearning is a trend driven by technological tools, which are not only supported by design but, fundamentally, by the production and distribution of educational proposals (Hug, 2005). An exercise in creation and recreation that reinvests in the quality and effectiveness of current education. An alternative rooted in contemporary society, where topics are presented in small capsules to promote the effectiveness and validity of the different content units.

A broad concept that is being redefined by the neologism "knowmad" (knowledge nomads), which brings together people who, driven by the desire to innovate, imagine, and be creative, are motivated by technological tools that revolve around ubiquity and connectivity (Roca, 2015). A liquid (Bauman, 2009), digitized, and flexible society and education system changes students' mindsets and ways of doing things based on the new skills and abilities of contemporary learning. And all of this is seasoned with, for example, an appealing variety, precision in design, and the possibility of reuse after categorization in a repository for search and access.

FINAL CONSIDERATIONS

It can be hasty, and even complicated, to reach conclusions in an educational and technological context that is constantly evolving. It no longer depends on current education or technological humanism itself, but also on a myriad of coordinates imposed by the commodification between the two frameworks. For this reason, we have chosen to discuss final considerations. Consideration has a profile that, to a certain extent, fits the intentions of this work, since a line of thought has been established based on analyzed realities. It is a way of inviting further reflection on everything noted in the previous paragraphs and encouraging the reader to draw their own conclusions.

We are currently experiencing a period of educational transformation that encompasses most of the tasks and responsibilities of education, with emerging artificial intelligence proving to be cross-cutting (Barrera, 2025). It is not only appropriate to speak of a digital transformation, which is evident, but also of one that encompasses all areas of education, as change has taken place both inside and outside the classroom, involving not only the teacher-student relationship but also others that extend to the family, school management, support staff, educational inspectors, collaborators, guests, etc. It is clear that initiatives are being taken to transform education, which is being modified by technological innovation (Moreira et al, 2024). Steps have been taken in the planning and design of educational objectives, training cycles have been carried out to include technologies in classroom dynamics with the call for digital skills, and learning has been personalized (more and better) thanks to technologies. Similarly, continuous assessment has been promoted, along with improved methodologies and teaching approaches designed to foster student development and progress, while the meaning of the current curriculum is being questioned, etc. To a large extent, the entire teaching and learning process has been redefined in the techno-evolution in the interests of techno-utopia (Re, 2021) and the development of ethics in the age of artificial intelligence (Coeckelbergh, 2021).

The change has not only taken place outside of school or educational environments, but also within the classroom and in schools, colleges, and universities themselves. We need only remember how teachers communicate with families or how families function, for example, through WhatsApp groups. De la Herrán (2024) proposes a radical modern education. Therefore, it is necessary to update all areas that could affect education in the 21st century, as well as to provide relevant teacher training, since "it is designed for the future, to pave the way for permanent renewal, to be prepared for the challenges of global society," (Zavala et al, 2024).

Students are sensory overloaded and may raise their hands to say that what they are being taught is better explained on a certain website, or that it is expressed in their native language in a way that is easier to understand. Similarly, the way of learning has also changed. Self-directed learning involves a significant degree of autonomy and self-esteem so as not to be overwhelmed by knowledge. They know how to search, select, update, and compare, and they also have the ally of artificial intelligence (Mateos, 2024; Muñoz de Luna et al., 2024). However, in this context, content has become more diverse. Microlearning has emerged as a benchmark, based on the presentation of fragmented and granular content, inspired by a mosaic approach and featuring brief, interactive, persuasive, and audiovisual discourses, with learning situations that promote dialogic learning (Amar et al., 2024). The narrative and its creator take center stage, inviting interaction between the sections that make up this context of technological humanism.

Areas of knowledge that use podcasts as a creative exercise that can be shared in a serialized and episodic format, as well as an educational one. A dramatized way of maintaining intention and attention. But, equally, it comes together with storytelling to teach and learn in a concise and effective way, moving away from superfluous, incomplete, or incorrect content and, where possible, presenting it in a customizable way (where teachers can adapt it to the level of difficulty required by their students); and, in most cases, proving to be an ally of virtual intelligence (Albarrán, 2023)... It is now necessary to vindicate poetry (promoting beauty through words), as well as poiesis (understood as a creative action). We can properly speak of self-learning, as well as of an action with educational purposes in the face of social knowledge, as opposed to researched knowledge linked to the pedagogy of understanding and mobile learning (Vázquez & Sáez, 2024).

However, grand narratives are becoming diluted and an innovative compendium of educational pills is emerging; these are ideal dosages that diversify knowledge. MOOCs (Massive Open Online Courses; open, participatory, and distributed courses) are becoming more accessible and versatile with SPOCs (Small Private Online Courses; an evolved version of MOOCs, now with fewer people... to achieve greater success in the training experience), or with NOOCs (Nano Open Online Massive Courses; with an option of small training pills that share the same educational philosophy as MOOCs, as well as having a very short duration). This represents an advance in the teaching-learning process, quality, and innovation, in addition to having generative artificial intelligence as a cross-cutting theme (Carbonell et al, 2024).

The debate continues, as we may be perpetuating the past by equipping it with tools from the present. In other words, ¿have we created a pastiche by introducing new tools into traditional or obsolete models? But we are facing a debate that is widening because it is focusing on today's education, which is evolving rapidly and using tools from the first third of the 21st century to train students who will develop personally and professionally in the second third of the 21st century, with substitute educational spaces. This debate focuses on the co-responsible and dynamic teacher, the architect of the ceremony of technological humanism and aware of the changes. However, it is not without conflicts, whether resolved or unresolved, more or less difficult, in the present or inherited from the past (Huxley, 2017) with glimpses of a solution.

This chapter does not seek to define concepts or present them as "fundamental," but rather to clarify them and make them understandable for further discussion.

All in all, we need to think and rethink education today so that it continues to be meaningful and useful.

REFERENCES

Accardi, Á. (2023). *La sociedad de la incertidumbre.* Acercándonos Ediciones.

Albarrán, E. (2023). *Hacia una educación personalizada y adaptativa: la disrupción de la inteligencia artificial.* Universidad Pedagógica Experimental Libertador.

Alonso, A. (2024). Hacia un marco ético de la inteligencia artificial en la educación. *Teoría de la Educación. Revista Interuniversitaria, 36*(2), 79–98. DOI: 10.14201/teri.31821

Alvariñas, M., Domínguez, S., Agrelo, M., & Pino, C. (2025). Are future teachers academically motivated? *Review of Education, 61*(1), 213–228. DOI: 10.5565/rev/educar.2136

Amar, V. (2020). Ideas sobre la pedagogía de la seducción en el profesorado universitario. *Review of Education, 44*(2), 426–440. DOI: 10.15517/revedu.v44i2.39535

Amar, V. (2022). Tecnología y educación: El resurgir del cuarto mundo. *Historia Actual Online, 8*, 175–182. DOI: 10.36132/hao.v0i8.126

Amar, V. (2024). Educación digital en el marco de los Objetivos de Desarrollo Sostenible. Una narrativa. *Revista Lusófona de Educação, 61*, 157–173. DOI: 10.24140/issn.1645-7250.rle61.10

Amar, V.; Romero, M. y Heredia, H. (2024). Presentación de la sección especial: Microaprendizaje y tecnología. Edutec, *Revista electrónica de tecnología educativa, 88*, 1–6. DOI: 10.21556/edutec.2024.88.3313

Andrade, L.; Portugal, R.; Sandoval. Y. y Labanda, C. (2024). Youtube e Instagram en educación superior: competencias mediáticas del docente universitario. *RIED: revista iberoamericana de educación a distancia. 27*(2), 339–356. DOI: 10.5944/ried.27.2.39080

Ardèvol, E., & Márquez, I. (2017). El youtuber como celebridad mediática: Entre la autenticidad y el mercado. *Rizoma, 5*(2), 72–87. DOI: 10.17058/rzm.v5i2.11288

Arrieta, B., & Meza, R. (2001). El currículum nulo y sus diferentes modalidades. *Revista Iberoamericana de Educación, 25*, 1-9. https://rieoei.org/RIE/article/view/3143/3947

Ayuso, D., & Gutiérrez, P. (2022). La Inteligencia Artificial como recurso educativo durante la formación inicial del profesorado. *RIED. Revista Iberoamericana de Educación a Distancia, 25*(2), 347–360. DOI: 10.5944/ried.25.2.32332

Bauman, Z. (2009). *El reto de la educación en la modernidad liquida*. Gedisa.

Bauman, Z. (2021). *Vida líquida*. Paidós.

Barrera, J. (2025). La influencia de la inteligencia artificial en la educación actual y los desafíos éticos que presenta. *Vida científica. Boletín científico de la escuela preparatoria 4, 13*(25), 1-5. DOI: 10.29057/prepa4.v13i25.14050

Bazarra, L. y Casanova, O. (2019). *influencers educativos: ¿cómo transformamos en adultos inspiracionales?* Ediciones Sm.

Beck, U. (2019). *La sociedad del riesgo*. Paidós.

Bertolosa, M. (2024). *Inteligencia artificial y humanismo tecnológico*. Digital Reasons.

Betancur, V., & García-Valcárcel, A. (2023). Características del diseño de estrategias de microaprendizaje en escenarios educativos: Revisión sistemática. *RIED-Revista Iberoamericana de Educación a Distancia*, *26*(1), 201–222. DOI: 10.5944/ried.26.1.34056

Bonaga, C., & Turiel, H. (2016). *Mamá, ¡quiero ser youtuber!* Temas de Hoy.

Brey, A. (2009). La sociedad de la ignorancia. En Antoni Brey, Daniel Innerarity y Gonçal Mayos. *La Sociedad de la Ignorancia y otros ensayos* (pp. 17-42). Infonomia.

Cabero, J., Rodríguez, M., & Llorente, C. (2025). Realidade mista, virtual e aumentada: tecnologias para aprendizagem. (2025). *Texto Livre, 18*, 1-19. DOI: 10.1590/1983-3652.2025.49561

Callejo, J. (2020). La sombra de la incertidumbre. In Ramón, R., & García, F. (Eds.), *Incertidumbres en las sociedades contemporáneas*. Centro de Investigaciones Sociológicas.

Cascone, K. (2000). The aesthetic of failure: "post-digital" tendencies in contemporary computer. [Massachusetts Institute of Technology] [MIT]. *Computer Music Journal*, *24*(4), 12–18.

Carbonell, A., Sánchez, A., Benítez, N., & Gertrudix, M. (2024). Impacto de la Inteligencia Artificial Generativa en la eficiencia, calidad e innovación en la producción de Recursos Educativos Abiertos para MOOCS. *Comunicación y Sociedad*, *22*, 1–31. DOI: 10.32870/cys.v2025.8784

Cassidy, D., Le Borgne, Y., Bellas, F., Vuorikari, R., Rondin, E., Sharma, M., Niewint, J., Gröpler, J., Gilleran, A., & Kralj, L. (2023). *Use Scenarios & Practical examples of AI Use in Education.* European Commission. https://doi.org//arXiv .2309.12320DOI: 10.48550

Cendoya, R. (2018). *Revolución. Del Homo sapiens al Homo digitalis.* Sekotia.

Cerezo, B., Gutiérrez, M., Figueredo, L., & Gallardo, K. (2023). La construcción del conocimiento a pequeña escala: El impacto del microaprendizaje en la era digital. *Journal of Science and Research, 8*, 102–115. https://revistas.utb.edu.ec/index.php/sr/article/view/2984

Coeckelbergh, M. (2021). *Ética de la Inteligencia artificial.* Cátedra.

Cortejoso, D. (2019). Mamá, quiero ser 'youtuber. *Eroski Consumer, 7*, 62-67. https://cutt.ly/SYGMZt4

Cortina, A. (2024). *Ética o ideología de la inteligencia artificial?* Paidós.

De la Herrán, A. (2024). ¿Qué es la innovación educativa radical? *Cuadernos de pedagogía, 550*, 30-36.

Fernández, S., & Roussos, A. (2023). La aplicación de tecnologías digitales en tratamientos para el trastorno obsesivo compulsivo: Una revisión sistémica. *Praxis Psy, 24*(40), 1–15. DOI: 10.32995/praxispsy.v24i40.254

Fernández-Enguita, M. (2023). *La Quinta Ola. La transformación digital del aprendizaje, de la educación y de la escuela.* Morata.

French, G. (2023). Microlearning in the Digital Age: The Design and Delivery of Learning in Snippets. *The Alberta Journal of Educational Research, 1*(69), 141–143. DOI: 10.11575/ajer.v69i1.76120

Gabelas, J., Marta, C., & González, P. (2015). El factor relacional en la convergencia mediática: Una propuesta emergente. *Anàlisi. Quaderns de Comunicació i Cultura, 53*, 20–34. DOI: 10.7238/a.v0i53.2509

Gardner, J., O'Leary, M., & Yuan, L. (2021). Artificial intelligence in educational assessment: 'Breakthrough? Or buncombe and ballyhoo?'. *Journal of Computer Assisted Learning, 37*(5), 1207–1216. DOI: 10.1111/jcal.12577

García. (2016). *Inteligencia artificial. Fundamentos, práctica y aplicaciones.* Libros RC.

García, F., Llorens, F., & Vidal, J. (2024). La nueva realidad de la educación ante los avances de la inteligencia artificial generativa. *RIED. Revista Iberoamericana de Educación a Distancia, 27*(1), 9–39. DOI: 10.5944/ried.27.1.37716

García, N., Rincón, M., & Lantarón, B. (2025). Docentes y tecnología: ¿Cómo enfrenta el futuro profesorado el uso de la Inteligencia Artificial? *Revista Electrónica Interuniversitaria de Formación del Profesorado, 28*(1), 155–168. DOI: 10.6018/reifop.638431

Gascón, P., Morte, T., & Manrique, L. (2024). *El factor relacional en la era de la IA*. Dykinson.

Gil, J. (2023). *Educación y comunicación en una sociedad postdigital: Investigación documental y análisis de perspectivas.* Octaedro.

Giró, X., & Sancho, J. (2021). Artificial Intelligence in Education: Big Data, Black Boxes and Technological Solutionism. *Seminar.net, 17*(2). DOI: 10.7577/seminar.4281

Gómez, M., & Zelmalman, H. (2005). *Conocimiento social. El desafío de las ciencias sociales para la formación de profesores en América Latina.* Pax México.

González. E. y Rojas E. (2024). Docentes influencers: Innovación digital y desafíos éticos en la educación del futuro. *Innovaciones educativas, 26*, 6-10. DOI: 10.22458/ie.v26iespecial.5521

Gutiérrez, M. y Ramírez, A. (2022). El deseo de los menores por ser youtuber y/o influencer. Narcisismo como factor de influencia. *Pixel Bit. Revista de medios y educación. 63*, 227-255. DOI: 10.12795/pixelbit.92341

Gutiérrez, M.; Ramírez, A. y Reifs, R. (2022). La generación Z desea ser youtuber y/o influencer. Factores que determinan esta tendencia. *ICONO 14. Revista científica de comunicación y tecnologías emergentes, 20*(2). DOI: 10.7195/ri14.v20i2.1882

Gracián, B. (2003). *Oráculo manual y arte de prudencia.* El Cid editor.

Guerschberg, L., & Gutiérrez, Y. (2025). Microaprendizaje en Educación Superior: Impacto en el Desarrollo del Proceso de Aprendizaje. *Sapiens in Higher Education, 2*(1), 1-20. https://revistasapiensec.com/index.php/Sapiens_in_Higher_Education/article/view/85

Gunkel, D. (2018). The other question: Can and should robots have rights? *Ethics and Information Technology, 20*, 87–99. DOI: 10.1007/s10676-017-9442-4

Habermas, J. (1998). *Escritos sobre moralidad y eticidad.* Paidós.

Han, B. (2017). *La sociedad del cansancio*. Herder.

Hariri, Y. (2024). *Nexus. Una breve historia de las redes de información desde la Edad de Piedra hasta la IA*. Debate.

Hartung, C., Ann, N., Albury, K., Johnston, S., & Welch, R. (2023). Teachers of TikTok: Glimpses and gestures in the performance of professional identity. *Media International Australia, 186*(1), 81–96. https://doi.org/10.1177/1329878X211068836

Hug, T. (2005). Microlearning: A new approach to learning and education. European *Journal of Open. Distance and E-Learning, 8*(1), 1–10. DOI: 10.1515/eje.2005.8.1.1

Huxley, A. (2017). *Literatura y ciencia. El humanismo frente al progreso científico y tecnológico*. Página Indómita.

Ibanez, M., Limón, M., & Ruiz, C. (2022). Retos virales: Análisis del impacto de TikTok para los vínculos familiares. *Revista de Ciencias Sociales, 28*(3), 42–54. DOI: 10.31876/rcs.v28i3.38449

Innerarity, D. (2024). *La sociedad del desconocimiento*. Galaxia Gutenberg.

Innerarity, D., & Robledo, E. (2024). *La humanidad amenazada*. Gedisa.

Kay, J., & King, M. (2020). *Radétiical Uncertainty. Decision-making for an unknowable future*. The Bridge Street Press.

Kissinger, H., Schmidt, E., & Huttenlocher, D. (2023). *La era de la Inteligencia Artificial y nuestro futuro humano*. Anaya.

Knox, J. (2019). What does the "postdigital" mean for education? Three critical perspetives on the digital, with implications for educational reserch and practice. *Postdigital science and education, 1*(2), 357-370. DOI: 10.1007/s42438-019-00045-y

Korres A. y Elexpuru, I. (2022). Youtubers: Identificación y motivos de agrado de la audiencia. *Revista ICONO 14. Revista científica de comunicación y tecnologías emergentes, 20*(1), 1-19. .DOI: 10.7195/ri14.v20i1.1761

Lipovetsky, G. (2022). *La sociedad de la decepción*. Anagrama.

López, A. (2022). Todos los ODS empiezan en la educación. En J. Benavides; A. Díaz y J. Camacho (Coords.). *ODS, las voces de la universidad y la empresa* (pp. 81-83). Editorial Kolima.

Marcelo, C., Yot, C., Marcelo, P., Murillo, P., & Mayor, C. (2022). No me llames influencer. Nuevos artesanos digitales en educación. *Campus Virtuales, 11*(2), 133–145. DOI: 10.54988/cv.2022.2.1150

Márquez, I., & Ardèvol, E. (2018). Hegemonía y contrahegemonía en el fenómeno youtuber. *Desacatos: Revista de Ciencias Sociales, 56*, 34–49. DOI: 10.29340/56.1876

Marta-Lazo, C., & Gabelas-Barroso, J. (2023). *Diálogos postdigitales. Las TRIC como medios para la transformación social.* Gedisa.

Mateos, J. (2024). La inteligencia artificial como tecnología educativa. En Jesús Flores (coord.). *Comprender la Inteligencia Artificial: Hermenéutica, herramientas y experimentalidad de la IA en la Educación y Comunicación* (p.p. 165-191). Fragua.

Mitchel, M. (2024). *Inteligencia artificial. Guía para seres pensantes.* Capitán Swing Libros.

Moreira, C., López, Y., Holguín, B., Mero, E., Vélez, Y., & Macías, N. (2024). La inteligencia artificial y su incidencia en la educación: Un análisis desde un rol transformador. *Revista de Desarrollo del Sur de Florida, 5*(7), 1–13. DOI: 10.46932/sfjdv5n7-031

Muñoz de Luna, A., Martín, S., & Cabezuelo, F. (2024). *Los retos de la inteligencia artificial en contextos educativos.* Fundación Universitaria San Pablo CEU.

Naval, C., Bernal, A., Jover, G., & Fuentes, J. (2020). *Perspectivas actuales de la condición humana y la acción educativa.* Dykinson.

Nowotny, H. (2016). The Cunning of Incertainty. *Polity.*

Paguay, M., Jiménez, D., Quiliguango, V., Maynaguez, M., Coello, C., & Coello, S. (2024). La ética en el uso de la inteligencia artificial en los procesos educativos. *Revista Científica Retos De La Ciencia, 1*(4), 145–158. DOI: 10.53877/rc.8.19e.202409.12

Piscitelli, A. (2009). *Internet: la imprenta del siglo XXI.* Gedisa.

Puelles, M. (2004). *Política y Educación en la España Contemporánea.* UNED.

Re, A. (2021). *Tecno_Evo: Manuale d'istruzioni per un ventennio sospeso.* Agenzia X.

Ribera, M., & Díaz, O. (2024). *ChatGPT y educación universitaria: posibilidades y límites de Chat GPT como herramienta docente.* Octaedro.

Roca, R. (2015). *Knowmads, los trabajadores del futuro.* Lid Editorial Empresarial, S.L.

Rodríguez, J. (2022). *Educación siglo XXI: Nuevos retos, nuevas soluciones.* Dykinson.

Rossellini, R. (2001). *Un espíritu libre no debe aprender como esclavo: escritos sobre cine y educación.* Paidós.

Santoveña, S. (2021). *Cartografía de la sociedad y educación digital, (investigación y análisis de perspectivas).* Tirant lo Blanch.

Torres, J. (2024). *La transformación de la inteligencia artificial.* Editorial Bosch.

UNESCO. (2019). *Preliminary study on the ethics of artificial intelligence.* UNESCO. https://unesdoc.unesco.org/ark:/48223/pf0000367823/PDF/367823eng.pdf.multi

Vázquez, E., & Sáez, J. (2024). *Tecnologías emergentes y activas en educación.* Dykinson.

Zavala, L., Reyes, G., Rodríguez, S., & Rabanal, V. (2024). Formación docente y actualización académica permanente: Desafíos ante los paradigmas del siglo XXI. *Revista de Ciencias Sociales, 30*(10), 130–142. DOI: 10.31876/rcs.v30i.42833

Chapter 9
Comparing the European Right to Good Administration and the US Hard Look Doctrine in the Context of Behavioral Law and Economics

Juli Ponce
https://orcid.org/0000-0002-1977-5063
University of Barcelona

ABSTRACT

The work provides a comprehensive analysis of the concept of good administration, which is connected with the idea of the common interest or good, its legal framework, and its practical implications, drawing comparisons between the European and U.S. legal traditions. The core argument is that good administration is not merely a desirable moral goal, how it was until the end of the 20th century, but a current legal requirement that can be enforced through various mechanisms, including judicial review and administrative procedures. The document also explores the relationship between good administration, transparency, and the need to address cognitive biases in regulatory decision-making.

DOI: 10.4018/979-8-3373-2332-9.ch009

INTRODUCTION: WHAT IS THE RIGHT TO GOOD ADMINISTRATION? LIMITS OF JUDICIAL REVIEW OF ADMINISTRATIVE DECISIONS: THE *CHEVRON* AND *LOPER BRIGHT* LEADING CASES. LAW AND POLITICAL SCIENCE: IMPARTIALITY IS NECESSARY BUT LIMITED[1]

I want to analyze the reflections that from the end of the 20th century have emerged in the field of the right to good administration which has a strong link with the topic of the common interest or good. I will do it by making some considerations about the concepts of good governance, good government and specially (the right to) good administration.

The existence of good governance, good government and good administration has been a fundamental human concern since time immemorial, likely emerging alongside the formation of communities where an individual—whether a tribal chief or a petty king—exercised power, that is, since the establishment of public authority. This age-old concern, deeply rooted in human life, has transcended both Law and Political Science, drawing attention from Philosophy and Art alike.

From a philosophical perspective, the notion that rulers should be bound by a "duty of good governance" can already be found in various classical authors, such as Solon, with his poem *Eunomia*, as well as Plato, Socrates, Aristotle, and Cicero, among others. Throughout the centuries, these thinkers—each with their own nuances—expressed the conviction that rulers should seek the happiness of all their subjects rather than just a privileged few, ordering what was necessary to achieve that end (De Asís Roig, 2000).

However, these approaches remained at a high level of abstraction, often grounded in Natural Law but lacking any foundation in formal legal norms. It was not until the 19th century that various scholars emphasized that the Administration should not only act within the boundaries of the legal system but also strive to govern well, in accordance with "principles of good administration," to which the Spanish professor of Administrative Law Posada Herrera had already referred (Posada-Carbó, 1997). In French legal thought, Hauriou articulated a similar idea, stating: *"L'Administration ne doit pas se borner à être correcte et respectueuse de la légalité; elle doit s'efforcer d'être habile"* (Hauriou, 1893). Hauriou would go on to develop this concept throughout various works, consistently emphasizing the idea of *bonne administration*, albeit from the perspective of administrative morality rather than as a set of legally binding duties or obligations (Hauriou, 2025).

It was only at the end of the 20th century and in the early decades of the 21st that the concepts of good governance and good administration transitioned from metaphysical discourse to concrete legal technique—a shift aptly described by García (1995) when discussing the role of modern public law. This transformation has been driven by legal scholarship, jurisprudence, and various legislative measures, as will be examined below. In this regard, Cassese (2009) already characterizes the 21st century as *the century of good administration*, a concern that, he argues, did not predominate in earlier times.

In this transition to concrete legal technique, the role of Administrative Law in relation to good administration has been key since the end of the 20th century, after new developments that have changed the traditional perspectives of this science.

In that sense, it has been said that Administrative Law has to do essentially with discretionary powers (Garcia De Enterría, 2000, quoting Schwartz, 1984). The traditional concept of discretionary powers entails two common aspects: choice and general interest. Academic writers agree that discretion means public administration is empowered by Law to choose from among several legal possibilities, taking into account non juridical criteria. This choice implies balancing public and/or private interests, by using extra-legal values to define a general interest which is not established by statutes (e.g. in Spain, Garcia De Enterria, E. & Fernández, 2002, 454, in Vedel and Devolvé, 1990, 524, in the UK, Craig, 1994, 384, in Italy, Giannini, 1939)[2].

The core of discretion, i.e. the choice between alternatives, has been something odd in traditional Administrative Law which does not encompass it, except for just *designing limits* for the selection that cannot be breached. The choice itself is considered a matter of politics, not a legal issue. In the traditional paradigm, Administrative Law provides, above all, a defence for individuals, a shield against arbitrary decisions.

From the classical point of view, *where law ends, tyranny begins* (Davis, 1976) and the only effective protection against tyranny is judicial review. Traditional Administrative Law *is not interested in good administrative decisions but just in the judicial review of illegal decisions*, to protect citizens against public arbitrariness. This is a negative approach, in the sense that it is against arbitrariness, not in favour of good decisions serving the general interest, and it is possible to link this point of view with Harlow's and Rawlings' metaphor of red-light theorists (Harlow and Rawlings, 1997). In my opinion, for example, this approach has been common in Spain for a long time, as well as in other European Countries, as testified by Cassese's explanation on the principle of legality as a "fetish."

But a new viewpoint is growing around the world, which can be considered an element of the so called Global Administrative Law. CASSESE has underlined that "si può dire che il nucleo essenziale del principio di buona amministrazione contituisca il nucleo principale del diritto amministrativo globale" (Cassese, 2009; see in that sense Cassese, 2012, and Ponce, 2010). This second approach is concerned with the quality of decisions. The discretionary choice itself is relevant for Administrative Law, because it is concerned with good decisions, with good administration. It is important that Public Administration makes both the legal and the *right* decisions because people demand good decisions, together with proper reasons to back them, and they want to be heard and to have a say in the matter (e.g. about where the highway should be constructed or the nuclear plant built).

As Mr Braibant has graphically pointed out "even when public authorities are allowed to do what they want, they cannot do whatever," (Braibant, 1970). That is, the proper use of discretionary powers matters to public law. It has been said that the 21st century is the century of good administration (Cassese, 2009, 1098, quoting the European Ombudsman). Actually, "there can be little doubt that the central purpose of Administrative Law is to promote good administration" (Elliott, Beatson & Matthews, 2011).

However, this new approach raises a problem. Traditional administrative law has underlined the judicial perspective. In fact, administrative law can be understood traditionally, in many countries such as Spain, as being almost synonymous with judicial review. And the problem is that judicial review cannot guarantee *per se and by itself* alone good administration. The reason is the *principle of separation of powers* (Hesse, 1983) a common idea in European legal systems (and in the United States[3]). Judges cannot substitute discretionary administrative decisions for the sake of a different opinion about the *best* solution, on the basis of social or economic ideas[4].

In the case of the US, for example, the American Supreme Court stated in 1984 in the *Chevron* case:

"Judges are not experts in the field [being regulated], and are not part of either political branch of government. Courts must, in some cases, reconcile competing political interests, but not on the basis of the judges' personal policy preferences... While agencies are not directly accountable to the people, the Chief Executive [and Congress] is, and it is entirely appropriate for [the political branches of government] to make such policy choices".

However, the U.S. Supreme Court's ruling in *Loper Bright* (June 28, 2024) seems to overturn the deference doctrine established in the *Chevron* case, as we will see in detail in the last part of this article.

In conclusion, there is currently a new increasing sensitivity in modern Administrative Law that judicial review is not the best legal tool to develop it on its own. Does this mean that good administration is just a desirable *moral* goal with no legal effects?[5] Or are there other legal elements that may make it compulsory and effective? Must we just ignore this or must we, as jurists, fight for good administration using the Law?

In short, can Administrative Law foster good administration? The answer is yes (Macmillan, 2009). Judicial review of administrative decisions is not the whole administrative law but just part of it. Administrative law is a branch of the legal science devoted to achieving *lawful and good* decisions. Judicial review is just an important tool which can guarantee by itself the former but not the latter, although it can contribute to achieving this goal, as we will see below.

There are several other important legal tools that can help to achieve good administration, besides judicial review (ethical codes, citizen´s charters, etc., Ponce, 2013). We are not going to study all of them here but we will focus on the role of *administrative procedure* and the *duty of giving reasons*[6]. By administrative procedure the study implies a way of developing administrative powers, the manner in which Public Administration carries out its functions, as underlined in the interesting dynamic view outlined by Benvenuti (1952). Thus, Administrative procedure is understood as the normal and suitable way of developing the *funzione amministrativa* of "service to general interests", to use the beautiful expression in art. 103 of the Spanish Constitution.

The main idea is that "better substantive results will be achieved in the everyday conduct of state government by improving the process by which those results are attained," (Bonfield, 1986). Therefore, the idea of procedure is linked to the idea of good use of powers, especially in the case of discretionary powers (Woehrling, 1988, refers to rules of "bonne utilization" of discretionary powers established by French case law).

On the other hand, the need to express the grounds supporting a decision will be proof that public authorities have complied with due administrative procedure, weighing up all the relevant interests and taking into account all the data collected.

This kind of behaviour is especially important whenever officials exercise discretionary power. In these cases, statutes do not intend to nor can they define the public interest to be implemented by public administration. Take the case of areas of public intervention where the concept of risk plays a relevant role (e.g. environment, public health...). Legislators are not able to assess and manage the risk. Thus, the "belt transmission" theory, as a formal model of explaining administrative activity and consequently of *legitimating* it (Stewart, 1975, Frug, 1984), does not work on its own all the time. In all these cases and in others (where there is a sphere of discretion) a new rationale behind public administrations is necessary; in other words, *a different source of legitimacy is needed*, besides the traditional view of the automatic implementation of statutes (Luhmann, 1969). As pointed out earlier, procedures can be a way of rationalising value judgements and a complementary source of legitimation in our complex and modern societies (Alexy, 1989).

Therefore, the idea of good administration leads us to a new way of understanding administrative legitimacy, to a new paradigm. If during the last century we moved from the Weber bureaucratic paradigm to New Public Management (NPM, which did not give all that it promised, Hood & Ruth, 2015), and from NPM to Governance

(PRATS, 2005), now in the 21st century the next step will be moving towards good government and good administration.

Thus, the right to good administration should force the change of paradigms regarding the administrative activity and their replacement for other new ones, more adapted to current necessities. Good administration, as a concept of necessary technical accuracy - but radically opposed to the indifference of the Law regarding the exercise of discretionary powers-, and the articulation of concrete legal mechanisms to implement it, like administrative procedures, can help to achieve better public decisions. Cerulli Irelli (1997) feels that even the production of formal legal decisions (regulations, permits...) as a result of exercising public powers is a service to citizens, just like managing hospitals or schools is, and that these decisions can and must be evaluated, taking as a reference standards of effectiveness, efficiency or economy, which can be implemented through the administrative procedure. This author says that this way of thinking is a "real revolution" for authorities, judges and even citizens.

In short, there is an increasing sensitivity concerning good administration. Moreover, administrative procedure and the duty to give reasons are considered, among others, useful legal tools in order to implement principles of good administration which can help to provide better decisions. This view explains a growing interest in the literature on these topics related to the idea of good governance[7], the right to a good administration and their connections with transparency.

As article 15 of the Treaty on the Functioning of the EU establishes:

"In order to promote good governance and ensure the participation of civil society, the Union institutions, bodies, offices and agencies shall conduct their work as openly as possible."

But there are still many doubts about the relationship between good governance and good administration and the meaning, usefulness and contents of a right to good administration (Trimarchi, 2011). Sometimes both expressions (good governance and good administration) are used in a similar way and also with good government. It depends on each legal tradition and on the language used (Addink, 2014). Whilst good governance is more used by Political Science in a broad and political context (including all public powers and private ones that are involved in public decisions) the right to good administration must have a precise legal meaning because it has been included in legal texts, as we will see[8], and it is used to establish administrative obligations which are enforceable by means of judicial review.

Therefore, the challenge is to understand the right to good administration and make it available for better control and improvement of administrative decisions. As an interesting Swedish report underlines (Swedish Agency for Public Management, Statskontoret, 2005, 78)[9]:

"The general idea behind a law on good administration is that if public administrations follow proper procedures, the probability of making good decisions increases dramatically. Designing procedures that ensures that the official considers all relevant facts, balances all relevant interests and ensures that all parties can hold him/her accountable during the process by transparent procedures and forcing the public authority to explicitly state the grounds for their decision, will ensure a minimum level of rational reflexivity in the process"

HOW IS THE RIGHT TO GOOD ADMINISTRATION REGULATED BY PUBLIC LAW?

Focusing now on the European arena, we should distinguish between the supranational institutions (the Council of Europe and the European Union) and the national legal systems.

The Council of Europe has been active in the field of good administration. First of all, it is noteworthy to mention the resolution of 28 September 1977 on the Protection of individuals with regard to actions of administrative authorities. Although in its text there is no specific reference to the term "good administration", this idea is implicit.

Secondly, the Recommendation number R (80)2, adopted by the Committee of Ministers on 11 March 1980, concerning the exercise of discretionary powers by the administrative authorities, does not refer to "good administration" either, but there are a number of principles designed to achieve this end. Finally, the Recommendation CM/Rec (2007) 7 of the Committee of Ministers to member states on good administration contains a number of interesting references to good governance and its relationship with regulatory quality, social needs and the weight of the interests of social and individual interests, good governance, other non-legal mechanisms (organizational quality, adequate human resources and governance), the requirements of the right to good administration (legality, equality, impartiality, proportionality, legal certainty, adopting decisions within a reasonable period, participation, respect of privacy and transparency) and its connections to administrative procedures. This Recommendation also includes several suggestions to Member States to promote good governance. Among them, there is one on the adoption of the standards established in a model code which is attached as an appendix to the Recommendation itself.

As evidence of the existence of a common European background in relation to the administrative procedure and good administration, the consecration of the Charter of Fundamental Rights should be noted:

"Right to good administration

1. Every person has the right to have his or her affairs handled impartially, fairly and within a reasonable time by the institutions and bodies of the Union.
2. This right includes:
   – the right of every person to be heard, before any individual measure which would affect him or her adversely is taken;
   – the right of every person to have access to his or her file, while respecting the legitimate interests of confidentiality and of professional and business secrecy;
   – the obligation of the administration to give reasons for its decisions.
3. Every person has the right to have the Community make good any damage caused by its institutions or by its servants in the performance of their duties, in accordance with the general principles common to the laws of the Member States.
4. Every person may write to the institutions of the Union in one of the languages of the Treaties and must have an answer in the same language."

This article refers to the right to a diligent performance as part of good administration in the first section and in the second specifies *a number of* consequences stemming from this right to good administration ("in particular", as the text clarifies, so as not to limit possibilities): the right of access to information contained in the file, the right to be heard (the *audi alteram partem* rule) and the duty of giving reasons for the decisions made.

Jacqué (2002), in a study on the Charter, argues that by means of this decision "la charte fait son entrée dans les principes généraux du droit par le biais des traditions constitutionnelles communes aux Etats membres", and he points out that "si cette solution était confirmée par la Cour, la voie paraît toute tracée par la Convention. En effet si serait aisé d´argumenter, face à ceux qui seraient hostiles à une référence a la charte dans les traités, que cette référence ne ferait que confirmer la jurisprudence et d´ajouter au minimum à l'article 6 l'indication que l'Union respecte les traditions constitutionnelles communes aux États membres telles qu´elles son confirmées par la Carte des droits fondamentaux de l'Union européenne".

The text from article 41 presents *few novelties* regarding what is set out in the Treaty or in case law and contains a number of loopholes[10]. For example, it is surprising to note a lack of reference to the institution of the European Ombudsman, mentioned in an independent reference in art. 43, referring specifically to his work controlling maladministration.[11]

The lack of an explicit connection between arts. 41 and 43 must be underlined, especially due to the fact that the European Ombudsman has been a fervent instigator of the existence of *Codes of Good Administration* in the setting of European organisms. It is known that the European Ombudsman launched his own initiative inquiry about the existence of and public accessibility to such codes, recommending the adoption of rules concerning good administrative behaviour. In 1999 the European Ombudsman recommended a draft Code of Good Administrative Behaviour to the Community institutions and bodies, drawing up guidelines for making the adoption of such a Code easier. The European Ombudsman's efforts finally crystallised in the Resolution of the European Parliament, adopted September 6, 2001. This Resolution approved the Code of Good Administrative Behaviour and called on the European Commission to submit a proposal for a future regulation of EU administrative´s procedure beyond this soft law (a new impulse of that idea can be found in the recent ReNEUAL works, ReNEUAL, 2014)

Art. 41 in the Charter does not mention anything on the thorny subject of the transcendence of procedural defects which give rise to a breach of the duty of good administration and the possible existence of irrelevant procedural defects for the final decision, the so-called "harmless error principle," (Trimarchi, 2011). Another important aspect is the individualistic perspective of the article regarding procedural participation, which boils down to a hearing "before any individual measure which would affect him or her adversely is taken". Thus, public participation –through devices like public hearings or similar - in procedures for elaborating general decisions (e.g., regulations) is not considered. This is a disappointing loophole because participation is a sensitive issue as regards developing the community's public policies, which includes transparency, equality, objectivity, democracy and accountability. As some authors have underlined, the European and American trajectories diverge notably in relation to this aspect, and a more detailed regulation should be established (Shapiro, 1990)

The right in the Charter concerning good administration implies the explicit and visible confirmation of the existence of a legal duty for public authorities to be in the best position to be able to make appropriate decisions, absorbing this way a common European inheritance[12]. Therefore, this implies important support to the procedural issues which have now passed to a higher position. The initial limited scope of the Charter (see art. 51[13]) does not affect the importance that procedural matters will command in the future of Europe, nor does it seem that a process of a national filtration of this procedural relevance may be prevented, since it seems difficult to imagine that a national judge would be able to apply a certain standard of good administration in compliance with EC Laws and other procedural standards when applying national Laws for the internal public authorities (about this problem, Gordon, 2002, in general, and take into account the Spanish case that we will explain immediately).

The right to good administration could be specially relevant in some European countries, in the sense that this would imply a positive shake-up of case law and scholars who could (and should) become more sensitive to the importance of administrative procedures as regards a factor of quality, linked to the relevance of procedural defects.

Although art. 41 can be considered a simple umbrella including previous existing procedural rights and making easier to citizens to know them, it is possible to identify something new in that article (SERIO, 2008). In that sense, the most characteristic element in article 41 is the duty of due care or due diligence. Although this duty existed in some countries, in one or another way (eg. reasonableness, used in the well-known case *Associated Provincial Pictures Houses, Ltd. V. Wednesbury Corporation* [1948] 1 KB 223 in the UK, or rinciple of proper administration used in Belgian law, LUST, 2002), in others cases, like Spain, it was not included in the legislation nor stated by case law.

Therefore, when this article is criticized because it is mainly rhetorical (Bousta, 2013), we should be aware of that relevant duty which has been established by the Charter, following the EU case law which extracted it from some legal national traditions.

This reflection moves us to the national level to check the role of good administration and the impact of art. 41 of the Charter. The duty of due care or due diligence can be found in the legal systems of the EU member states. An interesting Swedish report (Swedish Agency for Public Management, Statskontoret, 2005) identifies the *right to have ones affairs handled impartially and fairly* as one of the ten principles of good administration embraced by a majority of the EU Member States[14].

This report underlines that this right is "in one way or another, constitutionally guaranteed. They may also be laid down in statutes, most often in an Administrative Procedure Act. The exact wordings vary: "impartiality" and "fairness" is for instance sometimes replaced by the duty of the public administration to act with "objectivity" or to "treat everyone on an equal basis"[15]. This Swedish report seems to identify impartiality with objectivity and focuses its analysis on the general rules on disqualification of biased officials. But in my opinion impartiality (i.e. the absence of bias) is necessary but not enough to achieve objectivity if we understand (as I do) that acting with objectivity implies a duty of care or due diligence.

It could be interesting to research the common roots of the duty of care in the European legal (in that sense, Ponce Solé, 2001). For example, in the French case, the *Conseil d´État*'s case law has established that when the administrative authorities are exercising discretionary powers they must take into account all the relevant circumstances carefully before deciding. Public authorities must avoid an apparent or a merely formal study of the case before taking a decision: the analysis "ne doit être formel, mais loyal et complet", Isaac, 1968). This study must take into account costs and benefits and make and assessment of them (*bilan*, Conseil d´Etat, May 28, 1971, Ville Nouvelle-Est).

The same idea can be found in German public law (e.g. in the field of urban planning), where the public authority in charge of making decisions must take into account and balance all the public and private interests involved according to the German case law (Gromitsaris, 2007).

British efforts to build several principles of good administration are also worthy of mention. The Committee of the Justice—All Souls, a nongovernmental institution, published two reports that contained a draft of principles of good administration (Committee of Justice, 1971; 1988). Among them we can find principle number three which states that "It shall be the duty of an authority in proceeding to a decision to take all reasonable steps to ascertain the facts which are material to the decision".

This document clarifies that "all reasonable steps" means measures by way of inquiry, verification, deliberation or otherwise as are in all circumstances of the case necessary according to good administrative practice. The English case law has underlined the existence of a public duty when exercising discretion. Discretionary powers must be developed taking into account the specific circumstances of the case. The general rule is "that anyone who has to exercise a statutory discretion must not "shut his ears" to an application" (case *British Oxygen v. Board of Trade*). According to the famous concept of unreasonableness (used in the well-known case *Associated Provincial Pictures Houses, Ltd. V. Wednesbury Corporation* [1948] 1 KB 223) there is an administrative duty of taking into account all the relevant aspects before deciding[16]. This decision set up a standard of judicial review used by other countries in the common law sphere (In relation to the use of the reasonableness in Australia as a judicial standard of control, Dawnes, 2008)

As regards the Italian situation, the 1947 Italian Constitution establishes that Italian agencies must be organized so as to achieve administrative impartiality and *buon andamento*. The last words have been considered by many Italian scholars to be a duty of good administration (*buona amministrazione*). The *Corte Costituzionale* has declared that this duty obliges legislators to design proper administrative structures and procedures to carry out administrative functions. On the other hand, the principle imposes on public administration the duty of making sound decisions by gathering necessary information and balancing the relevant factors in each case before deciding (Falzone, 1953; Trimarchi, 2011, 8).

Regarding the situation in Holland, art. 3:2 of the Dutch *Algemene wet bestuursrecht* provides that:

> *"When preparing an order an administrative authority shall gather the necessary information concerning the relevant facts and the interests to be weighed"*

The consequences of this provision could be different in Dutch public law, according to the various authors participating in a collective book, (Graaf et al., 2007). Tolsma believes that "an important component of the requirement of due care is the duty to hear the parties involved before taking a decision". The administrative authority must "take an active approach and should not regard the hearing as a formality during which it merely listens to what is brought forward". And this administrative duty to investigate "leads to several indications that in certain circumstances it should strive toward consensus in the administrative decision-making process". The requirement of due care "provides a basis for this duty to try to reach an amicable settlement" and, generally speaking, to be active and open-minded during the development of the administrative procedure (Tolsma, 2007).

Regarding Spain, the current Spanish Constitution of 1978 is especially interesting in relation to the duty of care or due diligence. It provides in Articles 31 and 103 that public administration must act with objectivity and impartiality, in accordance with the principles of effective action, efficiency, economy and coordination; it also establishes a prohibition of arbitrariness.[17]

Scholars and case law use the words *buena administración* (good administration) in relation to the duty of achieving good administrative decisions. On the other hand, in the last few years, the need for statements of reasons to guarantee a good use of discretionary powers has been emphasized.

All the principles previously mentioned may be included in a more general concept, the duty of good administration, established initially by Spanish legislation regarding contracts, and later by case law. But until some years ago this legal concept suffered from a lack of consistent theoretical construction. Therefore, Spanish jurisprudence and case law are trying to define the meaning of such a duty and its legal consequences, in connection with the key role of administrative procedure. Here are some of the basic conclusions achieved.

The Spanish Constitution of 1978 contains a series of principles referring to the development of the activity of service to general interests.[18] This is a group of principles of *buena administración*—to use the traditional expression from Spanish legislation that refers to contracts—that guides the way of conducting administrative activity and, therefore, indirectly, though undoubtedly, conditions the content of its result.

Among them, the duty of objectivity has been defined by Spanish case law. Several Spanish Supreme Court decisions have pointed out that the duty of acting objectively before deciding means that public authorities must take into account all the relevant elements of the case, analyzing all the relevant facts (including the law to be applied) and interests (public and private) involved in the exercise of discretionary powers (Spanish Supreme Court´s decision of November 29, 1985, among others).

If a balance does not exist between of all the relevant interests and relevant facts involved in the case, the administrative decision will be illegal. The existence of this balance and good reasons supporting the discretionary decision can only be proved by a proper file and by reason based on the documents included in this file (Decisions of September 21, 1990 and June 1, 1999, among others).

Therefore, the duty of due diligence or due care which is extracted from the right to good administration (as a common standard in different European legal traditions) is different from the principle of proportionality. It is true that the prohibition included in the third level of the principle of proportionality (proportionality *stricto sensu*) regarding the need of avoiding an improper balance of costs and benefits in the exercise of discretion has a connection with the duty of care. Without the latter the principle of proportionality could not be achieved. In order to avoid an improper balance, it is clearly necessary to balance these principles (a comparative approach about this principle in Ranchordas and De Waard, 2015).

But taking care and acting with due diligence when balancing is not the equivalent to acting proportionally. The public authority can respect the duty of care and break the principle of proportionality. Both are linked but are different: the duty of care is a positive obligation (to find the facts and interests and to balance them) whilst the principle of proportionality is a negative limit (do not trespass the proportionality line). As Downes (2010) has said from the common law perspective:

"Reasonableness covers a wider field than proportionality. A measure might be proportionate, but its adoption unreasonable, because, for example, of a lack of consultation. It is not clear to me that the tests are the same, or even that they will yield the same result. They are quite different tests. One is a test of rationality; the other is a relationship test. One is an overall and general test; the other is a precise test applied negatively to a previously identified relationship".

A good example of the meaning of the good administration standard can be found in the decision of the General European Court of the European Union of April 29, 2015, T-217/11, Claire Staelen vs. European Union Ombudsman.[19]

Therefore, the right to good administration should encompass:

-a duty of collecting all relevant factors (facts, interests, law, rights) (a),

- a duty of considering the reasonable alternatives which rise during the procedure (b)

-a duty of taking into accounts all the relevant factors and dismissing all the irrelevant factors (c)

-a duty of keeping a rational relationship between the final decisions and those factors explaining the fulfilling of the three other duties through the duty of giving reasons. These reasons are the evidence that a careful consideration existed (d) (see Cane, 2015, about the relationship between records, reasons and racionality in several countries, including the US case that we will consider later)

HOW ARE THE LEGAL MECHANISMS OF GOOD ADMINISTRATION WORKING AND BEING REGULATED.?

As regards the mechanisms regulated by law for making possible the right to good administration, we mentioned before the administrative procedure and the duty of giving reasons, but they are not alone. It is impossible here to analyze all the related legal tools. In the Spanish case, for example, a new generation of recent legislation regarding good government and good administration has established several tools to promote quality in administrative decisions, including principles of good government, regulation of conflict of interests, ethical codes, citizen´s charters for the public services (*Cartas de servicios*) or regulatory impact assessments when passing new regulations (e.g. State Act 19/2013 and Catalan Act 19/29014).

At the moment, indicators of good administration have not been developed, although recent legislation makes a call for creating them in the future (e.g. Catalan Act 19/2014 which imposes its future *ex post* evaluation by the Catalan Ombudsman).

Nowadays, due to the lack of indicators of good administration, the easiest (but erratic and limited) way of checking how the right administration is working is case law.

Judicial Protection of the Right to a Good Administration in the European Level

In that sense, the case law of the ECHR has built the notion of good administration[20]. and good governance, applying it to resolve conflicts both in the administrative and in the judicial field. Several decisions that use the concept of good governance to control public activity are of special interest [21].

Regarding the European Union, references to the principle of good administration have been found in the case law since the 60`s. It is important to underline the well-known case C-260/90 *Technische University München* v. *Hauptzollamt München-Mitle* (1991) ECR I-546 in which the duty of due care is connected to the right to be heard and to the duty of giving reasons[22].

The first application of the right to good administration as included in the ECFR, was made by the European Court of First Instance in a decision of January 30, 2002. The Court analyses the obligation of the Commission to examine with diligence and impartiality the accusations presented in relation to art. 90.3 of the Treaty[23].

Since then, the EU Courts have used art. 41 several times to control administrative activity[24]. One recent example is the aforementioned decision of the General European Court of the European Union of April 29, 2015, T-217/11, Claire Staelen vs. European Union Ombudsman.

The Role of National Legislation

Although the Spanish constitution does not include the words good administration, as we saw before, the Spanish legislator (eg. 2013 Transparency Act) uses the term good government and the regional legislators have included the right to good administration in the *Estatutos de Autonomía*, Administrative Procedure Acts (e.g. Catalan Act of 2010) and legislation on transparency (e.g. Catalan act of 2014, Ponce, 2013). Iin relation to the Italian case and the role of the legislator, article 1 of the Italian Administrative Procedure Act that provides for administrative activity to be governed by the principles of EU law and therefore makes art. 41 of the Charter applicable in relation to Italian citizens in front of the national public administration (Trimarchi, 2011, 4).

Judicial Protection at the National Level

Moreover, the Charter of Fundamental Rights has been quoted in judgments by the Spanish Constitutional Court (decision 53/2002), the Spanish Supreme Court and the Spanish regional courts. In the two last cases, many judicial decisions allude to art. 41 of the Charter of Fundamental Rights of the European Union in the resolution of strictly internal conflicts and that case law establishes the same standard that the EU level. Actually, EU case law guides the interpretation of Spanish Courts in relation to the right to good administration, according art. 10.2 of the Spanish Constitution and several legal provisions (Spanish Organic Act 2/2008 and Catalan Administrative Procedure Act of 2010, additional clause number 14th).

Most of these Spanish judicial decisions include the reference to the right in a rhetorical way to support the national duty of giving reasons. But some of them are quite interesting because they use the right to good administration to check the fulfillment of the duty of due care or due diligence, analyzing:

(a) The administrative procedure
(b) The record, where all the activities are put down on paper making them "visible"
(c) The final decision itself, and
(d) The grounds that support it.

All of them are elements of a global system with different interactions. And this system is ruled by the idea of consistency, an expression of the principle of rationality. Thus, the documents included in the record (e.g., the answers to comments or observations made by the public), the content of the final decision, and the reasons given must be consistent and follow a rational link (e.g. in the field of rulemaking, decision of the Spanish Supreme Court of July 15, 2010, number of appeal.: 25/2008; in the field of adjudication, decision of the Catalan High Court number. 262 of 2011, March 30)

From that judicial perspective, the record and the reasons stated are similar to the black box in planes, but in relation to administrative procedures: a place where everybody (including the judge in the event of controls) can check what has happened, what was well done, and what was overlooked, or done badly. In other words, officials must prove that good administration has been conducted by means of records kept and reasons given, and this means that public administration has the burden of proof as with regard to good administration (Migliari and Ponce, 2015).

WHAT ARE THE POSSIBILITIES AND LIMITS OF REGULATION OF GOOD ADMINISTRATION BY PUBLIC LAW?

The legal development of the right to good administration could be a good antidote against corruption. If Klitgaard´s corruption formula (Klitgaard, 1998) is

C = M + D – A, or (to put this back into words): "Corruption equals monopoly plus discretion minus accountability."

Then the antidote that we propose is

D+B+T+P or Discretion+good administration+transparency+participation.

In that sense, the obligations of good administration (e.g. due process, duty of giving reasons and duty of due diligence or due care) are linked to transparency (and participation) in the sense that transparency and access to information can help to get a good administration.

But, obviously, the law has its limits. At the end of the day the final decisions are a human responsibility and their quality depends on the quality of who takes the decision. This does not mean that law is irrelevant. Smart regulations can design organizational systems and procedures to back good administration as we will develop immediately.

DEBIASING REGULATORS THROUGH OBLIGATIONS OF GOOD ADMINISTRATION AND JUDICIAL REVIEW

An interesting trend can be identified in relation to avoiding risks of maladministration and corruption: a more sophisticated regulation of procedures and organizations to promote good administration, using scientific developments about the human mind.

Probably, we will be able to rely in the future on cognitive psychology to detect cognitive illusions, structure better the administrative procedure and suggest the proper standard of judicial review in relation to the duty of due care. In that sense, a derivative of good administration, the so called better or smart regulation, is relying more and more on developments in behavioral sciences (especially Psychology and Economics). The combination of law and science in the research for good regulations is opening the door to the *nudging* developments (Thaler & Sunstein, 2009). *Nudging* implies the use of behavioral sciences to improve the effectiveness of regulation. The UK and the US have been very active in this area, creating special units to develop research in the field[25]. Obama's recent executive order of September 2015 ("Using Behavioral Science Insights to Better Serve the American People") is a good example of this trend.

In that sense, one aspect of interest to be developed in the future is the relationship between good administration, administrative procedure and *cognitive limitations* following the latest jurisprudential developments *connecting cognitive psychology and law* (Rachlinski & Farina, 2002). According to some opinions, maladministration and bad administrative decisions could be the result of flaws in human judgment and choice among governmental actors. The core premise of cognitive psychological theory is an understanding that the human brain is a limited information processor that cannot possibly manage successfully all of the stimuli crossing its perceptual threshold. Good decision-making by government officials requires learning to allocate scarce cognitive resources well. This learning is made difficult due to two primary strategies that people (including public officials) use to make the most of their cognitive abilities: mental shortcuts (heuristics) and organizing principles (schemas).

The heuristics consist largely of simple rules of thumb that facilitate rapid, almost reflexive, information processing. Schemas consist of a scripted set of default information and organizational themes that help people focus on the information most likely to be relevant, thereby allowing them to ignore information likely to be irrelevant.

Reliance on heuristics and schemas allows people to process an amazing array of complex stimuli efficiently. Although these devices serve people well most of the time, they can lead to systematic errors in judgment, which psychologists often refer to as "cognitive illusions".[26] Although introducing expertise in decision-making can help to avoid these kinds of cognitive illusions, experts can still fall prey to illusions of judgment. Experts tend to be overconfident about their decisions and to myopically focus on issues within their area of expertise and thereby fail to recognize that a decision would benefit from accessing other bodies of knowledge or ways of thinking.

When decisions are made in an organizational setting institutional design can counter the effect of cognitive limitations. A government that seeks to avoid maladministration and bad decisions must be structured carefully to avoid predictable error in judgment (IP EC, 2017).

For example, public participation and judicial supervision could be useful cures for an administrative authority pursuing its public-interest mandate in good faith, but predictably vulnerable to expert myopia and overconfidence. Serious judicial review of record and reasons forces a public authority to articulate the factors it considers relevant to its decision, engage in some perceptible assessment of alternative courses of action, and respond to meaningful comments by outsiders avoiding undue influence from *lobbies* (Ponce, 2015).

A COMPARISON BETWEEN THE RIGHT TO GOOD ADMINISTRATION AND THE US HARD LOOK DOCTRINE

Finally, that previous point leads us to our last remark. There should be expected in the future an increasing level of judicial review of the duty of due care or due diligence (including regulations) in Europe, to avoid formalistic approaches to the due process, and of the duty of giving reasons, as a way of guaranteeing good administration.

In that sense, the American experience can be of interest in both its positive and negative aspects (Ponce Solé, 2009). Although US public law does not recognize the legal term "good administration", American case law and American jurisprudence use a similar concept when understanding that administrative procedures are important for the quality of decisions.

In the United States, the Administrative Procedure Act (APA) plays an important role, but in relation to informal adjudication procedures, the APA is virtually silent. Informal procedures comprise a high percentage of all administrative procedures; in relation to those procedures, the due process requirements will not work at any time. Its influence depends on the type of decision (it is applied in the case of adjudication not in the case of rule-making), on the existence of entitlement, and on whether life, liberty or property are at stake. But in all cases, the main actor is judicial power because it defines ultimately the standard of review of administrative action. Thus, it has the last word about the level of exigency in relation to the good development of public functions through administrative procedures.

The limits in the review of discretionary powers make administrative procedures important. Courts can defend individual rights and collaborate in good administration without breaching the principle of functional distinction by reviewing administrative procedural aspects.

In that sense, we mentioned at the beginning of this analysis the well-known case *Chevron* of 1984, which has been impacted by the 2024 case *Loper Bright.* This new ruling maintains the importance of the judicial role in ensuring a "reasoned decision-making process", citing the *State Farm* decision of 1983, a leading case that we will consider below.

On the legal level, the APA establishes a procedural framework for federal agencies. In relation especially to rulemaking (but with similar reasoning in the case of formal and informal adjudications), where the discretionary power is wider, case law has expanded the requirements necessary in order to achieve good decisions. Since the 1970s, the courts, even the U.S. Supreme Court, have demanded that agencies act carefully, paying special attention to the relevant factors and interests involved. Case law has established the duty to listen to citizens, the duty to answer their comments by means of a statement of reasons, and the duty to study carefully the regulation before deciding, as a framework for ensuring sound rules (Mathews, 2015)

This judicial approach is known as the "hard look" doctrine (Breyer & Stewart, 1992) Although the expression "hard look" originally meant the careful scrutiny that an agency was expected to give to the issues, today is more commonly used to refer to the detailed and intensive inquiry that the courts often conduct as they review exercises of administrative discretion. The hard look doctrine, also known as the "reasoned decision making" standard is widely employed and shows how in modern American public law "the emphasis on arbitrariness review has shifted towards scrutiny of the *quality of the agency's reasoning*" (Levin & Gellhorn, 2007).

The APA 706 (2) (A) instructs a reviewing court to "hold unlawful…agency action…found to be…arbitrary, capricious, an abuse of discretion…".The arbitrary and capricious standard applies to all agency actions, including all formal adjudications, all informal adjudications and all kind of rulemaking.

In the adjudication sphere, the leading case is Citizens to Preserve Overton Park v. Volpe, 401 US 402 (1971). In that decision, the US Supreme Court held that an informal action, such as the Secretary of Transportation´ highway funding decision, should be based on a consideration of the relevant factors without a clear error of judgment.

In the rule-making field, the leading case is Motor Vehicle Manufacturers Ass´n v. State Farm Mutual Automobile Insurance Co., 463, U.S. 29 (1983), which involved a challenge to a decision by the National Highway Traffic Safety Administration to rescind a rule in which the agency had required every auto maker to include in every car marketed in the US after a specified date one or two safety devices (air bags or automatic seat belts). In this decision, the Supreme Court stated the arbitrary and capricious test in the following manner:

> *"Normally an agency rule would be arbitrary and capricious if the agency has relied on factors which Congress has not intended it to consider, entirely failed to consider an important aspect of the problem, offered an explanation for its*

decision that runs counter to the evidence before the agency, or is so implausible that it could not be ascribed to a difference in view or the product of expertise".

In relation to rule-making, the hard look doctrine is also referred to as the adequate consideration test. Lower courts regularly apply it as the basis for conclusions that an agency rule is arbitrary and capricious because an agency did not consider "adequately" comments critical of its proposed rule, potential alternatives to that rule, and studies inconsistent with the factual predicates for the rule. Since the 1970´s courts have required agencies to include in their statements of basis and purposes detailed discussions of their reasons supporting the exercise of discretion and showing the existence of due care when considering findings and comments submitted during the public hearing provided by article 553 of the APA (Auby & Perraud, 2013).

The *Loper Bright* ruling of 2024, above mentioned, ends the deference that courts were required to show towards administrative agencies' interpretations, as per the *Chevron* case. Despite overturning the deference doctrine, *Loper Bright* emphasizes the need for administrative decisions to result from sound and transparent reasoning. This aligns with the concept of a "reasoned procedure," where agencies are expected to justify their actions based on a careful consideration of relevant factors. *Bright* signals a shift towards more rigorous scrutiny of the quality of administrative reasoning, meaning that courts will more closely monitor the justification and rationality of decisions made by agencies. The ruling does not imply that courts will exercise a full review (*full jurisdiction*) of agency decisions, but they will more closely supervise the arguments and rationality of the decisions taken. This shift towards greater scrutiny of administrative reasoning in the U.S. parallels the trend observed in the European Union regarding the right to good administration, as we will see. In both cases, the aim is to ensure that public decisions are made in an informed, transparent, and responsible manner.

In summary, *Loper Bright* marks a transition from judicial deference towards a more active control of administrative reasoning, where agencies are expected to justify their decisions based on a careful and transparent analysis of relevant factors. This ruling also reinforces the idea that courts have a crucial role in ensuring that administrative power is exercised responsibly and in accordance with the principles of good administration.

SOME FINAL THOUGHTS

After our previous considerations, we cand finish by underlining some final considerations.

In the European arena, future EU case law could build a more specific definition of due diligence or due care, following the US example. However, future EU case law should take into account that judicial pressure has burdened the U.S. administrative law system, as pointed out by many authors. Rules have a high rate of judicial challenges and a high rate of being overturned. Courts are establishing heavy procedural burdens and demanding more than a hundred pages of explanation in order to uphold a rule, changing the meaning of article 553 APA that asks for a "concise general statement of its bases and purposes.

Some voices have emphasized that there is judicial activism and that the necessary self-restraint, which is required by the principle of separation of powers, has disappeared. Several professors claim that judicial review is causing delays and is a waste of time and money, paralyzing public policy in some sectors and threatening public interests like health and environmental protection. This phenomenon is known as ossification or paralysis by analysis (McGarity, 1992, Seidenfeld, 2009). On the other hand, other opinions believe that the benefits of the hard look approach outweigh the costs, although they are not denied. This is the case of Shapiro (2003), who thinks that new judicial requirements have "made rule-making more time-consuming and expensive, but the costs seemed worthwhile not only in terms of democratic benefits but in terms of improving the rationality of outcomes. An administrator faced with meeting judicial demands for transparency and participation will almost automatically end up doing the regulatory cost-benefit analysis demanded by the rationality school"

The U.S. example shows that judicial review is important and necessary to guarantee good administration, but, at the same time, paradoxically, it can be a contributing factor in generating maladministration. Therefore, regarding regulation and judicial review of scope and consequences of procedural defects the virtue lies in the middle.

It is necessary to balance procedural fairness and efficiency, avoiding unnecessary delays and costs but guaranteeing protection and good administration. This should be an important challenge for legislators and courts.

REFERENCES

Addink, G. H. (2014), "Three legal dimensions of good governance. Some recent developments", in CASTRO, A., (Ed.), *Buen Gobierno y Derechos Humanos*, PUCP, available at:

Alexy, R. (1989). *Teoría de la Argumentación Jurídica*. CEC.

Auby, J.-B., & Perroud, T. (2013), "Introduction", in AUBY, J-B and PERROUD, T. (Eds.), *Regulatory Impact Assesment*, INAP, GLP

Benvenuti, F (1952)., "Funzione amministrative, procedimento, proceso", *RTDP*, 1952, ff. 118.

Bonfield, A. E. (1986). *State Administrative Rulemaking*. Little Brown and Company.

Bousta, R. (2013), "Who said There is a "Right to Good Administration? A Critical Analysis of Article 41 of the Charter of Fundamental Rights of the European Union", *European Public Law*, 19, num. 3, p. 481 ff.

Braibant (1970), "CE", 13 November, 1970, Sieur Lambert, *AJDA*, 1971

Breyer, S & Stewart, R. (1992), *Administrative Law and Regulatory Policy: Problems, Text and Cases,* Little Brown & Co Law & Business

Cane, P. (2015): "Records, Reasons and Rationality in Judicial Control of Administrative Power: England, the US and Australia", *Israel Law Review*, volume 48, issue 3, November, pp. 309ff.

Cassese, S. (2009). "Il diritto a la buona amministrazione", *ERPL*, vol. 21, no. 3.

Cassese, S. (2012). New Paths for Administrative Law: A Manifesto. *International Journal of Constitutional Law*, *10*(3), 605.

Cerulli Irelli, V. (1997) "La simplificación de la acción administrativa", *Documentación Administrativa*, n. 248-249, ff 339

Committee of JUSTICE, (1971), Keith Goodfellow, Chairman, *Administration under law*

Committee of JUSTICE, (1988) Patrick Neill Chairman, *Administrative Justice: Some Necessary Reforms*

Craig, P. P. (1994). *Administrative Law* (3rd ed.). Sweet & Maxwell.

Davis, K.C.(1976) *Discretionary Justice. A preliminary Inquiry*, University of Illinois Press, 3rd printing.

Dawnes, G. (2008), “Reasonableness, Proportionality and Merits Review”, Paper delivered to the New South Wales Young Lawyers Public Law CLE Seminar, The Law Society, Sydney 24 September, available at

De Asís Roig, R. (2000). *Las paradojas de los derechos fundamentales como límites al poder.* Google Books. https://books.google.com/books?hl=en&lr=&id=s12WXRoycS0C&oi=fnd&pg=PA6&dq=De+As%C3%ADs+Roig

Downes, G. (2010) “Looking Forward Administrative Decision Making in 2020”, Paper presented to the Australian Corporate Lawyers Association, 2010 Government Law Conference, Canberra, 20 August 2010, available at:

Downes, G. (2011), “Future directions in administrative law: Part 2”, (2011) 67 AIAL FORUM 35, available at

Falzone, g.,(1953), il dovere di buona amministrazione, giuffrè

Elliott, M. J Beatson, & Matthews, M. H. (2011). *Beatson, Matthews, and Elliott’s administrative law : text and materials.* Oxford University Press.

Frug, G. (1984), "The ideology of bureaucracy in American Law", *Harvard Law Review*, vol. 97, p 1312 ff.

Garcia De Enterria, E. (2000), Democracia, Jueces y control de la Administración, Civitas, 5th ed, Civitas

Garcia De Enterria, E., & Fernandez, T. R. (2002). *Curso de Derecho Administrativo* (11th ed., Vol. I).

García, E. (1995). *La lucha contra las inmunidades del poder en el derecho administrativo.*

Giannini, M. S. (1939). *Il potere discrezionale della pubblica amministrazione: concetto e problemi.* Giuffrè.

Gordon, A. (2002). *UK Public Law & European Law. The Dynamics of Legal Integration.* Hart Publishing.

Graaf, K. J. D., Jans, J. H., Marseille, A. T., & Ridder, J. D. (2007). *Quality of Decision-Making in Public Law.* Europa Law Publishing.

Gromitsaris, A. (2007). Administrative law within the Legal System an in Relation to Practice. In Ruffert, M. (Ed.), *The transformation of Administrative Law in Europe.* European Law Publishers.

Hariou (1893), prelude to DE VELASCO´ s book *El acto administrativo*, Madrid, Revista de Derecho Privado

Hauriou. (2025). *La jurisprudence administrative de 1892 à 1929*. Google Books. https://books.google.com/books?hl=en&lr=&id=9BytAAAAMAAJ&oi=fnd&pg=PA1&dq=Hauriou

Harlow, C., & Rawlings, R. (1997). *Law and Administration* (2nd ed.). Butterworths.

Hesse, K. (1983). *Escritos de Derecho Constitucional*. CEC.

Hood, C. & Ruth, A (2015). Government that Worked Better and Cost Less?

Ip, E. C. (2017). Debiasing regulators; The behavioral economics of US Administrative Law. *Common Law World Review*, *46*(3), 171–197.

Isaac, G. (1968), La procédure ad Hood ministrative non contentieuse, Librairie générales de droit et jurisprudence, Paris

JACQUÉ, J-P (2002)., "La protection juridictionnelle des droits fondamentaux dans l'Union européenne". Dialogue entre le juge et le "constituant"", *AJDA,* June.

Klitgaard, R. (1998). *Controlling Corruption*. University of California Press.

Luhmann, N (1969), *Legitimation durch Verfahren*, Neuwied: Luchterhand

Lust, S. (2002) "Administrative Law in Belgium" in RENÉ SEERDEN.F. A. M. STROINK (eds), *Administrative Law of the European Union, Its Member States and the United,* Groningen.

MacMillan. J., (2009) "Can Administrative Law Foster Good Administration?", The Whitmore Lecture, available at: https://www.ombudsman.gov.au/files/16_September_2009_Can_administrative_law_foster_good_administration.pdf

Mathews, J. (2015): "Searching for Proportionality in US Administrative Law", Legal Studies Research Paper number 1-2015, Penn State Law, available at:

Mcgarity, T.O., (1992), *Some Thoughts on "Deossifying" the Rulemaking Process*, 41 Duke L.J. 1385

Migliari, W., & Ponce, J. (2015), "El derecho a una buena administración y su protección judicial. La contribución del Derecho y de los juristas al buen funcionamiento de las instituciones públicas", available at: http://blocs.gencat.cat/blocs/AppPHP/eapc-rcdp/

Millet, (2002) "The Right to Good Administration in European Law", Public Law, summer 2002.

Ponce, J. (Coord.) (2010). *Derecho Administrativo Global*, Marcial Pons, 2010. First pages available at:

Ponce, J. (2013), "Transparencia, innovación y buen gobierno", *Blog de la Revista Catalana de Derecho público*, available at:

Ponce, J. (2015). *Negociación de normas y lobbies.* Thompson Reuters Aranzadi.

Ponce Solé, J. (2001). *Deber de buena administración y derecho al procedimiento administrativo debido.* Lex Nova.

Ponce Solé, J. (2009) "Quality of Decision-Making in Public Law. Right to Good Administration and Duty of Due Care in European Law and in US Law", *European Review of Public Law,* 21_3 (73),

Posada-Carbó, E. (1997). Limits of Power: Elections Under the Conservative Hegemony in Colombia, 1886-1930. *The Hispanic American Historical Review, 77*(2), 245–279.

Prats, J. (2005). *De la burocracia al "management", del "management" a la gobernanza. Las transformaciones de las administraciones públicas de nuestro tiempo.* INAP.

Levin Gellhorn, E., (2007), *Administrative law and process in a nutshell,* 5th Edition

Rachlinski and Farina. (2002). "Cognitive Psychology and Optimal Government Design", 87. *Cornell Law Review*, •••, 549–615. http://library2.lawschool.cornell.edu/facbib/faculty.asp?facid=1

Ranchordas, S., & De Waard, B. (2015): The Judge and the Proportionate Use of Discretion: A Comparative Administrative Law Study, Routledge, 2015

ReNEUAL. (2014), *ReNEUAL model rules 2014*, available at: http://www.reneual.eu/publications/main_publications.html

Schwartz, B. (1984), Administrative Law, 2n Edition, Little, Brown and Company, Toronto and Canada

Seidenfeld, M. (2009). *Why Agencies Act: A Reassessment of the Ossification Critique of Judicial Review.* HeinOnline.

Serio, A. (2008). *Il principio di buona amministrazione procedurale.* Edizioni Scientifiche Italiane.

Shapiro, M. (1990) "Equality and Diversity", *European Review of Public Law*, vol. 11, n 2, summer, ff 400

Shapiro, M. (2003). Trans-Atlantic: Harlow Revisited. In Craig, P., & Rawlings, R. (Eds.), *LAW AND ADMINISTRATION IN EUROPE. ESSAYS IN HONOUR OF CAROL HARLOW, Oxford University Press.*

Stewart, R. B. (1975). The reformation of American Administrative Law. *Harvard Law Review*, *88*(8), •••.

SWEDISH AGENCY FOR PUBLIC MANAGEMENT (STATSKONTORET). (2005): *Principles of Good Administration in the Member States of the European Union*,(https://www.statskontoret.se/upload/Publikationer/2005/200504.pdf)

Thaler, R. H., & Sunstein, C. R. (2009). *Un pequeño empujón (nudge)*. Taurus.

Tolsma. (2007), "How can mediation be implemented in the current administrative decision-making process?", chapter 5 included in Graaf, K. J. D., Jans, J. H., Marseille, A. T. & Ridder, J. D., *Quality of Decision-Making in Public Law.* Groningen, Europa Law Publishing

Trimarchi, M. (2011), "The Impact of Article 41 of the EU Charter of Fundamental Rights on Italian Administrative Law: Some Observations", Ius Publicum, num. 3, available at:

Vedel, G., & Devolvé, P. (1990). *Droit Administratif* (11th ed., Vol. I). PUF.

Woehrling, J. M. (1988). "Le controle jurisdictionnel du pouvouir discretionnaire en France", in VERA PARISIO (Ed.), *Potere discrezionale e controllo giudiziario*, Giuffrè editore, 1998,p. 65 ff.

ENDNOTES

1 Some of the ideas included in this work were previously presented in the book *Preventing Corruption and Promoting Good Government and Public Integrity*, published by Bruylant in 2017 and edited by Professors Cerrillo and Ponce. For this edition, some perspectives have been reformulated, data has been updated, and new considerations related to behavioral insights have been added.

2 In the field of EU Law, see the Recommendation n. R (80) 2, Concerning the Exercise Of Discretionary Powers by Administrative Authorities (Adopted by the Committee of Ministers on 11 March 1980 at the 316th meeting of the Ministry's deputies). In its appendix this Recommendation defines "discretionary power" as a "power which leaves an administrative authority some degree of latitude as regards the decision to be taken, enabling it to choose from among several legally admissible decisions the one which it finds to be the most appropriate".

3 Translation made by the Spanish Ministry of Justice in 2015, available on internet: http://www.mjusticia.gob.es/cs/Satellite/Portal/1292427560225?blobheader=application%2Fpdf&blobheadername1=Content-Disposition&blobheadervalue1=attachment%3B+filename%3DAct_on_the_Jurisdiction_for_Judicial_Review_(Jurisdiccion_Contencioso_Administrativa).PDF

4 This idea may be found in the European context, for example, the Spanish Supreme Court has established in several decisions that when there is discretionary power judicial review cannot change administrative assessment. See, among others, the decision of the Supreme Court of July 24, 1987. The idea is included in article 71.2 of the Act 29/1998 of 13 July regulating the Jurisdiction for Judicial Review: "Judicial authorities may not determine how the precepts of a provision must be worded to replace quashed general provisions and may not determine the discretionary contents of quashed acts "

5 Historically, several scholars have argued in favor of the existence of a *moral* duty of good public behavior (that is the case of PLATO, among others). More recently, the great French scholar HARIOU believed that Public Law had its roots in old *moral* guidelines of good administration which became binding thanks to legal evolution (HARIOU, 1926)

6 Lord MILLET (2002, 310) explains that "By good administration is meant good administrative procedures". We agree with this statement but must add a nuance: good administration means good administrative procedures *and* good reasons to back the final decision, as we will see shortly.

7 See the 2001 European Commission white´s paper on Governance, available at: https://europa.eu/rapid/press-release_DOC-01-10_en.htm

8 As it is known, now it is included in Article 41 of the Charter of Fundamental Rights of Thc Europcan Union

9 Available at: https://www.statskontoret.se/globalassets/publikationer/2000-2005-english/200504.pdf . We will consider again this report later.

10 It mentions nothing about transparency, good faith or unjustifiable failure to exercise powers, besides the problems with its defensive approach, as will shortly be explained.

11 "The Ombudsman: Any citizen of the Union and any natural or legal person residing or having a registered office in a Member State has the right to refer to the Ombudsman of the Union cases of maladministration in the activities of the Community institutions or bodies, with the exception of the Court of Justice and the Court of First Instance acting in their judicial role".

12 In which art. 6 of the European Convention of Human Rights is relevant too.

13 “The provisions of this Charter are addressed to the institutions, bodies, offices and agencies of the Union with due regard for the principle of subsidiarity and to the Member States only when they are implementing Union law. They shall therefore respect the rights, observe the principles and promote the application thereof in accordance with their respective powers and respecting the limits of the powers of the Union as conferred on it in the Treaties”. See for exemple: See judgment of the Court (Grand Chamber) 26 February 2013 In Case C-617/10, judgment of the court (Grand Chamber) 26 February 2013 In Case C-617/10 (“the fundamental rights guaranteed in the legal order of the European Union are applicable in all situations governed by European Union law, but not outside such situations. In this respect the Court has already observed that it has no power to examine the compatibility with the Charter of national legislation lying outside the scope of European Union law”) or judgment of the court (Fourth Chamber) 8 May 2014 In Case C-604/12 (an example of application of the right to good administration to national authorities: “the right to good administration do not preclude a national procedural rule, such as that at issue in the main proceedings, under which an application for subsidiary protection may be considered only after an application for refugee status has been refused”)

14 The core set of principles of good administration in EU member states is the following (p. 71): 1.The principles of lawfulness, non-discrimination, proportionality 2.The right to have ones affairs handled impartially and fairly and 3.Within a reasonable time.4.The right to be heard before any individual measure is taken that would affect the citizen adversely.5.The right to have access to his or her file, regarding any individual measure that would affect him or her.6.The right of access to documents.7.The obligation to state reasons in writing for all decisions.8.The obligation to give an indication of remedies available to all personsconcerned.9.The obligation to notify all persons concerned of a decision.10.The obligation to be service-minded.

15 Id. p. 25, adding that in 1999 the OECD Public Management Committee (PUMA) launched a survey on managing ethics in the public service in all OECD countries. It is perhaps interesting to note that impartiality/neutrality/objectivity was the most frequently stated core public service value in the OECD countries.

16 Associated Provincial Picture Houses Ltd v Wednesbury Corporation [1948] 1 KB 223 at 229 per Lord Greene MR: "It is true that discretion must be exercised reasonably. Now what does that mean? ... [T]here may be something so absurd

that no sensible person could ever dream that it lay within the powers of the authority. Warrington LJ in Short v Poole Corporation gave the example of the red-haired teacher, dismissed because she had red hair. That is unreasonable in one sense. In another sense it is taking into consideration extraneous matters. It is so unreasonable that it might almost be described as being done in bad faith; and, in fact, all these things run into one another."(...)"

17 . *Id.* sec. 9, cl. 3.

18 . Constitución Española de 1978 sec. 9, cl. 3; pt. I, ch. 2, div. 2, sec. 31, cl. 2; pt. IV, sec. 103, cl. 1 (Sp.).

19 81: Article 41(1) of the Charter of Fundamental Rights, which establishes a right to good administration, provides that every person has the right to have his or her affairs handled impartially, fairly and within a reasonable time by the institutions, bodies, offices and agencies of the Union. Article 41(2) of the Charter states that that right includes the right of every person to be heard, before any individual measure which would affect him or her adversely is taken, the right of every person to have access to his or her file, while respecting the legitimate interests of confidentiality and of professional and business secrecy, and the obligation of the administration to give reasons for its decisions. 82: The word 'includes' in that latter provision shows that the right to good administration is not confined to the three abovementioned guarantees. This is also clear from the Explanations relating to the Charter of Fundamental Rights (OJ 2007 C 303, p. 17), according to which Article 41 is based on the existence of the Union as subject to the rule of law whose characteristics were developed in the case-law which enshrined inter alia good administration as a general principle of law. 83: The Explanations relating to the Charter of Fundamental Rights refer in particular to the case-law according to which, where a Union institution has a wide discretion, the review of observance of guarantees conferred by the Union legal order in administrative procedures is of fundamental importance. Those guarantees include respect for the principle of diligence, that is to say, for the competent institution, the obligation to examine carefully and impartially all the relevant elements of the individual case (see, to this effect, judgments of 21 November 1991 in Technische Universität München, C 269/90, ECR, EU:C:1991:438, paragraph 14; 6 November 2008Netherlands v Commission, C 405/07 P, ECR, EU:C:2008:613, paragraph 56; and 9 September 2011Dow AgroSciences and Others v Commission, T 475/07, ECR, EU:T:2011:445, paragraph 154). 84: It should be stated in this regard that compliance with the duty of the competent institution to gather, in a diligent manner, the factual elements necessary for the exercise of its broad discretion

as well as the review thereof by the European Union Courts are all the more important because the exercise of that discretion is only subject to a limited judicial review of the merits, confined to examining whether a manifest error has been committed. Thus, the obligation for the competent institution to examine carefully and impartially all the relevant elements of the individual case is a necessary prerequisite to enable the European Union Courts to ascertain whether the elements of fact and of law on which the exercise of that broad discretion depends were present (see, to this effect, judgments of 15 October 2009 in Enviro Tech (Europe), C 425/08, ECR, EU:C:2009:635, paragraphs 47 and 62; 11 September 2002Pfizer Animal Health v Council, T 13/99, ECR, EU:T:2002:209, paragraphs 166 and 171; and 16 September 2013ATC and Others v Commission, T 333/10, ECR, EU:T:2013:451, paragraph 84)." 20 See decision of September 20, 1997, Case Erstas Aydin and others vs. Turky, or decision of May 2005, case Intiba contra Turquía.

21 This is the case of the decisions Cazja vs. Poland, October 2, 2012, Rysovskyy vs. Ucrania, October 20, 2011, or Öneryildiz vs. Turkey, November 30, 2004. For example, in the first of them the ECHR (paragraph 70) says that: "In examining the conformity of these events with the Convention, the Court reiterates the particular importance of the principle of good governance. It requires that where an issue pertaining to the general interest is at stake, especially when it affects fundamental human rights, including property rights, the public authorities must act promptly and in an appropriate and above all consistent manner (see Beyeler v. Italy [GC], no. 33202/96, § 120, ECHR 2000-I; Öneryıldız v. Turkey [GC], no. 48939/99, § 128, ECHR 2004-XII; Megadat.com S.r.l. v. Moldova, no. 21151/04, § 72, 8 April 2008; and Rysovskyy v. Ukraine, no. 29979/04, § 71, 20 October 2011). It is desirable that public authorities act with the utmost care, in particular when dealing with matters of vital importance to individuals, such as welfare benefits and other such rights. In the present case, the Court considers that having discovered their mistake, the authorities failed in their duty to act speedily and in an appropriate and consistent manner (see Moskal, cited above, § 72)."

22 This decision states that:"13. It must be stated first of all that, since an administrative procedure entailing complex technical evaluations is involved, the Commission must have a power of appraisal in order to be able to fulfil its tasks. 14. However, where the Community institutions have such a power of appraisal, respect for the rights guaranteed by the Community legal order in administrative procedures is of even more fundamental importance. Those guarantees include, in particular, the duty of the competent institution to examine carefully and impartially all the relevant aspects of the individual case,

the right of the person concerned to make his views known and to have an adequately reasoned decision. Only in this way the Court verify whether the factual and legal elements upon which the exercise of the power of appraisal depends were present"

23 Max.mobil Telekommunikation Service GmbH v Commission of the European Communities. This important decision pointed out that: "Since the present action is directed against a measure rejecting a complaint, it must be emphasised at the outset that the diligent and impartial treatment of a complaint is associated with the right to sound administration which is one of the general principles that are observed in a State governed by the rule of law and are common to the constitutional traditions of the Member States. Article 41(1) of the Charter of Fundamental Rights of the European Union proclaimed at Nice on 7 December 2000 (OJ 2000 C 364, p. 1, hereinafter 'the Charter of Fundamental Rights) confirms that '[e]very person has the right to have his or her affairs handled impartially, fairly and within a reasonable time by the institutions and bodies of the Union."

24 According to a limited and not very sophisticated research made at the web page https://eur-lex.europa.eu/, we found 305 judgements, covering from 1960 to 2015, in which the term sound or good administration has been used . This use has increased dramatically in the last years: from 12 decisions in 2011 to 31 in 2015.

25 The Behavioural Insights Team in UK (http://www.behaviouralinsights.co .uk) and the Social and Behavioral Sciences Team in the US. (https://www .whitehouse.gov/sites/default/files/microsites/ostp/sbst_2015_annual_report _final_9_14_15.pdf)

26 I would like to offer just a couple of examples. As a consequence of relay on the "availability heuristic", people often overestimate the frequency of disasters, such as airplane crashes, tend to get extra attention from the news media. Schema also can lead people astray. Due to the so-called "framing effects" people have the tendency to treat potential gains differently from potential losses (and public authorities can prefer one or another option under sanitary emergencies according to these effects).

Chapter 10
Some Paradigm Shifts in Spanish Administrative Law:
Good Administration and its Consequences

Josep Ochoa Monzó
https://orcid.org/0009-0004-4112-0671
University of Alicante, Spain

ABSTRACT

This paper analyses good administration in Spanish law, exploring its development in legislation and some implications. It is assumed that good administration is a new or third generation right, of fundamental right in the European Union. It is a new generation right, whose function is to permeate the functioning of public administrations, and citizens. In construing the right to good administration, we recognize it as a subjective right and we align ourselves is a new or third-generation right. This right has acquired the category of a new generation fundamental right, as stated by the Supreme Court. It is a basic and essential right of citizens, which includes, as a minimum, the right of the individual to have public administrations respond within a reasonable period of time to the requests made to them, responding to them in an explicit, consistent and well-reasoned manner. It is also a cross-cutting right.

DOI: 10.4018/979-8-3373-2332-9.ch010

INTRODUCTION

Administrative Law as a Dynamic Law

In the sphere of Public Law (Administrative Law), several transformations have affected public administration and its role provided for in the Spanish Constitution (EC) of 1978. Since the passing of the constitution, there have been transformations of models or "patterns" that, together with genuine paradigm shifts, have influenced the area: it is within this context that the right to good administration emerges (Ponce 2019). Thus, examples of the latter highlighted in the literature include the control of the inactivity of the Administration in the administrative litigation process, in public procurement and good administration (Gimeno Feliú 2024), in the protection of personal data and its interrelation with the digital society[1] or in urban law[2]. All of these are linked to the way in which the management of matters of general interest is exercised, and the need for democratic legitimization with greater citizen participation, which is enhanced precisely, among other things, by increasing transparency (Blanes Climent, 2016), and by the creation of frameworks or a system of institutional integrity and of ethical public infrastructure in order to have an advanced administrative culture.

It is possible to distinguish between specific regulatory changes or modifications within Administrative Law and more profound transformations that constitute genuine paradigm shifts. This is unsurprising if we assume "there is no static and permanent Administrative Law, but a dynamic, undulating and changing administrative law," (Chaves García, 2021).

However, in relation to the dynamism of Administrative Law and the role of Administration, some modifications go beyond a one-off change in the legal-administrative structures and institutions. Among these, it has been said that Administrative Law must update its scientific system and commit to greater transdisciplinarity, seeking an epistemological and methodological renewal, insofar as globalization and social complexity generate so-called *wicked* problems, whose resolution is not possible with a single approach, demanding multiple perspectives and methodologies drawn from different fields of knowledge.

Paradigm Shifts

The above reflections allow us to affirm that, not only are there specific changes, but there are also more substantial ones what could be described as "paradigm shifts" in Public Law and Administrative Law in Spain, related to good governance and the right of citizens to good administration. We use the expression paradigm not so much in the sense defined by the *Real Academia Española de la Lengua* (RAE) as a variation in the model, example or concrete pattern applied to our discipline, but rather to refer to a mutation in the *theory or set of theories whose central nucleus is accepted without question and which provides the basis and model for solving problems and advancing knowledge*, as espoused in the reflections of Thomas Khunn[3]. Such paradigms are seen as the "universally recognized scientific achievements which, over a period of time, provide models of problems and solutions to a scientific community", as "the whole constellation of beliefs, values, techniques, etc., shared by the members of a given community"[4]. One of them is administrative transparency, which serves to measure the behavior of the administrative system and the necessary adaptation of the public administration to the demands of an advanced democratic society, in which the right to good administration and the democratic principle are integrated, (Barnés, 2019).

Another radical change is linked to good administration, which is taken as one of the greatest examples of a paradigm shift in 21st century administrative law, as noted in outstanding works[5], where the debate is sometimes home to significantly opposing affirmations or opinions. Thus, while some hold that "good administration is an illusion" (Blanes Climent, 2016)[6], this proposition was duly addressed and refuted by Ponce Sole[7], an essential figure in the doctrinal development of the concept, who affirms that there is an "incontestable reality of the principle and right to good administration." Meanwhile, Gómez Díaz (2024) in her *"¿Para qué sirve la buena administración?" (What is good administration for?)* starts by assuming it as a general guideline and stresses the need for it to be imposed on the actions of the public authorities. Vaquer Caballería (2023)[8] assumes that "... the concept of good administration is a general guideline. Although it is already profusely used by legislation and case law, we still have doubts about its legal nature - principle, right or both - and, more importantly, its content and scope: is it only a macro concept integrating the main requirements already in force of the administrative regime in a State governed by the rule of law (such as the hearing of interested parties, the resolution within a reasonable time or the motivation of acts) or is it a mandate for optimizing due administrative diligence, whose potential content is practically unlimited?"

Let us state for now, echoing the Spanish Supreme Court, Judgment of 15 October 2020, as a doctrine of cassation that *the principle of good administration is implicit in the Spanish Constitution (Articles 9.3, 103 and 106), has been enshrined in the Charter of Fundamental Rights of the European Union (Articles 41 and 42), and, according to the best doctrine, constitutes* ***a new paradigm of 21st century law*** *referring to a mode of public action that excludes negligent management and - as this same Chamber has pointed out on previous occasions - does not consist of a pure formula empty of content. Rather, it is imposed on public administrations, such that the set of rights derived from that principle (hearing, timely resolution, motivation,* *efficient, equitable treatment of matters and good faith) has - must have - effective expression and therefore entails a correlative set of duties fully enforceable by the citizen on public bodies".* For Fernández Rodríguez (2021), in this constitutional framework, the right to good administration allows us to glimpse its depth and its long history, as well as its potential for transformation, in which judicial decisions have played an important role. Moreover, in which, despite being to numerous to mention, we must highlight the judgments of the Supreme Court (STS) of 18 December 2019 (appeal number 4442/2018 with cassation doctrine) which states that *"the right to good public administration derives a series of rights of citizens with effective embodiment. It is not, therefore, a mere formula empty of content, but is imposed on public administrations in such a way that these rights are followed by a correlative list of enforceable duties, among which are, of course, the right to effective administrative protection and, in what is of interest here, above all, to an administrative resolution within a reasonable period of time".* A further example is the Judgment of the Supreme Court (STS of 4 November 2021).

SOME EXAMPLES OF PARADIGM SHIFTS IN SPANISH ADMINISTRATIVE LAW

The Quality of Public Services

The idea of paradigm shifts in Administrative Law is not new. As early as 1994, Martín Mateo published in the *Revista de Administración pública* (no. 134, pp. 7-27) an illustrative work entitled "*El sistema administrativo clásico y su permeabilidad a los nuevos paradigmas de la calidad total*" and reflected at an early stage on whether it was possible to incorporate criteria from the private sector into the public administration. He referred to the "total quality" of the service, seen as "a change of mentality of the components of the organisation .... calling for the incorporation of new management systems, receptiveness towards technological progress and the replacement of traditional labor control mechanisms with a human relations policy integrating the workforce," (Martín Mateo, 1994).

Additionally, if there were doubts in the 20th century as to whether the total quality management strategy could be applied to public services, albeit with nuances and adaptations, in 21st century administrative law, the debate has been overcome. There are clear connections between the quality of public services and good administration, in perfectly identified frameworks[9]. The demand for quality in administrative activity has been progressively extended since Royal Decree 951/2005, of 29 July, which established the General Framework for Quality Improvement in the General State Administration, the reference standard, and the generalization of Service or

Quality Charters in Public Administrations, for which a "Common Framework" was drawn up (2015). This seeks continuous improvement of services, with the quality commitments of the services that are managed in response to the needs and expectations of citizens and users; in short, service capability that connects quality with due diligence standards and effective service to citizens, for example, in the face of the digital divide[10] or administrative vulnerability[11].

There is no doubt that good administration, understood as the good performance of administrative functions, entails a concern for the quality of the organization Therefore, the right to good administration does not go beyond the right to legality, but rather forms part of it by demanding quality management, as well as the possibility of a legal reaction against bad administration, (Ponce Solé, 2019). Good administration must be able to consider objective parameters previously set or determined according to certain purposes, where the idea of due diligence or due care can be incorporated, as a mechanism to guarantee good governance and good administration, (Ponce Solé, 2019), which should be extended to good *e-administration* or good digital administration[13], and to the use of artificial intelligence[14].

Technological Innovations and Artificial Intelligence

Another enduring paradigm shift lies in what new technologies can do (or have already done) in administrative law and public administration, which extends to the impact of artificial intelligence (AI). The advent of digital or electronic administration and overcoming paper-based administration is a subject on which there is growing reflection[16], allowing us to speak of *good e-administration*[17].

Classic administrative law has been transformed into an administrative law with an open and diffuse texture (Chaves García 2021), with the undeniable impact of AI. In this context, we already speak with propriety of digital or electronic Administration, both in internal, material or technical, non-formalized administrative activity, and in legal or formalized activity, to create an electronic administration, *e-Administration* and an electronic administrative procedure[18] and the use of artificial intelligence or the use of automated systems for decision making, (Gamero Casado, 2023; Miranzo Díez, 2023). The generalization of digital administration that aspires to abandon the use of paper is another of these paradigm shifts that the Legal System and, evidently, Administrative Law, have been undergoing since Law 30/1992 of 26 November.

In short, we are immersed in a digital society in which the debate on AI and its possible impact of fundamental rights is central, (Presno Linera, 2022). Additionally, the discussion addresses how to define artificial intelligence itself, its risks, how and under what assumptions it acts in order to generate or collaborate in the production of administrative (or judicial) acts and whether a reserve of humanity should be preserved, (Ponce Solé 2023; Miranzo Díez, 2023). In addition, we have the question of the judicial control of automated administrative decisions and/or those adopted with artificial intelligence, with special attention to the discretionary ones[19]. For example, Regulation (EU) 2024/1689 of the European Parliament and of the Council of 13 June 2024 lays down harmonized rules in the field of artificial intelligence and amends Regulations, entailing a new way of thinking and acting in Public Administrations[20]; in short, a new paradigm shift.

Institutional Integrity

Preventing risks of maladministration and corruption is linked to the creation of regulatory frameworks of public or institutional integrity, in which the right to good administration is embedded. Here we have a new public administration, the 21st century one, which places the legal system in a different scenario from that of the Spanish Constitution of 1978. Indeed, there are references to Public Administration (among others, Art. 9, 97, 103, 105 and 106), but these are far from the evident change in Public Law (Administrative Law) today, linked to the amplification of ethics or public integrity, and its multiple connections or derivations in Public Administrations, whether from the international, European or state sphere.

We assume, following the *OECD* (2017), that "public integrity" is the consistent positioning of, and adherence to, common ethical values, as well as to the set of principles and rules aimed at protecting, maintaining and prioritizing the public interest over private ones. Within this framework, there are a number of connections between integrity and public ethics; between ethics and good administration, good government or good governance and in clear relation to the transparency of public activity. Moreover, it has been said that good administration is a prerequisite for ethics, although it does not wholly encompass ethics, without delving into the differences between good government and good administration. This fits with such institutional and procedural designs to guarantee good government, which is not indifferent to Law.

The purpose of these integrity systems or frameworks is to avoid the risks of malpractice and corruption and to foster an ethical climate in the organization, (Villoria Mendieta & Sánchez, 2016). The vocation is holistic and integrates instruments, processes and structures into a global system designed such that each element accommodates and reinforces the others, without forgetting that their ultimate goal is good governance (and therefore good administration), while at the same time providing the law with mechanisms to prevent and combat corruption, allowing the integrity of public administration to be measured.

The evident reinforcement of the creation of these institutional integrity systems is consubstantial with a new administrative culture and the redefinition of public policies and management, i.e. the role of administration and of administrative law itself.

Administrative Transparency

An essential element of integrity frameworks is that they naturally integrate administrative transparency, which is another major change in Spanish law. To speak of transparency (without going into the grammatical definition) is to speak of a multifaceted concept in which a distinction must be made between transparency in the decision, in the procedure (which includes specific procedures with their own substantive nature, such as public procurement) and transparency in the content of the rule and transparency in the exercise of public responsibility. This is undoubtedly linked to the right of access to public information (and to the obligation of active publicity that public administrations have) and to another core element that makes up the so-called "good governance" connected to the values inherent to the principle of good administration and to the logic of a modern administrative law with guarantees.

In Spain, there were no major advances in transparency until the approval of State Law 19/2013, of 9 December, on Transparency, Access to Public Information and Good Governance (LTAIBG), which arrived late compared to the legislative advances that already existed in other countries in our environment and also in some Autonomous Communities. Examples of the latter range from the pioneering Law 4/2006, of 30 June, on Transparency and good practices of the Galician public administration to the modern Law 1/2022, of 13 April, on Transparency and Good Governance of the Valencian Community, which enshrines the transparency of public activity in its dual aspect of active publicity and the right of access to public information. In addition, it contains novel regulations such as algorithmic transparency.

Nonetheless, it was Law 19/2013, of 9 December, which introduced a new paradigm in administrative law, the principle of transparency elevated to the same level as the principle of equality or efficiency, (Fernández Ramos, 2019). This is linked to how administrative activity and the role of the administration itself should be developed, and with a correlative right of citizens to access public information, to a right "to know" what happens within the public authorities, which has sometimes been graphically described as a third-generation right, (Blanes Climent, 2016). It is precisely since the first decade of the 21st century that there has been a genuine regulatory explosion, a paradigm shift in terms of the right of access to public information, of which not even the European Union was unaware (Fernández Ramos 2019). In addition, Spain ratified the Council of Europe Convention on Access to Public Documents in Tromsø on 18 June 2009 (*BOE*, Boletín Oficial del Estado, no. 253, 23 October 2023).

We must leave aside the exact configuration and legal nature of administrative transparency, which has undoubtedly restructured the relationship between the public administration and citizens since the Spanish Constitution of 1978 was approved, even though it is not mentioned in the Constitution. It does connect, however, with certain articles, such as art. 20. 1 d) and art. 105 b) of the Spanish Constitution (SC), which stipulated that a law would regulate the "right of access to administrative archives and registers". It is in art. 105 b) SC where the legislator anchors the right of access to public information and not in art. 20.1 d) where it should be placed according to leading scholars (Rollnert Liern 2014; Cotino Hueso, 2014; Sánchez Ferri 2023). The Supreme Court has argued on several occasions that the right of access to public information is configured in our legal system with a *"broad formulation" both in its recognition and in its legal regulation, which requires a strict interpretation of its limitations (STS of 16 October 2017) "... the right of access to public information enjoys broad recognition in our legal system and that, consequently, any restriction of its effectiveness must be based on a strict interpretation of the limits and expressly and proportionately justify its application. ... "The broad formulation in the recognition and legal regulation of the right of access to information requires a strict, if not restrictive, interpretation of both the limitations to this right contemplated in Article 14.1 of Law 19/2013 and the grounds for refusal of requests for information ... without accepting limitations that entail an unjustified and disproportionate impairment of the right of access to information"*. In the same vein, see the Supreme Court Rulings of 31 May and 2 June 2022.

In short, the legislator chose to assume the right of access to public information, and the right to transparency, as a subjective right of legal configuration, (Martín Delgado, 2019). This is based on the fact that Law 39/2015, of 1 October, in line with the LTAIBG, enshrines a clear principle of transparency in the formalized activity of the administrative procedure, which expressly protects the principle of "transparency and publicity" of the administrative procedure. This principle of transparency is undoubtedly connected with the requirements of good governance and good administration, (Martín Delgado, 2019) and the open government, as will be addressed later.

THE RIGHT TO GOOD ADMINISTRATION AS A MAJOR PARADIGM SHIFT IN SPANISH ADMINISTRATIVE LAW

Previous Ideas

To speak of good administration is to speak of something tangible (Ponce Solé, 2019) in contrast to "maladministration". The former is an "umbrella concept[21]" that encompasses any desired component of administrative activity, superimposed, in fact, on other already existing general rights and principles, such as those of legality, good faith, legal certainty, prohibition of arbitrariness, proportionality, equality, effectiveness, efficiency, good government, good governance, transparency, participation, quality, ethics and integrity. This concept is, however, too broad and somewhat operational if limited to encompassing a set of principles and rights relating to due process. It is necessary to seek a more technical, precise and restricted concept in which the right to good administration applies to the exercise of administrative powers and functions that in fulfilment of their obligations of good administration imply that they should act with the due diligence of a careful public servant.

Good administration is the specific obligation imposed on Public Administrations (and the people who compose them and provide their services therein), to maximize diligence in the exercise of their competences, which means that "such a principle demands, beyond strict compliance with the procedure, the full effectiveness of the guarantees and rights recognized legally and constitutionally and orders those responsible for managing (...), to observe the duty of care and diligence in the exercise of their competences, which means that such a principle demands, beyond strict compliance with the procedure, the full effectiveness of the guarantees and rights recognized legally and constitutionally and orders those responsible for managing (...), to observe the duty of care and diligence in the exercise of their competences.), to observe the duty of care and due diligence to [achieve] its effectiveness and (...) guarantee the necessary legal protection of citizens," (STS of 21/12/2023).

When seeking to understand what good administration entails, it is common to start by considering the meaning of the words that make up this expression, especially in contrast to "bad administration". Thus, it is necessary to explain that "good" should not be linked here to moral aspects or values, but means something "of positive value, in accordance with the qualities that can be attributed to it by its nature", such as something "useful and purposeful for something". Good administration has also been spoken of as "a polymorphic right with four powers which, in nature and structure, is "generic, indefinite and uncertain"[22].

From this point of view, although it has been described as a weak construction, the right to good administration is useful insofar as it is a right that is essentially attached to the way the administrative organization behaves, which is, by definition, evolving and changing. It serves as a basis for measuring the way things are done, where not only the principle of legality matters, but also the very heart of the administrative organization and a duty of conduct in accordance with a predefined standard of quality, (Carrillo Donaire, 2010) or a certain diligence.

Substantial Implications. Good Administration and Open Government

It is worth underlining that good administration is not limited to the rights that directly emanate from Article 41 of the European Charter of Fundamental Rights (2000), which are fundamental rights of the citizens of the European Union[23], in many cases already recognized in the majority of state legislation before their elevation to fundamental rights by Community law. The Charter does assume good administration as a "new right" in terms of its autonomous formulation for the first time in a catalogue of rights, which gives unity to other recognized rights (at national or Community level) and in Community jurisprudence, enshrining the right to good administration as a kind of right-guarantee or instrumental right, which favors the defense of other rights, (Tomás Mallen, 2004). Some of these are included in Law 39/2015, of 1 October or in Law 40/2015, of 1 October, as there is no doubt of the direct relationship with the rights in the administrative procedure, with the qualitative leap given by art. 41 of the European Charter not only from the philological viewpoint, but also by consolidating good administration as more than a mere concept, by including it within the list of fundamental rights, (Martín Retortillo Baquer, 2015).

Transparency and its role in public management connects with a more open administration and, in short, with open government, which is heralded as another paradigm shift. Law 1/2022, of 13 April, of Transparency and Good Governance of the Valencian Community, defines open government as "that which public administrations must promote in order to foster a framework of permanent, two-way relations and dialogue with citizens that guarantees the transparency and accountability of public activity and facilitates citizen participation and collaboration in public policies and management," (art. 2).

Open government is a management model that makes it possible to "open up" the management of public affairs to citizens via the Internet, so that they can, on the one hand, have greater knowledge, information and control over the actions of politicians and public managers, and on the other, intervene, collaborate and participate in this management, thus recovering the proximity between public management and citizens. Therefore, it is not only limited to what is known as e-administration (Blanes Climent 2016); open government or, where appropriate, open administration, is related to how to guarantee principles such as: (a) improving levels of transparency and access to information through the disclosure of public data (to exercise social control and accountability) and the reuse of public sector information (to promote innovation and economic development); b) facilitating citizen participation in the design and implementation of public policies (and influence decision-making); and c) favoring the generation of spaces for collaboration between different actors, particularly between public administrations, civil society and the private sector, to co-design and/or co-produce public value, (Ramírez-Alujas, 2013). Undoubtedly, one of the key aspects of open government, and a necessary one, is transparency in administrative activity, as open government "opens up", offering information to citizens about what it does, how it does it and with what means, (López Pagán, 2016). The commitment to open government seen as a "policy lever," (Moya-Clemente, Ribes-Giner, & Pantoja-Díaz, 2019) also allows for the fulfilment of Sustainable Development Goal (SDG) 16, which refers to the promotion and achievement of just, peaceful and inclusive societies ( ), within a framework that enables the regeneration of public life and the fight against corruption.

Open government seeks to be more transparent, trustworthy, participatory and collaborative (López Pagán 2016), for which it requires the use of information and communication technologies, which is also where the reuse of information and data, public participation -and collaboration- can be found, all thanks to the internet and web 2.0, (Cotino Hueso, 2014). Therefore, transparency, open data, citizen participation and collaboration go hand in hand, (López Pagán, 2016), such that there can be no open government or administration without open, accessible and reusable data. This leads to another paradigm shift that postulates promoting an Administration for data[24]. Such access contributes to the development of the Public Integrity System, strengthening ethical values and mechanisms to bolster the integrity of public institutions, ultimately supporting the overall concept of good administration.

Indeed, according to the OECD (2017), open government is fundamental to building citizen trust and is a key contributor to achieving different policy outcomes in various domains including public sector integrity and anti-corruption, public sector modernization, civic freedom, digital government, public procurement, public sector innovation, public financial management and human resource management.

In short, speaking of open government or open administration signifies another paradigm shift in representative democracy, towards a more conversational and open model of democracy, taking advantage of the possibilities provided by ICTs for citizens to participate in government decision-making processes beyond the exercise of the right to vote or participation in traditional social organizations.

THE LEGAL NATURE OF GOOD ADMINISTRATION

This paper has identified (specific and paradigm) changes in Administrative Law, and it is appropriate to focus now on what the right to good administration means. There are references to this in the doctrine and in some normative regulations[25], to the extent that it has been said that there was a need to address "good administration" from the perspective of administrative law: its meaning, its scope and, above all, the consequences of its legal recognition, (Meilán Gil, 2013). The concern with this issue lies in how public power, or government, is exercised, (Ponce Solé, 2019; Moreno Molina, 2024), or how general interests are managed.

It has conventionally been assumed that the 21st century is the "century of good administration" (Matilla Correa 2018)[26], with many authors making a doctrinal contribution to develop a useful concept, including the pioneering reflections of Ponce Solé (2019), who spoke precisely of the paradigm shift of good administration.

Gómez Díaz (2024) is a powerful exponent of the growing attention to the subject, focusing on a detailed analysis of the most recent jurisprudence, on the basis that "the formula of good administration intuitively contains positive or beneficial values. Nevertheless, it was affirmed that "the right to good administration is not a new right, nor an expression of "quintessence" of the rights it contains, but rather it brings a new dimension, a re-reading of pre-existing rights, giving them a more incisive aspect," (Carrillo Donaire, 2010). This concept has its origin as a counterpoint to the "maladministration" that developed between 1992 and the European Ombudsman's Report (1996), which defined it as "that which occurs when a public entity does not act in accordance with a rule or a principal binding on it," (Sanz Larruga, 2009). The case law clearly indicates that "the right to good administration derives a series of rights of citizens with effective embodiment, as it is not a mere formula empty of content, but is imposed on public relations, so that these rights follow a correlative list of enforceable duties, among which are, of course, the right to effective judicial protection" (among others, STS 3264/2020, 15 October).

With regard to its configuration, it should be noted that good administration is taken as a subjective right, as a value of the legal system and as a principle of administrative action. Importantly, it can also be seen as "an impalpable guideline from which one does not really know what to expect, which can develop in multiple directions and whose content, because it is unpredictable, can be very diverse... it is necessary to see what it consists of and what can be done with it," (Gómez Díaz, 2024).

Indeed, the right to good administration is enshrined in Article 41 of the European Charter of Fundamental Rights and is specified in particular in the following: a) the right of every person to be heard before an individual measure adversely affecting him is taken against him, b) the right of every person to have access to the file concerning him, while respecting the legitimate interests of confidentiality and professional and commercial secrecy; c) the obligation of the administration to give reasons for its decisions. It also includes the right of every person to have the Community make good any damage caused by its institutions or by its servants in the performance of their duties, in accordance with the general principles common to the laws of the Member States.

Additionally, in the "Ibero-American Charter of the Rights and Duties of the Citizen in Relation to Public Administration" (2013), Article 25 states that "citizens are entitled to the fundamental right to good public administration, which consists of ensuring that matters of a public nature are dealt with fairly, justly, objectively and impartially, and that they are resolved within a reasonable period of time in the service of human dignity"[27]. It then goes on to describe a series of guarantees or rights that are of a strong procedural nature[28].

A basic interpretation of Art. 41 of the European Charter makes it clear that its recognition establishes it as a fundamental and instrumental right with respect to other rights held by citizens in their relations with public administrations. This is because good administration includes a list of sub-rights and guarantees that serve from a formal point of view to guarantee other rights and legal situations of the citizen vis-à-vis the Administration, (Lara Ortiz, 2023). As stated by Tomás Mallen (2004), "the right to good administration is configured as a generic right, in turn integrated by other "sub-rights" that correlatively correspond to the obligations of the administrative bodies in this respect, which gives grounds to delimit the scope of the aforementioned constitutional principles of action and functioning of the Public Administration[29].

From this, we can say *prima facie* that there is a clear substantive connection between the right to good administration and, as Barnés (2019) said, the relationship with the democratic principle insofar as the right to good administration is integrated into a set of clearly procedural rights and ultimately of defence[30]. However, this should not involve equating good administration and good government[31], despite the border areas and the relations between ethics and good administration or good government, or good governance[32], or the relationship with the transparency of public activity, to the extent that it has been said that good administration *is a prerequisite* of ethics, although it does not exhaust it[33]. As Ponce[34] highlights, *"the idea of good governance refers to the way in which one part of the executive power, the government, carries out its functions, while good administration refers to the way in which the executive power carries out its administrative tasks, the concepts of maladministration (negligent) and corruption (malicious maladministration) being its opposites".*

Good administration is, secondly, a constitutional value, insofar as it is linked to constitutional legal values, since the EC assumes "freedom, justice, equality and political pluralism" as superior values of its legal system, and, evidently, none of those explicitly affirmed are possible with bad administration.

Thirdly, from the individual's perspective, it is a genuine and authentic subjective public right, from which derive, as recognized by the European Charter of Fundamental Rights, concrete and instrumental rights that define the status of the citizen in their relationship with public administrations, and which are aimed at underlining human dignity[35]. In other words, the expression "good administration" has ceased to be a merely programmatic aspiration to become a fundamental right, in the case of Article 41 of the Charter of Fundamental Rights of the European Union, which has procedural consequences, (Meilán Gil, 2013).

In the Spanish Constitution, the right to good administration is not expressly recognized as a subjective and singular right. However, according to the doctrine, it is included in some constitutional precepts with which it is connected. Nonetheless, the fact that the Magna Carta does not literally include the right or principle of good administration has no negative connotation, (Gómez Díaz, 2024), as some authors have seen that it is implicit in constitutional postulates, as stated in the STS of 15 October 2020, which catalogues it as a new paradigm of 21st century law. Therefore, it has been clearly stated that the right to good administration is "a new subjective right under the sun," (Ponce Solé, 2019) which is not directly enshrined in any state regulation (Laws 39/2015 and 40/2015[36]) but is provided for in certain Organic Laws that have approved diverse Statutes of Autonomy, as well as in other ordinary law.

Indeed, it should be remembered that many Spanish laws have enshrined the right to good administration, (Ponce Solé, 2019)[37], being a category of strong jurisprudential construction, both in Europe and in Spain[38].

In the *Obudsmen's* document-decalogue, which we will quote later, there are precise ideas about what good administration is, stating that:

A) Good administration requires placing citizens at the center of the actions of public administrations, guaranteeing fair and equitable treatment in all their interactions.
B) Good administration also requires that all administrative actions be carried out with due diligence, avoiding dysfunctions, and using resources in an optimal manner to achieve the desired results.
C) Good administration requires transparency in administrative actions and requires citizen participation in decision-making processes. Citizens have the right to relate to the administration in a comprehensible manner, which requires clear and accessible language in regulatory texts, documents and resolutions.
D) Good administration is incompatible with a lack of response (administrative silence), insufficient motivation and administrative inaction.
E) Good administration is essential to foster confidence in public institutions and the proper functioning of the rule of law.
F) Good administration requires the incorporation of technological innovation in order to improve the efficiency and accessibility of public services and the digitalization of the administration.
J) Good governance also needs to harness the benefits of artificial intelligence to improve the quality of public services.

In construing the right to good administration, we recognize it as a subjective right and we align ourselves once more to the words of the *Síndic de Greuges* of the Valencian Community[40] in that the right to good administration is a new or third-generation right. This right has acquired the category of a new generation fundamental right, as stated by the Supreme Court. It is a basic and essential right of citizens, which includes, as a minimum, the right of the individual to have public administrations respond within a reasonable period of time to the requests made to them, responding to them in an explicit, consistent and well-reasoned manner. It is also a cross-cutting right, whose function is to permeate the functioning of public administrations, redefining their relationship with citizens. It imposes additional obligations when addressing and resolving the requests and needs of individuals, thereby facilitating the exercise and satisfaction of their rights, since, as STS 5036/2023 of 17 November states, *the development of the principle of good administration is very strongly articulated on the basis of equity and the justice of the specific case*[41].

We end with Fernández Rodríguez (2021) affirmation that "the procedure, the form, can only be separated from the substance in a conventional way; form and substance are aspects of the same thing, of the same reality, the same thing. Moreover, Gimeno Feliú (2024) holds that "public management in the 21st century must be oriented towards good governance and good administration as a standard for the promotion of different public policies......", with the "right to good governance and good administration being the hallmarks of a democratic public administration at the service of citizens".

CONCLUSIONS

Admitting the paradigm shift that good administration entails, it should be recognized that it is directly linked to the democratic rule of law and strengthens the higher values of the legal system proclaimed in article 1 of the Spanish Constitution, namely, freedom, justice, equality and political pluralism. Additionally, if "the search for the right to good administration, formulated as such in an autonomous manner, in the Spanish Constitution of 1978 constitutes a futile task," (Tomás Mallen, 2004)[42]. We can therefore draw some conclusions:

First

The right to good administration is a subjective public right that entails a legal obligation of the duty of due diligence or due care in considering all the relevant facts in order for Public Administrations to make a decision. It can, in turn, be seen as a general principle of law and as a constitutional value. In any event, it is necessary to characterize the obligation of good administration and the link to the exercise of administrative functions with due diligence and with full submission to the principles of effectiveness and efficiency, in order to distinguish it from other concepts, with which it is often confused and identified, such as good governance or good government.

Second

Good administration is linked to, and forms part of, the framework of institutional integrity or public integrity, which plays an important role as a mechanism or safeguard against bad administration or corrupt practices. Good administration is not only administrative action with respect for certain rights, as is clear from Article 41 of the Charter of Fundamental Rights of the European Union, but it is also an administrative structure and organization that must serve to realize the general interest.

Thirdly

The right to good administration connects with other expressly enshrined rights, such as transparency and the right to public information, the right to participation, and with public ethics, which should not obscure its meaning as a concept *per se,* (Ponce Solé, 2019). It integrates the right to due process, including at least the rights established in Art. 41 of the European Charter of Fundamental Rights.

Fourth

Good administration, related to good governance, has a distinct nature and a different foundation, being enshrined in Spanish laws that proclaim genuine subjective rights. Such rights must be protected by the courts, which directs our attention to the guarantees of good administration, since the legal framework in which it is enshrined is primarily the result of jurisprudential development in both in European and Spanish case law. The national *Ombudsmen* and the European Ombudsman play an essential role in this area.

Fifth

Insofar as good administration must stem from good administrative action, it necessitates obliging and specifying that the administration fulfil legally transcendent parameters that guide its procedures and the scope of its purposes, (Matilla Correa, 2020). Therefore, it would be reasonable for the legislator to seek to define the right to good administration by incorporating due diligence (Ponce Solé, 2019). The above connects good administration with regulatory quality, including the regulatory footprint of both formal and informal activity[43] and with the "right to understand" the administration, i.e. the right to understand all administrative acts and documents.

REFERENCES

Ávila Rodríguez, C. M., & Gutiérrez Rodríguez, F. (Coord.). (2011). *El derecho a una buena administración y la ética pública*. Tirant lo Blanch, València.

Barnés, J. (2019). Buena administración, principio democrático y procedimiento administrativo. *Revista Digital de Derecho Administrativo, 21*, 77–123.

Beltrán Castellanos, J. M. (2024). *La brecha digital en las relaciones de la ciudadanía con las Administraciones Públicas*. Tirant lo Blanch.

Blanes Climent, M. Á. (2016). Transparencia y gobierno abierto. *Cuadernos de Derecho Local, 42*, 147–169.

Bousta, R. (2010). *Essai sur la notion de bonne administration en droit public*. L'Harmattan.

Campos Acuña, M. ª C. (2021). "La proyección de la gestión pública en la "Carta de Derechos Digitales": el derecho a una buena administración digital". *El Consultor de los Ayuntamientos*, 16 July, accessible at https://elconsultor.laley.es/Content/Documento.aspx?params=H4sIAAAAAAAEAMtMSbF1jTAAAkMzE2NjA7Wy1KLizPw8WyMDI0MDc0MzkEBmWqVLfnJIZUGqbVpiTnEqAGoWRSE1AAAAWKE (Accessed 7 July 2025).

Carrillo Donaire, J. A. (2010). *Buena administración, ¿Un principio, un mandato o un derecho subjetivo? Los principios jurídicos del Derecho Administrativo, Santamaría Pastor, J. A. (Dir.)*. La Ley.

Cotino Hueso, L. (2015). *El paradigma del gobierno abierto: retos y oportunidades de la participación, transparencia y colaboración*. Universidad Complutense de Madrid.

Cotino Hueso, L. (2014). El derecho fundamental de acceso a la información pública, la transparencia de los poderes públicos y el Gobierno Abierto. Retos y Oportunidades. In J. Valero Torrijos & M. Fernández Salmerón, *Régimen jurídico de la transparencia del sector público* (pp. 37-71). Navarra: Thomson-Reuters Aranzadi.

Criado Grande, J. I. (Coord.). (2022). *Gobierno abierto, innovación pública y colaboración ciudadana.* Madrid: INAP.

Criado Grande, J. I., & Ruvalcaba Gómez, E. (2016). *¿Qué es y qué se entiende por Gobierno Abierto. Análisis de la percepción e implementación del Gobierno Abierto en el ámbito local español*. Madrid: Novogab, Universidad Autónoma de Madrid.

Chaves García, J. R. (2021). *Derecho Administrativo vivo*, digital edition.

Chica Vélez, S. A., & Salazar Ortiz, C. A. (2021). Posnueva gestión pública, gobernanza e innovación. Tres conceptos en torno a una forma de organización y gestión de lo público. *Opera, 28*, 17–51.

Dodds Berger, A. (2011). Paradigmas del derecho, reflexión y derechos sociales. *Derecho y humanidades, 18*, 99-111.

Fernández Ramos, S. (2019). La transparencia pública: Pasado, presente y futuro. *Revista Aragonesa de Administración Pública, 51*, 213–243.

Fernández Rodríguez, T. R. (2021). Derecho a una buena administración. Una nueva mirada a la administración y el Derecho Administrativo. In J. Ponce Solé, & M. Villoria (Dirs.), *Anuario del buen Gobierno y de la calidad de la regulación* (pp. 81 & ff.).

Gamero Casado, E. (2023). Sistemas automatizados de toma de decisiones en el Derecho Administrativo Español. *Revista General de Derecho Administrativo, 63.*

Gamero Casado, E. (2019). *Actas del XIV Congreso de la Asociación Española de Profesores de Derecho Administrativo*. Madrid, 463-476. https://www.comunidad.madrid/sites/default/files/aud/justicia/eduardo_gamero_mediacion_intrajudicial_1.pdf (Accessed 2 October 2025)

Gimeno Feliú, J. M. (2024). *Hacia una buena administración desde la contratación pública. De la cultura de la burocracia y el precio a la de la estrategia y el valor de los resultados*. Marcial Pons.

Gómez Díaz, A. B. (2024). ¿Para qué sirve la buena administración? Análisis de la reciente jurisprudencia del Tribunal Supremo. *Revista de Administração Pública,* (223), 181–214.

Gutiérrez Rodríguez, F. (Coord.). (2011). *El derecho a una buena administración y la ética pública*. València: Tirant lo Blanch.

Khun, T. (1992). *La estructura de las revoluciones científicas* (Original work published 1961).

Lara Ortiz, M.ª L. (2023). Buena administración para la efectividad de los derechos sociales. *Revista de Derecho Administrativo*, (22), 38.

Litago Lledó, Rosa (20924*), La revisión jurisdiccional de la inactividad de la administración tributaria conforme a los principios de tutela judicial efectiva y buena administración,* Aranzadi.

López Pagán, J. (2016). Gobierno abierto y transparencia frente a la corrupción en el ámbito local. En VV. AA., *La corrupción en España. Ámbitos, causas y remedios jurídicos* (pp. 365–387).

Malaret, E. (2017). Bon govern, transparència i rendició de comptes. Reforçant i completant la legitimitat democràtica dels poders públics. *Revista Catalana de Dret Públic*, (55), 23–47.

Marín Gallego, J. D. (2007). Del concepto de paradigma en Thomas Kuhn, a los paradigmas de las ciencias de la cultura. *Magistro, 1*, 73–88.

Martín Delgado, I. (Dir.). (2019). *Transparencia y acceso a la información pública: de la teoría a la práctica*. Iustel.

Martínez Gutiérrez, R. (2023). Reforma para una Administración de datos. *Revista Catalana de Dret Públic*, (67), 67–81.

Martín Mateo, R. (1994). El sistema administrativo clásico y su permeabilidad a los nuevos paradigmas de la calidad total. *Revista de Administração Pública*, (134), 7–27.

Martín-Retortillo Baquer, L. (2015). La Carta Europea, el derecho a una buena administración y el procedimiento administrativo. In M. Rebollo Puig, M. López Benítez & E. Carbonell Porras (Coords.), *Régimen jurídico básico de las Administraciones Públicas. Libro homenaje al Profesor Luis Cosculluela* (pp. 135–150). Iustel.

Matilla Correa, A. (2023). Sobre la idea jurídica de buena administración. In J. Ponce Solé & M. Villoria Mendieta (Dirs.), *Anuario del buen gobierno y de la calidad de la regulación*. Fundación Democracia y Gobierno Local.

Matilla Correa, A. (2020). *La buena administración como noción jurídico-administrativa*. Dykinson.

Matilla Correa, A. (2018). La buena administración como principio jurídico: Una aproximación conceptual. *Revista de Derecho en Acción*, (19), 110–160.

Meilán Gil, J. L. (2013). El paradigma de la buena Administración. *AFDUC*, (17), 233–258.

Menéndez Sebastián, E. M. (2021). *De la función consultiva clásica a la buena administración. Evolución en el Estado social y democrático de Derecho*. Marcial Pons.

Menéndez Sebastián, E. M. (2019). Función consultiva y tutela administrativa efectiva: Procedimiento administrativo y buena administración. *Revista Española de la Función Consultiva*, (32), 105–126.

Miranzo Díez, J. (2023). *Inteligencia artificial y Derecho Administrativo*. Tecnos.

Moreno Molina, J. A. (2024). El derecho a una buena administración. *Lección inaugural del solemne acto de apertura del Curso Académico 2022/2023 de la Universidad de Castilla-La Mancha.* https://prodigital.web.uclm.es/wp-content/uploads/2024/03/LIBRO-DCHO-BUENA-ADMINISTRACION-1.pdf

Nogueira López, A. (2023). Una Administración para el 99 %. Reforma administrativa para la igualdad real. *Revista Catalana de Dret Públic*, (67), 18–35.

Palomar Olmeda, A. (1995). La utilización de las nuevas tecnologías en la actuación administrativa. *Revista Española de Derecho Administrativo*, (87), 361–384.

Pinazo Hernandis, J. (2013). *Administración Pública y Gobernabilidad. De los orígenes a los nuevos paradigmas.* València.

Ponce Solé, J. (2023). Seres humanos e inteligencia artificial: discrecionalidad artificial, reserva de humanidad y supervisión humana. In *E. Gamero Casado (Dir.) & F. L. Pérez Guerrero (Coord.), Inteligencia artificial y sector público. Retos, límites y medios* (pp. 195–253). Tirant lo Blanch.

Ponce Solé, J. (2019). Inteligencia artificial, Derecho administrativo y reserva de humanidad: algoritmos y procedimiento administrativo debido tecnológico. *Revista General de Derecho Administrativo*, (50).

Ponce Solé, J. (2001). *Deber de buena administración y derecho al procedimiento administrativo debido. Las bases constitucionales del procedimiento administrativo y del ejercicio de la discrecionalidad.* Lex Nova.

Presno Linera, M. Á. (2022). *Derechos fundamentales e inteligencia artificial.* Marcial Pons.

Ramírez-Alujas, Á. (2014). Gobierno abierto. *Eunomía. Revista en Cultura de la Legalidad*, (5).

Razquín Lizárraga, M. (2024), "La gobernanza de la IA", en *Derecho Digital e Innovación. Digital Law and Innovation Review*, nº. 21 (julio-septiembre).

Rodríguez Arana, J. (2012). *El ciudadano y el poder público. El principio y el derecho al buen gobierno y la buena administración.* Reus.

Rollnert Liern, G. (2014). El derecho de acceso a la información pública como derecho fundamental: Una valoración del debate doctrinal a propósito de la ley de transparencia. *Teoría y Realidad Constitucional*, (34), 349–368.

Sánchez Acevedo, M. E. (2015). *El derecho a la buena administración electrónica* (Doctoral Thesis, Universitat de València). Cotino Hueso, L. (Dir.). https://roderic.uv.es/rest/api/core/bitstreams/4cbe8ac2-f9eb-49c2-b5ee-70ae9b4dfbf0/content

Sánchez Ferri, R. (2023). La transparencia como derecho deber y sus relaciones con el derecho fundamental a ser informado. De nuevo, discrepando. [UNED]. *Teoría y Realidad Constitucional*, (51), 159–186.

Sánchez Vázquez, R. (Coord.). (2024). *Los paradigmas del Derecho*. València: Tirant lo Blanch.

Sanz Larruga, F. J. (2009). El Ordenamiento europeo. El Derecho Administrativo español y el derecho a una buena administración. [AFDUDC]. *Anuario da Facultade de Dereito da Universidade da Coruña*, (13), 729–751.

Sarasíbar Iriarte, M. (2023). *La integración de la Inteligencia Artificial en la Administración Pública. Derecho Digital e Innovación. Digital Law and Innovation Review, (17)*. July–September.

Tomás Mallen, B. (2004). *El derecho fundamental a una buena administración*. INAP.

Valero Torrijos, J. (2019). Las garantías jurídicas de la inteligencia artificial en la actividad administrativa desde la perspectiva de la buena administración. *Revista Catalana de Dret Públic*, (58), 82–96.

Vaquer Caballería, M. (2023). The humanism of contemporary administrative law. *Revista de Administração Pública*, (222), 33–64.

Villoria Mendieta, M., & Izquierdo Sánchez, A. (2016). *Public Ethics and Good Governance*. Tecnos.

Zapata Sevilla, J. (2024). The right to good administration: A developing right in EU and Spanish law. *Revista de Estudios Europeos*, (83), 395–427.

ENDNOTES

1 This is the title of the doctoral thesis of Domínguez Álvares, José Luis (2022), supervised by Fernando Pablo, Marcos, available at https://gredos.usal.es/bitstream/handle/10366/152599/PDAHJES_DominguezAlvarezJL_Datos.pdf?sequence=1&isAllowed=y(Accessed 2 October 2025).

2 Martín Valdivia, Salvador María, (2022), (Dir.), Un nuevo paradigma en el urbanismo andaluz. Análisis de la Ley 7/2021, de Impulso para la Sostenibilidad del Territorio en Andalucía), Thomson-Reuters.

3 In *La Estructura de las Revoluciones Científicas*, 1961, translated into Spanish in 1992. Although it was sometimes criticised, for example, an analysis can be

found at Marín Gallego, José Duván (2007). Sánchez Váquez, Rafael (Coord.), (2024).

4 For Dodds Berger (2011).

5 Vid. among the most recent Gimeno Feliú, José María (2024) on p. 58 will say that "in the 21st century the function of public law and public procurement (increasingly globalised) must be based on the pillar of good administration". Ponce Solé, Juli (2024b). Likewise, the excellent reflections of Litago Lledó (2024), in the case of tax administration, where there are many judicial decisions on good administration. In this sector, where the consolidation of the right to good administration has been key from the jurisprudential point of view, vid. *La proyección de la buena administración sobre los procedimientos de aplicación de los tributos*, Luchena Mozo, Gracia María and Sánchez López, María Esther (2023), (Dir.), Tirant lo Blanch. As for the jurisprudential analysis (Gómez Díaz, 2024).

6 https://www.hayderecho.com/2024/05/23/buena-administracion-ilusion/ (Accessed 6 July 2025).

7 https://www.hayderecho.com/author/juli-ponce/ (Accessed 2 October 2025).

8 Vaquer Caballería, Marcos, (2023), "El humanismo del derecho administrativo de nuestro tiempo", *Revista de Administración Pública*, núm. 222, 33-64.

9 Sánchez Blanco, Ángel, "Marcos de mejora de la calidad de las administraciones públicas", in Ávila Rodríguez and Gutiérrez Rodríguez (cit., pp.107 ff.).

10 See the work of Beltrán Castellanos (2024) who on p. 229 attributes this quality or "principle of quality" to the performance of the administration with electronic means. The same author assumes on p. 251 that the new paradigm of Administrative Law in the 21st century is good administration and public ethics. Good administration, in which, he continues, "citizens' access the Administration, must be clear, simple and close".

11 Nogueira López, Alba, (2023).

12 I refer to Gómez Díaz (2024).

13 See the thesis of Sánchez Acevedo, Marcos Emilio, (2015). The subject has its own derivations and substantivity, among others, if it is connected with the *Charter of Digital Rights*, which is *soft law*, as is well known. Thus, section XVIII Digital rights of citizens in their relations with public administrations. Campos Acuña, M.ª Concepción, (2021), De La Sierra Morón, Susana, "Una

introducción a la Carta de derechos digitales", in Cotino Hueso, Lorenzo (2022), *La Carta de Derechos Digitales, (*Coord.), Tirant lo Blanch, pp. 27-52.

14 Ponce (2024 b), and Razquín Lizarraga (2024).

15 I take part of the following reflections from my monograph *Administración digital y derechos lingüísticos* (2024).

16 Vestri, Gabriele (2024). *La inteligencia artificial en el sector público. Retos pendientes,* El Consultor de los Ayuntamientos, or the open text *Inteligencia artificial y Una visión comparada in Cerrillo i Martínez, Agustí; Di Lascio, Francesca; Martín Delgado, Isaac and Velasco Rico, Clara I. (Directors), (2024), Inteligencia artificial y Administraciones Públicas: una triple visión en clave comparada,* Iustel, accessible at https://www.iustel.com/editorial/90024094-IA-y-Administraciones-Públicas.pdf. (Accessed 3 July 2025).

17 This expression is in the prologue (p. 9) that Rodríguez Arana makes to the work of Miranzo Díez (2023), where we also read that "as a consequence of scientific advances, a new public administration appears before us all as a result of the rise of new technologies, more transparent, more participatory and closer to a new digital citizenship... An Administration that must be more focused on human dignity and the fundamental rights deriving from it". Valero Torrijos (2019) speaks of "the legal guarantees of artificial intelligence in administrative activity from the perspective of good administration". And Razquin (2024) in a specialised journal with interesting contributions. Other connections are in Ponce (2019: 169 et seq.), who also speaks of a paradigm shift towards the prevention of corruption risks, where technology can provide a remarkable element of effectiveness, in which the role of information technologies can be an essential aid to good administration.

18 Delving into this distinction is unnecessary here. I adopt the consolidated distinction already made by Palomar Olmeda (1995: 361).

19 Ponce Sole, Juli (2024 a).

20 Among others Sarasíbar Iriarte, Míren, (2023). It is essential to read, among others, the monographic issue 34 of the *Revista de Privacidad y Derecho Digital*, May-August 2024, accessible at https://www.rdu.es/articulos/libro/LIB-MON-REG-IA(Accessed 2 October 2025).

21 Menéndez Sebastian (2019: 112), speaks of the concept of "coat hanger".

22 All expressions in quotation marks are quoted from Carrillo Donaire (2010).

[23] Among others, Martín Retortillo, Lorenzo, "de los derechos humanos a una buena administración", in Ávila Rodríguez and Gutiérrez Rodríguez (2011). https://www.europarl.europa.eu/charter/pdf/text_es.pdf

[24] Martínez Gutiérrez (2023).

[25] See those cited by Moreno Molina (2022: 17), when distinguishing good administration from good government and governance. Also, Matilla Correa (2023: 70). The bibliography is abundant, with *ad hoc* studies on occasion, as in the case of Lara Ortiz, M.ª Lidón, (2023).

[26] Cassesse (2009), in his work "Il diritto a la buona amministrazione", *European Review of public Law*, no. 3.

[27] In Latin America, there are interesting works that we can only mention briefly. In Chile, Linazasoro Espinoza, Izaskun (2020), for the case of Chile. In Colombia, Esned Diaz Perilla, Viviana and Valencia Tello, Diana Carolina, (2023), *El derecho a la buena administración pública. Reflexiones para la construcción de un nuevo derecho administrativo de cara al ciudadano,* Tirant lo Blanch. In Mexico in Arroyo Cisneros, Edgar Alán (2017), "El derecho a una buena administración como principio constitucional y deber del Estado: el caso de la Constitución de la Ciudad de México", in *XXII Congreso Internacional del CLAD sobre la Reforma del Estado y de la Administración Pública, Madrid, Spain, 14 - 17 Nov. 2017.* For an analysis of Ibero-America, see also Ponce (2016 b): 234 et seq.

[28] In our case, those included in Law 39/2015, of 1 October, or in Law 40/2015. In addition to sectoral regulations such as the LTAIBG, among others.

[29] These include the right to a hearing and participation in the drafting of administrative provisions and acts, the right of access to administrative archives and records, the right to impartial, fair and reasoned administrative action and carried out within a reasonable period of time. For an analysis, see also Zapata Sevilla (2024). and Martín Retortillo (2015). Other succinct reflections can be found in Baena Del Alcázar, Manuel, "Sobre la idea europea de "buena administración", *Noticias de la Unión Europea*, nº 247-248, 2005, pp. 61-66.

[30] Barnés (2019). An example of this is in the case law itself when analysing the consequences for the administrative decision regarding the duty of good administration and the duty of diligence, the duty to resolve within a reasonable period of time or due process and linked to this the possible lack of defence, or the expiry of time, which is analysed by Gómez Diez (2024), among others.

31 Paraphrasing NIETO, in his famous *La organización del desgobierno*, we can assume that there is no "good government without good administration". On the differences between "good government" and "good administration", among others Meilán Gil (2013). See Malaret (2017).

32 It is almost impossible to refer to the abundant doctrine, apart from that cited by Gómez Díaz (2024). We refer, among others, to Rodríguez Arana, Jaime, "Sobre la ética en la Administración Pública", *Actualidad Administrativa*, no. 21-22, 1995. By the same author *El ciudadano y el poder público: el principio y el derecho al buen gobierno y la buena administración*, Reus, Madrid, 2012. González Pérez, Jesús, *Corrupción, ética y moral en las Administraciones Públicas*, Thomson-Reuters, Civitas, Cizur Menor, 2nd edition, 2014. Villoria Mendieta, Manuel and Izquierdo Sánchez, Agustín, (2016). See also the monograph in *Dilemata. International Journal of Applied Ethics*, No. 27, 2018: *El buen gobierno y la transparencia, a caballo entre la Ética y el Derecho.*

33 Ponce (2015).

34 Ponce, "La discrecionalidad no puede ser arbitrariedad y debe ser buena administración", in *Revista Española de Derecho Administrativo*, no. 175, 2016, p. 65. However, the subject is well known and extensively dealt with in the doctrine, for example, Rodríguez Arana, Jaime, "El derecho fundamental a la buena administración en la Constitución Española y en la Unión Europea", in *Revista Galega de Administración Pública*, no. 40, 2010, p. 253-264. Meilán IL, José Luis, "La buena administración como institución jurídica", in *Revista Andaluza de Administración Pública*, no. 87, 2013, pp. 13-50. Malaret, Elisenda (2017).

35 I take the long quotation from Fernández Ruiz, Jorge, in "Inserción del principio de buena administración en la nómina de derechos fundamentales", in *Paradigmas*, cit.

36 For Gómez Díaz (2024: 191) it seems reasonable to assume the hypothesis that this silence is not so much due to ignorance, but to the fact that the drafters of both laws considered it unnecessary, since the rights arising from the right to good administration were already enshrined.

37 Among the authors we follow, Sanz Larruga (2009: 738) indeed speaks of a "new right" when talking about good administration.

38 Ponce Solé (2019: 89), and on jurisprudence, Gómez Díaz (2024). Or once again Ponce and Cuerdo Blas, Jesús, in the aforementioned *Anuario de Buen*

Gobierno 2023, p. 239 et seq. Also earlier in Carrillo Donaire (2010: 1139 et seq.).

39 Sanz Larruga (2009).

40 In the Report of the *Síndic de Greuges de la Comunitat València* of 2023, violation of the right to good administration is introduced for the first time as a complaint procedure (p. 137 ff.). Moreover, in the "General considerations on the situation of the Catalan Ombudsman's rights and actions", the institution's position on the right to good administration has already been developed, where we can read "...". https://www.elsindic.com/wp-content/uploads/2024/03/Informe-anual-2023_CASTELLANO_AL.pdf (Accessed July 6, 2025).

41 Vid. the "Conclusions of the Meeting of Autonomous Ombudsmen", held in June 2024 in Alicante, under the slogan *The work of the Ombudsman's Offices in the promotion of good administration.* This work has been added to the XXXVII Conference on Coordination of Ombudsman's Offices held on 29 and 30 October in Vitoria-Gasteiz under the title *The work of the Ombudsman's Offices in promoting the right to good administration*, which has given rise to an accessible Decalogue, as well as the document that follows, at https://www.ararteko.eus/es/xxxvii-jornadas-de-coordinacion-de-defensorias-del-pueblo(Accessed 2 October 2025).

42 It is a recurrent assertion in the doctrine, among others, Ruiz-Rico Ruiz, "El derecho a una buena administración: dimensión constitucional y estatutaria", in Ávila Rodríguez and Gutiérrez Rodríguez (2011: 55).

43 I also follow in part, by courtesy of its author, Ponce Solé, the work "Documento de bases para una futura ley de buena administración de la Comunitat Valenciana", presented at the *II Encuentro de la II Encuentro de la Red Española de Cátedras de Transparencia e Institutos Universitarios de Gobierno Abierto* (University of Alicante, 24 May 2024).

Chapter 11
The Impact of Artificial Intelligence on the Development of Strategies and Policies in the Field of Education

Dimitrios Liovas
https://orcid.org/0009-0002-4156-9810
University of Alicante, Spain

ABSTRACT

Artificial Intelligence (AI) has begun to significantly influence the shaping of strategies and policies in the field of education, offering new opportunities and challenges. One of the main impacts of AI is its ability to enable personalized learning. Through adaptive learning systems, AI can analyze the needs and abilities of each student, providing tailored educational material and support. This not only improves educational outcomes but also helps reduce inequalities, as students with different skill levels can progress at their own pace. Moreover, AI assists in improving the management of educational institutions. By automating tasks such as grading, attendance tracking, and resource management, educators can focus more on teaching and creating quality educational experiences. At the same time, AI can be used to predict trends and analyze data, helping schools and policymakers make informed decisions about resource allocation and the development of new curricula.

DOI: 10.4018/979-8-3373-2332-9.ch011

INTRODUCTION

Artificial Intelligence (AI) has emerged as a transformative force in the field of education, fundamentally reshaping how knowledge is delivered, accessed, and governed. Initially introduced through narrow applications such as automated grading systems and intelligent tutoring platforms, AI has evolved into a complex ecosystem of technologies capable of influencing strategic decisions, institutional planning, and policy formulation. Its core functionalities—machine learning, natural language processing, predictive analytics, and adaptive algorithms—enable the analysis of vast datasets to identify patterns and generate insights that inform both micro- and macro-level educational practices (Zawacki-Richter et al., 2019; Holmes et al., 2019). AI not only enhances administrative efficiency and pedagogical innovation but also introduces new modes of personalized and data-driven learning tailored to individual needs and trajectories (Luckin et al., 2016; Chen et al., 2020). The relevance of investigating AI in education lies in its dual capacity to offer unprecedented opportunities for educational advancement while simultaneously posing ethical, social, and governance-related challenges. As governments, international organizations, and institutions increasingly integrate AI technologies into their strategic agendas, it becomes imperative to critically assess how these systems affect issues of equity, access, accountability, and human agency in educational contexts (UNESCO, 2021; Selwyn, 2019). A nuanced understanding of AI's implications is therefore essential not only for maximizing its benefits but also for safeguarding democratic and inclusive educational values in the face of rapid digital transformation.

The purpose of this chapter is to critically examine the multifaceted impact of Artificial Intelligence (AI) on the development of strategies and policies within the educational sector. In doing so, the chapter seeks to provide an integrative framework that connects the technological capacities of AI with broader questions of educational governance, policy innovation, and ethical responsibility. The central aim is not merely to document technological change but to interrogate how AI is embedded within institutional practices and policy discourses, and how it reconfigures power relations, decision-making processes, and pedagogical norms. To guide this inquiry, the chapter is structured around several key research questions:

(1) In what ways is AI currently being utilized to inform and shape educational strategies at institutional, national, and international levels?
(2) What are the potential benefits and risks associated with the integration of AI in educational policy development?
(3) How do ethical, political, and socio-economic considerations influence the implementation and governance of AI in education?

(4) What frameworks or mechanisms exist—or should be developed—to ensure that AI technologies contribute to inclusive, equitable, and democratic education systems?

In addressing these questions, the chapter is organized into seven interrelated sections. Following the introduction, the second section provides an overview of the evolution and current applications of AI in educational contexts. The third section explores the opportunities and innovations introduced by AI, particularly in relation to personalization and institutional efficiency. The fourth section discusses the ethical challenges and risks posed by AI technologies. The fifth section delves into the role of AI in strategic planning and policy-making, with an emphasis on stakeholder engagement and methodological triangulation. The sixth section addresses AI's potential to foster global collaboration and intercultural learning. Finally, the chapter concludes with a synthesis of key findings and proposes recommendations for responsible and impactful integration of AI in educational policy.

THE LANDSCAPE AND EVOLUTION OF AI IN EDUCATION

The integration of Artificial Intelligence (AI) into educational settings has followed a gradual but transformative trajectory, evolving from discrete operational tools to broader instruments of strategic governance and policy development. Early implementations of AI in education were predominantly focused on automating routine tasks and enhancing instructional delivery. Technologies such as computer-assisted instruction, automated grading systems, and rule-based tutoring engines were designed to increase efficiency and reduce administrative burdens, offering educators time-saving mechanisms for assessment and content management (Roll & Wylie, 2016; Luckin et al., 2016). These applications, while functionally limited, laid the groundwork for more sophisticated AI systems that emerged with advances in machine learning and natural language processing. Over time, AI's role expanded beyond classroom-level functions to more systemic applications, including data analytics for institutional planning, predictive modeling for student retention, and algorithmic insights for curriculum reform (Chen et al., 2020; Baker & Smith, 2019). This transition from operational support to strategic influence has been marked by the growing use of AI to inform high-level decision-making processes within ministries of education, regional authorities, and international policy bodies. AI-powered platforms now contribute to evidence-based policymaking by analyzing large-scale educational data, forecasting trends, and simulating the potential outcomes of various policy interventions (UNESCO, 2021; Zawacki-Richter et al., 2019). As a result, AI has shifted from being a back-end utility to a front-line actor in shaping the goals, structures, and equity considerations of contemporary education systems. This evolving landscape necessitates a critical examination of not only the technical capabilities of AI but also its governance, ethical orientation, and alignment with the broader public interest in education.

International organizations have played a pivotal role in shaping the normative, strategic, and ethical contours of Artificial Intelligence (AI) integration in education. Bodies such as UNESCO, the OECD, and the European Commission have not only issued technical guidelines but also contributed to framing global discourses around the responsible and equitable use of AI in educational systems. UNESCO, for instance, has been at the forefront of promoting a human-centered approach to AI, most notably through its Recommendation on the Ethics of Artificial Intelligence (2021), which establishes a global standard emphasizing transparency, inclusivity, and sustainability in AI deployment across sectors, including education. Its complementary report AI and Education: Guidance for Policy-makers (2021) offers specific strategies to member states for integrating AI into curricula, teacher training, and policy design, while stressing the need for data governance and the protection of human rights in digital learning environments. Similarly, the OECD has advanced an agenda centered on AI's implications for skills development, workforce readiness, and institutional innovation. The AI and the Future of Skills initiative frames AI as both a challenge and an enabler of lifelong learning, advocating for agile policy mechanisms and evidence-based approaches to align educational outcomes with emerging labor market demands (OECD, 2021). The European Commission, through its White Paper on Artificial Intelligence (2020) and the Digital Education Action Plan, has emphasized a "trustworthy AI" model grounded in ethical AI ecosystems, digital infrastructure investment, and the upskilling of educators and learners. These organizations collectively contribute to a multilateral governance architecture that promotes convergence around shared values, while also recognizing the necessity of local contextualization.

Emerging trends in AI policy and governance reflect a growing recognition that technical advancement alone is insufficient to ensure equitable and sustainable educational transformation. Among these trends is the movement toward regulatory clarity and ethical standardization, as evidenced by proposals such as the European Union's AI Act, which seeks to classify AI applications by risk level and mandate corresponding safeguards in sensitive areas like education. There is also an increasing emphasis on participatory governance, where educators, students, civil society actors, and technical experts are involved in shaping AI-related policies to avoid top-down impositions and algorithmic opacity. Another significant development is the push toward open and interoperable AI systems that prevent vendor lock-in and support transparency in educational data flows. Furthermore, the convergence of AI with other data-driven technologies, such as learning analytics and biometric systems, has heightened the urgency for cross-sectoral data governance frameworks. These trends underscore the shift from viewing AI solely as a technological instrument to understanding it as a sociotechnical assemblage that demands interdisciplinary scrutiny, democratic oversight, and long-term policy foresight. The growing involvement of supranational actors in articulating ethical AI principles signals not only the global nature of AI's educational impact but also the shared responsibility for steering its development in line with public interest and social justice goals.

INNOVATIONS AND OPPORTUNITIES

The integration of Artificial Intelligence (AI) into education has ushered in a paradigm shift toward personalization, transforming both pedagogical practices and institutional processes. One of the most widely discussed innovations is the rise of adaptive learning systems, which leverage AI algorithms to deliver tailored educational experiences based on individual learner profiles. These systems dynamically adjust content, pacing, and feedback by analyzing real-time performance data, cognitive patterns, and learning preferences (Luckin et al., 2016; Holmes et al., 2019). This level of customization enables learners to engage with material at their own pace, receive targeted interventions when difficulties arise, and build competencies in a more self-directed manner. AI-powered platforms such as Knewton, Squirrel AI, or Century Tech exemplify how data-driven instructional models can shift the focus from standardized curricula to learner-centered pathways. Such systems have proven particularly beneficial in supporting students with diverse needs, linguistic backgrounds, or learning disabilities, offering differentiated instruction that would be challenging to achieve in traditional, one-size-fits-all environments (Chen et al., 2020). Moreover, the deployment of virtual tutors, chatbots, and natural language processing tools enhances engagement outside formal classroom settings, allowing students to access assistance, review content, or explore supplementary material autonomously. These innovations not only democratize access to learning but also contribute to cultivating skills such as metacognition and self-regulation, which are critical for success in 21st-century knowledge economies.

In addition to pedagogical transformations, AI has introduced significant operational efficiencies within educational institutions. Administrative automation represents a major area of opportunity, reducing the burden of repetitive and labor-intensive tasks through the use of intelligent systems. AI-driven tools can handle a range of functions—such as attendance tracking, exam scheduling, admissions processing, and even real-time translation of administrative content—allowing staff and faculty to reallocate their time toward higher-order, student-facing activities (Roll & Wylie, 2016; Baker & Smith, 2019). Machine learning algorithms can also assist with enrollment forecasting, financial planning, and facility management, offering predictive insights that support strategic resource allocation. In higher education, for example, AI-based student information systems have been employed to anticipate course demand, identify at-risk students based on behavioral patterns, and streamline academic advising processes. These applications extend beyond simple efficiency gains; they contribute to more responsive, data-informed institutional governance. Furthermore, AI enables enhanced quality assurance and institutional benchmarking through the analysis of learning analytics and performance indicators across departments or institutions, facilitating continuous improvement and accountability (Zawacki-Richter et al., 2019). When implemented responsibly, these technologies help cultivate agile, resilient, and learner-centered educational environments that can adapt to changing societal demands and technological landscapes.

Beyond personalization and administrative efficiency, AI has also catalyzed new forms of pedagogical innovation that are reshaping the nature of teaching and learning. Among the most prominent tools are AI-powered virtual assistants and chatbots, which offer scalable, real-time academic support and extend learning beyond the physical classroom. These systems can respond to students' questions, guide them through assignments, deliver micro-content, and provide feedback with minimal human intervention (Chen et al., 2020). Unlike static learning management systems, conversational AI technologies are capable of simulating interactive dialogue, fostering learner engagement, and promoting autonomy through continuous access to support. Notably, the use of chatbots has also been instrumental in bridging communication gaps in multilingual or multicultural contexts, where linguistic barriers might otherwise hinder understanding. In parallel, the integration of AI with immersive technologies such as Augmented Reality (AR) and Virtual Reality (VR) has introduced new experiential dimensions to education. AI-enhanced AR/VR environments create interactive, simulated learning spaces where students can experiment, manipulate variables, and visualize abstract concepts—particularly in complex fields such as science, engineering, and medicine (Holmes et al., 2019; Roll & Wylie, 2016). These environments facilitate situated learning and encourage deeper cognitive engagement by allowing learners to explore scenarios that would be inaccessible or unsafe in physical settings. Such technologies are not merely supplementary tools; they represent a reconceptualization of pedagogy wherein learners become active agents in constructing knowledge through inquiry and interaction.

Equally transformative is AI's potential to contribute to the development of essential skills for the future workforce. In contrast to deterministic narratives that frame AI as a substitute for human labor, more nuanced perspectives emphasize the complementary role of AI in cultivating higher-order competencies that machines cannot replicate. Educational systems are increasingly tasked with preparing students for a labor market characterized by volatility, complexity, and rapid technological change. In this context, AI-enabled educational platforms can be designed to foster skills such as critical thinking, creativity, adaptability, and collaborative problem-solving—competencies widely recognized as vital for navigating the 21st-century knowledge economy (OECD, 2021; UNESCO, 2021). For example, AI-based learning analytics can provide real-time insights into students' cognitive processes, enabling instructors to intervene with tasks that promote reflection, synthesis, and innovation. Similarly, adaptive simulations and game-based learning environments can cultivate creative decision-making and iterative reasoning in authentic contexts. By shifting instructional focus from content acquisition to process-oriented learning, AI supports pedagogical frameworks that emphasize lifelong learning, self-directed inquiry, and intellectual resilience. These developments challenge traditional hierarchies of knowledge and authority in the classroom, advocating for a more distributed model of education that is responsive to both technological evolution and human potential. However, realizing this promise requires intentional design, inclusive access, and ethical governance to ensure that skill-building opportunities are equitably distributed and pedagogically sound.

In practice, several national education systems have begun to operate personalized learning on a scale through AI-based platforms. For example, in China, Squirrel AI has been deployed in over 2,000 learning centers to deliver adaptive tutoring in subjects such as mathematics and science. The system analyzes student input in real time, identifying learning gaps and adjusting instructional sequences accordingly, which has reportedly led to substantial gains in student retention and engagement. In Finland, the AI-based tool "Eduten Playground," developed in collaboration with the University of Turku, is used in primary schools to individualize math learning. It collects over 1,000 data points per student per hour, enabling real-time formative assessment and targeted feedback. These implementations demonstrate the scalability of adaptive learning when supported by institutional commitment and ethical oversight. Similarly, in Singapore's "Future Ready Education" strategy, AI-powered learning analytics are being integrated into the national school system to support data-informed instructional design, with a particular emphasis on student agency and socio-emotional development. Such examples highlight not only the technical viability of AI personalization but also the importance of aligning its use with pedagogical values, teacher empowerment, and localized curriculum goals. These case studies offer valuable insights into how adaptive learning environments can be embedded within broader systemic reform efforts, contributing to both individual learning gains and institutional innovation.

RISKS AND ETHICAL CONSIDERATIONS

While Artificial Intelligence (AI) offers unprecedented opportunities for educational enhancement, its deployment also carries substantial risks, particularly in relation to social justice, equity, and ethical governance. One of the most pressing concerns is the potential of AI to exacerbate existing digital divides and reproduce structural inequalities. Although AI technologies are often framed as neutral tools capable of democratizing access to education, their implementation is deeply shaped by unequal distributions of infrastructure, funding, and technical expertise. In low-resource contexts, schools and educational systems may lack the necessary digital connectivity, trained personnel, and maintenance support required to effectively integrate AI systems into teaching and administration (UNESCO, 2021; Selwyn, 2019). Even within high-income countries, disparities persist along socioeconomic, geographic, and demographic lines, with marginalized communities—such as rural students, migrants, and students with disabilities—often excluded from AI-driven innovations due to limited access to devices or broadband connectivity. This digital exclusion not only limits students' learning opportunities but also risks entrenching a two-tiered educational system, wherein privileged groups benefit from personalized, data-rich environments while others are left with under-resourced and outdated methods. Moreover, algorithmic models trained on biased or incomplete data sets may reinforce pre-existing inequities by misclassifying students, predicting poor performance based on historical patterns, or recommending limited educational pathways (Zawacki-Richter et al., 2019; Holmes et al., 2019). Without deliberate efforts to design inclusive systems and monitor their impacts, AI can inadvertently reproduce the very disparities it is often intended to mitigate.

Closely linked to these equity issues are growing concerns around data protection, surveillance, and student privacy. AI systems in education are typically fueled by large volumes of learner data, including behavioral logs, biometric indicators, geolocation data, and personal identifiers. While this data may be used to optimize learning outcomes and inform policy decisions, its collection and processing raise fundamental ethical questions about consent, transparency, and ownership. In many cases, students and their guardians are either unaware of the extent to which data is being collected or unable to opt out of such systems without compromising access to educational resources. This lack of agency is particularly problematic when AI technologies are deployed through third-party platforms or commercial vendors, whose data practices may not align with institutional or national data protection standards (Chen et al., 2020; Baker & Smith, 2019). Furthermore, the integration of AI with surveillance technologies—such as facial recognition, emotion detection, and keystroke tracking—poses significant threats to students' autonomy and psychological well-being. These tools, often justified in the name of classroom management or academic integrity, risk normalizing surveillance cultures that undermine trust and create high-stress environments for learners. The long-term implications are particularly concerning, as early profiling and constant monitoring can shape how students are perceived, evaluated, and disciplined throughout their educational trajectories. Ensuring robust data governance frameworks—grounded in the principles of minimal data use, purpose limitation, and algorithmic transparency—is therefore essential to protecting students' rights and maintaining the integrity of educational spaces (UNESCO, 2021; OECD, 2021). Ultimately, the ethical use of AI in education requires more than technical compliance; it necessitates a broader commitment to democratic accountability, equity-centered design, and the safeguarding of human dignity in digital learning ecosystems.

Another critical area of concern in the educational use of AI is the presence of algorithmic bias, the lack of system transparency, and the widespread absence of accountability mechanisms. AI systems, far from being neutral or objective, often encode the values, assumptions, and limitations of the datasets on which they are trained. In educational contexts, this can result in the reproduction of discriminatory patterns that disproportionately affect vulnerable student populations. For example, predictive analytics tools used to assess performance or risk of dropout may rely on historical data shaped by systemic inequalities—such as socioeconomic status, racial background, or linguistic diversity—thereby reinforcing the very disparities they purport to address (Zawacki-Richter et al., 2019; Selwyn, 2019). Such biases are not always immediately visible, especially when decision-making processes are embedded in "black-box" algorithms whose internal logic is opaque to both educators and students. The lack of transparency not only impedes informed consent but also makes it difficult to challenge or appeal decisions generated by AI systems, such as course recommendations, admissions outcomes, or disciplinary actions. In cases where AI tools are developed or operated by private entities, proprietary software restrictions often further obscure the basis on which educational judgments are made. The absence of explainability in AI decision-making is particularly problematic in high-stakes educational settings, where outcomes can influence a student's academic trajectory, self-concept, and future opportunities (Roll & Wylie, 2016; Holmes et al., 2019). Without built-in mechanisms for auditing, contestability, and redress, AI risks shifting educational governance away from democratic deliberation and toward technocratic determinism.

In light of these challenges, the development and implementation of comprehensive ethical frameworks and regulatory safeguards has become an urgent priority. While general-purpose data protection laws such as the General Data Protection Regulation (GDPR) in the European Union provide a foundational legal context, they are not always adequate for the specific dynamics of AI in education. What is needed is a multilayered governance model that combines international ethical principles with national policies and institution-level guidelines tailored to the educational sector. UNESCO's Recommendation on the Ethics of Artificial Intelligence (2021) offers a starting point, emphasizing values such as human oversight, non-discrimination, and sustainability. However, translating such principles into operational standards requires clear protocols for data governance, impact assessment, and stakeholder participation. For instance, regulatory frameworks should mandate that AI systems used in education be subject to rigorous testing for bias, undergo regular audits, and provide accessible explanations for their outputs. In parallel, ethical guidelines must promote inclusivity in design processes, ensuring that diverse voices—including those of students, teachers, parents, and marginalized communities—inform the development and deployment of AI tools. Moreover, accountability must extend beyond the software itself to include the institutions and decision-makers who adopt these technologies. Ultimately, safeguarding the public mission of education in an AI-mediated era entails resisting the normalization of opaque and unaccountable systems, and instead fostering environments where transparency, equity, and democratic participation are integral to technological innovation.

AI IN POLICY AND STRATEGY FORMATION

Artificial Intelligence (AI) is increasingly positioned as a strategic asset in educational policymaking, offering new modalities for evidence-based decision-making and long-term planning. Traditionally, educational strategies and policies were shaped through iterative consultation, statistical analyses, and human expertise. While these methods remain essential, AI introduces new capacities for processing large-scale, multidimensional data in real time, thereby transforming how policymakers and institutional leaders understand educational systems and formulate interventions. AI-based analytics tools can detect emerging trends, forecast future outcomes, and model complex scenarios by integrating diverse data sources—ranging from student demographics and performance indicators to infrastructure availability and teacher evaluations (OECD, 2021; UNESCO, 2021). These capabilities allow decision-makers to simulate the potential effects of policy changes before implementation, optimize resource allocation, and respond more rapidly to dynamic educational challenges. For instance, ministries of education in countries like China, Singapore, and the United Arab Emirates have leveraged AI-driven dashboards to monitor student progress at scale, identify areas of systemic underperformance, and adapt strategic priorities accordingly (Chen et al., 2020). Similarly, institutional leaders in higher education increasingly rely on predictive analytics to inform enrollment strategies, assess program effectiveness, and align academic offerings with labor market demands.

In addition to augmenting strategic foresight, AI significantly influences key components of educational planning—most notably curriculum design, equity planning, and governance models. AI-powered tools enable curriculum developers to analyze vast bodies of academic literature, labor market trends, and learner behavior to design content that is both relevant and future-oriented. This allows for more dynamic, adaptable curricula that reflect evolving technological competencies and societal needs. Moreover, AI facilitates the granular analysis of learner data to identify content gaps, learning bottlenecks, and regional disparities, thereby informing decisions about curriculum differentiation, local adaptation, and personalized instruction pathways (Luckin et al., 2016; Holmes et al., 2019). From an equity perspective, AI tools can assist in the detection of patterns of exclusion and marginalization—such as disparities in academic outcomes across gender, ethnicity, or socioeconomic status—by cross-referencing indicators that might otherwise go unnoticed. When integrated with geographic information systems (GIS), for example, AI can help identify resource deserts and support data-informed decisions around school placement, funding prioritization, and infrastructure development. Furthermore, AI's influence extends to governance structures themselves. In some educational systems, algorithmic tools have begun to mediate aspects of school accountability, performance monitoring, and teacher evaluations, prompting a shift toward more technocratic forms of governance (Williamson & Piattoeva, 2022). While this may yield efficiency gains, it also raises critical questions about the delegation of authority to algorithmic systems and the role of human judgment in educational leadership. As AI becomes embedded in the infrastructure of educational governance, it is essential to maintain a reflexive stance that balances technological efficiency with democratic legitimacy, ensuring that strategic planning remains aligned with ethical, pedagogical, and social objectives.

The effective integration of AI into educational policy and strategy requires the coordinated engagement of multiple stakeholders, each playing a distinct and complementary role. Governments, as the primary architects of national education systems, are responsible for establishing regulatory frameworks, funding priorities, and long-term strategic agendas. Their role is especially critical in setting standards for ethical AI use, overseeing procurement processes, and ensuring equitable distribution of technological resources across diverse regions and populations. Ministries of education in countries such as Finland and Singapore, for example, have developed national strategies that explicitly embed AI within their digital education policies, often in collaboration with academic and civil society actors. Educational institutions—ranging from schools to universities—act as both implementers and co-creators of AI applications, often tailoring general frameworks to suit local needs and pedagogical cultures. Institutional leadership must balance innovation with accountability, cultivating internal expertise and ensuring that educators are equipped to engage with AI tools critically and effectively. Meanwhile, private sector developers and e-tech companies drive technological innovation, designing and deploying AI platforms used across educational settings. Their influence is profound, yet often under-regulated, raising questions about transparency, data ownership, and alignment with public values. As such, sustained dialogue and collaboration between public authorities, educators, developers, and communities are essential to ensure that AI systems serve pedagogical rather than purely commercial interests (Williamson & Piattoeva, 2022).

In this context, methodological triangulation becomes not only a research imperative but also a governance necessity. Relying solely on quantitative performance data or algorithmic outputs risk oversimplifying the complexities of educational realities and overlooking the human dimensions of teaching and learning. To counteract this, the triangulation of multiple data sources—such as semi-structured interviews with stakeholders, surveys of practitioner perceptions, and analysis of official policy documents—offers a more nuanced and comprehensive understanding of how AI is shaping educational strategy. Interviews with school leaders and policymakers, for instance, can reveal tacit values, implementation challenges, and institutional constraints that are not captured in formal datasets. Surveys can surface broader trends in teacher and student attitudes toward AI, highlighting areas of resistance, enthusiasm, or uncertainty. Document analysis of national AI strategies, curriculum reforms, and institutional planning reports enables researchers to trace the normative assumptions and discursive frameworks that underlie policy shifts. This mixed-methods approach also facilitates the triangulation of actor perspectives, allowing for the identification of gaps or misalignments between top-down policy intentions and bottom-up educational experiences. A preliminary example of such triangulation can be observed in Estonia's AI-driven education policy, which combines national policy directives, school-level data infrastructures, and active consultation with local educators to ensure contextual responsiveness and ethical alignment. Similarly, Canada's pan-provincial approach integrates public engagement forums, institutional pilots, and iterative policy evaluation to inform the scaling of AI tools in education. These cases illustrate how robust, multi-actor engagement and layered data collection are vital not only for informed decision-making but also for sustaining public trust in AI-mediated educational governance.

GLOBAL COLLABORATION AND CULTURAL EXCHANGE

One of the most compelling yet underexplored dimensions of Artificial Intelligence (AI) in education is its capacity to facilitate global collaboration and intercultural exchange. As digital platforms increasingly transcend national borders, AI functions as a mediating infrastructure that enables real-time interaction, knowledge sharing, and collective problem-solving among students and educators across geographical, linguistic, and cultural divides. AI-driven translation services, adaptive content delivery, and intelligent matchmaking algorithms now allow for the creation of multilingual and multicultural virtual classrooms where learners from diverse contexts can engage with shared educational content while receiving individualized support (Chen et al., 2020; Holmes et al., 2019). These technologies help reduce the friction of cross-border learning by offering personalized access to global knowledge resources, enabling asynchronous collaboration, and fostering peer-to-peer learning across time zones and continents. For instance, international platforms that integrate AI—such as Coursera, Edmodo, or UNESCO's Global Education Coalition—provide opportunities for learners and instructors to co-create educational experiences in digitally mediated environments that reflect a plurality of perspectives. In this way, AI not only expands access to content but also reconfigures the social architecture of education by making it more inclusive, participatory, and globally connected.

The potential of AI to promote intercultural dialogue and foster global citizenship is particularly significant in an era marked by rising nationalism, social polarization, and geopolitical fragmentation. AI-powered learning platforms can be intentionally designed to support cross-cultural understanding by curating diverse content, highlighting marginalized voices, and creating collaborative spaces that encourage empathy, critical reflection, and mutual respect. For example, AI can analyze learner interactions to identify moments of cultural misunderstanding and offer contextualized feedback or content designed to bridge conceptual and linguistic gaps. Such functionality can be further enriched through sentiment analysis, discourse modeling, and socio-linguistic pattern recognition, enabling more nuanced and constructive communication across cultural boundaries. By embedding ethical and global learning objectives into algorithmic design, AI can help cultivate competencies associated with global citizenship—such as intercultural communication, digital literacy, and social responsibility (UNESCO, 2021). Moreover, these platforms can empower educators to co-develop intercultural curricula, share pedagogical practices across borders, and collectively address global challenges such as climate change, inequality, and misinformation through collaborative inquiry.

At a systemic level, AI holds promises for building inclusive, networked education ecosystems that transcend the limitations of nation-bound educational infrastructures. By enabling interoperability across platforms and institutions, AI can facilitate the development of global learning networks where students, educators, policymakers, and researchers are embedded in dynamic knowledge flows. These ecosystems can support distributed innovation, allowing best practices to circulate and adapt across diverse contexts while also creating feedback loops for continuous improvement. However, achieving this vision requires deliberate governance to ensure that the benefits of global connectivity do not reinforce existing asymmetries of power, language, or technological access. Open standards, ethical design principles, and equitable data governance must guide the development of these networks to prevent the marginalization of underrepresented communities and ensure meaningful participation from the Global South. When inclusively governed and pedagogically oriented, AI-mediated global education ecosystems offer a transformative opportunity to reimagine education as a collaborative, transnational, and justice-oriented endeavor.

Several international initiatives exemplify how AI is being leveraged to promote global collaboration and intercultural education. One notable example is UNESCO's *Global Campus of Human Rights*, which integrates AI-powered translation and content recommendation systems to support inclusive participation in its MOOCs and collaborative learning activities. These technologies allow students from diverse linguistic and cultural backgrounds to engage with shared content while receiving contextualized support tailored to their regions. Another case is the European Commission's *SELFIE for TEACHERS* project, which, although not solely AI-based, is being increasingly linked with AI-enhanced analytics to offer feedback to educators across Europe on their digital competence. Through multilingual platforms that employ AI-driven personalization, the tool helps teachers from different countries understand and compare their practices, fostering a sense of shared pedagogical reflection. In addition, cross-national research consortia such as *AI4EDU*—a collaborative initiative involving institutions from the Global North and South—explore how AI can be co-designed to reflect diverse epistemologies, pedagogical traditions, and cultural norms. These efforts demonstrate that when AI is implemented with a commitment to linguistic diversity, equity of access, and cultural sensitivity, it can act as a powerful vehicle for international understanding and the co-construction of global knowledge commons. Such examples not only validate the theoretical promise of AI-enabled intercultural dialogue but also provide practical models for developing globally networked, ethically grounded education systems.

CONCLUSIONS AND RECOMMENDATIONS

The integration of Artificial Intelligence (AI) into education marks a critical juncture in the evolution of both pedagogical practice and educational governance. As this chapter has demonstrated, AI holds substantial potential to personalize learning, optimize institutional management, foster global collaboration, and inform evidence-based policy. Adaptive learning systems and intelligent tutoring technologies enable differentiated instruction that meets the needs of diverse learners, while administrative automation enhances operational efficiency and frees educators to focus on pedagogy. At a strategic level, AI contributes to policy development by enabling predictive analytics, trend forecasting, and more targeted equity interventions. Simultaneously, AI expands the global reach of education, facilitating cross-cultural dialogue and supporting the formation of inclusive, networked learning ecosystems. However, these opportunities are paralleled by significant risks—ranging from deepening digital inequalities to violations of student privacy and the perpetuation of algorithmic bias. As AI systems become increasingly embedded in educational decision-making and strategic planning, the urgency to govern their deployment ethically and inclusively intensifies.

In light of these insights, several key recommendations can be made for stakeholders at multiple levels. For policymakers, it is imperative to develop clear, sector-specific regulatory frameworks that define acceptable uses of AI in education, mandate impact assessments, and enforce accountability for algorithmic harms. Policies should promote equitable access to AI infrastructure, particularly in underserved regions, and ensure public oversight of private technology providers. For educators and institutional leaders, professional development in AI literacy is essential—not only to use AI tools effectively but also to critically evaluate their pedagogical and ethical implications. Institutions must adopt AI in ways that complement rather than replace human judgment and should actively involve educators and students in decision-making processes related to AI integration. For developers and technology firms, ethical design must become a non-negotiable standard. This includes ensuring transparency in algorithmic operations, providing explainable outputs, addressing data bias, and engaging in participatory co-design processes with educators and learners. Commercial priorities should not supersede the pedagogical integrity or democratic function of educational systems.

More broadly, responsible AI use in education must be guided by a set of cross-cutting ethical and practical principles: transparency, equity, inclusivity, accountability, and human-centeredness. These principles must be embedded in the full lifecycle of AI—from design and deployment to evaluation and revision. Educational institutions and governments should establish ethical review boards or AI oversight committees to monitor the ongoing impacts of AI systems and address emergent concerns. Additionally, efforts must be made to improve data literacy among all stakeholders, ensuring that AI-generated insights are interpreted accurately and used responsibly.

Finally, future research should pursue interdisciplinary approaches that combine technical expertise with insights from education, ethics, sociology, and critical data studies. Longitudinal studies are needed to assess the sustained impacts of AI on learning outcomes, institutional practices, and equity dynamics. Comparative case studies can illuminate best practices and context-specific challenges across different national or regional settings. Moreover, greater international collaboration—through research consortia, global pilot programs, and multilateral policy dialogues—will be vital for harmonizing ethical standards and fostering innovation that serves the public good. As education systems worldwide grapple with digital transformation, a reflexive, inclusive, and ethically grounded approach to AI will be essential for ensuring that technological progress advances rather than undermines the core values of education.

Key Action Steps for Policymakers

To ensure the ethical, effective, and equitable integration of Artificial Intelligence in education, policymakers should consider the following strategic actions:

1. **Develop sector-specific AI regulations for education**, distinct from general data protection laws, that define acceptable uses, mandate bias audits, and require algorithmic explainability in high-stakes decision-making.
2. **Invest in national AI strategies for education** that include capacity-building for teachers and administrators, infrastructure development in under-resourced areas, and incentives for inclusive, open-source AI solutions.
3. **Mandate stakeholder consultation in all phases of AI deployment**, including participatory design processes with educators, students, parents, and civil society representatives to ensure contextual relevance and social accountability.
4. **Establish independent AI ethics boards or oversight committees** within educational systems to monitor long-term impacts, adjudicate disputes, and review vendor compliance with public standards.
5. **Promote international collaboration and knowledge exchange**, particularly between the Global North and South, to reduce global disparities in AI access and co-create culturally responsive AI tools.
6. **Ensure public ownership and transparency of educational data**, including clear guidelines on consent, data minimization, and secure infrastructure to prevent misuse or commercialization of student information.
7. **Support interdisciplinary research and pilot programs** that examine the pedagogical, social, and psychological impacts of AI in education, using mixed-method approaches to inform iterative policy refinement.

These steps are not exhaustive but represent foundational elements of a forward-looking AI governance agenda in education—one that balances innovation with responsibility and places human dignity, democratic participation, and social justice at the core of technological transformation.

REFERENCES

Baker, T., & Smith, L. (2019). *Educ-AI-tion rebooted? Exploring the future of artificial intelligence in schools and colleges*. Nesta Foundation.

Chen, L., Chen, P., & Lin, Z. (2020). Artificial intelligence in education: A review. *IEEE Access : Practical Innovations, Open Solutions*, *8*, 75264–75278. DOI: 10.1109/ACCESS.2020.2988510

Holmes, W., Bialik, M., & Fadel, C. (2019). *Artificial intelligence in education: Promises and implications for teaching and learning*. Center for Curriculum Redesign.

Luckin, R., Holmes, W., Griffiths, M., & Forcier, L. B. (2016). *Intelligence unleashed: An argument for AI in education*. Pearson Education.

OECD. (2021). AI and the Future of Skills, Volume 1: Capabilities and Assessments. OECD Publishing. https://doi.org/DOI: 10.1787/5f7c8a44-en

Roll, I., & Wylie, R. (2016). Evolution and revolution in artificial intelligence in education. *International Journal of Artificial Intelligence in Education*, *26*(2), 582–599. DOI: 10.1007/s40593-016-0110-3

Selwyn, N. (2019). *Should robots replace teachers? AI and the future of education*. Polity Press.

UNESCO. (2021). *AI and education: Guidance for policy-makers*. United Nations Educational, Scientific and Cultural Organization.

UNESCO. (2021). Recommendation on the Ethics of Artificial Intelligence. United Nations Educational, Scientific and Cultural Organization. https://unesdoc.unesco.org/ark:/48223/pf0000381137

UNESCO. (2021). AI and Education: Guidance for Policy-makers. United Nations Educational, Scientific and Cultural Organization. https://unesdoc.unesco.org/ark:/48223/pf0000376709

Williamson, B., & Piattoeva, N. (2022). Education governance and datafication: Reimagining education policy and practice. In Williamson, B., & Piattoeva, N. (Eds.), *Education Governance and Datafication* (pp. 1–18). Bloomsbury Academic.

Zawacki-Richter, O., Marín, V. I., Bond, M., & Gouverneur, F. (2019). Systematic review of research on artificial intelligence applications in higher education–where are the educators? *International Journal of Educational Technology in Higher Education*, *16*(1), 1–27. DOI: 10.1186/s41239-019-0171-0

Chapter 12

The Common Good Toward the Crucial Role of Myanmar Migrant Workers in Thailand Through the Prisms of Utilitarianism and Distributive Justice

Tin Maung Htwe
https://orcid.org/0009-0002-3002-169X
Chiang Mai University, Thailand

ABSTRACT

The dual philosophical frameworks of Utilitarianism and Distributive Justice, This chapter critically examines the indispensable contributions of Myanmar migrant workers to Thailand's socio-economic structure through. Chapter argues that improving labor conditions to ensure equitable wages, and grant legal protections to migrant workers do not merely benefit the workers themselves but also serve the broader common good. By strengthening economic productivity, fostering social cohesion, and promoting sustainable development, Myanmar migrants could play a pivotal role in labor-intensive industries such as agriculture, construction, and manufacturing sectors of Thailand in long term. Depend on Thailand's economic growth in Migrant workers, paper argue that precarious working conditions and limited legal protections are still a matters for migrant development.

DOI: 10.4018/979-8-3373-2332-9.ch012

INTRODUCTION

The movement of Myanmar migrant workers into Thailand is not merely a function of economic necessity but a reflection of deeper structural forces shaping the region. In a rapidly globalizing world, the demand for cheap and mobile labor has created a complex (Stalker, 2000). It is often exploitative system in which millions of workers find themselves indispensable yet unprotected (Harrod and Power 1987). Nowhere is this more apparent than in Thailand, where Myanmar migrants constitute a significant portion of the labor force, occupying essential roles in agriculture, construction, manufacturing, and services (Mostafanezhad et al. 2022). Their contributions sustain Thailand's economic vitality (Anantanasuwong, 2021), yet their legal and social standing remains tenuous, with protections failing to keep pace with their economic indispensability (Warr, 2024).

This Dilemma is not unique to Thailand but rather a recurring phenomenon in capitalist economies reliant on migrant labor (Campbell, 2018) because economic dependence coexists with political and social exclusion. The structure of the Thai labor market positions Myanmar workers in a precarious status (Khai, 2023). The United Nations Development Programme (2024) assesses migration's role in Thailand's human development. It endure exploitative labor practices, wage discrimination, and restricted access to essential services such as healthcare and education (Musikawong, 2022). Despite their role as an economic backbone, they remain largely outside the framework of rights and protections afforded to Thai workers (Tungjiewlee, 2023). This condition raises fundamental questions about economic justice, the role of the state and the ethical obligations of host societies.

The persistence of Myanmar migrant labor in Thailand is a product of both push and pull factors. Political instability, economic stagnation and ethnic conflicts in Myanmar continue to drive migration, while Thailand's economic expansion has created an insatiable demand for low-wage labor in industries suffering from domestic shortages (International Organization for Migration, 2024). Thailand transitions toward an upper-middle-income economy, labor market policies and migration management have become pivotal in sustaining long-term growth, maintaining global competitiveness, and addressing structural challenges. (World Bank 2023). Provinces such as Samut Sakhon, Mae Hong Son, Tak, Bangkok, Chiang Mai, and Ranong have emerged as key hubs in Thailand. It is reflecting the intersection of economic necessity and labor stratification (Palmgren, 2022). Although Thailand's 13th National Economic and Social Development Plan (2023–2027) aims to align national growth with sustainability, innovation, and inclusivity, addressing economic resilience, social equity, and environmental challenges (Office of the National Economic and Social Development Council, 2023). Despite their economic centrality, these migrant workers still remain marginalized, caught in a system that simultaneously requires and excludes them (Alberti & Sacchetto, 2024).

This phenomenon is not merely an economic issue but a political one. Raising broader questions about state capacity, legal frameworks and the normative foundations of labor policy, the absence of robust protections for migrant workers signals both an unwillingness and an inability to integrate them into Thailand's social contract. The International Organization for Migration (IOM) (2024) presents economic and social aspects (IOM 2024). In many ways, the Thai state replicates patterns as if economic pragmatism takes precedence over human rights considerations. Thailand's political and economic structures reflect a broader authoritarian logic, where democratic rhetoric is strategically employed to mask underlying mechanisms of control (Cardin 2021). The result is a dual system in which migrants perform indispensable labor yet remain systematically disadvantaged. Migrant workers in Thailand often face informal employment and precarious migration status (Ducanes, Engblom, & Ramos, 2023), leaving them vulnerable to exploitation and legal uncertainty. At the same time, Thailand's labor market aspires to align with regional human rights standards through seeking to balance economic demands with dignity and fair treatment for all workers (Crocco, 2021). However, the gap between policy aspirations and on-the-ground realities underscores the challenges of achieving equitable labor governance in the region (Diller, 2022).

This study draws on Utilitarianism and Distributive Justice to examine the long-term implications of Myanmar migrant labor in Thailand. Utilitarianism (Bentham, 1789/1948; Mill, 1863/2001) compels an assessment of whether Thailand's current labor system maximizes societal benefits or merely entrenches economic disparities under the guise of efficiency. The classical liberal perspective on market efficiency (Smith, 1776/2003) must be weighed against the realities of wage suppression and labor exploitation (Arnold & Hewison, 2005). It is questioning whether the existing model creates sustainable prosperity or merely perpetuates inequality. Meanwhile, Distributive Justice (Rawls, 1971; Sen, 2009) challenges us to confront how structural inequities in wages, legal protections, and access to social services undermine the ethical legitimacy of Thailand's labor policies. A system that benefits from a workforce while systematically excluding it from the very rights and protections afforded to domestic labor cannot claim to be just.

Methodologically, this research employs discourse analysis (Fairclough, 2003) to uncover how labor policies, economic strategies, and migration governance shape the lived realities (De Genova, 2002) of Myanmar migrant workers. This approach moves beyond economic indicators to prioritize the voices of workers, labor unions, policymakers, and industry representatives. In the long run, Thailand's ability to sustain its economic growth depends not on labor exploitation but on aligning efficiency with fairness, ensuring that economic pragmatism and moral responsibility are not mutually exclusive but mutually reinforcing. Thus, this paper argues that the treatment of Myanmar migrant workers in Thailand is not merely a localized issue but rather a manifestation of broader dynamics that define modern labor markets within global capitalism. It illustrates the inherent contradictions where economic imperatives demand labor mobility, yet political and legal frameworks often inhibit the full integration of migrant workers. This study employs the ethical frameworks of Utilitarianism and Distributive Justice to evaluate these contradictions and advocate for comprehensive reforms.

LITERATURE REVIEW

The concept of the common good occupies a central position in ethical, political and economic discourses surrounding labor migration (Tyler, 2017). Gilodi, Albert, and Nienaber (2024) critique existing vulnerability models in migration studies and propose a nuanced, integrative conceptual model to better capture the complex realities of migrants' experiences. Reflecting the imperative, social and economic structures ought to be designed to foster the collective flourishing of individuals and communities (Hosseini, 2023). The presence of Myanmar migrant workers in Thailand's labor market raises profound questions about labor policies and the ethical obligations of host societies. The presence of Myanmar migrant workers in Thailand's labor market underscores the need for ethical labor policies (Pouryousefi & Freeman, 2021), which can be critically examined through the lenses of utilitarianism, focusing on the greatest good for the greatest number (Mill, 1863/2001), and deontology, which emphasizes the moral duty towards workers as ends in themselves (Kant, 1785/2012). Ethical labor policies address the vulnerabilities faced by migrant workers, including exploitation, unsafe working conditions, and limited access to legal protections (Harkins et al., 2017; International Labour Organization [ILO], 2021). Therefore, the integration of migrant workers into Thailand's economy highlights the importance of balancing economic benefits with human rights considerations.

Utilitarianism emphasizes the maximization of overall happiness and economic efficiency (Bentham, 1789; Mill, 1863), while Distributive Justice focuses on the fair distribution of resources and the safeguarding of human rights (Rawls, 1971; Petcharamesree, 2023). The ethical implications of valuing lives in decision-making processes, emphasizing trade-offs in public policy (Broome 2004). Rooted in the works of Jeremy Bentham (1789) and John Stuart Mill (1863), utilitarianism posits that ethical policies should aim to achieve the greatest good for the greatest number. Both Peter Singer (1972) and Will MacAskill (2015) have expanded this framework to address global labor and poverty challenges. From this perspective, Myanmar migrant workers play a critical role in sustaining Thailand's economic stability by addressing labor shortages in essential industries, maintaining competitive production costs, and enhancing overall productivity. Derek Parfit (2011)'s utilitarian ethics further reinforce the argument that labor migration serves as a mechanism for economic optimization. The broader societal benefits frequently outweigh the individual hardships faced by migrants. Migrant workers play a vital role in filling low-skilled and labor-intensive positions that are often avoided by local workers, thereby supporting industrial growth and economic development (Battistella, 2014). Labor migration aligns with utilitarian principles (Singer, 1972) by alleviating global poverty and promoting overall well-being (MacAskill, 2015). Remittances sent by migrants to Myanmar not only contribute to economic development in their home country but also stimulate Thailand's consumer economy (Htwe, 2025), creating a mutually beneficial dynamic (Vigneswaran, 2020).

Thailand's demographic trajectory poses significant challenges through an aging workforce and declining birth rates. These structural shifts highlight the increasing dependence on migrant labor as a vital mechanism for maintaining economic stability. In physically demanding sectors such as construction, fisheries, and other labor-intensive industries, migrant workers act as a critical stabilizing force to alleviate the pressures of demographic decline (Anukul, 2024: Marshall, Taylor, & Tödt, 2023). Their presence is not just a temporary solution but an integral part of Thailand's economic and social framework, shaping the nation's long-term labor dynamics. Public economics suggests that migrant labor enhances economic resilience. It can mitigate inflationary pressures that arise from workforce shortages (Broome, 2004). Toby Ord (2020)'s work on utilitarian ethics and public policy mentions that the benefits of integrating migrants into health and social welfare systems and lead to preferable public health outcomes. Policies that facilitate access to healthcare for migrants reduce the risk of disease transmission (World Health Organization, 2023) and enhance workplace productivity (Evagora-Campbell et al., 2022). Healthcare barriers affect majority of Myanmar migrants in Thailand based on accessibility issues (Positive Destinations, 2025). Similarly, inclusive labor policies promote social stability and cultural integration, fostering mutual understanding across diverse communities.

Nevertheless, critics of utilitarianism argue that its emphasis on economic efficiency can lead to the exploitation of migrant workers. While migrants contribute significantly to economic growth, they often face wage suppression, exploitative working conditions, and legal precarity (Bauböck & Ruhs, 2022). Shelly Kagan's critiques of utilitarianism underscore the ethical dilemmas inherent in prioritizing collective welfare at the expense of individual rights. The limits of morality in ethical decision-making still be a gap in conventional moral constraints (Kagan, 1989). Existential risks to humanity is still matter for long-term planning in global governance (Ord 2020). In contrast, the framework of Distributive Justice have rooted in the works of John Rawls and Amartya Sen. They advocates for the equitable distribution of economic and social benefits. This perspective insists that marginalized groups, such as migrant workers, must be afforded adequate legal protections, (McKee, 1981) fair wages and social security benefits (Rawls, 1971; Sen, 1999). Rawls' Theory of Justice (1971) asserts that justice should be evaluated from the standpoint of the least advantaged. His view can imply that labor policies should aim to uplift Myanmar migrant workers rather than merely optimize economic outcomes. Policies that guarantee minimum wage protections and safe working conditions not only enhance economic stability but also uphold human dignity. Amartya Sen (2009)'s capability approach further refines this argument by asserting that economic justice should be measured not solely by income levels but also by individuals' ability to achieve basic well-being. Access to legal employment status and social security benefits, for instance, can enhance long-term economic mobility and foster social cohesion (Chang et al., 2014). Addationally, Education for migrants and their family memebrs emerges as a critical factor in achieving intergenerational social mobility (Chang et al., 2023). Restricted access to education exacerbates economic inequality. It can perpetuate the cycles of poverty among migrant families (Stokke et al., 2018). Philip Pettit's work on political freedom and justice emphasizes that legal barriers preventing access to education violate fundamental rights and perpetuate social exclusion (Pettit, 1997). Despite the ethical imperatives of distributive justice, structural and political obstacles often impede its realization.

The concept of responsibility in justice emphasizes addressing structural inequalities and ensuring accountability (Young, 2011). In Thailand, employers often oppose policies that raise labor costs due to concerns over reduced profitability (Tödt et al., 2023). Chantavanich and Jitpong (2023) have critically examined labor migration in the Thai seafood industry, highlighting its implications for labor rights and worker protections. Additionally, inconsistent migration policies create legal vulnerabilities for migrant workers, resulting in systemic violations of their rights. Compounding these challenges, nationalist sentiments and political rhetoric hinder efforts to integrate migrants (Manatschal, 2022), further marginalizing them socially and economically (Stokke et al., 2018) both in policy implementation and in practice.

A comprehensive labor policy must navigate the tension between maximizing economic efficiency and upholding principles of fairness and equity. Labor, globalization, and governance are central to addressing socio-economic inequality and fostering social justice, particularly in post-communist states. Nae, Florescu, and Bălă oiu (2024) stress the importance of equitable labor policies and inclusive governance to reduce disparities. McClain et al. (2022) advocate for rights-based migration policies that balance state sovereignty with human rights, especially in climate and economic migration contexts. Wanjiru (2023)critiques restrictive border controls, showing how governance failures deepen exclusion. On one hand, the economic contributions of migrant workers and their role in stabilizing labor markets are critical to sustaining productivity and growth (Borjas, 2019; International Labour Organization [ILO], 2021). On the other hand, there is an ethical obligation to ensure fair treatment, equitable labor rights, and strong social protections for all workers (Sen, 1999; Heymann & McNeill, 2013).

The ethical framing of migrant labor policy hinges on core theoretical distinctions. Utilitarianism (Bentham, 1789; Mill, 1863; Singer, 1972) justifies policies that maximize net societal welfare, risking minority exploitation for the greater good (Bauböck & Ruhs, 2022). In contrast, Deontology (Kant, 2012) holds that migrant rights are inviolable ends in themselves, demanding dignity regardless of economic cost. Distributive Justice (Rawls, 1971) requires institutions to prioritize the worst-off via a fair distribution of rights and resources. Sen's Capability Approach (Sen, 1999) refines this, arguing justice is measured not by resources held, but by individuals' real freedoms to achieve well-being, such as health or social inclusion. Achieving this balance is vital for fostering both economic progress and social cohesion, as it aligns with the broader goal of building inclusive institutions that promote trust and stability within society (Acemoglu & Robinson, 2012) Joseph Stiglitz and Thomas Piketty argue that unregulated labor migration can exacerbate income inequality, necessitating policy interventions that safeguard human dignity (Stiglitz, 2012; Piketty, 2013).

THE HISTORICAL AND POLICY CONTEXT OF MYANMAR MIGRANT LABOR IN THAILAND

Migration from Myanmar to Thailand has unfolded in successive waves. Each had shaped by the broader forces of economic transformation, state repression (Weig, 2024) and labor market imperatives (Khemanitthathai, 2022). This movement is not simply a matter of individual agency but rather the product of structural conditions that have defined both Myanmar's domestic landscape and Thailand's demand for cheap, expendable labor (Mortensen, 2024). The origins of this migration can be traced back to the 1980s and early 1990s, a period when Myanmar's military regime oversaw economic stagnation and political repression (Waters et al., 2021). In parallel, Thailand's rapid economic expansion—driven by industrialization and the opening of its economy—created an insatiable need for low-wage workers (World Bank, 2024). The porous border between the two countries, coupled with weak regulatory oversight, allowed tens of thousands to cross into Thailand, often without documentation, to take on physically demanding and low-paid jobs (International Organization for Migration [IOM], 2023).

By the 1990s and early 2000s, Thailand had entered an era of accelerated economic growth, marked by urbanization, infrastructure expansion, and an increasing reliance on foreign labor (Huguet & Punpuing, 2005). Myanmar's political and economic conditions, meanwhile, remained fragile. The inability of the state to provide employment opportunities, combined with persistent armed conflicts in Karen, Mon, and Shan States, reinforced migration as a survival strategy (Vungsiriphisal, 2017). The Thai government had oscillated between tolerance and crackdowns. To manage the unexpected scale of the influx, they implemented a controlled migration framework (Chantavanich, 2014). Therefore, the 2003 Memorandum of Understanding (MoU) between Thailand and Myanmar signified a belated recognition that migrant labor was no longer a temporary phenomenon but a structural necessity for Thailand's economy (Huguet, 2015). The 2017 Royal Ordinance on the Management of Employment of Foreign Workers was an attempt to standardize labor protections, prevent trafficking, and enforce stricter documentation requirements (Royal Thai Government, 2017). As Myanmar embarked on a period of economic and political liberalization in the 2010s, migration patterns became more dynamic. Some migrants returned home, lured by economic reforms and nascent job opportunities (Arnold & Pickles, 2011). Yet, this period of optimism was short-lived.

The migration of Myanmar nationals to Thailand has surged in recent years, driven by political instability and economic collapse following the 2021 military coup. The 2021 military coup marked a turning point, triggering another mass exodus as thousands fled both political persecution and economic collapse. By 2023, approximately 1.7 million Myanmar migrant workers were documented in Thailand, highlighting the Thai economy's reliance on this labor force (Statista, 2023). The coup also triggered a refugee crisis, with at least 45,000 individuals fleeing to Thailand, exacerbating humanitarian challenges in border regions (Human Rights Watch, 2023). By March 2024, the number of registered Myanmar migrant workers in Thailand had risen to 2.3 million, reflecting both the scale of displacement and efforts to regularize migrant status (IOM Thailand, 2024). Concurrently, Thailand hosted over 82,000 refugees in border camps and 5,300 urban refugees, underscoring the protracted nature of Myanmar's crisis (United Nations High Commissioner for Refugees [UNHCR], 2024). Looking ahead, further displacement is expected due to Myanmar's ongoing instability, though precise projections remain uncertain (UNHCR, 2024). These trends highlight the intersection of political fragility, economic interdependence, and humanitarian need in the region. The 2021 military coup exemplified this dynamic. Thousands of Myanmar migrants, long tolerated as an economic necessity, suddenly found themselves the targets of a harsh immigration purge. The COVID-19 pandemic further exposed the fragility of migrant labor's position in Thailand's economy. Border closures and lockdowns left thousands jobless, stranded, and excluded from government relief programs, underscoring the extent to which they remain an expendable workforce rather than a protected labor class (United Nations Development Programme [UNDP], 2023).

Myanmar migrant workers sustain Thailand's economic stability in four key sectors: agriculture (Musikawong, 2022), fisheries, construction (Tun Shein, 2021), manufacturing and services (Htun, 2022). In rural Thailand, they have become indispensable to food production, filling gaps left by an aging and shrinking domestic workforce. Their presence in rice farming, plantations, and fisheries ensures the continued operation of Thailand's agrarian economy (Chaichanavichakit, 2024). Yet, despite their role in maintaining food security, these workers endure grueling conditions long hours, exploitative wages, and unsafe working environments without the protective oversight that domestic laborers might expect (Amfori, 2025). In urban centers, Myanmar migrants have played an equally critical role in Thailand's construction boom. From high-rise developments to public infrastructure projects, they have been instrumental in transforming the country's physical landscape (Karim, 2024). Thailand's manufacturing sector also relies heavily on Myanmar migrant labor, particularly in food processing, garment production, and electronics assembly. These workers form the backbone of Thailand's export-oriented economy, keeping costs low and production high (Palmgren, 2024). Yet, their employment is often characterized by excessive working hours, limited labor rights, and discrimination. The service sector, particularly domestic work and hospitality, has seen a growing influx of Myanmar migrant women. As domestic helpers, cleaners, hotel general staff, and retail workers, they sustain Thailand's tourism and service industries, providing essential (Association of Southeast Asian Nations [ASEAN], 2022) yet invisible labor. Their work extends beyond economic productivity, as they support Thai households through childcare, elderly care, and other domestic duties. However, the absence of formal labor protections leaves them vulnerable to exploitation, harassment, and abuse, a condition exacerbated by the social and legal invisibility of domestic workers (United Nations Thailand, 2022).

Thailand's approach to migrant labor mirrors a global phenomenon as reliance on foreign workers for economic growth without granting them corresponding rights or security. The central challenge lies in whether Thailand will continue to view Myanmar migrants as a temporary, disposable workforce or embrace them as essential contributors to its long-term economic and social framework. Meaningful reform will demand more than policy changes. It require a transformative shift in public perception, seeing migrant workers not as transient outsiders but as individuals whose labor, dignity, and well-being are deeply intertwined with Thailand's prosperity. Therefore, the paradox of Myanmar migrant labor in Thailand highlights a tension between necessity and exclusion. This dynamic reflects broader global patterns of labor mobility, where economic priorities frequently overshadow human rights and social inclusion.

RESEARCH FINDINGS

Economic Output With and Without Migrant Labor

The economic argument for migrant labor is straightforward. A stable, low-cost, and reliable workforce enables businesses to maintain efficiency, expand operations, and remain globally competitive. This benefits multiple stakeholders in a cascading effect: businesses reduce production costs and increase profitability. It is allowing reinvestment in growth. Thai workers gain opportunities in managerial and supervisory roles that offer upward mobility and consumers enjoy lower prices as industries operate with optimal labor efficiency. That are not only labor-intensive but increasingly avoided by local Thai workers. A 45-year-old rice farmer in Nakhon Sawan said "Without migrant workers, our farms would struggle. Many young Thais don't want to work in the fields anymore. They prefer jobs in offices or cities, but someone has to grow the food." Their role, therefore, is not an accident of economic convenience but a fundamental condition for stability and growth. A 30-year-old garment factory worker in Mae Sot: "We make the clothes that are sold everywhere, but nobody thinks about who sews them. Factories need us, but we are treated like we don't belong."The labor-intensive nature of these industries particularly seafood, manufacturing, and construction demands a workforce that Thailand's domestic labor pool is both unwilling and unable to supply at the required scale. Consider the seafood industry, one of Thailand's most globally competitive sectors (Stringer, Burmester, & Michailova, 2022). From a 35-year-old Myanmar seafood worker in Mahachai:, "We clean, cut, and pack seafood every day. If we stopped working, the factories would slow down, and the markets wouldn't have enough supply." Without Myanmar migrant workers, the industry would experience severe labor shortages, leading to declining exports, reduced output, and economic contraction. The same logic applies to manufacturing, agriculture, and construction. Each of these sectors relies on a steady labor supply to sustain Thailand's export-driven economy.

The counterfactual scenario reveals the magnitude of their contribution. A sudden contraction in the workforce would push wages upward, driving production costs higher. Businesses in labor-intensive sectors would respond either by raising prices or by cutting output, with both scenarios negatively impacting consumers (Rodchan, 2024). The resulting inflation would disproportionately harm lower-income households. Further, it is widening economic inequality. Additionally, foreign investors, facing increased labor costs, might seek alternative destinations such as Vietnam or

Malaysia (Rahim & Ab Rahman, 2024), reducing Thailand's long-term economic attractiveness (Ullah, Lee, & Hassan, 2024). Therefore, beyond economics, the utilitarian logic of migration policy is clear. Maximizing overall societal well-being necessitates the continued presence and fair treatment (Yazdiha, 2023) of Myanmar migrant workers. Their integration into the labor force ensures economic stability, supports business growth, sustains job creation, and maintains consumer purchasing power (International Organization for Migration [IOM], 2023). The alternative leads to inefficiency, economic decline, and greater hardship for all segments of society. This creates a compelling moral obligation for policymakers to construct a labor migration framework that is not only economically rational but also ethically sound (United Nations, 2024).

The Rationals of Welfare Maximization of Migrant Labor in Thailand

Based on a foundational tenet of utilitarian thought, the principle of maximizing welfare provides a compelling lens through which to assess labor policies (Bauböck & Ruhs, 2022), affecting Myanmar migrant workers in Thailand. The question at hand is not merely one of abstract ethical obligations but of tangible economic and social consequences. Policies that ensure fair treatment of these workers serve not only to enhance individual well-being but to bolster the broader system in which they participate (Parello & Ikhenaode, 2021).

Economic efficiency lies at the core of this rationale. A labor force that enjoys fair wages, legal protections, and safe working environments is inherently more productive and less susceptible to instability (Seubert, Hopfgartner, & Glaser, 2021). Where exploitation persists by manifesting in substandard wages, exclusion from legal recourse, or exposure to hazardous conditions inefficiency inevitably follows. High turnover, absenteeism, and low morale become endemic, eroding the very foundation of economic output (Corimanya, 2025). By contrast, when workers feel secure and valued, they contribute more effectively to industries critical to Thailand's economy (World Bank, 2023).

The aggregate gains from a stable, motivated workforce vastly outweigh the short-term advantages that some employers may reap from exploitative practices. A 32-year-old Myanmar construction worker in Bangkok stated that "Many of us leave jobs because the wages are too low and the work is dangerous. If we were treated better, we would stay and do our jobs well." Yet the impact of improved labor conditions extends beyond productivity alone, fostering social cohesion, reducing inequality, and promoting sustainable development (United Nations, 2023). Higher wages increase the purchasing power of migrant workers, injecting capital into local economies. Their expenditures on housing, food, and services create a ripple effect, driving demand and generating employment for local Thai citizens (Pholphirul & Rukumnuaykit, 2010). A 38-year-old Thai market vendor in Chiang Mai:, "Migrant workers spend their earnings on rent, food, and goods. When they have stable jobs and better pay, local businesses like mine benefit too". This dynamic may contradict the simplistic notion that migrant labor displaces domestic workers. Instead, it highlights the interdependence between economic growth and inclusive labor policies, demonstrating that migrants serve as catalysts for broader economic expansion rather than as a drain on resources.

Migrant-led organizing has consistently emerged as the first line of defense against exploitation, offering immediate support where state institutions fall short. Interviews with Myanmar workers highlight how community-based organizations function not only as service providers but also as vital spaces of solidarity and empowerment. "We understand the problems because we live them," explained, a 34-year-old coordinator of the Migrant Workers Rights Network (MWRN) who migrated from Mon State in 2005. "When someone is cheated out of wages, they do not trust a Thai lawyer immediately—they come to us first. Our experience gives us credibility." His words reveal the cultural and linguistic accessibility of grassroots groups compared to formal institutions. Established in 2009 in Samut Sakhon, Thailand's seafood-processing hub, MWRN began as an informal initiative to combat wage theft and abusive supervisors. Over time, it has grown into a network of more than 20,000 members with a formalized structure and elected representatives. Its guiding principle, "by migrants, for migrants," emphasizes self-determination. MWRN provides legal support, facilitates healthcare access, and assists with documentation, while cultivating collective strength and agency among its members. These grassroots initiatives challenge the simplistic binary of migrants as either passive victims or fully empowered actors. Instead, Myanmar workers construct alternative infrastructures of survival that blur the boundaries between informal welfare systems and political activism. Through organizations such as MWRN, migrants create subaltern counter-publics where rights discourses are not imposed from above but rather emerge organically from lived experience. Such practices demonstrate that Myanmar migrants in Thailand are far from invisible laborers. They are active rights-bearing agents who mobilize collectively, navigate legal systems, and strategically leverage transnational networks to advance their interests.

Employer attitudes toward these developments remain deeply ambivalent. Some businesses, particularly those seeking stability in highly competitive industries acknowledge the long-term advantages of a documented and loyal workforce. As one seafood processor in Mahachai explained: "It is cheaper in the long run to have a loyal workforce that you treat well than to constantly deal with workers running away." Yet, this recognition is not universal. In many low-margin industries, resistance persists, as compliance with minimum wage laws, overtime payments, and safety standards imposes immediate costs. In such contexts, employers often externalize these burdens onto already precarious labor, reinforcing cycles of informality and exploitation rather than addressing structural issues. Governments, meanwhile, reinforce this tension through contradictory policies. On one hand, Thailand's economy depends heavily on migrant labor, particularly in sectors such as seafood, construction, and agriculture. On the other hand, officials feel compelled to respond to anti-migrant sentiments through periodic crackdowns, deportations, and bureaucratic hurdles. An official from the Ministry of Labour, interviewed anonymously, admitted: "We need the workers, but we cannot be seen as opening the gates too wide. The public fears being overwhelmed. So, policy always has to balance economic need with political image." This illustrates the broader "migration management paradox": states both depend on migrant labor and simultaneously constrain migrants' rights, producing a governance system that is at once inclusionary and exclusionary.

The Structural Vulnerability of Thailand's Migrant-Dependent Economy

Emblematic of many Global South nations (Prabhakar, 2025), Thailand's economic ascendancy hinges on a precarious contradiction. Part of its economy reliance on migrant workforce Migrant workers enable Thailand to sustain low production costs and global competitiveness (Wailerdsak & Suehiro, 2025). However, this "flexibility" in labor markets, often lauded under neoliberal economic models, masks systemic exploitation (Standing, 2021). Migrant workers in Thailand more or less face and endure chronic precarity. They are suffer from substandard wages, legal invisibility and exclusion from labor protections. While Thailand's economic growth thrives on their disposability (Carr, 2023), this discourse interrogates the ethical and structural tensions between market efficiency and human dignity. The ILO (2022) discusses the challenges and opportunities for achieving decent work conditions for migrant workers in Thailand. Thailand's labor market exemplifies neoliberalism's central Discrepancy (Saad-Filho & Johnston, 2005).

Employers capitalize on their undocumented status to suppress wages and evade regulatory oversight. This model mirrors global patterns of labor extraction, where groups subsidize economic growth. It is framing this exploitation as economic necessity. Yet this system creates a self-reinforcing cycle of vulnerability. Workers, denied legal recognition, lack bargaining power to demand safer conditions or fair pay, trapping them in a liminal space where their labor is essential but their humanity is erased (van Nierop, Schönenberg, & Terziev, 2021).

Thailand's short-term gains in cheap labor, export competitiveness are undermined by long-term risks, while underinvestment in human capital stifles innovation. Unlike Japan (Kalleberg, Hewison, & Shin, 2021) or South Korea (Fleckenstein, Lee, &

Park, 2024), which coupled worker protections with industrial upgrading, Thailand's growth remains tethered to wage suppression rather than productivity gains. The result is a brittle economy, reliant on a transient underclass whose exclusion from social safety nets exacerbates inequality and instability. A purely utilitarian view, which reduces their value to cost-saving metrics, ignores the moral bankruptcy of a system that profits from dehumanization (Upegui, 2021). True economic efficiency cannot coexist with structural violence toward a fundamental workforce. Access to quality healthcare, education, and fair labor rights is essential. For instance, restricted healthcare access for migrants heightens public health risks (e.g., disease outbreaks in overcrowded fisheries), while educational exclusion perpetuates intergenerational poverty, stifling potential economic contributions (Office of the United Nations High Commissioner for Human Rights [OHCHR], 2014).

As the country faces demographic shifts, global economic competition, and rising ethical labor standards, the treatment and integration of migrant workers will increasingly shape Thailand's economic resilience, social cohesion,and international standing (International Organization for Migration [IOM], 2024). This systemic exclusion, while long tolerated under the guise of market efficiency, represents a growing strategic vulnerability. As Thailand's workforce shrinks in its working-age population projected to decline by 11 million by 2040, the failure to formalize and integrate migrant labor could create severe economic bottlenecks (World Bank, 2021). Without proactive measures to incorporate migrant workers into the formal economy, Thailand risks stalling economic growth and losing its edge in key sectors such as manufacturing, agriculture, and construction.

The social dimension is equally significant. Much of the public skepticism toward migration stems from anxieties about economic displacement and cultural tensions. However, history provides ample evidence that integrating migrant workers into the economic system enhances social cohesion, rather than marginalizing them. Societies that have enacted policies to protect migrant workers have observed declines in crime, stronger social trust, and increased civic engagement. From a 40-year-old economist at a Thai labor research institute from Chiang Mai University pointed that "Exploitation doesn't just harm workers. It undermines entire industries. Low morale and high turnover lead to inefficiencies that cost businesses more in the long run." The distribution of economic benefits and the fostering of social cohesion reinforce the conclusion that migrant-inclusive labor policies are not merely ethical imperatives but strategic necessities. In this sense, the logic of utilitarianism converges with pragmatic statecraft, pointing toward a model in which inclusive growth and national stability become mutually reinforcing pillars of long-term prosperity. Thailand's economic trajectory is often framed in terms of macroeconomic trends, trade partnerships, and technological advancements (Jongwanich, 2022). Yet beneath these visible indicators lies an overlooked but fundamental determinant of long-term stability of labor policy (Nae, Florescu, & Bălă oiu, 2024).

DISCUSSION: A COMMON GOOD FRAMEWORK FOR THAILAND'S MIGRANT LABOR SYSTEM

The Common Good framework offers a corrective. Equitable policies integrate migrants into society strengthen economic resilience. Public health investments, such as universal healthcare access, reduce long-term costs and enhance productivity. Education for migrant children disrupts cycles of exploitation, cultivating a skilled workforce. Social cohesion initiatives—anti-xenophobia campaigns, cultural exchange programs (Mazzucato, 2023) can mitigate tensions that arise from systemic marginalization. These measures are not altruistic but strategic and align with ethical responsibility and sustainable growth. Thailand's crossroads demands a reimagining of "flexibility." Current policies prioritize employer interests, framing migrant labor as a disposable input. Yet transitioning to an equity-centered model enhance competitiveness. Formalizing migrant labor could curb black-market exploitation, increase tax revenues and foster innovation through workforce diversification in the long term. South Korea's Employment Permit System, which grants migrants equal labor rights, demonstrates that ethical integration bolsters, rather than hinders, economic dynamism (Won, 2024). However, such reforms require confronting entrenched power structures. Industries reliant on exploitative practices, such as fisheries and agriculture, wield significant political influence. Additionally, nationalist narratives framing migrants as "outsiders" (Hackl, 2022) complicate public support for inclusion. Overcoming these barriers demands coalition-building such as uniting pro-labor activists, forward-thinking businesses, and international partners to reframe migrants as stakeholders in national development.

Thailand's economic future hinges on dismantling the false binary between efficiency and ethics. Migrant labor is not antithetical to growth but foundational to it; recognizing this necessitates systemic reforms that replace extraction with equity. By investing in human capital through legal protections, education, and healthcare, Thailand can transition from a low-cost labor model to a high-value, innovation-driven economy in globle market. This shift is not merely pragmatic but a moral reckoning: sustainable prosperity cannot be built on the backs of an invisible underclass. Flexibility, redefined as dignity in adaptability, must become the cornerstone of Thailand's next chapter of distribute justices.

A just society is one that ensures fairness, respects human dignity, and upholds the rights of all individuals, regardless of nationality or legal status (Wanjiru 2023). The plight of Myanmar migrant workers in Thailand exposes a stark contradiction between legal principles and lived realities. While Thailand has labor laws and international commitments that ostensibly protect workers, the gap between policy and enforcement reveals deep structural inequities (Palmgren, P. 2022). While economic benefits are disproportionately distributed, perpetuating cycles of marginalization rather than fostering inclusive growth (Andrews et al., 2021). Distributive justice demands that economic benefits and burdens be shared equitably across society (McKee, 1981). Yet, Myanmar migrant workers rarely reap the rewards of their labor. They endure long hours in hazardous conditions for wages far below those of their Thai counterparts. While industries benefit from cost efficiencies, workers remain economically vulnerable. Interviews stated that employers and authorities often exploit regulatory loopholes and weak enforcement mechanisms to suppress wages, deny benefits and circumvent labor protections. This imbalance reflects a governance failure where market efficiency is prioritized over human dignity (Magnuson, 2023), and economic growth is achieved at the expense of the most vulnerable.

Thailand's labor laws, including minimum wage regulations, social security provisions, and workplace safety standards, exist in theory (Musikawong, 2022) but are inconsistently enforced. Many migrant workers operate under informal agreements or temporary permits, leaving them without stable legal protections. Without formal contracts, they lack recourse to challenge exploitation, demand unpaid wages, or seek compensation for workplace injuries. In high-risk sectors like construction and fisheries, inadequate safety measures are not mere oversights but calculated trade-offs that prioritize cost-cutting over worker welfare. When enforcement of laws is inconsistent, they tend to function more as symbolic gestures rather than substantive tools for change. Thereby enabling systemic exploitation to continue unchecked. This phenomenon is evident in the context of symbolic policymaking in the UK during the 1960s, where restrictive immigration policies were frequently designed to create an illusion of control over irregular migration rather than tackling its underlying causes. Due to those factors, the legal status of migrant workers further exacerbates their vulnerability. Many navigate a precarious existence under temporary work permits or informal arrangements, making them easy targets for exploitation. The absence of a clear path to permanent residency or long-term employment stability leaves even long-term workers in legal limbo, unable to integrate fully into society or secure lasting protections. These structural inequalities are embedded in a system that views migrant labor as a temporary, expendable resource rather than a cornerstone of national development. International labor conventions emphasize the rights of all workers to fair wages, safe conditions, and freedom from coercion (Sengenberger, 2005). Yet, the stark contrast between these guarantees and the realities of Myanmar migrant workers in Thailand reveals a significant enforcement gap. Without meaningful oversight, labor protections remain theoretical, failing to shield workers from systemic vulnerabilities. A just labor system requires active institutional mechanisms to ensure accountability, prevent abuses, and empower workers to claim their rights (Reinecke & Donaghey, 2021).

To move toward a fairer and more sustainable economic model, Thailand must bridge the gap between legal principles and real-world protections. Strengthening enforcement mechanisms, ensuring equal pay for equal work, and providing a legal pathway for long-term employment stability are not just moral imperatives—they are economic necessities. A system that prioritizes fairness, dignity, and justice strengthens nationalcompetitiveness by fostering a labor market built on stability rather than exploitation. Myanmar migrant workers are integral to Thailand's economic and social fabric. From a utilitarian perspective, their indispensable role in sustaining economic productivity and labor market stability is evident, as they fill critical labor shortages and contribute to key industries such as construction, agriculture, and manufacturing (Harkins, 2019; Huguet, 2014). At the same time, principles of distributive justice emphasize the moral imperative of ensuring fair treatment, equitable labor rights, and access to social protections for these workers (Rawls, 1971). Therefore, a coherent national policy for Myanmar migrant workers, grounded in the Common Good, must integrate utilitarian efficiency with distributive justice to ensure sustainable development. The government should prioritize comprehensive legal integration, transitioning from short-term work permits to a transparent pathway for long-term residency. This policy shift formalizes the workforce, expands the tax base, and enhances productivity—maximizing societal utility. Concurrently, mandatory inclusion in social safety nets, including health insurance and access to public education, fulfills distributive justice by equitably sharing the benefits of growth. Furthermore, public-private partnerships should be incentivized to fund vocational training and anti-xenophobia initiatives, fostering social cohesion and building a skilled, stable workforce. These measures collectively reframe migration from a temporary expediency into a strategic investment, aligning economic pragmatism with the ethical imperative of dignity and rights.By integrating economic pragmatism with ethical labor reforms, Thailand can build a sustainable, inclusive labor system that benefits both its society and Myanmar migrant workers. Such an approach aligns with the broader goal of fostering social cohesion and inclusive growth, ensuring that the contributions of migrant workers are recognized and their rights protected (Acemoglu & Robinson, 2012). Ultimately, a nation's prosperity is measured not only by its economic output but by the extent to which it recognizes, protects, and values those who sustain its industries as integral members of society.

CONCLUSION

The presence of Myanmar migrant workers in Thailand embodies both economic necessity and socio-political complexity. As a vital labor force across agriculture, construction, manufacturing, and services, they underpin Thailand's economic competitiveness while simultaneously exposing deep structural vulnerabilities in its labor governance. This chapter has sought to bridge normative theory with applied policy analysis by demonstrating how ethical frameworks in utilitarianism and distributive justice can illuminate the contradictions between economic imperatives and the lived realities of migrant workers. Whereas utilitarian reasoning highlights the aggregate benefits of migrant labor for Thailand's growth, the lens of distributive justice reveals persistent inequities in wages, legal status, and access to social protections, underscoring the moral insufficiency of a purely efficiency-driven approach.

By integrating these normative perspectives with grounded policy analysis, the study highlights the need for structural reforms that move beyond narrow economic logics. Ensuring stronger legal protections, fair wage policies, and equal access to healthcare and education would not only enhance productivity but also affirm migrants' dignity and rights. In this sense, the chapter contributes to wider global debates on labor migration and justice, positioning the Thailand–Myanmar migration corridor as a critical case for rethinking the balance between growth, rights, and fairness in transnational labor markets. Ultimately, safeguarding the rights of Myanmar migrant workers is not merely a matter of domestic reform; it is integral to constructing a more ethical and sustainable model of labor governance that resonates with international human rights norms and advances global discussions on just migration standards.

REFERENCES

Acemoglu, D., & Robinson, J. A. (2012). *Why nations fail: The origins of power, prosperity, and poverty*. Crown Business.

Alberti, G., & Sacchetto, D. (2024). Enclaves of differentiated labour. In *The politics of migrant labour* (pp. 83–114). Bristol University Press., https://bristoluniversitypressdigital.com/display/book/9781529227765/ch003.xml DOI: 10.2307/jj.9692612.9

Amfori. (2025, March 3). Protecting Myanmar migrant workers in Thailand: Ethical recruitment and labour migration in focus. Amfori. https://www.amfori.org/en/news/protecting-myanmar-migrant-workers-in-thailand-ethical-recruitment-and-labour-migration-in-focus

Anantanasuwong, D. (2021). Population ageing in Thailand: critical issues in the twenty-first century. Education for the Elderly in the Asia Pacific, 31-56. https://doi.org/DOI: 10.1007/978-981-16-3326-3_3

Andrews, C., de Montesquiou, A., Sánchez, I. A., Dutta, P. V., Paul, B. V., Samaranayake, S., & Chaudhary, S. (2021). *The state of economic inclusion report 2021: The potential to scale*. World Bank Publications. DOI: 10.1596/978-1-4648-1598-0

Anukul, C. (2024). Labor policy responses to ageing society: How Thailand achieve human security with economic growth? *Social Justice and Inequality Journal, 5*(1), 18–29. DOI: 10.14456/sjij.2024.2

Arnold, D., & Hewison, K. (2005). Exploitation and empowerment in the Thai-Burmese border economy. *Journal of Contemporary Asia*, *35*(4), 521–540. DOI: 10.1080/00472330580000291

Arnold, D., & Pickles, J. (2011). Global work, surplus labor, and the precarious economies of the border. *Antipode*, *43*(5), 1598–1624. DOI: 10.1111/j.1467-8330.2011.00899.x

Association of Southeast Asian Nations (ASEAN). (2022, December). Women migrant workers in the laws and policies of ASEAN member states. ASEAN Secretariat. https://asean.org/wp-content/uploads/2023/02/ASEAN_REPORT_Final.pdf

Battistella, G. (Ed.). (2014). Global and Asian perspectives on international migration (Vol. 4). Springer. ht https://doi.org/DOI: 10.1007/978-3-319-08317-9

Bauböck, R., & Ruhs, M. (2022). The elusive triple win: Addressing temporary labour migration dilemmas through fair representation. *Migration Studies*, *10*(3), 528–552. DOI: 10.1093/migration/mnac021

Bentham, J. (1789). *An introduction to the principles of morals and legislation.* Clarendon Press. DOI: 10.1093/oseo/instance.00077240

Bentham, J. (1948). *An introduction to the principles of morals and legislation.* Hafner. (Original work published 1789)

Borjas, G. J. (2019). *Immigration economics.* Harvard University Press.

Broome, J. (2004). *Weighing lives.* Oxford University Press. DOI: 10.1093/019924376X.001.0001

Campbell, S. (2018). Migrant waste collectors in Thailand's informal economy: Mapping class relations. *European Journal of East Asian Studies, 17*(2), 263–288. DOI: 10.1163/15700615-01702003

Cardin, P. R. (2021). Democracy, Rhetoric, Authoritarianism: Democratic Rhetoric in Authoritarian Thailand (Doctoral dissertation, Purdue University Graduate School). https://hammer.purdue.edu/articles/thesis/Democracy_Rhetoric_Authoritarianism_Democratic_Rhetoric_in_Authoritarian_Thailand/15060591

Carr, S. C. (2023). Slavery wage. In *Wage and well-being: Toward sustainable livelihood* (pp. 89–116). Springer International Publishing., DOI: 10.1007/978-3-031-19301-9_4

Chaichanavichakit, A. (2024). Undercurrent forces beneath a long-standing migration corridor: A case study of Burmese workers in Thailand. *The International Journal of Interdisciplinary Organizational Studies, 19*(2), 1–26. Advance online publication. DOI: 10.18848/2324-7649/CGP/v19i02/1-26

Chang, A., Cheah, J., & Vigneswaran, D. (2023). Education and social mobility among migrant communities in Southeast Asia. *Journal of Migration Studies, 45*(2), 123–145. DOI: 10.3390/ijerph19095685

Chantavanich, S. (2014). Managing international labor migration in ASEAN: Thailand case. International Organization for Migration (IOM). https://tdri.or.th/wp-content/uploads/2013/07/h117.pdf

Chantavanich, S., & Jitpong, W. (2023). Precarity and social protection of migrant fishers in Thailand: Case studies of death and disappearance at sea. *Marine Policy, 155*, 105743. Advance online publication. DOI: 10.1016/j.marpol.2023.105743

Corimanya, E. (2025). THE FREE MARKET MYTH: Unveiling the Illusions of Economic Justice: Exploring Failures, Inequalities, and Alternative Futures in a Globalized World. Alternative Perspectives. https://www.everand.com/book/815229735/The-Free-Market-Myth-Unveiling-the-Illusions-of-Economic-Justice

Crocco, O. S. (2021). *Developing Human Resources in Southeast Asia.* Springer International Publishing., DOI: 10.1007/978-3-030-79697-6

De Genova, N. (2002). Migrant "illegality" and deportability in everyday life. *Annual Review of Anthropology, 31*(1), 419–447. DOI: 10.1146/annurev.anthro.31.040402.085432

Diller, J. M. (2022). Protecting the vulnerable: migration, work, and human rights due diligence. In *Handbook on Globalisation and Labour Standards* (pp. 84–106). Edward Elgar Publishing., https://ideas.repec.org/h/elg/eechap/18768_5.html DOI: 10.4337/9781788977371.00010

Ducanes, G. M., Engblom, A., & Ramos, V. J. R. (2023). Informal employment and irregular migration status: A double whammy for migrant workers in Thailand. *Asian and Pacific Migration Journal, 32*(2), 234–262. DOI: 10.1177/01171968231188135

Evagora-Campbell, M., Zahidie, A., Buse, K., Rabbani, F., & Hawkes, S. (2022). Promoting labour migrant health equity through action on the structural determinants: A systematic review. *Journal of Migration and Health, 5*, 100082. DOI: 10.1016/j.jmh.2022.100082 PMID: 35199076

Fairclough, N. (2003). *Analysing discourse: Textual analysis for social research.* Routledge. DOI: 10.4324/9780203697078

Fleckenstein, T., Lee, S. C., & Park, J. (2024). Skills and training in hierarchical capitalism: The rise and fall of vocational training in South Korea. *Journal of Contemporary Asia, 54*(2), 260–281. DOI: 10.1080/00472336.2023.2168207

Gilodi, A., Albert, I., & Nienaber, B. (2024). Vulnerability in the context of migration: A critical overview and a new conceptual model. *Human Arenas, 7*(3), 620–640. DOI: 10.1007/s42087-022-00288-5

Hackl, A. (2022). Good immigrants, permitted outsiders: Conditional inclusion and citizenship in comparison. *Ethnic and Racial Studies, 45*(6), 989–1010. DOI: 10.1080/01419870.2021.2011938

Harkins, B. (2019). Thailand's migration dilemma. International Organization for Migration (IOM). https://thailand.un.org/sites/default/files/2020-06/Thailand-Migration-Report-2019.pdf

Harkins, B., Lindgren, D., & Suravoranon, T. (2017). Risks and rewards: Outcomes of labour migration in South-East Asia. International Labour Organization. https://www.ilo.org/publications/risks-and-rewards-outcomes-labour-migration-south-east-asia

Harrod, J., & Power, P. (1987). the Unprotected Worker. Columbia University.

Heymann, J., & McNeill, K. (2013). Changing children's chances: New findings on child policy worldwide. UCLA World Policy Analysis Center. https://www.worldpolicycenter.org/sites/default/files/Childrens%20Chances%20Report%20-%20English.pdf

Hosseini, S. H. (2023). The well-living paradigm: Reimagining quality of life in our turbulent world. *Discover Global Society*, *1*(1), 19. DOI: 10.1007/s44282-023-00022-8

Htun, H. T. (2022). Unpacking gender inequality for inclusive development: A case study of Myanmar female migrant workers in Samut Sakhon Province, Thailand (Master's thesis, Chulalongkorn University). Chulalongkorn University Digital Repository. https://digital.car.chula.ac.th/chulaetd/5913/

Htwe, T. M. (2025). The roles of livelihood, remittances, and social capitals of Myanmar migrants in Mae Sot, Thailand post-2021 coup. YCU Research Institute. Retrieved from https://yri-mm.org/the-role-of-livelihood-remittances-and-social-capitals-of-myanmar-migrants-in-mae-sot-thailand-post-2021-coup/

Huguet, J. W. (2015). Thailand migration report 2014. United Nations Thematic Working Group on Migration in Thailand. https://thailand.iom.int/sites/g/files/tmzbdl1371/files/documents/EN%2520-%2520Thailand%2520Migration%2520Report%25202014.pdf

Huguet, J. W., & Punpuing, S. (2005). International migration in Thailand. International Organization for Migration. https://publications.iom.int/system/files/pdf/intl_migration_thailand.pdf

Human Rights Watch. (2023). Thailand: Recent refugees pushed back to Myanmar. https://www.hrw.org/news/2023/11/29/thailand-recent-refugees-pushed-back-myanmar

International Labour Organization [ILO]. (2021). World employment and social outlook: The role of digital labour platforms in transforming the world of work. ILO. https://www.ilo.org/publications/flagship-reports/role-digital-labour-platforms-transforming-world-work

International Organization for Migration (IOM). (2023, March). Labour migration in Asia: What does the future hold?IOM Asia-Pacific. https://roasiapacific.iom.int/sites/g/files/tmzbdl671/files/documents/2023-07/iom_labour-migration-in-asia_what-does-the-future-hold.pdf

International Organization for Migration (IOM). (2023). Thailand response plan for cross-border flows from Myanmar (September 2023 – August 2024). IOM Thailand. https://thailand.iom.int/sites/g/files/tmzbdl1371/files/documents/2024-07/iom-thailand-myanmar-appeal_2023.pdf

International Organization for Migration (IOM). (2024). Thailand migration report 2024. IOM Thailand. https://thailand.iom.int/sites/g/files/tmzbdl1371/files/documents/2024-12/thailand-migration-report-2024.pdf

International Organization for Migration (IOM) Thailand. (2024). Overview of Myanmar nationals in Thailand – March 2024. https://thailand.iom.int/sites/g/files/tmzbdl1371/files/documents/2025-03/myanmar_migrants_thailand_jan25_final-1.pdf

Jongwanich, J. (2022). *The economic consequences of globalization on Thailand.* Routledge., DOI: 10.4324/9781003144076

Kagan, S. (1989). *The limits of morality.* Oxford University Press., DOI: 10.1093/0198239165.001.0001

Kalleberg, A. L., Hewison, K., & Shin, K. Y. (2021). Precarious Asia: Global capitalism and work in Japan, South Korea, and Indonesia. Stanford University Press. https://doi.org/DOI: 10.1515/9781503629837

Kant, I. (2012). *Groundwork of the metaphysics of morals* (Gregor, M., & Timmermann, J., Trans.). Cambridge University Press. (Original work published 1785), https://cpb-us-w2.wpmucdn.com/blog.nus.edu.sg/dist/c/1868/files/2012/12/Kant-Groundwork-ng0pby.pdf

Karim, M. U. H. F. (2024). Irregular migration and informal employment status: A human rights dichotomy shifted from migrant worker parents to migrant children in Thailand's construction project. *Journal of Human Rights and Peace Studies, 10*(1). https://so03.tci-thaijo.org/index.php/HRPS/article/view/276621

Khai, T. S. (2023). A socio-ecological barrier to regular migration, regularization and healthcare access for Myanmar irregular migrant workers in Thailand. https://commons.ln.edu.hk/otd/200/

Khemanitthathai, S. (2022). Emigration state in transition: Foreign policy goals in Myanmar's emigration policies and practices (Doctoral dissertation, SOAS University of London). SOAS Research Online. https://eprints.soas.ac.uk/37407/

MacAskill, W. (2015). *Doing good better: How effective altruism can help you help others, do work that matters, and make smarter choices about giving back.* Gotham Books.

Magnuson, W. (2023). The failure of market efficiency. BYU Law Review, 48(3), Article 7. https://digitalcommons.law.byu.edu/cgi/viewcontent.cgi?article=3417&context=lawreview

Manatschal, A. (2022). Framing matters: Pathways between policies, immigrant integration, and native attitudes. In *Handbook on Migration and Welfare* (pp. 195–209). Edward Elgar Publishing., DOI: 10.4337/9781839104572.00018

Marshall, S., Taylor, K., & Tödt, S. (2023). Gendered distributive injustice in production networks: Implications for the regulation of precarious work. *Industrial Law Journal, 52*(1), 107–148. DOI: 10.1093/indlaw/dwab039

Mazzucato, M. (2023). Governing the economics of the common good: From correcting market failures to shaping collective goals. *Journal of Economic Policy Reform, 27*(1), 1–24. DOI: 10.1080/17487870.2023.2280969

McClain, S. N., Bruch, C., Daly, E., May, J., Hamada, Y., Maekawa, M., Shiiba, N., Nakayama, M., & Tsiokanou, G. (2022). Migration with dignity: A legal and policy framework. *Journal of Disaster Research, 17*(3), 292–300. DOI: 10.20965/jdr.2022.p0292

McKee, A. F. (1981). WHAT IS "DISTRIBUTIVE" JUSTICE? *Review of Social Economy, 39*(1), 1–17. https://www.jstor.org/stable/29769043. DOI: 10.1080/758528118

Mill, J. S. (1863). *Utilitarianism*. Parker, Son, and Bourn.

Mill, J. S. (1863). *Utilitarianism*. Parker, Son, and Bourn.

Mill, J. S. (2001). *Utilitarianism* (2nd ed.). Hackett Publishing. (Original work published 1863)

Mortensen, S. (2024). Rightless rurality: The illegalization of Myanmar migrant laborers in Thailand's agro-industry. *The Journal of Peasant Studies, 51*(2), 1–22. DOI: 10.1080/03066150.2024.2340648

Mostafanezhad, M., Sebro, T., Prasse-Freeman, E., & Norum, R. (2022). Surplus precaritization: Supply chain capitalism and the geoeconomics of hope in Myanmar's borderlands. *Political Geography, 95*, 102561. DOI: 10.1016/j.polgeo.2021.102561

Musikawong, S. (2022). Understanding the gaps between the bilateral regularization of migration and workers' rights: The case of agricultural migrant workers in Thailand. *Theoretical Inquiries in Law, 23*(2), 289–325. DOI: 10.1515/til-2022-0020

Nae, T. M., Florescu, M. S., & Bălă oiu, G. I. (2024). Towards social justice: Investigating the role of labor, globalization, and governance in reducing socio-economic inequality within post-communist countries. *Sustainability (Basel), 16*(6), 2234. DOI: 10.3390/su16062234

Office of the National Economic and Social Development Council. (2023). The thirteenth national economic and social development plan (2023–2027). Office of the Prime Minister, Thailand. https://www.nesdc.go.th/en/the-national-economic-and-social-development-plan/the-thirteenth-plan-2023-2027/

Office of the United Nations High Commissioner for Human Rights (OHCHR). (2014). The corporate responsibility to respect human rights: An interpretive guide. United Nations. https://www.ohchr.org/sites/default/files/Documents/Publications/HR.PUB.12.2_En.pdf

Ord, T. (2020). *The precipice: Existential risk and the future of humanity*. Hachette Books., DOI: 10.1007/s10677-021-10181-9

Palmgren, P. (2024). Infrastructures of social reproduction: Migrant survival and economic development at the Thailand-Myanmar border. *The International Migration Review*, 01979183241287465. Advance online publication. DOI: 10.1177/01979183241287465

Palmgren, P. A. (2022). *Reactive Control: Development, Governance, and Social Reproduction in Thailand's Regimes of Labor Migration*. University of California., https://escholarship.org/uc/item/3q57g7vn

Parello, C. P., & Ikhenaode, B. I. (2021). Migration, community networks and welfare in neoclassical growth models. *Journal of Macroeconomics, 70*, 103369. DOI: 10.1016/j.jmacro.2021.103369

Parfit, D. (2011). *On what matters*. Oxford University Press.

Petcharamesree, S. (2023). Ethical frameworks in social policy: Utilitarianism and distributive justice. Publisher.

Petcharamesree, S. (2023). Migration and the common good: Ethical perspectives on labor policies in Thailand. *Journal of Southeast Asian Ethics, 18*(1), 34–52.

Pettit, P. (1997). *Republicanism: A theory of freedom and government*. Oxford University Press.

Pholphirul, P., & Rukumnuaykit, P. (2010). Economic contribution of migrant workers to Thailand. *International Migration (Geneva, Switzerland), 48*(5), 174–202. DOI: 10.1111/j.1468-2435.2009.00553.x

Piketty, T. (2013). *Capital in the twenty-first century.* Harvard University Press.

Positive Destinations. (2025, January 30). Thailand: Exploring the impact of healthcare barriers on Myanmar migrants in Thailand. Retrieved from https://www.positivedestinations.info/news/17371-thailand-exploring-the-impact-of-healthcare-barriers-on-myanmar-migrants-in-thailand/

Pouryousefi, S., & Freeman, R. E. (2021). Ethical labor policies in global markets: A framework for migrant workers. *Journal of Business Ethics*, *174*(3), 567–582. DOI: 10.1007/s10551-020-04620-3

Prabhakar, A. (2025). A Sustainable and Inclusive Economic Development: A Global Imperative: A Global Imperative. *Journal of Recycling Economy & Sustainability Policy*, *4*(1), 1–16. https://respjournal.com/index.php/pub/article/view/36

Rahim, H. A., & Ab Rahman, A.Hafizah Abdul RahimAsmak Ab Rahman. (2024). Towards positive peace: Malaysia's strides in well-functioning government and sustainable economic development. [JoHDeC]. *Journal of Human Development and Communication*, *13*, 99–109. DOI: 10.58915/johdec.v13.2024.1835

Rawls, J. (1971). *A theory of justice.* Harvard University Press. DOI: 10.4159/9780674042605

Rawls, J. (1971). *A theory of justice.* Harvard University Press. DOI: 10.4159/9780674042605

Reinecke, J., & Donaghey, J. (2021). Towards worker-driven supply chain governance: Developing decent work through democratic worker participation. *The Journal of Supply Chain Management*, *57*(2), 14–28. DOI: 10.1111/jscm.12250

Rodchan, K. (2024). An analysis of the spatial structure of foreign investment in Thailand: Foreign investors; To invest; Space; distribution. *Lao Social Sciences Journal*, *1*(2), 22–31. DOI: 10.71026/lss.2023.02003

Royal Thai Government. (2017). Royal Ordinance Concerning the Management of Employment of Foreign Workers, B.E. 2560 (2017). Retrieved from https://natlex.ilo.org/dyn/natlex2/natlex2/files/download/107728/THA107728%20Eng.pdf

Saad-Filho, A., & Johnston, D. (Eds.). (2005). *Neoliberalism: A critical reader.* Pluto Press.

Sen, A. (1999). *Development as freedom.* Oxford University Press.

Sen, A. (2009). *The idea of justice.* Harvard University Press.

Sengenberger, W. (2005). *Globalization and social progress: The role and impact of international labour standards* (2nd rev. ed.). Friedrich-Ebert-Stiftung., https://library.fes.de/pdf-files/iez/02980.pdf

Seubert, C., Hopfgartner, L., & Glaser, J. (2021). Living wages, decent work, and need satisfaction: An integrated perspective. *International Journal of Human Resource Management, 32*(16), 808–823. DOI: 10.1080/09585192.2021.1964098

Singer, P. (1972). Famine, affluence, and morality. *Philosophy & Public Affairs, 1*(3), 229–243.

Smith, A. (2003). *The wealth of nations*. Bantam Classics. (Original work published 1776)

Stalker, P. (2000). Workers without frontiers: the impact of globalization on international migration. International Labour Organization. Pp 121-232 https://unesdoc.unesco.org/ark:/48223/pf0000198692

Standing, G. (2021). *The corruption of capitalism: Why rentiers thrive and work does not pay*. Biteback Publishing.

Statista. (2023). Number of Burmese migrant workers in Thailand 2023. https://www.statista.com/statistics/1551849/thailand-number-of-burmese-migrant-workers/?srsltid=AfmBOopOytyKXoRIwUxhHBUCuZi7a4kdTH0h5F1Q6ZTEKUMUsqtDyjRu

Stiglitz, J. (2012). *The price of inequality: How today's divided society endangers our future*. W.W. Norton & Company.

Stokke, K., Tödt, D., & Vigneswaran, D. (2018). Migration and inequality in Southeast Asia. *The Journal of Asian Studies, 77*(4), 987–1009.

Stringer, C., Burmester, B., & Michailova, S. (2022). Modern slavery and the governance of labor exploitation in the Thai fishing industry. *Journal of Cleaner Production, 371*, 133645. DOI: 10.1016/j.jclepro.2022.133645

Tun Shein, N. (2021). Why Myanmar migrant workers flee to Thailand? (Doctoral dissertation, Mahidol University). Mahidol University Archive. https://archive.cm.mahidol.ac.th/handle/123456789/4464

Tungjiewlee, R. (2023). Assessing human rights due diligence for migrant workers in an SME business: A focus on the agricultural supply chain (Doctoral dissertation, Mahidol University). Mahidol University Archive. https://archive.cm.mahidol.ac.th/handle/123456789/5465

Tyler, C. (2017). Economic Migration, Social Justice and the Common Good: A Public Lecture. In: Common Good Politics. Palgrave Macmillan, Cham. DOI: 10.1007/978-3-319-32404-3_10

Ullah, A. A., Lee, S. C. W., & Hassan, N. H. (2024). *Southeast Asia in pre-and post-COVID-19: Economy, society, mobility and religion.* Taylor & Francis., DOI: 10.4324/9781003464051

United Nations. (2024). Report of the Secretary-General on the Global Compact for Safe, Orderly and Regular Migration. United Nations Network on Migration. https://migrationnetwork.un.org/sites/g/files/tmzbdl416/files/sg-report-2024/SG_Report_GCMpdf.pdf

United Nations Development Programme (UNDP). (2023, November). Seeking opportunities elsewhere: Exploring the lives and challenges of Myanmar migrant workers in Thailand. UNDP. https://www.undp.org/sites/g/files/zskgke326/files/2023-12/undp-mmr_seeking-opportunities-elsewhere_nov_2023_final.pdf

United Nations High Commissioner for Refugees (UNHCR). (2024). Thailand Multi-Country Office: Situation Report. https://www.unhcr.org/where-we-work/countries/thailand

United Nations Thailand. (2022, July 12). Opinion: Domestic workers have rights too. United Nations Thailand. https://thailand.un.org/en/191709-opinion-domestic-workers-have-rights-too

Upegui, D. (2021). *Social Justice and Evolutionary Biology: A Natural Fit.* University of Rhode Island.

van Nierop, P., Schönenberg, L., & Terziev, P. (2021). Counteracting undeclared work and labour exploitation of third-country national workers. European Labour Authority (ELA). https://www.ela.europa.eu/sites/default/files/2023-12/counteracting-undeclared-work-labour-exploitation-third-country-national-workers.pdf

Vigneswaran, D. (2020). *Migration and development: A global perspective.* Routledge.

Vungsiriphisal, P. (2017). *Labor migration in Thailand: Policy and practice.* Chulalongkorn University Press.

Wailerdsak, N., & Suehiro, A. (2025). Impacts of external shocks and domestic change on Thailand's economy and social policies. Journal of Contemporary East Asia Studies, 1-22. DOI: 10.1080/24761028.2024.2434299

Wanjiru, D. (2023). The intersection of immigration policies and human rights. *American Journal of Law and Policy, 1*(1), 1–12. https://forthworthjournals.org/journals/index.php/AJLP/article/view/21

Warr, P. (2024, January 25). Thailand's economy remains beset by low productivity and slow growth. East Asia Forum. https://eastasiaforum.org/2024/01/25/thailands-economy-remains-beset-by-low-productivity-and-slow-growth/

Waters, T., South, A., Vaddhanaphuti, C., & Corbin, L. (Eds.). (2021). Moving around Myanmar: Migration in, from, and back to Burma. Regional Center for Social Science and Sustainable Development (RCSD), Chiang Mai University. https://rcsd.soc.cmu.ac.th/wp-content/uploads/2022/03/Moving-Around-Myanmar_web.pdf

Weig, A. (2024). (De-)constructing 'migrant illegality': A critical examination of narratives of irregular migration among Westerners in Thailand [Master's thesis, Uppsala University]. DiVA Portal. https://www.diva-portal.org/smash/record.jsf?pid=diva2:1875840

Won, S. Y. (2024). *Immigrants as 'new' precariats in the Korean immigration policy regime: Navigating identity, rights, and governance.* Taylor & Francis. DOI: 10.4324/9781003566762

World Bank. (2021). Aging and the labor market in Thailand: Labor markets and social policy in a rapidly transforming and aging Thailand. International Bank for Reconstruction and Development. https://www.worldbank.org/en/country/thailand/publication/aging-and-the-labor-market-in-thailand

World Bank. (2023). Thailand economic monitor: Migration and labor market dynamics. Washington, DC: World Bank Group. https://www.worldbank.org/en/country/thailand/publication/temdec2023

World Bank. (2024). Thailand economic monitor July 2024: Unlocking the growth potential of secondary cities.International Bank for Reconstruction and Development. https://documents1.worldbank.org/curated/en/099062924133030977/pdf/P50100914f725005f1b9211803e7e17020a.pdf

World Health Organization. (2023). Promoting the health of refugees and migrants: experiences from around the world. World Health Organization. https://www.who.int/publications/i/item/9789240067110

Yazdiha, H. (2023). Bridging the Sociologies of Morality and Migration: The Moral Underpinnings of Borders, Policies, and Immigrants. In *Handbook of the Sociology of Morality* (Vol. 2, pp. 399–412). Springer International Publishing., DOI: 10.1007/978-3-031-32022-4_28

Young, I. M. (2011). *Responsibility for justice*. Oxford University Press. DOI: 10.1093/acprof:oso/9780195392388.001.0001

Chapter 13
Contemporary Political Theories and Their Impact on the Administration of Vocational High Schools (EPAL) in Greece

Angeliki Ntinieraki
https://orcid.org/0009-0002-4156-9810
University of Alicante, Spain

ABSTRACT

The administration of Vocational High Schools (EPAL) in Greece has undergone significant transformations due to the influence of contemporary political theories. These theories have shaped the policies and governance models adopted by school administrators, affecting decision-making processes, leadership styles, and institutional priorities. The impact of these theories can be observed in areas such as democratic governance, neoliberal reforms, inclusivity, and social justice. One of the most prominent political theories influencing the administration of EPALs is democratic governance. Rooted in liberal democratic thought, this approach emphasizes participatory decision-making, accountability, and transparency. School administrators are expected to involve teachers, students, and parents in the governance process, ensuring that policies are developed through consultation and collective input. This participatory model aligns with broader European Union directives that encourage stakeholder engagement in educational administration.

DOI: 10.4018/979-8-3373-2332-9.ch013

INTRODUCTION

Vocational education in Greece, primarily delivered through Vocational High Schools (EPAL), occupies a critical yet contested space within the national educational system. Historically perceived as a second-tier pathway, EPALs have often been associated with students from lower socio-economic backgrounds, serving as institutional mechanisms for labor market integration rather than academic advancement (Rodokanakis & Vlachos, 2019). Despite recent policy reforms aimed at modernizing vocational training and aligning it with European standards—such as the introduction of modular curricula, work-based learning schemes, and upgraded certification frameworks—EPALs continue to operate under complex structural constraints, including limited autonomy, resource scarcity, and entrenched social stigma (Gounari & Grollios, 2012). Situated within a highly centralized bureaucratic system, the administration of these schools is governed by top-down directives issued by the Ministry of Education, leaving limited room for contextual adaptation or innovative leadership at the school level. At the same time, EPALs are increasingly expected to fulfill diverse roles: addressing youth unemployment, promoting social inclusion, and contributing to the digital and green transitions dictated by European policy agendas.

In this context, the study of contemporary political theories becomes essential for understanding the evolving dynamics of school administration within vocational education. Educational institutions do not function in a political vacuum; rather, they reflect and reproduce dominant ideological frameworks that shape governance models, leadership practices, and institutional priorities (Pagoulatos, 2003). Theories such as democratic governance, neoliberalism, critical social justice, and post-bureaucratic management each offer distinct lenses through which educational administration can be analyzed and critiqued. Their influence is evident in policy formulations that emphasize stakeholder participation, performance-based accountability, inclusion of marginalized groups, and responsiveness to global labor market demands. In the case of EPALs, these political currents often coexist in tension, producing contradictory expectations and layered administrative challenges. Exploring how these theories manifest in school-level governance provides critical insights into both the limits and possibilities of reform, particularly in systems marked by socio-political volatility, economic constraint, and institutional inertia. Thus, this chapter aims to examine the impact of contemporary political theories on the administration of EPALs in Greece, illuminating the ideological forces that underlie policy discourse and administrative practice, and assessing their implications for equity, efficiency, and democratic governance in vocational education.

This chapter is guided by a central analytical concern: how do contemporary political theories influence the administration of vocational education in Greece, particularly within the context of Vocational High Schools (EPAL)? More specifically, it interrogates the ways in which governance practices, leadership logics, and institutional objectives are shaped by competing ideological frameworks—ranging from participatory democratic ideals to technocratic and neoliberal imperatives. The inquiry is situated at the intersection of educational administration, political sociology, and critical policy studies, drawing on theoretical perspectives to unpack how policy discourse materializes within administrative structures and everyday decision-making. Key research questions include: (1) In what ways do political ideologies such as democratic governance, neoliberalism, and social justice manifest in the administration of EPALs? (2) How do bureaucratic and institutional constraints mediate the implementation of politically informed reforms? (3) What tensions arise between policy rhetoric and administrative practice, and how are these negotiated by school leaders? (4) To what extent do transnational policy pressures and national political currents reshape the mission, identity, and operational logic of vocational education in Greece? These questions aim to reveal not only the structural forces that condition school administration but also the ideological contestations that define the governance of educational space.

To address these questions, the chapter is organized into seven interrelated sections. Following this introduction, the second section outlines the historical and institutional development of EPAL within the broader Greek education system, emphasizing the legacy of centralization and the evolving role of vocational education in socio-economic planning. The third section provides a theoretical mapping of contemporary political ideologies—democratic governance, neoliberalism, social justice, technocracy, intersectional feminism, and nationalism—and discusses their operational manifestations in educational policy and administration. The fourth section turns to transnational policy influences, particularly those emanating from the European Union and international organizations and examines their impact on EPAL reform agendas. The fifth section synthesizes the preceding analysis by exploring the tensions, contradictions, and practical dilemmas encountered by school administrators who must reconcile conflicting policy imperatives within constrained institutional settings. An optional sixth section offers illustrative case reflections or vignettes that ground the theoretical discussion in practical realities. Finally, the seventh section draws conclusions and presents forward-looking recommendations for policymakers, practitioners, and researchers. Through this structure, the chapter aims to contribute to a deeper understanding of the political underpinnings of educational administration and to highlight the strategic challenges facing vocational education in the contemporary Greek context.

HISTORICAL AND INSTITUTIONAL BACKGROUND OF EPAL IN GREECE

The institutional evolution of Vocational High Schools (ΕΠΑΛ) in Greece reflects a long-standing tension between the state's developmental priorities and the persistent marginalization of vocational education within the broader educational hierarchy. Historically, vocational training in Greece has been characterized by institutional instability, limited prestige, and an ambivalent policy orientation. Since their formal establishment under Law 3475/2006, EPALs replaced the former Technical Vocational Education Schools (TEE), in an effort to rationalize and modernize the fragmented system of secondary-level vocational education. The reform aimed to integrate general and technical subjects, strengthen connections with the labor market, and offer clearer pathways to tertiary education. Despite these intentions, the vocational track continues to be perceived as a "residual" option, frequently associated with students of lower academic performance and limited socio-economic capital (Rodokanakis & Vlachos, 2019). The dual mission of EPALs—preparing students for immediate labor market entry while also enabling vertical educational mobility—has produced structural contradictions that are reflected in policy, pedagogy, and institutional identity.

The role of EPALs within the Greek education system is further complicated by the deeply centralized nature of educational governance. The Ministry of Education exercises direct control over school curricula, staffing, budgeting, and strategic planning, leaving minimal discretionary power to local educational authorities or individual school leaders. This vertical model of administration, rooted in Weberian bureaucratic traditions, prioritizes standardization and formal equity across regions, but it also constrains responsiveness to local needs and impedes context-sensitive innovation (Gounari & Grollios, 2012). School principals in EPALs function primarily as implementers of ministerial directives, with limited authority to adapt programs, manage resources autonomously, or build external partnerships that could enhance institutional relevance and flexibility. This administrative rigidity is compounded by the procedural complexity of state regulations and the slow pace of policy implementation, which collectively undermine efforts toward decentralization and institutional differentiation.

Moreover, the vocational education system in Greece has been repeatedly shaped—and often destabilized—by alternating political agendas and abrupt legislative interventions. Policy reforms affecting EPALs have tended to be top-down, fragmented, and frequently reversed with changes in government, resulting in limited continuity and long-term strategic coherence. For example, while some reforms have emphasized work-based learning and dual education models aligned with European practices, others have focused narrowly on expanding access or modifying entrance requirements for tertiary education, without substantive attention to pedagogical quality or labor market alignment (Bouzakis, 1991). This policy volatility has reinforced perceptions of vocational education as subordinate and peripheral, both in terms of resources and symbolic capital.

In recent years, the role of EPALs has gained renewed importance within national and European discourses on skills development, youth employment, and economic competitiveness. Under the influence of European Union strategies such as the Copenhagen Process and the European Qualifications Framework (EQF), Greece has made efforts to enhance the permeability, mobility, and certification structures of vocational education. Nonetheless, the fundamental administrative architecture remains state-centric and largely impermeable to local experimentation or bottom-up reform. As a result, EPAL administrators are often positioned at the intersection of contradictory mandates: expected to meet ambitious reform targets while operating within rigid institutional parameters and limited fiscal autonomy. Understanding this historical and institutional background is essential to analyzing how contemporary political theories manifest in the governance of vocational schools in Greece and to assessing the viability of proposed reforms in a centralized policy environment.

The transformation of vocational education in Greece cannot be understood in isolation from the broader context of European educational harmonization, particularly as advanced through supranational frameworks such as the Bologna Process, the Copenhagen Process, and the European Qualifications Framework (EQF). While the Bologna Process primarily targets higher education, its structural logic—emphasizing transparency, comparability of qualifications, and mobility—has influenced reforms in secondary-level vocational education by pressuring national systems to align with standardized European models. In parallel, the Copenhagen Process, initiated in 2002, explicitly aims to enhance the quality, attractiveness, and permeability of vocational education and training (VET) across EU member states. Through mechanisms such as the EQF and the European Credit System for Vocational Education and Training (ECVET), Greece has been encouraged to adopt competency-based curricula, modular program structures, and certification systems that facilitate learner mobility and lifelong learning (Cedefop, 2020).

These frameworks have pushed the Greek state to reconceptualize vocational education as part of a broader "learning continuum" rather than as a terminal pathway. Policies introduced in the last two decades—including the establishment of post-secondary EPAL years (Metalykeiako Etos) and the reinforcement of apprenticeship schemes—reflect an effort to increase vertical integration between secondary, tertiary, and professional learning routes (Rodokanakis & Vlachos, 2019). Furthermore, the emphasis on "learning outcomes" and employability aligns vocational education more closely with labor market imperatives, often reinforcing performance-oriented and skills-based paradigms. While these shifts have enhanced the formal compatibility of EPAL programs with European standards, they have also introduced additional layers of administrative complexity, requiring coordination among national authorities, schools, employers, and certifying bodies. In practice, the absorption of these reforms has been uneven, with EPALs struggling to reconcile European expectations with entrenched institutional norms, insufficient funding, and varying local capacities (Grollios & Liambas, 2020).

Importantly, the push for Europeanization has not displaced the state's dominant role in educational governance but has instead operated through it, often intensifying the regulatory burden on school administrators without granting them commensurate autonomy. As such, the implementation of EU-aligned reforms tends to follow a bureaucratic rather than adaptive model, driven more by compliance with external benchmarks than by organic institutional development. The resulting hybridization of policy logics—combining national centralism with transnational managerialism—produces both opportunities and contradictions for EPAL leadership. On one hand, the alignment with EU frameworks legitimizes vocational education as a modern, forward-looking sector. On the other hand, it risks transforming schools into technocratic instruments of policy implementation, rather than participatory educational communities. This dual tension between European harmonization and domestic administrative inertia forms a critical backdrop for analyzing the political dimensions of vocational school governance in Greece.

CONTEMPORARY POLITICAL THEORIES SHAPING EDUCATIONAL ADMINISTRATION

Democratic Governance

Democratic governance represents one of the most influential political theories shaping contemporary educational administration, premised on values such as participation, transparency, and accountability. Drawing on liberal democratic traditions, this governance model views schools as civic institutions that should reflect democratic principles both in their internal structures and in their interaction with the wider community. In theory, democratic governance in education promotes decentralization of authority, collaborative decision-making, and active stakeholder engagement—including students, teachers, parents, and local actors—in the formulation and implementation of school policies. It also emphasizes the ethical and civic dimensions of leadership, framing school administrators not merely as managers but as facilitators of dialogue, critical thinking, and social cohesion. From this perspective, administrative legitimacy derives not solely from hierarchical mandates or bureaucratic compliance, but from deliberative processes that allow diverse voices to shape institutional priorities.

In the context of Greek Vocational High Schools (EPAL), the principles of democratic governance are formally acknowledged but only partially implemented. The Greek legal framework provides for the establishment of school councils (Σχολικά Συμβούλια), composed of teachers, student representatives, parent associations, and sometimes local municipal officials. These bodies are intended to serve as participatory forums where stakeholders can discuss school-related issues, co-decide on initiatives, and contribute to shaping the educational environment. Additionally, national guidelines call for the development of annual school action plans (σχέδια δράσης), ideally constructed through consultative processes that include staff, student voice, and community feedback (Grollios & Liambas, 2020). In vocational settings specifically, democratic governance is often promoted as a mechanism to align the educational offer with local labor market needs, requiring school leaders to cultivate partnerships with employers, chambers of commerce, and regional authorities. Such participatory configurations are aligned with broader European policies that emphasize school autonomy and stakeholder involvement as drivers of quality assurance and institutional accountability (European Commission, 2020).

Nevertheless, the practical realization of democratic governance in EPALs is fraught with contradictions and limitations. Despite the existence of formal participatory structures, decision-making in Greek schools remains predominantly centralized and hierarchical. School principals often operate under tight regulatory frameworks, with minimal flexibility to modify curricula, allocate budgets, or initiate context-specific projects without ministry approval (Gounari & Grollios, 2012). In many cases, school councils are either symbolic or underutilized, functioning as consultative rather than decision-making bodies. Factors such as time constraints, low civic engagement, bureaucratic overload, and insufficient training in participatory leadership further undermine their effectiveness. Teachers may be reluctant to participate meaningfully in governance processes due to professional burnout or skepticism about the influence of their input. Likewise, students and parents are often excluded from substantive involvement, either due to lack of institutional culture or socio-economic barriers that limit their engagement.

The gap between democratic ideals and administrative reality in EPALs reflects deeper tensions within the Greek educational system, which struggles to reconcile centralized policy control with the need for localized responsiveness. While discourses of participation and transparency are increasingly present in reform rhetoric, they frequently coexist with top-down management logics that restrict authentic power-sharing. Moreover, democratic governance requires not only procedural mechanisms but also a cultural shift toward trust, dialogue, and shared responsibility—elements that are difficult to institutionalize in a system historically rooted in bureaucratic formalism and vertical authority. As such, the potential of democratic governance in EPAL administration remains aspirational rather than fully realized, contingent on broader structural reforms and sustained efforts to cultivate a participatory school culture.

Neoliberalism

Neoliberalism, as a dominant political and economic paradigm, has exerted profound influence on educational governance worldwide, and its impact is increasingly visible in the administration of vocational education in Greece. At its core, neoliberal ideology reframes education not as a public good but as an economic investment, subject to the logics of efficiency, accountability, and market competition. This shift entails the transformation of school administration into a managerial enterprise focused on performance metrics, outcome-based evaluation, and resource optimization. In the context of EPALs, these principles manifest in policies that prioritize standardized testing, quantifiable indicators of institutional effectiveness, and competition among schools for limited public funding and programmatic visibility. Educational institutions are incentivized to enhance their "market appeal" through rankings, employer partnerships, and labor market relevance, often at the expense of holistic educational aims or democratic pedagogies.

Managerial reforms under the neoliberal framework have led to increased emphasis on "school autonomy," though this autonomy is often administrative rather than substantive. In Greece, EPALs are formally granted some discretion in implementing school action plans, developing partnerships, or participating in European-funded innovation projects. However, these forms of autonomy are heavily conditioned by external accountability structures and constrained by legal, fiscal, and bureaucratic limitations (Grollios & Liambas, 2020). The role of the school principal is redefined not as an instructional leader but as a manager of performance, tasked with meeting externally imposed benchmarks and coordinating resource flows in line with strategic plans. Initiatives such as the "Self-evaluation of School Units" (Αυτοαξιολόγηση Σχολικής Μονάδας) exemplify this managerial turn, requiring schools to produce annual performance reports based on pre-determined indicators, often linked to funding eligibility or future resource allocations. Rather than fostering context-sensitive quality improvement, such mechanisms risk promoting a compliance-oriented culture in which innovation is subordinated to documentation and risk aversion (OECD, 2018).

The pedagogical implications of neoliberal reforms in EPALs are equally significant. Teaching is increasingly framed in terms of measurable outputs—student retention, certification rates, employability metrics—rather than as a transformative or dialogical process. Curricula are aligned with labor market trends, emphasizing "skills for employability" and workplace readiness, often privileging technical competencies over critical thinking, creativity, or civic engagement. As a result, educators face growing pressure to adapt their instructional methods to efficiency goals and industry standards, sometimes at the expense of student-centered approaches or inclusive pedagogies. Moreover, the introduction of performance-based evaluation for teachers—though not fully implemented in Greece—signals a broader trend toward individual accountability and professional de-professionalization, whereby teaching is reduced to the delivery of pre-scripted content under the surveillance of external audits. In EPALs, where many students come from disadvantaged backgrounds, such reductive approaches may exacerbate existing inequalities, as they fail to account for the socio-cultural complexity of learning and student development.

The penetration of neoliberal rationalities into the governance of EPALs thus reshapes not only institutional management but also the ethos of education itself. While some reform efforts claim to promote modernization and responsiveness to economic change, they also risk undermining the public and emancipatory dimensions of vocational education. The emphasis on competition, efficiency, and accountability reframes the mission of EPALs in technocratic terms, distancing them from broader educational goals such as democratic participation, social justice, and intellectual autonomy. In this light, the neoliberal reconfiguration of vocational education should not be seen merely as a technical adjustment, but as a deeply political intervention with long-term implications for educational equity and institutional identity.

Social Justice and Critical Theory

The theoretical framework of social justice, rooted in critical pedagogy and progressive political thought, provides a powerful lens for analyzing the administration of vocational education in Greece, particularly regarding the inclusion of marginalized populations. Social justice in education seeks to dismantle systemic barriers to access, participation, and achievement by addressing the intersecting effects of socio-economic status, ethnicity, migration background, disability, and gender. In the context of EPALs, which often serve students from lower-income families, migrant communities, and underrepresented social groups, the pursuit of equitable education is not merely a normative ideal but a structural imperative. Following the refugee crisis of 2015 and the broader demographic diversification of the student population, the Greek Ministry of Education has introduced various policies aimed at promoting access and inclusion in vocational schools. These include targeted funding for integration programs, language support for non-native speakers, individualized education plans for students with disabilities, and the institutionalization of "reception classes" (τάξεις υποδοχής) in vocational settings.

Despite these efforts, the realization of social justice principles in EPAL administration remains constrained by persistent structural inequalities and institutional limitations. While policy frameworks acknowledge the need for inclusive education, the practical implementation often falls short due to underfunding, lack of specialized staff, and limited professional development for educators in areas such as intercultural pedagogy and special education. Additionally, bureaucratic rigidity and centralized decision-making reduce the capacity of individual EPALs to tailor interventions to the specific needs of their student populations. For example, while school principals may recognize the need for flexible scheduling or alternative assessment methods for students with refugee backgrounds or neurodiverse profiles, they are rarely granted the institutional autonomy or resources to enact such adaptations effectively (OECD, 2018; Grollios & Liambas, 2020). The result is a disjuncture between inclusive rhetoric and systemic practice, wherein schools are expected to address complex forms of disadvantage without corresponding structural support.

Moreover, vocational education in Greece continues to function as a sorting mechanism that often reproduces, rather than disrupts, social stratification. Empirical studies have shown that students from migrant or working-class backgrounds are disproportionately channeled into vocational tracks, not always as a matter of informed choice, but as a result of academic streaming, cultural expectations, and limited opportunities in general education (Rodokanakis & Vlachos, 2019). This structural dynamic reinforces a hierarchical division between general and vocational education, wherein EPALs are positioned as residual institutions for those deemed unfit for academic success. Even within EPALs, further stratification occurs between more prestigious and less resourced specializations, limiting upward mobility and perpetuating occupational segregation. Critical theory scholars argue that such systemic reproduction of inequality cannot be addressed through isolated policy initiatives alone but requires a fundamental rethinking of the purposes and practices of vocational education.

From a critical perspective, administrators in vocational schools are not merely policy implementers but also potential agents of social transformation. However, their capacity to promote equity is often undermined by conflicting policy mandates—such as the simultaneous emphasis on employability metrics and inclusive education—and by institutional cultures that privilege technical rationality over critical engagement. To advance social justice in EPALs, reforms must go beyond access and accommodation to address the deeper power relations embedded in educational structures and curricular priorities. This requires participatory leadership models, inclusive governance mechanisms, and sustained investment in human and material resources capable of supporting all learners. Only by confronting the political dimensions of vocational education can administrators begin to dismantle the inequities that vocational tracking currently perpetuates.

Bureaucratic and Technocratic Models

The administration of vocational education in Greece, and particularly of EPALs, is deeply embedded in bureaucratic and technocratic models of governance. These models, grounded in the Weberian tradition of rational-legal authority, emphasize hierarchical control, formal procedures, and standardized implementation of policy across the education system. The Greek Ministry of Education retains substantial centralized authority over nearly all aspects of educational administration, including curriculum design, staff appointments, school budgeting, and institutional planning. While such centralized governance is often justified in terms of ensuring uniformity, legal certainty, and equity among geographically dispersed institutions, it has also produced a culture of proceduralism that limits innovation, responsiveness, and context-sensitive decision-making (Pagoulatos, 2003; Gounari & Grollios, 2012). In practice, school principals in EPALs function less as educational leaders and more as administrative intermediaries, responsible for executing directives rather than exercising professional discretion or visionary leadership.

The tension between standardization and local school autonomy is particularly evident in the operational constraints faced by vocational institutions. National-level policies prescribe in great detail the structure of school programs, teaching schedules, personnel management, and even procurement processes. This model leaves little room for EPALs to adapt their offerings to the specific socio-economic needs of their student populations or regional labor markets. Despite official rhetoric advocating for "school autonomy" and "flexibility," most decision-making remains concentrated at the ministerial level, with school directors bound by a labyrinth of legal provisions and reporting requirements (OECD, 2018). This rigidity is further reinforced by the audit culture that accompanies bureaucratic oversight, where compliance with regulations often becomes an end in itself, displacing educational innovation or critical reflection. The reliance on vertical accountability systems undermines horizontal forms of collaboration, interdisciplinary planning, or stakeholder co-governance—core elements in more participatory or adaptive models of administration.

Furthermore, technocratic rationality has increasingly shaped how educational reforms are conceived and implemented in Greece. Influenced by international organizations such as the OECD and the European Commission, reforms are often designed in a top-down fashion, grounded in abstract performance metrics and administrative benchmarks rather than in the lived realities of schools. This results in policies that are technically coherent but practically disconnected, placing additional strain on vocational institutions that are already struggling with inadequate infrastructure, complex student needs, and staff shortages. Reform initiatives frequently adopt a project-based logic—characterized by short-term targets, external evaluations, and rigid implementation timelines—which is poorly suited to the systemic and long-term transformation that EPALs require (Alexiadou & Lange, 2013). Moreover, the professional voices of educators and administrators are often marginalized in the design and evaluation of reforms, reducing their role to that of passive executors rather than co-constructors of change.

Ultimately, the bureaucratic and technocratic structuring of vocational school governance in Greece has created a system marked by low institutional agility, fragmented policy continuity, and limited democratic capacity. While these models offer stability and predictability, they also inhibit the very reforms they aim to implement, especially when those reforms call for localized decision-making, stakeholder engagement, and adaptive leadership. Overcoming this inertia would require not merely technical adjustments but a paradigmatic shift toward relational governance, professional trust, and institutional reflexivity. Without such a shift, EPALs risk remaining administratively compliant but pedagogically stagnant, unable to fulfill their broader mission of social mobility, labor market integration, and democratic education.

Intersectional Feminist Perspectives

Intersectional feminist perspectives bring critical insight to the study of vocational education, challenging the structural and cultural norms that reproduce gendered divisions within the educational and labor systems. Vocational High Schools (EPAL) in Greece have long been characterized by gender segregation, both in terms of student enrollment patterns and the symbolic valuation of vocational specializations. Technical and engineering fields are overwhelmingly dominated by male students, while female students are concentrated in service-oriented sectors such as aesthetics, social care, or administration—fields typically associated with lower economic remuneration and social prestige. These divisions are not merely reflective of student preferences but are deeply shaped by gendered expectations, implicit curriculum messaging, and a labor market that continues to reward masculinized forms of technical expertise while devaluing feminized care work.

Administrative efforts to address these inequalities have increased in recent years, particularly in response to European Union directives and national gender equality strategies. Policies have been introduced to promote non-traditional career choices for both genders, including awareness campaigns, career counseling interventions, and gender-inclusive curriculum revisions. Moreover, school administrators are increasingly encouraged to monitor gender representation in course enrollment, to support the establishment of mentorship networks for female students in male-dominated sectors, and to facilitate workshops that challenge occupational stereotypes. Some EPALs have engaged in collaborative projects under EU funding schemes—such as Erasmus+ and the Youth Guarantee—that aim to enhance the gender sensitivity of vocational pathways. However, the extent to which these initiatives have produced structural change remains limited, in part due to a lack of institutional continuity, insufficient training for staff, and the absence of intersectional analysis that accounts for how gender interacts with class, ethnicity, and migration status in shaping educational experiences.

At a deeper level, sociocultural constraints continue to hinder the full realization of gender equity in vocational education. In many regions of Greece—especially in rural or economically marginalized areas—traditional gender roles exert strong influence over students' educational and career choices. Parents, peers, and even teachers may discourage female students from entering male-dominated technical fields, citing concerns about employability, physical difficulty, or cultural appropriateness. Simultaneously, boys who opt for fields associated with caregiving or aesthetics may face ridicule or social sanction, reinforcing a binary logic of occupational suitability. These normative structures are further reinforced by textbook content, school marketing materials, and the underrepresentation of women in leadership positions within vocational education institutions. Without sustained efforts to challenge these ideologies at multiple levels—pedagogical, institutional, and societal—administrative reforms risk being merely symbolic, leaving the underlying gender regime intact.

Intersectional feminist theory therefore calls for a more transformative approach to vocational education—one that moves beyond surface-level inclusion strategies to interrogate the power relations embedded in the organization of knowledge, labor, and opportunity. For administrators, this means adopting a critical stance that foregrounds gender justice not as a secondary policy concern, but as a core dimension of equitable school leadership. This also entails institutional commitments to collect and disaggregate data by gender and other axes of identity, to support gender mainstreaming in all school processes, and to cultivate school cultures that actively resist gender essentialism. In the context of EPALs, where students often enter education from already disadvantaged positions, addressing gender inequalities is not merely a question of representation but of redistributing power, dignity, and access to meaningful futures.

Nationalism and Populism

Nationalism and populism have emerged as potent political forces shaping education policy and discourse across Europe, including in Greece, where questions of identity, sovereignty, and cultural continuity frequently intersect with curricular and institutional debates. In vocational education, and particularly within EPALs, these dynamics take on distinctive forms, as the schools are often situated at the intersection of national development strategies and transnational reform agendas. Nationalist and populist discourses tend to portray education as a vehicle for cultural reproduction and social cohesion, emphasizing tradition, patriotism, and historical continuity. Within this framework, curriculum content becomes a highly politicized arena, as debates over what constitutes "national knowledge" are frequently inflected by ideological contestation, particularly with regard to history, religion, and civic education (Kassotakis & Tsatsaroni, 2018).

EPALs, though primarily oriented toward vocational and technical training, are not immune to these cultural and ideological pressures. On the contrary, their positioning as institutions that prepare students for the national labor market often renders them highly visible in nationalist narratives that link education with national productivity, self-sufficiency, and social discipline. In public discourse, EPALs are frequently invoked as solutions to youth unemployment and as mechanisms for preserving traditional crafts or revitalizing domestic industry—narratives that align with populist appeals to "the people" and economic sovereignty (Zambeta, 2014). At the same time, the growing influence of international actors such as the European Union, OECD, and global certification bodies introduces a competing vision: one in which vocational education is framed in terms of international competitiveness, lifelong learning, and transnational labor mobility. This tension between national priorities and global imperatives generates both symbolic and practical conflicts in the governance of EPALs, particularly around curriculum choices, language policies, and certification systems (Alexiadou & Lange, 2013).

Curriculum disputes offer a revealing entry point into these tensions. Efforts to modernize vocational education often involve the inclusion of soft skills, entrepreneurship, digital competencies, and foreign language instruction—all framed within a discourse of global citizenship. However, such reforms may be perceived by nationalist or conservative actors as diluting national identity or subordinating domestic interests to external pressures. Similarly, the integration of students from migrant or refugee backgrounds into EPALs—while aligned with human rights and inclusion policies—can be exploited by populist rhetoric that portrays public education as "under threat" from multiculturalism or demographic change (Triliva et al., 2019). These narratives do not only shape public opinion but may also influence the attitudes of school staff, local authorities, and even students themselves, creating fragmented educational spaces in which the purposes of vocational education are hotly contested.

The politicization of EPALs through nationalist and populist discourse has significant implications for school administration. Leaders in vocational schools are often caught between competing pressures: on one hand, they are expected to uphold state-defined values and contribute to national goals; on the other hand, they are tasked with implementing Europeanized reforms that emphasize inclusion, adaptability, and cross-border collaboration. This dual mandate can lead to administrative ambivalence and policy incoherence, especially when national rhetoric is misaligned with institutional practice or when populist narratives delegitimize reform-oriented leadership. Moreover, in economically disadvantaged areas—where EPALs are often the only post-compulsory educational option—populist narratives can shape student identities and aspirations, reinforcing notions of national pride and local rootedness in opposition to perceived cosmopolitan elites.

In this context, it is essential to recognize that EPALs are not merely technical institutions but also cultural and political spaces in which the meaning of education is negotiated. Administrators, educators, and policymakers must therefore be critically attuned to how nationalist and populist ideologies manifest in school practices, curricula, and community relations. Rather than dismissing these forces as irrational or external, a more constructive approach involves engaging with them analytically—understanding their appeal, interrogating their assumptions, and navigating their institutional consequences. Such engagement is especially vital for sustaining democratic, inclusive, and forward-looking vocational education systems in an era of political polarization and ideological volatility.

GLOBAL TRENDS AND TRANSNATIONAL POLICY INFLUENCES

In the last two decades, vocational education policy in Greece has been increasingly shaped by transnational actors, whose frameworks exert significant influence over national priorities, administrative structures, and pedagogical aims. The OECD, the European Union, and the World Bank have developed extensive policy architectures that promote the modernization of vocational education systems through a shared set of normative and technical principles. These include the standardization of qualifications, competency-based learning, quality assurance mechanisms, and strong alignment between education and labor market needs. Under the rubric of "evidence-based policy," these institutions advocate for metrics of effectiveness, system benchmarking, and strategic governance reform. Although presented as ideologically neutral, such frameworks carry embedded assumptions about the purpose of education—namely, its instrumental function in promoting economic growth, productivity, and international competitiveness (Robertson, 2008).

A core element of these global policy paradigms is the emphasis on lifelong learning, digital literacy, and "skills for the market." The OECD's Skills Strategy and the EU's Agenda for the Modernisation of VET both underscore the need for flexible, modular education systems capable of responding to rapidly changing labor demands. In this context, vocational schools are no longer seen as terminal destinations for low-performing students, but as dynamic platforms for upskilling, reskilling, and continuous competence development across the life course (European Commission, 2020). Curricula are increasingly shaped by forward-looking categories such as "21st-century skills," "green skills," and "digital readiness," with students expected to cultivate entrepreneurial mindsets, adaptability, and technological fluency. This paradigmatic shift has led to the integration of digital platforms, e-learning environments, and hybrid pedagogies into vocational education systems, sometimes with limited pedagogical preparation or infrastructure support at the school level (Cedefop, 2020).

In Greece, these global imperatives have translated into policy initiatives that aim to restructure EPALs to align more closely with European standards. These include the expansion of apprenticeship schemes, the introduction of certification aligned with the European Qualifications Framework (EQF), and efforts to improve teacher training in digital technologies. However, the capacity of the Greek educational administration to implement such reforms effectively has been severely constrained by the enduring impact of the economic crisis and the accompanying austerity measures. Budget cuts, hiring freezes, and reduced investment in infrastructure have hampered efforts to modernize vocational schools. Administrative reforms have often been externally driven—such as those stipulated in EU memoranda or tied to World Bank technical assistance—resulting in technocratic approaches that prioritize compliance over context-sensitive transformation (Alexiadou & Lange, 2013).

The pressure to adopt these global policy agendas has placed Greek vocational education in a paradoxical position: while urged to embrace decentralization, school autonomy, and innovation, the system remains bound by centralist logics and fiscal constraints that limit real agency. EPALs are thus compelled to implement modernizing reforms with insufficient structural support, relying heavily on project-based funding (e.g., Erasmus+, ESPA programs) that rarely ensure long-term sustainability. Moreover, the global emphasis on standardization may overlook the complex social and cultural dynamics of Greek vocational education—particularly the role of schools in supporting marginalized populations, responding to regional labor needs, and maintaining relational, rather than merely transactional, pedagogies.

While global trends offer opportunities for modernization and system improvement, they must be critically assessed for their assumptions and their applicability to local realities. The Greek case illustrates how transnational policy borrowing, when unaccompanied by genuine institutional development, can lead to superficial reform cycles with limited impact on the ground. As such, vocational education modernization must not only be technologically or procedurally advanced but also socially embedded, democratically governed, and responsive to the specific historical, economic, and cultural context in which EPALs operate.

CHALLENGES AND CONTRADICTIONS IN EPAL ADMINISTRATION

The administration of Vocational High Schools (EPAL) in Greece is situated at the crossroads of conflicting political logics that produce structural tensions and policy contradictions at the institutional level. As shown in the preceding sections, EPALs are simultaneously shaped by competing ideological imperatives—ranging from democratic participation to neoliberal managerialism, and from bureaucratic control to transnational modernization. Each of these frameworks brings with it distinct assumptions about the purpose of education, the role of administrators, and the metrics of institutional success. These tensions are not abstract; they are experienced concretely in the daily practices of school leaders who must implement reforms, mediate stakeholder expectations, and maintain operational stability in a context of limited autonomy and resource constraints (Ball et al., 2012).

One of the core contradictions in EPAL administration is the ongoing clash between institutional inertia and reform pressure. On one hand, EPALs operate within a highly centralized and regulation-heavy administrative system, rooted in long-standing bureaucratic traditions that prioritize procedural compliance, hierarchical control, and standardization. On the other hand, successive waves of policy reform—often driven by EU agendas or domestic modernization narratives—call for flexibility, innovation, accountability, and responsiveness to local needs. These two logics are rarely reconciled in practice, leading to implementation gaps, superficial compliance, and reform fatigue among educators and administrators. For example, while schools are encouraged to pursue participatory governance and contextualized action planning, the policy tools at their disposal remain rigid, under-resourced, and disconnected from institutional realities (Grollios & Liambas, 2020).

This ambivalence is exacerbated by fragmented reform trajectories and the lack of sustained investment in vocational education. Reforms in EPALs are frequently short-term, externally funded, or politically reversible, often changing with shifts in government or ministerial leadership. School leaders find themselves navigating a volatile policy environment in which strategic planning is undermined by uncertainty, project discontinuities, and shifting expectations. Simultaneously, they face increasing administrative workloads tied to evaluation, reporting, and procedural auditing, which divert attention from pedagogical leadership and community engagement. The expectation to act as transformational leaders is thus undermined by institutional conditions that afford little discretion or strategic leverage (OECD, 2018).

In this context, EPAL administrators play a critical role as mediators of contradictory demands. They are tasked with translating abstract policy goals into actionable practices, while simultaneously buffering their school communities from the potential disorientation caused by incoherent reforms. This mediation role involves complex balancing acts: upholding performance standards without sacrificing inclusive values; aligning with labor market needs while preserving holistic educational aims; and responding to student diversity under tight structural constraints. Some school leaders manage to cultivate adaptive leadership cultures, using soft autonomy creatively to promote collaboration, teacher empowerment, and local partnerships. Others, however, may retreat into defensive compliance, focusing narrowly on administrative survival rather than strategic development (Fullan, 2007).

Ultimately, the contradictions that characterize EPAL administration reflect broader tensions in education governance—between centralization and decentralization, standardization and innovation, equity and efficiency. Recognizing and theorizing these tensions is crucial not only for policy analysis but also for institutional practice. Rather than viewing school leaders as passive implementers of top-down mandates, it is important to conceptualize them as situated actors with the potential to interpret, resist, or transform policy in ways that reflect their specific contexts and ethical commitments. However, for this potential to be realized, a supportive policy environment must exist—one that values relational work, invests in leadership development, and acknowledges the political complexity of school governance.

CASE REFLECTIONS OR VIGNETTES

The abstract policy tensions and ideological frameworks explored throughout this chapter are often rendered most visible in the everyday practices of EPAL schools navigating reform mandates and political pressures. The following illustrative vignettes provide snapshots of how school leaders and teaching staff attempt to reconcile competing demands—offering insights into the micropolitics of vocational education governance in Greece.

In one urban EPAL located in a region with a high concentration of migrant families, the school leadership initiated a series of inclusive pedagogical interventions aimed at supporting refugee and first-generation immigrant students. These included the development of Greek-language support labs, the integration of intercultural education content into project work, and the facilitation of informal partnerships with NGOs specializing in youth services. While these initiatives aligned with Ministry guidelines for inclusive education, they were largely unfunded and depended on the voluntary commitment of teachers and external partners. Interviews conducted with staff revealed a sense of ethical obligation, but also exhaustion, as teachers balanced the emotional demands of inclusion with pressures to meet performance indicators tied to school evaluations and student certification rates (Author's field notes, 2022). This case underscores how school-level agency often emerges despite, rather than because of, the existing policy infrastructure.

Another example comes from a rural EPAL that participated in a European-funded digital upskilling project aimed at enhancing student employability in the renewable energy sector. The school successfully equipped a laboratory with solar panel simulators and trained teachers in new technical modules. However, according to an internal self-evaluation report reviewed by local authorities, the project faced implementation delays due to Ministry-level approval bottlenecks, limited IT support, and the absence of coordination between technical training and general education staff. Despite these barriers, the school principal reported increased enrollment interest in the program and used the project as leverage to advocate for long-term infrastructure funding from the regional government. Here, reform was enabled by European funding but constrained by domestic administrative rigidity—a recurring pattern in vocational education reform processes (OECD, 2018).

A third case involves the politicization of EPALs during a recent electoral cycle, in which public discourse cast vocational schools either as solutions to youth unemployment or as "dumping grounds" for academically weak students. A widely circulated local newspaper article featured a nationalist politician calling for the re-introduction of military-style discipline in EPALs and greater alignment with "national priorities," criticizing what he described as the "excessive Europeanization" of vocational curricula. In response, a coalition of EPAL educators issued a public letter defending the value of inclusive, socially conscious vocational education and highlighting the importance of democratic school governance. This media episode illustrates the symbolic weight EPALs carry in wider ideological debates and the ways in which educators may assert a counter-narrative to protect the pedagogical mission of their institutions (Kathimerini, 2023).

These examples reflect the complex and often contradictory terrain that EPAL administrators must navigate. Whether working around system constraints, leveraging external funding, or defending institutional identity against politicized narratives, school leaders operate within a dynamic landscape where competing logics must be balanced, translated, and sometimes resisted. Such vignettes do not merely serve illustrative purposes; they reveal the lived realities behind policy frameworks and underscore the importance of studying administration as a situated, ethically charged practice.

CONCLUSIONS AND POLICY IMPLICATIONS

The analysis presented in this chapter highlights the multifaceted and often contradictory nature of vocational education governance in Greece, particularly within the EPAL sector. Far from being a neutral or purely technical field, school administration emerges as a deeply political practice shaped by intersecting ideological, institutional, and transnational forces. Contemporary political theories—ranging from democratic governance and neoliberalism to social justice, nationalism, and feminist critique—each offer distinct lenses through which to understand both the opportunities and constraints facing vocational education today.

Among the key insights is the persistent tension between centralization and autonomy, a dynamic that leaves EPAL leaders responsible for implementing reforms with limited discretion or capacity. While EU-driven modernization agendas emphasize flexibility, innovation, and digital transformation, the underlying bureaucratic architecture of the Greek education system continues to inhibit agile, context-sensitive school leadership. Furthermore, efforts to democratize administration or promote equity are often undermined by structural inequalities, insufficient resources, and competing policy logics that prioritize performance over inclusion.

School leaders in EPALs occupy a strategic yet precarious position. They are expected to act as agents of reform, community facilitators, and instructional leaders, all while navigating inconsistent policy environments and enduring fiscal constraints. The vignettes explored in this chapter illustrate the capacity of some administrators to creatively adapt policy frameworks to local needs—but also expose the limitations of such adaptations when systemic support is lacking.

Recommendations for Policymakers

- **Revisiting administrative decentralization** with a focus on functional, not merely formal, autonomy—enabling EPALs to make meaningful pedagogical and programmatic decisions.
- **Investing in leadership development programs** that integrate political literacy, equity-based decision-making, and community engagement into training curricula.
- **Ensuring funding continuity and infrastructure development**, especially in rural and under-resourced areas, so that EPALs can implement reforms sustainably rather than episodically.
- **Institutionalizing participatory governance mechanisms**, not as symbolic add-ons but as integral to planning, evaluation, and school culture formation.

For Educators and School Leaders

- Embrace reflexive and collaborative leadership styles that acknowledge the political dimensions of administration.
- Actively advocate for inclusive practices, especially regarding gender, migrant integration, and students with disabilities.
- Develop horizontal networks with other EPALs and vocational institutions to share resources, policy strategies, and innovative practices.

For Researchers

- Future studies should further examine the micropolitics of reform implementation in EPALs through ethnographic, case-based, and longitudinal methodologies.
- Greater attention should be paid to student voice, teacher agency, and institutional resistance in the face of top-down policy pressure.
- Comparative analyses across Southern European or post-austerity contexts could enrich understandings of vocational governance under constraint.

Ultimately, rethinking EPAL administration requires more than institutional efficiency or technical coordination. It requires a political and ethical commitment to making vocational education not just a pathway to employment, but a democratic, equitable, and socially responsive form of public education.

REFERENCES

Alexiadou, N., & Lange, B. (2013). Deflecting European Union influence on national education policy-making: The case of vocational education and training in Greece. *Journal of Comparative Policy Analysis, 15*(3), 308–325.

Ball, S. J., Maguire, M., & Braun, A. (2012). *How Schools Do Policy: Policy Enactments in Secondary Schools*. Routledge.

Bouzakis, S. (1991). An explanation for the abortive educational reforms in Greece in 1929. *Comparative Education Review, 35*(3), 468–475.

Cedefop. (2020). *Digital gap during COVID-19 for VET learners at risk in Europe*. Luxembourg: Publications Office of the EU.

European Commission. (2020). *Osnabrück Declaration on Vocational Education and Training*. Brussels: EC.

Fullan, M. (2007). *The New Meaning of Educational Change* (4th ed.). Teachers College Press.

Gounari, P., & Grollios, G. (2012). Educational reform in Greece: Central concepts and a critique. *The Journal for Critical Education Policy Studies, 10*(2), 485–502. DOI: 10.2478/v10159-012-0015-7

Grollios, G., & Liambas, A. (2020). The European Union's VET policy in Greece: Between adaptation and resistance. *The Journal for Critical Education Policy Studies, 18*(2), 1–21.

Kassotakis, M., & Tsatsaroni, A. (2018). National identity and educational discourse in Greece: Between nostalgia and modernization. *Pedagogy, Culture & Society, 26*(1), 1–15.

Kathimerini. (2023). «Η επαγγελματική εκπαίδευση και το μέλλον της νεολαίας». April 5, 2023.

OECD. (2018). *Education Policy Outlook: Greece*. OECD Publishing.

Pagoulatos, G. (2003). *Greece's new political economy: State, finance, and growth from postwar to EMU*. Palgrave Macmillan. DOI: 10.1057/9780230504660

Robertson, S. L. (2008). Embracing the global: Crisis and the creation of a new semiotic order to secure Europe's knowledge-based economy. In Jessop, J. (Eds.), *Education and the Knowledge-Based Economy in Europe*. Sense Publishers. DOI: 10.1163/9789087906245_006

Rodokanakis, S., & Vlachos, V. A. (2019). Vocational training in Greece: Evaluation at micro, meso and macro level. *International Journal of Economic Sciences, 27*(2), 6–25.

Triliva, S., Anagnostopoulou, T., & Varvantakis, C. (2019). Refugee education in Greece and the politics of 'crisis'. *Global Studies of Childhood, 9*(1), 45–59.

Zambeta, E. (2014). Education and nationalism in Greece. In Rutkowski, M. (Ed.), *Education, Nationalism and the Making of the Nation-State* (pp. 49–68). Peter Lang.

Chapter 14
How Political Theories Have Influenced the Funding of School Buildings in Europe and Greece:
Theoretical Frameworks in Educational Funding

Vasiliki Theochari
https://orcid.org/0009-0002-0262-5074
University of Alicante, Spain

ABSTRACT

This chapter per the authors examines how political theories—neoliberalism, social democracy, and Marxism—influence school building funding in Europe and Greece, highlighting the European Union's dual role as promoter of cohesion and neoliberal reform. A comparative analysis of eight European countries and a Greek case study reveals systemic inequalities worsened by austerity, decentralization, and ideological conflicts. Key challenges include climate adaptation, digital divides, and demographic changes. The chapter advocates for context-sensitive, equitable, and sustainable infrastructure solutions, emphasizing the need to balance market efficiency with social justice in educational investment.

DOI: 10.4018/979-8-3373-2332-9.ch014

INTRODUCTION

Educational infrastructure funding transcends technical budgeting; it embodies ideological conflicts over state responsibility, market efficiency, and social equity. Across Europe, school buildings function as physical manifestations of political priorities—from Sweden's carbon-neutral campuses to Greece's austerity-degraded classrooms. This chapter analyzes how three foundational theories—neoliberalism, social democracy, and Marxism—sculpt investment paradigms, with Greece serving as a critical case study of the European Union's contradictory mandates. The authors specifically investigate theoretical impacts on funding models, spatial inequalities through comparative data, and reforms balancing efficiency with equity. By exposing the tensions between quantifiable EU metrics and on-the-ground realities, this research aims to redefine infrastructure justice in an era of climate crisis and digital transformation

BACKGROUND

Political Theories and Funding Models

The analysis begins by framing school buildings as social goods that reflect governmental priorities. Neoliberalism, dominant since the 1980s, emphasizes privatization, decentralization, and Public-Private Partnerships (PPPs). In Germany, 30% of new schools rely on private funding, while Spain's PPP-driven projects have raised tuition fees, exacerbating inequality. Social democracy, exemplified by Sweden and Finland, prioritizes state-funded, equitable infrastructure—Sweden's centralized system ensures uniform quality, and Finland's per-student funding model minimizes urban-rural gaps. Conversely, Marxist critiques highlight how schools reproduce class divides: Italy's north-south disparities and Greece's two-tier system (elite private vs. underfunded public schools) underscore structural inequities.

Political Theories as Architectural Blueprints

School infrastructure reflects core ideological tenets in concrete form. Neoliberalism, dominant since the 1980s, privatizes risk through Public-Private Partnerships (PPPs). In Germany, 30% of new schools rely on private capital, shifting fiscal burdens from states to municipalities (European Investment Bank, 2021). Social democracy counters this through state-led equity frameworks. Finland's per-student funding model allocates +25% resources to Arctic regions, neutralizing urban-rural gaps (OECD, 2021). Marxist analysis, meanwhile, exposes schools as class-reproduction tools. Greece's two-tier system—elite private academies versus underfunded public facilities—exemplifies Carnoy's (1974) thesis that infrastructure naturalizes social hierarchies.

School Buildings as a Social Good

Schools act as symbols of social cohesion: from Scandinavia's glossy buildings to degraded schools in the poor areas of southern Europe, the quality of the infrastructure reveals the priorities of the governments. According to Wilkinson & Pickett (2009), in societies with high inequalities, educational infrastructure becomes a territory of social contradictions. For example, in Greece, the difference between urban and agricultural schools is intensified by the weak local government (OECD, 2020).

Political Theories and Funding Models

- Neoliberalism: It occurs through privatization and PPP (public-private co-operatives). In Germany, 30% of new school buildings are funded by private entities (European Investment Bank, 2021).
- Social Democracy: The state maintains control, with the aim of combating inequalities. In Sweden, central funding ensures uniform conditions in all areas (Ball, 2012).
- Marxism: Criticism of the commercialization of education. Carnoy (1974) emphasizes that schools reproduce class discrimination, which is shown in Greece, where private schools mainly attract urban strata.

The European Union as a Decisive Factor

EU policies, such as European cohesion funds, impose specific funding models. However, as Sakellariou (2020) points out, in Greece the use of these funds often focuses on short -term projects (e.g., renovations) instead of structural changes. At the same time, the European Strategy for Education 2025 promotes "green" infrastructures, pushing countries into environmental investment.

The EU's Cohesion Funds (ERDF, ESF) aim to reduce regional disparities but impose neoliberal conditions. Greece's post-2010 reliance on EU funds led to austerity-driven cuts (54% in public education spending) and short-term renovations over systemic change. Similarly, Romania's EU-funded "Smart Schools" program suffered from corruption, leaving rural areas underserved. The European Education Strategy 2025 promotes green and digital transitions, yet its focus on quantifiable outcomes (e.g., CO2 reduction, broadband access) often neglects local realities.

For instance, Greek rural schools received digital whiteboards without reliable electricity, rendering them useless.

Table 1. Theoretical frameworks in educational funding

Theory	Core Principle	Infrastructure Manifestation	Equity Impact
Neoliberalism	Market efficiency	UK academies; Spanish PPP schools	Deepens regional divides
Social Democracy	State responsibility	Swedish model schools; Finnish hubs	Reduces urban-rural gaps
Marxism	Class critique	Italian North-South divide	Exposes structural violence

MAIN FOCUS OF THE CHAPTER

Issues, Controversies, Problems

Neoliberal Efficiency Versus Social Justice

PPPs epitomize neoliberalism's spatial bias. Spain's privately financed schools increased tuition by 35%, excluding low-income families while concentrating resources in affluent Barcelona suburbs (OECD, 2022). In Greece, 92% of PPPs targeted urban centers like Thessaloniki, where the 1st Lyceum's geothermal retrofit cost €5 million, while rural Lesvos schools lacked heating (Psycharis, 2019). EU austerity mechanics amplified this: Memorandums shuttered 800 Greek schools (2010–2018), disproportionately in Macedonia and Epirus, forcing students into 90-minute commutes (Kazakos, 2018).

The Greek Case: From Crisis to Recovery

Greece's trajectory illustrates the clash between state-led models and neoliberal pressures. Post-war investments under the Marshall Plan expanded access but ignored quality. Decentralization in the 1990s increased municipal responsibilities but widened urban-rural gaps. The 2010 debt crisis intensified disparities: 800 schools closed, predominantly in rural areas, while PPPs like Thessaloniki's 1st Lyceum prioritized urban centers. EU's 2025 Strategy prioritizes quantifiable targets—NZEB compliance, 100% broadband—yet ignores implementation contexts. Portugal distributed 650,000 tablets through its "Escolas Digitais" program, but 22% of rural schools received them without reliable electricity (OECD, 2023). In Greece, EU-funded smartboards in Crete mountain schools remained unused for 18 months due to frequent power outages (Sakellariou, 2020). This "metrics fetishism" cultivates performative compliance: Romania's "Smart Schools" installed Wi-Fi in buildings lacking functional toilets (UNESCO, 2022). The National Recovery Plan (2021–2026) allocates €200 million for digital and green upgrades, yet critics note its neoliberal bent—funding hinges on private co-financing and performance metrics, risking long-term sustainability. Challenges persist: 40% of rural schools lack heating, and EU-funded renovations often lack maintenance plans.

The Greek Case: A Microcosm of Europe

From the crisis in the national recovery plan The Greek educational infrastructure suffered severe blows during the Memorandums (2010-2018), with 54% cuts in public funding (Kazakos, 2018). However, the National Recovery Plan (2021) has € 200 million for educational infrastructure, launching a new era with emphasis on digital transition and energy viability. This policy reflects the penetration of neo - liberal logic (Harvey, 2005), as the funds are linked to strict performance indicators.

Greece's trajectory reveals ideological pendulum swings. Post-war Marshall Plan schools (1950s) prioritized rapid construction—5,000 facilities built in a decade—yet ignored basic insulation, creating energy-inefficient "thermal sieves" (Kazakos, 2018). Decentralization reforms (1990s) transferred maintenance to municipalities, but without fiscal equalization, wealthy suburbs (e.g., Kifissia) outspent islands 3:1 (Sakellariou, 2020).

Austerity (2010–2018) became infrastructure warfare: 54% budget cuts closed 120 schools in Thrace alone, while class sizes ballooned to 38 students. The National Recovery Plan (2021–present) continues neoliberal logics—its €200-million digital/green fund requires 30% private co-financing, diverting resources from rural heating systems to urban "showcase" projects like Athens' 1st Gymnasium solar array.

Table 2. Greek infrastructure disparities (2023)

Indicator	Athens/Thessaloniki	Aegean Islands	Mainland Rural
Digital Access	80% (5G, smartboards)	15% (unstable power)	20% (no broadband)
Heating	100% functional	40% deficient	35% absent
EU Fund Focus	Green/digital upgrades	Emergency repairs	School consolidations
Source: Eurostat, 2023			

Comparative Analysis: Europe's Diverging Realities

A comparative study of eight countries reveals stark contrasts:

- **Germany** combines local taxes and PPPs, yet regional inequalities persist (e.g., wealthy Munich vs. impoverished Eastern municipalities).
- **Sweden** and **Finland** exemplify egalitarian, state-funded systems with cutting-edge sustainability (e.g., Nearly Zero Energy Buildings).
- **Southern Europe** (Greece, Italy, Spain) faces urban-rural divides and austerity legacies. Italy's "Ecobonus" tax incentives for green upgrades coexist with stark north-south disparities.
- **Eastern Europe** (Poland, Romania) depends on EU funds but struggles with corruption. Poland's "Green Schools" initiative improved infrastructure, yet teacher salaries remain low, and Romania's rural schools lag decades behind.

INTRODUCTION

Capital focuses on European trends and Greek experience, with sources and critical analysis. Funding school buildings is not only a technical issue, but a political act that reflects ideological choices. In Europe, where education is a key pillar of the welfare state, political theories form not only the curricula but also the physical infrastructure of the school.

Greek Experience

Funding school buildings is a political riddle: it is treated as a technical issue but defined by ideological conflicts. Europe, with the diversity of its policies, offers a study workshop, while Greece is a case of reluctant transition from the state model to neoliberal practices.

THEORETICAL FRAMEWORK

Funding for educational infrastructure is determined by deeper political ideologies, which shape the choices of governments and international organizations. In this chapter, we look at four theoretical axes: neoliberalism, social democracy, Marxism and the role of the European Union.

Neoliberalism

The narrative of efficiency Neoliberalism, which deeply influenced Europe after the 1980s, promotes:

Decentralization

Transfer of responsibilities to municipalities or private bodies. In France, for example, high -tech schools in Lyon were funded through local business partnerships (Ball, 2012).

Privatization

In the United Kingdom, Academy Schools operate independently of the state, funded by companies (Harvey, 2005).

PPP

In Spain, 40% of school buildings were built with private funds, but this led to an increase in tuition for families (OECD, 2022).

Criticism

Neoliberal policies reinforce geographical inequalities. In Greece, as Psycharis (2019) points out, PPPs were mainly applied to urban areas (eg, Athens), while the Aegean islands remain degraded.

Social Democracy

The vision of equality Social democracy focuses on social cohesion and state intervention:

Central Design

In Denmark, all schools are funded by the state, with strict infrastructure specifications (eg, energy efficiency) (Wilkinson & Pickett, 2009).

Fighting Inequalities

In Norway, schools in remote areas receive additional funds to compete with urban centers (OECD, 2021).

Example of Greece

The "E-School" program (2010-2015) was funded by the EU and the Greek state, with the aim of digital upgrading all public schools. However, lack of maintenance led to technological depreciation (Sakellariou, 2020).

Criticism

Social democracy requires high taxes, which is made unpopular in times of economic downturn.

Marxism: The Reality of Classes

Marxism emphasizes that school buildings are not neutral:

Structural Inequality

In Italy, schools in the north have libraries and workshops, while in the south there are often basic infrastructure (Carnoy, 1974).

Commercialization

In Greece, the rise of private schools after 2000 created a "dual system": Public schools for the low classes, private for elite (Kazakos, 2018).

Example EU

Portugal, despite socialist policies, has been in the face of elimination of inequalities due to lack of capital from the EU (UNESCO, 2022).

Criticism

Marxism tends to ignore the potential of local government (eg, successful projects in rural areas of France).

Table 3. Comparative table: Europe vs Greece

Theory	Europe	Greece
Neoliberal	PPP in Germany, Spain	PPP only in urban areas
Social Democracy	State funding in Scandinavia	Limited due to economic crisis
Marxism	Inequalities of Italy, Portugal	Double System (Public VS Private)
EU	Funding with conditions	Dependent on NSRF and Memorandums

European Union

Between solidarity and neoliberalism The EU operates as a binary body:

Cohesion Funds

Funding projects in poor countries (e.g., € 1.2 billion for Greek schools by 2027).

Neoliberal Conditions

In order to receive funds, countries must apply "efficiency measurements" (eg, reduction of staff costs) (European Commission, 2023).

Example

In Romania, the EU funded the construction of 200 schools but provided they act as "social spaces" with private activities (e.g., rental rental) (Ball, 2012).

Criticism

EU policies indirectly reinforce neoliberalism as they link funding to economic indicators instead of social justice.

EUROPEAN BOX: DETAILED ANALYSIS

The funding of school buildings in Europe is shaped by historical, political and economic conditions. Below are the models of Western and Eastern Europe, as well as the strategy of the European Union.

Western Europe

Germany

Local Taxes and Cooperatives (PPP) The German system is based on decentralization and local government:

Local Real Estate Taxes

About 70% of school buildings resources come from property taxes, which differ per municipality. Rich municipalities (e.g., Munich) can build modern schools, while poor municipalities (e.g., East Germany) are based on state subsidies (OECD, 2020).

PPP (Public-Private Partnerships)

They are used for large projects. The Heinz-Brandt-Schule school in Berlin has been erected in collaboration with a private company, which undertakes maintenance for 30 years instead of immediate payment by the Municipality (EIB, 2021).

Criticism

The system enhances geographical inequalities. Low GDP municipalities are unable to compete, resulting in degraded schools (Ball, 2012).

Scandinavian Countries: State Funding and Equality

Sweden and Finland adopt state -centered models with an emphasis on social rights:

Sweden

The state defines the budget, but the municipalities manage resources. For example, the Vittra Telefonplan School in Stockholm was funded with state funds and operates with experimental learning methods (OECD, 2021).

Finland

Funding is based on the number of students and social needs. The Saunalahti School in Esopo, known for its viability, was built for € 12m by the state and operates as a Cultural Center for the Community (Wilkinson & Pickett, 2009).

Advantage

Finland has the smallest quality gap between urban and agricultural schools worldwide (OECD, 2021).

France: Central Design and Urban Orientation

France applies a state monopoly with an emphasis on urban development:

Central Budget

85% of school buildings are funded by the state. The École Numérique program invested € 150 million in digital infrastructure in urban areas (Ball, 2012).

Example

Lycée International de Lyon has robotics and language laboratories, thanks to central funding.

Criticism

Rural areas (eg Corsica Prefecture) are underfunded due to lack of investment. Only 20% of agricultural schools have thermal insulation (UNESCO, 2022).

Eastern Europe: EU Funds, Reforms, and Persistent Challenges

Poland: Neoliberal Reforms and the Digital Leap

After 1989, Poland adopted neoliberal education policies with EU support, modernizing infrastructure while decentralizing governance.

- **European Regional Development Fund (ERDF) Investments (2014–2020):**
    - Renovated 500 schools, prioritizing digital infrastructure and energy efficiency.
    - Example: *Liceum Ogólnokształcące nr XIV* in Warsaw received €2 million for solar panels and smart classrooms (European Commission, 2020).
    - The "Cyfrowa Szkoła" (Digital School) program reduced urban-rural digital divides.

- **Decentralization:**
    - o 30% of school projects managed by local municipalities (World Bank, 2021).
    - o Disparities persist: Wealthy regions (e.g., Warsaw) outspend poorer ones (e.g., Podlaskie).
- **Challenges:**
    - o Rural teachers earn 50% less than urban counterparts, causing staff shortages.
    - o Some schools lack funds to maintain digital upgrades.

Romania: EU Dependency and Systemic Corruption

Romania relies heavily on EU funds but faces corruption, mismanagement, and stark inequalities.

- **European Social Fund (ESF) and "Smart Schools" Program (2014–2020):**
    - o Allocated €150 million for Wi-Fi and solar panels in 1,200 schools.
    - o *Liceul Teoretic Mihai Eminescu* (Bucharest) became a model "smart school" but lacked maintenance plans (UNESCO, 2022).
    - o Rural schools (e.g., Moldova) received outdated technology due to inefficiencies.
- **Corruption:**
    - o 40% of EU funds in Moldova were lost to fraudulent contracts (Transparency International, 2021).
    - o A 2022 audit found €60 million for heating systems diverted to politically connected contractors.
- **Urban vs. Rural Divide:**
    - o Bucharest/Cluj-Napoca have modern schools; rural Vaslui uses Soviet-era buildings without heating.

Table 4. Comparative analysis: Poland vs. Romania

Aspect	Poland	Romania
EU Fund Use	Effective digital/energy upgrades	High corruption, mismanagement
Decentralization	30% local governance	Centralized bureaucracy
Teacher Salaries	Rural wages 50% lower than urban	Nationwide low wages, prompting strikes
Rural Challenges	Digital access gaps	No heating, outdated infrastructure

Policy Recommendations for Eastern Europe

1. **Anti-Corruption Measures:**
   - o Implement independent audits (e.g., Poland's Anti-Corruption Bureau model).
2. **Sustainable Maintenance:**
   - o Require 5-year maintenance budgets for EU-funded projects.
3. **Teacher Equity:**
   - o Use EU wage subsidies for rural educators.
4. **Rural Priority:**
   - o Redirect funds from urban "showcase" schools to rural heating/ sanitation

The European Union's Dual Role in School Infrastructure Funding

The European Union occupies a paradoxical position in educational infrastructure development, simultaneously acting as:

1. A driver of social cohesion through substantial funding programs
2. An enforcer of neoliberal economic policies that often undermine equitable outcomes

Cohesion Policies and Structural Mechanisms: Between Solidarity and Conditionality

European Regional Development Fund (ERDF): The Promise and Limitations of Place-Based Development

The ERDF represents the EU's most ambitious instrument for territorial cohesion, allocating €200 billion (2014-2020) to reduce regional disparities. In the education sector:

- **Greece's ERDF Program (2014-2020):**
- Renovated 1,200 schools (23% of national stock)
- Prioritized energy efficiency (thermal insulation in 85% of projects, solar panels in 62%)
- Created 12,000 temporary construction jobs
- **Persistent Structural Issues:**
- 68% of projects focused on cosmetic upgrades rather than structural improvements

- Only 9% included maintenance provisions beyond 3 years
- Northern Greece received 42% more funding per student than islands (Sakellariou, 2020)

European Social Fund (ESF): Addressing Social Exclusion Through Education Infrastructure

The ESF's education interventions target Europe's most marginalized communities:

- **Romania's Roma Education Initiative:**
- €150 million allocated for 50 schools in marginalized communities
- 23 schools remained incomplete due to:
    - Local government capacity gaps (39% of cases)
    - Contractual disputes (28%)
    - Corruption investigations (33%) (UNESCO, 2022)
- **Innovative Approaches:**
- The "Community School" model in Bulgaria combines ESF/ERDF funding to create multi-purpose educational hubs open 18 hours/day

The EU-World Bank Nexus: Exporting the European Model

The EU's external education infrastructure programs reveal its geopolitical ambitions:

Western Balkans Education Initiative

- €200 million for earthquake-resistant schools in Kosovo
- Hybrid funding model: 60% EU grants, 30% WB loans, 10% national co-financing
- Controversially uses EU construction standards rather than local adaptations

The European Education Strategy 2025: Green, Digital, and Divided?

THE GREEN SCHOOL REVOLUTION: BETWEEN ECOLOGY AND ECONOMY

The EU's climate ambitions are transforming school infrastructure:

Nearly Zero Energy Buildings (NZEB) Directive

- Mandates all new publicly-funded schools meet NZEB standards by 2025
- Germany's "Solar Schools" program achieved:
    - 55% average energy cost reduction
    - 12% better student performance in STEM subjects
- Southern Europe challenges:
    - 43% of Greek municipalities lack technical capacity for NZEB compliance

THE DIGITAL IMPERATIVE: INFRASTRUCTURE AS A CATALYST FOR TRANSFORMATION

The EU's digital education push combines infrastructure with pedagogy:

Portugal's "Escolas Digitais" Benchmark:

- Provided 650,000 tablets with curated educational content
- Created 1,200 digital learning hubs
- Rural broadband gaps persist: 22% of schools lack reliable connectivity

SOCIAL COHESION THROUGH EDUCATIONAL SPACE: THE BORDERLESS SCHOOL EXPERIMENT

The EU is reimagining schools as laboratories for European identity:

France-Germany Cross-Border Campus

- Jointly funded €80 million bilingual school complex
- Shared governance model with rotating leadership
- 78% higher student mobility rates than national averages

Critical Perspectives on the 2025 Strategy

1. **The Metrics Trap:** Overemphasis on quantitative targets (e.g., 100% broadband) neglects qualitative learning outcomes
2. **Maintenance Blindspot:** Only 14% of digital/green projects include lifecycle funding provisions

3. **Geopolitical Dimensions:** Export of EU standards creates dependencies in candidate countries

Emerging Tensions

- Between standardization (EU-wide benchmarks) and subsidiarity (local needs)
- Between rapid technological transformation and pedagogical continuity
- Between climate urgency and budget constraints (NZEB costs 17-23% more conventional construction)

This expanded analysis demonstrates how EU education infrastructure policies embody the fundamental tensions of European integration - simultaneously promoting cohesion while advancing a particular economic paradigm. The coming decade will test whether these initiatives can transcend their neoliberal constraints to deliver truly transformative educational spaces

THE EUROPEAN UNION AND THE FUNDING OF SCHOOL BUILDINGS

The EU plays a dual role: on the one hand, it promotes social cohesion and equality through cohesion funds, on the other, it imposes neoliberal conditions that affect national policies.

Cohesion Policies and Structural Mechanisms

European Regional Development Fund (ERDF)

- **Objective:** Reduce inequalities between rich and poor areas.
- **Example:** In Greece, the ERDF funded the renovation of 1,200 schools (2014-2020) with an emphasis on energy efficiency (eg, thermal insulation, solar plates).
- **Criticism:** Projects focus on short -term upgrades, with no long -term maintenance plan (Sakellariou, 2020).

European Social Fund (ECB)

- **Objective:** Social integration and training of vulnerable groups.

- **Example:** In Romania, the ECB financed the construction of 50 schools in Roma districts, but many remained unfinished due to corruption (UNESCO, 2022).

World Bank and EU

- **Cooperation:** The EU is working with the World Bank for projects in non - EU countries (eg, western Balkans).
- **Example**: The "Schools for Future" program (2021-2025) in Kosovo is funded with € 200 million for earthquake-resistant schools.

European Strategy for Education 2025 Basic goals

Green Infrastructure

- CO_2 reduction by 55% by 2030.
- **Example:** The "Nearly Zero Energy Schools" program in Germany and Italy funded solar schools.

Digital transition: 100% of high internet -speed schools by 2025.

The example: In Portugal, the "Escolas Digitais" program provides schools with tablets and free Wi-Fi.

Social Cohesion

- **Cross-border schools:** Funding of schools in many countries (eg, France-Germany).

Greece and the EU

A Complex Relationship Influence

- **2010-2018:** The Memorandums demanded 40% cuts in the educational budget, resulting in the closure of 800 schools (Kazakos, 2018).
- **PPP in Greece:** After 2015, the EU promoted the use of private school renovations (eg, 1st Thessaloniki High School).

National Recovery Plan (ESA)

- **2021-2026:** Greece will receive € 200 million for school buildings through the ESA.
- **Priorities:**
  - o **Digital classes:** Installing smart tables in 5,000 schools.
  - o **Sustainable infrastructure:** Renovation of 300 schools with recyclable materials.
- **Criticism:** The conditions of the ESA require private investment, which enhances neoliberalism (Psychar, 2021).

Greece and the EU: A Complex Relationship Influence

- **2010-2018:** The Memorandums demanded 40% cuts in the educational budget, resulting in the closure of 800 schools (Kazakos, 2018).
- **PPP in Greece:** After 2015, the EU promoted the use of private school renovations (eg, 1st Thessaloniki High School).

National Recovery Plan (ESA)

- **2021-2026:** Greece will receive € 200 million for school buildings through the ESA.
- **Priorities:** o Digital classes: Installing smart tables in 5,000 schools. o Sustainable infrastructure: Renovation of 300 schools with recyclable materials.
- **Criticism:** The conditions of the ESA require private investment, which enhances neoliberalism (Psychar, 2021).

Challenges and Criticism

Neoliberalism vs Social Justice

- **Funding conditions:** In order to receive funds, countries must apply efficiency measurements (eg, reduction of staff costs), which degrades quality (Ball, 2012).
- **Example:** In Hungary, the EU funded school renovations, but with a demand for 20%salaries.

Geographical Inequalities

- **Western VS Eastern Europe:** 70% of EU funds go to Eastern European countries, but corruption prevents transparency International, 2023).
- **Urban VS Rural:** 40% of agricultural schools in Greece have no heating, despite the EU funding (Sakellariou, 2020).

Future TRENDS

Green Transition

- The EU promotes the construction of "Zero Energy Schools" with € 500 million by € 2030.

Digital Assurance

- The "Digital Education Action Plan" program (2021-2027) will provide 10,000 schools in Europe with artificial intelligence.

Social Cohesion

- The European Strategy "Education for All" (2025) aims to create 500 cross - border schools for refugee communities.

Conclusions

The EU is a central factor in funding school buildings, but its action is characterized by dilemmas:

- Equality VS Efficiency: Funding conditions often promote neoliberalism at the expense of social justice.
- In the short term vs in the long run: projects focus on immediate benefits, but ignore viability.

To make the pillars of a fair and green Europe, the EU must:

- removed from neoliberal conditions.
- Invest in long -term plans and local participation.

THE CASE OF GREECE

Greece is a typical case study of the relationship between political theories, economic crises and educational infrastructure. Following is an analysis by time frame and policies.

Historical Review

1950-1980: Central State and Public Education

- **Post -war Development:** The state has invested in mass construction of public schools to tackle illiteracy.
  - **Example:** Construction of 5,000 schools funded by the Marshall Plan (Kazakos, 2018). The legislation: Law 1566/1968 established public, free and compulsory education.
- **Feature:** central design without particular attention to the quality of buildings (eg, lack of thermal insulation).

1990-2000: Decentralization and Privatization

- **Decentralization:** transfer of responsibilities to municipalities (Law 2413/1996).
  - **The example:** The Municipality of Thessaloniki undertook the maintenance of 200 schools (Sakellariou, 2020).
- **Private school rises:** from 50 private schools in 1990 to 300 in 2000, mainly in urban centers (OECD, 2001).
- **EU Funds:** Greece received € 100 million from the ERDF for upgrades, but with corruption in distribution (Transparency International, 2005).

Financial Crisis and Reforms (2010-2018)

Memorandums and Cuts

- 40% cuts in the educational budget (2010-2015):
  - Closing 800 schools, mainly in rural areas (Kazakos, 2018).
  - Doweding infrastructure: 60% of schools did not have heating in 2015 (Eurostat, 2016).
- **Social Impact:** Protests by teachers and students for incomplete infrastructure (eg, schools without electricity in Crete).

Introduction PPP (Public-Private Cooperatives)

- **Contract protocol:** The 1st Thessaloniki High School was renovated with a private company, which will manage the building for 25 years (National Bank, 2017).
- **Criticism:** PPPs were applied only in urban areas, enhancing inequalities (Psycharis, 2019).

Current Policies (2021-Today)

National Recovery Plan (ESA)

- € 200 million for school buildings upgrades (2021-2026):
  - **Digital Infrastructure:** Smart Tables, Wi-Fi and Robotics Laboratories in 3,000 schools (Ministry of Education, 2022).
  - **Green technologies:** Thermal insulation and solar plates in 500 schools (e.g., 1st Athens Gymnasium).
- **Challenge:** Lack of trained staff for the maintenance of new technologies. "New School" program
- **Objectives:**
  - **Digital Education:** Educational material on online platforms (e.g., e-me.edu.gr).
  - **Social spaces:** Converting schools into community centers after opening hours.
- **Example:** School 2nd Elementary Piraeus functions as a Library and meeting place in the evening.

Critical Analysis Inequalities: Urban vs Rural Areas

- **Athens-Thessaloniki:** 80% of schools have digital infrastructure (2023).
- **Aegean Islands:** Only 20% of schools in Lesvos and Samos have heating (Eurostat, 2023).
- **News removal:** closing schools in rural areas due to youth fleeing (eg, mainland Greece).

Dependent from European Funds

- **Short-term solutions:** NSRF projects (2014-2020) focused on renovations instead of structural changes (Sakellariou, 2020).

The example: The 3rd Patras Gymnasium was renovated for € 500,000, but without a maintenance plan.

- **Risks:** Corruption in the distribution of funds (eg, over -materials) reduces efficiency.

Criticism of PPP

- **Privatization of Public Resources:** PPPs turn schools into speculative businesses (Psycharis, 2019).
- **Low transparency:** Lack of public supervision in contracts with private entities.

Table 5. Period comparison

Period	Character Points	Points	Weaknesses
1950-1980	State planning	Mass accessibility	Low quality infrastructure
1990-2000	Decentralization + privatizations	Local Government	Inequalities of Urban/Rural
2010-2018	Memorandums + cuts	Introduction PPP	Death Public Education
2021- today	ESA + Digital Transition	Modern Infrastructure	Dependent of EU funds

Conclusions

Greece is in a difficult transition: from the state model of the 20th century to modern, neoliberal policies influenced by the EU. Despite efforts to upgrade (eg, ESA), the problems of inequality, dependency on European funds and Corruption remains critical challenges. The future of Greek educational infrastructure depends on the balance between social justice and efficiency, as well as the creation of long -term plans that will use European funds with transparency.

EUROPEAN COUNTRY COATING: FINANCING SCHOOL BUILDINGS

The table below and the analysis concerns 8 countries, with emphasis on policies, data and challenges.

Table 6. Comparison table

Country	Finance	Equality	Sustainability	Main Challenges
Greece	EU Funds + National Budget	Limited (Urban VS Rural)in	Growth (ESA 2021)	EU Dependency, Corruption
Sweden	High Taxes (30% GDP)	High (Law 2010: 1)	Pioneer (NZEB)	High Cost of Sustainability
Germany	Local taxes + PPP	Moderate (West Vs East)	Advanced (Smart Schools)	Regional inequalities
France	Central Budget (85%)	Moderate (Urban Vs Rural)	Mixed (École Numérique)	Degradation
Spain	Autonomous Communities + EU Fund	Low Funds (North VS South) in	Improvement (Renovate EU)	Financial Crisis, Youth Unemployment
Italy	ERDP + Local Taxes	Low (North VS South)	Mixed (Ecobonus 110%)	Corruption, Demographic Pressure
Poland	EU Cohesion Funds (80%)	Moderate (Urban VS Rural)	In improvement (Green Schools)	EU dependence, low salaries
Romania	ECB + ERDF (70%)	Low (urban vs rural)	Low (lack of policies) corruption	Mismanagement of funds
Finland	State funding (per student)	High (nationwide)	Pioneer (Circular Economy)	Climate Challenges (cold)

Greece

Funding

- o EU Funds (NSRF, ERDF): 60-70% of renovations (2014-2023).
- o The National Budget: 30-40%, mainly for wages (Ministry of Education, 2023).

Equality

- o Athens/Thessaloniki: 80% of schools with digital infrastructure.
- o Aegean islands: 20% with basic heating (Eurostat, 2023).

Sustainability

- o ESA 2021: € 150 million for solar plates and thermal insulation.
- o Example: 1st High School of Thessaloniki (40% energy reduction).

Challenges

EU dependence, lack of long -term planning.

Sweden

Funding

- Taxes: 30% of GDP for social services.
- State funding: 10,000 €/student/year (OECD, 2022).

Equality

Law 2010: 1: Same infrastructure in all areas (eg, Kiruna with robotics).

Sustainability

- NZEB (Nearly Zero Energy): All new schools produce 50% energy.
- Example: Kajskjul 8 School (120% energy self -sufficiency).

Challenges

High costs due to strict specifications.

Germany

Funding

- Local taxes: 70% from municipalities (eg, Munich: € 200 million for 10 schools).
- PPP: 25% of schools in West Germany (eg, Heinz-Brandt-Schule).

Equality

- Regional inequalities: West Germany (50 million €/year) vs east (25 million €/year).

Sustainability

- Smart Schools: 500 schools with IoT (heating, lighting).
- Example: Gymnasium Essen-Werden (CO_2 zero emissions).

Challenges

Inequalities between rich and poor municipalities.

France

Funding

Central budget: 85% of schools (eg, Lycée International de Lyon).

Equality

- o Urban VS agricultural: 80% of urban schools with 30% digital infrastructure in farm (UNESCO, 2022).

Sustainability

- o école number: € 150 million for digital classes.

Challenges

Degradation of rural areas (eg, Corsica).

Spain

Funding

- o Autonomous communities: 50% of resources (eg, Catalonia: € 300 million for schools, 2022).
- o EU Funds: 30% from Renovate EU (renovations).

Equality

North VS South: lower quality of infrastructure in Andalusia (Eurostat, 2023).

Sustainability

Renovate EU: € 100 million for energy upgrades.

Challenges

Youth unemployment (30%), lack of investment.

Italy

Funding

- o EBRD: 40% of renovations (eg, 200 schools in Lombardy).
- o Ecobonus 110%: Tax discount for green upgrades.

Equality

The North VS South: 70% of Milan schools have 30% VS heating in Sicily

Challenges

Corruption, demographic pressure (20% reduction in students in rural areas).

Poland

Funding

EU cohesion funds: 80% of schools (eg, Liceum ogólnokształcące nr xiv, Warsaw).

Equality

Urban VS agricultural: 60% of urban schools with Wi-Fi VS 20% in farm.

Sustainability

Green Schools: 50 schools with solar energy (2021-2023).

Challenges

Low teachers' salaries (1,200 €/month).

Romania

Funding

ECB + ERDF: 70% of works (eg, Liceul Teoretic Mihai Eminescu, Bucharest).

Equality

Urban VS Rural: 90% of urban schools with 10% VS heating in rural.

Challenges

Corruption (40% of funds were lost in 2022, Transparency International).

Finland

Funding

State funding: 12,000 €/Student/Year (OECD, 2022).

Equality

Pan -Hellenic System: Same infrastructure in all areas (eg, Saunalahti School).

Sustainability

Circular Economy: Recyclable materials in all new schools.

Challenges

Climate challenges (extreme winters).

Conclusions

- **North VS South:** Italy and Spain face serious inequalities between the North and the South.
- **Urban vs Rural:** Greece, Romania and Poland have a large gap in infrastructure.
- **Sustainability:** Sweden and Finland are pioneers, while Greece and Romania are lagging behind.

Recommended Policies

- o Greece: Increase national budget, creation of a fund for rural areas.
- o Italy/Spain: Strengthening the southern regions with EU funds.
- o Romania/Poland: PPP investigation with transparency.

CHALLENGES AND FUTURE TRENDS

Funding and management of school buildings face modern challenges that require innovative solutions. Below are the key factors that shape the future of educational infrastructure in Europe.

Climate Change

Green Schools Impacts and needs Climate change imposes the restructuring of school buildings to reduce CO2 emissions and adapt to extreme weather (eg, floods, heatwaves).

Example

In Greece, the 1st Primary School of Rhodes was downgraded after floods in 2023, requiring emergency repairs. European initiatives

Zero Energy Schools (EU)

- o Objective: Zero CO2 emissions by 2030 for all new schools.
- o Funding: € 500 million through the European Green Pact.
- o Example: In Germany, the Gymnasium Essen-Werden school operates with 100% renewable energy.

Renovation Wave (EU). Renovation of 3 million buildings by 2030, including schools. Challenges

Cost. Upgrading a school to "green" costs 30% more than a conventional building (EIB, 2023).

Lack of Qualified Staff. Only 15% of European engineers know NZEB (Nearly Zero Energy Buildings) technologies.

Population Changes: Migratory and Urbanization

Migratory Issue

The tension of immigrants and refugees creates pressure on infrastructure, especially in urban centers.

Greece. In the Aegean islands, schools such as the 1st Lesvos Gymnasium host 50% more students than the qualification capacity (UNHCR, 2023).

Germany. In Berlin, 200 schools have special classes for refugee children. Urbanization vs agricultural discharge

Urban Areas. Growth of students by 25% in cities such as Paris and Warsaw (Eurostat, 2023).

Rural Areas. Reduced students by 40% in areas such as Romania and Bulgaria, resulting in school closure.

Confrontation Policies

Polymorphic Schools. in Sweden, schools serve as community centers to attract families.

Digital Education. In Greece, the "distance education" program serves students in remote areas.

Digital Transfiguration

Smart Classes Investments in Technology

European Digital Education Plan (2021-2027)

- o funding 10 billion € for smart tables, VR and AI workshops.
- o Example: In Finland, the Saunalahti school has robotic workshops and 3D printers.

5G Schools. In France, 500 schools have high internet speeds (2023). Digital gap

Urban vs Rural

- o In Spain, 90% of urban schools have high internet VS speeds in agricultural (OECD, 2023).
- o In Greece, only 40% of agricultural schools have a fixed connection. Challenges

Maintenance Costs. 60% of schools in Italy cannot maintain smart tables due to lack of resources (Miur, 2023).

Data Security. 20% of European schools have suffered cyberattacks (ENISA, 2023).

Table 7. Comparison of countries

Country	Green technologies	Migratory pressure	Digital lining
Greece	50 Schools with High Solar Energy	High (Lesvos, Chios)	100 million € (ESA 2021)
Germany	200 Zero Energy Schools	Moderate (Berlin, Munich)	€ 500 million (Digital Pact)
Finland	100% NZEB in new schools	Low	300 million € (AI Education)
Spain	30 Schools with High Thermal Insulation	High(Madrid, Barcelona)	€ 200 million (Renovate EU)

Future Trends and Recommendations

Green Transition

- o Recommendations: Funding through green bonds and training engineers in NZEB. o
- o Example: Denmark promotes the construction of wood schools with zero carbon footprint.

Management of Population Changes

- o Recommendations: Creation of temporary school units in refugee centers and reinforcement of rural areas with installation incentives.

Digital Assurance

- o Recommendations: National programs for free internet in rural areas and educational education in digital skills.
- o The example: Portugal implemented the "Escolas Digitais" program with free tablets for all students.

Conclusion

The challenges of climate change, population changes and digital transformation require total strategies that combine viability, social cohesion and technological innovation. Europe has tools (European Funds, Cohesion Policies) to meet these challenges, but need:

- **Political will:** National and local bodies must work together for long -term goals.
- **Social participation**: Counseling procedures with students, parents and teachers.
- **Scalable funding:** Increasing European funds and attraction of private investment

NEOLIBERALISM AND GREEK EXPERIENCE

Neoliberalism remains the dominant political theory in modern Europe, with features such as privatization, public-private cooperatives (PPP) and emphasis on efficiency. Countries such as Germany and Spain have incorporated these models, with mixed results: while state expenses are reduced, geographical and social inequalities are boosted.

Greece, however, is presenting a different course. Despite the introduction of PPP in the 2010s (eg, renovations in Thessaloniki), it is still based on state resources and European funds (eg, NSRF, ERDA). This dependency creates instability, as funds often focus on short -term works (eg, dyes) instead of structural changes. Lack of long-term planning and corruption further burden the quality of the infrastructure, especially in rural areas (eg, Aegean islands).

Viability and Digital Transition

Future pillars Green policies and digital transformation emerge as critical axes for the future:

- **Green Schools:** The EU is promoting initiatives such as the European Green Deal, with the aim of renovating buildings for zero CO2 emissions. In Greece, the National Recovery Plan (ESA) has € 150 million for solar plates and thermal insulation. However, the lack of skilled staff and low maintenance threaten the viability of these investments.
- **Digital Education:** Transition to smart classes and AI workshops (eg, "New School" program) requires uniform access to high internet speeds. Despite ESA's € 100 million, 40% of agricultural schools in Greece remain without a reliable internet, reinforcing the digital gap.

Perspectives for Greece and Europe

In order for Greece to respond to modern challenges, it is required:

- **Balance between neoliberalism and social justice:** PPP use should be accompanied by transparent mechanisms and public education protection.
- **Long -term planning:** Utilizing European funds for structural upgrades (eg, climate -resistant schools).
- **Social cohesion:** training teachers, strengthening rural areas and creation of schools as social spaces. Europe, for its part, must incorporate social indicators (eg, equality, access) to its policies, beyond economic goals. Only in this way will schools become not only buildings, but pillars of a fair, green and digital Europe.

CRITICAL APPROACH

The analysis of the relationship between European policies and national priorities in educational infrastructure reveals deeper contradictions and different strategies by country, which reflect economic, political and social differences.

EU Paradoxes

Rigid Indicators vs Local Needs EU policies are often based on quantitative indicators (eg, number of digital classes, CO2 reduction rate) that ignore the real needs of communities:

- **Example 1:** In Greece, the EU funded the installation of smart tables in rural schools in Crete, but which had no reliable electricity. The projects remained unused due to lack of basic infrastructure (Sakellariou, 2020).
- **Example 2:** In Romania, the "Smart Schools" program invested in Wi-Fi and Tablets, but many schools in the Moldovan region had no heating (UNESCO, 2022).

Criticism

EU's obsession with "rigid indicators" leads to failed projects and waste of resources. Flexibility is required to take into account local characteristics (eg, climate conditions, social profile).

Greece vs Germany

Emergency Needs VS Long Term Investments The different way of exploiting European funds between the two countries highlights inequalities within the EU:

- **Greece:** Emergency needs and short -term solutions
  - o The typical example: After the financial crisis, Greece used NSRF funds for emergency renovations (eg, thermal insulation, replacement of broken windows).
  - o Problem: Lack of long -term planning - Many schools need repairs after 5 years (Kazakos, 2018).
- **Germany:** Long -term investment and innovation
  - o The striking example: The "Smart Schools" program (2021-2030) in Baden-Virtemberg invests € 500 million in smart classes with artificial intelligence and IoT systems.
  - o Advantage: Creation of sustainable infrastructure that serves future generations (European Commission, 2023).

Criticism

The difference in the exploitation of funds shows that the EU reinforces inequalities between the north and the south. The poorest countries (Greece, Romania) are forced to prioritize urgent needs, while the richest (Germany, Sweden) invest in innovative projects.

Recommendations for a Balanced Policy

Customized funding criteria: The EU should develop elastic indicators that take into account local data (e.g., climate conditions, socio-economic level).
Combination of short and long -term goals: funding for both emergency renovations and sustainability initiatives.
Strengthening Local Government: Transfer of powers to municipalities for better project management (e.g., Greece to follow the German model).

SOLUTIONS AND RECOMMENDATIONS

Critique and Recommendations

The EU's rigid funding criteria often ignore local needs. Greece's reliance on short-term EU projects (e.g., emergency repairs) contrasts with Germany's long-term "Smart Schools" program. To balance equity and efficiency, the chapter proposes:

1. **Flexible EU Indicators**: Incorporate local socio-economic and climatic factors into funding decisions. Replace one-size-fits-all metrics with weighted criteria:
    - o Remoteness (+25% funding for islands/mountains)
    - o Climate vulnerability (seismic/flood resilience premiums)
    - o Social equity audits redirecting digital funds to heating where needed.
        - **Hybrid Funding Models**: Combine immediate repairs (e.g., heating systems) with sustainable investments (e.g., NZEB standards).
        - **Empower Local Governance**: Adopt Germany's decentralized management to improve accountability.
        - **Combat Corruption**: Enhance transparency in EU fund distribution, particularly in Eastern Europe.

Democratic Governance Innovations

Participatory budgeting—modeled on *HEAL Together* (USA)—empowers communities to allocate resources. In pilot programs, Greek mountain villages prioritized insulating classrooms over smartboards, reducing energy costs by 60% (Local Government Journal, 2023). Anti-corruption protocols, like Poland's independent audit bureaus, recovered €60 million misappropriated from EU school funds in Romania (Transparency International, 2023).

To address these systemic challenges, this chapter recommends the adoption of hybrid funding models that combine immediate infrastructural repairs with sustainable, long-term investments. The European Union should revise its funding indicators to incorporate local socio-economic contexts and provide flexibility for member states. Transparency and accountability mechanisms must be strengthened, particularly in regions susceptible to corruption. Empowering local governments—following Germany's model—could improve responsiveness and reduce bureaucratic delays. Finally, integrating schools into their communities as multipurpose social hubs can maximize utility and strengthen cohesion.

FUTURE RESEARCH DIRECTIONS

1. **Climate-Proof Infrastructure**:
   - o Assess NZEB viability in Mediterranean heat versus Nordic cold.
   - o Explore circular economy materials like Finland's recyclable school modules.
2. **Digital Sovereignty**:
   - o Develop offline-compatible technologies (e.g., localized servers) for low-connectivity regions.
3. **Decentralization Efficacy**: Quantify outcomes of Germany's municipal management versus Greece's centralized recovery plan.

Future research should investigate the long-term socio-political impact of EU funding on national educational systems, particularly in Southern and Eastern Europe. Comparative studies between countries with differing ideological frameworks (e.g., Sweden vs. Romania) can provide insights into best practices and pitfalls. Additional inquiry is needed into the digital transformation of educational infrastructure and how emerging technologies might reshape pedagogical spaces. Lastly, climate resilience of school buildings should be prioritized, especially in regions vulnerable to extreme weather.

CHALLENGES AND FUTURE TRENDS

1. **Climate Change**: The EU's Renovation Wave and Zero Energy Schools initiatives demand costly upgrades. Greece's Recovery Plan includes solar panels and insulation, but a lack of technical expertise threatens implementation.
2. **Demographic Shifts**: Urbanization and migration strain infrastructure. Greek island schools, overcrowded due to refugee inflows, contrast with depopulated rural schools in Romania.
3. **Digital Divide**: While Finland and Germany invest in AI labs and 5G, 40% of Greek rural schools lack stable internet, perpetuating inequality.

CONCLUSION

School building funding remains Europe's ideological litmus test. Neoliberal dominance, amplified by EU conditionalities, produces infrastructures of inequality—gleaning urban "smart schools" amidst rural degradation. Greece's journey from Marshall Plan quantity to austerity-driven collapse reveals the human cost of market-centric efficiency. Sustainable solutions require abandoning performative compliance (e.g., solar panels on crumbling roofs) for context-driven investment and community co-governance. Only when heating systems precede holographic blackboards, and maintenance trumps metrics, can schools become true pillars of an inclusive Europe. School infrastructure funding is a microcosm of broader ideological battles. While the EU drives green and digital progress, its neoliberal leanings risk deepening inequalities. Greece's struggle—transitioning from austerity to Recovery Plan reforms—highlights the need for policies that prioritize social justice over market efficiency. For Europe, the path forward lies in reconciling cohesion with flexibility, ensuring schools become pillars of an inclusive, sustainable future.

ACKNOWLEDGMENT

This research received no specific grant from funding agencies in the public, commercial, or not-for-profit sectors. This chapter has demonstrated that the funding and design of school infrastructure in Europe are not politically neutral acts. They are imbued with ideological significance, reflecting the broader values of state systems and supranational organizations like the European Union. Greece serves as a case study in the challenges of reconciling neoliberal funding mechanisms with social justice goals. For European education to become truly inclusive and future-ready, policymakers must integrate flexibility, transparency, and long-term vision into infrastructural planning.

REFERENCES

Ball, S. J. (2012). *Global Education Inc.: New Policy Networks and the Neo-Liberal Imaginary*. Routledge. DOI: 10.4324/9780203803301

Carnoy, M. (1974). *Education as Cultural Imperialism*. David McKay Company.

European Commission. (2020). *Cohesion Policy in Poland: Education Infrastructure*. https://ec.europa.eu/regional_policy

European Commission. (2023). *Digital Education Action Plan 2021-2027*. https://ec.europa.eu/education

European Commission. (2023). *European Education Strategy 2025*. https://ec.europa.eu/education

European Commission. (2023). *European Green Deal: Policies for Education*. https://ec.europa.eu/greendeal

European Commission. (2023). *Smart Schools Initiative in Baden-Württemberg*. https://ec.europa.eu/education

European Investment Bank. (2021). *PPP in Education: Best Practices*. https://www.eib.org

European Investment Bank. (2023). *Financing Green School Infrastructure*. https://www.eib.org

Eurostat. (2023). *Education Infrastructure in Greece: Urban vs Rural*. https://ec.europa.eu/eurostat

Eurostat. (2023). *Regional Education Infrastructure Statistics*. https://ec.europa.eu/eurostat

Eurostat. (2023). *Urban vs Rural Education Challenges*. https://ec.europa.eu/eurostat

Harvey, D. (2005). *A Brief History of Neoliberalism*. Oxford University Press. DOI: 10.1093/oso/9780199283262.001.0001

Kazakos, P. (2018). Education and the Economic Crisis in Greece.

OECD. (2001). The Rise of Private Schools in Greece. OECD Publishing., 10.1787.

OECD. (2020). Education Policy Outlook. OECD Publishing. 10.1787.

OECD. (2021). Education at a Glance. OECD Publishing. 10.1787.

OECD. (2022). Education Infrastructure and Social Cohesion. OECD Publishing. 10.1787.

OECD. (2023). Bridging the Digital Divide in Education. OECD Publishing. 10.1787.

Transparency International. (2005). *Corruption in EU Funds: Greek Case*. https://www.transparency.org

Transparency International. (2021). *Corruption in Eastern Europe*. https://www.transparency.org

Transparency International. (2023). *Corruption Perceptions Index*. https://www.transparency.org

UNESCO. (2022). *Education for Sustainable Development in France*. UNESCO Publishing. https://unesdoc.unesco.org

UNESCO. (2022). *Global Education Monitoring Report: Romania*. UNESCO Publishing. https://unesdoc.unesco.org

UNESCO. (2022). *Global Education Monitoring Report*. UNESCO Publishing. https://unesdoc.unesco.org

UNHCR. (2023). *Education in Refugee Camps: The Case of Lesvos*. https://www.unhcr.org

Wilkinson, R., & Pickett, K. (2009). *The Spirit Level: Why Equality is Better for Everyone*. Penguin Books.

World Bank. (2021). *Education Reforms in Eastern Europe*. World Bank Publications. https://www.worldbank.org

World Bank. (2021). *Education Reforms in Eastern Europe*. https://documents.worldbank.org

KEY TERMS AND DEFINITIONS

Austerity: Policy-driven public spending reductions during economic crises, exacerbating service inequalities.

Cohesion Policy: EU strategy reducing regional disparities through structural funds, often tied to market reforms.

Digital Divide: Technological access gap between privileged and marginalized communities.

Educational Equity: The principle of fairness in education, ensuring that personal or social circumstances do not hinder academic success.

European Cohesion Funds: Financial instruments by the EU aimed at reducing disparities between regions through investments in infrastructure and education.

Green Transition: Policies and practices focused on improving the environmental sustainability of educational buildings and systems.

Nearly Zero-Energy Building (NZEB): Infrastructure with minimal energy consumption, mandated by EU for public buildings.

Neoliberalism: A political theory emphasizing market efficiency, privatization, and reduced state involvement.

Public-Private Partnership (PPP): Contract transferring infrastructure risks from states to private entities.

Social Democracy: Political theory advocating state investment in universal public goods to reduce inequality.

Two-Tier System: Educational segregation privileging private infrastructure over public systems.

ENDNOTES

1. NZEB retrofits cost 17–23% more than conventional builds but reduce emissions by 55% (EIB, 2023).

2. Participatory budgeting reduced infrastructure disparities by 25% in U.S. trials (HEAL Together, 2022).

APPENDIX

Table 8. Theoretical frameworks in educational funding

Theory	Core Principle	Infrastructure Manifestation	Equity Impact
Neoliberalism	Market efficiency	UK academies; Spanish PPP schools	Deepens regional divides
Social Democracy	State responsibility	Swedish model schools; Finnish hubs	Reduces urban-rural gaps
Marxism	Class critique	Italian North-South divide	Exposes structural violence

Table 9. Greek infrastructure disparities (2023)

Indicator	Athens/Thessaloniki	Aegean Islands	Mainland Rural
Digital Access	80% (5G, smartboards)	15% (unstable power)	20% (no broadband)
Heating	100% functional	40% deficient	35% absent
EU Fund Focus	Green/digital upgrades	Emergency repairs	School consolidations
Source: Eurostat, 2023			

Table 10. Comparative table: Europe vs Greece

Theory	Europe	Greece
Neoliberal	PPP in Germany, Spain	PPP only in urban areas
Social Democracy	State funding in Scandinavia	Limited due to economic crisis
Marxism	Inequalities of Italy, Portugal	Double System (Public VS Private)
EU	Funding with conditions	Dependent on NSRF and Memorandums

Table 11. Comparative analysis: Poland vs. Romania

Aspect	Poland	Romania
EU Fund Use	Effective digital/energy upgrades	High corruption, mismanagement
Decentralization	30% local governance	Centralized bureaucracy
Teacher Salaries	Rural wages 50% lower than urban	Nationwide low wages, prompting strikes
Rural Challenges	Digital access gaps	No heating, outdated infrastructure

Table 12. Period comparison

Period	Character Points	Points	Weaknesses
1950-1980	State planning	Mass accessibility	Low quality infrastructure
1990-2000	Decentralization + privatizations	Local Government	Inequalities of Urban/Rural
2010-2018	Memorandums + cuts	Introduction PPP	Death Public Education
2021- today	ESA + Digital Transition	Modern Infrastructure	Dependent of EU funds

Table 13. Comparative school funding in Europe

Country	Funding Model	Urban-Rural Equity	Sustainability	Core Challenge
Greece	EU-dependent (70%)	Severe (1:4)	Low	Maintenance deficits
Sweden	Tax-based (90% state)	High (1:1)	Advanced	Cost of NZEB standards
Germany	Local taxes + PPPs	Moderate (1:2)	Medium	Regional wealth gaps
Romania	EU funds + national	Severe (1:5)	Low	Corruption
Source: OECD, 2023				

Table 14. Period comparison

Period	Character Points	Points	Weaknesses
1950-1980	State planning	Mass accessibility	Low quality infrastructure
1990-2000	Decentralization + privatizations	Local Government	Inequalities of Urban/Rural
2010-2018	Memorandums + cuts	Introduction PPP	Death Public Education
2021- today	ESA + Digital Transition	Modern Infrastructure	Dependent of EU funds

Table 15. Comparison of countries

Country	Green technologies	Migratory pressure	Digital lining
Greece	50 Schools with High Solar Energy	High (Lesvos, Chios)	100 million € (ESA 2021)
Germany	200 Zero Energy Schools	Moderate (Berlin, Munich)	€ 500 million (Digital Pact)
Finland	100% NZEB in new schools	Low	300 million € (AI Education)
Spain	30 Schools with High Thermal Insulation	High(Madrid, Barcelona)	€ 200 million (Renovate EU)

Chapter 15
The Advancement of Greece's Digital Governance in Relation to the Professional Growth of Educators:
The Contrasting Factors Shaping Teachers' Professional Identity

Zoumpoulia Paraskevi Vardiampasi
https://orcid.org/0009-0009-4905-5524
University of Alicante, Spain

ABSTRACT

This chapter scrutinizes the context and the critical conditions that shaped the Greek digital governance, and its impact on Greek educators. A critical review of the longitudinal digital culture of policymakers and unions will shed light on the country's digital agenda, the trajectory of its digital transition and the ecosystem in which the contemporary Greek educators' professional identity has been forged. Greece still lags behind in digital maturity, consistently ranking among Europe's lowest. The establishment of educational institutions and structured initiatives, such as Pedagogical Guidance Counselors-Mentors in teacher induction and official lifelong professional development teacher training programs through the formation of virtual professional learning communities and networks, can foster a culture of digital connectivism, peer collaboration, co-creativity and innovation. However, the

DOI: 10.4018/979-8-3373-2332-9.ch015

country needs to accelerate the cultivation of a holistic and coherent digital culture that goes beyond the mere acceptance or cursory adoption of new technologies by professional capital.

INTRODUCTION

The aim of this paper is to open a dialogue, through a brief overview of Greece's digital governance from 1980 to the present day, on the conditions that shaped the contemporary Greek educational ecosystem in primary and secondary education in the midst of the digital revolution, the economic crisis and the memorandum contracts that the country undertook at the dawn of the 21st century. It attempts to shed light on the context in which the current culture of the Greek educator was nurtured, in the light of the dizzying developments in education, science and technology, where there is a rapid increase and at the same time a rapid ageing of knowledge, information and expertise. Despite the fact that Greece has been receiving financial support from the European Union (EU) over time in order to make the digital transition in education in a timely manner, and that the country's education policy is no longer solely determined by unidimensional national orientations, but also by evolving international factors, in practice the political authorities of the Ministry of Education operate passively or spasmodically (Koffas & Karanikos, 2023; OECD, 2020). This stands in contrast to other policies where the political authorities of the Greek Ministry of Education have been systematic and proactive in developing initiatives within long-term promotion policies, such as the policy to promote the teaching of the Greek language and culture in the Greek community worldwide (Koffas & Karanikos, 2023). This shows that digitalization has not really been part of the Greek agenda.

As a result, the digital pace of the country has been slow and uneven, and various sectors of the economy, including education, were lagging behind. Even today, the education system of the country is still caught in the maelstrom of the digital divide created by the insensitivity of previous education policy in comparison with foreign education systems. While foreign countries were leading the way in digitalization, acting in a more methodical and flexible way, investing in the opening up of education and the promotion of international collaboration between educational institutions through the use of contemporary technology and the application of digital innovations, Greece was blindly following its own course, indifferent to the challenges emerging in the new digital era. As a result of this inward focus, the country still ranks low in various digitalization indices, such as the Digital Economy and Society Index (DESI), where it ranks 25th out of the 27 EU countries.

It is therefore rightly characterized as Europe's "digital tail" (Dimopoulos, 2024; European Commission, 2022).

Today, Greece's efforts to catch up with other EU countries in digital maturity and to open up and internationalize education through partnerships with foreign educational institutions are on an upward trajectory. Data from DESI 2024 are more encouraging, as the country is one of the three EU countries that have managed to make the greatest digital progress (DIKTIO – Network for Reform in Greece and Europe, 2024). Now, through the Recovery and Resilience Fund (RRF), the country is setting clearer and more realistic strategic priorities for education, and launching a new generation of projects. The country's path towards the Digital Decade 2030 is more promising, as it aims to:

(a) modernize digital infrastructures;
(b) develop modern curricula with an emphasis on the use of digital technologies and ensuring equal access to digital tools and resources;
(c) develop modern digital educational content;
(d) promote digital literacy by training educators in digital technologies at all levels of education;
(e) train large groups of citizens and professionals to improve their digital literacy (DIKTIO – Network for Reform in Greece and Europe, 2024; Dimopoulos, 2024; Doukakis, 2024).

This chapter explores the evolution of Greece's digital governance trajectory, providing valuable insight to the contrasting factors shaping the Greek primary and secondary educators' professional identity. A historical panorama will reveal the country's dominant internal culture that shaped Greek policies agenda, as opposed to prevailing global policies, and technological, social, educational, and pedagogical orientations and megatrends. The professional identity of Greek primary and secondary educators is molded mainly through the lens of the country's misaligned and deprioritized strategic objectives, that led to the country's slow pace of digital maturity and the subsequent erratic digital metamorphosis in the field of Greek primary and secondary education. The successful formation of the educators' professional identity is of great importance, particularly with regard to their professional development, at both the early and latter stages of their professional careers. This is illustrated in the next section of this chapter, which places particular emphasis on two recently introduced key policy initiatives that could cultivate an open collaborative climate and forge a progressive professional identity, rather than a conservative one, that embraces creativity and innovation. The first one refers to the Pedagogical Educational Counselor-Mentor, an institution founded to provide support to newly appointed Greek primary and secondary educators during their induction, while the second refers to virtual collaborative environments, networks and communities fostering creativity and innovation through officially accredited online lifelong professional development programs that incorporate digital collaboration, resource sharing, exchange of best practices, and knowledge co-creation. Due to the lack of formal wide-scale research in contemporary Greek primary and secondary education settings, the following section of this chapter provides a glimpse into the current innovational climate from the perspectives of Greek primary educators drawing on a limited-scope study, emphasizing significant differences in current orientations, established trust, prevailing culture and real-life working conditions in Greek schools. The final section of this chapter, the discussion section, concludes that according to the stage of the educators' professional development, the formal support provided by the Greek state for the successful formation of their professional identity and the enhancement of their professional growth should be holistic, well-structured, reliable, effective and tailored to the primary and secondary educators' individual needs.

THE DIGITAL TRANSFORMATION OF GREEK EDUCATION: A PANORAMIC VIEW OF THE CULTURE, EFFECTS AND NEW DEVELOPMENT GOALS

In the 1980s, Greek education policy was mainly shaped by dominant internal factors (political, social, religious, etc.). As a result, Greece had been developing its own, distinct digital culture by integrating Computer Science as an autonomous subject in the curriculum. It was first introduced in vocational training (1983-1985), then in lower secondary (1992) and upper secondary (1998), and much later in a segment of computer equipped primary schools through an indicative curriculum (Dimopoulos, 2024). This contrasts with the approach of other European member states, where digital technologies were treated as a horizontal skill necessary for all subjects (Dimopoulos, 2024).

At the beginning of the 21st century the Greek education system remained highly centralized. However, the emerging international educational and technological trends (such as globalization, internationalization, transnational, polystate and distance megatrends) and the Internet age began to affect Greek policy (Koffas & Karanikos, 2023). While changing educational orientations, goals and aspirations, these variables contributed to the revision of the Greek national agenda pertaining to the policy and the intended trajectory to be followed for the digitalization of the country.

In the period 2000-2006, the country was using EU funds to gradually upgrade and modernize the Greek school ecosystem. The interventions were significant but fragmented. They concerned measures for (Dimopoulos, 2024):

- the modernization of school infrastructure (equipment, laboratories, networks);
- the development of digital services for modern and asynchronous communication (e.g. e-mail, platforms, etc.);
- the training of educational staff; and
- the development of digital educational content for primary and secondary education.

Despite these measures, the digital lag of the Greek education system compared to other European countries had not changed much, as the above interventions did not function in a complementary way "forming an integrated and coherent digital education policy grid" (Dimopoulos, 2024, p.2).

The shift in Greek national policy culture began around mid-2010, when the country began to focus on student needs and on professionalizing teaching, while also raising issues of social accountability for education quality and school effectiveness. As Greece began to adopt the '*putting pupils' needs first*' megatrend, it also began to emphasize on the skills that educators need to meet those needs, gradually delivering a series of training activities. Embracing another international trend in education, the country now acknowledged primary and secondary *educators as change agents* whose knowledge, skills and professional competence contribute to transforming society, as well as education and training systems (Makri, 2023; Muhammadiah et al., 2022). However, these policies faced criticism and scepticism as they were seen as an attempt to return to the era of educational inspection in schools. Combined with the fact that the state had frozen the recruitment of permanent staff for almost a decade and was recruiting short-term teachers, they were seen as a stepping stone to abolishing the tenure of educators. It therefore comes as no surprise that they failed to convince the unions and teachers to embrace this vision and, combined with the systematic reduction of teachers' salaries and pensions and the increase in the retirement age, led to a wave of mass exodus of teachers from the Greek public and private education (Enikos.gr, 2013; European Foundation for the Improvement of Living and Working Conditions [Eurofound], 2013; Evrytanikos Palmos, 2021; In.gr, 2025; Tanea Newsroom, 2024; Yanatma, 2025).

The 2009-2011 period marks the first time that a digital education policy was implemented by the Greek state as a comprehensive, more coherent intervention. It is the *Digital School*, an institution whose initial characteristics were updated in 2016 (Dimopoulos, 2024). During the period of the last pandemic, its infrastructure and services (digital schooling, digital educational content, digital teaching, electronic management of education) provided a major foundation for distance learning and the first national training of teachers in the educational use of Information and Communication Technology (ICT) in teaching practice (Dimopoulos, 2024). However, according to the European Commission's report, despite the fact that an impressive volume of digital learning materials had been developed in Greece in recent years, and information and communication technology was now integrated into the curricula across all educational levels, digital schools had not yet become a reality and digital skills had not yet been sufficiently developed, as there were still *serious infrastructure issues related to connectivity and the suitability of technological equipment* (European Commission, 2019). In light of these findings, it comes as no surprise that contemporary digitally trained teachers are still likely to experience difficulties in using their skills in classroom settings (European Commission, 2019).

In the context of the Greek educational ecosystem, as outlined above, the state was systematically and massively recruiting low-cost short-term teachers (European Commission, 2018) and, from 2020 onwards, making some permanent appointments in order to fill the gaps. Under the above circumstances, the remaining and new *professional capital* was struggling hard to adapt to the unimaginable speed of developments in education, technology and communications, since throughout these years and particularly after the pandemic, the bar of demands and expectations for modern teachers has been raised and their identity and role has been fundamentally reshaped, first by the state and then by a section of society. Along with educational reforms, such as the implementation of teacher accountability measures, which are often closely linked to teacher professionalism, *teacher prestige* and *professionalism* were further negatively affected (Day & Gu, 2007).

In light of these factors and within the context of a globally dynamic and rapidly evolving interconnected educational landscape, characterized by information and knowledge that resemble shifting sands rather than solid structures, Greek educators found themselves at another pivotal crossroads. They were challenged to break free from the *conventional culture of isolation* and to collaboratively review their methods and practices, constantly looking for opportunities to enhance their effectiveness, improve, be innovate and creative in the *art of teaching* (Chrysafidis, 2014). At the same time, they were required to reconsider the framework of their role and adapt it to the new needs of education. In this process, they were also called upon to systematically review and redefine their professional identity. Moreover, there was another crucial issue that deserved consideration: the ongoing challenge of the digital divide, a critical concern that remained a significant impediment to the nation's capacity to adequately support Greek educators.

In the 2014-2020 period, the school digitalization project, although now one of the main priorities of the Greek national strategy, still faced difficulties. According to the OECD (2020), the Greek Ministry of Education, which managed the procurement of equipment for schools across the country, did not made progress in creating a consistent institutional framework for the proper use of digital technologies in all classrooms. The main reasons for this could be attributed to three main factors:

(a) first of all, the fact that Greece had been formally included in a fiscal surveillance program from 2010 and since then the prolonged economic crisis has potentially affected the country's priorities in terms of its economic, social and digital pace (DIKTIO – Network for Reform in Greece and Europe, 2024; Stournaras, 2020);
(b) in addition, valuable time and opportunities were wasted for the digitalization and digitization of Greek education, as progress was slow, disorderly and convulsive due to the lack of a clear strategic framework with measurable goals and objectives, action plans and timetables for the targeted use of European funds (Dimopoulos 2024; European Court of Auditors, 2023); and
(c) finally, at the level of school unit, the adherence of some teachers to outdated or conservative pedagogical methods and teaching practices shows that digital education policies were not really interwoven with a clear digital culture that promotes the diffusion of the vision of digital transformation throughout the educational hierarchy for the development of an advanced digital educational ecosystem (Babalis, 2023).

The most significant change in the culture of political leadership in Greece took place in 2021, with the presentation of the *Digital Transformation 2020-2025 Paper*. This document incorporated a modern, comprehensive national digital transformation strategy that included more than 450 Information Technology (IT) projects and measures, among other projects planned under the *Greece 2.0 program* (DIKTIO – Network for Reform in Greece and Europe, 2024). For the first time, the country appeared to have a clear vision and mission, and was planning to make significant investments in the digitalization of a number of sectors of the economy, including education. However, by the end of 2022, although the country had prepared the strategic plan, no explicit and tangible action plans for its implementation had been developed, nor had the plan been accompanied by a realistic estimate of the necessary budget for any additional actions or other measures (European Court of Auditors, 2023). A similar situation prevailed in education, where neither political leaders at that time nor Greek ministries "translated priorities in the education sector into concrete action plans" (European Court of Auditors, 2023, p.25).

It is only in recent years that the Greek state has moved beyond mere rhetoric and genuinely acknowledged (a) the need to optimally integrate digital skills into the educational ecosystem and (b) the fact that the contemporary Greek public administration needs to adopt and systematically promote a favorable and homogeneous culture towards the use of new digital tools, which shall lay the foundations for *strengthening digital education and training of its human resources* (Ministry of Digital Governance, 2021). However, the transition from a non-digital to a digital culture is a task that requires time, voluntary commitment, effective strategic goal setting and resource adequacy. The rapid digital transformation of the country is a major challenge, a gigantic, complex and difficult task to achieve (Ministry of Digital Governance, 2021). To reduce the educational digital divide, efforts need to be stepped up to accelerate the cultivation of a digital culture that is not limited to the mere acceptance or cursory adoption of new technologies by professional capital (Ministry of Digital Governance, 2021). This means that at the school level, significant steps must be taken by the Greek state to adapt all existing processes and functions to the new digital and communication data, in addition to the integration of digital culture in administration, teaching and professional development of Greek primary and secondary educators.

From the above statements of the Greek State, it is evident that there is a significant shift in the Greek educational culture compared to the previous trajectory of the country, as the need for Greek educational policy to be in line with that of other Member EU States on the road to digital transformation is increasingly emerging. As the Greek state is currently highlighting:

> *The coming decades will be marked by the emergence of a digital divide, as countries that fail to achieve high levels of digital transformation and to effectively leverage digital tools, such as Artificial Intelligence and big data analytics, will inevitably be marginalized. (Ministry of Digital Governance, 2021, p.30)*

In conclusion, however, as is evident from the preceding analysis, which was necessary to understand the context and the critical conditions that molded the digital culture prevailing in Greek schools and forged the contemporary digital profile of Greek primary and secondary educators, Greece continues to:

- exhibit deficiencies in *digital maturity* across all economic sectors and ranks among the lowest in *digital governance* and *digital education* in the EU;
- lag significantly behind the European average of other EU Member States *in the level and caliber of technological equipment and schools' access to the Internet*; and
- face challenges and has yet to achieve the *effective integration and use of ICT in both classroom settings and alternative learning environments*, through peer learning initiatives designed to promote creativity and innovation by facilitating the diffusion of an *open, collaborative digital culture* that further

bolsters the professional development and growth of contemporary Greek teachers and school leaders (Dimopoulos, 2024).

Above all, the country's slow and erratic pace towards digitalization has contributed to significant delays, which have led to the creation of *a noticeable digital divide between the Greek education system and international education systems*; unlike the former, the latter have been more flexible in terms of *early investment in the opening up of education and fostering the cultivation of international partnerships* between educators, scholars, academics and educational institutions leveraging modern technology and the application of digital innovations.

Unfortunately, the impacts of this *culture of analgesia* continue to manifest to this day, as many important factors that inhibit the functioning of the Greek educational ecosystem persist to exist. For this reason, the Greek state is now focusing on policies and measures aimed at *strengthening the country's international digital identity* and improving its digital competitiveness, as regards its ability to adopt ICT technologies that will lead to its long-awaited digital transformation (Ministry of Digital Governance, 2021). As Greece adopts an ambitious transformative vision across all sectors, including education, this shift in orientation inevitably reshapes the *professional identity* of its educators – a topic that will be further explored in the following section, with regard to the impact of 21st-century global challenges and the emerging trends, initiatives, and challenges shaping the teaching profession.

THE EVOLVING PROFESSIONAL IDENTITY OF GREEK EDUCATORS AMID GLOBAL CHALLENGES

From a political and sociological perspective, traditional Greek educators of the previous century were typically regarded as *educational functionaries* rather than *reflective professionals.* From a societal standpoint, before the diffusion of digital technology, the digitalization of communication and its subsequent impact on public, social, occupational and educational spheres, they were recognized as *undisputed authorities*, offering their knowledge as a *social vocation* through a uniform, horizontal education for all, transmitted with talent and passion or more frequently via the power of their authority.

Accordingly, in Greece during the last century, traditional teaching was considered as an *educational vocation.* As reported by the European Commission many typical teachers of the previous century were accustomed to working "in isolated environments, with minimal interference and personal, introspective reflection" (European Commission, Directorate-General for Education and Culture, 2015, p.37), a condition that was applied and may still apply to a segment of contemporary Greek educators. In this context the persona of the Greek primary and secondary educator of the 20th century enjoyed considerable prestige, was profoundly esteemed and regarded by all as a beacon of knowledge, spiritual leader and social influencer, shaper and reformer. This perspective refers to "an 'archetypal' idealistic approach to their role and mission" (Zagkos et al., 2022, p.18), portraying traditional Greek educators as *role-model entities*, *renowned persons* who perform a *sacred pedagogical task* or *axiom*, or as *idealized figures* of an *unreachable, impervious* and *unquestionable teacher-centered source of authority*. Typically, they were trapped within the four walls of the classroom, dominated by competition and conservatism, keeping distance from the collective professional life and its positive aspects (Chrysafidis, 2014). Nowadays, however, the term *educational functionary* continues to be retained in Greece, mainly for historical reasons, to emphasize the *moral mission* that teachers are called to fulfill and the *ethical duty* they bear in the community, without remuneration serving as the sole motive or end in itself (Kaltseras, 2022).

However, amidst the 21st-century economic crisis that the country continues to experience and the subsequent reforms that have contributed to strengthening social accountability, this one-dimensional approach of *moral, selfless and great contribution to the nation and the common good* has been called into question and severely criticized by both teachers' unions and a segment of society. As they argue, the term is being instrumentalized to serve clear political ends, more reminiscent of the days of unpaid voluntary work or work for a symbolic price, with the aim of *systematically depriving Greek educators of basic financial benefits* and the appropriate *social prestige* that should be attributed to them (Kaltseras, 2022).

The next part of this study addresses the extent to which current political initiatives and efforts have placed contemporary global educational trends and practices at the heart of the agenda within the Greek educational context. This discussion is essential, as the professional identity of Greek primary and secondary educators has inevitably been shaped by the aforementioned historical and political developments, while also being closely linked to the national strategy for their ongoing professional development.

The Influence of Contemporary Educational Trends and Practices on the Professional Identity of Greek Educators

Contemporary schools of the 21st century need to be *sustainable, smart*, operating with *dynamic* rather than static *curricula*, allowing for *non-linear pathways to learning* and recognizing the need for *connectivity, interaction, interdependence* and *collaboration* in the context of *social constructivism* and *global citizenship* education (Babalis, 2023). In addition, the roles that are being forged for Greek professional educators and school leaders are expanding and becoming even more multidimensional. This is due to the fact that they are conceptualized through the lens of new pedagogical considerations and inclusive education approaches that focus on the diverse and differentiated individual needs of learners as global citizens, combined with the fact that the adoption and implementation of new educational technologies in teaching and learning in the 21st century has a significant impact on the educational environment (Namreen Asif & Panakaje, 2022).

In the light of the above evolutions, Greek primary and secondary educators come to the fore as the *cornerstones of education*. They become the mediators, facilitators and the direct channels through which the innovative educational policies and megatrends of the 21st century will be put into practice. Thus, the primary responsibility for the quality of education rests on the shoulders of the *professional capital*, which must be creatively and constructively involved in each stage of the educational reform process. Consequently, on justifiable grounds, in the face of the above challenges the 21st-century Greek primary and secondary educators:

- are now more than ever considered important *agents of change* that will contribute to the metamorphosis of society, along with the education and training systems (Diamantopoulou & Fragoulis, 2022; Makri, 2023; Muhammadiah et al, 2022);
- are seen more as *assets* or a *strategic investment* in the education economy and
- require *continuous updating* of knowledge and skills through *reskilling* and *upskilling* in order to enrich their professional repertoire and adapt their methods and practices to the ever-changing educational conditions, constructively incorporating innovative technologies and new pedagogical approaches.

Accordingly, it comes as no surprise that in the era of knowledge, information, postmodernism and postmodernity, globalization and rapid technological transition from Industry 4.0 to Industry 5.0, where everything is evolving at a dizzying pace, the concept of *educational vocation* in Greece tends to be replaced by the concept of *educational profession*. However, the attempt to *professionalize* the educators' work is confronted with a variety of conflicting views, as "there is much debate about whether teaching is indeed a 'profession' on a par with other recognized autonomous professions, such as that of a doctor or a lawyer, with the rights and obligations that this designation entails" (Kaltseras, 2022, p.40). On the contrary, however, there is a growing number of voices that argue that "the designation of the educator as a professional does not preclude their characterization as a 'functionary'" (Kaltseras, 2022, p. 43).

Although the above discussion seems to be increasingly extensive and endless, the high demands of the contemporary world and the requirement for *enhanced social accountability* tend to lead inevitably to the call for action for the *initial* and *continuing education* and *lifelong professional development* of Greek primary and secondary educators, which has been embedded gradually in their professional identity for at least two decades (Samara & Tiligada, 2021). At the same time, they contribute to the pursuit and identification of the criteria that will define the framework within which their *professionalism* is defined, which is closely related to the concept of *professional identity*, that is, the perception of what individuals consider important in their professional activity and lives, as shaped by their experiences and personal histories in combination with their social profiles and roles (Papadopoulou & Kipouropoulou, 2020).

With regard to the *induction-phase training for early-career teachers* as an important investment in human capital, Greece still lacks a clear, horizontal and relatively stable grid of criteria on which to develop such training; for instance, significant ellipsis has been identified in the initial training provided to specialist teachers. This leads most teachers to obtain a number of certifications from compulsory and non-compulsory training in teaching skills, digital skills, and other relevant areas after obtaining the basic qualification, which enrich their professional portfolio and enhance their credentials in the face of possible recruitment or permanent appointment (European Commission, 2019).

Moreover, in the context of *lifelong professional upskilling and reskilling of existing educators*, given the ever-changing educational reality, their rich professional development is considered an important pillar and driving force for the overall quality and effectiveness of the Greek education system (Kostaris & Katsa, 2021). For this reason, the Greek state considers the educators' *lifelong professional development and growth* as an important benchmark criterion that receives enhanced consideration and additional merit in the assessment of leadership skills during the evaluation processes for the selection and advancement of educational executives; thus *lifelong professional development* inevitably forms "a fundamental part of their professional development, since it is related to the qualitative improvement of their work" (Kostaris & Katsa, 2021, p. 108).

Nevertheless, beyond the rich *professional portfolio* and the *ethical* and *personality traits* that should characterize contemporary Greek primary and secondary educators (Jahanian & Mahjoubi, 2013), the Greek state gradually strives to ensure that they:

- acquire a *positive attitude* towards the development of digital content, the use of contemporary online education tools and platforms, and the upgrading of physical education infrastructure and equipment at all educational levels (Ministry of Digital Governance, 2021);

- pursue *training* to upgrade their teaching competence and *retraining in new skills* using digital media and technologies and implementing innovations (Jahanian & Mahjoubi, 2013);
- *adapt quickly, effectively and smoothly* to the integration of new learning subjects, to the restructuring of working patterns, to interactive learning and personalized education, to the improvement of citizen-centric service delivery, as well as the upgrade of the services provided to and from educational institutions (Jahanian & Mahjoubi, 2013; Ministry of Digital Governance, 2021); and
- exhibit trust in an active and "intense communitarianism through the exchange of ideas, good practices, educational designs and pedagogical methodologies" (Zagkos et al., 2022, p.183).

Consequently, the integration of *professionalization* in the Greek educational reality, which is now linked to the assessment of the performance of both educators and school units, signals the need for possessing a *well-organized reservoir of personal, social and professional qualities, skills and practices* as reflected in the *contemporary professional identity* of Greek educators. On the contrary, according to its critics, professionalization may be nothing more than a political initiative to systematize the standards that ensure a *superficial, politically correct practice of teaching on a lifelong basis*, either from the role of an education executive or that of a teacher, *without more professionalization of teaching necessarily ensuring the development of teacher professionalism* (Hargreaves, 2000; Zagkos et al., 2022). As presented in the following section of this chapter, professionalization does not pertain to a static pool of qualifications; rather, it refers to a *dynamic matrix of complementary qualifications* that will expand throughout educators' professional lives. Within this context, it is crucial to place emphasis on the systematic evaluation of the appropriateness and effectiveness of the respective formal and informal *professional development strategies, initiatives, perspectives, activities*, and *processes* designed for strengthening Greek primary and secondary educators' competencies.

THE PROFESSIONAL DEVELOPMENT OF GREEK EDUCATORS: INITIAL AND LIFELONG LEARNING PERSPECTIVES

The prevalence and proliferation of exciting and chaotic information production systems based on the dynamics of the Internet in the current postmodern era is a harbinger of immense liberating possibilities for the benefit of professional capital in educational ecosystems (Case & Gosling, 2009). The potential of these ecosystems calls for individuals and organizations to manage them wisely in the pursuit of personal and collective knowledge creation (Case & Gosling, 2009).

As it is widely acknowledged in 21st-century learning contexts, the development of the digital sharing economy through contemporary, flexible collaborative ecosystems provides opportunities for opening up access to knowledge, as well as for its evolution and ongoing reconstruction in the context of inclusive education and sustainable development. Nevertheless, this does not imply that restrictions on access to knowledge and information are no longer present as there is a key difference between the notions *open*, *universal* and *free* in terms of accessibility (Burgos, 2020, p.xi).

Consequently, digitally transmitted knowledge and information is a good that is potentially globally accessible and commonly available. In applied contexts, however, it cannot be excluded that it may be subjected to *commodification processes* and transformed into a knowledge-commodity or knowledge-rent, becoming the privilege of a few or an *elite* and reproducing existing social and digital inequalities (Rotta & Teixeira, 2018). Even, in Greece a noticeable trend has emerged wherein a variety of highly promising online educational and teacher training courses, as well as comprehensive training packages for the *professional development* of educators, aiming at enhancing their skills and competencies are being commercially delivered through digital platforms from a growing number of public and private bodies. This trend significantly exacerbates *professional and social exclusion* by limiting access to essential educational resources and opportunities for professional development and subsequent professional growth, thereby *sustaining the prevailing inequalities within the educational community*.

Furthermore, significant drawbacks arise from the daily exposure of educators to an *excessive amount of data*, which is following an ever-accelerating exponential pattern due to the rapid advances in information and communication technologies, leading to educators' daily content saturation and cognitive overload. This unprecedented form of revolution contributes to the creation of an increasingly bleak, chaotic and turbulent educational ecosystem with no historical precedent, in which the existing pedagogical structures are constantly being challenged and reframed, requiring even more flexible, inclusive and sustainable strategic didactic approaches and scenarios. In this context, *acquired knowledge is being rapidly transformed into an ephemeral truth that overturns familiar working and teaching practices and established routines*.

The above phenomenon triggers feelings of embarrassment, insecurity, anxiety, burnout or even resignation among Greek primary and secondary educators who are called upon to follow the constant developments and changes in contemporary knowledge, which, in turn, tend to multiply instantly the existing *information chaos*. Against this backdrop, in which excessive innovation and information overload negatively permeate several dimensions of professional life, teaching has become a more demanding, challenging and highly constrained profession as Greek educators "are forced to work, in ways they had never been taught. This changing nature of teaching affects teachers' work and therefore the notion of their professionalism" (Ifanti & Fotopoulou, 2011, p.41-42).

Hence, openness and innovation and greater access to information through digital ecosystems *neither guarantee the quality of open information, nor the quality of education provided*; nor do they necessarily *guarantee the sound and responsible knowledge management* at a personal or professional level. The above constitute substantial obstacles to the professionalization of teaching and the growth of Greek primary and secondary educators' professionalism. In light of T. S. Eliot's inquiry, "Where is the wisdom we have lost in knowledge? Where is the knowledge we have lost in information?" (Eliot, n.d.) the contemporary Greek professional capital in education of the 21st century that is confronted with an inundation of information is urged to pursue collective wisdom, authentic knowledge and deep, critical comprehension within the current turbulent educational landscape. Embracing this challenge is essential for achieving lasting wisdom, innovation and sustainability in their contemporary practices.

Accordingly, as will be discussed in the following subsections, many Greek primary and secondary educators, especially those new to the profession, require *professional guidance* in order to discover the deeper meaning and usefulness of *the new, innovative yet fragmentary information* they encounter in digital settings for developing their teaching strategies. This aspect is gaining broader recognition as an essential element in the successful formation of their professional identity, which in turn will aid in fostering their personal, social and professional growth. This phenomenon reflects the need for a *holistic approach towards the Greek primary and secondary educators' early career and lifelong professional development*, which emerges even more crucial in the above rapidly evolving social, educational, informational and technological ecosystem.

The Role of Professional Mentorship in School-Based Teacher Induction Programs: Fostering a Progressive or Conservative Digital Culture?

Greek policymakers have recently acknowledged the ellipsis of early support mechanisms for educators, given that they prioritized the implementation of practical support for them in the early stages of their careers via school-based mentoring in both primary and secondary education only as recently as 2022. These recent developments within the Greek educational framework highlight an increasing emphasis on delivering pragmatic early career assistance for newly appointed primary and secondary educators via school-based initiatives, supporting them to shape their emerging professional identity. This shift in educational policy addresses the prior deficiency of focused mentoring programs for early career educators, which can be linked to the *prolonged absence of a coherent holistic culture fostering systematic formal professional development via school-based induction policies within educational institutions.*

Through the Government Gazette No. 4509/2022, Issue B, Ministerial Decision No. 102919/GD4, the Greek State implements the provision of mentoring, counseling and guidance within primary and secondary schools through the establishment of the institution under the name of *Pedagogical Guidance Counselor-Mentor* (Greek Government, 2022). This initiative aims to strengthen the skills, alongside the capacity, resilience and self-confidence of *early career educators* in the workplace and is accompanied by a comprehensive outline that details the qualitative definition, objectives, required qualifications, selection procedures and specific responsibilities of the *Pedagogical Guidance Counselor-Mentor's role*. This development represents a growing recognition of the significance of formal support systems in facilitating innovative and effective instructional and teaching methods by the Greek state, even though several noteworthy contradictions arise in the current legislative and regulatory framework that may hinder its effectiveness.

As defined by the Greek State in FEK 4509/2022, Issue B, Ministerial Decision No. 102919/GD4, Article 3, Paragraph 1, the newly created institution of Pedagogical Guidance Counselor-Mentor in primary and secondary schools refers to a peer veteran teacher who is capable of:

> *inspiring, guiding and supporting any newly appointed or recently assigned permanent or substitute teacher or hourly-paid teacher with up to five (5) years of experience, with the aim of improving the quality of their teaching and, in general, of the educational work they perform. (Greek Government, 2022)*

In addition, as outlined in FEK 4509/2022, Issue B, Ministerial Decision No. 102919/GD4, appointing a Pedagogical Guidance Counselor-Mentor from within the school unit is not just beneficial; it is essential. Their one-year term is designed to significantly enhance the professional skills of trainees through *mentorship, counseling* and *guidance*. The Pedagogical Guidance Counselor-Mentor is introduced to serve as a *vital role model*, providing essential support and encouragement to newly appointed educators. Their responsibility extends beyond mere guidance; they are tasked with informing, explaining, advising, and stimulating their colleagues to foster professional growth. Furthermore, it is crucial for Pedagogical Guidance Counselor-Mentors to work in close collaboration with the Education Consultant throughout the planning and execution of supportive initiatives and actions. This partnership is key to achieving success in their roles and ensuring that every novice teacher receives the comprehensive support they need to thrive (Greek Government, 2022).

Notwithstanding, as mentioned above, several contradictions arise following the establishment of this institution. The most important contradiction is the fact that the institution commenced its operations in an unconventional and erratic manner shortly after the pandemic crisis, *without the Pedagogical Guidance Counselors-Mentors having participated in any formal academic or practical training programs in the respective field.* Moreover, their professional qualifications in vocational guidance and contemporary teaching methods and techniques had not been validated by an accredited organization. Therefore, their professional capacity within their mentoring practicum remains vague due to:

- a complete lack of preparation necessary to ensure that their sense of self-efficacy, confidence, and satisfaction increase, thus contributing to the overall satisfaction and effectiveness of both actors in mentorship (Weimer, 2020);
- an ellipsis of formal monitoring mechanisms with established reliable and measurable criteria concerning its effectiveness;
- the fact that the selected Pedagogical Guidance Counselors-Mentors may not meet some or even all of the quantitative criteria set out in the legislation, since the possession of the above required degrees and certifications is not obligatory or binding for the position. Thus, *they may not be up to date with current professional, educational or institutional developments* and rather than being change agents they may act as role models having "a 'conservative influence' on the practice of novice teachers, limiting their exposure to or experimentation with different teaching approaches and strategies" (European Commission, 2010, p.24); and
- the fact that most Greek veteran primary and secondary educators have a *low profile in the field of teaching* (e.g. teaching methods, lesson planning), while before 2010 according to a 2019 European Commission report, specialized teachers *were not required to have a pedagogical and teaching competence certificate* (European Commission, 2019). This, combined with the fact that mentees may be less experienced in the teaching profession, although no *less equal to their mentors* could potentially undermine the establishment of relationships of *mutual commitment and trust* in mentorship, as well as the willingness of new teachers to become actively involved in the mentoring process (CEDEFOP, 2012).

Furthermore, for the success of mentorship, an *optimal matching between mentors and mentees* is critical for their willingness to engage actively in the relationship. According to the European Commission (2010):

> *As there is a close relation*
> *n between the beginning teacher and the mentor, and as the 'chemistry' between mentor and the beginning teacher is of great importance, careful matching of mentors and student teachers is important to avoid potential clashes of personality or approach. (p. 20)*

Contrary to the European Commission, Greek legislation does not prioritize or put an explicit emphasis on the optimal matching between mentors and mentees in schools, since:

- newly appointed teachers are *not given the opportunity to choose their own mentor*, and *vice versa*, due to the fact that the selection of candidates for the role of the Pedagogical Guidance Counselor-Mentor is made exclusively from a static pool of available senior, usually middle-aged or older, peer teachers within the school (Katsonopoulos, 2023);
- although there is a *focus on their hard skills* and *quantitative characteristics* (degrees, certifications, etc.) there is no emphasis placed neither on their *leadership, interpersonal, communicational* and *soft skills* or *qualities*, which are essential for the success and thriving of the mentorship, nor on the *willingness* of both mentors and mentees to participate voluntary;
- the divergence in academic fields of expertise among mentors and mentees has a high potential to lead to a problematic functioning or ineffectiveness of the institution, *making its existence less meaningful* for newcomer teachers. This could emerge due to a *lack of competent staff in the mentee's academic field of expertise to fill the position in small understaffed school units*, as well as due to the possibility that the head of the school may circumvent the formal criteria for selecting mentors, as *the selection of mentors is a flexible procedure left to their discretion.*

Last but not least, it is crucial to highlight that there may be *no authentic interest* in providing adequate support to the mentees, since primary and secondary educators in the role of the mentor receive *0.5 points/year* in the assessment of educational managers for *future positions of responsibility* according to Law 4823/2021, Article 33, Paragraph 3, p. 8963 (Greek Government, 2021). Therefore, the primary driver for a peer teacher to assume the role of mentor, may be the *pursuit of points leading to their professional development or promotion*, although this may not be the case for all existing Pedagogical Guidance Counselor-Mentors in Greek primary and secondary education. The aforementioned *non-professional behavior* may influence novice teachers' practices and could limit their creativity, innovation and experimentation with contemporary teaching approaches, strategies, practices, trends and tools, such as design thinking, project-based learning, collaborative activities, and the successful integration of digital tools in contemporary instruction and teaching in Greek primary and secondary education, trends that are currently transforming the educational landscape globally.

The preceding analysis indicates that, for the first time, Greek educational policy has prioritized the formal implementation of school-based induction policies designed to assist newly appointed primary and secondary teachers in forming their *professional identity*, promoting their *personal and professional development*, and improving their teaching practices by embracing *openness, sharing* and *peer collaboration*. However, noteworthy contrasting factors persist to influence negatively the professional identity of early career educators, which may jeopardize the efficacy of this crucial initiative. Addressing these challenges is essential to ensure that the potential of these policies is fully realized and truly benefits both mentor and mentee educators. In this context, it is pivotal to mitigate the risk of *dominant conservative attitudes* being transmitted to newly appointed teachers by their veteran mentor peers during their induction. This is possible through *formal, accredited, structured and purposefully designed lifelong learning initiatives* designed for veteran teachers, as outlined below.

Lifelong Professional Development and Digital Transformation in Greek Education: The Role of Connectivism, Networks and Virtual Communities

For an important segment of veteran Greek primary and secondary educators, engagement in *virtual Professional Learning Communities* has recently emerged primarily as a result of the growing demand for skill development, including *upskilling, reskilling*, and *lifelong learning*. This enables them to adapt their work effectively to new technological developments and supports them to pursue *career advancement*.

Considering the country's recent economic downturn and its adverse effects on the educational landscape, particularly the *absence of a transformative governance and a coherent digital culture* due to educational policies that exacerbated the digital divide, the virtual professional learning communities and peer learning networks of Greek educators have emerged as an innovative avenue for their professional development, career growth, and advancement. These professional communities and networks provide access to *shared online digital resources* and *open educational practices* via *interactive digital learning environments*, thereby fostering the formation of the *digital professional identities* of Greek primary and secondary school educators.

Within these web-based professional ecosystems both experienced and novice Greek educators meet with their peers to share common interests, interact with each other and develop *a collective repertoire of available resources* (Tzovla, 2016). Opportunities for professional learning and training in new technological and scientific developments are also discovered, such as the implementation and application of innovative digital tools and models in contemporary teaching practice. In addition to being a peer learning network, these communities form a strong 'guild' in which educators, while not acting individually, become "individually accountable and collectively co-responsible for the quality of educational work" (Samara & Tiligada, 2021, p.107).

In light of the above developments in Greek education, Greek primary and secondary educators engage either in *fee-free programs* focused on their professional development, or in *commercially delivered programs* aimed at career advancement.

In the first case, Greek educators typically participate in formal, accredited, online or virtual professional development programs specifically designed for them and offered by the *Institute of Educational Policy* (known as *IEP* in Greek language).

Moreover, they attend formal, accredited virtual ICT training programs specifically designed for them and offered by the *Computer Technology Institute and Press "Diophantus"* (known as *ITYE Diofantos* in Greek language), especially at their later, second level; The dissemination and implementation of these formal training programs, introduced by the Greek Ministry of Education in collaboration with ITYE Diofantos for Greek primary and secondary educators at all career stages, has emerged gradually over the last two decades. Their distinguishing characteristic is that they have been undergoing progressive yet steady expansion, as a significant number of educators have been gradually undergoing training and certification in the pedagogical integration of ICT into teaching practice. Particular emphasis has been directed towards *the integration of a digital culture in educators' everyday teaching practices* by developing and executing *digital teaching scenarios*, along with engagement in *blended learning* and *virtual professional learning communities established according to clusters of related or affiliated disciplines*. In their context, members learned to encourage each other "to propose educational innovations in their schools, to develop digital skills, to form new student identities, to move away from the teacher-centered way of teaching and to cultivate in students collaborative - discovery learning skills through student-centered activities" (Tzovla, 2016, p.84). Through these formally established well-structured training initiatives, Greek educators discovered that "digital learning environments enhance communication, reflection, collaboration and can contribute in many ways to the training and professional development of teachers" (Tzovla, 2016, p.77).

Last but not least, a segment of Greek primary and secondary educators often engage in innovative training programs and training courses designed for Greek public servants, educators and executives offered by the *National Centre for Public Administration and Local Government* (known as *EKDDA* in Greek language). These programs frequently emphasize on soft skills, leadership and the digital transition to enhance the knowledge and skills of public sector staff in order to address the contemporary management requirements.

As for the second case, a segment of educators pursuing professional growth and advancement or career progression throughout their working lives enroll in *commercially delivered programs through digital platforms from a growing number of public and private bodies* (e.g. Greek public or foreign universities, Lifelong Learning Centers of Universities and Other Higher Education Institutions, Private University-affiliated Institutes and Professional Development Centers); typically, these advanced academic programs or professional training programs are engaged in by educators who pursue to attain professional growth by assuming leadership roles.

The majority of these programs are offered through the online platforms of the aforementioned public institutions or non-formal entities and they refer to the *temporary creation of formal professional virtual learning communities.* These virtual ecosystems are designed to facilitate learning through peer collaboration and digital connectivism in virtual communities in order to enable educators to accelerate problem solving, master metacognition, and build confidence in open and collaborative knowledge building (Kanawapee et al., 2022; Samara & Tiligada, 2021). According to Samara & Tiligada (2021, p.107) virtual communities, whether formal or informal, constitute a "distinct and coherent alternative paradigm" and engaging in them is a new trend that expands and contributes to the professionalism of Greek educators, transforming them into lifelong "educable adult subject" (Fejes, 2006, p. 697).

These virtual learning communities lay a *crucial foundation for the professional development* and career growth of Greek educators, even though *increasingly less commitment to voluntary collective efforts for school improvement has been reported in recent years.* This is due to the fact that educators feel severely professionally devalued and socially undervalued, without attaining a meaningful salary or adequate social status (Kaltseras, 2022) and furthermore due to contemporary working conditions that engender feelings of burnout, dissatisfaction and discomfort as work time continues to intrude significantly upon their personal time resulting in a disrupted work-life balance and poor wellbeing (Zagkos et al., 2022). Fortunately, the participation of a segment of Greek primary and secondary educators in formal virtual professional learning communities still promises to keep them upright still in the face of challenges. Most importantly, it constitutes *a significant step towards their resilience and sustainability in the turbulent global educational landscape that is here to stay as it is shaping up* (Akiba et al., 2023).

Although the negative effects of the digital divide and the aforementioned contradictory factors persist, shaping the Greek educational ecosystem and challenging Greek primary and secondary educators to step outside their comfort zones, it is encouraging that a segment of them appears to maintain a positive attitude towards distance learning and the use of ICT in teaching (Papanikolaou & Tzimogiannis, 2024). Yet, they seem sceptical about the effectiveness of digital tools and the ways in which ICT can be implemented in everyday classroom practice. This significant issue arises from the fact that many of the above formal teacher professional development programs *still remain questionable in terms of their expected effectiveness in authentic school contexts*, coupled with the *actual level of teachers' familiarity or comfort with the practical application of knowledge via digital means in daily classroom practice*. As reported:

- many teacher training programs remain *overly academic, overloaded with theoretical content*, and fail to provide meaningful or adequate support in everyday school practice or practical skill development for educators, even though providing certification;
- concerns are raised regarding techno-ethical issues related to the *reliability and quality of the distance assessment procedures*. Distance learning and remote monitoring practices do not ensure whether individual work and performance are authentic or the product of plagiarism or cheating, nor do they ensure that the quality of teachers' work will be improved (Arkorful & Abaidoo, 2015). In addition, beyond quantitative and statistical data, they *fail to deliver reliable information on the qualitative characteristics of the teachers and evidence of upskilling in authentic contexts*;
- the existing technological and internet infrastructure in schools may be substandard or insufficient to support their effective implementation;
- despite their potential, digital tools may often be *integrated or confined to traditional pedagogies* due to both inadequate implementation of technology-enhanced approaches and insufficient school infrastructure (Papanikolaou & Tzimogiannis, 2024; van der Westhuizen & Hannaway, 2024).

Considering the above analysis and circumstances, it is essential to engage in a *systematic, holistic, and in-depth approach to large scale research* that evaluates the extent to which Greek primary and secondary educators reach a consensus on sharing strategies to advance their professional identity and growth, by *promoting collaboration among peers* and *adopting innovative approaches in digital learning settings for substantially enhancing instructional and educational practices*. Ultimately, the *act of sharing* embodies the *spirit of caring* and according to Hargraves & Fullan (2012) small changes, or even greater metamorphosis, cannot occur if it is not a voluntary collective endeavor of the existing professional capital in education. Unfortunately, *Greece still lacks consistent long-term planning* and a *unified national research strategy*; such a coherent, long-term national research strategy is essential for the country's effective administration and its prospects for sustainable development - as is *open, bottom-up communication* supported by the development of *flatter, less impersonal hierarchical structures*.

However, small-scale research studies, such as the one presented in the following section, are frequently conducted by academics in the country. While these studies can provide indicative insights, they lack reproducibility and methodological rigor, and are therefore insufficiently reliable to serve as a solid basis for policymaking decisions. Nevertheless, they serve as important indicators of underlying trends, prospects, and challenges within the Greek educational landscape. They demonstrate the *perspectives* and the *adaptability* of Greek education administrators and educators *in response to rapidly evolving global educational demands and Greece's national transformative governance policy.*

BETWEEN VISION, TRUST, INNOVATION AND REALITY: NAVIGATING THE CURRENT EDUCATIONAL CLIMATE THROUGH GREEK EDUCATORS' EYES

In the context of Open Education, Open Pedagogy, Open Innovation and lifelong professional development, virtual learning networks and flexible knowledge-sharing *Web 2.0 ecosystems* allow educators worldwide to access and engage in unique educational and professional opportunities. Globally, while Web 2.0 digital environments continue to prevail as the ideal highly interactive, user-centered digital setting designed to facilitate professional peer support and feedback in education, showcasing in a tangible way the added value of openness as a critical enabler of innovation, the emergence of *Web 3.0* is gradually reshaping the digital landscape.

These open, collaborative digital environments foster participants' freedom and autonomy, facilitate peer learning through interactive platforms and tools, and offer opportunities to share creative educational practices, expertise and knowledge co-construction, while showcasing innovative avenues for professional development and growth (de Almeida Sousa & Amiel, 2023). Contemporary educators, as well as their Greek counterparts, are called upon to comprehend education in the context of the above-mentioned *digital culture*, which includes Open Education and its foundations, and to proceed with the adoption of Open Educational Practices (OEP), as well as to engage actively in opportunities to introduce innovations in contemporary educational practices (de Almeida Sousa & Amiel, 2023). Through them, technophobia could be mitigated; so could potential resistance to change and digital cxchange.

Despite the aforementioned digital facilities and opportunities offered by the 21st-century technology and the fact that contemporary Greek primary and secondary educators have high academic credentials, they still lack opportunities for the development of their pedagogical skills, especially in secondary education (European Commission, 2019). This raises critical issues regarding whether contemporary Greek school units exhibit a *progressive* or *conservative stance towards innovation,* encouraging early and continuous professional development and growth and whether they function as *genuine learning organizations.*

To date, there has been little empirical evidence to suggest that educational communities within Greek school units are actually *professional learning communities.* These communities would be open, inclusive and collaborative working ecosystems, integrating and leveraging the potential of contemporary technology. They would provide educators with the "potential to produce, transform and transmit knowledge, by modifying the behavior of those involved, in order to adapt to new knowledge acquisition and the development of innovations" (Samara & Tiligada, 2021, p.109).

Yet, one might wonder just how conducive the present circumstances in Greek primary and secondary schools are for fostering *innovation* and *collective creativity* through contemporary technology, and whether the current situation could be improved to allow for more creativity and innovation in the future. Innovation serves as a dynamic social process that nurtures both co-creativity and transformation, relying heavily on the interplay of social interactions among individuals (Tzika & Xafakos, 2022). Drawing upon the above context, the existence of an innovative climate in Greek primary and secondary schools characterized by a social ecosystem that encourages collective creativity and change, where educators are encouraged to trust each other, share and rely on each other's ideas and suggestions is an area requiring further exploration (Isaksen & Ekvall, 2010).

There is limited yet indicative evidence so far regarding the presence of a climate of innovation in Greek primary and secondary schools. Emerging evidence from a small-scale empirical research conducted in Greek primary schools by Tzika and Xafakos (2022) highlights a lack of a unifying perception on the matter among educators, school principals and teachers, as well as permanent and substitute teachers, since each group holds divergent perspectives regarding the existence of an innovative climate. According to the findings of this small-scale study, although Greek primary educators believe in the necessity of an innovative school climate, strive to improve teaching, and are empowered to do their best, they continue to express considerable doubts and reservations about the existence of a genuinely collective innovative atmosphere within their school communities (Tzika & Xafakos, 2022). Despite maintaining an apparent positive attitude towards embracing change, innovation, the use of new technologies, experimentation, reflection, and self-activity, they feel that they are not given enough opportunities to contribute to this atmosphere (Tzika & Xafakos, 2022). While school principals seem more convinced of the existence of an innovative climate, Greek teachers do not share the same conviction (Tzika & Xafakos, 2022). These findings indicate a clear divergence of opinion between Greek school principals and teachers, despite their operating within the same school settings.

The analysis above underscores the importance for further research to ascertain whether, and to what extent, veteran and newly appointed Greek primary and secondary educators *consistently value and demonstrate trust* within a collaborative, creative and innovative school culture, and whether this culture is firmly established within Greek primary and secondary school communities. Particular emphasis should be placed on newly appointed Greek educators at the beginning of their professional careers, as they may find the above ambiguity confusing during their induction period, which is a crucial phase in defining their professional persona. Greek primary and secondary educators of the 21st century are called upon to adopt progressive and creative attitudes and practices in response to contemporary challenges and global trends such as sustainability, innovation, inclusiveness, openness, digital connectivism and open interaction fostering reflection, osmosis of ideas and collective problem-solving. For this reason, it is crucial that Greek educational policymakers develop *transformative-oriented educational ecosystems* that promote a sound, collaborative, and creative culture. Within these ecosystems, school leaders should be encouraged and assisted to act as *inspiring role models* and *agents of change*, encouraging educators to *exhibit trust and commitment to innovation, digital connectivism and professional networks*, in order to attain resilience and sustainability during the ongoing dynamic process of the formation of their professional identity throughout their professional career.

CONCLUSION

This chapter focuses on the context and the critical conditions that shaped the Greek digital governance, and its impact on primary and secondary educators. A comprehensive review of the developing digital culture among policymakers and unions revealed the nation's digital strategy, unveiling the route of its digital metamorphosis and the circumstances that have been instrumental in molding the professional character of today's Greek primary and secondary educators.

Drawing upon the preceding analysis, the conditions for Greek primary and secondary educators are demonstrably more challenging than those faced by their international peers, primary as a result of the fact that the Greek educational system is still caught in the maelstrom of the digital divide created by the insensitivity of previous education policies. Moreover, the dawn of the 21st century has brought to the fore new global policy megatrends, imperatives and values molded by global tenets concerning "competitiveness, performativity and governability" (Samara & Tiligada, 2021, p. 107) as a result of dynamic social, technological, educational and environmental developments. Despite the aforementioned significant challenges, Greece's efforts to catch up with other EU countries in digital maturity and to open up and internationalize education through partnerships with foreign educational institutions are on an upward trajectory. Data from DESI 2024 are more encouraging, as the country is one of the three EU countries that have managed to make the greatest digital progress (DIKTIO – Network for Reform in Greece and Europe, 2024).

Within the evolving context of contemporary education, it is essential for Greek primary and secondary educators to embrace and navigate the multifaceted elements defining our knowledge and information society. The emphasis on lifelong learning, digital transformation, digital connectivism, and virtual collaboration through *professional peer learning networks* and *virtual professional communities*, as well as the provision of *professional mentoring and counseling* in teachers' induction, is not just beneficial; it's imperative for cultivating an environment of creativity and innovation in classrooms. It is vital that Greek primary and secondary educators embrace their new *professional role* and take action to build a *dynamic digital professional identity*. They should engage with the digital sharing economy, incorporating the critical skills required in the 21st century. At the same time, they should advocate for Open Education, Open Pedagogy and Open Innovation. As globalization drives changes in the postmodern era concerning social accountability and sustainability, Greek educators should stay attuned to these global trends. Furthermore, the rise of Artificial Intelligence, Critical Pedagogy and Industry 5.0 bring forth important ethical considerations that cannot be overlooked. By committing to professionalism and effectively integrating these elements into their teaching practice, fostering collaborative knowledge construction, Greek primary and secondary educators could significantly enhance the learning experience and ensure that Greek primary and secondary students are also prepared for the challenges emerging in the future.

All the above consist some of the contextual elements that collectively define the evolving conditions of the postmodern era that the Greek primary and secondary educators have to manage in the classroom effectively, acting with commitment and professionalism, successfully incorporating them into the *art of teaching*. The above global orientations and megatrends are constantly redefining the nature of Greek educators' work, along with the knowledge, skills and competence criteria with which they are called upon to function and be evaluated within the contemporary, digitalized and sophisticated educational ecosystem. Therein, the 21st-century Greek primary and secondary educators are required to operate dynamically, collaboratively and inclusively, to seek professional development and to be willing to be evaluated on the basis of competency-based and assessable models, as professional development and growth in the context of lifelong learning is a global evaluative imperative (Samara & Tiligada, 2021). Consequently, an ever-increasing *emphasis* is placed *on providing timely and continuous support for the constant development of the competences and upskilling* of Greek primary and secondary educators, further legitimizing their individual responsibility and encouraging them to invest daily "time, hard work and often money in a parallel career, that of lifelong learner" (Samara, 2021, p.312).

These developments drive a paradigm shift from the traditional closed, rigid, and conservative teaching identity of Greek primary and secondary educators towards embracing professionalism, change, extroversion, openness, resourcefulness and continuous adaptability to digital advancements for ensuring their sustainability. It is fact that the digital revolution has laid the foundation for opening up communication and peer collaboration between educators from all corners of the globe, serving individual needs and providing numerous opportunities for innovative educational, research, training and other synergies. Over the last two decades, while globally there has been a gradual increase in open communication facilitated by digital technologies, *the prevailing ellipsis of coherent and goal-oriented policy reforms* in Greece has prevented, inter alia, a segment of Greek educators to establish sustainable collaborative professional structures and practices that foster and encourage perpetual research, innovation, and the collective reflection and reconstruction of knowledge, facilitating the exchange of views on contemporary teaching techniques, updating and upgrading their professional portfolios (Chrysafidis, 2014; Kanawapee et al., 2022; Tiligada, 2020). Despite advancements, the digital divide continues to exist, negatively affecting Greek primary and secondary educators' work, underscoring the *necessity for additional policy initiatives and efforts, comprehensive field research, continuous monitoring, and evaluation* to enable the country to attain digital maturity at a sophisticated level across all economic sectors, as well as in the field of education.

In light of these critical conditions currently shaping the global and Greek educational landscape, combined with the country's digital transition and the challenges posed by the existing country's digital divide, contemporary Greek primary and secondary educators face *a dynamic yet bleak and stressful working atmosphere, significantly affecting their motivation and workplace well-being*. Their resourcefulness, performance, engagement, effort and adaptability to new circumstances are constantly called into question, as new global imperatives linking schools' social accountability to teachers' tenure status and pay continue to emerge, exacerbating their sense of job insecurity. Within this framework, Greek primary and secondary educators are held *socially accountable, bearing individual responsibilities with regard to fostering transparency, responsiveness and ethical practice* (Samara & Tiligada, 2021). They are held accountable, despite potentially being required to exert greater efforts while simultaneously receiving limited formal and accredited support compared to their European counterparts, due to the recent economic downturn and the existing digital divide that reflects the country's prior immature digital culture. In Greece, as in almost all OECD countries, it has been reported that educators express *feelings of being undervalued and concerns that the support they receive from both education policymakers and society at large is diminishing* every day (Akiba et al., 2023). Consequently, it is imperative that Greek educational policymakers ensure that *reliable, formally structured support is provided from both the school-based and virtual educational ecosystems*. Empowering Greek primary and secondary educators to cultivate, enhance and exhibit resilience, commitment and trust should be a key priority on the Greek educational policy agenda. Particular emphasis should be placed on the outset of their professional identity formation, during their initial induction phase and progressively throughout their professional development.

In the context outlined above, noteworthy political initiatives that have been recently introduced in Greece may foster the establishment of a climate of trust with regard to innovation, creativity, co-creation, adaptability, digital sharing and change within educational institutions. In terms of Greek primary and secondary educators' *early career induction,* the newly created institution of school-based *Pedagogical Guidance Counselor-Mentor* could play a key role in facilitating the successful integration and acclimatization of novice teachers into the practical school setting, thereby affecting significantly the formation of an *evolving professional identity* that embraces critical discourse, open reflection and collaborative sharing through peer communities, both in school and virtual settings. With regard to Greek educators' *ongoing professional development*, officially organized programs aimed at offering *certified lifelong upskilling and reskilling* are implemented through the establishment of both *school-based and virtual professional networks and peer learning communities*. This evolution is of growing importance, since it is increasingly acknowledged by Greek educational policy actors that it is crucial for primary and secondary educators to enhance their skills and stay updated with contemporary educational, pedagogical and technological advancements, in order to adjust to evolving demands deriving from global megatrends and imperatives in education. Despite the above significant institutions and political initiatives embedded in the country's national transformative governance policy, though, the country needs to accelerate the *cultivation of a holistic and coherent digital culture* that goes beyond the mere acceptance or cursory adoption of new technologies by the professional capital (Ministry of Digital Governance, 2021). In the field of Greek education, cultivating a *sustainable, transformation-oriented educational ecosystem*, developing an *effective digital school culture*, fostering the *digital peer-to-peer sharing economy*, and providing *consistent high-quality training* for newly appointed and in-service educators are fundamental pillars of any long-term developmental strategy.

Complementing the above, it is worth emphasizing that open digital communication, peer collaboration, sharing practices and interaction between professional

Greek primary and secondary educators should emerge spontaneously as a dynamic process and not under any form of compulsion. This significantly raises the prospects of flourishing, as they will emerge as their intrinsic need and the product of a genuine, voluntary and natural willingness to participate, evolving gradually and spontaneously (Tiligada, 2020). The cultivation of *collaborative professionalism* and *innovation* will not be enhanced by an abrupt and imposed attempt to join face-to-face and digitally mediated professional groups and communities that is not driven by a personal necessity or an intentional decision to pursue and embrace change. Instead, if the relationships being developed are a consequence of *administrative enforcement* rather than a genuine expression of Greek primary and secondary educators, this may lead to a *violent, coercive*, and *contrived collegiality* that could potentially undermine genuine collaboration and professional development among them, in both traditional and virtual educational contexts (Hargreaves & Dawe, 1990).

REFERENCES

Akiba, M., Byun, S., Jiang, X., Kim, K., & Moran, A. (2023). Do Teachers Feel Valued in Society? Occupational Value of the Teaching Profession in OECD Countries. *AERA Open*, *9*(1), 1–21. DOI: 10.1177/23328584231179184

Arkorful, V., & Abaidoo, N. (2015). The role of e-learning, advantages and disadvantages of its adoption in higher education. *International Journal of Instructional Technology and Distance Learning*, *12*(1), 29–42. https://www.itdl.org/Journal/Jan_15/Jan15.pdf#page=33

Babalis, Th. (2023). Ζητήματα στην εκπαίδευση των εκπαιδευτικών: Από το όραμα στην πράξη [Issues in teacher education: From vision to practice]. In V. Karamanolakis (Ed.), *Εκπαίδευση και Εκπαιδευτική Πολιτική* [*Education and educational policy*] (pp. 91–102). Τράπεζα Πειραιώς και Εθνικό και Καποδιστριακό Πανεπιστήμιο Αθηνών [Piraeus Bank and National and Kapodistrian University of Athens].

Burgos, D. (2020). About Open Science and Open Education [Editorial]. In D. Burgos (Ed.), *Radical Solutions and Open Science: An Open Approach to Boost Higher Education* (pp. xi–xiv). Springer. https://doi.org/DOI: 10.1007/978-981-15-4276-3

Case, P., & Gosling, J. (2009). *Where is the wisdom we have lost in knowledge? A stoical perspective on personal knowledge management* [Paper presentation]. Sixth International Critical Management Conference, Warwick Business School, University of Warwick, UK. https://www.researchgate.net/publication/237216310

CEDEFOP. (2012). *The Mentor Handbook: A Practical Guide for VET Teacher Training*. European Centre for the Development of Vocational Training. https://www.cedefop.europa.eu/files/MENTORING_HANDBOOK_final_version.pdf

Chrysafidis, K. (2014). Ο ρόλος των πρακτικών ασκήσεων στη διαμόρφωση κατάλληλων συνθηκών για το «Νέο Σχολείο» [The role of practical exercises in shaping appropriate conditions for the "New School"] [Research in Education]. *E (Norwalk, Conn.)*, *1*(2), 86–104. DOI: 10.12681/hjre.8939

Day, C., & Gu, Q. (2007). Variations in the conditions for teachers' professional learning and development: Sustaining commitment and effectiveness over a career. *Oxford Review of Education*, *33*(4), 423–443. DOI: 10.1080/03054980701450746

de Almeida Sousa, J., & Amiel, T. (2023). Open Educational Practices from the perspective of open educators: Contributions to teacher professional development. *Edutec Revista Electrónica de Tecnología Educativa*, *85*(85), 85–102. DOI: 10.21556/edutec.2023.85.2853

Diamantopoulou, M., & Fragoulis, I. (2022). Η αποτελεσματικότητα του προγράμματος Επιμόρφωσης Β2 Επιπέδου στις Τεχνολογίες Πληροφορίας και Επικοινωνιών [The effectiveness of the B2 Level Training program in Information and Communication Technologies]. Απόψεις εκπαιδευτικών Δευτεροβάθμιας Εκπαίδευσης των Περιφερειακών Ενοτήτων Αχαΐας και Κορινθίας. *Epistimoniko Ekpaideftiko Periodiko "εκπ@ιδευτικός κύκλος", 10*(2), 495–558. https://educircle .gr/wp-content/uploads/2020/01/teyxos_10_2_26.pdf

DIKTIO – Network for Reform in Greece and Europe. (2024, May). *Η Ε.Ε. και η Ελλάδα: Ψηφιακή Δεκαετία 2030* [The EU and Greece: Digital Decade 2030]. https://todiktio.eu/wp-content/uploads/2024/05/Digital-Decade_GR.pdf

Dimopoulos, K. (2024, January). *Το έλλειμμα της ψηφιακής εκπαίδευσης στην Ελλάδα: Πηγαίνοντας από το 0 στο 1* [The digital education deficit in Greece: Going from 0 to 1] (Policy Brief No. 2). Center for Liberal Studies (KEFiM). https://kefim.org/wp-content/uploads/2020/07/Policy-Brief-2-2024-3.pdf

Doukakis, S. (2024, September 9). Πρόεδρος ΙΕΠ: Οι τρεις προκλήσεις στο ψηφιακό οικοσύστημα των εκπαιδευτικών βαθμίδων. *ESOS*. Retrieved from ESOS

Eliot, T. S. (n.d.). *Where is the wisdom we have lost in knowledge? Where is the knowledge we have lost in information?* In *The Rock*. Retrieved May 31, 2025, from https://www.goodreads.com/quotes/115907-where-is-the-wisdom-we-have-lost-in -knowledge-where

Enikos.gr. (2013, August 17). *Μαζικές αποχωρήσεις στην εκπαίδευση* [*Mass resignations in education*]. https://www.enikos.gr/politics/mazikes-apoxoriseis-stin -ekpaidefsi/220882/

European Commission. (2010). *Developing coherent and system-wide induction programmes for beginning teachers: A handbook for policy makers* (Staff Working Document SEC (2010) 538 final). European Commission. Retrieved from https:// ec.europa.eu/education/policy/school/doc/handbook0410_en.pdf

European Commission. (2018). *Education and training monitor 2018: Greece*. Publications Office of the European Union. https://education.ec.europa.eu/sites/ default/files/document-library-docs/et-monitor-report-2018-greece_en.pdf

European Commission. (2019). *Education and training monitor 2019: Greece*. Publications Office of the European Union. https://education.ec.europa.eu/sites/ default/files/document-library-docs/et-monitor-report-2019-greece_en.pdf

European Commission. (2022). *Digital Economy and Society Index (DESI) 2022 – Greece.* Shaping Europe's Digital Future. https://digital-strategy.ec.europa.eu/en/policies/desi-greece

European Commission, Directorate-General for Education and Culture. (2015). *A guide on policies to improve Initial Teacher Education. Education & Training 2020 - Schools Policy.* Publications Office of the European Union. https://www.cedefop.europa.eu/files/2_13_4_teacher_careers_en.pdf

European Court of Auditors. (2023). *EU support for the digitalisation of schools: Significant investments, but a lack of strategic focus in the use of EU financing by member states* (Special Report No. 11/2023). Publications Office of the European Union. https://www.eca.europa.eu/Lists/ECADocuments/SR-2023-11/SR-2023-11_EN.pdf

European Foundation for the Improvement of Living and Working Conditions. (2013). *Impact of the crisis on working conditions in Europe* (Report No. TN1212025S). European Foundation for the Improvement of Living and Working Conditions. https://www.eurofound.europa.eu/sites/default/files/ef_files/docs/ewco/tn1212025s/tn1212025s.pdf

Evrytanikos Palmos. (2021, March 25). *Μαζικές αποχωρήσεις εκπαιδευτικών* [*Mass resignations of teachers*]. https://www.evrytanikospalmos.gr/μαζικές-αποχωρήσεις-εκπαιδευτικώ

Fejes, A. (2006). The planetspeak discourse of lifelong learning in Sweden: What is an educable adult? *Journal of Education Policy*, *21*(6), 697–716. DOI: 10.1080/02680930600969266

Greek Government. (2021). *Law 4823/2021: Upgrading the school, empowerment of teachers, and other provisions* [Government Gazette, Issue A, No. 136/03-08-2021]. https://www.kodiko.gr/nomothesia/document/739038/nomos-4823-2021Academia

Greek Government. (2022). *Ministerial Decision No. 102919/GD4: Criteria for appointment, number of Pedagogical Advisors - Mentors, and term of service* [FEK 4509/2022, Issue B]. *Government Gazette.* https://www.e-nomothesia.gr/kat-ekpaideuse/ya-102919-gd4-2022.html

Hargreaves, A. (2000). Four ages of professionalism and professional learning. *Teachers and Teaching*, *6*(2), 151–182. DOI: 10.1080/713698714

Hargreaves, A., & Dawe, R. (1990). Paths of professional development: Contrived collegiality, collaborative culture, and the case of peer coaching. *Teaching and Teacher Education*, *6*(3), 227–241. DOI: 10.1016/0742-051X(90)90015-W

Hargreaves, A., & Fullan, M. (2012). *Professional capital: Transforming teaching in every school.* Teachers College Press.

Ifanti, A. A., & Fotopoulou, V. S. (2011). Teachers' perceptions of professionalism and professional development: A case study in Greece. *World Journal of Education, 1*(1), 40–51. DOI: 10.5430/wje.v1n1p40

In.gr. (2025, January 28). *Εκπαιδευτικοί: Δραματική μείωση των μισθών τους στην Ελλάδα – Έχασαν το ένα τρίτο μέσα σε 18 χρόνια* [*Teachers in Greece face dramatic salary cuts – losing one third over 18 years*]. https://www.in.gr/2025/01/28/economy/oikonomikes-eidiseis/ekpaideytikoi-dramatiki-meiosi-ton-misthon-tous-stin-ellada-exasan-ena-trito-mesa-se-18-xronia/

Isaksen, S. G., & Ekvall, G. (2010). Managing for innovation: The two faces of tension in creative climates. *Creativity and Innovation Management, 19*(2), 73–88. DOI: 10.1111/j.1467-8691.2010.00558.x

Jahanian, R., & Mahjoubi, S. (2013). Education in 21st Century. *International Journal of Learning and Development, 3*(6), 19–25. DOI: 10.5296/ijld.v3i6.4607

Kaltseras, D. (2022). *Ο εκπαιδευτικός ως «επαγγελματίας»: θεωρητικές αναζητήσεις και προβληματισμοί* [The teacher as a "professional": Theoretical inquiries and concerns]. *Erkyna, Educational-. Scientific Review (Singapore)*, (24), 40–58. https://erkyna.gr/e_docs/periodiko/dimosieyseis/ekpaideytika/t24-01.pdf

Kanawapee, C., Petsangsri, S., & Pimdee, P. (2022). The importance of sharing, caring and collaboration in Thai teacher competency development through online professional learning communities. *Journal of Positive Psychology and Wellbeing, 6*(1), 3674–3689. https://journalppw.com/index.php/jppw/article/view/5900

Katsonopoulos, Th. (2023, March 17). *Χαρτογράφηση της δευτεροβάθμιας εκπαίδευσης: Αριθμητικά δεδομένα για το έτος 2023-2024* [Mapping secondary education: Statistical data for the year 2023–2024] [Web article]. https://www.esos.gr/arthra/88932/hartografisi-tis-deyterobathmias-ekpaideysis-arithmitika-dedomena-gia-etos-2023-2024

Koffas, S., & Karanikos, A. (2023). Εκπαιδευτική πολιτική και παγκοσμιοποίηση. Διαμόρφωση πολιτικών [Educational policy and globalisation: Policy formation]. *In Proceedings of 8o Diethnes Synedrio gia tin proothisi tis ekpaideftikis kainotomias*, (Vol. B, pp.460–467), Larisa, Greece.

Kostaris, Ch., & Katsa, M. (2021). Ο ρόλος της εξ αποστάσεως εκπαίδευσης στην επιμόρφωση των εκπαιδευτικών [The role of distance education in teacher training]. *MusEd: Μουσείο–Σχολείο–Εκπαίδευση*, 2(1), 99-112. https://pasithee.library.upatras.gr/mused/article/view/4217/4167

Makri, I. (2023). Ψηφιακή εκπαίδευση: Η ταξινόμηση των ψηφιακών δεξιοτήτων μέσω του Ευρωπαϊκού πλαισίου για την ψηφιακή ικανότητα των πολιτών (DigComp) [Digital education: The classification of digital skills through the European framework for citizens' digital competence (DigComp)] [PDF]. *Informative Notes, IME GSEVEE*, No. 25. https://imegsevee.gr/wp-content/uploads/2023/07/makri_n25.pdf

Ministry of Digital Governance. (2021). *Βίβλος Ψηφιακού Μετασχηματισμού 2020–2025* [*Digital Transformation Bible 2020–2025*]. Hellenic Republic. https://digitalstrategy.gov.gr/website/static/website/assets/uploads/digital_strategy.pdf

Muhammadiah, M., Hamsiah, A., Muzakki, A., Nuramila, N., & Fauzi, Z. A. (2022). The role of the professional teacher as the agent of change for students. *Al-Ishlah: Jurnal Pendidikan, 14*(4), 6887–6896. DOI: 10.35445/alishlah.v14i4.1372

Namreen Asif, V. A., & Panakaje, N. (2022). Paradigm Shift - The role of educational technology and internet in Indian education system. *International Journal of Case Studies in Business, IT, and Education, 6*(2), 930–944. DOI: 10.5281/zenodo.7508889

OECD. (2020). *Education Policy Outlook in Greece*. OECD Publishing., DOI: 10.1787/f10b95cf-

Papadopoulou, V., & Kipouropoulou, E. (2020). Όψεις της επαγγελματικής ταυτότητας υποψήφιων εκπαιδευτικών: Η περίπτωση των τελειόφοιτων φοιτητών του Π.Τ.Δ.Ε. Φλώρινας [Aspects of the professional identity of prospective teachers: The case of final-year students of the Department of Primary Education, Florina] [Diadrasi Publications.]. *Paidagogiki Epitheorisi, 37*(69), 120–135.

Papanikolaou, G., & Tzimogiannis, A. (2024). Το έργο «Επιμόρφωση εκπαιδευτικών στην αξιοποίηση των Τεχνολογιών της Πληροφορίας και των Επικοινωνιών στην εκπαίδευση»: Μια αποτίμηση της υλοποίησής του στο νομό Ιωαννίνων [The project "Teacher training in the use of Information and Communication Technologies in education": An evaluation of its implementation in the Ioannina region]. *Proceedings of the Hellenic Scientific Association for Information and Communication Technologies in Education, 1*, 395–404. https://eproceedings.epublishing.ekt.gr/index.php/cetpe/article/view/6296

Samara, A. (2021). Education governance in the era of lifelong learning: The construction of the lifelong learning teacher. In V. Chiou, L. Geunis, O. Holz, N. Orucg Ertiürk, & F. Shelton (Eds.), *Voices from the classroom: A celebration of learning* (Vol. 1, pp. 307–317). Waxmann.

Samara, A., & Tiligada, E. (2021). Επαγγελματικές κοινότητες μάθησης και διαρκής επαγγελματική συνανάπτυξη των εκπαιδευτικών [Professional learning communities and continuous professional development of teachers]. In S. X. Pantazis, E. P. Maraki, E. D. Beledakis, G. E. Striligas, I. A. Tzortzakis, Ch. S. Droumpogiannis, E. Markaki, & E. Psaltaki (Eds.), *Πρακτικά του 7ου Διεθνούς Συνεδρίου IAKE, τ. Β'* [Proceedings of the 7th International IAKE Conference, Vol. B] (pp. 107–114). Ινστιτούτο Ανθρωπιστικών και Κοινωνικών Επιστημών IAKE [Institute of Humanities and Social Sciences IAKE].

Stournaras, G. (2020, February 24). *Διδάγματα από την ελληνική οικονομική κρίση, οι προκλήσεις και οι ευκαιρίες για το μέλλον* [*Lessons from the Greek economic crisis, challenges and opportunities for the future*]. Speech at the Gennadius Library, Athens. Bank of Greece. https://www.bankofgreece.gr/enimerosi/grafeio-typoy/anazhthsh-enhmerwsewn/enhmerwseis?announcement=fc915812-ab24-47ab-9e60-a566653a1f42

Tanea Newsroom. (2024, September 11). *Teachers resign en masse in private schools – What they report* [*Σχολεία: Μαζικές παραιτήσεις εκπαιδευτικών και στα ιδιωτικά – Τι καταγγέλλουν*]. https://www.tanea.gr/2024/09/11/greece/sxoleia-mazikes-paraitiseis-ekpaideytikon-kai-sta-idiotika-ti-kataggelloun/

Tiligada, E. (2020). Συνεργατικές πρακτικές επαγγελματικής μάθησης και συνανάπτυξης εκπαιδευτικών: Περιπτώσεις Ιδιωτικών Σχολείων Δευτεροβάθμιας Εκπαίδευσης Αττικής [Collaborative practices of professional learning and co-development of teachers: Cases of private secondary schools in Attica]. *Συγκριτική και Διεθνής Εκπαιδευτική Επιθεώρηση* [Comparative and International Educational Review], *20*, 147–167.

Tzika, V., & Xafakos, E. (2022). Διερεύνηση των αντιλήψεων των εκπαιδευτικών για το καινοτομικό σχολικό κλίμα: μία έρευνα μεικτών μεθόδων [Exploring teachers' perceptions of innovative school climate: A mixed methods study]. In S.-G. Soulis & M. Liakopoulou (Eds.), *Education in the 21st century: Contemporary challenges and reflections. Proceedings of the International Conference of the Department of Primary Education, University of Ioannina* [Στο Σούλης, Σ.Γ. & Λιακοπούλου, Μ. (Επιμ.). *Πρακτικά Διεθνούς Επιστημονικού Συνεδρίου Εκπαίδευση στον 21ο αιώνα: σύγχρονες προκλήσεις και προβληματισμοί*]. (Vol. B, pp. 1157–1169). Ioannina, Greece.

Tzovla, I. (2016). Εξ αποστάσεως επαγγελματική ανάπτυξη εκπαιδευτικών και χρήση του παραγόμενου εκπαιδευτικού υλικού στη σχολική εκπαίδευση [Distance professional development of school teachers and usage of the produced training material in school education]. *Open Education: The Journal for Open and Distance Education and Educational Technology, 12*(1), 76–86. DOI: 10.12681/jode.10241

van der Westhuizen, L., & Hannaway, D. (2024). Authentic caring in online professional development for early childhood teachers in South Africa. *South African Journal of Childhood Education, 14*(1), 1574. Advance online publication. DOI: 10.4102/sajce.v14i1.1574

Weimer, K. R. (2020). Mentor identification, selection, preparation, and development: A literature review. *Update - University of South Carolina. Dept. of Music, 39*(3), 20–28. DOI: 10.1177/8755123320965138

Yanatma, S. (2025, January 27). *Εκπαιδευτικοί στην Ευρώπη: Ποιες χώρες δίνουν υψηλές αυξήσεις – πολύ χαμηλοί οι μισθοί στην Ελλάδα* [*Teachers in Europe: Which countries give high raises – very low salaries in Greece*]. Euronews Greece. https://gr.euronews.com/business/2025/01/27/ekpaideytikoi-stin-eyropi-poies-xores-dinoyn-ipsiles-ayxiseis-xamiloi-misthoi-stin-ellada

Zagkos, C., Kyridis, A., Kamarianos, I., & Fotopoulos, N. (2022). Working conditions of university teachers during the pandemic-the case of Greek universities. *European Journal of Open Education and E-learning Studies, 8*(1).

ADDITIONAL READING

Giannarou, G., & Alexandropoulos, G. (2019). *Η εισαγωγή του e-mentoring ως θεσμού υποδοχής-υποστήριξης των νεοεισερχόμενων εκπαιδευτικών στην πρωτοβάθμια εκπαίδευση: Μια μελέτη περίπτωσης* [The Introduction of E-Mentoring as an Induction and Support Mechanism for Newly Appointed Primary School Teachers: A Case Study]. *Anoikti Ekpaidefsi: to periodiko gia tin Anoikti kai ex Apostaseos Ekpaidefsi kai tin Ekpaideftiki Technologia, 15*(1), 92. https://doi.org/DOI: 10.12681/jode.16367

Joynes, C., Rossignoli, S., & Fenyiwa Amonoo-Kuofi, E. (2019). *21st century skills: Evidence of issues in definition, demand and delivery for development contexts* (K4D Helpdesk Report). Institute of Development Studies. https://assets.publishing.service.gov.uk/media/5d71187ce5274a097c07b985/21st_century.pdf

Koutsoukos, M. (2022). In search of a model of mentoring adult educators. *Adult Education Critical Issues*, *2*(1), 86–111. DOI: 10.12681/aeci.30861

Markovits, Y., Boer, D., Gerbers, S., & van Dick, R. (2017). The impact of a lasting economic crisis on employee attitudes: A follow-up and extension. *Athens Journal of Business & Economics*, *3*(2), 85–100. DOI: 10.30958/ajbe.3.2.1

Owusu-Ansah, A., & Kyei-Blankson, L. (2016). *Going back to the basics: Demonstrating care, connectedness, and a pedagogy of relationship in education. World Journal of Education,* *6*(3), 1–9. https://doi.org/ Press+4DOI: 10.5430/wje.v6n-3p1SciEdUp

Pinjani, A., Pasha, A., Bijani, A., & Aslam, A. A. (2017). Promoting culture of sharing through teacher professional development. *Literacy Information and Computer Education Journal*, *8*(2), 2592–2597. DOI: 10.20533/licej.2040.2589.2017.0343

Rotta, T. N., & Teixeira, R. A. (2018). *The commodification of knowledge and information* (GPERC Working Paper No. 60). Greenwich Political Economy Research Centre. https://research.gold.ac.uk/id/eprint/26883/1/Rotta%20and%20Teixeira%20(2018)%20-%20The%20Commodification%20of%20Knowledge%20and%20Information%20-%20%5B20june2018%5D%20-%20GPERC%20wp3.pdf

Rusman, A., Mas'udi, M. M., & Hermoyo, R. P., Yarno, Yunianti, S., & Rafsanjani, H. (2023). *Education transformation in 5.0 society development era.* In Proceedings of the 5th International Conference on Innovative Design, Analysis & Development Practices in Aerospace & Automotive Engineering (I-DAD'22) (Surakarta, Indonesia, December 20–21, 2021). *AIP Conference Proceedings*, 2727(1), 020050. https://doi.org/DOI: 10.1063/5.0141657

Sakkoulis, D., Asimaki, A., & Vergidis, D. (2017). Η επιμόρφωση των εκπαιδευτικών: ζητήματα ορισμού και τυπολογίας. Η ελληνική εμπειρία και οι διεθνείς τάσεις [Teacher training: Issues of definition and typology. The Greek experience and international trends]. *Εκπ@ιδευτικός Κύκλος, 5*(1), 104–126. https://educircle.gr/wp-content/uploads/2017/06/teuxos_5_1_5.pdf

KEY TERMS AND DEFINITIONS

Agent of Change: Any individual, group or organization who actively promotes, encourages and supports change, innovation, advancement and positive metamorphosis for the common good to occur within a group, organization, or society. If they function not only as change agents, but also as role models, their impact tends to be more significant and widespread, as they lead change not only through their actions but also by inspiring others to emulate their behavior.

Digital Culture: The prevailing practices, values, rules and cognitive frameworks that mold the ways in which individuals, organizations, institutions and society at large act in digital environments; It affects the way they communicate, interact and behave when integrating digital technologies into their everyday lives and practices.

Digital Maturity: The extent to which individuals, organizations, systems or ecosystems successfully adopt, incorporate, adapt and leverage current, contemporary, emerging or evolving digital technologies within their operations, culture, and strategic frameworks in order to enhance performance and adaptability in the current digital landscape; In other words, it is how effectively persons, teams, systems, entities, etc. adopt and utilize modern digital technology in their work, the kind of atmosphere they foster, and their overall strategy for improvement and adjustment to the current digital landscape.

Digital Professional Identity [of educators]: The digital version of the educators' professionals identities, formed and evolved by their online presence in the digital sphere; it evolves alongside digital culture through web-based social interactions by leveraging online professional platforms and digital tools for professional networking, knowledge co-creation and sharing, alongside skill development.

[Global] Educational Megatrends: The prevailing global directions, priorities, advancements, popular movements and forces that challenge, influence and reshape teaching, learning, and the frameworks of educational systems. These powerful, dynamic, long-term trends, which come in response to emerging innovations, technological advancements, societal shifts, groundbreaking research outcomes, and changes in policy and pedagogical approaches, influence the nature and orientation of education systems at a global scale.

Induction: A plethora of structured processes and specialized practices for the professional development and socialization of newcomer teachers, through which they are gradually introduced to the teaching profession, address challenges and seize opportunities. Chronically, this sense-making experience it may occur after having completed initial teacher education and preparation, during the first years of teaching. It has an early and decisive impact on the development of their personal, social, digital and professional identity.

Pedagogical Guidance Counselor-Mentor: A veteran, senior or experienced peer primary or secondary teacher whose role is to inspire, guide and support every newly appointed or recently appointed permanent, substitute or hourly paid teacher with less experience, with the aim of improving the quality of their teaching and, more broadly, the overall educational work they do.

Virtual Professional Peer Learning Networks [in education]: Vibrant virtual professional learning communities where educators from various specialties engage with one another, sharing insights and collaborating to enhance their professional capacity, alongside their skills. These networks are purposefully structured to promote ongoing professional development and career growth of educators by facilitating the sharing of experiences, exchanging valuable knowledge, and providing reciprocal support among members.

Chapter 16

The Idea of Good Governance in the Collection Greek Tales on Papyrus: Reading, Playing, and Learning

María Paz López Martínez
https://orcid.org/0000-0002-8564-7780
Universidad de Alicante, Spain

Aramis Enrique López
https://orcid.org/0000-0003-4331-597X
Facultat de Belles Arts, University of Barcelona, Spain

Olimpia Navarro López
University of Alicante, Spain

ABSTRACT

Among the protagonists the collection Greek Tales on Papyrus are members of legendary lineages from great empires. These sagas encompass several successive members of each family. The younger rulers learn from and inherit from their ancestors a series of fundamental values, among which lie the principles of good governance within the realm. This ideal constitutes one of the primary treasures of the legacy passed from parents to their children. Ninus, Semiramis, Sesonchosis, Parthenope and Calligone and their families have been transformed into playing card characters.

DOI: 10.4018/979-8-3373-2332-9.ch016

INTRODUCTION

"Little reader, welcome to the world of tales inspired by very, very ancient Greek novels. They were written more than two thousand years ago on papyrus scrolls that remained hidden under the desert sands. You too can discover the enigmas hidden in these pages by accessing the secret codes. You will learn fascinating things from the protagonists, do you feel like travelling to distant lands and living fantastic adventures?"

With these words, we open each copy of our collection *Greek Tales on Papyrus*, a project that was born as a result of the transfer of tales inspired by ancient Greek texts found in Egypt and written on papyrus that appeared among the rubble and ruins of ancient cities that were built along the banks of the Nile. (Kussl, 1991; Stephens & Winkler, 1995; López Martínez, 1998, Bastianini & Casanova, 2010; Henrichs, 2010; Gargiulo, 2013). Over the centuries, these towns were abandoned by their inhabitants and buried by the desert sand. Thanks to archaeological campaigns, these papyri containing the novels that inspired the plot of these tales have been found. The complete originals of these works were lost very early, in antiquity itself, and for many centuries we knew nothing about these novels. Now, thanks to the studies of María Paz López Martínez, we have been able to recover them. Her work has consisted of editing, translating, studying and reconstructing all these texts.

The originals were written in Greek in the early Imperial period, from around the 1st century BC to the 4th century AD, and are novels of love and adventure. The genre of the novel is an exquisite literary product that was born in the time of Augustus, around the 1st century BC, and covers the whole of the Imperial Age. It is projected into the Byzantine world and from there, through the medieval monasteries, it reaches the entire Western tradition, which converges with the Persian world in translations made in the Library of Wisdom in Baghdad. Hence we can find them in Arabic, Armenian, Ethiopian and other language versions, from East to West.

The origin of these novels can be explained in the globalised world that arose from Alexander's conquests. Its characters come from diverse peoples and travel all over the known world, from the Mediterranean, to the Black Sea, the Red Sea and other seas, from India to Iberia and from Ethiopia to the island of Tule.

Its characters include Greek warlords, Assyrian monarchs, Persian satraps and pharaohs. Exotic characters, eunuchs, ghosts. Also rogues, villains and pirates. There is no lack of intellectuals, poets, philosophers, magicians and priests, or princesses, queens, Amazons, witches, corsairs, courtesans, freedwomen, philosophers, readers and intellectuals who set out on journeys in search of knowledge, as highlighted by studies on the ancient novel (Konstan, 1994; Ruiz Montero, 2006; Stramaglia, 2000; Tilg, 2010).

The project *Greek Tales on Papyrus* was launched in 2021 and was inspired by a specific group of novels, whose protagonists are members of legendary lineages and leaders of great empires. Consequently, they appear in works by Greek historians such as Herodotus, Thucydides, Diodorus Siculus and Polybius, to name but a few. In other cases, it is the events they narrate that are cited in literary, archaeological or other sources. This group of novels constituted a specific type of novel, known as the "historical novel", which was very successful in antiquity itself, as it is today (Dostálová, 1991).

The protagonists are Greek rulers, but also monarchs of Eastern peoples with whom the Greeks had contact: Trojans, Assyrians, Egyptians, Phoenicians, Persians, Scythians, Macedonians and more. The heroines, and in many cases protagonists of the novel, are especially interesting and courageous. As such queens or princesses, they receive the same education as if they had been boys.

The young learn and inherit a set of values from their ancestors, through a long chain of transmission of knowledge that includes the wisdom and experience of grandparents, paternal and maternal advice, together with their exemplary attitude, formal education in reading and writing, knowledge of the literary, oral and written tradition that also provides positive and negative behavioural references. This whole set of learning mechanisms constitutes the paideia (παιδεία), the Greek ideal of education, which enables young people to excel in word and deed.

Initiatory travel narratives are prevalent and can be identified across a wide range of traditional stories. These narratives typically depict a prince or heroine completing a period of youth and embarking on a transformative journey that underscores the necessity of personal development. Through these experiences, the protagonist comes to understand their social role in the adult world and prepares to assume the responsibilities their birthright entails.

In contrast, contemporary adventure narratives frequently omit these formative dimensions. They no longer center on the protagonist's internal growth or preparation for leadership roles such as kingship, governance, or command. A salient example can be found in the *Epic of Gilgamesh*, in which the youthful king of Uruk initially behaves irresponsibly and must undergo a series of trials. These challenges ultimately enable his return as a wiser, more just ruler. Comparable processes of moral and psychological development are evident in the labors of Hercules, the voyage of the Argonauts, and the legendary exploits of Alexander the Great—all of which reflect narratives of personal struggle, acquisition of knowledge, and the attainment of mature identity.

Such imperatives for individual growth have largely receded from the contemporary cultural imagination. Modern heroes are more often depicted as seekers of external objects, wealth, or symbolic trophies. In popular cinema, for instance, superheroes—who function as contemporary mythic figures—tend to inherit only the physical attributes of ancient gods. These powers are employed to avert global catastrophe, but the characters themselves frequently undergo little or no internal transformation.

By contrast, in traditional narratives, young protagonists strive to cultivate the personal virtues and qualities necessary to fulfill the roles history or fate has assigned to them. These stories foreground the importance of self-knowledge, ethical development, and societal responsibility as essential components of heroic identity.

Once the theoretical framework is in place and the time has come, the prince or princess must take the lead alone. These are difficult times, there are no second chances. The lives of his or her family and fiefdoms depend on his or her success. He or she will face battles, land expeditions, but also sea voyages. He will have to know how to deal with the members of the court, to avoid the insidiousness of his rivals to the throne, to block the attacks of enemy peoples, but also to manage human, civic and war conflicts, to harangue and raise the morale of the troops, especially in moments of decay. The dangers and difficult situations that occur in these novels include meteorological phenomena, sea storms and shipwrecks, which cast a shadow over the spirits of the crew and lead to uncertain destinations. Among the main treasures that these apprentice monarchs will receive, as a legacy from their ancestors, are the keys to the proper administration of their kingdom, what we know as the "good governance" of the kingdom.

In the case of the tyrants, they will display a generous management of their patrimony, inviting philosophers and artists to their respective courts. The reason for the journey has a lot to do with all these processes. They are characters called to hold power, and their journey opens the way to knowledge of the mechanisms of power. In any case, this is a host country where they come into contact with other forms of good government.

The young princesses receive the same training as the boys, both in the use of words and in the military, and are, like them, able to handle bows, arrows, swords and all kinds of weapons, ride horses and lead armies. But there is also another, more conventional model of woman. They all enjoy art, culture and good food in times of peace.

The plot of the Greek novels and, consequently, of the tales presents a similar structure and covers different stages in the life of these heroes: 1) Childhood and adolescence; 2) Educational process, for, as befits the heir to a kingdom, the protagonist receives a complete education, oratory and literature, but also horsemanship, handling of weapons and military strategy; 3) Paternal advice on good government; 4) On reaching youth, he must demonstrate his ability to face military campaigns and sea voyages alone; 5) To complete his maturing process, love appears. Eros, in fact, is a fundamental and differentiating ingredient in these novels. Unlike what happens in most of the myths and stories of the previous tradition, in the novels, there is a reciprocated love between both members of the couple; 6) On the death of his progenitor, the young prince, the hero will become the leader of a great empire.

These patterns are very concrete in the case of Greek novels inspired by the leaders of great empires and, in order to exemplify what has been said, we are going to take a closer look at two of them, starring a prince and a princess. They are Nino and Calligone. These novels are the basis of their stories, as well as the characters of the Assyrian and Greek families of Pontus in the deck of cards accompanying the last work of López and Navarro (2025).

NINUS

We begin with the oldest, which is probably the first novel in the Western tradition. It is *Ninus*, of which two papyri have come down to us from the beginning or middle of the 1st century AD (*P.Berol.* 6926 + *P.Gen.* 85 and *PSI* 1305) and from which the story Nino, the adventures of the king of Nineveh (2021) and the cards of the Assyrian family are inspired. The plot of the novel narrates the adventures and experiences in love and war of the young Assyrian prince after whom the novel is named. The novel may have been written in the middle of the 1st century BC and the literary quality of the work is exceptionally high (Fernández Garrido, 2022).

The character Nino may be inspired by the historical Bronze Age (1243-1207) king Tukulti-Ninurta I, who was probably a contemporary of the Trojan War. He is considered the mythical founder of the city of Nineveh and is mentioned in the Bible. He had border disputes with Urartu (Armenia), the Hittite kingdom and Babylon. Sources report that one of his sons, in collaboration with some Assyrian nobles, provoked a revolt and was killed in the capital he himself had founded. His figure may have met a fate parallel to that of Queen Semiramis herself and the Egyptian Pharaoh Sesostris: a native legend developed around the historical Tukultī-Ninurta I, enriched with elements from oral and written tradition and perhaps crystallising episodes and traits of several historical Assyrian kings. *The Deed of Tukultī-Ninurta* has been found to have been used in Mesopotamian education in the 1st millennium.

This legend may have reached the first millennium BC and reached the ears of classical Greek writers such as Herodotus or Ctesias (regardless of the language in which they heard it), who eventually incorporated in their works a literary biography of the character under the Hellenised form of the name, Νίνος. In the 1st century BC, Diodorus Siculus would have composed his *Bibliotheca historica* from a collection of Persian accounts included in the work of the Greek Ctesias of Cnidus (second half of the 5th century to the first decades of the 4th century BC), who was a physician at the Persian court of Artaxerxes II. Ctesias' work, *τ Περσικά*, was inspired by a universalist principle and aimed to tell the story of the empires of Asia from their origins to the Persian king Artaxerxes II -398/397 BC. The complete text has not been preserved, but some fragments have come down to us and it would cover the history of the Assyrian, Median and Persian kingdoms, Diodorus himself openly acknowledging the dependence of his work on that of the physician of Cnidus and stating that it was Ninus who was the first native Assyrian king of whom history and memory are preserved (D.S. II 1, 3-4).

Both the novelistic character and Diodorus' description of Ninus underline that Ninus corresponds to the archetype of the great founding king and universal conqueror, traits that we also find in other leaders of great ancient powers such as Sesostris in Egypt or Alexander in Greece, protagonists, in turn, of two Greek novels, which serve as the basis for the stories about the legendary pharao as well as future publications about the life of Alexander the Great. In his biography of Ninus, Diodorus summarises his foreign policy successes: alliance with the king of Arabia, campaigns against Babylon, Armenia, Media, Egypt, Phoenicia and a whole host of peoples between Asia Minor and Asia, between the Nile and the Tanais, with the exception of India and Bactria. It was precisely there in Bactria that his first failure led to his return to his homeland, where he founded a walled city and began a major construction activity.

Another *topos* in the training of the young apprentice ruler is the journey, which becomes a space for learning about other peoples and customs. Such experiences in inhospitable lands and even in enemy territories also provide life lessons. After the conquest of Armenia, Ninus probably embarks on a ship sailing across the Euxine Pontus, with the intention of further expanding his Assyrian kingdom. Indeed, archaeological evidence supports the existence of trade routes from Urartu to Colchis for the exchange of luxury goods, further emphasising Colchis as a significant mythical setting. However, despite the expertise of the ship's captain, the ship becomes stranded on sandbanks and eventually wrecks on the banks of the Hippos River, now probably identified as the Kodori. The crew abandon ship and try to salvage their belongings. Nino feels even more desperate than his sailors and curses his luck, for changes of fortune are typical of the vicissitudes encountered by the protagonists of the novels. However, in the midst of his present misfortune, the young prince is able to overcome it.

In several cities in Asia Minor, we have a series of testimonies from the end of the 1st century AD. In several cities in Asia Minor, we have a series of testimonies from the end of the 1st century AD - specifically from 90 AD - in which Ninus is depicted, together with his wife, Queen Semiramis, as the founding hero of several cities. The most important of these is the relief that adorns the basilica of Aphrodisias in Caria. The city was also called Λελέγων πόλις, Μεγάλη Πόλις and Νινόλις and worshipped Zeus Nineudios. On the relief, he is depicted with hiton, himátion and a long sceptre in his hand. He is celebrating a sacrifice or libation next to an altar on which rests an eagle. There is also a dry tree with three long branches and, next to Ninus, a male figure dressed in the clamid deposits offerings on a smaller altar. Both Ninus and Semiramis have the noble and respectable appearance of those who embody civic virtues. These relief images are consistent with the evidence presented on coins from the 2nd-3rd century AD from the city of Aninetta, on the border between Caria and Lydia. In all these Minorasian materials the figures are depicted standing, in official activity, in active tension, exercising their function as city founders. The intention is to transfer to the most remote times, to that space on the border between myth and history, the origin of a series of cities that lack noble ancestors. To the political, in the case of Aphrodisias, we could add the economic interest: to justify the privileged treatment the city receives from Rome. A very different attitude is presented by the characters in some mosaics that have been found in localities very close to each other in the province of Syria (Alexandretta - Iskenderum and Antioch of Orontes - Daphne) and which date from the end of the 2nd or beginning of the 3rd century AD, where Nino is comfortably seated, in a melancholic attitude and contemplating a portrait. While the reliefs and coins from Aphrodisias, Aninetta and Thyatira present our protagonist in his public and official dimension, however, in the mosaics from Antioch and Alexandretta, which come from private houses in Syria, Nino appears in an intimate scene, enjoying *otium*.

SESONCHOSIS

Sesonchosis is a lost Greek novel inspired by the life of an Egyptian pharaoh known from the works by Herodotus (2.102-110), Diodorus (1.53-58) and Pseudo-Chalisthenes (1.34.2). The original text has come down to us in five papyri, all from the city of Oxyrhynchus and dating between the 2nd to 4th centuries AD. They are now in the Sackler Library in Oxford and in the British Museum in London.

The name of the protagonist of the novel is inspired by the Greek forms of the names of several pharaohs of the 12th Dynasty and of the Pharaoh Sheshonq of the 22nd Dynasty and of Berber origin (ca. 943 BC to 922 BC). Variants appear in Greek sources as έ ω τρι and ε όγχω ι . The character of the Greek novel is a literary construction amalgamating several historically documented kings. The pharaoh Sesostris or Senusert intervenes in fictional narratives that have come down to us in papyri of the demotic period, whose plots are inspired by legends concerning characters connected with the 12th Dynasty. A recent monograph on this figure has been published (Hoffmann & Schoske, 2024).

The creation of a Greek novel from the narrative around the life of the leader of a great empire also occurs in another lost Greek novel, Ninus, and Alexander. The historical setting also equates *Sesonchosis* with other fragmentary lost novels we mentioned here, such as *Ninus*, *Parthenope* or *Calligone*, which can be considered "historical novels" proper.

We offer here a hypothesis of the plot of the novel. In *P. Oxy*. 1826 is a very short and vague text. It could give an account of the military training that Sesonchosis acquires at the hand of his father. The scene points to a conversation. Amenhemath would give him useful advice and warnings about the treachery and intrigues that await him when the protagonist occupies the throne. Demotic papyri can be placed in the first part of the novel, while the father was still alive. In a native context, we must also consider *The Teachings of King Amenhemhat*, whose purpose was to teach the prince. In Greek context, Diodorus also refers to the instruction given by the pharaoh to his son. The literary topic is present in the *Cyropaedia*, one of Nino's references, and in *Parthenope*.

P. Oxy. 2466. While Sesonchosis was still a child, the Arabs attacked Egypt under the command of a certain Arab leader named Webelis, of whom we have no record in the sources. Nor do we have any record of the Arab invasion, perhaps a literary pretext to justify later Egyptian hostility. Reinforcements arrive on the battlefield from all over the kingdom, from both Upper and Lower Egypt. There are heavy casualties among the Arab troops and they begin to flee in panic. In the midst of the turmoil, the enemies trample each other and many are killed. Themos, a friend of the protagonist and a frequent name in inscriptions, including those found in Egypt, Nubia, Syria and Arabia, tells Sesonchosis all that is happening and the young prince resolves that one day he will conquer this territory. Webelis, the enemy leader, manages to escape with his life and return to Arabia.

P. Oxy. 5262 is a very brief and vague fragment. From the mention of the Red Sea we could place the action in some oasis in the Arabian Peninsula. Caution should be exercised, for other areas, such as the lands on the other side of the Red Sea, occupied by legendary kingdoms of the Horn of Africa, such as the so-called Kingdom of Aksum or Sheba, should not be completely ruled out.

Diodorus (1.53.5-6) helps to continue the story: once the instruction was completed, Pharaoh Amenhemhat I sent his son on a military expedition to Arabia. The time had come for Sesonchosis to fulfil the dream he had conceived as a child. The demotic papyri mention a mission to Arabia and refer to Sesonchosis as 'the king's son'. The plot of the novel probably takes up a moment in the protagonist's life when Amenhemhat is still alive and sends his son to these lands in the company of his faithful friend and adviser Pamunis. Sesonchosis would emerge victorious from this conflict which occurred prior to his father's death. In the 20th year of his reign, 1918 BC, Amenhemhat appointed Senwosret I, his son, as co-regent. Under the historical Amenhemhat I the copper mines in the Sinai were exploited and punitive raids were carried out against the local Bedouin tribes.

After the Arabian episode, we assume that the protagonist launches an attack on Libya, with the aim of extending control as far as Nubia. He erects fortifications at strategic points and reaches as far as the Second Cataract. The historical Amenhemhat I dies during a military campaign by his son against the Libyans in the western desert. On his return from this expedition, Sesonchosis receives the news of his father's death and considers some kind of return strategy, like Odysseus in the Odyssey, bearing in mind his father's advice and his warnings of possible intrigues that members of his own court might plot against him. Perhaps, he is informed of such plots by a loyal member of his court or by the Egyptian Themos. In Parthenope something similar occurs: Methiocus, the son of the famous Miltiades, arrives at Samos, at the court of Polycrates, fleeing from the intrigues of his stepmother Hegesipilla because she intends to benefit her own sons in dynastic rights. Both situations would be in line with the machinations of Penelope's suitors in the Odyssey against Telemachus.

Sesonchosis decides to take refuge in Arabia, because it is an already pacified and allied territory: the Arab warlord Webelis, at the time of the defeat, would have promised Sesoncosis the hand of his daughter.

P. Oxy. 5262 refers to “the man” with article (δ νθρω̣[πο], line 6). He could be Pamounis, the friend who accompanies Sesonchosis in papyrus P. Oxy. 3319, or the Egyptian Themos.

P. Oxy. 3319 is an erotic episode that takes place in Arabia, in an oasis close to the one described in the previous papyrus. The young Meameris, along with other members of her circle, are in a room presided over by Webelis. This could be a tent, as the Arabs are a nomadic people. Other possible enclaves are Hegra or Taima, which became important hubs on the trade routes for silk, spices and perfumes, especially Boswellia Sacra. Webelis holds a banquet or feast attended by his daughter Meameris. Meanwhile, Sesonchosis hides with Pamounis by a nearby fountain. Following the Homeric model, he would have arrived incognito at the court.

Meameris leaves the party and stops. At that moment, their eyes meet and the daughter of Webelis is captivated by the beauty of the protagonist. It is not surprising that the girl does not recognize her fiancé: neither does Penelope recognize Odysseus when he arrives in Ithaca. Quite disturbed, the Arabian princess returns to the party, but is no longer able to enjoy the reunion. This is the end of the text. We assume that, after this meeting, the handsome young man would make himself known to his father-in-law, the couple would marry and together they would return to Egypt where, victorious in the Arabian and Libyan campaigns, Sesonchosis would be proclaimed Pharaoh.

P. Oxy. 5263 After his accession to the throne, Sesonchosis reigned alone and a new era of prosperity and prosperity began in Egypt, according to the testimony of Greek authors, including Herodotus. Mention is made of a king, πρ τ ν βα ι[λέα], perhaps Sesonchosis himself, already proclaimed pharaoh. A messenger arrives to announce what has happened: he speaks of grief at someone's death, ships being loaded, parents or ancestors and Sesonchosis' actions or deeds.

Everything suggests that the protagonist, after his victories in Arabia and Libya, then embarks on a sea voyage. In the novel of the same name, Ninus also sets out on a sea expedition after his successful land campaign against Armenia. Besides the commercial interest, the journey would have an ethnographic purpose.

P. Oxy. 5263 narrates a sea voyage. Sesonchosis departs by ship from Egypt, most probably from the port of Alexandria, to trace an itinerary that includes several stops, of which an account is given in the first column: Italy, Dacia, Germania. He would also visit other towns and lands. We could even think that the pharaoh intended to go round the world.

An itinerary that starts in Alexandria, stops in Italy and, from there, heads west and reaches the Iberian Peninsula is the journey undertaken by the protagonists of another lost novel, Incredible Things beyond Thule, of which four papyri have been preserved. The Sesoncosis voyage is therefore comparable to other novelistic journeys. Antonio Diogenes' novel is a choral work, featuring, among other characters, a certain girl called Derkyllide, who travels from Naples to Iberia, where she comes into contact with Celts, Aquitans, Artabrians and Asturians, learns about the incredible customs of these peoples and, after enjoying her stay, returns to Sicily, crossing Gaul and Italy. The monograph by Schmedt (2020) is currently considered fundamental.

The plot twist includes a possible storm at sea, which would be a frequent topic in the novels. The reading of the papyrus is difficult and it is possible to complete with an eruption of Vesuvius, or a polar night in the Arctic, to which I myself would add a fourth: a total eclipse, along the lines of the one described by Archilochus: "Once Zeus, father of the Olympians,/ made night in the middle of the day,/ hiding the light of the bright sun". Lines after in the papyrus, we read "cyclical world", "circular universe". There could be several interesting interpretations. Perhaps, the novelist has recomposed a cyclical image of the world map, along the lines of that already elaborated by Strabo and based on the earlier geographical tradition. Next, there is talk of saving a girl. Rather, it would be a new character, along the lines of Xen. *Cyr*. 6.3.14, Char. 5.8.9 and 6.8.1 and even *Parthenope* (*P. Oxy*. 435.6-7).

The traveler sets course for the western regions of the earth. In the following line, it is specified with the information that these are the untrodden places. The journey continues to a point where the travelers catch sight of an impressive atmospheric phenomenon: "some rocks that emit fire from or by lightning... that fall into the sea". This could be a description of a real phenomenon: an episode of volcanic activity or even meteorites. In the same line of striking spectacles, the papyrus describes a bird landing on the ground. It is large, with colored wings and a head covered with hair that looks like rays and is compared to the mythical bird "that [they] call the "Phoenix"".

Ps. Callisthenes explicitly equates Alexander with the pharaoh Sesonchosis, the Macedonian is a "new Sesonchosis (νέο ε όγχω ι)". Also fundamental are the data provided by certain sources, especially Diodorus, who refers to certain plans Alexander had to sail westwards and to reach the Pillars of Hercules (18.4.4).

In fact, Arrian (*An.* 7.1.2), Plutarch (*Alex.* 78) and Curtius claim that Alexander would have wanted to reach Gades, which he considered an island situated between Africa and Hispania (10.1.17-18). Also according to the sources, Alexander himself is said to have recorded this desire in a will which, at his death, was ignored by his successors, so that the western dreams of the Macedonian conqueror were never realized. Alexander's connection with Gades is also evidenced by certain reports mentioning the existence of a statue of Alexander in the Heracleion in Cadiz (Dio Cassio (*Historia Romana* 37.52.2). Also, in Suetonius (*Caesar* 7).

At the end of the column, the papyrus presents a beautiful vision: the description of a very beautiful bird that resembles, according to the papyrus itself, the Phoenix bird. The origin of the mythical phoenix is obscure and explicitly referred to in the text, as it is also present in the novelist Achilles Thacius (3.25.2). My opinion is that the novelist could refer to any of the real migratory birds with which this mythical being has been associated due to its colorful plumage and also to the appendage that grows from its head in some cases.

If so, this is a realistic depiction of a large, stylized and colorful-looking nomadic bird or a flock of them, the ibis, which in Egypt was considered a beneficent being, or the flamingo, which is pink or even deep pink in color. Both are migratory birds: from North Africa and even from the eastern Mediterranean, they arrive on the Iberian Peninsula and disperse to different wetlands.

The pace of the story quickens at this point. It is possible that the last lines of the papyrus comprise a diegesis by way of a summary of the chapter or the novel itself. Unfortunately, at this point the papyrus is interrupted. The journey would therefore reach the Iberian Peninsula, perhaps as far as the area of Cadiz or Huelva, and then move northwards towards Dacia and Germania.

PARHENOPE

We will see that the ideal of "good government" is also welcomed if the protagonist is a woman. We believe it is interesting and even necessary to introduce a gender perspective into the analysis of the data provided by the papyrus fragments of the Greek novel, focusing on the topos of good government. The first question is to assess the extent to which the women who appear in these stories correspond to the parameters of the reality of the time in which they were written. The fragmentary nature of the texts conditions the research, but it also makes the task very attractive. Given the age of the protagonists, an essential figure is that of νύμφη βασιλίς, i.e., the marriageable princess, using the term employed by Euripides to refer to Creusa or Glauce in (*Medea*, 1003). In addition to the daughters of kings, we also include in this group the daughters of aristocrats or local tyrants, etc. The literary archetype of these princesses is, of course, Nausicaa in the Odyssey, but there are also other important references such as Iphigenia in Euripides' *Iphigenia in Aulis*. We are particularly interested in the heiresses to the throne, that is, those young female protagonists with military training and, therefore, the ability to wield weapons and lead armies, such as the Pontic Caligone. Within these stories, there are other examples, such as the indomitable Parthenope, daughter of the tyrant Polycrates. Alongside them, as allies, are the queen mothers and consorts, whose stereotypes could be Hecuba, the Trojan queen in the Iliad, and Arete, the queen of the Phaeacians, in the *Odyssey*.

Shortly after Nino's success, the vicissitudes of the anonymous daughter of the tyrant Polycrates of Samos (6th century BC), as recounted by Herodotus, captured the imagination of a prose writer who, echoing the aesthetic innovations of his time – in particular the ποικιλία of genres – designed a new heroine for an innovative literary genre. An anonymous prose writer of literary culture and skill comparable to that of Nino, at the end of the 1st century BC or the beginning of the 1st century AD, was inspired by Herodotus' words 'she prefers to remain unmarried' (HDT. 3, 124, 2: βούλεσθαι γ ρ παρθενεύεσθαι). He also had in mind the ancient names of the island of Samos, Παρθενία, and its river, the Παρθένιος, which was later called μβρασος. There was also a siren named Partenope, which is why some sources confuse the names and adventures of the tyrant's daughter, the siren, and the city on whose beach the waves left her body, now known as Naples. The monograph by Hägg and Utas (2003) remains fundamental.

With all these elements, she constructed a novel using characters from historical sources, but she does not strictly follow the chronology of historians and mixes some details from the myth. We have three papyri from *Parthenope*, the young woman 'with the maiden's gaze': *P.Berol.* inv. 7927 + 9588 + 21179 (2nd to 3rd centuries AD), *P.Mich.* inv. 3402v (3rd century AD) and *P.Oxy.* III 435 (2nd century AD). The Berlin papyrus consists of three fragments and appears to be a professional work, copied with little care, on the verso and in two sizes of writing, with all kinds of errors, corrections and letters *supra lineam*. On the recto, it contains rental contracts. We also have an *ostracon*, *O.Bodl.* II 2175, from the early 1st century AD, which could contain a fragment of the novel or a text of school origin inspired by its plot, as may have been the case with Nino. The rhetorical level of both novels is exceptionally high (Fernández Garrido, 2022).

The starting point of Partenope is set during the second half of the 6th century BC, in Samos, one of the Eastern Sporades, near the coast of Asia Minor. Its protagonist is the anonymous daughter of the tyrant Polycrates of Samos, patron of philosophers and poets such as Anacreon and Ibycus, who also appear in the novel (Hdt. 2.39.121, 3.39-140 and 6.41). The ancient name of this island is Παρθενία, where the river μβρασος is located, which was also known as Παρθένιος. In Herodotus, the young woman is an anonymous character who expresses her desire to remain unmarried (Hdt. 3, 124, 2). According to the myth, Partenope is also a siren, whose name and story are confused, according to the authors, with that of the fictional heroine and with that of the city, on whose beach the waves abandoned the siren herself. Parthenope is an independent heroine with initiative. Her education included sports, poetry and weaponry, as if she were a boy.

Her partner is Metiochus, a character also mentioned by Herodotus (VI.39-41), who is the son of the historical Miltiades, governor of the Thracian Chersonesus. His father combines two very famous historical Miltiades (Ephorus, IV BC): The first, the Athenian Miltiades the Elder (590-528 BC), ο κιστ and ruler of the Thracian Chersonese, who died without an heir. The second is the victor of Marathon, Miltiades the Younger, a descendant, but not the son, of the former. On an uncertain date (523 BC, according to some authors, and 516 BC, according to others), he assumed the government of the Thracian Chersonese, where he reigned armed with an escort of 500 mercenaries. Miltiades the Younger first married an Athenian woman from the family of Hippias, the mother of Metiochus, and then married the princess Hegesipyle (Ηγησιπύλη), daughter of the Thracian king Oloro. Due to a Scythian attack, he was forced to flee, but he was able to return and regain the throne. He launched a fleet bound for Athens, which was attacked by Phoenician pirates as it was sailing along the coast of Chersonesus. Four ships managed to reach safety, but the fifth, captained by Metiochos, the eldest of his sons, was captured. Upon learning his identity, thinking they could collect a large ransom, the pirates took Metiochos before the Persian king Darius, but the king did not harm him and, moreover, showered him with gifts, gave him a house, property and a Persian wife, with whom Metiochos had children who were considered full-fledged Persians.

Parthenope's father also played an important role in the history of Greece, as we know from Herodotus' account (III, 40-43 and 124). Polycrates, 'very powerful, most powerful', πολύς + κράτος, was rich, powerful and undertook a major public works campaign: an aqueduct, walls and a palace where he received and hosted great artists and intellectuals, such as the poet Ibycus and the philosopher Anaximenes. He also rebuilt a temple dedicated to the goddess Hera. He also established alliances with other peoples, first with Egypt and then with the Persians. When Polycrates was about to embark on a sea voyage to visit the neighbouring satrap Oroetes in Sardis, in Asia Minor, soothsayers, friends and even his own daughter advised him not to do so. When Polycrates was embarking, the maiden (παρθένος, with no other name given) begged him not to go because she had had bad omens in a dream (πρ ς δ κα δούσης τ ς θυγατρ ς ψιν νυπνίου τοιῆνδε). Polycrates was annoyed and threatened her in the following terms: 'If you are wrong and I return safe and sound, you will remain unmarried for a long time.' The threat of remaining unmarried did not matter to the daughter of Samos, who, contrary to expectations, implored the gods that the punishment be fulfilled, for she would rather be single than an orphan: δ ρήσατο πιτελέα τα τα γενέσθαι· βούλεσθαι γ ρ παρθενεύεσθαι πλέω χρόνον το πατρ ς στερ σθαι (Herododotus III.124.2). Polycrates ignored his daughter and ended up being assassinated in Sardis around 522 BC.

The adventures of these historical figures captured the imagination of an anonymous prose writer in the early 1st century AD, who, echoing the aesthetic innovations of his time, coined a model of heroine for an innovative literary genre, the novel, still very much attached to history, intertwined with certain ingredients of myth: a historical novel set during the 6th century BC, at the height of the tyrannies, in Samos, one of the Eastern Sporades, near the coast of Asia Minor (Hdt. 2.39.121, 3.39-140 and 6.41). The anonymous prose writer writes a historical novel, ignoring the chronology of historians, and invents a romance between two young aristocrats who come from similar backgrounds.

The unnamed daughter of Polycrates is now called Parthenope, "she who has the face or gaze of a maiden", because of the way Herodotus refers to her, παρθένος, and because of the ancient name of her island, Παρθενία. *Parthenio*s, 'of the maiden', is also the alternative name of a river in Samos, the Imbraso. It was also called Parthenios, because the γνος is the chaste tree or vitex (Vitex agnus castus). This is the bush with which our protagonist was identified in ancient times was the chaste tree or black cohosh. It grows along rivers, in steep places and gullies and its flower is white or purple. In ancient times, women celebrated a festival called the Thesmophoria and scattered chaste tree branches on their beds.

The name of the plant itself is very eloquent and intertwines myth, history and fiction. It is a shrubby plant that grows along rivers, in steep places and gullies; its flower is either white with a hint of purple or purple. Asio of Samos (6th century BC) says that Ancaeus, lord of the Leleges, was the founding hero of the island. He was the son of Poseidon and Astipalea and accompanied Jason on the ship Argos, distinguishing himself for his skill at the helm. Parthenope is also a siren, whose story is confused, depending on the authors, with the fictional character and with references to Naples, on whose beach the waves abandoned her body.

She will be accompanied by a partner of her own standing, Metíoco, also an aristocrat and son of a tyrant. The Greek novel must have been a resounding success: a different heroine for a new literary genre. Its fame spread to different parts of the empire, from Egypt to Syria, and in various formats. Along with the papyri and the ostracon, we have quotations from other authors and archaeological remains. In addition to the papyri, the other testimonies of the characters in the work are fundamental, mixing facts from the lives and legends of the different Parthenopes known in Antiquity, from the mythical siren to the city in southern Italy, the local goddess, the lover of Metiochus and the heroine of the novel.

As we have explained before, with all these elements, the ancient author constructed a novel, using characters from historiographical sources, but he does not strictly follow the chronology of historians and mixes some details from myth. The result is Parthenope: an independent heroine with initiative. As a princess and heir to the throne, her education was the same as that of a boy: it included sports, poetry and weaponry.

However, one day she falls in love. Her partner is Metiochus, a character also mentioned by Herodotus, who is the son of the historical Miltiades, governor of the Thracian Chersonesus. He arrives at the court of Polycrates in Samos, fleeing the intrigues of his stepmother, who is trying to benefit her sons in the dynastic rights. The tyrant organized a welcome banquet, attended by artists, intellectuals, philosophers and his daughter. The young people fell in love, but they had to part. It was then that Partenope set out alone in search of her beloved across the Mediterranean. On her solo journey, Partenope faces all kinds of dangers and, in particular, unwanted suitors. On the island of Corcyra, she is about to get married but manages to escape and resume her search for her lover. She wanders as far as Persia, where she discovers that Metiochus is perfectly settled, has married a Persian woman with whom he has children and an important estate. Parthenope, broken with grief, symbolically cuts her hair and sets sail for home. Finally, she returns to Samos, where she regains her father's power. The fundamental hypotext is the *Odyssey*, but the Platonic component is also fundamental. The language and style are very cultured.

Parthenope, the novel, is innovative but includes the above elements: the story of her childhood and youth, her formative years, and, although she is a woman, she receives the education befitting someone who is to inherit the throne. We do not know if the novel includes military conflicts, but in any case, the heroine has military training. Of course, we have the fundamental ingredient: symmetrical, requited love. Partenope is a learned young woman, with military training and in love. Perhaps she served as a model for other novels featuring women with great leadership skills, such as Calligone (cf. infra), and perhaps a comic version was also developed.

As in the case of Nino, all this reflects that Partenope was also very successful: there are also references to her by Lucian and mosaics that have appeared in Daphne and Zeugma, which are Syrian cities bathed by important rivers and for which the river and sea elements are fundamental. One of the mosaics decorates a cubicle where the couple Psyche and Eros are also represented.

The novel was so popular that, centuries later, it became a Coptic martyrdom and in the 9th century a Persian poem was written that is a fairly faithful translation of the text and helps us to reconstruct the plot of the novel. The Coptic martyrdom adapts the life of the protagonist to the Christian faith. Parthenope, instead of being a girl from Samos, is a young woman from Constantinople.

In our collection *Cuentos griegos en papiro* (*Greek tales on papyrus*), the story is based on this martyrological account of Saint Parthenope. The protagonist is a powerful and cultured girl, such as the Byzantine empresses Theodora and Irene.

Saint Parthenope never existed. The action takes place in the 4th century. In this story, human love has become divine love. The young woman enters a convent and loses her life in order to remain a virgin, because, as a nun, she has married God.

The Parthenope's suitors are two historical figures. The first is Constantine, the first emperor to support Christianity and founder of the city of Constantinople, and the second is Cosroes, one of the most important Persian monarchs who welcomed the last pagan philosophers from the closed Academy of Athens founded by Plato. he biographies of Constantine and Cosroes, do not coincide in time, but that does not matter to novelists. Despite the insistence of both monarchs, the protagonist prefers to give herself up to martyrdom rather than lose her virginity. In the final scene, Parthenope's body returns to the convent.

CALLIGONE

We now focus on another novel, whose protagonist is a also woman. Her name is Calligone. The characters could be inspired by historical figures such as Hypsicrates, the last wife of Mithridates VI. In Crimea, Armenia and in the Kurgans of Kazakhstan, tombs of women from the 6th to 3rd centuries BC have been found, whose grave goods include arrows, quivers, swords, daggers, objects related to horse training and tusk pendants symbolising courage. One of these female individuals also has an arrowhead stuck in her ribcage, evidence of a violent death in combat.

The original papyri of this work were found in the city of Oxyrhynchus and date from the 2nd and 3rd centuries AD, i.e. they were copied at a time when Egypt was already part of the Roman Empire, so the novel was written before this date (*PSI* 981 and *P.Oxy*. 5355). The protagonist is a princess of a Greek colony on the Black Sea. From the 7th century BC onwards, there is evidence of the existence of Greek colonies on the banks of the Euxine Pontus and, as time went by, cities were founded around its coasts, whose population spoke Greek and were educated in the paradigm of the Greek *paideia*.

Calligone is the daughter of King Eubotheus and grows up in her father's palace in the city of Boristhenes. Her name means 'beautiful by birth' or 'of good family'.

As crown princess, as a child and adolescent, she would receive the same training as if she were a boy: in addition to literary culture, she would have military and equestrian training. Of course, she would also receive paternal advice to learn how to deal with the court intrigues that could take the throne away from her. Faced with a situation complicated by internal insidiousness or by an attack from an external enemy, such as the Scythians, her father Eubiotus decided to put her on a ship to save her life or for Calligone to ask for help from another Greek city on the neighbouring coasts. However, his ship is shipwrecked in the land of the Amazons. The queen's name is Themisto, who receives her and asks her about the intentions of her visit. Calligone wins the confidence of the warriors, whom he helps to organise their army for war against the Scythians.

Calligone is brave on the battlefield, but she is also a woman soldier in love. During the war, at the military camp, Calligone enters her tent, sword in hand, cursing her lover Erasinus and the goddess Artemis.

SEMIRAMIS

It is possible that the Assyrian queen starred in her own novel Semiramis (*P.Oxy.* 5264 and *P.Köln* VI 248). As we know, Semiramis in Greek sources is associated with the historical Sammu-rāmat, who ruled as regent upon the death of her husband Šamšiadad V (824-811 BC), while her son Adad-nirari III was still a minor (811-783 BC). There are cuneiform inscriptions engraved on statues and steles that mention the queen's name alongside those of kings (her husband, her son or her father-in-law). These testimonies are considered evidence of her presence on the battlefield and her direct participation in the war. In the Greek form of the name, Σεμίραμις, the character became an archetype of exotic queens married to kings from distant lands and, from there, was applied to other historical Assyrian queens of great renown, in particular Naqi'a-Zakutu, second wife of Sennacherib, whose name also appears in inscriptions attesting to her active participation in public life.

As for the papyri, *P. Köln* Gr. 6 248 is a very early copy (3rd century BC), whose text describes the amusing reaction of a queen while reading a letter and about to organise her army. The scene has been compared to the moment when Semiramis laughs upon receiving the letter from the Indian king Estabrobates, also in a war context (Diodorus 2.18.2). In the case of *P.Oxy.* 5264 (2nd-3rd centuries AD), she undertakes the construction of pyramids after conquering Egypt.

The aftermath of this story can be found in the *History of Armenia* by Moses of Corene (5th century AD) or in the Persian poem *osrow o Širin* by Ne āmi (12th century AD), as in the case of Parthenope, the one I referred to before and which appears in quotations from the Persian story Dārāb-nāmah and, especially, the epic poem *Vāmiq u dhrā* by 'Un υrī, dated to the 11th century. In Moses of Corene, Shamiran is the widow of King Nino and falls in love with Prince Ara the Beautiful, founder of the Armenian people. When her love is not reciprocated, she invades Armenia with the intention of kidnapping him. Finally, Ara dies on the battlefield and Shamiran transports his body to Lake Van, where she founds a city and builds a palace in which she places his remains. Centuries later, the Persian Ne āmi may also have been inspired by the Assyrian queen to create Širin, the protagonist of his poem.

We could go on analysing the protagonists of the first European historical novels, but we are going to stop at this point to deal with a recent process of metamorphosis, one more, in their long trajectory from Antiquity to the present day, that the protagonists of these lost Greek novels have undergone.

THE PLAY

We have delved into the family nucleus of each protagonist and traced the line of succession marked by the last links: grandparents, parents and children. All of them, with their respective partners, form the following mosaic:

I. Assyrian family: 1.Adadnirari, 2.Yaba, 3.Salmanasar, 4.Thambe, 5.Ninus, 6.Semiramis.
II. Egyptian family: 1.Senusret, 2.Neferet, 3.Amhenemet, 4.Neferitachenen, 5.Sesoncosis, 6.Meameris.
III. Greek family from the Pontus Euxinus in Classic period: 1.Mithridates, 2.Laodice, 3.Eubiotos, 4.Dinamis, 5.Erasinos, 6.Calligone.
IV. Byzantine familiy: 1.Eutropios, 2.Parthenope, 3.Dioclecianus, 4.Helena, 5.Constantinus, 6.Irene.
V. Carthaginian family: 1.Barca, 2.Dido, 3.Amilcar, 4.Sophonisba, 5.Anibal, 6.Himilce.
VI. Familia troyana: 1.Laomedotes, 2.Estrimos, 3.Priamus, 4.Hecuba, 5.Hector, 6.Andromacaa.
VII. Macedonian: 1.Amintas, 2.Euridice, 3.Philippos, 4.Olimpias, 5.Alexander, 6.Barsine.

Each of these characters corresponds to a playing card and all together they form a set of 42 cards, grouped into 7 families. Each family is identified by a different colour and is made up of 6 members. In each family, where the main characters of the old lost novels and tales of our collection are represented.

For the most part, they are real characters and their family relationships are also real, hence the complexity of the onomastics. There are very few cases in which a character has been created out of nothing without the support of a historical, literary or archaeological source to document his or her real existence.

The female links in the family chain have been more difficult to find, as they have often been anonymous and we have no trace of their name or their existence. In such cases, we have researched until we have found the possible historical reference or at least a plausible or coherent hypothesis of such a member of this family. There may be other reasons, but they are the fewest and we do not have space here to explain them.

Very briefly, the context of each of the families that make up the deck would be as follows:

Assyrian Family

Nino is identified with the mythical founder of the city of Nineveh, who probably refers to the historical Assyrian Bronze Age king Tukulti-Ninurta I. His fiancée is Semiramis, the historical Assyrian monarch Sammu-ra Sammu-ra mat of the 9th century BC. His betrothed is Semiramis, historical Assyrian monarch Sammu-rā mat of the 9th century BC. Reference story: Nino, the Adventures of the King of Nineveh.

Figure 1. Illustration by Luis David Gómez Delgado (López & Navarro 2025) [Playing cards]. Venal edition ISBN: 979-13-990309-0-7

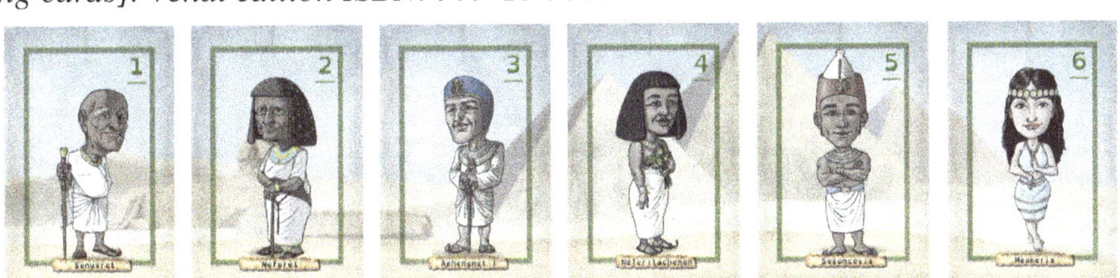

Egyptian Family

Sesoncosis is a literary figure that amalgamates several historical pharaohs of the 12th Dynasty, a period in which important literary texts were composed, such as Sinuhe or the Instructions of Amenemhat. Reference story: The Papyrus of the Seafarer Sinuhe.

Figure 2. Ilustration by Luis David Gómez Delgado (López & Navarro 2025) [Playing cards]. Venal edition ISBN: 979-13-990309-0-7

Classical Greek Family of Pontus

Calligone is a fictional princess who lives in a Greek colony on the shores of the Black Sea, a region located near barbarian territories. The protagonist comes into contact with the Amazons, a mythical tribe of women. Reference story: The Adventures of Calligone and the Amazons.

Figure 3. Ilustration by Luis David Gómez Delgado (López & Navarro 2025) [Playing cards]. Venal edition ISBN: 979-13-990309-0-7

Byzantine Family

The pagan novel has evolved into martyrdom and recalls the story of St. Patricia. Human love has become divine love. The Christian emperor Constantine and the Persian king Cosroes are the suitors but the protagonist has consecrated her life to God. Reference story: The martyrdom of Saint Parthenope.

Figure 4. Ilustration by Luis David Gómez Delgado (López & Navarro 2025) [Playing cards]. Venal edition ISBN: 979-13-990309-0-7

Carthaginian Family

The Phoenicians were great sailors and sowed the Mediterranean with rich colonies. The ports of Tyre or Byblos are frequent settings in Greek novels. We have focused on the legend surrounding the kings of Carthage. Reference story: In preparation.

Figure 5. Ilustration by Luis David Gómez Delgado (López & Navarro 2025) [Playing cards]. Venal edition ISBN: 979-13-990309-0-7

Trojan Family

The characters of the Iliad are well known to us. The Trojan kings are a family of losers, yet Greek literature treats them with admiration. Reference story: In preparation.

Figure 6. Ilustration by Luis David Gómez Delgado (López & Navarro 2025). [Playing cards]. Venal edition ISBN: 979-13-990309-0-7

Macedon

The Story of Alexander is a biographical novel about the son of Philip of Macedon. It has become one of the most influential works of world literature throughout the ages. Reference story: In preparation.

Figure 7. Ilustration by Luis David Gómez Delgado (López & Navarro 2025). [Playing cards]. Venal edition ISBN: 979-13-990309-0-7

Through the images that we include in the cards and in the stories, we show the data and the research behind the reconstructions of the novels that we have just presented. The information on literary, iconographic, historical and cultural aspects of the period in which the novel is set. Almost everything is documented. We have worked closely with the artist Luis David Gómez Delgado, who has great experience in historical illustration and has done a beautiful job, following our guidelines.

The rules of the game are quite well known, at least in Spain. Besides the ludic aspect, these cards are an interesting tool to work on specific aspects of clinical linguistics, as the typography is especially adapted to readers with dyslexia. This game is entertaining, but it can also help us to broaden our knowledge of history and culture and to develop strategy, memory, as well as linguistic skills, etc.

The contents of this collection are aimed at pupils at various stages, primary, secondary and baccalaureate. Ultimately, we like to say that they are accessible to children of all ages. We propose a space for play, in the classroom or at home, to open a parenthesis of shared time between adults and/or children, whatever their age. We open a space to enter a realm of imagination and adventure, but also of exchange of knowledge, reflection, discussion and learning about issues that can have great significance. The whole arsenal that we have inherited from the classical world: the idea of democracy, the exercise of power and its limits, geographical borders, the differences between languages and cultures or the condition of the foreigner, to give just a few examples. In addition, the cards are interesting instruments for working on specific aspects of clinical linguistics, as the typography is especially adapted to readers with dyslexia.

TO CONCLUDE

In conclusion, in the history of Greek literature, reflection on the excesses and limits of power, the relationship of the subject and, later, citizen with the ruler, is one of the main threads of many of its arguments throughout antiquity. In particular, the idea of good government is already present in Homer, in Sophocles, with his Antigone, for example, and in fact it is a concern in authors of all periods and genres.

Those of us responsible for the collection *Cuentos griegos en papiro* (*Greek Tales on Papyrus*) are aware of all this, and we understand the power of the game to transmit all this knowledge today. Stories, like the deck of cards, are entertaining instruments that, in addition to amusing us, can help us to broaden our knowledge of a heritage that has its roots in the East, crosses Europe and reaches America. We would like to think that *Los héroes de Cuentos griegos en papiro juegan en familia* (*The Heroes of Greek Tales on Papyrus Play as a Family*) could become an instrument that, albeit very modestly, contributes to making us all aware of the significance that the fundamental values of Humanism still have today and, in a very special way, those by which geographically and politically distant cultures shared aesthetic codes, religious beliefs, social models and languages at other times in history.

REFERENCES

Bastianini, G., & Casanova, A. (Eds.). (2010). *I papiri del romanzo antico: Atti del convegno internazionale di studi (Firenze, 11–12 giugno 2009)*. Firenze.

Dostálová, R. (1991). *Il romanzo greco e i papiri.*

Fernández Garrido, R. (2022). Ninus and Metiochus in the school of rhetoric: The first Greek novels. *Ancient Narrative, 18*, 58–75. DOI: 10.21827/an.18.37380

Gargiulo, T. (2013). Papiri letterari e nuove cronologie. *Studi Ellenistici, 10*, 99–115.

Hägg, T., & Utas, B. (2003). *The virgin and her lover: Fragments of an ancient Greek novel and a Persian epic poem.* Brill.

Henrichs, A. (2010). Missing pages: Papyrology, genre, and the Greek novel. In Obbink, D., & Rutherford, R. (Eds.), *Culture in pieces: Essays on ancient texts in honour of Peter Parsons* (pp. 302–322). Oxford University Press.

Hoffmann, F., & Schoske, S. (Eds.). (2024). *Sesostris – Scheschonq – Sesonchosis.* Brill. DOI: 10.1163/9789004712393

Konstan, D. (1994). *Sexual symmetry: Love in the ancient novel and related genres.* Princeton University Press.

Kussl, R. (1991). *Papyrusfragmente griechischer Romane: Ausgewählte Untersuchungen.* Gunter Narr Verlag.

López, M. P., & Navarro, O. (2025). *Los héroes de Cuentos griegos en papiro juegan en familia: Una propuesta de gamificación de los saberes clásicos.* Alicante: Ficción en papiro.

López Martínez, M. P. (1998). *Fragmentos papiráceos de novela griega.* Editorial Universidad de Alicante.

Ruiz Montero, C. (2006). *La novela griega.* Akal.

Schmedt, H. (2020). *Antonius Diogenes, Die unglaublichen Dinge jenseits von Thule.* De Gruyter. DOI: 10.1515/9783110600148

Stephens, S. A., & Winkler, J. J. (1995). *Ancient Greek novels: The fragments.* Princeton University Press. DOI: 10.1515/9781400863389

Stramaglia, A. (Ed.). (2000). *ρως. Antiche trame greche d'amore.* Levante.

Tilg, S. (2010). *Chariton of Aphrodisias and the invention of the Greek love novel.* Oxford University Press. DOI: 10.1093/acprof:oso/9780199576944.001.0001

Chapter 17

The Need for Adult Informatics Educators in the Greek and European Public Sector: Through the Lens of Political Theories

Christos Lalos
https://orcid.org/0009-0002-4156-9810
University of Alicante, Spain

ABSTRACT

The need for adult educators in the field of Informatics in the Greek and European public sector is a vital issue, especially within the framework of modern political theories that emphasize the importance of lifelong learning and digital transformation. In an era where technology evolves at an exponential pace, the need to inform and educate adults becomes increasingly urgent, both for individual development and for the prosperity of society as a whole. According to political theories, adult education is not merely a tool for individual growth but also a mechanism for social cohesion and economic development. The theory of human capital argues that investment in education and training leads to increased productivity and economic growth. In this context, adult educators in Informatics play a critical role, as they help workers adapt to the new technological demands of the labor market.

DOI: 10.4018/979-8-3373-2332-9.ch017

INTRODUCTION

In the contemporary European context, the urgency of adult informatics education has become increasingly pronounced, particularly within the evolving framework of the digital transition and the structural modernization of public administration. Greece, like many other EU member states, faces the dual challenge of responding to rapid technological advancements while addressing enduring deficits in digital literacy among adult populations, particularly within the public sector. As the European Commission's Digital Economy and Society Index (DESI) repeatedly demonstrates, a significant proportion of the Greek workforce lacks the necessary digital skills to participate meaningfully in e-governance, data management, and digital service delivery (European Commission, 2023). This digital skills gap is particularly acute among civil servants and public employees, whose roles are now shaped by digital platforms, automated systems, and algorithmically mediated workflows. Consequently, the development of structured, inclusive, and pedagogically sound adult informatics education programs has become not only a technical imperative but also a socio-political necessity.

Adult education, especially in the domain of informatics, cannot be approached merely as a matter of upskilling or technical instruction. Rather, it must be situated within broader political and educational frameworks that shape how knowledge is constructed, distributed, and legitimized. Two dominant theoretical paradigms are especially relevant in this regard: human capital theory and critical pedagogy. Human capital theory, as articulated by Becker (1993), conceptualizes education as an economic investment that enhances individual productivity and contributes to national competitiveness. Within this framework, adult informatics education is seen as a tool to optimize labor market efficiency, institutional performance, and economic growth. While this approach has informed much of the EU's policy discourse—particularly through strategies such as the Lisbon Agenda and the Digital Education Action Plan—it tends to reduce learners to economic units and overlooks the broader emancipatory functions of education.

In contrast, critical pedagogy, rooted in the work of Paulo Freire (2000), foregrounds education as a transformative practice aimed at cultivating critical consciousness and democratic agency. From this perspective, adult informatics education is not merely about technical adaptation, but about empowering citizens to engage with technology reflexively and ethically. It challenges the instrumental logic of digital training by advocating for dialogical learning, social inclusion, and resistance to the commodification of knowledge. As such, critical theory compels us to reimagine the role of the adult informatics educator—not as a transmitter of predefined content, but as a co-constructor of meaningful learning experiences that respond to learners' lived realities.

These theoretical tensions are particularly salient in the Greek context, where economic austerity, administrative centralization, and fragmented policy implementation have constrained the development of comprehensive adult education systems. At the same time, EU policy alignment has created opportunities for reform and innovation, especially in vocational and lifelong learning sectors. Within this evolving landscape, the adult informatics educator emerges as a pivotal figure—at once a facilitator of digital inclusion, an agent of administrative modernization, and a mediator of contested political values. This chapter explores these roles through a multidisciplinary lens, examining how political theory, institutional policy, and pedagogical practice intersect in shaping the future of adult informatics education in the Greek and European public sector.

In light of the growing demand for digitally competent professionals within the public sector and the broader imperative of fostering democratic and inclusive digital societies, this chapter aims to critically examine the multifaceted role of adult informatics educators in Greece and the European Union. It explores how digital education intersects with political theory, public administration, and lifelong learning policy, highlighting both the strategic significance and the normative implications of adult informatics training in a rapidly digitizing world. By situating this analysis within the broader frameworks of human capital theory and critical pedagogy, the chapter offers a theoretically grounded and policy-relevant perspective on the design, implementation, and governance of informatics education for adults.

The chapter pursues three primary objectives. First, it seeks to map the institutional and political terrain in which adult informatics education is embedded, with particular emphasis on EU policy frameworks, national strategies, and digital transformation agendas. Second, it investigates the pedagogical identity and professional requirements of the adult informatics educator, examining the competencies, values, and challenges associated with this emerging role. Third, it identifies systemic obstacles—such as funding limitations, institutional fragmentation, and sociocultural resistance—that hinder the effective integration of digital literacy into public administration training programs. Throughout, the chapter foregrounds the ethical and democratic dimensions of adult education, emphasizing the need for inclusive, critical, and context-sensitive approaches.

Methodologically, the chapter adopts an interdisciplinary perspective that combines political theory, policy analysis, and educational thought. While primarily conceptual, it draws on selected empirical reports and case-based examples from the Greek and broader European context to illustrate the application of theory to practice. The scope includes formal and non-formal education settings, with a focus on public sector training but with implications for wider adult learning ecosystems. By bridging theory and policy, this chapter aims to inform scholars, educators, and policymakers about the strategic and normative stakes involved in cultivating a digitally competent and civically empowered adult population in Europe.

THEORETICAL AND POLICY FOUNDATIONS

The design and implementation of adult informatics education in the public sector cannot be dissociated from the political and ideological frameworks that shape educational priorities, governance mechanisms, and normative expectations. Political theory provides the conceptual architecture through which the aims and effects of education can be interpreted—not merely as technocratic interventions, but as politically charged practices embedded within broader socioeconomic systems. In the context of adult informatics education, three major theoretical paradigms are particularly salient: Human Capital Theory, Critical Pedagogy, and contemporary theories of digital and democratic education. Each offers distinct insights into the rationale, structure, and implications of educating adults in the digital age.

Human Capital Theory, primarily associated with the work of Gary Becker (1993), conceptualizes education as an investment in individuals' productive capacities. Within this framework, skills acquisition is viewed as a means to enhance economic efficiency, improve labor market outcomes, and stimulate national economic growth. Education is reduced to a functional input within the broader machinery of economic development. From this perspective, adult informatics education is justified insofar as it yields measurable returns in terms of increased workplace productivity, better service delivery in public institutions, and greater adaptability to technological change. Human capital theory has profoundly influenced EU policy discourse, as evidenced in strategies such as the Lisbon Agenda, the European Skills Agenda, and the Digital Education Action Plan. These policy instruments prioritize employability, competitiveness, and innovation as central objectives of adult learning systems. While human capital logic has facilitated the integration of digital competencies into mainstream educational policy, it also risks narrowing the purpose of education to utilitarian and market-driven outcomes.

In contrast, Critical Pedagogy, most famously articulated by Paulo Freire (2000), challenges the reductionist logic of education-as-instrumentality and foregrounds the emancipatory potential of learning. Freirean theory views education as a dialogical, transformative process through which learners become conscious of their socio-political realities and are empowered to act upon them. In the context of adult informatics education, critical pedagogy shifts the focus from mere technical proficiency to critical digital literacy: the ability not only to use digital tools but to question their design, governance, and social consequences. Rather than treating adult learners as passive recipients of knowledge or mere economic actors, Freirean-informed pedagogies position them as subjects capable of reflective thinking and collective agency. This perspective is especially relevant in a public sector increasingly shaped by algorithmic decision-making, datafication, and platformization—processes that demand not only technical understanding but also critical insight into the values, exclusions, and power asymmetries embedded in digital systems.

Complementing these paradigms are contemporary theories of digital and democratic education, which build on and extend earlier traditions to address the complex realities of the networked society. Scholars such as Castells (2010) and Selwyn (2019) have examined how digital technologies reconfigure the social functions of education, alter institutional hierarchies, and transform the nature of public knowledge. Castells's notion of the "network society" emphasizes the structural centrality of information and communication technologies (ICTs) in shaping all aspects of economic, political, and cultural life. In this view, digital literacy becomes a prerequisite for meaningful social participation, democratic engagement, and personal autonomy. Selwyn (2019), meanwhile, interrogates the political economy of digital education, highlighting issues of data surveillance, educational inequality, and the commodification of learning. His work urges educators to adopt a critical stance toward the often-celebrated "digital transformation," emphasizing the need for ethically grounded, socially responsive pedagogies.

Together, these theoretical perspectives offer a multidimensional understanding of adult informatics education: human capital theory emphasizes economic functionality; critical pedagogy centers on emancipation and civic agency; and digital-democratic theories contextualize digital skills within broader socio-technical systems. A robust educational policy must draw from all three, balancing the demands of economic development with the imperatives of equity, critical consciousness, and democratic sustainability. In the European and Greek policy landscape, these tensions are often visible in competing goals: the push for upskilling and standardization coexists with rhetorical commitments to inclusion and lifelong learning. Understanding and negotiating these theoretical foundations is essential for designing adult informatics education that is not only effective but also just, inclusive, and future-oriented.

The theoretical paradigms discussed above acquire concrete policy relevance when situated within the broader strategic shift toward lifelong learning and digital transformation at both national and supranational levels. Lifelong learning, once understood primarily in terms of adult literacy or vocational retraining, has evolved into a comprehensive framework that encompasses formal, non-formal, and informal modes of learning across the entire life course. In the context of the digital transition, lifelong learning has acquired renewed urgency, as individuals must continuously update their digital competencies to adapt to evolving technologies, labor market shifts, and changing institutional demands. Adult informatics education thus represents a critical pillar of the digital inclusion agenda, particularly for public sector employees who are expected to interface with e-governance systems, manage digital records, and deliver services through online platforms.

This vision is formalized at the European level through initiatives such as the Digital Decade 2030 strategy, which sets ambitious targets for digital skills, digital infrastructure, and public sector digitalization. Among its four cardinal objectives, the strategy includes the commitment that by 2030, at least 80% of the EU population should have basic digital skills, and that all key public services be accessible online (European Commission, 2021). These targets underscore the inseparability of digital transformation and inclusive lifelong learning systems, emphasizing the need to equip not only youth but also mid-career and older adults with the necessary capabilities to thrive in an increasingly digitalized society. Within this policy context, adult informatics educators are positioned as essential actors in operationalizing the digital rights and capacities enshrined in the EU's vision of digital citizenship.

Parallel frameworks by the OECD and UNESCO reinforce this orientation. The OECD's Skills Outlook series (2019, 2021) highlights the role of adult education in closing digital divides, promoting economic resilience, and enabling agile labor force adaptation. The OECD emphasizes "skills ecosystems" that combine individual learning opportunities with systemic support structures—an approach that demands not only targeted training programs but also institutional coordination, inclusive pedagogy, and responsive governance. Similarly, UNESCO frames digital literacy as a core component of the human right to education, advocating for equitable access to digital learning tools, especially for vulnerable and marginalized populations. UNESCO's Futures of Education report (2021) calls for a renewed social contract in which technology is leveraged not merely for economic competitiveness but for social justice, ecological sustainability, and democratic vitality.

These policy frameworks, though distinct in emphasis, converge in recognizing adult digital education as a foundational requirement for 21st-century citizenship and institutional efficacy. They also share an implicit recognition of the complex political and pedagogical tasks involved in building digitally literate societies. Moving beyond a purely instrumental view of informatics, they call for systemic approaches that integrate human-centered pedagogy, inclusive access, and ethical governance. In this respect, the adult informatics educator becomes more than a technical trainer: they are an intermediary between global policy ambitions and local realities, responsible for cultivating not only skills, but also digital confidence, critical awareness, and civic participation.

THE DIGITAL TRANSFORMATION OF THE PUBLIC SECTOR

The digital transformation of the public sector represents a profound restructuring of administrative, operational, and service delivery systems across Europe. In the past decade, European governments have increasingly adopted digital technologies not merely to improve internal efficiency, but to redefine the relationship between state institutions and citizens. The shift towards e-governance, open data, cloud infrastructure, and interoperable information systems signals a move from hierarchical, paper-based administration to agile, data-driven governance. Within this context, the public sector is no longer a passive adopter of technology but an active domain of innovation, standard-setting, and ethical contestation. The transformation is guided by European strategies such as the Digital Europe Programme, the eGovernment Action Plan, and the EU Interoperability Framework, which aim to foster "digital-ready" administrations capable of providing user-centric, secure, and inclusive services (European Commission, 2022).

Greece, historically characterized by administrative centralization and technological lag, has made notable strides in recent years under the dual pressure of EU directives and domestic modernization imperatives. The Greek government's Digital Transformation Bible 2020–2025 lays out a comprehensive plan for automating bureaucratic processes, integrating digital identification systems, expanding online public services, and improving interoperability among state entities. Flagship initiatives such as the gov.gr portal, digital prescriptions, and online tax services have significantly altered citizen-state interactions. However, the digitalization of the Greek public sector remains uneven, with disparities across regions, agencies, and professional cohorts. Crucially, the success of these reforms hinges not only on technological infrastructure but on the digital competence of the human capital managing and delivering these services—highlighting the central role of adult informatics education.

As public administration increasingly relies on complex digital systems, new skill demands are emerging that extend well beyond basic ICT literacy. One such demand is artificial intelligence (AI) literacy, particularly in the context of algorithmic decision-making tools used for fraud detection, public health monitoring, or predictive analytics in welfare systems. While AI adoption in Greece is still nascent, the EU's coordinated plan on AI and its AI Act will gradually mandate the integration of algorithmic systems into administrative domains—raising questions about transparency, accountability, and digital ethics. Public employees will need the capacity to both understand and critically engage with AI-driven workflows, including the ethical implications of automated decision-making.

Another pressing domain is cybersecurity. With the expansion of digital services comes heightened vulnerability to cyber threats, data breaches, and identity theft.

Public institutions, particularly those handling sensitive health, taxation, or social security data, are increasingly targeted by malicious actors. As a result, cybersecurity awareness and risk management are no longer the exclusive domain of IT professionals; they must become integral components of public sector training curricula at all levels. The EU Cybersecurity Act and the NIS2 Directive (Directive on Security of Network and Information Systems) underscore the legal and institutional obligations of states to build cybersecurity capacity among public employees. In the Greek case, coordination between the Ministry of Digital Governance, national cybersecurity centers, and education providers is still in early stages, pointing to the need for structured educator-led interventions in this field.

Closely linked to these developments is the imperative of data literacy. Public administrators are now expected to interpret, manage, and ethically use large volumes of data generated through digital platforms, citizen interactions, and interagency systems. Data-driven decision-making is presented as a means to enhance efficiency, transparency, and policy responsiveness. However, without adequate training in data analysis, visualization, and critical interpretation, the benefits of digital governance risk being undermined by misuse or misapprehension of data. This challenge is particularly pronounced in smaller municipalities or understaffed agencies, where digital upskilling has not yet reached operational depth.

Taken together, these emerging demands suggest that digital transformation in the public sector is not a purely technical process but a deeply pedagogical one. The shift from analog to digital governance requires new forms of adult learning—targeted, flexible, and reflective—capable of equipping civil servants with not only procedural knowledge, but also ethical judgment, critical awareness, and technological adaptability. The adult informatics educator, therefore, is no longer a peripheral figure, but a central actor in shaping the digital public sector of the future.

The digital transformation of the public sector has fundamentally altered the nature of administrative labor, redefining the roles, expectations, and professional identities of public employees. As digital technologies become embedded in day-to-day operations, the public servant is increasingly expected to function as a technologically fluent, data-literate, and client-responsive actor. This shift entails not only the adoption of new digital tools but also profound changes in workflow organization, communication patterns, and accountability structures. Processes that were once linear, paper-based, and manually executed are now automated, decentralized, and mediated through digital platforms. From online citizen portals and digital signatures to real-time document tracking and virtual inter-agency communication, the pace and complexity of administrative work have increased substantially (OECD, 2020).

For many public employees, especially those who entered the workforce before the digital turn, these changes have been both disorienting and demanding. Job roles that previously relied on tacit knowledge, institutional memory, or procedural repetition are now subject to continual retraining and technological updating. Employees are expected to adapt rapidly to new systems, comply with cybersecurity protocols, and manage digital interactions with citizens—all while maintaining the procedural integrity and legal responsibilities of their positions. In this environment, digital competence becomes not merely an asset, but a prerequisite for employability, task execution, and professional development within the public sector. Yet, the transition has not been uniformly supported by institutional mechanisms for digital training and reskilling.

The result is a pervasive skills gap—both in terms of basic digital literacy and more advanced data and systems competencies. Studies by the European Commission and the Hellenic Ministry of Administrative Reconstruction indicate that a substantial proportion of civil servants in Greece lack the digital skills necessary to navigate new administrative tools with confidence and competence (European Commission, 2023; National Centre for Public Administration and Local Government, 2022). These gaps are most acute in local government, small municipalities, and among older employees, many of whom did not receive formal ICT training during their education or early professional development. The absence of coherent and inclusive training frameworks exacerbates this divide, creating disparities in administrative performance and deepening digital inequalities within the public workforce.

Beyond individual skill shortages, the lack of a digital culture within institutions further complicates transformation efforts. Resistance to change, fear of technological obsolescence, and hierarchical inertia often impede the effective integration of digital tools into organizational routines. In some cases, digital systems are formally adopted but poorly used, either due to inadequate training or lack of contextual alignment with existing workflows. Moreover, professional development opportunities—where they exist—are often short-term, fragmented, and generic, failing to address the specific challenges faced by diverse categories of public employees. These deficits suggest the need for sustained, context-sensitive, and pedagogically grounded adult learning strategies that move beyond one-size-fits-all approaches.

In this regard, the role of the adult informatics educator becomes indispensable. These professionals are not only responsible for transmitting technical knowledge, but also for facilitating organizational learning, mediating resistance, and promoting digital confidence among learners. Their pedagogical strategies must account for the anxieties, expectations, and prior experiences of adult learners, many of whom approach digital tools with skepticism or apprehension. Effective adult digital education in the public sector thus demands more than instructional expertise; it requires emotional intelligence, critical engagement with institutional cultures, and an understanding of how power and hierarchy operate within bureaucratic systems. Addressing digital skill gaps and workflow challenges is not merely a technical endeavor—it is a deeply human and political process that hinges on the quality, relevance, and inclusiveness of adult education practices.

THE ROLE AND PROFILE OF ADULT INFORMATICS EDUCATORS

The evolving digital landscape of public administration has redefined not only the technical requirements of civil service work, but also the pedagogical and professional profiles of those tasked with equipping adults to meet these demands. In this context, the adult informatics educator has emerged as a critical actor in mediating the transition from traditional bureaucratic routines to data-driven, platform-based governance. However, the educator's role is far more complex than that of a conventional ICT trainer. They must possess a unique blend of technological expertise, pedagogical acumen, and social-emotional competence, allowing them to respond to the diverse needs, prior experiences, and institutional contexts of adult learners.

To fulfill this role effectively, adult informatics educators must meet a range of formal and informal qualifications. At a minimum, they are expected to have a solid academic background in informatics, computer science, or educational technology, often complemented by postgraduate training in adult education, instructional design, or digital learning methodologies (Zawacki-Richter et al., 2019). In the European context, alignment with the European Qualifications Framework (EQF) and national professional standards ensures a baseline of technical proficiency. However, formal credentials alone are insufficient. Given the heterogeneity of adult learners—ranging from digitally illiterate public employees to those requiring advanced data management training—educators must also develop situational flexibility and adaptive teaching strategies to address diverse cognitive, emotional, and institutional variables.

Equally important are pedagogical skills rooted in the principles of andragogy, or adult learning theory. According to Knowles (1980), adult learners bring with them a wealth of lived experiences, established identities, and internal motivations, which must be acknowledged and integrated into the learning process. Effective adult informatics educators design learning environments that are collaborative, problem-centered, and relevant to learners' immediate professional contexts. They foster a climate of respect, build on learners' prior knowledge, and encourage reflective engagement with both the content and the medium through which it is delivered. These pedagogical approaches contrast sharply with didactic or standardized training models, which often fail to resonate with adult learners and may reinforce resistance to digital change (Brookfield, 2013).

Moreover, the profile of the adult informatics educator must include a robust portfolio of digital competencies, in line with frameworks such as the DigCompEdu model developed by the European Commission. These competencies encompass more than basic ICT skills. They include the ability to use digital tools for instructional design, assess learning outcomes through technology, engage in collaborative knowledge construction, and critically evaluate the ethical dimensions of digital pedagogy. For example, an educator must be able to design a blended learning module using a learning management system (LMS), embed data privacy considerations into instructional content, and support learners in developing both functional and critical digital literacies. In environments characterized by rapid technological change, educators are also expected to continuously upskill themselves through communities of practice, professional networks, and ongoing professional development initiatives (UNESCO, 2020).

Beyond their technical and instructional functions, adult informatics educators are increasingly called upon to act as facilitators of organizational change. They occupy a liminal space between top-down digital reform agendas and the lived realities of public employees, many of whom are skeptical of or alienated by these transformations. In this facilitative role, educators not only transmit knowledge, but also interpret policy, negotiate expectations, and mediate between institutional constraints and individual aspirations. They must be able to recognize the sources of resistance—be they technological, generational, or cultural—and develop pedagogical strategies that transform resistance into engagement. This entails cultivating trust, fostering dialogue, and creating learning spaces that are psychologically safe and socially responsive. In short, the adult informatics educator is as much a cultural broker and emancipatory guide as a transmitter of digital competencies.

An effective approach to adult informatics education must be firmly grounded in the principles of adult learning, which differ significantly from traditional pedagogical models aimed at children or adolescents. These principles, as developed by Knowles (1980) and further refined by adult education theorists, emphasize the learner's autonomy, accumulated life experience, goal orientation, and practical problem-solving focus. Interactivity is foundational to this process; adult learners benefit most from dialogical engagement and collaborative problem-solving, rather than passive content reception. Informatics education, in this context, should emphasize experiential learning—through simulations, case studies, and peer exchange—rather than abstract instruction or rote memorization.

Equally vital is the practical relevance of content. Adult learners, especially those in professional or institutional settings, are acutely attuned to whether what they are learning has immediate applicability to their daily tasks and responsibilities. Informatics educators must therefore tailor their content to specific professional environments—be it data handling in social services, digital documentation in municipal governance, or cybersecurity protocols in health systems. This alignment between instructional material and occupational relevance is essential not only for retention and motivation but also for institutional buy-in and long-term cultural change. Moreover, educational interventions must remain adaptable, responding flexibly to learners' pace, prior exposure to digital tools, and shifting technological demands. This is particularly important in the public sector, where learners may range from highly skilled IT staff to frontline clerical workers with minimal digital experience.

However, the responsibilities of adult informatics educators do not end at the successful transmission of functional skills. In today's complex digital societies, educators are also entrusted with a broader ethical and democratic mission: to cultivate critically aware, socially responsible digital citizens. As Selwyn (2019) has argued, digital education must equip learners not only with the ability to operate systems, but also with the reflexivity to question their design, implications, and governance. This entails fostering awareness of data privacy, algorithmic bias, surveillance risks, and the socio-political consequences of digital technologies in public life. For instance, public servants who manage citizen data must not only know how to use software correctly but also understand the ethical frameworks surrounding data protection and equity in algorithmic decision-making.

Moreover, the educator's task includes promoting democratic values within digital learning environments. This involves not only respecting the voices and experiences of adult learners, but also modeling inclusive, participatory, and non-hierarchical forms of instruction. In doing so, the educator contributes to building a digitally literate public workforce capable of upholding the principles of transparency, accountability, and service equity in a digital governance ecosystem. Given the increasing role of ICT in democratic participation—from e-voting to digital petitions and online public consultations—informatic competence must be framed as a condition for full democratic engagement, not just administrative efficiency.

Thus, the adult informatics educator emerges not merely as a transmitter of competencies, but as a facilitator of transformation: helping institutions modernize, supporting individuals in adapting to change, and embedding technology within an ethically and democratically grounded educational framework. Their role is both pedagogical and political, requiring technical mastery, emotional intelligence, and normative vision. In designing training programs and public policies, these multidimensional responsibilities must be recognized and supported—through ongoing professional development, institutional autonomy, and meaningful collaboration across sectors.

BARRIERS AND CHALLENGES

Despite the strategic importance of adult informatics education for the digital transformation of the public sector, its implementation is often constrained by a range of structural and cultural barriers that undermine both its effectiveness and sustainability. These challenges are particularly evident in Greece but resonate across multiple European contexts where adult education remains under-resourced, undervalued, and insufficiently integrated into broader administrative reform agendas. Understanding these impediments is essential for developing viable solutions and realistic expectations regarding the role of educators and institutions in building digital capacity.

One of the most persistent structural barriers is the chronic underfunding of adult education, especially in the domain of digital training for public sector employees. While significant resources have been allocated to digital infrastructure—such as the creation of e-government portals or the deployment of administrative software—corresponding investments in human capital development have lagged behind. Training programs are often project-based, short-term, and externally funded, relying on European Structural and Investment Funds (ESIF) or ad hoc national initiatives. This funding model creates cycles of discontinuity, in which innovative efforts lack the long-term financial support required for institutional embedding and impact (OECD, 2020).

Furthermore, the organizational architecture of public administration frequently lacks the institutional coherence necessary for effective adult learning strategies. Responsibilities for training are dispersed across ministries, local authorities, and semi-autonomous institutions such as Greece's National Centre for Public Administration and Local Government (EKDDA), often without clear coordination mechanisms. This fragmentation results in overlapping mandates, inconsistent standards, and inefficient use of resources. Moreover, strategic alignment between digital transformation plans and adult training initiatives is often superficial, with training treated as a secondary or reactive component rather than a core pillar of reform. In many cases, educational needs assessments are either absent or conducted without stakeholder consultation, leading to curricula that are misaligned with workplace realities and learner needs (UNESCO, 2020).

Equally significant are the cultural barriers that limit engagement with adult informatics education. Many public employees, particularly those from older age cohorts or lower educational backgrounds, display resistance to digital training, perceiving it as irrelevant, burdensome, or threatening to their professional identity. This resistance is often rooted in experiences of prior exclusion, a lack of confidence in using technology, or skepticism about the purpose and outcomes of training initiatives. For some, participation in digital training programs is seen less as an opportunity for empowerment and more as an imposed obligation that exacerbates existing anxieties about job security and organizational change.

The intergenerational divide further complicates these dynamics. While younger employees may adapt more quickly to digital environments due to prior exposure and formal education, older workers may struggle to keep pace, particularly when training is delivered in a standardized or fast-paced manner. Without differentiated instruction and contextual sensitivity, these generational gaps can foster resentment and deepen inequalities within the workplace. In extreme cases, they may even lead to informal divisions between "digital insiders" and "analog holdouts," fragmenting institutional cultures and reducing the efficacy of teamwork.

Adding to these difficulties is the prevalence of technophobia—not merely as a psychological condition, but as a culturally reinforced pattern of avoidance and disengagement from digital tools. Technophobia can be fueled by poor instructional design, inaccessible interfaces, or prior experiences of failure, and it is often exacerbated when public discourse frames digital transformation as an inevitable, dehumanizing, or punitive process. If digital training is perceived as a top-down imposition with little regard for learners' autonomy or dignity, resistance will likely persist, regardless of the technical quality of the instruction.

To address these structural and cultural challenges, adult informatics education must be supported by comprehensive policy reforms, adequate and stable funding, and pedagogically informed approaches that center the learner's needs, context, and aspirations. Without such interventions, even the most technologically advanced systems will fall short of their potential, undermined by institutional inertia and human disengagement.

In addition to structural and cultural obstacles, policy-level gaps continue to hinder the institutionalization and efficacy of adult informatics education within the public sector. Despite high-level policy commitments—such as Greece's Digital Transformation Bible 2020–2025 or the European Commission's Digital Education Action Plan—the translation of strategy into coherent and sustained implementation remains inconsistent. While national digital strategies articulate ambitious targets for upskilling the workforce and promoting lifelong learning, these visions are rarely matched by detailed operational roadmaps, sufficient funding allocations, or monitoring mechanisms. In many cases, initiatives remain at the declarative level, resulting in fragmented interventions, overlapping mandates, and variable implementation across regions and agencies (European Commission, 2023).

One of the key weaknesses in current policy design is the absence of mechanisms for stakeholder engagement, particularly at the local or institutional level. Public servants, educators, and learners are often not meaningfully involved in shaping curricula, identifying needs, or evaluating outcomes. As a result, training programs tend to reflect centralized assumptions rather than on-the-ground realities. This top-down orientation reinforces a compliance-based culture, where training is seen as an external requirement rather than an internally driven process of professional development and organizational learning. The disconnection between policy rhetoric and practical implementation not only reduces effectiveness but also undermines trust in public education systems and reform agendas (OECD, 2020).

Closely related are issues of access and equity, which remain under-addressed in many adult education strategies. Although digital transformation is frequently promoted as a democratizing force, it often reinforces existing inequalities unless specific measures are taken to reach and support marginalized populations. In the public sector, this includes not only employees in remote or rural areas, but also women returning to work, older adults, persons with disabilities, and staff from lower socio-economic or educational backgrounds. These groups face multiple barriers to participation, ranging from lack of access to high-speed internet and devices, to limited prior exposure to digital tools, to structural discrimination within their workplaces.

Furthermore, training programs rarely account for the intersectional nature of disadvantage. For instance, a woman over 55 working in a small municipal office may face compounded challenges—limited institutional support, gendered assumptions about technological competence, and physical barriers to participation in training. Addressing such inequalities requires not only targeted outreach and inclusive instructional design but also policy frameworks that incorporate equity as a core principle, rather than a secondary concern. Initiatives such as flexible learning schedules, modular content, hybrid learning models, and context-sensitive assessments can help reduce these access barriers—but they require deliberate planning, adequate resourcing, and institutional commitment.

In sum, the success of adult informatics education hinges not only on technical or pedagogical quality, but on the alignment of strategic intent with inclusive, participatory, and well-resourced implementation mechanisms. Without attention to policy coherence and social justice, digital training initiatives risk reproducing the very exclusions they are meant to overcome. To realize the transformative potential of digital governance, adult education must be embedded in a broader vision of democratic institutional change—one that recognizes learners not as passive recipients of skill acquisition, but as active agents of civic and organizational renewal.

CASE STUDIES OR GOOD PRACTICES

The implementation of adult informatics education within the public sector has been bolstered by various national and European initiatives aimed at enhancing digital competencies among civil servants. These programs not only address the technical aspects of digital literacy but also emphasize pedagogical innovation and institutional collaboration, thereby serving as models for effective practice.

National and EU-Funded Training Programs

In Greece, the National Centre for Public Administration and Local Government (EKDDA) plays a pivotal role in the continuous professional development of public sector employees. EKDDA offers a range of training programs, including modules on digital governance, information systems, and e-government services. These programs are designed to align with national digital transformation strategies and are often supported by EU funding mechanisms, ensuring both relevance and sustainability.

At the European level, the Digital Skills and Jobs Coalition, an initiative by the European Commission, brings together Member States, companies, social partners, non-profit organizations, and education providers to tackle the digital skills gap. Through this coalition, numerous projects have been launched to upskill public sector workers, such as the development of Massive Open Online Courses (MOOCs) tailored to public administration needs and the establishment of digital competence centers across various regions.

Effective Educator-Led Interventions in Public Administration

Educators have been instrumental in designing and delivering training that transcends traditional instruction methods. For instance, in several municipalities, trainers have adopted blended learning approaches, combining face-to-face sessions with online modules to accommodate diverse learning preferences and schedules. These interventions often incorporate real-life scenarios and problem-solving exercises, enabling learners to apply digital tools directly to their work contexts.

Moreover, some programs have emphasized peer-to-peer learning, where participants share experiences and solutions, fostering a collaborative learning environment. This approach not only enhances engagement but also builds a community of practice that supports ongoing digital competence development.

Profiles of Institutions or Municipal Initiatives Demonstrating Impact

Municipalities have also taken proactive steps to enhance digital literacy among their staff. For example, the city of Aarau in Switzerland implemented a data-driven approach to participatory policymaking, which required training public employees in data analysis and digital engagement tools. This initiative led to more informed decision-making processes and increased citizen participation.

Similarly, in Poland, the LivingLab PJAIT project focused on empowering seniors through ICT education. By involving older adults in the development and testing of digital solutions, the project not only improved their digital skills but also ensured that public services were more accessible and user-friendly for this demographic.

These case studies underscore the importance of context-specific, educator-led initiatives in advancing digital competencies within the public sector. They highlight how targeted training programs, supported by institutional commitment and innovative pedagogical approaches, can effectively address the challenges of digital transformation.

CONCLUSIONS AND RECOMMENDATIONS

This chapter has critically examined the role of adult informatics education in the digital transformation of the public sector, with particular emphasis on Greece and the broader European context. Through a multidisciplinary and policy-oriented approach, it has argued that equipping public sector employees with digital skills is not a merely technical task, but a pedagogical, ethical, and political imperative. Digital literacy—understood as both competence and consciousness—is foundational to the functioning of modern public institutions and to the democratic participation of citizens in a digitized society. In this regard, the adult informatics educator emerges as a central figure, not only in transmitting skills but also in shaping the values, attitudes, and critical perspectives of learners within the state apparatus.

Drawing on a range of theoretical frameworks—including Human Capital Theory, Critical Pedagogy, and contemporary notions of digital citizenship—the chapter has shown that adult informatics education must navigate competing logics: efficiency and inclusion, innovation and equity, standardization and contextual responsiveness. Educators must operate at this intersection, translating policy aspirations into meaningful learning experiences that reflect the lived realities of adult learners. This requires high levels of technical fluency, instructional adaptability, and socio-political awareness. Without this complex professional identity, digital training risks becoming procedural, superficial, or even alienating for the very populations it seeks to empower.

At the same time, the chapter has identified significant barriers to effective implementation. These include fragmented institutional structures, underinvestment in training infrastructures, lack of strategic policy integration, and persistent cultural resistance. Digital transformation, while often celebrated rhetorically, is unevenly experienced and inequitably distributed. Vulnerable groups—such as older employees, those in remote areas, or persons with limited educational attainment—remain at risk of digital exclusion unless proactive, equity-oriented measures are taken. Furthermore, policy documents often remain aspirational, failing to deliver coherent, inclusive, and long-term strategies that prioritize human development alongside technological innovation.

To address these challenges and actualize the potential of adult informatics education, several key policy recommendations are offered:

1. **Invest in sustained, pedagogically rich educator training**: Educators should be equipped with interdisciplinary skill sets that include digital tools, adult learning theory, inclusive pedagogy, and ethical awareness. This investment should not be limited to one-time seminars, but embedded within national qualification frameworks, professional development systems, and communities of practice.
2. **Integrate informatics education into comprehensive adult learning ecosystems**: Digital competence must be recognized as a lifelong requirement and embedded across public administration curricula, from basic onboarding to executive leadership training. Modular, stackable learning formats and blended delivery models can help reach diverse learner profiles.
3. **Advance inclusive policy frameworks**: Equity should be central to digital education policy. This includes developing outreach strategies to marginalized workers, providing accessible learning environments, supporting multilingual instruction where needed, and ensuring that training content is culturally and socially responsive.
4. **Foster inter-institutional coordination and participatory governance**: Cross-sector collaboration between ministries, municipalities, training providers, unions, and civil society organizations is essential for scaling good practices and ensuring relevance. Participatory planning mechanisms should empower educators and learners to co-shape digital training agendas.
5. **Promote critical digital literacy as a democratic goal**: Beyond functionality, adult informatics education should enable learners to interrogate the technologies they use—understanding the risks of algorithmic bias, surveillance, and data misuse, while cultivating ethical practices and civic responsibility.

In conclusion, digital transformation must not be seen as a purely managerial undertaking, nor should it reinforce existing hierarchies or exclusions. Instead, it offers a unique opportunity to reimagine public administration as a site of innovation, inclusion, and democratic renewal. Adult education—when delivered critically, inclusively, and competently—can help realize this vision. By foregrounding the role of educators as agents of both skill development and civic empowerment, this chapter calls for a revaluation of adult informatics education not merely as a policy instrument, but as a cornerstone of just and forward-looking governance.

REFERENCES

Becker, G. S. (1993). *Human capital: A theoretical and empirical analysis, with special reference to education* (3rd ed.). University of Chicago Press. DOI: 10.7208/chicago/9780226041223.001.0001

Brookfield, S. D. (2013). *The Skillful Teacher: On Technique, Trust, and Responsiveness in the Classroom* (3rd ed.). Jossey-Bass.

Castells, M. (2010). *The rise of the network society* (2nd ed.). Wiley-Blackwell.

European Commission. (2021). *2030 Digital Compass: The European way for the Digital Decade*. Publications Office of the European Union., DOI: 10.2759/011713

European Commission. (2022). *Digital Europe Programme* and *eGovernment Action Plan 2016–2020*. Brussels.

European Commission. (2023). *Digital Economy and Society Index (DESI) – Greece Country Report*. Brussels.

Freire, P. (2000). *Pedagogy of the oppressed* (30th anniversary ed.). Continuum.

Knowles, M. (1980). *The Modern Practice of Adult Education: From Pedagogy to Andragogy*. Cambridge Books.

Ministry of Digital Governance (Greece). (2020). *Digital Transformation Bible 2020–2025*. Athens.

National Centre for Public Administration and Local Government (EKDDA). (2022). Retrieved from https://www.ekdd.gr/en/

OECD. (2019). *Getting skills right: Future-ready adult learning systems*. OECD Publishing., DOI: 10.1787/9789264311756-

OECD. (2020). *The Digital Transformation of the Public Sector: Helping Governments Respond to the Crisis*. OECD.

Selwyn, N. (2019). *Should robots replace teachers? AI and the future of education*. Polity Press.

UNESCO. (2020). *Education in a post-COVID world: Nine ideas for public action*. United Nations Educational, Scientific and Cultural Organization.

UNESCO. (2020). *Digital Competency Framework for Educators*. UNESCO Institute for Information Technologies in Education.

Wellings, T., Majumdar, S., Fricker, R. H., & Pournaras, E. (2023). Improving City Life via Legitimate and Participatory Policy-making: A Data-driven Approach in Switzerland. *arXiv preprint arXiv:2306.13696*. DOI: 10.1145/3598469.3598472

Zawacki-Richter, O., Marín, V. I., Bond, M., & Gouverneur, F. (2019). Systematic review of research on artificial intelligence applications in higher education–where are the educators? *International Journal of Educational Technology in Higher Education*, *16*(1), 1–27. DOI: 10.1186/s41239-019-0171-0

About the Contributors

Antonio Cortijo Ocaña is Distinguished Professor at the University of California Santa Barbara. He is the author of over 60 books and monographs ranging from studies on classical culture to humanism, economic history, political theory, and religious persecution in the medieval and early modern period. He has also translated numerous Catalan works into English, from medieval classics to contemporary philosophers and poets. In addition, many of his publications are multidisciplinary and bridge the fields of humanities and applied psychology and education. He has received numerous awards and grants during his career. He is a member of the Royal Academy of Good Letters (Barcelona) and co-director of the Center for Medieval Studies (UCSB). Finally, he is the founder and director of the journal *eHumanista.*

Vicent Martines is a Professor at the University of Alicante. He is PI of ISIC-IVITRA and a member of the Reial Acadèmia de Bones Lletres de Barcelona, Institut d'Estudis Catalans, IULMA, IIFV. He is the Co-director of the Center For Catalan Studies (University of California at Santa Barbara [UCSB] / University of Alicante) and the Co-director of the Internationales Institüt für Iberische Studien (Universitat d'Alacant / Otto-Friedrich Universität Bamberg). He is the chief editor of Series IVITRA Research in Linguistics and Literature, John Benjamin (Amsterdam, The Netherlands / Philadelphia, USA) and co-editor of eHumanista/IVITRA (UCSB). He also co-directs Mirabilia/MedTrans. In addition, he is the director of the "Textes catalanes modernes" series of the Classiques Garnier (Paris, France) and of the "Textes catalans du Moyen Âge" series of the Textes littéraires du Moyen Âge (Paris, France). He has received the following awards: Rei En Pere el Catòlic d´Investigació (Institut d´Estudis Catalans, 1988), Premi d´Investigació Historicocultural Ibn Al-Abbar (Generalitat Valenciana, Ajuntament d´Onda, 1990), and the Premio de Ensayo de Catalán, Gallego y Vasco de la Fundación Ortega y Gasset (Fundació "La Caixa", 1993). He is the author of 280 publications, including 5 chapters and 3 books published by IGI-Global (he acting as coeditor): History of Catalonia and Its Implications for Contemporary Nationalism and Cultural Conflict (Ed. with A. Cortijo, 2021), Handbook of Research on Historical Pandemic Analysis and the Social Implications of COVID-19 (Ed. with A. Cortijo), Managing Pandemic Isolation With Literature as Therapy (Ed. with A. Cortijo & V. Orazi, 2023).

***

Jacek Adamczak is a lawyer, economist and academic lecturer associated with the Institute of Finance of the Warsaw School of Economics, where he obtained his doctorate under the scientific supervision of the Supervisor, prof. SGH dr hab. Zbigniew Grzymała. Circular Economy Expert, and his research areas are the legal and economic aspects of enterprise restructuring related to the transformation of the Polish economy towards a circular economy (CE) in the field of waste management and packaging management in enterprises. He specializes in designing and implementing economically justified business models in the process and operational activities of enterprises in their restructuring towards a circular economy (CE), implementing dedicated solutions in waste and packaging management in the e-commerce industry on European Union markets and introducing Polish enterprises to the German market in terms of their functioning and reporting resulting from the obligations of entrepreneurs related to packaging and waste management in Germany directly related to the German VerpackG/VerpackG2 Act and the German register for entrepreneurs LUCID. Internal auditor ISO 9001 and ISO 14001. Expert of the "Climate Leadership" Program and industry expert of the "Polish Cleaner Production Movement" Association, the sozosfera.pl portal in the field of waste and packaging management and the wesele.pl portal in the field of introducing and operating low-emission vehicle fleets in enterprises.

Lavinia Bianchi is an Associate Professor of General and Social Pedagogy in the Department of Education Sciences at Roma Tre University. She teaches Intercultural and Communication Pedagogy. Her research interests include critical, intercultural and gender pedagogy, decolonial and intersectional perspectives.

Aurora Bulgarelli is a Researcher in General and Social Pedagogy at the Department of Human Sciences, Link Campus University. She holds a Ph.D. in Educational Theory and Research from the Department of Education at Roma Tre University, with a dissertation focused on migration and linguistic educational pathways for adult migrants. Her research explores general and social pedagogy, with particular attention to intercultural, decolonial, and intersectional approaches in the analysis of educational and social phenomena.

Alessandra Casalbore is a teacher in kindergarten. She is currently a research fellow at the Department of Educational Sciences, University of Rome Tre. My interests focus on intercultural and social pedagogy

Francesca Gabrielli is a Research Fellow at the Department of Economic, Psychological, Communication, Educational and Motor Sciences at Niccolò Cusano University, Rome. She holds a PhD in Educational Theory and Research from Roma Tre University. Her research interests lie in the fields of intercultural and social pedagogy, with a particular focus on equity and social justice.

Zbigniew Grzymala is a PhD, DSc, Associate Professor, Institute of Finance, Department of Enterprise. Number of years of work in the current company: at the Warsaw School of Economics – 33 years. For 12 years he was the head of the Department of Economics and Finance of Local Government. Key qualifications: ratio analysis of the company (balance sheet, income statement, employment and wages, fixed assets, etc.); strategic analysis of the organization (creating strategies for the development of organizations, especially local government units), analysis of the commune budget (income, expenses); analysis and evaluation of the effectiveness of capital expenditures in infrastructure, including logistics infrastructure, cost-benefit analysis, business plan and feasibility studies of investment projects, life cycle of products in municipal industries, economics of the public sector, economic policy, spatial policy, spatial management, restructuring of the municipal sector, ecologist – Circular Economy, including energy transformation of municipal economy, management property. Participation in many research projects on urban economy and the SME sector. Author of numerous publications on the issues of local government, municipal management, including the waste management industry. The classes with the students will be about " Circular economy models in the enterprises".

|**Marco Iori**, PhD in Reggio Childhood Studies, is currently a research fellow at the Department of Education, University of Roma Tre. His research focuses on the relationship between education and ethics, reflective thinking and, in general, the relationship between collective and individual instances in education. His study interests range from critical pedagogy to the training of the educational professions, especially of the pedagogist, from outdoor education to the relationship between theatre and early childhood and children's literature.

Christos Lalos was born in Athens. Graduate of Informatics in Management and Economics, holder of two Master's Degrees in Digital Systems and Business Administration, graduate of ASPAITE and adult trainer. He is a Doctor in the field of Informatics and Lifelong Learning. He has worked in various private companies in the field of Plirifics and education, while in recent years in the public sector.

Marco Leggieri is a teaching assistant in General and Social Pedagogy (PAED-01/A) at the University of Tuscia in Italy. He also is a teacher of legal and support subjects in secondary schools and a PhD student in the international jointly supervision at the Universities of Alicante and Roma Tre, conducting research on hate speech. He holds degrees in Law and Political Science. Marco has participated in national and international conferences and has numerous publications in national and international journals to his name. His research interests include hate speech, gender issues, intercultural education, and educational perspectives in schools.

Olimpia Navarro is a professor in the General Linguistics Area of the Department of Spanish Philology, General Linguistics and Literary Theory at the University of Alicante.

María López Martínez is a Professor of Greek Philology. Her research focuses on papyri containing lost novels and the papyri of the Life of Alexander the Great. She also studies Herculaneum papyrology, female literacy, and the staging of Greek drama. In collaboration with a team of specialists in Classics, Linguistics, the Arts, History, and Roman Law, she created the website Ficción en papiro), where she publishes the digital versions of many of her works. The site aims to facilitate access to ancient texts that tell fascinating stories. The website also features a podcast, Fragmentos. Ficción en papiro; a collection of videos, Documentos visuales y sonoros; and a digital version of the Greek Tales on Papyrus collection, also available in print. The currently available titles include: Nino, the Adventures of the King of Nineveh; The Adventures of Caligone and the Amazons; Partenope; The Papyrus of Sinuhe the Sailor; and The Martyrdom of Saint Partenope. These stories are adaptations of her reconstructions of fragmentary novels and are printed as die-cut editions, evoking the style of vintage children's books. Through their pages, readers can explore the literary, iconographic, historical, and cultural contexts of the periods in which these novels are set. She also conducts research on the status of women in the ancient world and its representation in literature, as well as on the Herculaneum papyri—particularly the aesthetic treatises of Philodemus of Gadara. Additionally, she has worked on translating and staging Greek drama, especially tragedy. She has served, and continues to serve, as Principal Investigator on several research projects and have delivered lectures and seminars around the world.

Josep Ochoa Monzó is a Professor of Administrative Law. PhD in Law in 1995 with a pioneering thesis titled El régimen jurídico de los riesgos mayores. La protección civil ('The legal regime of major risks. Civil protection', director: Ramón Martín Mateo, PhD). He is also interested in other lines of research related to environmental issues, urban planning or social responsibility, among others. He has participated in national and international conferences (Mexico, Peru, Costa Rica or Brazil) and in numerous research projects, both public and private. He studied at the Centre de Recherches Interdisciplinaires en Droit de l'Environnement, de l'Aménagement et de l'Urbanisme (CRIDEAU) in Limoges, France and at the Scuola di Specializzazione in Studi sull'Amministrazione Pubblica in Bologna, Italy. He has combined his teaching work in undergraduate and Master's degrees at the Faculty of Law and others with other positions, working as an authorised legal representative of the state (Alicante Office of the State Legal Service, 2006-2007) and as a substitute senior judge (Contentious-Administrative Division of the High Court of Justice of the Valencia Region, 2007-2013). Furthermore, he was Director General for Social Responsibility and Self-Government Promotion within the Valencia Region Government's Department of Transparency, Social Responsibility, Participation and Cooperation (2015-2019), a position that allowed him to advance social responsibility policies in the Valencia Region or promote the creation of the Valencia Region Government's Research Chair in Social Responsibility at the University of Alicante. During this period, he was also director of Revista Valenciana de Estudios Autonómicos and vice chair of the Valencia Region's Civil Law Codification Committee.

Veronica Riccardi is an Associate Professor in the Department of Educational Sciences at Roma Tre University, where she teaches General Pedagogy and Intercultural and Social Pedagogy. She is particularly interested in the integration of students with migrant backgrounds in Italian educational contexts, with a specific focus on primary schools, services for children, lifelong learning and adult education, the history of pedagogy, peace education, and global citizenship.

Lisa Stillo is a Researcher in General and Social Pedagogy at the Department of Education in Roma Tre University. Her research explores general and social pedagogy, with particular attention to intercultural education, decolonial, and intersectional approaches, pupular education in the formal and informal context.

Vasiliki Theochari is an economics teacher in special education with a strong interest in inclusive practices, digital transformation, and career guidance. They have coordinated Erasmus+ and eTwinning projects, developed accessible educational content, and actively participate in national and European conferences.

Zoumpoulia Paraskevi Vardiampasi is a PhD candidate at University of Alicante in Spain. She serves as a secondary school principal and has previously held positions as principal and vice principal at a Vocational High School, as well as department head at a Laboratory Center. She holds a degree in Business Administration and has completed postgraduate studies in Educational Leadership, as well as in Digital and Soft Skills in Educational Sciences. She studies and authors scientific articles and books, and delivers presentations at academic conferences.

Agnieszka Wójcik-Czerniawska, the PhD of Economics field- Management, MBA in Spanish- ICEX-CECO- Madrid, DBA (Doctor of Business Administration,), LL.D (Doctor of Laws), DPH (Doctor of Public Health). Visiting Professor at many foreign Universities in Europe (Italy, Spain, France) and World (Peru, Kenya, Turkey, Georgia). The area of research are connected with: modern finance, finance technology, digital currency, financial isolation, silver generation, circular economy, innovative marketing, society in digitalization world. The participant in many international conferences in all around the world. The keynote speaker in world conferences in: Milan, Turkey, Republic of South Africa, Ireland, Bahrain. The polyglot with more than twelve languages.

Index

H

I

J

L

M

N

P

www.ingramcontent.com/pod-product-compliance
Lightning Source LLC
LaVergne TN
LVHW062334300926
849161LV00007B/1693

* 9 7 9 8 3 3 7 3 2 3 3 2 9 *